THE CHARLTON STANDARD CATALOGUE OF CANADIAN BANK NOTES

3RD EDITION

**W.K.CROSS
PUBLISHER**

The Charlton Press

Birmingham, Michigan • Toronto, Ontario

COPYRIGHT NOTICE AND TRADEMARK NOTICE

COPYRIGHT © 1996 CHARLTON INTERNATIONAL INC.

All Rights Reserved.

No part of this publication, including the CHARLTON CATALOGUE NUMBERING SYSTEM used herein, may be reproduced, stored in a retrieval system, or transmitted in any form or by any means, electronic, mechanical, photocopying, recording, or otherwise, without the prior written permission of the copyright owner.

No copyright material may be used without written permission in each instance from Charlton International Inc. Permission will be liberally given for the use of the CHARLTON CATALOGUE NUMBERING SYSTEM and initials for all notes and varieties by anyone wishing to do so, including their use in advertisements of notes for sale provided Charlton receives proper acknowledgement in each instance.

Permission is hereby given for brief excerpts to be used for the purpose of reviewing this publication in newspapers, magazines, periodicals and bulletins, other than in the advertising of items for sale, provided the source of the material so used is acknowledged in each instance.

The terms Charlton, Charlton's, The Charlton Press, the Charlton Catalogue Numbering System, Charlton Numbers and abbreviations thereof, are trademarks of Charlton International Inc. and shall not be used without written consent from Charlton International Inc.

While every care has been taken to ensure accuracy in the compilation of the data in this catalogue, the publisher cannot accept responsibility for typographical errors.

Canadian Cataloguing in Publication Data

Main entry under title:

The Charlton standard catalogue of Canadian bank notes

3rd ed.
Includes index.
ISBN 0-88968-096-5

1. Bank notes - Canada - Catalogs.   I. Charlton Press.

HG657.C45 1996   769.5' 5971   C91-094003-7

**Printed in Canada
in the Province of Quebec**

The Charlton Press

**Editorial Office
2010 Yonge Street
Toronto, Ontario M4S 1Z9
Telephone: (416) 488-4653 Fax: (416) 488-4656
Telephone: (800) 442-6042 Fax: (800) 442-1542**

ACKNOWLEDGEMENTS

The Charlton Press wishes to thank all those who have assisted in the third and previous editions of the Charlton Standard Catalogue of Canadian Bank Notes.

Editorial

Editor	Walter D. Allan
Associate Editor	Robert J. Graham
Price Editors	Nick Gerbinski and
	Ian Laing
Editorial Assistant	Davina Rowan
Layout	Marc Rowan

Current Contributors

Walter Allen	Gary Becker	Harry M. Eisenhauer
Mike Findlay	Robert Graham	Ronald A. Greene
Richard Gross	Charles Moore	

Past Contributors

G.H. Bishop	Al Bliman	Sheldon S. Carroll
R.D. Lockwood	Ruth McQuade	Dr. S. Sarpkaya
R. Stewart Taylor		

Institutions

American Bank Note Company
Bank of Canada, National Currency Collection
Canadian Imperial Bank of Commerce
Bank of Nova Scotia
Toronto Dominion Bank

British American Bank Note Company
Canadian Bankers Association
Bank of Montreal
Royal Bank of Canada
Royal Bank of Canada

Corrections

The publishers welcome information, for future editions, from interested collectors and dealers concerning any aspect of the listings in this book.

TABLE OF CONTENTS

INTRODUCTION vii
How To Use This Catalogue: vii
   I. General vii
   II. Canadian Banks Section vii
   III. The Charlton Catalogue Numbering System viii
   IV. Grading ix
   V. Useful Terminology and Information ix
ABBREVIATIONS FOR BANK NOTE PRINTERS' IMPRINTS x
FRATERNAL ORGANIZATIONS xi

CANADIAN NOTE ISSUING BANKS

Acadia, The Bank of	1
Accommodation Bank, The	2
Agricultural Bank, The (Montreal)	3
Agricultural Bank, The (Toronto)	4
Arman's Bank	7
Barclay's Bank (Canada)	8
Boucherville, La Banque de	9
Brantford, The Bank of	10
British Canadian Bank, The	12
British Columbia, The Bank of	13
British North America, The Bank of	17
Canada Bank (Montreal)	48
Canada Bank, The (Toronto)	48
Canada, The Bank of (Montreal)	49
Canadian Bank of Commerce, The	53
Canadienne, Banque	65
Canadienne Nationale, Banque	66
Cataract Bank	69
Central Bank of Canada, The	69
Central Bank of New Brunswick	70
Charlotte County Bank	73
Charlottetown, Bank of	75
City Bank, The (Montreal)	76
City Bank (St. John)	82
City Bank of Montreal, The	84
Clifton, The Bank of	84
Colonial Bank of Canada, The	86
Colonial Bank of Chatham, The	89
Commercial Bank (Brockville)	90
Commercial Bank (Kingston)	91
Commercial Bank, The (Montreal)	92
Commercial Bank of Canada, The	92
Commercial Bank of Fort Erie, The	97
Commercial Bank of Lake Ontario, The	99
Commercial Bank of Manitoba, The	99
Commercial Bank of Montreal	100
Commercial Bank of New Brunswick, The	102
Commercial Bank of Newfoundland	105
Commercial Bank of the Midland District, The	109
Commercial Bank of Windsor, The	113
Commercial Branch Bank of Canada	115
Consolidated Bank of Canada, The	116
County of Elgin, The Bank of the	118
Crown Bank of Canada, The	119
Dominion Bank, The	120
Eastern Bank of Canada	128
Eastern Townships Bank, The	129
Exchange Bank, The	133
Exchange Bank Company of Chippewa, The	134
Exchange Bank of Canada, The (Montreal)	134
Exchange Bank of Canada, The (Windsor)	137
Exchange Bank of Toronto, The	137
Exchange Bank of Yarmouth, The	138
Farmer's Bank, The	139
Farmers Bank of Canada, The	140
Farmers' Bank of Malden, The	141
Farmer's Joint Stock Banking Co., The	142
Farmers J.S. Banking Co., The	145
Farmers Bank of Rustico, The	146
Farmers Bank of St. Johns, The	147
Federal Bank of Canada, The	149
Fredericton, The Bank of	151
Free Holders Bank of the Midland District, The	152
Goderich Bank	152
Gore Bank, The	153
Gore Bank of Hamilton, The	154
Grenville County Bank, The	155
Halifax Banking Company, The	156
Hamilton Bank, The	162
Hamilton, The Bank of	162
Hart's Bank	169
Hatley Bank, The	171
Henry's Bank	172
Hochelaga, Banque d'	173
Home Bank of Canada, The	183
Hull, The Bank of	184
Imperial Bank of Canada, The	184
International Bank of Canada, The	193
Internationale du Canada, Banque	198
Jacques Cartier, La Banque	199
Kingston Bank, The	203
Liverpool, The Bank of	203
London in Canada, The Bank of	205
Lower Canada, The Bank of	207
Lower Canada Bank	208
Macdonald & Co.	209
Maritime Bank of the Dominion of Canada, The	210
Mechanics Bank, The (Montreal, Canada East)	213
Mechanics Bank, The (Montreal, Lower Canada)	214
Mechanics Bank of St. John's, The	215
Mercantile Banking Corporation, The	217
Merchants Bank, The (Montreal, Lower Canada)	217
Merchants Bank, The (Toronto)	218
Merchants Bank, The (Montreal, Canada East)	219
Merchants Bank of Canada, The	221
Merchants Bank of Halifax, The	228
Merchants Bank of Prince Edward Island, The	234
Merchants Exchange Bank	236
Metropolitan Bank, The (Montreal)	237
Metropolitan Bank, The (Toronto)	238
Molsons Bank, The	240
Montreal Bank, The	251
Montreal Bank	251
Montreal, The Bank of	255
Nationale, La Banque	283
New Brunswick, The Bank of	289
Newcastle Banking Company, The	295
Newcastle District Loan Company, The	296
Niagara District Bank, The	297
Niagara Suspension Bridge Bank, The	300
Northern Bank, The	302
Northern Crown Bank, The	304
Nova Scotia, The Bank of	305
Ontario Bank, The	315
Ottawa, The Bank of (Montreal)	321
Ottawa, The Bank of (Ottawa)	323
People, The Bank of the	331
Peuple, La Banque du	333
People's Bank of Halifax, The	340
People's Bank of New Brunswick, The	343
Phenix Bank, The	347
Pictou Bank, The	348
Prince Edward Island, The Bank of	349
Provincial Bank, The	352
Provincial Bank of Canada, The	353
Provinciale du Canada, La Banque	354
Quebec, Bank, The	358
Quebec Lower Canada, Bank of	372
Royal Bank of Canada, The	373
Royal Canadian Bank, The	390
Saint Francis Bank, The	394
St. Hyacinthe, La Banque de	395
St. Jean, La Banque de	397
St. Jean Baptiste, Banque	399
St. Lawrence Bank, The	400
St. Lawrence Bank & Lumber Co., The	402
St. Stephens Joint Stock Banking Comp'y, The	402

St. Stephen's Bank, The	403
Saskatchewan, The Bank of	410
Sovereign Bank of Canada, The	411
Stadacona Bank, The	412
Standard Bank of Canada, The	414
Sterling Bank of Canda, The	418
Summerside Bank of Prince Edward Island, The	421
Toronto, The Bank of	424
Traders Bank of Canada, The	431
Union Bank, The	436
Union Bank of Canada, The	438
Union Bank of Halifax, The	445
Union Bank of Lower Canada, The	450
Union Bank of Montreal, The	453
Union Bank of Newfoundland	454
Union Bank of Prince Edward Island, The	458
United Empire Bank of Canada	461
Upper Canada, Bank of (Kingston)	462
Upper Canada, The Bank of (York)	464
Vancouver, The Bank of	475
Victoria, The Bank of	477
Ville Marie, La Banque	477
Western Bank of Canada, The	480
Western Canada, The Bank of	481
Westmorland Bank of New Brunswick, The	482
Weyburn Security Bank, The	484
Yarmouth, The Bank of	485
Zimmerman Bank, The	487
Private Banks and Bankers in Canada	492
Canadian Chartered Bank Notes Outstanding	505
Current Chartered Banks in Canada	506
Non-Note Issuing Banks	507
Bank Mergers & Amalgamations since July 1, 1867	508
INDEX	509
SOURCES	523

INTRODUCTION

Paper money in Canada has a much longer and more interesting history than many would suspect. During the early days of the French regime, North America's first paper money was made on the backs of ordinary playing cards or parts of them. The famous playing card money even preceded the notes of the American colonies to the south.

In those long distant days paper money was a new idea and it was only a representative of coined money. A note was a promise to pay real money (coins) if the note holder so desired.

In the last 50 years, however, it has assumed a greater place in our everyday lives. It has supplanted coins to a large extent and reduced coins to a change-making and machine slug function. The traditional "will pay (coins) to the bearer on demand" has been replaced by "this note is legal tender."

Collectors of Canadian paper money have much to chose from. The earliest banks, whether chartered or private, issued their own notes. Many merchants did as well. In addition to the private issues were government notes on the municipal, provincial and federal levels. This tradition of government vs. private issues has persisted to some degree right up to the present day.

Canada's bank notes begin with the short-lived Canadian Banking Company in Montreal in the 1790's and continue with the early issues of the Montreal Bank, the Quebec Bank and the Bank of Upper Canada. After the twentieth century, the number of banks was reduced through absorptions and mergers, leaving the familiar banks where we do our business today.

Bank notes not only reflect the fascinating history of our reputable financial institutions but of a number of fraudulent ones as well. Consequently, some notes have survived to be enjoyed by collectors because the bank that issued them ultimately failed, leaving them unredeemable, or because they were issued by a sham bank and were never redeemable at any time. Such losses to holders of notes of chartered banks ended with the 1890 Bank Act revision, which provided for a fund to guarantee the redemption of notes failed banks. Subsequently, notes of the few banks which failed after 1890 were sometimes redeemable at even more than their face value, because they gathered interest from the time of the bank's suspension of their redemption until redemption through the fund which was provided for.

Merchants' notes remain generally less appreciated and collected compared to the other types of Canadian notes. This situation will undoubtedly change with time as the other series become increasingly expensive to collect. The script issued by merchants is a large and important series. It includes crude notes issued prior to 1800, a large group of notes issued in Upper and Lower Canada in the late 1830's, fur trade issues by the Hudson's Bay Co. and modern pieces like Canadian Tire money. This field not only offers great collecting opportunities but it also offers an area where much research remains to be done.

Unquestionably the most popular Canadian notes are those issued by the various provincial governments and by the federal government after Confederation. The provincial issues begin with the French regime notes in the 1680's to the 1750's, followed by British colonial issues from the 1790's up to Confederation. The notes of the Province of Canada, dated 1866, are particularly popular with collectors. Their denominations range from $1 to $500 although notes above the $2 are practically never available.

Notes of the Dominion government, called Dominion notes, cover an even broader range of denominations, including the 25c note (shinplaster), the $4 note and the very rare $1000 note. Dominion notes were first issued in 1870 and remained in general circulation until about 1940.

Most of the paper money now in circulation is issued by our central bank, the Bank of Canada. In 1935, with the opening of the Bank of Canada, the withdrawal of Dominion notes was ordered and the chartered banks were required to gradually reduce the circulation of their own notes. It was the government's intention to essentially replace both types of notes with Bank of Canada notes by 1950. The latest date to appear on a chartered bank note is 1943 (the Royal Bank of Canada $5). In 1950 the chartered banks paid over to the Bank of Canada $13,302,046.60, the face value of their outstanding notes, and since that time the Bank of Canada has been responsible for their redemption. As the chartered bank notes are redeemable, the Bank of Canada credits the accounts of the banks that originally issued the notes.

The opportunities for specialization within the Canadian paper money series are numerous. In the chartered series some collectors attempt to assemble a collection of all notes issued by a particular bank or by a currently existing bank and all the banks that it absorbed along the way. Others save a single note from each bank. Still others collect notes payable in a particular section of the country, that is, they collect on a regional basis. Since the government series is smaller than the chartered series, collectors of government notes tend to save varieties as well as basic types of notes. They concentrate on signature differences, seal colour varieties and even series letters and plate number combinations. Clearly, the study and collecting of Canadian paper money offers a great number of challenges and something for all tastes.

It is interesting that only in the past twenty years has the collecting of Canadian paper money enjoyed its deservedly widespread appeal. Just as the establishment of the Canadian Numismatic Association in 1950 responded to and stimulated the interest in Canadian coins, tokens and medals, so the founding of the Canadian Paper Money Society in 1964 signalled the coming of age of Canadian paper money collecting. A major stimulus for this hobby came with the inclusion of paper money in a number of general and specialized catalogues in the sixties and early seventies. This book represents the new and growing interest in Canadian paper currency.

How To Use This Catalogue

I. GENERAL

Generally speaking this catalogue has been arranged in the same format as the paper money sections of the previous Charlton Standard Catalogues. Due to the enormous expansion which has occurred, a complete index has been provided for easy access to the information compiled. It is strongly suggested that the index be utilized as, for instance, banks quite often overlapped different designs of notes within the same time period. The index is found on page 510.

II. CANADIAN BANKS SECTION

A. Alphabetical Listing of Banks

As in previous editions the issuing banks are in alphabetical order with the words "THE," "BANK" and "OF" (or "LA," "BANQUE" and "DE") ignored. Thus, Molsons Bank is listed before the Bank of Montreal. Each note is assigned a set of numbers. The first set designates the individual bank. The following sets (up to three) designate further aspects of each note and provide a comprehensive, expandable bank note numbering system.

B. Introductory Information

At the beginning of the listing for each bank the period of operation and the location of the head office are stated. Below this the redeemability status of the notes and a brief historical sketch are given where such information is available.

C. Order of the Note Listings Within Each Bank

Generally speaking, a bank puts out its notes in issues or groups. An issue usually consists of a design set and thus several denominations linked through either a vignette (an engraved picture) or a common style. The present catalogue departs from previous editions in listing the bank notes first by design set (issue). Issues or design sets are denoted by two numbers for each design set section. An attempt has been made to indicate features common to each design set in the title, eg., "Randolph Portrait" Issue, "Blue Protector" Issue. Major alterations within the design sets are denoted by a third set of two(55-10-02) numbers. By using this system, it is much easier for the reader to appreciate the note issuing patterns of each bank and for the first time to construct a checklist of the basic designs for each bank. Although all notes with the same design are generally listed under a single issue number, in a few cases where an old design reappears after a long absence, a new issue number is used. Such cases are indicated in the issue titles.

D. Subsidiary Information

1. Designs and Colours: The main vignettes appearing on each note are described in the same order as they occur on the notes, with oblique lines separating descriptions, eg., beaver/ship/cattle. Where there is no vignette illustrated on a particular portion of the note, a slash (-) appears in place of the description. Where there are two main vignettes appearing on one portion of the note, they are described from top to bottom with a semi-colon (;) separating the descriptions, eg., beaver; ship; arm and hammer; cattle. Special knowledge is not required to understand the descriptions of most vignettes, however, the allegorical figures and human figures used to represent or personify abstract concepts, need some explanation. In the descriptions the following figures are usually described as they appear below rather than giving details of what the woman is holding, what she is wearing, and so on.

The exact details of these figures can vary slightly, but the following are the most commonly encountered:

"Justice" Figure: blindfolded woman, with a balance in one hand and a sword in the other.

"Commerce" Figure: woman holding a caduceus; usually seated amid bales, casks and/or goods.

"Agriculture" Figure: woman with sickle, sheaf and produce or cornucopia.

Britannia: helmeted woman, with a trident or spear and often a shield.

Mercury: man wearing a winged helmet, usually holding a caduceus.

Neptune: bearded man holding a trident, usually in or around the sea.

Quotation marks are also used in describing the vignettes in the following circumstances:

A. The name of the painting or other source from which the engraving was derived.

B. The actual name found on the engravings as originally done by the engraving companies.

2. Imprint: The bank note company imprint is given for each note or issue. The imprint indicates the company that engraved the plates and or printed notes from them. The dual imprint, eg. "ABNC and BABN," indicates plates originally engraved by the American Bank Note Company that were later used by the British American Bank Note Company for printing notes.

3. Signature: For each issue, all of the printed and some of the manuscript (mss.) (handwritten with pen and ink) signatures are given. There are two kinds of printed signatures: engraved (engr.), and typographed (typed).

Engraved signatures are engraved into the face plate and are printed at the same time as the face design. For notes printed from the same part of a plate the positions of the engraved signatures relative to the frame do not vary.

Typed signatures, however, are added after the rest of the note has been printed. Consequently, the signatures may be found to be in slightly different positions when the notes are compared. Typed signatures usually have flat, broad strokes in contrast to the thin strokes of the engraved signatures.

4. Issue Dating: Unlike the previous catalogue, dates are now listed, in most cases, almost exactly as they appear on the notes. Most manuscript dates are shown as written but in a few cases where the same date appears in more than one manner, eg. Jan 2, 2 Jan, only one has been shown.

5. Protectors: Protectors are coloured overprints which give the denomination of the note and serve as an anticounterfeiting device. They can occur either as a word (ONE) or numeral (1) type and usually appear on the face of the note, reading normally, as well as on the back, often in mirror image.

Sometimes protectors are found printed on only the face of the back.

6. Overprints and Stamps: Overprints, extra details added by a printing press after the notes have otherwise been completed, are listed for each issue. Stamps differ from overprints in being added by hand, with a rubber or wooden implement. If an overprint appears on separate lines on the note, this is indicated by an oblique (/), eg. PAYABLE AT/LONDON.

7. General Treatment of Varieties: Most engraved differences are given separate listings. Where branch names are engraved in the plates, subheadings are always formed. However, when a branch name has been added as an overprint, it is given separate treatment only in special cases like "DAWSON," "YUKON" and "Winnipeg." Usually, overprints are simply listed at the beginning of each issue.

8. Remainders(R), Essays(E), Proofs(P) and Specimens(S): Whenever possible, fully completed notes (those signed, numbered and dated) are listed. In cases where fully completed notes are not known or when other forms are much more common, remainders, proofs or specimens are listed.

A remainder is a regular note which has not had all of the blanks filled in. Remainders are sometimes encountered with spurious signatures and dates, etc.; this does not change their status.

Failing the availability of completed or remainder notes either specimens or proofs are listed.

A specimen is not intended for circulation, but is used to acquaint bank employees and others with the characteristics of the genuine notes. It is normally printed on banknote paper with face and back designs the same as the issued note; however, it usually has serial numbers consisting of all 0's and is overprinted or stamped "SPECIMEN," often in the signature areas.

Proofs are trial or sample impressions taken from the printing plates usually on very thin paper backed with card, but some are printed directly on card. They often have no serial numbers and may or may not be stamped with the word "SPECIMEN." "FACE PROOF" is indicated when the face impression only is printed (usually the case).

Essays are trial printings made to introduce new designs or test new manufacturing concepts. Essays might also test new papers and/or the construction of new bank notes such as the addition of foil or heliograms to the note. Essays are produced to gain approval or acceptance of new features before a note is officially authorized. Essays are extremely rare.

Models are paste ups, using lathework, counters and engravings or photographs, to illustrate a proposed note showing a design concept. It is an example and often the artist's or engraver's working stage before an essay.

9. Sheets of Notes: Notes were usually printed in sheets of four, which could be all the same denomination or a mixtrue of two or more denominations. The form for the listings is $1, 1, 3, 5, which for this example refers to a sheet consisting, from top to bottom, of a $1, a $1, a $3 and a $5 note.

III. THE CHARLTON CATALOGUE NUMBERING SYSTEM

Each note is assigned a set of numbers. The first set designates the individual bank. The following sets (up to three) designate further aspects of each note and provide a comprehensive, expandable bank note numbering system. A bank note is identified by a number in the following form:

55-10-02-02

The first set of numerals represents the bank number. The banks are numbered beginning with 5 for the Bank of Acadia and jump-numbered by five thereafter allowing for future expansion.

The second series of numerals represents the design concept or issue. This series consists of two numbers for the issue number, starting at 10 and jump-numbered by two, again to allow for expansion. Thus, for the example shown above, the note would be from the first issue or design set.

The third set of two numbers represents any major alteration that might occur within the design set. The numbers are again jump-numbered to allow for expansion. This set of numbers may be omitted if no major alterations occur.

The fourth set records all the varieties that are found. Following these numbers can be a series of upper or lower case letters indicating further information about the note.

The following table will help the collector in understanding the numbering system:

Bank Number
5, 10, 15, etc.

Design Concept 10, 12, 14	A design concept is a series of notes bound together by a common design concept, printer, denomination, theme, date or domicil\e. Examples are vignettes, a small bank crest, issue of 1860, overall green tint, Kingston Jamaica and pounds issue.
Major Alteration 02, 04, 06, etc.	A major alteration is when the design concept has been altered by a colour change addition or alteration of a back design domicile, etc. An example is the addition of an agency branch name or any significant change to the original design concept.
Variety 02, 04, 06, etc.	Varieties occur with different denominations, signatures, typefaces, major overprints and proctectors. They also occur when issue dates appear in manuscript and typography and when either the size or colour of a denomination is altered.

Type of Note Upper Case Letters (as required)	R-Remainder, S-Specimen, P-Proof, E-Essay, A-Altered. Issued notes will not have upper case letters.
Minor Variety Lower Case Letters (as required) a,b,c, etc.	Minor varieties are imprints, minor overprints, stamps and minor design changes. An example is a change in size or style of type face of "General Manager" or "President."

The major alteration number is dropped when not required. Bank numbers are generally jump-numbered by fives. Design concepts, major alterations and minor varieties are jump-numbered by a minimum of one.

IV. GRADING

When grading a note it is essential to first determine if the note may be safely removed from its holder without causing any damage due to brittleness, unseen tears, glue remnants, etc. Then, carefully remove the note and holding it lightly, consider the general appearance, amount of wear, the hue and intensity of the colour of both the face and back. Determine a preliminary grade. If the note is Fine or better it should be held obliquely in line with a good light source. Move it around at various angles, such that the light will reflect off the note highlighting any ripples, cointing creases, havey creases, pressed out creases, tears, pinholes, cancellations, repairs or fading. The mastering of this technique is mandatory in successfully grading paper money. When these have been carefully considered, one must decide if these are "normal" for the preliminary grade which was determined. If not, then the grade may have to be reduced depending on the number and severity of the defects, or the defects will have to be listed in addition to the overall grade of the note. It is generally better to state the overall grade, followed by any unusual defect, than to downgrade the note.

Careful inspection to detemine the correct grade will lead to greater trust and confidence between buyers and sellers of notes.

UNCIRCULATED, UNC — A perfect note. Crisp and clean as when printed and without any creases or pinholes. Colours have original hue and intensity.

ABOUT UNCIRCULATED, AU — Similar to Uncirculated, but it will have either a very light fold or ripple "counting creases," to the extent that the paper fibers are not broken. If any combination of the two is present, the note would fall into the extremely fine grade.

It has been common practice, by some, to add a "plus," "+," "about" or "almost" to infer a slightly higher or lower condition than the designated grade, eg. about VF, VF+ or almost EF.

EXTREMELY FINE, EF — Very crisp, clean and colourful as an uncirculated note, but has a major crease or several minor creases. The note may or may not show some slight evidence of wear.

VERY FINE, VF — A fairly crisp and clean note. It may have several major and minor creases and folds, some evidence of wear especially along the edges or at the corners. There may be some slight decrease in hue and intensity of the colours. The design in the creases should not be worn off.

FINE, F — A note with considerable evidence of circulation. Numerous creases and folds, but a small degree of firmness remaining. Usually fairly soiled and the hue and intensity of the colour are slightly reduced. There may be a slight amount of the design worn off along the major creases.

VERY GOOD, VG — A heavily circulated note but with all the major design still visible. Usually limp with no crispness or firmness, quite soiled, and the hue and design may be worn off along the major creases or in the "cointing crease" areas. Numerous other defects may apply (see list below).

GOOD, G — Similar to VG, but often with tears and small pieces missing. Usually some of the major design is worn off. Signatures and sheet numbers are often unreadable. The note is very limp and usually has numerous other defects.

FAIR, F — Similar to Good, but larger pieces missing. Signatures and sheet numbers entirely missing. Often has numerous tears and other defects.

POOR, P — As a Fair note, but with a major portion of the note torn off or the design obliterated. Often numerous tape repairs. Generally collectable only because of rarity.

In addition, to accurately grade a note it is necessary to consider any additional impairments. These should include:

1. Minor counting creases or edge defects, especially for UNC and EF grades.
2. Tears, pinholes or signature perforations.
3. Stains, smudges, crayon marks or writing.
4. Missing corners, cut and punch cancellations or edge defects.
5. Undesirable rubber stamps.
6. Any repairs, such as with sticky tape, scotch tape, stamp hinges, etc.
7. Chemical damage, paste or glue from attachment to a page.
8. Poorly centered or badly trimmed edges.

Proof, specimen and essay notes are commonly accepted as being in uncirculated condition, otherwise, they should be described as impaired with the type and degree of impairment stated.

V. USEFUL TERMINOLOGY AND INFORMATION
A. Kinds of Banks

1. Private Bank: A bank that operated without a charter, usually as a private partnership.

2. Chartered Bank: A bank that was incorporated by an act of Parliament and sold stock to the general public.

3. Spurious or Phantom Bank: A bank that had no legal existence, whose name is found on notes intended to deceive the unwary. Such spurious notes were often made in vague imitation of some legitimate bank's notes, using the colloquial name of such an institution, eg., The Kingston Bank or The Gore Bank of Hamilton.

4. Wildcat Bank: A bank with a legal existence, but whose main purpose was to "push" its notes on the public, with no intention of redeeming most of them, eg., The Bank of Clifton or The International Bank of Canada.

B. Kinds of Fraudulent Notes

1. Counterfeit: A facsimile copy of a note of a legitimate bank.

2. Spurious: A note that is of a design that does not correspond to any notes issued by a legitimate bank. Spurious notes can purport to be redeemable at a legitimate or phantom bank.

3. Altered: In the Canadian context, a genuine note on which the name of the bank has been fraudulently changed to that of another bank.

4. Raised: A note which has been fraudulently modified so as to appear to be of a higher denomination.

C. Parts of Notes

1. Face: The front of a note, sometimes incorrectly referred to as the obverse.

2. Back: The subordinate side of a note, sometimes incorrectly called the reverse. Many notes were printed with blank or "plain" backs.

3. Vignette: An engraved picture (portrait or scene) on a bank note.

4. Counter: A word, letter or number indicating the denomination of a note.

5. Payee: The person or organization to whom a note is made payable. The payee on many modern notes is simply referred to as "the bearer."

6. Domicile: The specific city or town where the note was made payable.

7. Tint: The background coloured design found on notes. The tint is printed before the face or back plate, as opposed to a protector, which is an overprint. In the 19th century tints were usually printed by the engraved plate method. Gradually, beginning in the late 19th century, banknote companies switched over to printing tints by lithography.

D. Printing Methods

1. Letterpress (or Typography): In this process the design is the highest part of the printing plate and is flat. When the plate is inked only the design receives the ink by virtue of its location. Letterpress results in a fairly thick and flat layer of ink on the note. Sheet numbers, protectors and most overprints were added by this method of printing.

2. Engraved Plate (or Intaglio): The design is cut into a flat sheet of metal, and in contrast to letterpress, the design is below the flat upper surface of the plate. The plate is inked and the flat surface wiped clean, leaving ink only in the recessed (engraved) areas which is then transferred to the paper during printing. The resulting image has a 3-dimensional character. Most notes were printed by this means since it made possible the highest resolution of fine lines and the most life-like portraits. This method also provided the best security against counterfeiting.

3. Lithography: In the latter part of the 19th century lithography was used to print the coloured background (tint) on some notes. As it was practised then, lithography involved the photography of a design and its transfer via a negative to the surface of a special stone coated with a layer of a photosensitive material. After treatment, only the image on the stone would pick up the ink. This type of printing resulted in the transfer of a thin flat layer of ink.

E. Printers

Printers' names, abbreviations or monograms will usually appear as part of the frame design or below it on the face and/or back. In some instances the engraver's name may also appear in a similar location of a note. The abbreviations below identify printers for many of the notes listed in this volume.

F. How Notes Were Numbered

1. Sheet Number: As a general rule, 19th century bank notes were printed in sheets. Within each sheet all of the notes were given the same number - the sheet number. Notes were generally given black or blue numbers. Occasionally when the first number reaches its limit, a new number series would start in a different colour.

2. Check Letter: Since more than one note in a sheet could bear the same number, each note was provided with a distinguished letter, a check letter.

3. Series Letter: For a particularly large issue of notes, where all the available sheet numbers had been used, the same numbers would be started over again, preceded or followed by a series letter. A new series letter would be used for each successive cycle of sheet numbers. Commonly, the first series would have no series letter and the second would have an "A," the third a "B," and so on.

4. Serial Number: From the above it should be clear that the serial number, the designation that uniquely defines a note, must include not only the sheet number but also the check letter and series letter if they are present.

ABBREVIATIONS FOR BANK NOTE PRINTERS' IMPRINTS

ABBREVIATION	IMPRINT
ABNC	American Bank Note Company
BABNC	British American Bank Note Co., Ltd.
Br Am BN	British American Bank Note Company
Britton & Co.	Lith. Britton & Co. S.F.
BFL	Barclay & Fry Ltd. (England)
BG	Burton and Gurley, New York
BGE	Burton, Gurley Edmonds, New York
BWC	Bradbury, Wilkinson & Co (England)
Canada BN	Canada Bank Note Company
CBC	Columbian Banknote Co.
CBNC	Canadian Bank Note Company
CDB & E	Casilear, Durand, Burton & Edmonds, New York
Con BN	Continental Bank Note Company
CS & E	Charles Skipper & East (England)
CWT	C.W. Torbett
DS & H	Danforth, Spencer & Hufty, New York
DTL	Draper, Toppan, Longacre & Co.
DU	Danforth, Underwood & Co., N.Y.
DW	Co. Danforth, Wright & Co., N.Y. & Phila.
EAW	Fairman, Draper & Underwood, N.Y.
FLBN	Franklin-Lee Bank Note Company
Graphic	Graphic
HLBNC	Homer Lee Bank Note Co.
HS	Harris & Sealey, Engravers, New York
HW	Hay & Whiting, New York
IBNC	International Bank Note Company
JBNC	Jeffries Bank Note Company
Jones	Jones
JDW	Jocelyn, Draper, Welsh & Co.

ABBREVIATION	IMPRINT
K McKenzie	Kenneth McKenzie, Printer, London
LR	Leney & Rollinfon
L Perrault	Louis Perrault, Montreal
NBNC	National Bank Note Company
NEBN	New England Bank Note Company, Boston
NYBN	New York Bank Note Company
PBC	Perkins, Bacon & Co. (England)
PB & P	Perkins, Bacon & Petch (England)
PH	Perkins, Heath
Reed, A	Reed
RS	Reed, Stiles & Co.
RWH	Rawdon, Wright, Hatch and Company
RWHE	Rawdon, Wright, Hatch & Edson
SBNC	Security Banknote Company
SH & D	Spencer, Hufty & Danforth, Phila.
SJHS	St. John & Halifax Steam Lith. Company
Starke & Co.	Starke & Co., Printers, Montreal
Star Office	Star Office
T dL R	Thomas de La Rue (England)
TP	Terry Pelton & Co., Boston and Prov.
TC	Toppan Carpenter & Company
UBS & H	Underwood, Bald, Spencer & Hufty, Phila.
Union BN	Union Bank Note Company
USBNC	United States Banknote Corp.
W & S	Waterlow & Sons Ltd. (England)
WBN	The Western Bank Note Company, Chicago
WH & W	Wellstood, Hay & Whiting, New York
Western	Western Printing & Lithographing Co. Ltd., Calgary
WWS	W.W. Sprague & Co. Ltd. (England)

FRATERNAL ORGANIZATIONS

Listed below are a number of organizations dedicated to the preservation, study and enjoyment of paper currency. All will be delighted to hear from collectors interested in any aspect of paper money collecting.

THE CANADIAN PAPER MONEY SOCIETY

Established in 1964 and incorporated in 1972, the society is a non-profit, historical and educational organization interested in Canadian bank notes, banking and other Canadian paper money. It publishes *The Canadian Paper Money Journal* quarterly and has library and other facilities available. The society is sustained by regular members' contributions of $25.00 per year or a $375.00 life membership donation to the Income Trust Fund. The official address of the Society is P.O. Box 562, Pickering, Ontario, Canada, L1V 2R7.

THE CANADIAN NUMISMATIC ASSOCIATION

The CNA was founded in 1950 and incorporated in 1963. It is a non-profit educational association which has members in every province in Canada, every state in the U.S. and many other countries. Its objective is to encourage and promote the science of numismatics by acquirement and study of coins, paper money, medals, tokens and all other numismatic items with special emphisis on material pertaining to Canada. Membership includes use of the associations library material as well as a subscription to *The Canadian Numismatic Journal,* a monthly magazine devoted to Canadian num,ismatics. Annual membership fees are $25.00 for those over 21 years of age, $12.50 for those under the age of 21, $35.00 for a family membership and $25.00 for a club, society, library or other non-profit organization. Life membership is $400.00. The current executive secretary is Mr. Kenneth B. Prophet and he may be reached at P.O. Box 226, Barrie, Ontario, Canada, L4M 4T2.

THE INTERNATIONAL BANK NOTE SOCIETY

The IBNS was founded in 1961 and now has a membership of over 1,500 with representation from over 60 countries. The current annual dues are as follows: regular membership $17.50, family membership $22.50, and junior membership $9.00. Life memberships are also available for $300.00 U.S. The society publishes the *IBNS Journal* quarterly which is distributed free of charge (by surface mail) to its members. The current general secretary is Mr. Milan Alusic, P.O. Box 1642, Racine, Wisconsin 53401, U.S.A.

SOCIETY OF PAPER MONEY COLLECTORS

In June of 1964 the society was incorporated as a non-profit organization under the laws of the District of Columbia. Membership now numbers approximately 2,300, the majority of which reside in Canada and the U.S. but there is representation throughout the world. The SPMC publishes *Paper Money* bimonthly in the odd months and sends it to its members. Dues are $12.00 (U.S.) per year. Those interested should contact Mr. Ronald Horstman, New Member Co-ordinator, P.O. Box 6011 St. Louis, Missouri 63139, U.S.A.

LANSA
Latin American Paper Money Society

This Society was organized in 1973. It publishes a small journal. For information write Peter G. Burkhart, P.O. Box 3467, Sarasota, Florida, 34230, U.S.A.

THE CHARLTON
STANDARD CATALOGUE OF
CANADIAN BANK NOTES

THE BANK OF ACADIA

1872-1873

LIVERPOOL, NOVA SCOTIA

BANK NUMBER 5   **NONREDEEMABLE**

Established in 1872 in Liverpool, Nova Scotia, The Bank of Acadia was in existence for only three months and twenty-six days, making it the shortest-lived bank in Canadian history. It re-opened for a few days after its failure to redeem some of its notes, but with the exception of the government, note holders not reimbursed at this time received nothing. The government held notes worth several thousand dollars but received only 25 cents on the dollar.

5-10.   ISSUE OF 1872

DESIGNS AND COLOURS

5-10-02
    $4 Face Design: —/cherubs and ornate 4/—
         Colour: Black with green tint

    Back Design: Lathework, counters and bank name
         Colour: Green

5-10-04
    $5 Face Design: —/ships "Clipper"/arm and hammer "muscle"
         Colour: Black with green tint

    Back Design: Lathework, counters and bank name
         Colour: Green

5-10-06
    $10 Face Design: —/cherubs and ornate X/—
         Colour: Black with green tint

    Back Design: Lathework, counters and bank name
         Colour: Green

5-10-08
    $20 Face Design: Sailing ship/"Steamboat Canada"
         Colour: Black with green tint

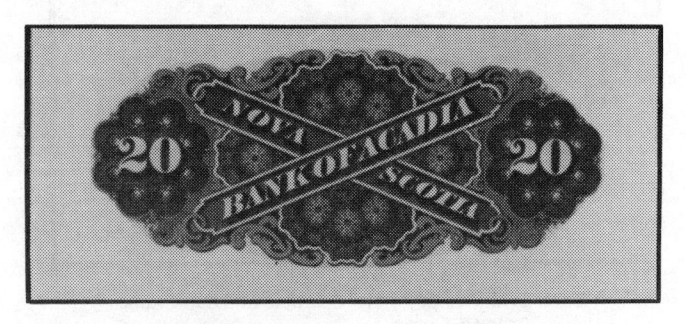

THE ACCOMMODATION BANK

Back Design: Lathework, counters; Bank of Acadia
Colour: Green

IMPRINT
British American Bank Note Co. Montreal & Ottawa

SIGNATURES
left	right
mss. G.E. Stevens	mss. T.R. Pattillo

ISSUE DATING
Engraved
2nd Dec. 1872

Cat.No.	Denom.	Date	G	VG	F	VF	EF	AU
10-02	$4	1872	135.	275.	400.	600.	1,000.	-
10-04	$5	1872	250.	500.	650.	900.	1,400.	-
10-06	$10	1872	250.	500.	650.	900.	1,400.	-
10-08	$20	1872	1,000.	2,000.	3,000.	4,000.	4,000.	-

THE ACCOMMODATION BANK

1836-1837

KINGSTON, UPPER CANADA

BANK NUMBER 10   **NONREDEEMABLE**

This bank appears to have been established in either Kingston or Bath in 1836 despite opposition by the local people. The British Whig of September 30, 1836, discusses its establishment in Kingston, however, both the Kingston Chronicle and the British Whig of January 7, 1837 report an Accommodation Bank established at Bath. This bank appears to be a "spurious bank."

10-10.   **ISSUE OF 1837**

IMPRINT
Rawdon, Wright, Hatch New-York

SIGNATURES
left	right
mss. J. Everitt	mss. J. Miller

ISSUE DATING
Partially Engraved__18__:
1837: Jany 26

Notes read "will pay to bearer twenty shillings twelve months after date."

2.   No "_____" above vignette

DESIGNS AND COLOURS

10-10-02-02R
$4 (20s) Face Design: —/seated "Justice" figure with lion at right/—
Colour: Black with no tint

Back Design: Plain

Cat.No.	Denom.	Date	Variety	G	VG	F	VF	EF	AU
10-02-02R	$4(20s)	185	Design 02*	75.	150.	200.	275.	475.	-

4. "Redeemable at the UPPER CANADA BANK at Kingston..." engraved above vignette.

DESIGNS AND COLOURS

10-10-04-02a
$4 (20s) **Face Design:** —/seated "Justice" figure with lion at right/—
Colour: Black with no tint

Back Design: Plain

Cat. No.	Denom	Date	Variety	G	VG	F	VF	EF	AU
10-04-02R	$4(20s)	185	Design 04**	75.	150.	200.	275.	475.	-
10-04-02a	$4(20s)	1837	Design 04***	300.	600.	900.	1,200.	2,000.	-

THE AGRICULTURAL BANK
1837
MONTREAL, LOWER CANADA

BANK NUMBER 15　　　　　　　　**NONREDEEMABLE**

Probably trading on the name of The Agricultural Bank in Toronto, The Agricultural Bank in Montreal was a phantom bank. In all probability, these notes were never issued by the "bank". Signatures and dates are likely spurious.

15-10.　　　　**BURTON & GURLEY.**
　　　　　　　　NEW YORK PRINTINGS

DESIGNS AND COLOURS

15-10-02
$1 **Face Design:** Indian/farmer ploughing with oxen; farm implements and sheaves below/ allegorical female
Colour: Black with no tint

Back Design: Plain

15-10-04
$2 **Face Design:** Farmer with grain under tree/seated "Agriculture" figure, sheaves and cattle; bear beside tree below/helmeted female
Colour: Black with no tint

Back Design: Plain

THE AGRICULTURAL BANK

15-10-06
   $3 Face Design: Women with rakes/seated "Agriculture" figure, tools, shield with "3"; crown below/ farmer ploughing with oxen
   Colour: Black with no tint
   Back Design: Plain

IMPRINT
   Burton & Gurley. New-York

SIGNATURES
left	right
mss. various	mss. various

ISSUE DATING
   Partially engraved__18__:
   Incomplete or various dates in the 1840's
   June 4, 1841
   Apr 10th, 1842
   May 3rd, 1842
   May 3rd, 1843
   June 7th, 1843
   Aug 2, 1846
   Feb. 1, 1847

Cat.No.	Denom.	Date	G	VG	F	VF	EF	AU
10-02	$1	18__	165.	325.	450.	600.	-	-
10-04	$2	18__	165.	325.	450.	600.	-	-
10-06	$3	18__	250.	500.	700.	1,000.	-	-

THE AGRICULTURAL BANK
1834-1837
TORONTO, UPPER CANADA

BANK NUMBER 20   **NONREDEEMABLE**

The first bank in Canada to pay interest on deposits. The Agricultural Bank was established in 1834 in Toronto as the private bank of Truscott, Green & Company, a joint-stock firm. Liquidated in November of 1837, a substantial portion of its notes and other liabilities were unprovided for, the partners having left the country. The bank's policy of paying interest was criticized in the beginning by other banks but became general practice soon afterwards.

The Agricultural Bank also began personal savings accounts on which cheques could be written, making it one of the first banks in Canada to do so.

There is a $1 note dated "1 April 1833". The date is presumably an error, either a clerical error in writing out the date which accidentally antedated the note, or the last 3 is a misinterpreted 5.

**20-10.   RAWDON, WRIGHT, HATCH & Co.
              PRINTINGS PAYABLE AT TORONTO**

DESIGNS AND COLOURS

20-10-04
   $1 (5s) Face Design: —/horse; beaver below/woman holding wheat
   Colour: Black with no tint
   Back Design: Plain

20-10-10
   $2 (10s) Face Design: Men with livestock/beehive, cornucopia, sheaf, spinning wheel; beaver below/ men with livestock
   Colour: Black with no tint
   Back Design: Plain

THE AGRICULTURAL BANK

20-10-15
$4 (20s) Face Design: Plough in oval (sideways)/woman and Indian, Crest; beaver below/sheaf in oval
Colour: Black with no tint
Back Design: Plain

20-10-18
$5 (25s) Face Design: Beaver/seated woman, sheaf and cattle/men with livestock
Colour: Black with no tint
Back Design: Plain

20-10-22
$10 (50s) Face Design: —/farmers cutting grain with cradles; beaver below/King William IV
Colour: Black with no tint
Back Design: Plain

20-10-24
$20 (£5) Face Design: —/King William IV; lion on crown below/farmer picking corn
Colour: Black with no tint
Back Design: Plain

IMPRINT
Rawdon, Wright, Hatch & Co. New York

SIGNATURES

	left	right
1834-1835:	mss. W. Fryer	mss. Geo Truscott
	mss. W. Fryer	mss. J.C. Green
	mss. F. Franklin	mss. J.C. Green
	mss. H.J.Hensleigh	mss. Geo. Truscott
1837:	mss. F. Franklin	mss. Geo. Truscott
1837:	mss. H.J.Hensleigh	mss. Geo. Truscott

ISSUE DATING
Partially Engraved : _18__ :

$1 (5s) 1834: 1 April, Aug. 8, Oct. 1, Oct. 20, Nov. 1, Dec. 1
1835: Feb. 2, July 1
$2 (10s) 1834: Aug. 8, Aug. 18, Sept. 1, 1 Oct,16th Oct, Nov. 1, Dec. 1
1835: Feb. 1, Feb. 2, May 1, July 1
1837: Sept. 21, mss. "One year after date"; Oct. 5
$4 (20s) 1833: 1st Apr.
1834: 30th Aug, 1 Sept, 1 Oct.
1837: 1 Mar., mss. "One year after date"
$5 (25s) 1834: Aug. 8 , 30 Aug., 1 Sept., Oct., Oct. 16, Nov. 1, 1 Dec.
1837: 1 Mar.
$10 (50s) 1834: Jan. 1, Feb. 1, Sept. 1
1835: Jan. 1
$20 (£5) 1834: Sept. 1, Nov. 1

OVERPRINTS
A,C,D,E,F,G,H,O,R,SS,U,V in black some notes have a purple stamp on the back "Harveys of Bristol" mirror image in a circle

Cat.No.	Denom.	Date	G	VG	F	VF	EF	AU
10-02	$1(5s)	1834	35.	70.	110.	175.	300.	-
10-04	$1(5s)	1835	35.	70.	110.	175.	300.	-
10-06	$2(10s)	1834	35.	70.	110.	175.	300.	-
10-08	$2(10s)	1835	35.	70.	110.	175.	300.	-
10-09	$2(10s)	1837	35.	70.	110.	175.	300.	-
10-10	$2(10s)	1837*	45.	90.	125.	200.	325.	-
10-12	$4(20s)	1833	85.	175.	250.	375.	575.	-
10-14	$4(20s)	1834	85.	175.	250.	375.	575.	-
10-15	$4(20s)	1835	85.	175.	250.	375.	575.	-
10-16	$4(20s)	1837*	100.	200.	300.	400.	800.	-
10-18	$5(25s)	1834	70.	140.	200.	275.	475.	-
10-19	$5(25s)	1837	70.	140.	200.	275.	-	-
10-20	$10(50s)	1834	400.	800.	1,100.	1,600.	-	-
10-22	$10(50s)	1835	400.	800.	1,100.	1,600.	-	-
10-24	$20(£5)	1834	750.	1,500.	2,000.	2,500.	4,000.	-

THE AGRICULTURAL BANK

20-12. NEW ENGLAND BANK NOTE CO. PRINTING PAYABLE IN MONTREAL

DESIGNS AND COLOURS

20-12-02-04
- **$1(5s) Face Design:** Portrait of girl/woman raking hay/deer below/sheaf and plough/cattle
- **Colour:** Black with no tint
- **Back Design:** Plain

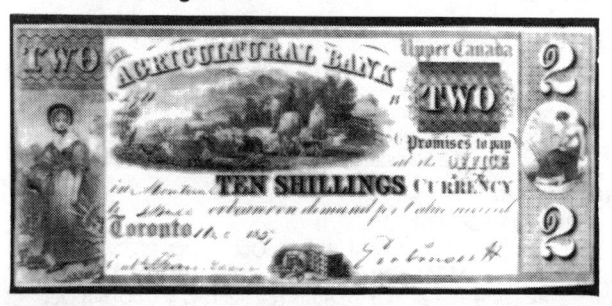

20-12-04-04
- **$2(10s) Face Design:** Milkmaid/pastoral scene; dog with key beside strongbox below/seated female with sickle, grain in oval
- **Colour:** Black with no tint
- **Back Design:** Plain

20-12-04-06
- **$4(20s) Face Design:** Boy with rake/cherubs/milkmaid; farm produce below/cherubs/smithy shoeing horse
- **Colour:** Black with no tint
- **Back Design:** Plain

20-12-02-14
- **$5(25s) Face Design:** Female group/haying scene; farm produce below/seated Britannia
- **Colour:** Black with no tint
- **Back Design:** Plain

IMPRINT
New England Bank Note Co. Boston

SIGNATURES

	left	right
1835:	mss. F.Franklin	mss. Geo. Truscott
	mss. H.J. Hensleigh	mss. J.C. Green
1836:	mss. H.J. Hensleigh	mss. J.C. Green
1837:	mss. F.Franklin	mss. Geo. Truscott

2. "FOR GEO. TRUSCOTT..." ENGRAVED AT BOTTOM 1835-1836

ISSUE DATING
Partially Engraved__18__:
- $1 (5s) 1835: Oct. 1, 1 Nov., 1 Dec.
- 1836: Jan. 1
- $2 (10s) 1835: Jan. 1, Oct. 1, 1 Nov., 1 Dec.
- 1836: Jan. 1
- $4 (20s) 1835: Oct. 1, 1st Nov., Dec. 1
- 1836: 1 Jany
- $5 (25s) 1835: Oct. 1, Nov. 1, 1 Dec.
- 1836: 1 Jan., October 1st

OVERPRINTS STAMP
- "B" in black, "C" in red
- "B" in black
- "H" in black
- "C" in red
- "A. Coulton/BOOKSELLER BRANTFORD" at right end in black
- "4 4" written over cherubs at both sides.

Cat.No.	Denom.	Date	VG	F	VF	EF	Unc
12-02-02	$1(5s)	1835	20.	30.	40.	70.	150.
12-02-04	$1(5s)	1836	20.	30.	40.	70.	150.
12-02-06	$2(10s)	1835	20.	30.	40.	70.	150.
12-02-08	$2(10s)	1836	20.	30.	40.	70.	150.
12-02-10	$4(20s)	1835	40.	60.	75.	100.	175.
12-02-12	$4(20s)	1836	40.	60.	75.	100.	175.
12-02-14	$5(25s)	1835	20.	30.	50.	70.	150.
12-02-14	$5(25s)	1835	20.	30.	50.	70.	150.

4. "FOR GEO. TRUSCOTT..." OMITTED, AND "THE" ADDED TO BANK NAME 1837

ISSUE DATING
Partially Engraved__18__:
1837: 1 Oct.

Cat.No.	Denom.	Date	VG	F	VF	EF	Unc
12-04-02	$1(5s)	1837	12.	20.	30.	45.	90.
12-04-04	$2(10s)	1837	12.	20.	30.	45.	90.
12-04-06	$4(20s)	1837	30.	45.	60.	90.	125.
12-04-08	$5(25s)	1837	12.	20.	30.	45.	90.

ARMAN'S BANK
1837
MONTREAL (LOWER CANADA)

BANK NUMBER 25   **NONREDEEMABLE**

25-10.   **ISSUE OF 1837**

DESIGNS AND COLOURS

25-10-02
- **5d (10 sous) Face Design:** —/numeral inside shaded circle; cornucopia/—
- **Colour:** Black with no tint
- **Back Design:** Plain

25-10-04
- **10d (20 sous) Face Design:** —/numeral inside shaded circle; cornucopia/—
- **Colour:** Black with no tint
- **Back Design:** Plain

25-10-06
- **15d (30 sous) Face Design:** —/numeral inside shaded circle; cornucopia/—
- **Colour:** Black with no tint
- **Back Design:** Plain

IMPRINT
None

SIGNATURES

left	right
mss. various	mss. various

ISSUE DATING
Engraved
1 August 1837

Cat.No.	Denom.	Date	VG	F	VF	EF	Unc
10-02	5d(10 sous)	1837	375.	525.	-	-	-
10-04	10d(20 sous)	1837	375.	525.	-	-	-
10-06	15d(30 sous)	1837	375.	525.	-	-	-

BARCLAY'S BANK (CANADA)

1929-1956

MONTREAL, QUEBEC

BANK NUMBER 30 **REDEEMABLE**

An important event in Canadian banking history occurred in 1929 with the entry of one of the leading British banks, Barclay's Bank, Limited. It became a new chartered bank, Barclay's Bank (Canada) with its head office in Montreal. Although the bank had a Canadian Board of Directors, its operations remained under the control of the parent institution in England. The Canadian bank's first president was Sir Robert Borden. A statement issued by the management noted that the object of the bank in Canada was, "to establish another link in the chain of their affiliations with a view of fostering trade with the Empire. "Branches were established in Toronto and Vancouver and paid-up capital reached $3 million by 1950. By this time deposits exceeded $30 million and in 1956 amalgamated with The Imperial Bank of Canada.

30-10. **ISSUE OF 1929**
LARGE SIZE NOTES

DESIGNS AND COLOURS

30-10-02
$5 **Face Design:** —/seated female with globe/—
Colour: Black with blue-green tint
Back Design: Lathework, counters, bank name and bank building
Colour: Green

30-10-04
$10 **Face Design:** —/seated female with globe/—
Colour: Black with orange tint
Back Design: Lathework, counters, bank name and bank building
Colour: Orange

30-10-06
$20 **Face Design:** —/seated female with globe/—
Colour: Black with blue tint

Back Design: Lathework, counters, bank name and bank building
Colour: Blue

IMPRINT
Canadian Bank Note Company, Limited

SIGNATURES
left	right
typed J.R. Bruce	typed R.L. Borden
typed F.H. Dickenson	typed R.L. Borden
typed H.A. Stevenson	typed R.L. Borden

ISSUE DATING
Engraved
Sept. 3rd 1929

Cat.No.	Denom.	Date	Variety	VG	F	VF	EF	Unc
10-02	$5	1929	Bruce, I	400.	560.	840.	1,425.	2,850.
10-02a	$5	1929	Dickenson, I	400.	560.	840.	1,425.	2,850.
10-02b	$5	1929	Stevenson, I	400.	560.	840.	1,425.	2,850.
10-04	$10	1929	Bruce, I	400.	560.	840.	1,425.	2,850.
10-04a	$10	1929	Dickenson, I	400.	560.	840.	1,425.	2,850.
10-04b	$10	1929	Stevenson, I	400.	560.	840.	1,425.	2,850.
10-06	$20	1929	Bruce, I	450.	630.	945.	1,600.	3,200.
10-06b	$20	1929	Stevenson, I	450.	630.	945.	1,600.	3,200.

30.12. ISSUE OF 1935 SMALL SIZE NOTES

DESIGNS AND COLOURS

30-12-02
- **$5 Face Design:** —/seated female with globe/—
- **Colour:** Black with blue-green tint
- **Back Design:** Lathework, counters, bank name and bank building

30-12-06
- **$10 Face Design:** —/seated female with globe/—
- **Colour:** Black with orange tint
- **Back Design:** Lathework, counters, bank name and bank building
- **Colour:** Orange

IMPRINT
Canadian Bank Note Company, Limited

SIGNATURES

left	right
typed H.A. Stevenson	typed R.L. Borden
typed H.A. Stevenson	typed A.A. Magee

ISSUE DATING
Engraved
Jan'y 2nd, 1935

Cat.No.	Denom.	Date	Variety	VG	F	VF	EF	Unc
12-02	$5	1935	Borden, r.	45.	65.	110.	225.	450.
12-04	$5	1935	Magee, r.			SPECIMEN		1,000.
12-06	$10	1935	Borden, r.	45.	65.	110.	225.	450.
12-08	$10	1935	Magee, r.	45.	65.	110.	225.	450.

LA BANQUE DE BOUCHERVILLE

1830's

BOUCHERVILLE, BAS CANADA

BANK NUMBER 35   **NONREDEEMABLE**

La Banque de Boucherville was established in 1836 or 1837 in Lower Canada on a "joint stock" basis. It did not flourish.

35-10. BOURNE PRINTING

DESIGNS AND COLOURS

35-10-02
- **$1 Face Design:** No vignette, French text.
- **Colour:** Black with no tint
- **Black Design:** Plain

IMPRINT
Bourne Sc.

SIGNATURES

left	right
none	none
A. Duquette	H. Haineault

ISSUE DATING
Partially Engraved__18__
1837: 23 Juin

Cat.No.	Denom.	Date	Variety	VG	F	VF	EF	Unc
10-02R	$1	18__	Remainder*	30.	60.	85.	120.	225.
10-02	$1	1837		30.	60.	85.	120.	225.

THE BANK OF BRANTFORD

THE BANK OF BRANTFORD

1857-1860's

BRANTFORD, CANADA WEST

BANK NUMBER 40   **NONREDEEMABLE**

Established in Brantford, Canada West in 1857, The Bank of Brantford, during its relatively short period of operation, managed to circulate a considerable number of notes. Most of their notes were released in the United States. In Ontario they were considered suspicious and not readily accepted.

40-10.   **PAYABLE AT BRANTFORD, OVERALL GREEN TINT**

DESIGNS AND COLOURS

40-10-02-02a
- **$1 Face Design:** St. George slaying dragon/ girl with calves/cattle scene
- **Colour:** Black with overall green tint
- **Back Design:** Plain

40-10-02-04
- **$2 Face Design:** Girl with sheaves/boat in locks, train/ man with hammer
- **Colour:** Black with overall green tint
- **Back Design:** Plain

40-10-02-06
- **$4 Face Design:** Portrait of Lord Elgin/ unloading wagon at canal, mill in back-ground/young girl
- **Colour:** Black with overall green tint
- **Back Design:** Plain

40-10-04-08
- **$5 Face Design:** Queen Victoria (Winterhalter portrait) train, boats and horses/Solomon Carvalho's "Child with rabbits"
- **Colour:** Black with overall green tint
- **Back Design:** Plain

40-10-02
- **Purple overprint on Back:** "Fred Westbrook 10 mile champion of Canada Hotel Belmont, Brantford, Ontario" Man on bicycle design, all in purple
- **Colour:** Purple

IMPRINT
American Bank Note Company

THE BANK OF BRANTFORD

2. PARTIALLY ENGRAVED DATE

SIGNATURES
left	right
mss. S.P. Stokes	mss. J.J. Kingsmill
mss. S.P. Stokes	mss. Peter Carroll

ISSUE DATING
Partially Engraved__18__:
1859: Nov. 1

OVERPRINT
Face: "ISSUED AND PAYABLE AT THE AGENCY IN/ HONITON, 1st May, 1862." in blue

Cat.No.	Denom.	Date	Variety	VG	F	VF	EF	Unc
10-02-02	$1	1859	No o/p	40.	50.	75.	125.	250.
10-02-02a	$1	1859	Kingsmill, Blue o/p	60.	75.	110.	175.	350.
10-02-02b	$1	1859	Carrole, Blue o/p	60.	75.	110.	175.	350.
10-02-04	$2	1859		40.	50.	75.	125.	250.
10-02-04a	$2	1859	Westbrook, Purple o/p	65.	110.	190.	-	-
10-02-06	$4	1859		60.	100.	150.	225.	300.
10-02-06a	$4	1859	Westbrook, Purple o/p	100.	175.	300.	-	-
10-02-08	$5	1859		40.	55.	75.	110.	200.
10-02-08a	$5	1859	Westbrook, Purple o/p	65.	110.	175.	-	-

4. ENGRAVED DATE

SIGNATURES
left	right
mss. S.P. Stokes	mss. Peter Carroll

ISSUE DATING
Engraved
Novr. 1st, 1859

OVERPRINT
Face: "ISSUED AND PAYABLE AT THE AGENCY IN/HONITON 1st May, 1862." in blue

Cat.No.	Denom.	Date	Variety	VG	F	VF	EF	Unc
10-04-02	$1	1859	No o/p	40.	50.	75.	125.	250.
10-04-02a	$1	1859	Blue o/p	40.	50.	75.	125.	250.
10-04-04	$2	1859	No o/p	40.	50.	75.	125.	250.
10-04-04a	$2	1859	Blue o/p	60.	75.	110.	175.	200.
10-04-06	$4	1859		60.	100.	150.	225.	300.
10-04-08	$5	1859		40.	55.	75.	110.	200.

40-12. PAYABLE AT SAULT ST. MARIE, OVERALL RED TINT

DESIGNS AND COLOURS

40-12-02R

40-12-04R

40-12-06R

40-12-08R

SIGNATURES
left	right
none	none

ISSUE DATING
Engraved
Novr 1st 1859

Cat.No.	Denom.	Date	Variety	VG	F	VF	EF	Unc
12-02R	$1	1859	Remainder*	-	-	-	50.	100.
12-04R	$2	1859	Remainder*	-	-	-	50.	100.
12-06R	$4	1859	Remainder*	-	-	-	100.	200.
12-08R	$5	1859	Remainder*	-	-	-	50.	100.

THE BRITISH CANADIAN BANK

THE BRITISH CANADIAN BANK

1883-1884

TORONTO, ONTARIO

BANK NUMBER 45   **NONREDEEMABLE**

Established in Winnipeg, Manitoba in 1882, The British Canadian Bank changed its name from the North Western Bank in 1883, but its charter was never used.

45-10.   **BABNC PRINTINGS**
                           1884

DESIGNS AND COLOURS

45-10-02P
    $5 Face Design: Train and ships at wharf/—/—
    Colour: Black with green tint

Back Design: Lathework, counters and bank name
Colour: Green

45-10-04P
    $10 Face Design: Youthful bust of Queen Victoria/—/
                          10 with seated Britannia, native child and lion
    Colour: Black with green tint

Back Design: Lathework, counters and bank name
Colour: Green

IMPRINT
    British American Bank Note Company, Montreal

SIGNATURES
    left   **right**
    none   none

ISSUE DATING
    Engraved
       September 15th, 1884
       Sept. 15th 1884

Cat.No.	Denom.	Date	Unc
10-02P	$5	1884	FACE PROOF 900.
10-04P	$10	1884	FACE PROOF 900.

12

THE BANK OF BRITISH COLUMBIA
1862-1901
VICTORIA, VANCOUVER ISLAND

BANK NUMBER 50　　　　　　　　　　**REDEEMABLE**

The Royal charter incorporating The Bank of British Columbia was granted on May 31, 1862 and ran for twenty years. In its prospectus, its preliminary advertising and the watermark of its earliest notes, the name of the institution appeared as The Chartered Bank of British Columbia and Vancouver Island. On July, 1862, the directors changed the name to correspond with the chartered name. The bank opened for business in Victoria within a few days of the change.

On May 11, 1883, the charter was renewed for one year, and in 1894 the ten year extension of the bank's charter obtained May 27, 1884 expired and was renewed under the same terms for another seven years. This charter was to expire July 1, 1901, with the understanding that it would not likely be renewed again, although the bank still had the option of a Dominion charter.

At a general meeting in July of 1900, The Canadian Bank of Commerce submitted a proposal of amalgamation to the shareholders and at a special meeting in December of that year, the shareholders of The Bank of British Columbia agreed to accept the offer and its shares were purchased by The Canadian Bank of Commerce on January 2, 1901.

There is no relation between this bank and the one currently chartered under the name of the Bank of British Columbia.

50-10.　　　　**"VICTORIA COIN" ISSUE**
1862-1863
LARGE SIZE NOTES
(20.8 x 12.3 cm.)

Notes of this issue were printed on paper watermarked "The Chartered Bank of British Columbia and Vancouver's Island" on first issues and later "Bank of British Columbia".

DESIGNS AND COLOURS

Notes of this issue have Queen Victoria facing left, as on the obverse of the British Indian rupee coin, at the left end of the note.

50-10-04
$5 Face Design: Victoria coin; miner swinging pickaxe/
　　　　　　　　Britannia and seated woman/ship's stern
Colour: Black with blue tint
Back Design: Plain

50-10-08
$20 Face Design: Victoria coin; miner pouring ore/
　　　　　　　　　Britannia and seated woman/
　　　　　　　　　miners walking
Colour: Black with blue tint
Back Design: Plain

50-10-10
$50 Face Design: Victoria coin; miner at crank/
　　　　　　　　　Britannia and seated woman/ship's stern
Colour: Black with blue tint
Back Design: Plain

50-10-12
$100 Face Design: Victoria coin; miner holding pickaxe/
　　　　　　　　　　Britannia and seated woman/man working
Colour: Black with blue tint
Back Design: Plain

IMPRINT
Rixon & Arnold

SIGNATURES
　　　　　　left　　　　　　　　　　right
　　　　mss. various　　　　　　mss. various

THE BANK OF BRITISH COLUMBIA

ISSUE DATING
Partially Engraved__18__:
1862: Nov. 28
1863: 6th Jany

VARIETIES
"Victoria" following left note number space
Blank tablet following left note number space

Cat.No.	Denom.	Date	Variety	VG	F	VF	EF	Unc
10-02	$5	1862	Victoria	-	-	5,250.	-	-
10-04	$5	1863	Victoria	-	-	5,250.	-	-
10-06	$5	1863	Blank tablet	-	-	5,250.	-	-
10-08	$20	1862		-	-	5,250.	-	-
10-10	$50	1862		-	-	5,250.	-	-
10-12	$100	1863		ALL REDEEMED				

50-12. "VICTORIA MEDALLION" ISSUE
1863-1875
SMALL SIZE NOTES

Some notes of this issue are printed on watermarked white, buff or pink paper.

DESIGNS AND COLOURS
Notes of this issue have a gothic portrait of Queen Victoria facing right, on a medallion without legend, at the left end of the notes.

50-12-02
 $1 Face Design: Victoria "medallion"; miner swinging pickaxe/ Britannia and seated woman/ship's bow
  Colour: Black with blue tint
 Back Design: Plain

50-12-04-02
 $5 Face Design: Victoria "medallion"; miner swinging pickaxe/ Britannia and seated woman/ship's bow
  Colour: Black with blue tint
 Back Design: Plain

50-12-04-04
 $10 Face Design: Victoria "medallion"; miner swinging pickaxe/ Britannia and seated woman/ship's bow
  Colour: Black with blue tint
 Back Design: Plain

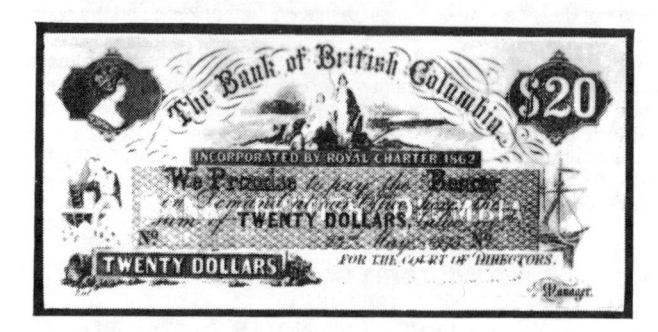

50-12-04-06
 $20 Face Design: Victoria "medallion"; miner swinging pickaxe/ Britannia and seated woman/ship's bow
  Colour: Black with blue tint
 Back Design: Plain

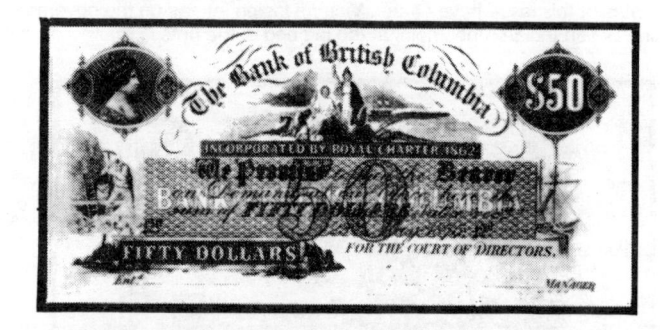

50-12-04-08
 $50 Face Design: Victoria "medallion"; miner swinging pickaxe/ Britannia and seated woman/ship's bow
  Colour: Black with blue tint
 Back Design: Plain

IMPRINT
Wm. Brown & Co. Sc. London

SIGNATURES
left	right
mss. various	mss. various

2. PARTIALLY ENGRAVED DATE 1863

ISSUE DATING
Partially Engraved __18__:
1863: 24 June, 30 June

STAMP
"NEW WESTMINSTER" in blue vertically at left end

Cat.No.	Denom.	Date	VG	F	VF	EF	Unc
12-02	$1	1863	4,000.	5,000.	6,000.	-	-

4. FULLY ENGRAVED DATE 1864 - 1875

ISSUE DATING
Engraved
March 31st 1864
15th May 1873
23rd May 1875

Cat.No.	Denom.	Date	VG	F	VF	EF	Unc
12-04-02	$5	1864	-	-	-	-	-
12-04-04	$10	1873	-	-	-	-	-
12-04-06	$20	1875	-	-	-	-	-
12-04-08	$50	1875	-	-	-	-	-

50-14. ISSUE OF 1879

DESIGNS AND COLOURS

50-14-02-02
 $5 **Face Design:** Sailing ship/Queen Victoria/mine
   Colour: Black with no tint
  Back Design: Lathework and counters with "PAYABLE AT VICTORIA"
   Colour: Green

50-14-02-04
 $10 **Face Design:** Sailing ship/Queen Victoria/mine
   Colour: Black with no tint
  Back Design: Lathework and counters with "PAYABLE AT VICTORIA"
   Colour: Green

50-14-02-06
 $20 **Face Design:** Sailing ship/Queen Victoria/mine
   Colour: Black with no tint
  Back Design: Lathework and counters with "PAYABLE AT VICTORIA"
   Colour: Green

50-14-02-08
 $50 **Face Design:** Sailing ship/Queen Victoria/mine
   Colour: Black with no tint
  Back Design: Lathework and counters
   See subheadings
   Colour: Green

50-14-02-10
 $100 **Face Design:** Sailing ship/Queen Victoria/mine
   Colour: Black with no tint
  Back Design: Lathework and counters
   See subheadings
   Colour: Green

IMPRINT
Wm. Brown & Co. 40 & 41 Old Broad St. London

SIGNATURES
 left   right
 mss. various   mss. various

ISSUE DATING
Engraved
1st June 1879

PROTECTOR
Green "word" on face only

THE BANK OF BRITISH COLUMBIA

2. RED SERIAL NUMBER ON FACE ONLY

Cat.No.	Denom.	Date	VG	F	VF	EF	Unc
14-02-02	$5	1879				EXTREMELY RARE	
14-02-04	$10	1879				EXTREMELY RARE	
14-02-06	$20	1879	4,500.	-	-	-	-
14-02-08	$50	1879				EXTREMELY RARE	
14-02-10	$100	1879				EXTREMELY RARE	

4. BLACK SERIAL NUMBER ON FACE, REPEATED ON BACK

Cat.No.	Denom.	Date	VG	F	VF	EF	Unc
14-04-02	$5	1879	4,000.	-	-	-	-
14-04-04	$10	1879	4,000.	-	-	-	-
14-04-06	$20	1879	4,000.	-	-	-	-
14-04-08	$50	1879	4,000.	-	-	-	-
14-04-10	$100	1879	4,000.	-	-	-	-

50-16.   ISSUE OF 1894

DESIGNS AND COLOURS

50-16-02
  $5 Face Design: —/Britannia and seated woman, mountains in background/—
  Colour: Black with pale yellow and green tint

Back Design: Lathework, counters and bank name
Colour: Green

50-16-04
  $10 Face Design: —/Britannia and seated woman, mountains in background/—
  Colour: Black with yellow and blue tint

Back Design: Lathework, counters and bank name
Colour: Blue

50-16-06
  $20 Face Design: —/miners/—
  Colour: Black with yellow and red-brown tint

  Back Design: Lathework, counters and bank name
  Colour: Dark brown

THE BANK OF BRITISH NORTH AMERICA
1836-1918

BANK NUMBER 55 **REDEEMABLE**

The Bank of British North America was formed in England in 1836 as a private institution to conduct business through branches in the various North American provinces. Each branch obtained a Provincial Charter. The bank began business with capital of œ1 million without double liability to shareholders. In 1840 the promoters of the bank secured a Royal Charter, which stipulated that no notes smaller than œ1 could be issued. Only The Bank of British North America, of all the chartered banks made use of the Free Banking Act of 1850 to enable it to again extend its issue to $1 and $2 notes, which it did until 1870. The expansion of this bank in Canada influenced the Canadian banking system through the infusion of large numbers of young British bankers who had received their early training in British banks. Once in Canada, these young bankers gradually joined other Canadian institutions and at one time no less than eleven Canadian banks were under the general management of former employees of The Bank of British North America.

In London the directors of the bank found it increasingly difficult to conduct operations in Canada during World War I. Although the bank was well managed and sound, the war had imposed restrictions on travel and communications, making it difficult for the directors to keep in touch with Canadian conditions. They concluded that a merger would be advantageous, and in April of 1918 the bank was absorbed by The Bank of Montreal. At the time of merger, the bank had a paid-up capital of nearly $5 million, a reserve fund of about $3 million, total assets of $78 million, and was represented by 92 branches.

55-10. **EARLY "BANK CREST" ISSUES**
1837 - 1847

DESIGNS AND COLOURS
  Face Design: various with "Bank Crest"
  Colour: Black with no tint

  Back Design: Plain

IMPRINT
  Perkins, Bacon & Petch, London

2. **"HALIFAX NOVA SCOTIA BRANCH" ISSUE**

55-10-02-02P

55-10-02-04P

ISSUE DATING
  Entire date added letterpress with serial numbers

Cat.No.	Denom.	Date	Unc
10-02-02P	£5	no date	PROOF 500.
10-02-04P	£7.10	no date	PROOF 500.

50-16-08
  $50 Face Design: —/Royal Crest/—
    Colour: Black with pale yellow and deep orange tint

  Back Design: Lathework, counters and bank name
    Colour: Red-orange

IMPRINT
  $5: American Bank Note Co. N.Y.
  $10, 20, 50: American Bank Note Co. New York

SIGNATURES
  left   right
  mss. various   mss. various

ISSUE DATING
  Engraved
  Jany 1st 1894

Cat.No.	Denom.	Date	VG	F	VF	EF	Unc
16-02	$5	1894	3,500.	-	-	-	-
16-02S	$5	1894		SPECIMEN		1500. - 2000.	
16-04	$10	1894					EXTREMELY RARE
16-04S	$10	1894		SPECIMEN		1500. - 2000.	
16-06	$20	1894					EXTREMELY RARE
16-06S	$20	1894		SPECIMEN		1500. - 2000.	
16-08	$50	1894					EXTREMELY RARE
16-08S	$50	1894		SPECIMEN		1500. - 2000.	

THE BANK OF BRITISH NORTH AMERICA

4. "MONTREAL LOWER CANADA" ISSUE

55-10-04-08P

55-10-04-10P

Photo not available
at
press time

55-10-04-12

55-10-04-20

SIGNATURES
Left	Right
mss. various	mss. various

ISSUE DATING
Entire date added letterpress with serial numbers:
$1: Septr. 1 1838

Partially Engraved__18__:

Cat.No.	Denom.	Date	VG	F	VF	EF	Unc
10-04-02	$1	1838	700.	800.	1,200.	-	-
10-04-02R	$1	1838	-	-	300.	500.	-
10-04-08P	$7	no date			PROOF		1,000.
10-04-10P	$9	no date			PROOF		1,000.
10-04-12P	$10	18__			PROOF		500.
10-04-20P	$50	no date			PROOF		500.

5. "MONTREAL" BRANCH ISSUE

55-10-05-20P

ISSUE DATING
Partially Engraved ___ 18___:

Cat.No.	Denom	Date	VG	F	VF	EF	Unc
10-05-12	$10				NOT CONFIRMED		
10-05-20P	$50	18__			PROOF		700.

6. "QUEBEC LOWER CANADA" ISSUE

55-10-06-02

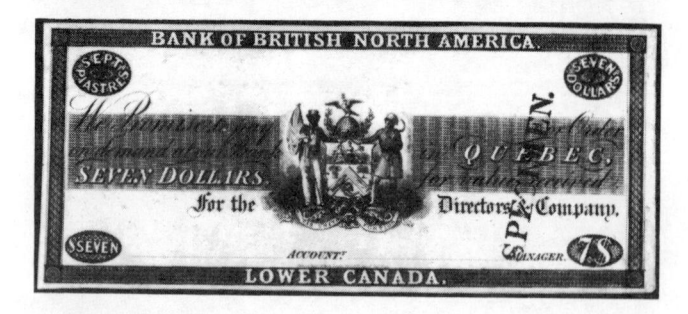

55-10-06-10

55-10-06-12

18

ISSUE DATING
   Entire date added letterpress with serial numbers:
   Sept. 1 1838

Cat.No.	Denom.	Date	VG	F	VF	EF	Unc
10-06-02	$1	1838	700.	800.	1,200.	-	-
10-06-10P	$7					PROOF	500.
10-06-12P	$9					PROOF	500.

7. "QUEBEC" BRANCH ISSUE

55-10-07-08

55-10-07-14

55-10-07-30P

ISSUE DATING
   Partially Engraved ___ 18 ___:

Cat.No.	Denom	Date	G	VG	F	VF	EF	Unc
10-07-08P	$5	18__					PROOF	500.
10-07-14P	$10	18__					PROOF	500.
10-07-30P	$50	18__					PROOF	500.

8. "ST. JOHN, NEW BRUNSWICK" ISSUE

55-10-08-02

55-10-08-04P

ISSUE DATING
   Entire date added letterpress with serial numbers:
   July 1 1837

Cat.No.	Denom.	Date	VG	F	VF	EF	Unc
10-08-02	$1(5s)	1837	800.	1,000.	1,500.	-	-
10-08-04P	$2(10s)	no date					PROOF 850.
10-08-06p	$4 (20s)	no date					PROOF 850.
10-08-08P	$5 (25s)	no date					PROOF 850.
10-08-14P	$10 (50s)	no date					PROOF 850.
10-08-20P	$50 (£12.10)	no date					PROOF 850.

10. "ST. JOHN'S, NEWFOUNDLAND" ISSUE
LARGE SIZE NOTES (21.5 x 14 cm.)

55-10-10-01P

THE BANK OF BRITISH NORTH AMERICA

55-10-10-02

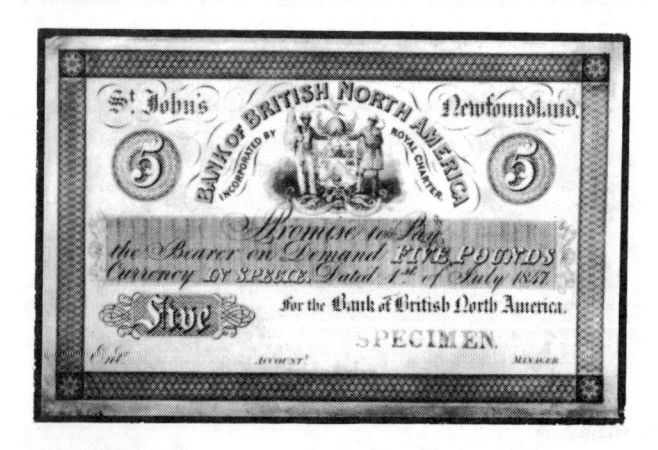

55-10-10-04P

ISSUE DATING
Partially Engraved__18__:
1837: Mar. 20
Engraved
1st of July. 1847

Cat.No. Denom.	Date	VG	F	VF	EF	Unc
10-10-01P 10s	18__				PROOF	600.
10-10-02 £1	1837	1,500.	2,000.	-		-
10-10-04P £5	1847				PROOF	600.
10-10-08P £20	18__				PROOF	600.

12.   "TORONTO, UPPER CANADA BRANCH" ISSUE

55-10-12-02P

55-10-12-04P

55-10-12-08P

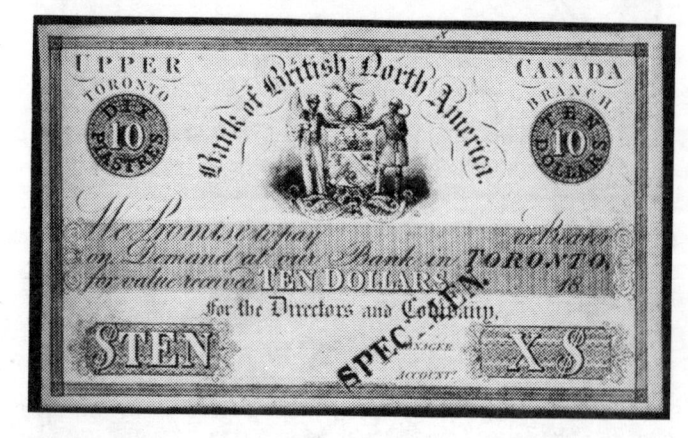

55-10-12-14P

ISSUE DATING
Partially Engraved__18__:

Cat.No. Denom.	Date	G	VG	F	VF	EF	Unc
10-12-02P $1	18__					PROOF	1,000.
10-12-04P $2	18__					PROOF	1,000.
10-12-08P $5	18__					PROOF	1,000.
10-12-14P $10	18__					PROOF	1,000.

55-12.   "MINIATURE ROYAL CREST" ISSUES
1841-1872

Notes of these issues have a miniature Royal Crest at the bottom centre and a complete frame.

2. "BRANTFORD" ISSUE

The branch name is engraved at the lower left centre and vertically inside the right and left vignettes.

DESIGNS AND COLOURS

55-12-02-02P
- **$4 (£1) Face Design:** Britannia/reclining "Commerce" figure/ Seated "Commerce" figure
- **Colour:** Black with no tint
- **Back Design:** Plain

55-12-02-04
- **$5(£1.5) Face Design:** Bank Crest/beehive/sheep, plough in foreground
- **Colour:** Black with no tint
- **Back Design:** Plain

IMPRINT
Perkins, Bacon & Petch, London

ISSUE DATING
Engraved
5th July 1852
1st July 1853

PROTECTOR
$5: (£1.5) Green "word and numeral" on face and back

Cat.No.	Denom.	Date	VG	F	VF	EF	Unc
12-02-02P	$4(£1)	1853					PROOF 400.
12-02-04	$5(£1.5)	1852	700.	800.	1,200.	-	-

4. "FREDERICTON NEW BRUNSWICK" ISSUE

The branch name is engraved at the lower left centre and vertically inside the right and left vignettes.

DESIGNS AND COLOURS

55-12-04-02p
- **£1 Face Design:** Britannia/beehive/seated "Commerce" figure
- **Colour:** Black with no tint
- **Back Design:** Plain

IMPRINT
Perkins, Bacon & Petch, London

ISSUE DATING
Engraved
1st Septr 1847

Cat.No.	Denom.	Date					Unc
12-04-02P	£1	1847					PROOF 500.

5. "HALIFAX" ISSUE

The branch name is engraved at the lower left of centre and vertically at the ends.

DESIGNS AND COLOURS

55-12-05-04P
- **£5 Face Design:** Seated Indian/ships/Britannia
- **Colour:** Black with no tint
- **Back Design:** Plain

IMPRINT
Perkins, Bacon & Co., London

ISSUE DATING
Partially Engraved __18__:

Cat.No.	Denom.	Date	VG	F	VF	EF	Unc
12-05-04P	£5	18__					PROOF 500.

THE BANK OF BRITISH NORTH AMERICA

6. HAMILTON "BRANTFORD" AGENCY ISSUE
DESIGNS AND COLOURS

55-12-06-02
$5(25s) **Face Design:** Bank Crest/beehive/
  sheep, plough in foreground
Colour: Black with no tint

Back Design: Plain

IMPRINT
  Perkins, Bacon & Co. London

ISSUE DATING
  Engraved
  1st March 1852

Cat.No.	Denom.	Date	VG	F	VF	EF	Unc
12-06-02	$5(25s)	1852	700.	800.	1,200.	-	-

8. HAMILTON "DUNDAS" AGENCY ISSUES
     1853 and 1856

The branch name is engraved at the lower left centre. The agency names are engraved at the upper right and vertically inside the right and left vignettes.

DESIGNS AND COLOURS

55-12-08-04P
$4 (£1) **Face Design:** Standing female with beehive and ship/
  Two allegorical females/Bank Crest
Colour: Black with no tint

Back Design: Plain

55-12-08-06P
$5 (£1.5) **Face Design:** Brittania/ships/seated "Commerce"
  figure in crowned frame
Colour: Black with no tint

Back Design: Plain

55-12-08-08P
$10 (£2.10) **Face Design:** Sheep, plough in foreground/
  cherubs/Indian camp
Colour: Black with no tint

Back Design: Plain

IMPRINT
  Perkins, Bacon & Co. London

ISSUE DATING
  Engraved
  1st March 1852
  2nd Feby 1853
  1st March 1856

Cat.No.	Denom.	Date	VG	F	VF	EF	Unc
12-08-04P	$4(£1)	18__				PROOF	400.
12-08-06P	$5(£1.5)	1852				PROOF	400.
12-08-08P	$5(£1.5)	1856				PROOF	400.
12-08-10P	$10(£2..10)	1853				PROOF	400.

10.   HAMILTON "SIMCOE" AGENCY ISSUE

The branch name is engraved at the lower left centre. The agency names are engraved at the upper right and vertically inside the right and left vignettes.

DESIGNS AND COLOURS

55-12-10-04P
- **$4 (£1) Face Design:** Seated "Agriculture" figure/reclining "Commerce" figure/seated "Agriculture" figure
- **Colour:** Black with no tint
- **Back Design:** Plain

Photo Not Available

55-12-10-06P
- **$5 (£1.5) Face Design:** Unknown
- **Colour:** Black with no tint
- **Back Design:** Plain

IMPRINT
Perkins, Bacon & Co. London

ISSUE DATING
Engraved
Jan.1, 1845
1st Jany 1848

Cat.No.	Denom.	Date	VG	F	VF	EF	Unc
12-10-02	$4(£1)	1845	700.	800.	1,200.	-	-
12-10-04P	$4(£1)	1848				PROOF	400.
12-10-06P	$5(£1.5)	1848				PROOF	400.

12.   "HAMILTON" BRANCH ISSUE

DEIGNS AND COLOURS
The branch name is engraved at the lower left centre and vertically at the ends.

55-12-12-04
- **$4 (£1) Face Design:** Reclining allegorical female/three seated allegorical women/seated Indian
- **Colour:** Black with no tint
- **Back Design:** Plain

55-12-12-08
- **$5 (£1.5.0) Face Design:** Bank Crest/seated allegorical female with one arm on beehive and the other around "Commerce" figure/ Queen Victoria on throne
- **Colour:** Black with no tint
- **Back Design:** Plain

55-12-12-12
- **$10 (£2.10) Face Design:** "Agriculture" figure in circle/sheep, plough in foreground/beehive/commerce figures
- **Colour:** Black with no tint
- **Back Design:** Plain

Photo Not Available

55-12-12-14P
- **$50 (£12.10) Face Design:** Seated "Justice" figure, fasces/Royal Arms/"Commerce" figure with lute
- **Colour:** Black with no tint
- **Back Design:** Plain

IMPRINT
Perkins, Bacon & Co., London

ISSUE DATING
Engraved
1st Novr 1845
1st Novr 1852
May 1, 1853
May 1, 1855
1st March 1856

PROTECTOR
- **Issued Notes of the 1850's:** Blue "word" across mock coins on the face only
- **$4 (£1) 1852:** Green "word" on face and back

THE BANK OF BRITISH NORTH AMERICA

OVERPRINT
$4 (£1) 1855: "PARIS" in blue

Cat.No.	Denom.	Date	VG	F	VF	EF	Unc
12-12-02	$4(£1)	1845	700.	800.	1,200.	-	-
12-12-04	$4(£1)	1852	700.	800.	1,200.	-	-
12-12-06	$4(£1)	1855	700.	800.	1,200.	-	-
12-12-08	$5(£1.5)	1845	700.	800.	1,200.	-	-
12-12-10	$5(£1.5)	1855	700.	800.	1,200.	-	-
12-12-12	$10(£2.10)	1853	700.	800.	1,200.	-	-
12-12-14P	$50(£12.10)	1856			PROOF	400.	

14. "KINGSTON ISSUE"

The Branch name is engraved at the lower left centre and vertically inside the right and left vignettes.

DESIGNS AND COLOURS

55-12-14-08
- **$4 Face Design:** Seated Indian/reclining "Commerce" figure/seated woman with cornucopia, corn and cattle in background
- **Colour:** Black with no tint
- **Back Design:** Plain

55-12-14-12
- **$5 Face Design:** Queen Victoria on throne/two seated allegorical women holding hands/seated Indian
- **Colour:** Black, with no tint
- **Back Design:** Plain

Photo Not Available

55-12-14-14P
- **$10 Face Design:** View of city and harbour/two seated allegorical women/Bank Crest
- **Colour:** Back with no tint
- **Back Design:** Plain

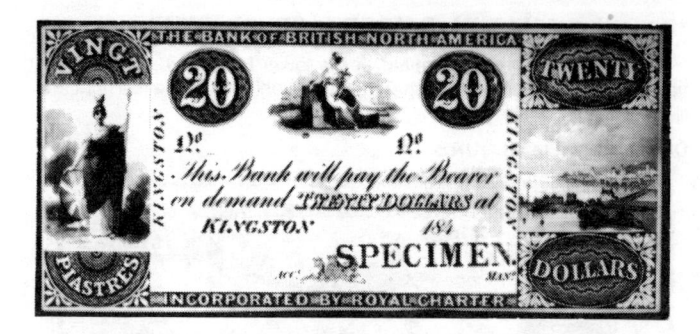

55-12-14-16P
- **$20 Face Design:** Britannia/small seated "Commerce" figure/view of city and harbour
- **Colour:** Black with no tint
- **Back Design:** Plain

55-12-14-18P
- **$50 Face Design:** Small "Commerce", Britannia and "Agriculture" figures in circle/seated allegorical woman with cornucopia and balance/Indians, canoe, teepee
- **Colour:** Black with no tint
- **Back Design:** Plain

IMPRINT
Perkins, Bacon & Co. London
Perkins, Bacon & Petch, London

ISSUE DATING
Partially Engraved:__18__:
Remainder of date added letterpress with serial numbers: __18__: Feb 1, 1852
Entire date added letterpress with seral numbers:
_____: July 1, 1853

Engraved
$4: 1st July 1853
$5: Aug. 4, 1852

PROTECTOR
Some Notes of the 1850's: Green "word" on face and back

Cat.No.	Denom.	Date	Variety	VG	F	VF	EF	Unc
12-14-02P	$4	184-				PROOF	400.	
12-14-02	$4	1852		700.	800.	1,200.	-	-
12-14-06P	$4	1853	No ptr.*			PROOF	400.	
12-14-08	$4	1853	Green ptr.	700.	800.	1,200.	-	-
12-14-10P	$5	184-				PROOF	400.	
12-14-12	$5	1852		700.	800.	1,200.	-	-
12-14-14P	$10	184-				PROOF	400.	
12-14-16P	$20	184-				PROOF	400.	
12-14-18P	$50	184-				PROOF	400.	

THE BANK OF BRITISH NORTH AMERICA

16. "LONDON" ISSUE

The branch name is engraved at the lower left and vertically inside the right and left end vignettes.

DESIGNS AND COLOURS

55-12-16-02P
$4 (£1) **Face Design:** Seated Britannia with lion and anchor/ Bank Crest/seated "Justice" figure, fasces
Colour: Black with no tint
Back Design: Plain

55-12-16-06
$5 (25s) **Face Design:** Sheep, plough in foreground/three seated allegorical women/small Britannia seated on shell in water
Colour: Black with no tint
Back Design: Plain

55-12-16-08
$10 (50s) **Face Design:** "Agriculture" figure with cornucopia/seated "Agriculture" figure with cornucopia/woman seated with hand on harp
Colour: Black with no tint
Back Design: Plain

55-12-16-10P
$20 **Face Design:** Commerce figure and ship/commerce allegory/Victoria on throne
Colour: Black with no tint
Back Design: Plain

55-12-16-12P
$50 **Face Design:** Agricultural figure/harvest figure/ commerce figure
Colour: Black with no tint
Back Design: Plain

IMPRINT
Perkins, Bacon & Co London.

ISSUE DATING
Engraved
1st March 1854
1st Jan'y 1855
1st Jan 1856

PROTECTOR
Issued Notes: Blue "word" on mock coins on face only

OVERPRINT
1856: "NAPANEE" in red

Cat.No.	Denom.	Date	VG	F	VF	EF	Unc
12-16-02P	$4(£1)	1854				PROOF	400.
12-16-04	$4(£1)	1856	700.	800.	1,200.	-	-
12-16-06	$5(25s)	1854	700.	800.	1,200.		
12-16-08	$10(50s)	1854	700.	800.	1,200.	-	-
12-16-10P	$20(£5)	1855				PROOF	400.
12-16-12P	$50(£12.10)	1855				PROOF	400.

THE BANK OF BRITISH NORTH AMERICA

17. MONTREAL "BYTOWN" AGENCY ISSUE

The branch name is engraved at the lower left centre. The agency name is engraved at the upper centre and vertically inside the left and right vignettes.

DESIGN AND COLOURS

55-12-17-06P
  $4 (20s) Face Design: Queen Victoria on throne/cherubs/agriculture figure, cornucopia
       Colour: Black with no tint
  Back Design: Plain

IMPRINT
  Perkins, Bacon & Co., London

ISSUE DATING
  Engraved
  1st May 1847

Cat.No.	Denom.	Date	VG	F	VF	EF	Unc
12-17-06P	$4(20s)	1847				PROOF	400.

18. "MONTREAL" ISSUE

The branch name is engraved at the lower left and vertically inside the right and left end vignettes.

DESIGN AND COLOURS

55-12-18-22
  $4 (20s) Face Design: Seated Indian/sailing ship/seated "Commerce" figure in crowned frame
       Colour: Black with no tint
  Back Design: Plain

55-12-18-52
  $5 (£1.5) Face Design: Brock's monument/sailing ship/Queen Victoria on throne
       Colour: Black with no tint
  Back Design: Plain

55-12-18-62P
  $10 (£2.10) Face Design: Indian camp/seated "Commerce" figure/view of harbour entrance
       Colour: Black with no tint
  Back Design: Plain

55-12-18-72P
  $20 (£5) Face Design: View of Montreal buildings/three allegorical women/monument, houses
       Colour: Black with no tint
  Back Design: Plain

55-12-18-82P
$50 (£12.10) **Face Design:** Bank Crest/steamship/
view of Montreal buildings
Colour: Back with no tint

Back Design: Plain

IMPRINT
Perkins, Bacon & Petch, London

ISSUE DATING
Partially Engraved __18__:
$4 (20s) 1841: Jan. 1
1847: Jan. 1

Partially Engraved __184__:
$4 (20s) & $5 (£1.5) 1841: Jan. 1
$20 (£5) 1847: Jan 1

Engraved
1st Decr 1851
1st Decr 1852
1st Jany 1854

PROTECTOR
1852 & 1854 Green "word" on face and back
Green "word" on mock coins, face only

OVERPRINT
$4 (20s): "BYTOWN" in black and red
$4 (20s): "PARIS" in black and red
$20 (£5): "PAYABLE IN OTTAWA" in red

Cat.No.	Denom.	Date	VG	F	VF	EF	Unc
12-18-02	$4(20s)	1841	700.	800.	1,200.	-	-
12-18-12	$4(20s)	1847	700.	800.	1,200.	-	-
12-18-22	$4(20s)	1851	700.	800.	1,200.	-	-
12-18-32	$4(20s)	1852	700.	800.	1,200.	-	-
12-18-42	$5(£1.5)	1841	700.	800.	1,200.	-	-
12-18-52	$5(£1.5)	1854	700.	800.	1,200.	-	-
12-18-62P	$10(£2.10)	184-				PROOF	400.
12-18-72P	$20(£5)	184-				PROOF	400.
12-18-72	$20(£5)	1847	700.	800.	1,200.	-	-
12-18-82P	$50(£12.10)	184-				PROOF	400.

20. "QUEBEC" ISSUE

The branch name is engraved at the lower left and vertically at the ends.

DESIGNS AND COLOURS

55-12-20-04
$4 (20s) **Face Design:** Seated "Commerce" figure in crowned frame/—/seated Indian
Colour: Black with no tint

Back Design: Plain

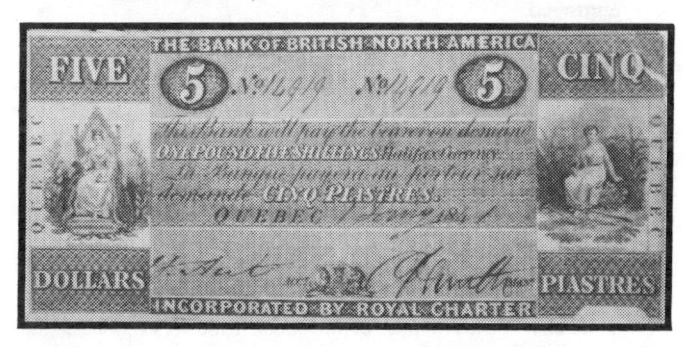

55-12-20-06
$5 (£1.5) **Face Design:** Queen Victoria on throne/—/seated "Commerce" figure with sickle, field in background
Colour: Black with no tint

Back Design: Plain

55-12-20-08
$10 (£2.10) **Face Design:** Sheep and plough/—/sailing ship
Colour: Black with no tint

Back Design: Plain

THE BANK OF BRITISH NORTH AMERICA

55-12-20-10P
 £5 Face Design: Falls/—/Britannia
 Colour: Black with no tint
 Back Design: Plain

IMPRINT
 Perkins, Bacon, Petch, London

ISSUE DATING
 Partially Engraved ___18___:
 $4:
 $5 & $10 1841: 1 Jany
 Partially Engraved ___184__:
 Engraved
 1 Jany, 1853

Cat.No.	Denom.	Date	VG	F	VF	EF	Unc
12-20-02P	$4(20s)	18__				PROOF	400.
12-20-04	$4(20s)	1853	700.	800.	1,200.	-	-
12-20-06	$5(£1.5)	1841	700.	800.	1,200.	-	-
12-20-08	$10(£2.10)	1841	700.	800.	1,200	-	-
12-20-10P	$20(£5)	184_				PROOF	400.

22. "ST. JOHN, NEW BRUNSWICK" ISSUE

The branch name is engraved at the lower left and vertically inside the right and left end vignettes.

DESIGNS AND COLOURS

55-12-22-02
 $1 (5s) Face Design: Seated "Justice" figure, fasces/
  "Bank Crest/Commerce" figure with lute
  "1" over "Dollar" in oval left,
  "5" over "Shillings" in oval right
 Colour: Black with no tint
 Back Design: Plain

55-12-22-04
 $1 (5s) Face Design: Seated "Justice" figure, fasces/
  Bank Crest/Commerce" figure with lute
 Colour: Black with no tint
 Back Design: Plain

55-12-22-06
 $2 (10s) Face Design: Small Britannia seated on shell in water/
  small seated "Commerce" figure/small
  "Commerce", Britannia and "Agriculture"
  figures in circle
 Colour: Black with no tint
 Back Design: Plain

55-12-22-08P
 $4 (£1) Face Design: Bank Crest/ship/woman with anchor and
  beehive
 Colour: Black with no tint
 Back Design: Plain

55-12-22-12
$5 (£1.5) **Face Design:** Bank Crest/ship/woman with anchor and beehive
Colour: Black with no tint
Back Design: Plain

Photo Not Available

55-12-22-14P
$20 (£5) **Face Design:** Queen Victoria (Chalon portrait)/two allegorical women/reclining women with ship in the distance
Colour: Black with no tint
Back Design: Plain

Photo Not Available

55-12-22-16P
$40 (£10) **Face Design:** Queen Victoria (Chalon portrait)/Bank Crest/—
Colour: Black with no tint
Back Design: Plain

IMPRINT
Perkins, Bacon & Co. London

ISSUE DATING
Engraved
1st Jany. 1853
2nd Jany. 1954
1st Decr. 1859
1st Decr. 1862
1st Sept. 1869
2nd Jany. 1871

PROTECTOR
Issued Notes: Green "word" on mock coins on face only

OVERPRINT
$5: "V V" in red

Cat.No.	Denom.	Date	VG	F	VF	EF	Unc
12-22-01	$1(5s)	1854				PROOF	500.
12-22-02	$1(5s)	1859	600.	850.	1,275	-	-
12-22-04	$1(5s)	1862	600.	850.	1,275	-	-
12-22-06	$2(10s)	1854	600.	850.	1,275	-	-
12-22-08P	$4(£1)	1853				PROOF	500.
12-22-10P	$4(£1)	1871				PROOF	500.
12-22-12	$5(£1.5)	1862	600.	850.	1,275	-	-
12-22-13P	$5(£1.5)	1869				PROOF	500.
12-22-14P	$20(£5)	18__				PROOF	500.
12-22-16P	$40(£10)	18__				PROOF	500.

24. "ST. STEPHEN NEW BRUNSWICK" ISSUE

The branch name is engraved at the lower left and vertically inside the right and left end vignettes.

DESIGNS AND COLOURS

55-12-24-02P
$4 (£1) **Face Design:** Bank Crest/ship/woman with anchor and beehive
Colour: Black with no tint
Back Design: Plain

IMPRINT
Perkins, Bacon & Petch, London

ISSUE DATING
Engraved
12th Augt 1872

Cat.No.	Denom.	Date			Unc
12-24-02P	$4(£1)	1872		PROOF	500.

26. "TORONTO" DOLLAR ISSUE

The branch name is engraved at the centre left and vertically at the ends.

DESIGNS AND COLOURS

Photo Not Available

55-12-26-02P
$4 **Face Design:** Unknown
Colour: Black with no tint
Back Design: Plain

55-12-26-04P
$5 **Face Design:** River, cliffs & tower/—/seated "Commerce" figure in crowned frame
Colour: Black with no tint
Back Design: Plain

THE BANK OF BRITISH NORTH AMERICA

55-12-26-06P
  $10 **Face Design:** Canadian Niagara Falls/—/Queen Victoria on throne
     Colour: Black with no tint
  Back Design: Plain

55-12-26-08P
  $20 **Face Design:** Bank Crest/—/Canadian Niagara Falls
     Colour: Black with no tint
  Back Design: Plain

55-12-26-10P
  $50 **Face Design:** Indian camp/—/Beehive with flowers
     Colour: Black with no tint
  Back Design: Plain

IMPRINT
  Perkins, Bacon & Petch, London.

ISSUE DATING
  Partially Engraved__184__:

Cat.No.	Denom.	Date		Unc
12-26-02P	$4	184-	PROOF	400.
12-26-04P	$5	184-	PROOF	400.
12-26-06P	$10	184-	PROOF	400.
12-26-08P	$20	184-	PROOF	400.
12-26-10P	$50	184-	PROOF	400.

28. "TORONTO" DOLLAR/ POUNDS AND SHILLINGS ISSUE

The branch name is engraved at the centre left and verticaly at the ends.

DESIGNS AND COLOURS

55-12-28-04

55-12-28-06P
  $5 (25s) **Face Design:** River, cliffs & tower/—/seated "commerce" figure in crowded frame
     Colour: Black with no tint
  Back Design: Plain

Photo Not Available

  $5 (25s) **Face Design:** Seated "commerce" figure/—/Bank Crest
     Colour: Black with no tint
  Back Design: Plain

Photo Not Available

55-12-28-10
  $10 (50s) **Face Design:** Canadian Niagara Falls/—/Queen Victoria on throne
     Colour: Black with no tint
  Back Design: Plain

ISSUE DATING
  Engraved
   1st Jany 1846
   1st Novr 1852
   Unknown, 1864
   Jan 4, 1865

Cat.No.	Denom.	Date	VG	F	VF	EF	Unc
12-28-02P	$4(£1)	1846				PROOF	350.
12-28-04	$4(£1)	1852	600.	800.	1,200	-	-
12-28-06P	$5(£1/5s)(25s)	1846				PROOF	350.
12-28-08P	$5(25s)	1865				PROOF	350.
12-28-10	$10(50s)	1864	600.	800.	1,200	-	-

30

55-13 LARGE ROYAL CREST ISSUE
1856

Notes of these issues have a large royal crest at the top centre and a complete frame.

10. HAMILTON "DUNDAS" AGENCY ISSUE
1856

The branch name is engraved at lower left of centre. The agency names are engraved at upper right and vertically inside the right and left vignettes.

DESIGN AND COLOURS

55-13-10-06
$5 (£1.5) Face Design: Britannia/Royal Crest/ seated "Commerce" figure in crowned frame
  Colour: Back with no tint

  Back Design: Plain

IMPRINT
  Perkins, Bacon & Co., London

ISSUE DATING
  Engraved
  1st March 1856

Cat.No.	Denom.	Date	VG	F	VF	EF	Unc
13-10-06	$5(£1.5)	1856				PROOF	500.

14. "HAMILTON" ISSUE

The branch name is engraved at lower left of centre and vertically inside the right and left vignettes.

DESIGNS AND COLOURS

55-13-14-20P
$50 (£12.10) Face Design: Seated "Justice" figure, fasces/Royal Crest/"Commerce" figure with lute
  Colour: Black with no tint

  Back Design: Plain

IMPRINT
  Perkins, Bacon & Co., London

ISSUE DATING
  Engraved
  1st March 1856

Cat.No.	Denom.	Date	VG	F	VF	EF	Unc
13-14-20P	$50(£12.10)	1856				PROOF	500.

26. "ST. JOHN, NEW BRUNSWICK" ISSUE

The branch name is engraved at the lower left of centre and vertically inside the right and left vignettes.

DESIGNS AND COLOURS

55-13-26-20P
$50 Face Design: Woman standing, cornucopia/Royal Crest/ Seated female "Commerce figure" with cask and bale, buildings
  Colour: Black with no tint

  Back Design: Plain

IMPRINT
  Perkins, Bacon & Co. London

ISSUE DATING
  Engraved
  1st September 1866
  1st January 1870

Cat.No.	Denom.	Date	Unc
13-26-20P	$50	1866	PROOF 500.
13-26-24P	$50	1870	PROOF 500.

55-14. "NO FRAME" $1 and $2 ISSUES
1852 - 1868

There are different designs for each place of issue. Notes of these issues lack a frame.

IMPRINT
  Perkins, Bacon & Co. London.

ISSUE DATING
  Engraved
  1st December 1852
  1st Decr, 1852
  1st January 1856
  1st Jany, 1856

THE BANK OF BRITISH NORTH AMERICA

2. "BRANTFORD" ISSUE

DESIGNS AND COLOURS
  $1: The branch names are located at the upper right and lower left.
  $2: The branch names are located at the lower left and one or two ovals at the top.

55-14-02-02
  $1 (5s) Face Design: Queen Victoria/Bank Crest/Prince Albert
  Colour: Black with no tint
  Back Design: Plain

55-14-02-04
  $1 (5s) Face Design: Similar to Toronto Issue, see 55-14-16.

Photo Not Available

55-14-02-08
  $2 (10s) Face Design: Queen Victoria/
  Bank Crest/Prince Albert
  Colour: Black with no tint
  Back Design: Plain

PROTECTOR
  1852: Red "numeral" on the face only on some notes.
  1856: Blue "word" on mock coins on the face only.

Cat.No.	Denom.	Date	VG	F	VF	EF	Unc
14-02-02	$1(5s)	1852	800.	1,200.	-	-	-
14-02-04	$1(5s)	1856	800.	1,200.	-	-	-
14-02-08	$2(10s)	1856	800.	1,200.	-	-	-

4. "HAMILTON" ISSUE

DESIGNS AND COLOURS
Similar to Brantford Issue, see 55-14-02.

55-14-04-06

PROTECTOR
  1852: Blue "numeral" on the face only
  1852: Blue "word" on mock coins on the face only
  1856: Blue "word" on mock coins on the face only

Cat.No.	Denom.	Date	Variety	VG	F	VF	EF	Unc
14-04-02	$1(5s)	1852	Blue "1 1"	600.	800.	1,200.	-	-
14-04-04	$1(5s)	1852	Blue "ONE"	600.	800.	1,200.	-	-
14-04-06	$1(5s)	1856		600.	800.	1,200.	-	-
14-04-10	$2(10s)	1856	Blue "TWO"	600.	800.	1,200.	-	-

6. "KINGSTON" ISSUE

DESIGNS AND COLOURS
Similar to Brantford Issue, see 55-14-02.

55-14-06-04

55-14-06-06P

PROTECTOR
  Blue "word" on mock coins on the face only

Cat.No.	Denom.	Date	VG	F	VF	EF	Unc
14-06-04	$1(5s)	1856	600.	800.	1,200.	-	-
14-06-06P	$2(10s)	no date				PROOF	400.
14-06-08	$2(10s)	1856	600.	800.	1,200.	-	-

8. "LONDON" ISSUE

DESIGN AND COLOURS
Similar to Brantford Issue, see 55-14-02.

Photo Not Available

PROTECTOR
Blue "word" on mock coins on the face only

Cat.No.	Denom.	Date	VG	F	VF	EF	Unc
14-08-04	$1(5s)	1856	600.	800.	1,200.	-	-
14-08-08	$2(10s)	no date				PROOF	400.

10. "MONTREAL" ISSUES

DESIGNS AND COLOURS
1852: The branch names are located at the upper right and lower left.
1856: The branch names are located at the top centre and lower left.

DESIGNS AND COLOURS

55-14-10-04
$1 (5s) Face Design: Bank Crest/—/Royal Arms
Colours: Black with no tint
Back Design: Plain

55-14-10-04a
$1 (5s) Face Design: Bank Crest/—/Royal Arms
Colour: Black with no tint
Back Design: Plain

55-14-10-06
$2 (10s) Face Design: Royal Arms/—/Bank Crest
Colour: Black with no tint
Back Design: Plain

55-14-10-08
$2 (10s) Face Design: Royal Arms/—/Bank Crest
Colour: Black with no tint
Back Design: Plain

IMPRINT
Perkins, Bacon & Co. London.

ISSUE DATING
Engraved
1st December 1852
1st January 1856

PROTECTOR
1852: Red "numeral" on the face only
1856: Blue "word" on mock coins face only

OVERPRINT
$2 1852: "BYTOWN" in black in the centre and at the end
$1 1856: "OTTAWA" in blue in the centre and vertically inside right and left vignettes.
$2 1856: "OTTAWA" in blue in the centre and vertically inside right and left vignettes. "PAYABLE IN OTTAWA" in red

Cat.No.	Denom.	Date	Variety	VG	F	VF	EF	Unc
14-10-02	$1(5s)	1852		600.	800.	1,200.	-	-
14-10-04	$1(5s)	1856		600.	800.	1,200.	-	-
14-10-04a	$1(5s)	1856	o/p Ottawa	600.	800.	1,200.	-	-
14-10-06	$2(10s)	1852		600.	800.	1,200.	-	-
14-10-08	$2(10s)	1856		600.	800.	1,200.	-	-
14-10-08a	$2(10s)	1856	o/p Ottawa	600.	800.	1,200.	-	-

THE BANK OF BRITISH NORTH AMERICA

12. "QUEBEC" ISSUE

DESIGN AND COLOURS
Similar to Montreal Issue, see 55-14-10.

55-14-12-04

55-14-12-05P

55-14-12-08

ISSUE DATING
Engraved
1st December 1852
1st January 1856

PROTECTOR
1852: Red "numeral" on the face only
1856: Blue "word" on mock coins on the face only

OVERPRINT
$1: "PAYABLE IN OTTAWA" in red

Cat.No.	Denom.	Date	VG	F	VF	EF	Unc
14-12-02	$1(5s)	1852			NOT CONFIRMED		
14-12-04	$1(5s)	1856	600.	800.	1,200.	-	-
14-12-05	$2(10s)	no date			PROOF	400.	
14-12-06	$2(10s)	1852	600.	800.	1,200.	-	-
14-12-08	$2 (10s)	1856	600.	800.	1,200.	-	-

14. "ST. JOHN, NEW BRUNSWICK" ISSUE

DESIGNS AND COLOURS
$1: The branch names are engraved at the upper right and lower left.
$2: The branch names are engraved at the lower left and twice at the top.

ISSUE DATING
Engraved
31 August 1866
15 July 1868
1 December 1868

55-14-14-02
1868 $1 Face Design: Queen Victoria (Chalon portrait)/
Bank Crest/Prince Consort
Colour: Black with no tint
Back Design: Plain

55-14-14-04
1868 $1 Face Design: Queen Victoria (Chalon portrait)/
Royal Arms/Prince Consort
Colour: Black with no tint
Back Design: Plain

55-14-14-08
$2 Face Design: Seated Indian/small Royal Arms/
Lion, Britannia, 2 in shield over anchor
Colour: Black with no tint

Cat.No.	Denom.	Date	VG	F	VF	EF	Unc
14-14-02	$1	1866	700.	900.	1,400.	-	-
14-14-04	$1	1868	700.	900.	1,400.	-	-
14-14-08	$2	1868	700.	900.	1,400.	-	-

THE BANK OF BRITISH NORTH AMERICA

16. "TORONTO" ISSUE
DESIGNS AND COLOURS

55-14-16-04
$1 (5s) Face Design: Queen Victoria (Chalon portrait) in oval/
Bank Arms/Prince Consort in oval
Colour: Black with no tint
Back Design: Plain

55-14-16-08
$2 (10S) Face Design: Queen Victoria (Chalon portrait) in oval/
Bank Arms/Prince Consort in oval
Colour: Black with no tint
Back Design: Plain

ISSUE DATING
 Engraved
  1st Jany 1856
PROTECTOR
 1852: Red "numeral" on face only
 1856: Blue "word" on mock coins on face only

Cat.No.	Denom.	Date	VG	F	VF	EF	Unc
14-16-02	$1(5s)	1852	600.	800.	1,000.	-	-
14-16-04	$1(5s)	1856	600.	800.	1,000.	-	-
14-16-08	$2(10s)	1856	600.	800.	1,000.	-	-

18. "VICTORIA VANCOUVER'S ISLAND" ISSUE
The branch names are engraved at the lower left and twice at the top.
DESIGNS AND COLOURS

55-14-18-02P
$1 Face Design: Queen Victoria (Chalon portrait) in oval/
seated Britannia with lion at left/—/counter
Colour: Black with no tint
Back Design: Plain

55-14-18-14R
$2 Face Design: Seated Indian/seated "Commerce" figure/
Britannia, counter
Colour: Black with no tint
Back Design: Plain

IMPRINT
 Perkins, Bacon & Co. London
ISSUE DATING
 Partially Engraved:__18__:
 Engraved
  1st December 1859
  2nd January 1860
  Dec. 2 1867
PROTECTOR
 Issued and Specimen Notes: Green "word" on mock coins on face and back

Cat.No.	Denom.	Date	VG	F	VF	EF	Unc
14-18-02P	$1	185				PROOF	500.
14-18-04	$1	1859	-	-	2,500.	3,500.	-
14-18-04	$1	1859	2,000.	2,500.	-	-	-
14-18-10P	$1	1867				PROOF	500.
14-18-14	$2	1860	-	-	2,500.	3,500.	-

THE BANK OF BRITISH NORTH AMERICA

55-16. COMMON DENOMINATION DESIGN PAYABLE AT SEPARATE BRANCHES
1859 - 1875

DESIGNS AND COLOURS

$4 Face Design: Seated Justice" figure/Royal Crest/ seated woman with sheaf and sickle
Colour: Black with no tint

Back Design: Plain

$5 Face Design: Seated Britannia, lion/Royal Crest/ Queen Victoria on throne
Colour: Black with no tint

Back Design: Plain

$10 Face Design: —/Royal Crest/—
Colour: Black with no tint

Back Design: Plain

$20 Face Design: sheep, beehive and tools
Colour: Black with no tint

Back Design: Plain

$20 Face Design: —/radiant Royal Crest/—
Colour: Black with no tint

Back Design: Plain

$50 Face Design: Seated woman with lute/Royal Crest/ seated "Commerce" figure
Colour: Black with no tint

Back Design: Plain

2. "BRANTFORD" ISSUE

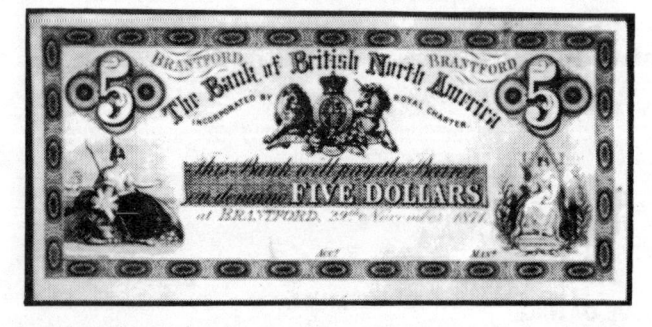

55-16-02-02

55-16-02-04P

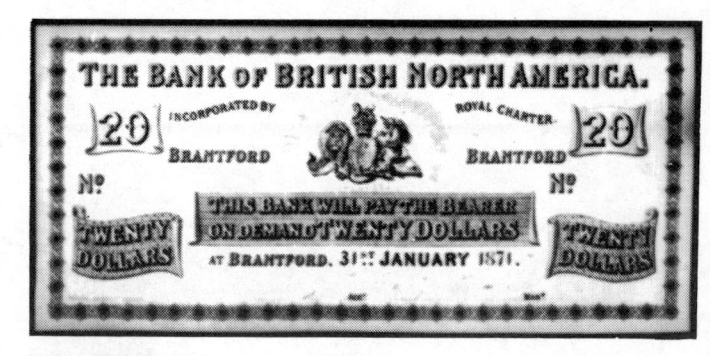

55-16-02-06P

ISSUE DATING
Engraved
$5: 31st January 1871
 29th November 1871
$5, $10 & $20: 31st January 1871

Cat.No.	Denom.	Date	VG	F	VF	EF	Unc
16-02-02	$5	1871	350.	500.	750.	-	-
16-02-04P	$10	1871				PROOF	350.
16-02-06P	$20*	1871				PROOF	450.

4. "HALIFAX, NOVA SCOTIA" ISSUE

55-16-04-14P

55-16-04-31

55-16-04-32P

36

THE BANK OF BRITISH NORTH AMERICA

55-16-04-46P

55-16-04-62P

IMPRINT
Perkins, Bacon & Co. London.

ISSUE DATING
Engraved

$4: 31 January 1871
Dec. 1, 1874

$5: 1st July 1870
2nd Jany 1871
1st July 1871
1st Novr 1871
1st Dec'r 1874
Dec. 1, 1874

$10: 1st July 1870
1st July 1871
July 1, 1871
Dec. 1, 1874

$20: 24th May 1865
1st July 1871
1 Nov'r 1871
1 Dec'r 1874

PROTECTOR
Issued Notes: Green "word" on mock coins face only

OVERPRINT
$5 1st July, 1871: "HALIFAX" at the ends and "PAYABLE IN DOMINION CURRENCY" across the top, both in red
$5 1st Novr. 1871: "Canada Currency" at both end in red

Cat.No.	Denom.	Date	Variety	VG	F	VF	EF	Unc
16-04-14P	$4	1872					PROOF	500.
16-04-18P	$4	1874					PROOF	500.
16-04-26P	$5	1870					PROOF	350.
16-04-30P	$5	1871	(2nd Jan)				PROOF	350.
16-04-31P	$5	1871	(1st July)	800.	1,000.	1,500.	-	-
16-04-32P	$5	1871	(1st Novr)				PROOF	350.
16-04-38P	$5	1874					PROOF	350.
16-04-46P	$10	1870					PROOF	400.
16-04-50P	$10	1871					PROOF	400.
16-04-58P	$10	1874					PROOF	400.
16-04-62P	$20*	1865					PROOF	450.
16-04-70P	$20	1871					PROOF	450.

6. "HAMILTON" ISSUE

55-16-06-01P

55-16-06-02P

55-16-06-06

THE BANK OF BRITISH NORTH AMERICA

ISSUE DATING
 Engraved
  $4: 1st June 1874
  $5: 1st June 1874
     May 1, 1875
  $10: 1st June 1874

Cat.No.	Denom.	Date	VG	F	VF	EF	Unc
16-06-01P	$4	1874				PROOF	300.
16-06-02P	$5	1874				PROOF	300.
16-06-04P	$5	1875				PROOF	300.
16-06-06	$10	1874	600.	800.	1,200.	-	-

8. "KINGSTON" ISSUE

55-16-08-02

55-16-08-08P

55-16-08-10P

ISSUE DATING
 Engraved
  $4: May 4, 1872, 1st May 1875
  $5: 1st May 1875
  $10: 6th May, 1872, 1 May 1875

Cat.No.	Denom.	Date	VG	F	VF	EF	Unc
16-08-02	$4	1872	600.	800.	1,200.	-	-
16-08-04	$4	1875				PROOF	300.
16-08-08P	$5	1875				PROOF	300.
16-08-10P	$10	1872				PROOF	350.
16-08-12P	$10	1875				PROOF	350.

10. "LONDON, CANADA WEST; LONDON ONTARIO" ISSUE

55-16-10-06P

55-16-10-10P

55-16-10-20P

55-16-10-30P

ISSUE DATING
Engraved
- **$4:** 3rd August 1875
- **$5:** 23rd April 1866
  1st August 1872
  3rd August 1875
- **$10:** 24th May, 1866
- **$20:** 3rd August, 1875

Cat.No.	Denom.	Date	VG	F	VF	EF	Unc
16-10-06P	$4	1875				PROOF	400.
16-10-10P	$5	1866				PROOF	300.
16-10-12P	$5	1872				PROOF	300.
16-10-14	$5	1875	500.	700.	900.	-	-
16-10-20P	$10	1866				PROOF	350.
16-10-30P	$20	1875				PROOF	450.

12. "MONTREAL" ISSUE

Photo Not Available

55-16-12-08

55-16-12-14P

55-16-12-22

55-16-12-30P

55-16-12-40P

ISSUE DATING
Engraved
- **$4:** Dec. 1, 1873
- **$5:** 1st August 1870
  8th April 1872
- **$10:** 30th November 1865
  1 August 1870
- **$20:** 1st December 1865
- **$50:** 1st January 1866

Cat.No.	Denom.	Date	VG	F	VF	EF	Unc
16-12-08	$4	1873	600.	800.	1,200.	-	-
16-12-14P	$5	1870				PROOF	300.
16-12-16P	$5	1872				PROOF	300.
16-12-20P	$10	1865				PROOF	350.
16-12-22	$10	1870	600.	800.	1,200.	-	-
16-12-30P	$20*	1865				PROOF	450.
16-12-40P	$50	1866				PROOF	450.

13. "NAPANEE" ISSUE

55-16-13-10

ISSUE DATING
Engraved
- **$4:** 1st Dec'r 1874

Cat.No.	Denom	Date	VG	F	VF	EF	Unc
16-13-10	$4	1874				PROOF	400.

THE BANK OF BRITISH NORTH AMERICA

14. "OTTAWA" ISSUE

55-16-14-08P

55-16-14-12P

55-16-14-24P

55-16-14-34P

ISSUE DATING
Engraved
- **$4:** 1st Dec'r 1871
  1st Decr 1873
- **$5:** 10th August 1865
  31st January 1871
  May 1, 1872
- **$10:** 1st September 1865
  31st January 1871
- **$20:** 23rd April 1867
  31st January 1871

OVERPRINT
1873: "ARNPRIOR" in blue at the ends

Cat.No.	Denom.	Date	VG	F	VF	EF	Unc
16-14-04	$4	1871				PROOF	400.
16-14-08	$4	1873	600.	800.	1,200.	-	-
16-14-12P	$5	1865				PROOF	300.
16-14-14P	$5	1871				PROOF	300.
16-14-16P	$5	1872				PROOF	300.
16-14-22P	$10	1865				PROOF	350.
16-14-24P	$10	1871				PROOF	350.
16-14-34P	$20*	1871				PROOF	450.

16. "QUEBEC" ISSUE

55-16-16-08

55-16-16-24P

ISSUE DATING
Engraved
- **$4:** 22 Nov'r 1871
- **$5:** 22nd Nov'r 1871
- **$10:** 22nd Nov'r 1871
- **$20:** 22nd Nov'r 1871
- **$50:** 22nd Nov'r 1871

Cat.No.	Denom.	Date	VG	F	VF	EF	Unc
16-16-08	$4	1871	600.	800.	1,200.	-	-
16-16-12P	$5	1871				PROOF	300.
16-16-16P	$10	1871				PROOF	350.
16-16-20P	$20	1871				PROOF	450.
16-16-24P	$50	1871				PROOF	550.

THE BANK OF BRITISH NORTH AMERICA

18.   "ST. JOHN, NEW BRUNSWICK" ISSUE

55-16-18-08

55-16-18-14P

Photo Not Available

55-16-18-20P

55-16-18-28P

55-16-18-34P

55-16-18-40P

ISSUE DATING
Engraved

- **$4:** 31 May, 1871
  31st May 1872
- **$5:** 1st May 1871
  1st May 1872
  1 Oct'r 1873
- **$10:** 1 Jan'r, 1870
  18th June, 1872
- **$20:** 1 Sept'r 1869
  29th April, 1871
  29th April, 1872
- **$50:** 1st Sept'r, 1866
  1st Jan'r, 1870
  18th June 1872

PROTECTOR
Green word on mock coins face only

OVERPRINT
$4 1872: "FREDERICTON" in blue at the ends
$4 1872: "MONCTON" in blue across the centre

Cat.No.	Denom.	Date	VG	F	VF	EF	Unc
16-18-06P	$4	1871				PROOF	500.
16-18-08	$4	1872	850.	1,200.	2,000.	-	-
16-18-14P	$5	1871				PROOF	350.
16-18-16P	$5	1872				PROOF	400.
16-18-17P	$5	1873				PROOF	400.
16-18-20P	$10	1870				PROOF	400.
16-18-24P	$10	1872				PROOF	450.
16-18-28P	$20	1869				PROOF	450.
16-18-30P	$20*	1871				PROOF	450.
16-18-32P	$20*	1872				PROOF	450.
16-18-34P	$50	1866				PROOF	500.
16-18-36P	$50	1870				PROOF	500.
16-18-40P	$50	1872				PROOF	500.

20.   "TORONTO" ISSUE

55-16-20-08P

41

THE BANK OF BRITISH NORTH AMERICA

55-16-20-14

55-16-20-22P

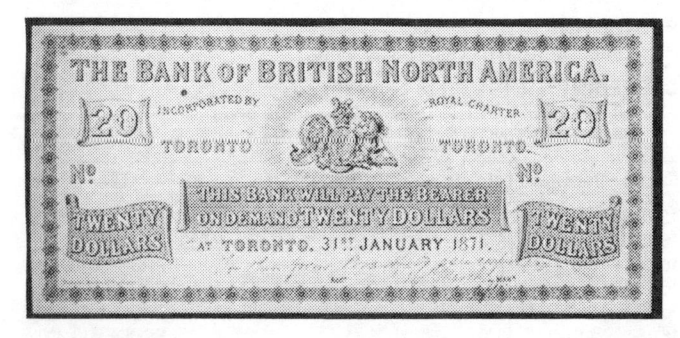

55-16-20-40P

ISSUE DATING
Engraved
- **$4:** 8th Decr. 1871
- **$5:** 4th January 1865
  1st January 1871
  31st January 1871
- **$10:** 23rd April, 1864
  31st January 1871
- **$20:** 31st January 1871

OVERPRINT
$5 1865: "DUNNVILLE" in red vertically near ends.

Cat.No.	Denom.	Date	VG	F	VF	EF	Unc
16-20-08P	$4	1871				PROOF	400.
16-20-14	$5	1865	450.	700.	1,000.	-	-
16-20-18P	$5	1871				PROOF	300.
16-20-22	$10	1864	600.	800	1,200.	-	-
16-20-28P	$10	1871				PROOF	350.
16-20-40P	$20	1871				PROOF	350.

22. "VICTORIA, VANCOUVER'S ISLAND" ISSUE

55-16-22-04R

55-16-22-20P

55-16-22-36R

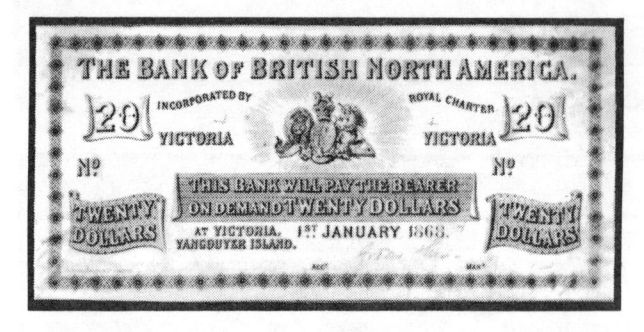

55-16-22-42P

Both varieties of the $20 face design are shown, but the individual branches used only one in their note issue.

THE BANK OF BRITISH NORTH AMERICA

ISSUE DATING
Remainder of date added letterpress:
$5__18__: 27th Septr. 1859
Engraved
$5: 23rd April 1867
$10: 3rd February 1860
Apr. 23, 1867
9th November 1867
16 October 1873
$20: 5th March 1860
1st January, 1868
16 October 1873

Cat.No.	Denom.	Date		VG	F	VF	EF	Unc
16-22-04	$5	1859		-	-	2,500.	3,500.	-
16-22-08P	$5	1867					PROOF	375.
16-22-16	$10	1860		-	-	2,500.	3,500.	-
16-22-18P	$10	1867	23rd April				PROOF	375.
16-22-20P	$10	1867	9th Nov				PROOF	375.
16-22-32P	$10	1873					PROOF	375.
16-22-36R	$20*	1860		-	-	2,500.	3,500.	-
16-22-42P	$20**	1868					PROOF	375.
16-22-48P	$20**	1873					PROOF	375.

24. BRANCH NAME TO BE FILLED IN MANUSCRIPT
1861 - 1872

DESIGNS AND COLOURS

55-16-24-02P
$100 Face Design: Cherubs/Royal Crest/cherubs
Colour: Black with no tint
Back Design: Plain

55-16-24-08P
$500 Face Design: Seated "Commerce" figure/Royal Crest/seated "Commerce" figure
Colour: Black with no tint
Back Design: Plain

55-16-24-10P
$1000 Face Design: Seated "Commerce" figures, cask, bale and ship/Royal Crest/Seated "Commerce" figures, cask, bale and ship
Colour: Black with no tint
Back Design: Plain

ISSUE DATING
Engraved
1 August 1861
15 August 1861
5 September 1861
15 August 1865
22 November, 1866
22 November 1871
Apr. 15, 1872
1 March 1875

PROTECTOR
Green word on face

Cat.No.	Denom.	Date		Unc
16-24-02P	$100	1861	PROOF	450.
16-24-03P	$100	1865	PROOF	450.
16-24-04P	$100	1866	PROOF	375.
16-24-05P	$100	1871	PROOF	375.
16-24-06P	$100	1872	PROOF	375.
16-24-07P	$100	1875	PROOF	375.
16-24-08P	$500	1861	PROOF	1,200.
16-24-10P	$1,000	1861	PROOF	1,500.

55-18. GENERAL ISSUES PAYABLE AT ALL BRANCHES
1876 - 1877

DESIGNS AND COLOURS

55-18-02
$4 Face Design: Seated Britannia, lion/Royal Crest Queen Victoria on throne
Colour: Black with green tint

THE BANK OF BRITISH NORTH AMERICA

Back Design: Lathework, counters and The Bank of British North America
Colour: Green

55-18-04
$5 Face Design: Seated Britannia and lion "Britannia No. 2"/ Royal Crest/Queen Victoria on throne
Colour: Black with green tint

Back Design: Lathework, counters; The Bank of British North America
Colour: Green

55-18-10
$10 Face Design: Seated Britannia, lion/Royal Crest/ Queen Victoria on throne
Colour: See varieties

Back Design: Lathework, counters and bank name
Colour: Green

55-18-14
$20 Face Design: Seated Britannia, lion/Royal Crest/ Queen Victoria on throne
Colour: Black with green tint

Back Design: Lathework, counters and bank name
Colour: Green

55-18-18
$50 Face Design: Seated Britannia, lion/Royal Crest/ Queen Victoria on throne
Colour: Black with green tint

THE BANK OF BRITISH NORTH AMERICA

Cat.No.	Denom.	Date	Variety	VG	F	VF	EF	Unc
18-02	$4	1877		1,000.	1,400.	2,200.	-	-
18-04	$5*	1877		500.	700.	950.	-	-
18-06P	$10	1876	Green tint				PROOF	500.
18-08	$10	1877	Green tint	700.	950.	1,400.	-	-
18-10	$10	1877	Red Brown tint	800.	1,150.	1,700.	-	-
18-12	$20	1877	Grindley,r.	700.	950.	1,400.	-	-
18-14	$20	1877	Stikeman,r.	700.	950.	1,400.	-	-
18-16	$50	1877	Grindley,r.	1,500.	2,000.	3,000.	-	-
18-18	$50	1877	Stikeman,r.	1,500.	2,000.	3,000.	-	-
18-20	$100	1877	Grindley,r.	1,500.	2,000.	3,000.	-	-
18-22	$100	1877	Stikeman,r.	1,500.	2,000.	3,000.	-	-

Back Design: Lathework, counters and bank name

55-18-22
$100 Face Design: Seated Britannia, lion/Royal Crest/ Queen Victoria on throne
Colour: Black with green tint

Back Design: Lathework, counters and bank name

IMPRINT
British American Bank Note Co. Montreal

SIGNATURES
	left	right
All denominations:	mss. various	mss. various
Some $20 - $100:	mss. various	engr. R.R. Grindley
	mss. various	engr. H. Stikeman

ISSUE DATING
Engraved
1st July, 1876
1st July 1877
3rd July, 1877

VARIETIES
$10 Face Colour: Black with green tint
$10 Face Colour: Blue with red-brown tint

55-20. $5 ISSUE OF 1884
DESIGNS AND COLOURS

55-20-02
$5 Face Design: —/Queen Victoria/—
Colour: Blue with orange tint (Five on mock coins)

55-20-04

Back Design: Lathework, counters and bank name
Colour: Black with orange tint

IMPRINT
Perkins, Bacon & Co. London. on face and back

SIGNATURES
left	right
mss. C. Deacon	mss. W. Collier

45

THE BANK OF BRITISH NORTH AMERICA

ISSUE DATING
 Engraved
  1st May 1884

Cat.No.	Denom.	Date		VG	F	VF	EF	Unc
20-02	$5	1884	Montreal	1,500.	2,000.	3,000.	-	-
20-04	$5	1884	Victoria			PROOF	500.	

55-22. ISSUE OF 1886 AND 1889
DESIGNS AND COLOURS

55-22-04
 $5 Face Design: Prince of Wales/Bank Crest/Queen Victoria
 Colour: Black with green tint

Back Design: lalthework, counters and bank name
Colour: Green

55-22-06
 $10 Face Design: St. George slaying dragon/
  Queen Victoria/Bank Crest
 Colour: Black with green tint

Back Design: lathework, counters, bank name and bank crest
Colour: Green

IMPRINT
 British American Bank Note Co. Ottawa
 British American Bank Note Co. Montreal

SIGNATURES
left	right
mss. various	mss. various
mss. various	engr. H. Stikeman

ISSUE DATING
 Engraved
  May 28th, 1886
  3rd July, 1889

Cat.No.	Denom.	Date	Variety	VG	F	VF	EF	Unc
22-02	$5	1886	Mss. signature,r.	100.	150.	200.	300.	-
22-04	$5	1886	Stikeman,r.	100.	150.	200.	300.	-
22-06	$10	1889	Mss. signature,r.	125.	200.	275.	425.	-
22-08	$10	1889	Stikeman,r.	125.	200.	275.	425.	-

55-24. ISSUE OF 1911
DESIGNS AND COLOURS

55-24-02
 $5 Face Design: Small Royal Crest/King George V/
  small Canadian Crest
 Colour: Back with green tint

Back Design: Lathework, counters, bank name and bank crest
Colour: Green

55-24-07
$10 **Face Design:** Small Royal Crest/Queen Mary/ small bank crest
  Colour: Black with blue-green tint
Back Design: Lathework, counters, bank name and bank crest
Colour: Blue

55-24-10
$20 **Face Design:** Small Royal crest/King Edward VII/ small Canadian crest
  Colour: Black with red-orange tint

Back Design: Lathework, counters; The Bank of British North American and Bank Crest
Colour: Brown

55-24-14S
$50 **Face Design:** —/Queen Alexandra/—
  Colour: Black with lilac tint

THE BANK OF BRITISH NORTH AMERICA

Back Design: Lathework, counters, bank name and bank crest
Colour: Purple

55-24-16S
$100 **Face Design:** Small Royal crest/Queen Victoria/ small bank crest
  Colour: Orange
Back Design: Lathework, counters, bank name and bank crest
Colour: Brown

IMPRINT
Waterlow & Sons Ld. London
Waterlow & Sons Ld. London Wall, London
Waterlow & Sons Limited, London Wall, London EC

SIGNATURES
left	right
mss. various	engr. H. Stikeman
mss. various	engr. H.B. Mackenzie

ISSUE DATING
  Engraved
  July 3rd, 1911

Cat.No.	Denom.	Date	Variety	VG	F	VF	EF	Unc
24-02	$5	1911	Stikeman,r.	200.	300.	450.	700.	-
24-04	$5	1911	Mackenzie,r.	200.	300.	450.	700.	-
24-06	$10	1911	Stikeman,r.	200.	325.	475.	800.	-
24-07	$10	1911	Mackenzie,r.	200.	325.	475.	800.	-
24-08S	$20	1911	Stikeman,r.				SPECIMEN	500.
24-10	$20	1911	Mackenzie,r.	900.	1,200.	2,000.	-	-
24-12S	$50	1911	Stikeman,r.				SPECIMEN	500.
24-14S	$50	1911	Mackenzie,r.				SPECIMEN	500.
24-14	$50	1911	Mackenzie,r.	900.	1,200.	2,000.	-	-
24-16S	$100	1911	Mackenzie,r.				SPECIMEN	500.
24-16	$100	1911	Mackenzie,r.	900.	1,200.	2,000.	-	-

CANADA BANK

1792

MONTREAL, LOWER CANADA

BANK NUMBER 60   **NONREDEEMABLE**

The Canada Bank may have been established in 1792 in Montreal as a private company. It is possible that it was established because of fur trade rivalry.

60-10.   ISSUE OF 1792

This issue comes in notes of two sizes: — shillings 11.2 x 8.2 cm and — pounds 20 x 12 cm. Both sizes were printed on watermarked paper.

DESIGNS AND COLOURS

60-10-04
_Shillings **Face Design:** Beaver gnawing at stump/—/— Engraved "For the Canada Banking Comp.y"
Colour: Black with no tint
Back Design: Plain

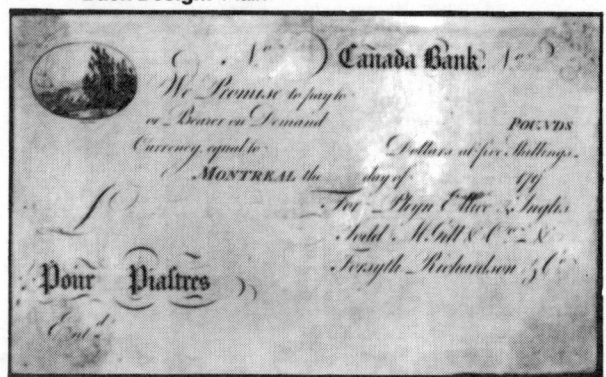

0-10-06R
_Pounds **Face Design:** Beaver gnawing at stump/—/— Engraved "For Phyn Ellis & Inglis"/Todd McGill & Co. &/Forsyth, Richardson & Co."
Colour: Black with no tint
Back Design: Plain

IMPRINT
Albby Sc., London

SIGNATURES
left only
mss. John Lilly Junior

ISSUE DATING
Partially Engraved __179_:
The 10th day of August, 1792

Notes 10-04 and 10-06 are remainders, * unsigned, undated and unnumbered.

Cat.No.	Denom.	Date	Variety	VG	F	VF	EF	Unc
10-02R	— shillings	179_	Remainder*	500.	700.	1,000.	1,800.	-
10-04	5 shillings	1792		700.	1,000.	1,500.	2,500.	-
10-06R	— pounds	179_	Remainder*	1,100.	1,550.	2,300.	3,900.	-

THE CANADA BANK

1855

TORONTO, CANADA WEST

BANK NUMBER 65   **NONREDEEMABLE**

This bank intended to operate under The Free Banking Act, but never opened for business under the name of The Canada Bank. It is the Bank of Canada in the Province of Canada, chartered in 1858, and which later operated as The Canadian Bank of Commerce. See "History of the Canadian Bank of Commerce" Vol. 2, Victor Ross, Pages 9 & 18.

65-10.   DANFORTH, WRIGHT & CO.
           PRINTINGS 1855

DESIGNS AND COLOURS

Photo Not Available

5-10-01P
$1 **Face Design:** Queen Victoria/Niagara Falls/Prince Albert
Colour: Black with no tint
Back Design: Plain

65-10-02P
$1 (5s) **Face Design:** Queen Victoria (Chalon portrait)/ Roebling Suspension Bridge/ Prince /Albert
Colour: Black with no tint
Back Design: Plain

65-10-04P
$2 (10s) **Face Design:** Woman with sickle and grain sprigs/ Royal Crest/—
Colour: Black with no tint
Back Design: Plain

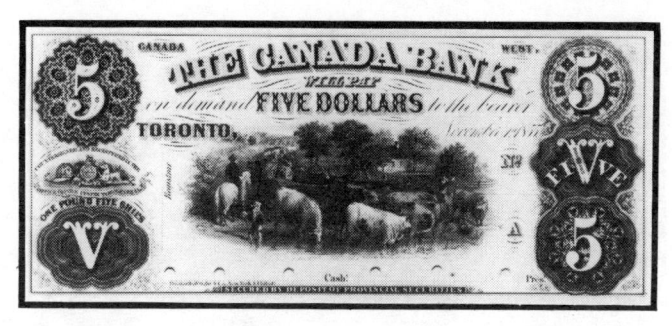

65-10-06P
  $5 (£1.5) Face Design: —/cattle standing in pond drinking/—
  Colour: Black with no tint
  Back Design: Plain

IMPRINT
  Danforth, Wright & Co. New York and Philad'a

SIGNATURES
  left   right
  none   none

ISSUE DATING
  Engraved
  November 1st, 1855

Cat.No.	Denom.	Date	Variety		Unc
10-01P	$1(5s)	1855	Falls	FACE PROOF	750.
10-02P	$1(5s)	1855	Bridge	FACE PROOF	750.
10-04P	$2(10s)	1855		FACE PROOF	750.
10-06P	$5(£1.5)	1855		FACE PROOF	750.

THE BANK OF CANADA

1818 - 1831

MONTREAL, LOWER CANADA

BANK NUMBER 70   **NONREDEEMABLE**

The Bank of Canada began business in 1818 as a private corporation. It submitted its first petition to incorporate in December of 1820, and obtained a charter in 1822. By 1825 a rapid decline had taken place in its business and the problems of the institution were compounded by the depression of 1826. By 1831 all business by the bank was discontinued and it was to be absorbed by The Bank of Montreal upon the lapse of its charter. There is no relation between this bank and the present Bank of Canada.

70-10.   **FIRST ISSUE 1818 - 1822**

DESIGNS AND COLOURS

70-10-02
  $1 Face Design: —/seated woman with cornucopia and left hand on 1, agricultural tools and sheaves below/—
  Colour: Black with no tint
  Back Design: Plain

70-10-04P
  $2 Face Design: Seated woman with sword and right hand on 2, small ship below/— Inscribed "AT THE MECHANICS' BANK IN THE CITY OF N. YORK." and 2's in top counters
  Colour: Black with no tint
  Back Design: Plain

THE BANK OF CANADA

70-10-06
  $2 Face Design: Seated woman with cornucopia and left hand on 2; agriculture tools and sheaves below/—and "2" "II" in counters at top
  Colour: Black with no tint
  Back Design: Plain

70-10-08P
  $5 Face Design: Five Spanish dollars/woman afloat with right hand on 5, paddlewheeler below/"Inscribed "AT THE MECHANICS' BANK IN THE CITY OF N.YORK."
  Colour: Black with no tint
  Back Design: Plain

70-10-10P
  $10 Face Design: Ten Spanish dollars/town and citadel on hill, Prince of Wales crest below/—
  Colour: Black with no tint
  Back Design: Plain

70-10-12P
  $20 Face Design: —/Royal Crest, shield against bales below/—Inscribed "AT THE MECHANICS' BANK IN THE CITY OF N. YORK"
  Colour: Black with no tint
  Back Design: Plain

70-10-14
  $50 Face Design: —/Crest, beaver below/—
  Colour: Black with no tint
  Back Design: Plain

70-10-16P
  $100 Face Design: —/Royal Crest, ships below/—
  Colour: Black with no tint
  Back Design: Plain

70-10-18P
  Post Note Face Design: Angel in clouds blowing trumpet, running deer at bottom
  Colour: Black with no tint
  Back Design: Plain

IMPRINT
   Reed

SIGNATURES
left	right
mss. R. Armour	mss. Tho. A. Turner
mss. R. Armour	mss. H. MacKenzie

ISSUE DATING
   Partially Engraved: __18__:
      $1   **1818:** Aug. 1
             1819: Nov. 6
      $2   **1822:** Feb. 1
      $50 **1818:** 25th Augt
   POST NOTE: 1818 17 Sept.
                     1822 17 Augt

VARIETIES
   $2 Face Design: —/seated woman with sword and right hand on 2, small ship below/— Inscribed "AT THE MECHANICS' BANK IN THE CITY OF N. YORK." and 2's in top counters
   $2 Face Design: —/seated woman with cornucopia and left hand on 2, agriculture tools and sheaves below/-and "2" "II" in counters at top

Note: Most signed and dated notes of the first issue are counterfeits.

Cat.No.	Denom.	Date	Variety	VG	F	VF	EF	Unc
10-02	$1	1818-19		200.	450.	800.	1,200.	-
10-04P	$2	18__	Sword vign				PROOF	500.
10-06	$2	1822	Cornucopia vign*	65.	85.	125.	225.	-
10-08P	$5	18__					PROOF	500.
10-10P	$10	18__					PROOF	500.
10-12P	$20	18__					PROOF	500.
10-14	$50	1818		350.	600.	950.	1,300.	-
10-16P	$100	18__					PROOF	500.
10-18P	Post Note	18__					PROOF	400.
10-18a	Post Note	1818					PROOF	400.
10-18b	Post Note	1822					PROOF	400.

*(counterfeit)

70-12.   SECOND ISSUE 1818 - 1823

DESIGN AND COLOURS

70-12-02-01
   $1 Face Design: —/Horse pulling couple in sleigh; coin below/—Payee engraved "J. Dewitt"
      Colour: Black with no tint
   Back Design: Plain

70-12-02-02
   $1 Face Design: —/Horse pulling couple in sleigh/— Inscribed "AT THE MECHANICS' BANK in the city of New York", and 1, ONE in top counters; Payee engraved "B. Throop"
      Colour: Black with no tint
   Back Design: Plain

70-12-02-03
   $2 Face Design: —/seated woman with sickle, two coins below/—Payee engraved "T. Fisher"
      Colour: Black with no tint
   Back Design: Plain

70-12-02-06
   $3 Face Design: —/boat, native and man, 3 on box/— Inscribed "AT THE MECHANICS' BANK in the city of New York", and 3, 111 in top counters. Payee engraved "J. Brown"
      Colour: Black with no tint
   Back Design: Plain

THE BANK OF CANADA

70-12-02-07
- **$5 Face Design:** —/boat, seated native with lion, five coins below/—Payee engraved "S. S. Keyes"
- **Colour:** Black with no tint
- **Back Design:** Plain

70-12-02-10
- **$10 Face Design:** —/Ship, X on box, three people, sheaves etc./—Inscribed "AT THE MECHANICS' BANK in the City if New York." Payee engraved "T.C. Bush"
- **Colour:** Black with no tint
- **Back Design:** Plain

IMPRINT
Graphic Company

SIGNATURES

left	right
mss. R. Armour	mss. Tho. A. Turner
mss. R. Armour	mss. H. Mackenzie

2. ENGRAVED DATE, ENGRAVED PAYEE'S NAME

ISSUE DATING
Engraved
1st October 1818

Cat.No.	Denom.	Date	Variety	VG	F	VF	EF	Unc
12-02-01R	$1	1818		250.	350.	500.	850.	-
12-02-02R	$1	1818	Mechanics Bank	250.	350.	500.	850.	-
12-02-03	$2	1818		250.	350.	500.	850.	-
12-02-04	$2	1818	Mechanics Bank	NOTE NOT CONFIRMED				
12-02-05	$3	1818		NOTE NOT CONFIRMED				
12-02-06R	$3	1818	Mechanics Bank	250.	350.	500.	850	-
12-02—07	$5	1818		250.	350.	500.	850.	-
12-02-08	$5	1818	Mechanics Bank	NOTE NOT CONFIRMED				
12-02-09	$10	1818		NOTE NOT CONFIRMED				
12-02-10R	$10	1818	Mechanics Bank	250.	350.	500.	850.	-

4. PARTIALLY ENGRAVED DATE, PAYEE'S NAME NOT ENGRAVED

70-12-04-02
- **$5 Face Design:** —/seated Indian with lion and 5, five coins below/—
- **Colour:** Black with no tint
- **Back Design:** Plain

ISSUE DATING
Partially Engraved__18__:
- **1820:** 6th January
- **1823:** June 4th

Cat.No.	Denom.	Date	VG	F	VF	EF	Unc
12-04-02	$5	1820-23	250.	350.	500.	850.	-

70-13   REED AND STILES ISSUE

DESIGNS AND COLOURS

70-13-30
- **$5 Face Design:** —/Ship building, woman,FIVE/—; five coins below
- **Colour:** Black with no tint
- **Back Design:** Plain

IMPRINT
Reed and Stiles

SIGNATURES

left	right
mss. R. Armour	mss. H. MacKenzie

ISSUE DATING
Partially Engraved: ___18___:
$5 1823: 1 June

Cat.No.	Denom.	Date	VG	F	VF	EF	Unc
13-30	$5	1823	150.	-	-	-	-

Note: These notes may all be counterfeit. Design is similar to Montreal Bank 550-14-08

70-14. GRAPHIC ISSUE OF 1822
DESIGNS AND COLOURS

70-14-02
- **$1 Face Design:** —/"coin" of George IV superimposed over produce/—
- **Colour:** Black with no tint
- **Back Design:** Plain

70-14-04
- **$2 Face Design:** —/two "coins" of George IV superimposed over flowers/—
- **Colour:** Black with no tint
- **Back Design:** Plain

IMPRINT
Graphic Company

SIGNATURES

left	right
mss. R.Armour	mss. Tho. A.Turner
mss. R.Armour	mss. H. Mackenzie

ISSUE DATING
Engraved
1st Janry, 1822

Cat.No.	Denom.	Date	VG	F	VF	EF	Unc
14-02	$1	1822	250.	350.	500.	850.	-
14-04	$2	1822	250.	350.	500.	850.	-

THE CANADIAN BANK OF COMMERCE
1867 - 1961
TORONTO, ONTARIO

BANK NUMBER 75 **REDEEMABLE**

In August of 1858 The Bank of Canada in the Province of Canada was incorporated and chose Toronto as its head office. However, this charter was bought by another group of investors, and the charter was amended by August 15, 1866, changing the name to The Canadian Bank of Commerce. On May 15, 1867, the bank opened for business in Toronto with an authorized capital of $1,000.000.

The bank showed rapid progress and by 1871 had 18 branches in Ontario and 1 in Montreal. In 1870 it absorbed The Gore Bank, an institution which at one time had shared a leading position with The Bank of Upper Canada and The Commercial Bank. Further expansion occurred following amalgamations with The Bank of British Columbia in 1901, The Halifax Banking Company in 1903, The Merchants Bank of P.E.I. in 1906 and The Eastern Townships Bank in 1912. Total assets of the bank had grown from $3 million in 1868 to $70 million in 1901, $113 million in 1906 and $246 Million in 1912.

Continuing to expand during World War I, the bank's assets reached $440 million by 1918, ranking it as the third largest bank in Canada. Like other banks, it gave considerable assistance to the government, and despite wartime operating conditions it continued to expand its business. In 1961 it amalgamated with The Imperial Bank of Canada to form the Canadian Imperial Bank of Commerce.

75-10. ISSUES OF 1867 - 1871
DESIGNS AND COLOURS

75-10-02
- **$1 Face Design:** Woman on shell pulled by dolphins/ small female head below/Indian maiden
- **Colour:** Black with green tint

- **Back Design:** Lathework, counters and bank name
- **Colour:** Green

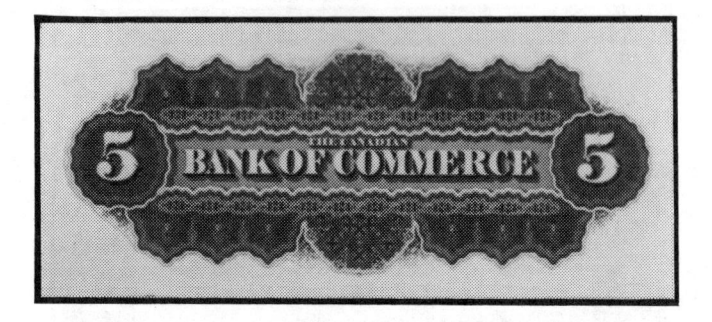

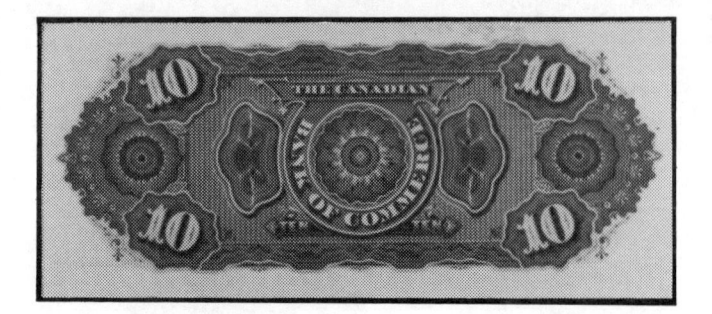

THE CANADIAN BANK OF COMMERCE

75-10-04
    $2 Face Design: Anchor, box and barrel "Exports"/
                    small beaver below/seated woman at wharf
    Colour: Black with green tint

    Back Design: Lathework, counters and bank name
    Colour: Green

75-10-06
    $4 Face Design: Old woman teaching girl to knit,
                    "The first lesson"/cattle/beehive
    Colour: Black with green tint

    Back Design: Lathework, counters and bank name
    Colour: Green

75-10-08
    $5 Face Design: —/Queen Victoria in "Window's weeds"/—
                    See varieties
    Colour: Black with green tint

    Back Design: Lathework, counters and bank name
    Colour: Green

75-10-14P
    $10 Face Design: —/Royal Crest/—
                     See varieties
    Colour: Black with green tint

    Back Design: Lathework, counters and bank name
    Colour: Green

THE CANADIAN BANK OF COMMERCE

75-10-22
    $50 Face Design: Seated allegorical female "Intelligence" /—/seated allegorical female holding torch, child "Science" See varieties
    Colour: Black with green tint

Back Design: Lathework, counters and bank name
Colour: Green

IMPRINT
    British American Bank Note Co. Montreal & Ottawa

SIGNATURES
left	right or below
mss. various	engr. Wm. McMaster

ISSUE DATING
    Engraved
    May 1st, 1867
    July 1st, 1870
    May 1st, 1871

OVERPRINT
    Some notes of 1867:
    "GUELPH" in blue
    "HAMILTON" in blue
    "LONDON" in blue
    "ST. CATHARINES" in blue
    "G" in red and "ST. CATHARINES" in blue

VARIETIES
    Face Design: "CAPITAL $4,000.000" printed at bottom
    Face Design: "CAPITAL $6,000.000" printed at bottom

Cat.No.	Denom.	Date	Variety	VG	F	VF	EF	Unc
10-02	$1	1867		600.	900.	1,500.	-	-
10-04	$2	1867		1,000.	1,600.	2,500.	-	-
10-06	$4	1870		600.	900.	1,500.	-	-
10-08	$5	1867		1,000.	2,000.	3,000.	-	-
10-10	$5	1871*	"CAPITAL $4,000.000"	1,000.	2,000.	3,000.	-	-
10-12	$5	1871*	"CAPITAL $6,000.000"	1,000.	2,000.	3,000.	-	-
10-14	$10	1867				EXTREMELY RARE		
10-16	$10	1871**	"CAPITAL $4,000.000"			EXTREMELY RARE		
10-18	$10	1871**	"CAPITAL $6,000,000"			EXTREMELY RARE		
10-20	$50	1870	"CAPITAL $4,000.000"			EXTREMELY RARE		
10-22	$50	1870	"CAPITAL $6,000.000"			EXTREMELY RARE		

*Beware of counterfeits, which have a poor rendering of the Queen's face and have the left-hand signature stamped on. Prices are for genuine notes.

**Beware of well done counterfeits. Prices are for genuine notes.
  Proofs exist at $500.00

75-12.   **ISSUES OF 1879 and 1887**
DESIGNS AND COLOURS

75-12-02P
    $5 Face Design: —/Hon. Wm. McMaster/—
    See varieties
    Colour: Black with green tint

    Back Design: Lathework, counters and bank name
    Colour: Green

75-12-04
    $5 Face Design: —/Hon. Wm. McMaster/—
    See varieties
    Colour: Black with green tint

    Back Design: Lathework, counters, bank name and Coat of Arms
    Colour: Green

75-12-06P
    $10 Face Design: —/Hon. Wm. McMaster/ship/ Henry W. Darling
    Colour: Black with green tint

55

THE CANADIAN BANK OF COMMERCE

Back Design: Lathework, counters and bank name
Colour: Green

IMPRINT
British American Bank Note Co. Montreal

SIGNATURES
	left	right
$5:	engr. Wm. McMaster	mss. various
$10:	mss. various	engr. Henry W. Darling

ISSUE DATING
Engraved
1st Jan. 1879
3rd Jan, 1887

VARIETIES
$5 Face Design: Rectangular frame around portrait
$5 Face Design: Oval frame around portrait

Cat.No.	Denom.	Date	Variety	VG	F	VF	EF	Unc
12-02	$5	1879	Rectangular	3,000.	-	-	-	-
12-04	$5	1879	Oval	3,000.	-	-	-	-
12-06	$10	1887		-	-	-	-	-

75-14. ISSUES OF 1888 - 1912

DESIGNS AND COLOURS
$5, $10 & 100: Amounts of capital printed under the bank seal.
$20 & $50: Amount of capital printed at top of note.

75-14-04b
$5 Face Design: Woman with books, lamp/—/ Bank Seal
Colour: Black with orange and yellow-brown tint

Back Design: Lathework, counters, bank name and bank building
Colour: Brown

75-14-24
$10 Face Design: Bank Seal/helmeted woman's head and cherubs/child painting
Colour: Black with yellow and rose tint

Back Design: Lathework, counters, bank name and bank building
Colour: Blue

75-14-42
$20 Face Design: Ships, child and dolphin/Bank Seal/ seated woman with globe and urn
Colour: Black with orange and green tint

Back Design: Lathework, counters, bank name and bank building
Colour: Orange

THE CANADIAN BANK OF COMMERCE

SIGNATURES

	left	right	Capital
1888:	engr. Henry W. Darling	mss. various	$ 6,000,000
1892:	engr. Geo. A. Cox	mss. various	$ 6,000,000
1893:	engr. Geo. A. Cox	mss. various	$ 6,000,000
1901:	engr. Geo. A. Cox	mss. various	$ 8,000,000
1906:	engr. Geo. A. Cox	mss. various	$10,000,000
1907:	typed B.E. Walker	mss. various	$10,000,000
1912:	typed B.E. Walker	mss. various	$15,000,000
	typed B.E. Walker	typed A.H. Ireland	$15,000,000
	typed B.E. Walker	typed John Aird	$15,000,000
	typed B.E. Walker	typed Alex Laird	$15,000,000

ISSUE DATING

Engraved

2nd January 1888   2nd January 1906
2nd January 1892   8th January 1907
3rd July 1893   1st May 1912
2nd January 1901

OVERPRINT

A. "D D" or "SS" in red
B. "YUKON" twice in blue, green or purple
C. "DAWSON" twice in red
D. "DAWSON" twice in red or green
E. "E E" or "H H" in red
F. "YUKON" twice in red, green or orange
G. "YUKON" Twice in brown

75-14-54S
  $50 Face Design: —/seated woman with urn, lyre/—
  Colour: Black with yellow and brown tint

  Back Design: Lathework, counters, bank name and bank building
  Colour: Brown

75-14-62
  $100 Face Design: —/seated woman with books, globe/—
  Colour: Black with orange and blue tint

  Back Design: Lathework, counters, bank name, bank building and griffens
  Colour: Green

IMPRINT
American Bank Note Co. New York
American Bank Note Company, Ottawa

Cat.No.	Denom.	Date	Variety	VG	F	VF	EF	Unc
14-02	$5	1888		600.	900.	1,200.	-	-
14-04	$5	1892		200.	300.	400.	-	-
14-04a	$5	1892	"D D" or "SS" o/p(A)		500.	700.	-	-
14-04b	$5	1892	"YUKON" (B) o/p	3,000.	4,200.	5,000		
14-06	$5	1901		200.	300.	400		
14-06a	$5	1901	"DAWSON" (C) o/p		3,000.	4,200.	5,000.	
14-08	$5	1906		200.	300.	400.		
14-08a	$5	1906	"E E" o/p	200.	300.	400.		
14-08b	$5	1906	"H H" o/p	200.	300.	400.		
14-10	$5	1907		115.	160.	295.	450.	
14-12	$5	1912	Mss. signature, r.	115.	160.	295.	450.	
14-14	$5	1912	Ireland, r.	115.	160.	295.	450.	
14-16	$10	1888		600.	1,000.	1,400.	-	-
14-18	$10	1892		200.	300.	400.		
14-18a	$10	1892	"YUKON" (B) o/p	3,000.	4,200.			
14-20	$10	1901		125.	175.	250.		
14-20a	$10	1901	"DAWSON" (C) o/p		3,000.	4,200.		
14-22	$10	1906		200.	300.	400.	550.	
14-24	$10	1907		115.	160.	225.	400.	
14-26	$10	1912	Mss. signature, r.	115.	160.	225.	400.	
14-28	$10	1912	Ireland, r.	115.	160.	225.	40-0.	
14-30	$20	1888		1,200.	1,700.	-	PROOF 500.	
14-32	$20	1892		1,200.	1,700.	-	PROOF 500.	
14-32a	$20	1892	"YUKON" (F) o/p	3,000.	4,200.	-	PROOF 500.	
14-34	$20	1901		500.	900.	-		
14-34a	$20	1901	"YUKON" (G) o/p	3,000.	4,200.	-PROOF 1,000.		
14-34b	$20	1901	"DAWSON" (D) o/p		3,500.	4,900.		
14-36	$20	1906		500.	1,600.			
14-38	$20	1907		500.	1,600.			
14-40	$20	1912	Mss. signature, r.	115.	160.	225.		
14-42	$20	1912	Aird, r.	115.	160.	225.		
14-44	$50	1893		1,500.	2,000.	-	PROOF 500.	
14-44a	$50	1893	"YUKON" (F) o/p			-	- RARE	
14-46	$50	1901		1,500.	2,800.		-	
14-46a	$50	1901	"DAWSON" (D) o/p				RARE	
14-48	$50	1906		1,500.	2,800.			
14-50	$50	1907		1,200.	1,700.			
14-52	$50	1912	Mss. signature, r.	1,000.	1,600.			
14-54	$50	1912	Laird or Aird, r.	1,000.	1,600.			
14-56P	$100	1888				FACE PROOF	500.	
14-57S	$100	1898				SPECIMEN	750.	
14-58P	$100	1901				FACE PROOF	500.	
14-60P	$100	1906				FACE PROOF	500.	
14-61p	$100	1907				FACE PROOF	500.	
14-62	$100	1912	Mss. signature, r.	700.	1,000.			
14-64	$100	1912	Laird or Aird, r.	700.	1,000.			

Yukon specimen note overprints exist 3,000. - 4,000. each.

THE CANADIAN BANK OF COMMERCE

75-16. **ISSUE OF 1917**

DESIGNS AND COLOURS

75-16-02-02
  $5 Face Design: Allegorical group: Mercury with "Agriculture" at left and "Inventor" to the right

  Back Design: Mercury/British Crown over Bank Seal/Ceres

75-16-04-12
  $10 Face Design: Pastoral landscape: Juno with bull, Ceres, goat herd

  Back Design: Mercury/British Crown over Bank Seal/Ceres

75-16-02-08
  $20 Face Design: Seascape: Neptune, sea-maidens, Mercury and maiden

  Back Design: Mercury/British Crown over Bank Seal/Ceres

75-16-04-22
  $50 Face Design: Industry: vulcan, herculean youths surrounded by symbols of science and industry

  Back Design: Mercury/British Crown over Bank Seal/Ceres

75-16-02-12
  $100 Face Design: Rocky wastes, mountains and forests, with Mercury and Manufacturing at left, three goddesses at centre left and a sturdy pioneer and explorer at the right

  Back Design: Mercury/British Crown over Bank Seal/Ceres

2. **WHITE BACKGROUND ON FACE, TINT CONSISTS OF SEAL ONLY**

  $5 Face Colour: See varieties
  Back Colour: Olive green
  $10 Face Colour: Black with blue, green, lilac and orange tint
  Back Colour: Blue
  $20 Face Colour: Black with blue, green, lilac and orange tint
  Back Colour: Blue
  $50 Face Colour: Black with blue, green, ochre and red tint
  Back Colour: Chocolate brown
  $100 Face Colour: Black with blue, olive, orange and brown tint
  Back Colour: Purple

IMPRINT
American Bank Note Co, Ottawa
Canada Bank Note Company Limited, Ottawa

SIGNATURES

	left	right
$5-$50	typed B.E. Walker	typed John Aird
$5	typed John Aird	typed S.H. Logan
$100	typed John Aird	typed S.H. Logan

ISSUE DATING
Engraved
2nd Jany. 1917

VARIETIES
$5 Face Colour: Black with green and red tint
(02-02) (numbers up to 505500)
$5 Face Colour: Black with blue, lilac, green and red tint
(02-04) (numbers over 505500)

Cat.No.	Denom.	Date	Variety	VG	F	VF	EF	Unc
16-02-02	$5	1917	Green and red seal	60.	100.	150.	275.	600.
16-02-04	$5	1917	Multicoloured seal	125.	175.	250.	400.	900.
16-02-06	$10	1917	White backgr.	60.	100.	140.	250.	600.
16-02-08	$20	1917	White backgr.	120.	175.	275.	400.	900.
16-02-10	$50	1917	White backgr.	250.	325.	425.	800.	1,600.
16-02-12	$100	1917	White backgr.	150.	200.	300.	450.	900.

4. OVERALL FACE TINTS WITH SEAL

DESIGNS AND COLOURS
$5. Face Colour: Black with overall green and blue, lilac, green and red tint
Back Colour: Olive green
$10 Face Colour: Black with overall orange and blue, lilac, green and red tint
Back Colour: Olive green
$10 Face Colour: Black with overall orange and blue, green, lilac and orange tint
Back Colour: Blue

Note: A few $10 notes with a cream coloured background have been seen, but are due to a chemical change of the orange tint. and do not constitute a separate variety.

$20 Face Colour: Black with overall yellow and blue, green, lilac and rose tint
Back Colour: Orange
$50 Face Colour: Black with overall olive green and blue, green, ochre and red tint
Back Colour: Brown

IMPRINT
American Bank Note Co. Ottawa
Canadian Bank Note Company Limited, Ottawa

SIGNATURES

	left	right
$5	typed B.E. Walker	typed John Aird
	typed John Aird	typed F.M. Gibson
	typed John Aird	typed S.H. Logan
$10	typed B.E. Walker	typed John Aird
	typed John Aird	typed C.W. Rowley
	typed John Aird	typed S.H. Logan
$20	typed B.E. Walker	typed John Aird
	typed John Aird	typed A.St.L. Trigge
	typed John Aird	typed S.H. Logan
$50	typed B.E. Walker	typed John Aird
	typed John Aird	typed S.H. Logan

*Variations occurs in the size and style of the Logan signature.

THE CANADIAN BANK OF COMMERCE

ISSUE DATING
Engraved
Jan. 2, 1917

VARIETIES
$5, $10, $20 Logan, R.: general manager in lower case, typed GENERAL MANAGER in capitals, engraved
$10 Walker, l.: Orange overall face tint, no CBN imprint bottom left margin
Orange overall face tint, CBN imprint bottom left margin

Cat.No.	Denom.	Date	Variety	VG	F	VF	EF	Unc
16-04-02	$5	1917	Green tint, Walker,l.	50.	70.	110.	200.	425.
16-04-04	$5	1917	Green tint, Gibson,r.	50.	70.	110.	200.	425.
16-04-06	$5	1917	Green tint, Logan,r. Gen. Man. lower case	55.	75.	140.	225.	450.
16-04-06a	$5	1917	Green tint, Logan,r. GEN.MAN.caps	30.	40.	60.	100.	250.
16-04-08	$10	1917	Orange tint, Walker,l., no CBN	50.	70.	110.	200.	425.
16-04-08a	$10	1917	Orange tint, Walker,l., with CBN	50.	70.	110.	200.	425.
16-04-10	$10	1917	Orange tint Rowley r., Gen Man lower case	50.	70.	110.	200.	425.
16-04-10a	$10	1917	Orange tint Rowley r., GEN MAN caps	50.	70.	110.	200.	425.
16-04-12	$10	1917	Orange tint Logan,r. Gen. Man. lower case	50.	70.	110.	200.	425.
16-04-12a	$10	1917	Orange tint Logan,r. GEN. MAN. caps	35.	55.	80.	150.	250.
16-04-16	$20	1917	Yellow tint, Walker,l.	125.	175.	250.	450.	900.
16-04-18	$20	1917	Yellow tint, Trigge,r.	200.	300.	450.	800.	1,700.
16-04-20	$20	1917	Yellow tint, Logan,r. Gen. Man., lower case	55.	80.	110.	200.	400.
16-04-20a	$20	1917	Yellow tint Logan,r GEN. MAN, caps	55.	80.	110.	200.	400.
16-04-22	$50	1917	Olive tint, Walker,l.	175.	225.	300.	600.	1,200.
16-04-24	$50	1917	Olive tint, Logan,r.	175.	225.	300.	600.	1,200.

Proofs of the 1917 series are common face proof $200.00 - $300.00.

THE CANADIAN BANK OF COMMERCE

75-18. ISSUE OF 1935
SMALL SIZE NOTES

DESIGNS AND COLOURS

75-18-04
- **$5 Face Design:** Allegorical group: Mercury with "Agriculture" at left and "Invention" to the right
- **Colour:** Black with overall green and blue, green, lilac and red tint
- **Back Design:** Mercury/British Crown over Bank Seal/Ceres
- **Colour:** Olive Green

75-18-06
- **$10 Face Design:** Pastoral landscape: Juno with bull, Ceres, goat herd
- **Colour:** Black with overall orange and blue, green, lilac and orange tint
- **Back Design:** Mercury/British Crown over Bank Seal/Ceres
- **Colour:** Blue

75-18-10
- **$20 Face Design:** Seascape: Neptune, sea-maidens, Mercury and maiden
- **Colour:** Black with overall yellow and blue, green, lilac and rose tint
- **Back Design:** Mercury/British Crown over Bank Seal/Ceres
- **Colour:** Orange

IMPRINT
Canadian Bank Note Company Limited

SIGNATURES

left	right
typed John Aird	typed S.H. Logan
typed John Aird	typed S.M. Wedd
typed S.H. Logan	typed A.E. Arscott

ISSUE DATING
Engraved
2nd Jany. 1935

Cat.No.	Denom.	Date	VG	F	VF	EF	Unc
18-02	$5	1935 Logan,l.	15.	20.	35.	60.	110.
18-04	$5	1935 Arscott,r.	20.	25.	45.	80.	200.
18-05	$5	1935 Wedd,r			UNIQUE SHEET KNOWN		
18-06	$10	1935 Logan,r.	40.	55.	90.	210.	
18-08	$10	1935 Arscott,r	35.	50.	65.	110.	225.
18-10	$20	1935 Logan,r.	40.	60.	90.	150.	325.

BRITISH WEST INDIES ISSUES

Trade relations between the province of Nova Scotia and the West Indies had always been active, as far back as the early days of The Halifax Banking Company, the business of which was acquired by The Canadian Bank of Commerce in 1903. The latter opened branches in Havana, Cuba, and Kingston, Jamaica, in 1920, followed by others in Barbados and Trinidad. After the opening of these branches, application was made to local authorities for note issuing privileges similar to those enjoyed by other banks doing business in these colonies. These privileges were granted, and specially designed notes were prepared for use in Jamaica, Trinidad and Barbados. The Jamaica issues appeared in 1 and 5 denominations and the Trinidad and Barbados issues appeared in local denominations of $5, $20 and $100.

75-20. BRIDGETOWN, BARBADOS
ISSUES OF 1922 and 1940
LARGE SIZE NOTES

DESIGNS AND COLOURS

75-20-04
- **$5 Face Design:** —/seated woman with lyre and spilling water jug/—
- **Colour:** Black with green and red-orange tint
- **Back Design:** Counters, lathework and Bank Crest
- **Colour:** Orange

75-20-06
- **$20 Face Design:** —/seated woman with globe, book and looking glass/—
- **Colour:** Black with red-brown and green tint
- **Back Design:** Counters, lathework and Bank Crest
- **Colour:** Green

75-20-10
- **$100 Face Design:** Seated woman with book and lamp/—/—
- **Colour:** Black with blue and olive tint
- **Back Design:** Counters, lathework and Bank Crest
- **Colour:** Chocolate brown

IMPRINT
American Bank Note Company, Ottawa or
Canadian Bank Note Company, Limited

SIGNATURES

	left	right
1922:	typed B.E. Walker	mss. various
	typed John Aird	mss. various
1940:	typed S.H. Logan	mss. various

ISSUE DATING
Engraved
2nd January, 1922.
1st July 1940.

Cat.No.	Denom.	Date	Variety	VG	F	VF	EF	Unc
20-02	$5	1922	Walker,l.	500	700.	1,500.	-	-
20-04	$5	1922	Aird,l.	500.	700.	1,500.	-	-
20-06S	$20	1922				SPECIMEN		500.
20-08S	$20	1940				SPECIMEN		500.
20-10	$100	1922		1,200.	1,600.	-	-	-

THE CANADIAN BANK OF COMMERCE

75-22. **BRIDGETOWN, BARBADOS**
ISSUE OF 1940
SMALL SIZE NOTES

DESIGNS AND COLOURS

75-22-02
  $5 Face Design: Allegorical group: "Architecture", Mercury, "Invention"
  Colour: Black with green and red-orange tint
  Back Design: Lathework, counters, bank name and Mercury/British crown over Bank seal/Ceres
  Colour: Orange

IMPRINT
  Canadian Bank Note Company Limited

SIGNATURES
  left   right
  typed S.H. Logan   typed A.E. Arscott

ISSUE DATING
  Engraved
  July 1, 1940

Cat.No.	Denom.	Date	VG	F	VF	EF	Unc
22-02	$5	1940	400.	525.	725.	1,200.	-

75-24. **KINGSTON, JAMAICA**
ISSUES OF 1921 and 1938
LARGE SIZE NOTES

DESIGNS AND COLOURS

75-24-02
  £1 Face Design: Allegorical group: "Architecture", Mercury, "Invention"
  Colour: Black with orange tint
  Back Design: Lathework, counters, bank name and Mercury/British crown over Bank seal/Ceres
  Colour: Brown

75-24-04
  £5 Face Design: —/seated woman holding fruit/—
  Colour: Black with green and red tint
  Back Design: Lathework, counters, bank name and Mercury/British crown over Bank seal/Ceres
  Colour: Green

75-24-06
  £5 Face Design: —/seated woman holding fruit/—
  Colour: Black with green and red tint
  Back Design: Lathework, counters, bank name and Mercury/British crown over Bank seal/Ceres
  Colour: Green

IMPRINT
  American Bank Note Company, Ottawa or
  Canadian Bank Note Company, Limited

SIGNATURES
  left   right
  1921: typed B.E. Walker   mss. various
  1938: typed S.H. Logan   typed A.E. Arscott

ISSUE DATING
  Engraved
  1st March 1921
  1st June 1938

Cat.No.	Denom.	Date	VG	F	VF	EF	Unc
24-02	£1	1921	700.	1,000.	1,400.	2,500.	-
24-04	£5	1921	650.	900.	1,300.	2,400.	-
24-06	£5	1938			SPECIMEN		750.

75-26. KINGSTON, JAMAICA
ISSUE OF 1938
SMALL SIZE NOTES

DESIGNS AND COLOURS

75-26-02
- **£1 Face Design:** Allegorical group: "Architecture", Mercury, "Invention"
- **Colour:** Black with orange tint
- **Back Design:** Lathework, counters, bank name and Mercury/British crown over Bank seal/Ceres
- **Colour:** Brown

IMPRINT
Canadian Bank Note Company, Ottawa

SIGNATURES
left	right
typed S.H. Logan	typed A.E. Arscott

ISSUE DATE
Engraved
1st June 1938

Cat.No.	Denom	Date	VG	F	VF	EF	Unc
26-02	£1	1938	400.	525.	750.	1,300.	-

75-28. PORT OF SPAIN, TRINIDAD
ISSUES OF 1921
LARGE SIZE NOTES

DESIGNS AND COLOURS

75-28-02
- **$5 Face Design:** —/seated woman with lyre and spilling water jug/—
- **Colour:** Black with green and ochre tint
- **Back Design:** Lathework, counters, bank name and Mercury/British crown over Bank seal/Ceres
- **Colour:** Green

75-28-04
- **$20 Face Design:** —/seated woman with globe, book and looking glass/—
- **Colour:** Black with green and red tint
- **Back Design:** Lathework, counters, bank name and Mercury/British crown over Bank seal/Ceres
- **Colour:** Blue

75-28-06S
- **$100 Face Design:** Seated woman with book and lamp/—/—
- **Colour:** Black with olive and red tint
- **Back Design:** Lathework, counters, bank name and Mercury/British crown over Bank seal/Ceres 
- **Colour:** Red

IMPRINT
American Bank Note Company, Ottawa

SIGNATURES
left	right
typed B.E. Walker	mss. various

ISSUE DATING
Engraved
1st March 1921

Cat.No.	Denom.	Date	VG	F	VF	EF	Unc
28-02	$5	1921	600.	800.	1,400.	-	-
28-04	$20	1921	900.	1,200.	1,900.	-	-
28-06S	$100	1921			SPECIMEN		750.

THE CANADIAN BANK OF COMMERCE

75-30.   **PORT OF SPAIN, TRINIDAD**
                    ISSUES OF 1939
                    SMALL SIZE NOTES

DESIGNS AND COLOURS

75-30-02
    $5 Face Design: Allegorical group: "Architecture", Mercury, "Invention"
    Colour: Black with ochre and green tint

    Back Design: Lathework, counters, the Canadian Bank of Commerce, Mercury/British crown over Bank seal/Ceres
    Colour: Green

75-30-04
    $20 Face Design: Seascape: Neptune, sea-maidens, Mercury and maiden
    Colour: Black with red-orange tint

    Back Design: Lathework, counters, the Canadian Bank of Commerce, Mercury/British crown over Bank seal/Ceres
    Colour: Blue

IMPRINT
    Canadian Bank Note Company Limited

SIGNATURES
    left   **right**
    typed S.H. Logan   typed A.E. Arscott

ISSUE DATING
    Engraved
    1st July 1939

Cat.No.	Denom.	Date	VG	F	VF	EF	Unc
30-02	$5	1939	275.	350.	500.	850.	1,700.
30-04	$20	1939	275.	350.	500.	850.	1,700.

Face proofs exist for most issues $400.00 - $500.00.

BANQUE CANADIENNE

1836 - 1838

ST. HYACINTHE, LOWER CANADA

BANK NUMBER 80   **NONREDEEMABLE**

Established in 1836 as a private corporation at St. Hyacinthe, Lower Canada, this bank failed in 1838 following the panic of 1837 and the suspension of specie payment, despite a measure of relief from the Legislature of Lower Canada.

80-10. DRAFT ISSUE OF 1836

Engraved: "Mssrs Archambault, Pacaud, De La Bruere"

DESIGNS AND COLOURS

80-10-02
- **$1 Face Design:** Men and livestock/cornucopia, sheaf and spinning wheel, beaver below/ man ploughing with horses
- **Colour:** Black with no tint

- **Back Design:** Lathework/habitant/lathework
- **Colour:** Blue-green

80-10-04
- **$2 Face Design:** Britannia, anchor/seated allegorical female, cattle and sheaves, beaver below/—
- **Colour:** Black with no tint

- **Back Design:** Lathework/habitant/lathework
- **Colour:** Blue-green

IMPRINT
Rawdon, Wright and Hatch, New York

SIGNATURES

left	right
none	mss. C.A. Pacaud
none	mss. A.A. Delphos

ISSUE DATING
Partially Engraved __18__:
1836: 23 Augt

Cat.No.	Denom.	Date	VG	F	VF	EF	Unc
10-02	$1	1836	200.	300.	450.	-	-
10-04	$2	1836	200.	300.	450.	-	-

80-12. NOTE ISSUE OF 1836

DESIGNS AND COLOURS

80-12-02
- **$5 Face Design:** Indian shooting arrow/sailing ship, deer below/train (sideways)
- **Colour:** Black with no tint

- **Back Design:** Lathework/habitant/lathework
- **Colour:** Green

80-12-04
- **$10 Face Design:** King William IV/train, produce and waterfall; man in canoe below/beehive
- **Colour:** Black with no tint

- **Back Design:** Lathework/habitant/lathework
- **Colour:** Green

IMPRINT
Rawdon, Wright and Hatch, New York

SIGNATURES

left	right
mss. L. Archambault	mss. Arch. Plu. De La Bruere & Cie.

ISSUE DATING
Partially Engraved __18__:
1836: Aug. 23

Cat.No.	Denom.	Date	VG	F	VF	EF	Unc
12-02	$5	1836	350.	500.	800.	-	-
12-04	$10	1836	350.	500.	800.	-	-

BANQUE CANADIENNE NATIONALE

1924 - 1979

MONTREAL, QUEBEC

BANK NUMBER 85 **REDEEMABLE**

La Banque Nationale, chartered in Quebec City, Canada East, in 1859 and Banque d'Hochelaga, established in Montreal, Quebec, in 1873, merged in 1924 to become the Banque Canadienne Nationale, although Banque d'Hochelaga did not change its name until Feb. 1, 1925.

The key event which set the stage for the merger of the two banks actually took place in Ontario in 1923. The Home Bank of Canada had failed, and in the same year, La Banque Nationale found itself in a difficult position. An attempt was made to merge the three major Francophone banks, the Nationale, Hochelaga and La Banque Provinciale du Canada. The latter declined, so the directors of the other two banks asked the Quebec Government for assistance. The government made the merger possible by the unusual step of conveying to Banque d'Hochelaga, in full ownership, its bonds for $15 million bearing interest at 5% and maturing in 40 years. Increasing its clientele as a result of the merger, the Banque d'Hochelaga became a much larger institution. The merger greatly increased the number of branches to be operated by the Banque Canadienne Nationale. The Banque d'Hochelaga had 197 branches, the new bank a total of 263. The new bank made such progress that, despite the depression of the 1930's, it was able to reimburse the Quebec Government within 20 years, instead of the stipulated 40.

The war years of 1939 - 1945 produced only token profits for the bank, while expenses and work loads were much greater. From 1945 onwards, the bank's business volume had continued to grow at about the same pace as the national economy. It was the sixth largest bank in Canada with large operations abroad when, on Nov. 1, 1979, it merged with La Banque Provinciale du Canada to form the National Bank of Canada.

85-10. ISSUE OF 1925

DESIGNS AND COLOURS

85-10-02
  $5 Face Design: J.A. Vaillancourt/monument/Beaudry Leman
  Colour: Black with green tint

  Back Design: Bank name, counters and Provincial Crests
  Colour: Green

85-10-04
  $10 Face Design: J.A. Vaillancourt/monument/Beaudry Leman
  Colour: Black with brown tint

  Back Design: Bank name, counters and Provincial Crests
  Colour: Brown

85-10-06
  $20 Face Design: J.A. Vaillancourt/monument/Beaudry Leman
  Colour: Black with blue tint

  Back Design: Bank name, counters and Provincial Crests
  Colour: Blue

85-10-08
  $50 Face Design: J.A. Vaillancourt/Maisonneuve monument/Beaudry Leman
  Colour: Black with olive tint

  Back Design: Bank name, counters and Provincial Crests
  Colour: Olive

85-10-10
  $100 Face Design: J.A. Vaillancourt/—/Beaudry Leman
  Colour: Black with purple tint

Back Design: Bank name, counters and Provincial Crests
Colour: Purple

IMPRINT
Canadian Bank Note Company Limited

SIGNATURES
left	right
typed J.A. Vaillancourt	typed Beaudry Leman

ISSUE DATING
Engraved
Le 1er Fev. 1925

Cat.No.	Denom.	Date	VG	F	VF	EF	Unc
10-02	$5	1925	50.	65.	100.	175.	-
10-04	$10	1925	50.	70.	120.	200.	-
10-06	$20	1925	125.	175.	250.	-	-
10-08	$50	1925	300.	450.	600.	-	-
10-10	$100	1925	450.	600.	900.	-	-

85-12 ISSUE OF 1929
LARGE SIZE NOTES

DESIGNS AND COLOURS

85-12-02
$5 Face Design: F.L. Beique/monument/Beaudry Leman
Colour: Black with green tint

Back Design: Bank name, counters and Provincial Crests
Colour: Green

85-12-04
$10 Face Design: F.L. Beique/monument/Beaudry Leman
Colour: Black with brown tint

Back Design: Bank name, counters and Provincial Crests
Colour: Brown

85-12-06
$20 Face Design: F.L. Beique/monument/Beaudry Leman
Colour: Black with blue tint

Back Design: Bank name, counters and Provincial Crests
Colour: Blue

85-12-08
$50 Face Design: F.L. Beique/Maisonneuve monument/Beaudry Leman
Colour: Black with orange tint

Back Design: Bank name, counters and Provincial Crests
Colour: Orange

BANQUE CANADIENNE NATIONALE

85-12-10S
 $100 Face Design: F.L. Beique/—/Beaudry Leman
 Colour: Black with purple tint

Back Design: Bank name, counters and Provincial Crests
 Colour: Purple

IMPRINT
 Canadian Bank Note Company Limited

SIGNATURES
left	right
typed F.L. Beique	typed Beaudry Leman

ISSUE DATING
 Engraved
 Le 1er Fev. 1929

Cat.No.	Denom.	Date	VG	F	VF	EF	Unc
12-02	$5	1929	50.	65.	100.	175.	-
12-04	$10	1929	50.	70.	110.	185.	-
12-06	$20	1929	150.	225.	300.	-	-
12-08	$50	1929	450.	600.	800.	-	-
12-10S	$100	1929			SPECIMEN		1,000.

85-14. **ISSUE OF 1935 SMALL SIZE NOTES**

DESIGNS AND COLOURS

85-14-02
 $5 Face Design: Hon. J.M. Wilson/monument/Beaudry Leman Esq.
 Colour: Black with green tint

Back Design: Lathework, counters, bank name and Provincial Crests
 Colour: Green

85-14-04
 $10 Face Design: Hon. J.M. Wilson/monument/Beaudry Leman Esq.
 Colour: Black with brown tint

Back Design: Lathework, counters, bank name and Provincial Crests
 Colour: Brown

IMPRINT
 Canadian Bank Note Company Limited

SIGNATURES
left	right
typed J.M. Wilson	typed Beaudry Leman

ISSUE DATING
 Engraved
 Le 2 Jan. 1935

Cat.No.	Denom.	Date	VG	F	VF	EF	Unc
14-02	$5	1935	30.	60.	65.	100.	250.
14-04	$10	1935	35.	50.	80.	125.	300.

Face proofs of all issues, large size $250.00 - $350.00, small size $200.00 - $300.00

CATARACT BANK

1855 - 1858

NIAGARA CITY

PROVINCE OF CANADA

BANK NUMBER 88   **NONREDEEMABLE**

Orders for bank-notes were placed with Danforth, Wright and Co. on June 6th 1855 and Aug. 25th, 1858. Whether any notes were actually printed or are still in existence is not known.

THE CENTRAL BANK OF CANADA

1883 - 1887

TORONTO, ONTARIO

BANK NUMBER 90   **NONREDEEMABLE**

This bank, incorporated in 1883 with its head office in Toronto, should not be confused with the Central Bank of Canada incorporated in 1873 in Montreal. The latter bank never used its charter or issued notes, and the history of the former is one of discreditable practice, scandalous mismanagement and dishonest diversion of its resources. its note holders were paid in full and other creditors received about 99% of their investment when the bank finally failed in 1887.

90-10.   **ISSUES OF 1884 and 1887**

DESIGNS AND COLOURS

90-10-02
    $5 Face Design: D. Blain/—-/allegorical female, V and cherubs
    Colour: Black with green tint

    Back Design: Lathework, counters, bank name and Horses at trough
    Colour: Green

90-10-04
    $10 Face Design: D. Blain/man ploughing with horses
    Colour: Black with green tint

CENTRAL BANK OF NEW BRUNSWICK

Back Design: Lathework, counters and bank name
Colour: Green

90-10-06P
$50 Face Design: D. Blain/—/A.A. Allen
Colour: Black with green tint

Back Design: Lathework, counters and bank name
Colour: Green

IMPRINT
British American Bank Note Co. Montreal

SIGNATURES
left	right
engr. D. Blain	mss. various

ISSUE DATING
Engraved
Jany. 1st, 1884
3rd Jan. 1887

Cat.No.	Denom.	Date	VG	F	VF	EF	Unc
10-02	$5	1884	500.	800.	1,200.	-	-
10-04	$10	1884	700.	1,000.	1,500.	-	-
10-06P	$50	1887			FACE PROOF		500.

Note: A $5 back proof exists with blue tint.

CENTRAL BANK OF NEW BRUNSWICK
1834 - 1866
FREDERICTON, NEW BRUNSWICK

BANK NUMBER 95   **NONREDEEMABLE**

This bank was established in Fredericton, New Brunswick in 1834. Its charter contained, for the first time in complete form in Canada, one of the most important requirements in that the shareholders should be liable for double the amount of their shares. The bank operated successfully for more than twenty years.

However, the business conditions in the province, affected adversely by those in Upper Canada following the collapse of the land boom, resulted in the failure of the bank in 1866. All creditors were paid in full and approximately 1% of its capital was available to divide among the shareholders.

95-10.   **ISSUE OF 1847 - 1857**
POUNDS SHILLINGS DOLLARS

DESIGNS AND COLOURS

95-10-06-02
$1 (5s) Face Design: Blacksmith at anvil/seated "Justice" figure, lion; cargo and ships below/-
Colour: See subheadings
Back Designs: See subheadings
Colour: See subheadings

95-10-02-04
£1 Face Design: Seated Indian with rifle/Royal Crest; paddlewheeler below/-
Colour: See subheadings
Back Design: See subheadings
Colour: See subheadings

95-10-10-06P
  £5 Face Design: King William IV/St. George slaying dragon; lion crown below/-
  Colour: See subheadings
  Back Design: See subheadings
  Colour: See subheadings

IMPRINT
  Rawdon, Wright, Hatch & Co. New York
  Rawdon, Wright, Hatch & Edson, New York

SIGNATURES
left	right
mss. illegible	mss. illegible

2. BLACK FACE AND BLUE LATHEWORK BACK 1847

ISSUE DATING
  Partially Engraved: __18__:
  1847: May 1

Cat.No.	Denom.	Date	VG	F	VF	EF	Unc
10-02-02	5s	1847	1,200.	1,600.	-	-	-
10-02-04	£1	1847	1,200.	1,600.	-	-	-
10-02-06	£5	1847	1,200.	1,600.	-	-	-

4. BLUE FACE AND GREY LATHEWORK BLACK 1847 - 1853

ISSUE DATING
  Partially Engraved: __18__:
  $1(5s) **1847:** Nov.1
  1853: 1 April
  £1 **1847:** Oct. 1
  £5 **1851:** Feb. 1
  £5 **1857:** 1 Nov.

Cat.No.	Denom.	Date	VG	F	VF	EF	Unc
10-04-02	$1 (5s)	1847	1,800.	2,200.	-	-	-
10-04-02a	$1 (5s)	1853	1,800.	2,200.	-	-	-
10-04-04	£1	1847	1,200.	1,600.	-	-	-
10-04-06	£5	1851	1,200.	1,600.	-	-	-
10-04-08	£5	1857	1,200.	1,600.	-	-	-

6. BLUE FACE AND ORANGE LATHEWORK BACK 1847 - 1853

ISSUE DATING
  Partially Engraved: __18__:
  1847: 1January, 1 Oct., 1Nov.
  1852: 1 Oct.
  1853: 1 May

Cat.No.	Denom.	Date	VG	F	VF	EF	Unc
10-08-02	$1(5s)	1852	1,000.	1,500.	-	-	-
10-08-04	$1(5s)	1853	1,000.	1,500.	-	-	-
10-08-06	£1	18__	1,400.	2,000.	-	-	-
10-08-08	£5	1853	1,200.	1,800.	-	-	-

8. BLUE FACE AND GREEN LATHEWORK BACK 1847-

ISSUE DATING
  Partially Engraved: __18__:
  1847: 10 Nov.

Cat.No.	Denom.	Date	VG	F	VF	EF	Unc
10-08-02	$1(5s)	1847	1,400.	2,000.	-	-	-

10. BLACK FACE AND PLAIN BACK 1856 - 1857

ISSUE DATING
  Partially Engraved: __18__:
  1856: 1 June
  1857: 1 Augt, 1 Oct.

Cat.No.	Denom.	Date	VG	F	VF	EF	Unc
10-10-02	$1(5s)	1856	1,400.	2,000.	-	-	-
10-10-04	£1	1857	1,000.	1,500.	-	-	-
10-10-06P	£5	18-				PROOF	900.

CENTRAL BANK OF NEW BRUNSWICK

95-12. ISSUE OF 1860
DESIGNS AND COLOURS

95-12-02
- **$1 Face Design:** Henry George Clopper/lion and shield/ Queen Victoria (Winterhalter portrait) in oval
- **Colour:** Black with green tint
- **Back Design:** Plain

95-12-04
- **$2 Face Design:** Henry George Clopper/seated allegorical women and ornate 2/Queen Victoria in oval
- **Colour:** Black with green tint
- **Back Design:** Plain

95-12-06
- **$3 Face Design:** Prince of Wales/allegorical female/ sailing ship/Henry George Clopper
- **Colour:** Black with green tint
- **Back Design:** Plain

95-12-08P
- **$5 Face Design:** Henry George Clopper/Royal Crest/sailboat
- **Colour:** Black with green tint
- **Back Design:** Plain

95-12-10R
- **$20 Face Design:** "Justice" figure/St. George slaying the dragon/Wellington in oval
- **Colour:** Black with green TWENTY

- **Back Design:** Lathework
- **Colour:** Green

95-12-12P
- **$20 Face Design:** "Justice" figure/St. George slaying the dragon/Wellington in oval
- **Colour:** Black with overall green tint
- **Back Design:** Lathework
- **Colour:** Green

95-12-14P
  $50 Face Design: Queen Victoria (Chalon portrait) in oval/
  female, ships and cornucopia/
  cattle, train on bridge "The Drove"
  Colour: Black with overall green tint

  Back Design: Green

IMPRINT
Rawdon, Wright, Hatch & Edson, New York
or American Bank Note Company

SIGNATURES
left	right
mss. illegible	mss. illegible
none	none

ISSUE DATING
  Partially Engraved: __18__:
  Novr 1st 18__
  Engraved
  November 1st 1860

VARIETIES
  $20: Green "Twenty" protector
  $20: "Twenty" outlined by overall green face tint

Cat.No.	Denom.	Date	Variety	VG	F	VF	EF	Unc
12-02	$1	1860		1,200.	2,000.	-	-	-
12-04	$2	1860		1,200.	2,000.	-	-	-
12-06	$3	1860		3,000.	4,000.	-	-	-
12-08P	$5	1860				FACE PROOF		900.
12-10R	$20	18__	*Green twenty	-	-			
12-12P	$20	18__	Green tint			FACE PROOF		900.
12-14P	$50	18__				FACE PROOF		900.

*unsigned, undated, unnumbered and remainder.

CHARLOTTE COUNTY BANK

CHARLOTTE COUNTY BANK
1825 - 1865
ST. ANDREWS, NEW BRUNSWICK

BANK NUMBER 100 **NONREDEEMABLE**

The Charlotte County Bank was established in 1825 at St. Andrew's, New Brunswick with a capital of 15,000. Its charter was for twenty years and its total liabilities were restricted to twice the paid-up capital. Although the bank ceased operations some time prior to 1865, during that year a final winding up was authorized by the government. All claims on the bank were paid but the shareholders lost their entire capital.

100-10. PERKINS AND HEATH PRINTINGS
1852 - 1859

DESIGNS AND COLOURS

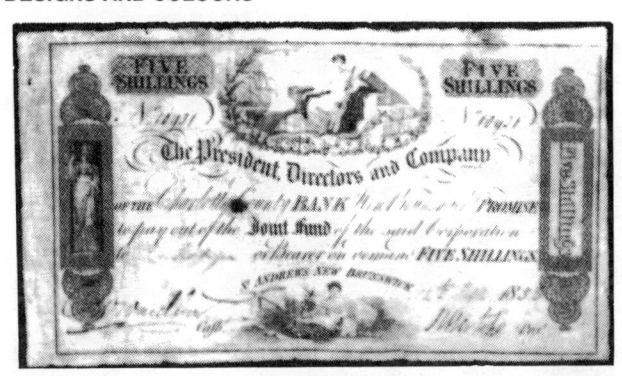

100-10-02
  5s Face Design: Britannia/seated allegorical female at seaside;
  seated allegorical female at seaside/—
  Colour: Black with no tint

  Back Design: Lathework, female portraits in corners
  and small vignettes top and bottom
  Colour: Red-brown or plain

100-10-08
  £1 Face Design: Britannia/seated allegorical female at seaside;
  allegorical female at seaside/—
  Colour: Black with no tint

  Back Design: Lathework, female portraits in corners
  and small vignettes top and bottom
  Colour: Red-brown

CHARLOTTE COUNTY BANK

100-10-10
- **£3 Face Design:** Britannia/seated allegorical female at seaside; seated allegorical female at seaside/—
- **Colour:** Black with no tint

- **Back Design:** Lathework, female portraits in corners and small vignettes top and bottom
- **Colour:** Red-brown

Photo Not Available

100-10-12P
- **£5 Face Design:** Britannia/seated allegorical female at seaside; seated allegorical female at seaside/-
- **Colour:** Black with no tint

- **Back Design:** Lathework, female portraits in corners and small vignettes top and bottom
- **Colour:** Red-brown

Photo Not Available

100-10-14P
- **£10 Face Design:** Britannia/seated allegorical female at seaside; seated allegorical female at seaside/-
- **Colour:** Black with no tint

- **Back Design:** Lathework, female portraits in corners and small vingettes top and bottom
- **Colour:** Red-brown

IMPRINT
Perkins and Heath, London

SIGNATURES

	left	right
1852:	mss. illegible	mss. illegible
1853-1854:	mss. C.W. Wardlaw	mss. illegible
1856:	mss. C.W. Wardlaw	mss. Geo. D. Street
1859:	mss. illegible	mss. illegible

ISSUE DATING
Partially Engraved: __18__:
- **1852:** 1 Sept.
- **1853:** 12 Sept.
- **1854:** 22 Augt.
- **1856:** 26 Augt.
- **1859:** Nov. 8

Cat.No.	Denom.	Date	VG	F	VF	EF	Unc
10-02	5s	1853	1,200.	-	-	-	-
10-04	5s	1854	1,200.	-	-	-	-
10-06	5s	1856	1,200.	-	-	-	-
10-07	£1	1852	1,200.	-	-	-	-
10-08	£1	1859	1,800.	-	-	-	-
10-10	£3	1852	1,800.	-	-	-	-
10-12P	£5	18__			FACE PROOF		700
10-14P	£10	18__			FACE PROOF		700

Note:: These notes are extremely rare in grades over VG

BANK OF CHARLOTTETOWN

1852

CHARLOTTETOWN, PRINCE EDWARD ISLAND

BANK NUMBER 105 **NONREDEEMABLE**

Established in 1852, the Bank of Charlottetown was a spurious bank. The notes and drafts were the concoctions of A. Sleigh, and circulation was attempted in New York. Sleigh's lifetime was devoted to fraud and swindling.

105-10. POUNDS, SHILLINGS & PENCE NOTE ISSUE

DESIGNS AND COLOURS

These notes carry three currencies, the first P.E.I., the second Canada, N.B. Halifax and NFLD. currency and the third U.S.

105-10-02P
 £5 (£4; 16 US)
 Face Design: Roses, shamrock and thistle/ Royal Crest/two ships and counter "Payable at/S. Draper's New York"
 Colour: Black with no tint
 Back Design: Plain

10-10-04P
 £5 (£4.3.4; 16.66 U.S.)
 Face Design: Roses, shamrock and thistle/Royal Crest/ two ships and counter "Redeemed at/S. Draper's, New York"/and at/Wm. Elliott & COS./British Consulate/Boston
 Colour: Black with no tint
 Back Design: Plain

IMPRINT
 Rawdon, Wright, Hatch & Edson, New York
 Rawdon, Wright, Hatch & Edson, New York
 and New England Bank Note co. Boston

SIGNATURES
left	right
none	mss. A.Sleigh

ISSUE DATING
 Partially Engraved __18__

Cat.No.	Denom.	Date		Unc
10-02P	£5 (£4; 16 US)	18__	PROOF	900.
10-04P	£5 (£4.3.4; 16.66 US)	18__	PROOF	900.

105-12. DOLLAR DRAFT ISSUE 1852

Engraved: "To Simeon Draper, New York"

DESIGNS AND COLOURS

105-12-02P
 Face Design: Floral panel/seated Britannia, with symbols of commerce/two small sailing ships.
 Colour: black with no tint
 Back Design: Plain

105-12-04
 $2 Face Design: Roses, shamrocks and thistles/ seated sailor/two small ships
 Colour: Black with no tint
 Back Design: Plain

105-12-06P
 $3 Face Design: Floral panel/seated female with farm produce/ships
 Colour: Black with no tint
 Back Design: Plain

THE CITY BANK

IMPRINT
Rawdon, Wright, Hatch & Edson New York
and New England Bank Note Co. Boston

SIGNATURES
left	right
none	mss. A. Sleigh

ISSUE DATING
Engraved
May 1st, 1852

Cat.No.	Denom.	Date	VG	F	VF	EF	Unc
12-02P	$1	1852				PROOF	900.
12-04	$2	1852	2,500.	-	-	-	-
12-06	$3	1852	3,500.	-	-	-	-

THE CITY BANK
1833 - 1876
MONTREAL, LOWER CANADA

BANK NUMBER 110   **NONREDEEMABLE**

On its second attempt, The City Bank received its charter and opened for business on October 14, 1833. The charter remained in effect until June 1, 1837, when it was again renewed.

By 1841 it was the fifth largest bank in terms of discounts and the fourth largest in terms of circulation.

However, in 1870, The City Bank was involved in an intricate court case regarding gold speculation which cost it $140,000. It was a severe blow in a period of impending depression. Public confidence was lost and in 1873 Sir Francis Hincks was asked to become president. A merger with The Royal Canadian Bank was completed in 1876 to form The Consolidated Bank of Canada.

110.10.   **BILINGUAL ISSUE 1833 - 1840's**
PAYABLE AT MONTREAL
DENOMINATIONS IN DOLLARS ONLY

DESIGNS AND COLOURS

110-10-02
$1 **Face Design:** King William IV/Indian shooting arrow/ Indian paddling canoe below/—
Colour: Black with no tint

Back Design: "Steel" over standing woman in panel/ "CITY BANK / MONTREAL"/"plate" over standing woman in panel, and overall lathework
Colour: Red

THE CITY BANK

110-10-04P
   $2 Face Design: —/Indian in canoe; beaver below/King William IV
   Colour: Black with no tint

   Back Design: Unknown

110-10-06P
   $5 Face Design: King William IV/Archimedes moving the earth/Arms (sideways)
   Colour: Black with no tint

   Back Design: Unknown

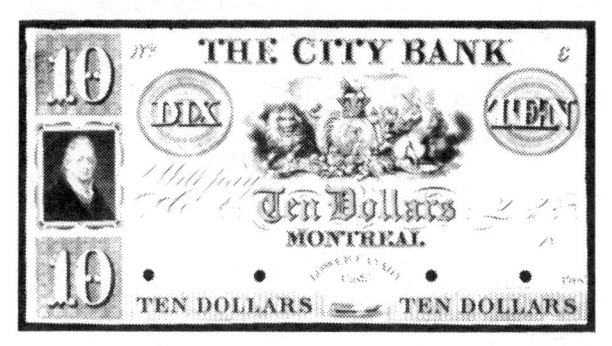

110-10-08P
   $10 Face Design: King William IV/Royal Crest; ship below/woman with sheaf of wheat
   Colour: Black with no tint

   Back Design: Unknown

110-10-10

Note: Beware of counterfeit $10 notes of 1836 which have "PARLIAMENT" at the left under the portrait.

   $10 Face Design: King William IV/Royal Crest; ship below/woman with sheaf of wheat, has misspelled word "Parliment" at left under portrait
   Colour: Black with no tint

   Back Design: Unknown

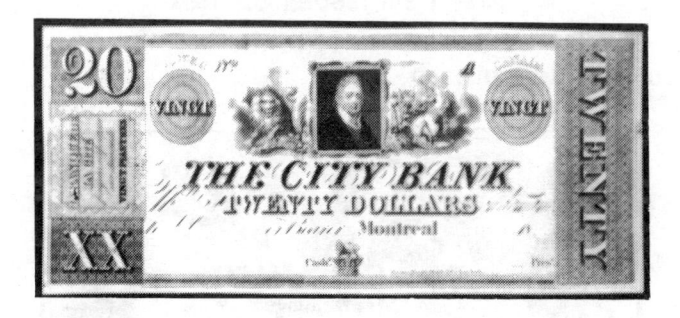

110-10-12P
   $20 Face Design: —/King William IV on Royal Crest; lion on crown below/—
   Colour: Black with no tint

   Back Design: Unknown

110-10-14P
   $100 Face Design: St. George slaying dragon King William IV; beaver below/St. George slaying dragon
   Colour: Black with no tint

   Back Design: Unknown

IMPRINT
   Rawdon, Wright, Hatch & Co. New York

SIGNATURES
left	right
mss. Chs. H. Castle	mss. J. Frothingham

THE CITY BANK

ISSUE DATING
Partially Engraved __18__:
1833: 10 Oct.
1834: 1 Augt

OVERPRINT
"EASTERN TOWNSHIPS" in large red letters across the face.

Cat.No.	Denom.	Date	Variety	VG	F	VF	EF	Unc
10-02	$1	1833		1,000.	1,500.	-	-	-
10-04P	$2	18__				PROOF		500.
10-06P	$5	18__				PROOF		500.
10-08P	$10	18__				PROOF		500.
10-10	$10*	18__	Counterfeit	100.	150.	225.	-	-
10-12P	$20	18__				PROOF		600.
10-14P	$100	18__				PROOF		600.

110-12. SEPARATE BRANCH ISSUES 1850 - 1865 DOLLARS/POUNDS & SHILLINGS

2. MONTREAL ISSUE 1851 - 1853

Branch name engraved at bottom.

DESIGNS AND COLOURS

110-12-02-02
$1 (5s) **Face Design:** Counter with lion and unicorn/bank building; crown on swords below/Britannia
Colour: Black with no tint
Back Design: Plain

Photo Not Available

110-12-02-04P
$2 (10s) **Face Design:** —/bank building/man and woman
Colour: Black with no tint
Back Design: Plain

112-12-02-06
$4 (£1) **Face Design:** Queen Victoria (Chalon portrait)/ bank building; ship below/—
Colour: Black with no tint
Back Design: Plain

110-12-02-08
$5 (£1.5) **Face Design:** Portrait of young woman/Indians and shield (like Bank of Montreal Crest); crown on swords below /bank building
Colour: Black with no tint
Back Design Plain

110-12-02-10P
$10 (£2.10) **Face Design:** —/bank building/—
Colour: Black with no tint
Back Design: Plain

Photo Not Available

110-12-02-12P
$20 (£5) **Face Design:** Woman/bank building/—
Colour: Black with no tint
Back Design: Plain

Photo Not Available

110-12-02-14P
$50 (£12.10) **Face Design:** —/bank building/—
Colour: Black with no tint
Back Design: Plain

Photo Not Available

112-12-02-16P
$100 (£25) **Face Design:** Prince Albert/bank building/ Queen Victoria (Chalon portrait)
Colour: Black with no tint
Back Design: Plain

IMPRINT
Rawdon, Wright, Hatch, New York
Rawdon, Wright, Hatch & Edson, New York

SIGNATURES

	left	right
1851:	mss. various	mss. W. Workman
1853:	mss. various	mss. W. Macdonald
	mss. Alex Ross	mss. W. Workman

ISSUE DATING
Partially Engraved __18__:
1851: 1 May, May 2
1853: 1 February, 1 Feby.

PROTECTOR
1851 & Proofs: Red "word" on face and back

Cat.No.	Denom.	Date	VG	F	VF	EF	Unc
12-02-02	$1(5s)	1851	900.	1,600.	-	-	-
12-02-04P	$2(10s)	18__				PROOF	500.
12-02-06	$4(£1)	1853	1,000.	1,500.	-	-	-
12-02-08	$5(£1.5)	1853	1,000.	1,500.	-	-	-
12-02-10P	$10(£2.10)	18__				PROOF	500.
12-02-12P	$20(£5)	18__				PROOF	600.
12-02-14P	$50(£12.10)	18__				PROOF	600.
12-02-16P	$100(£25)	185				PROOF	600.

TORONTO ISSUE 1850 - 1865

$1 & $2: Branch name engraved at bottom centre.
$5 - $20: Branch name engraved at bottom centre and on lower right.

DESIGNS AND COLOURS

110-12-04-02
$1 Face Design: —/seated woman looking left, shield/ Queen Victoria (Chalon portrait)
Colour: Black with no tint
Back Design: Plain

110-12-04-16
$2 Face Design: —/seated woman looking right, shield/ Queen Victoria (Chalon portrait)
Colour: Black with no tint
Back Design: Plain

110-12-04-26
$5 Face Design: Royal Crest (sideways)/Archimedes moving the earth; cask, bales and ship below/King William IV
Colour: Black with no tint
Back Design: Plain

110-12-04-30
$10 Face Design: King William IV/Royal Crest; ship below/"Justice" figure
Colour: Black with no tint
Back Design: Plain

Photo Not Available

110-12-04-40P
$20 Face Design: Allegorical woman/King William IV/—
Colour: Black with no tint
Back Design: Plain

IMPRINT
$1 & $2: Rawdon, Wright, Hatch, New York
$5 & $10: Rawdon, Wright, Hatch & Edson, New York

SIGNATURES

	left	right
$1 1850:	mss. Thos. Connolly (p.)	mss. W. Workman
	mss. Walter Ross (per)	mss. John Carter (p.)
$2 1850:	mss. Thos. Connolly (p.)	mss. W. Workman
	mss. Walter Ross (per)	mss. W. MacDonald (p.)
1852:	mss. F. Woodside (p.)	mss. W. Workman
$2 1854:	mss. F. Woodside (p.)	mss. W. MacDonald
$5 1856:	mss. F. Woodside (p.)	mss. John Carter (v.)
$10 1854:	mss. John Major (p.)	mss. John Carter (v.)
1861:	mss. J. Moat (per)	mss. W. Macdonald (p.)

ISSUE DATING
Partially Engraved __18__:
1850: 1 Oct., 1 October
1852: 31 Dec.
1854: 1 Sept.
1856: 1st, Augt
1861: Aug. 1
1865: Oct. 2

THE CITY BANK

PROTECTOR
  1861 & 1865: Green "word" on face and back

Cat.No.	Denom.	Date	VG	F	VF	EF	Unc
12-04-02	$1	1850-65	700.	900.	-	-	-
12-04-16	$2	1852-56	1,000.	1,500.	-	-	-
12-04-26	$5	1856	1,000.	1,500.	-	-	-
12-04-30	$10	18__	1,000.	1,500.	-	-	-
12-04-40P	$20	1854-61			PROOF	500.	

6. QUEBEC ISSUE

Branch name engraved at bottom centre

DESIGNS AND COLOURS

110-12-06-02P
  $2 Face Design: —/seated woman looking right, shield/Queen Victoria (Chalon portrait)
  Colour: Black with no tint
  Back Design: Plain

110-12-06-04P
  $4 (£1) Face Design: Queen Victoria (Chalon portrait) bank building; ship below/—
  Colour: Black with no tint
  Back Design: Plain

IMPRINT
  Rawdon, Wright & Hatch New York

SIGNATURES
  left   right
  none   none

ISSUE DATING
  Partially Engraved __18__:

PROTECTOR
  $4 (£1): Red "word" on face only

Cat.No.	Denom.	Date		Unc
12-06-02P	$2	18__	PROOF	500.
12-06-04P	$4(£1)	18__	PROOF	600.

110-14. COMMON BRANCH ISSUE OF 1857 PROVINCE OF CANADA

DESIGNS AND COLOURS

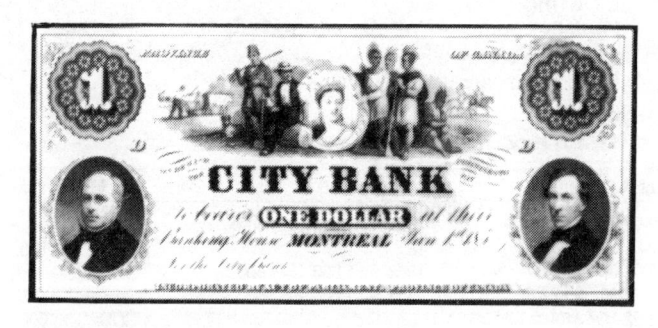

110-14-02-02
  $1 Face Design: Male portrait/Queen Victoria (Chalon portrait) on Crest/male portrait
  Back Design: See subheadings

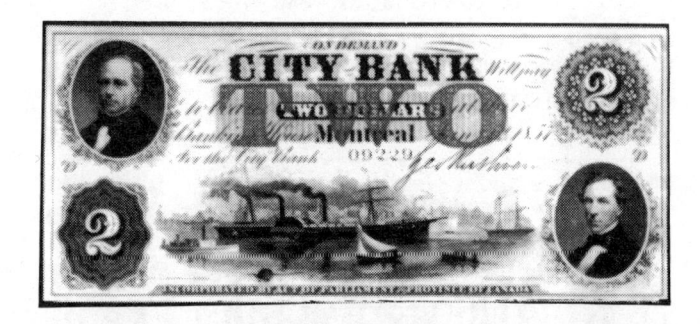

110-14-02-04
  $2 Face Design: Male portrait/paddlewheel steamship and boats, city in background/male portrait
  Back Design: See subheadings

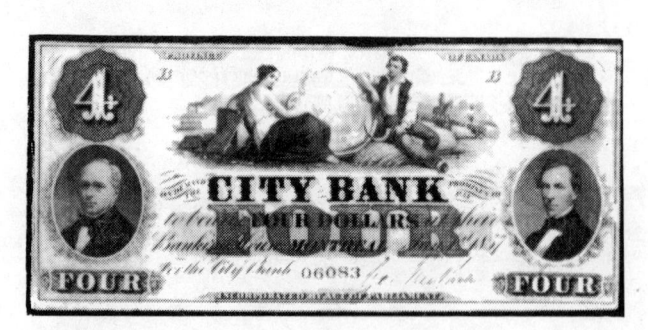

110-14-02-06
  $4 Face Design: Male portrait/crest with woman and farmer/male portrait
  Back Design: See subheadings

THE CITY BANK

110-14-02-08
$5 Face Design: Male portrait/farmers waving to passing train/male portrait
Back Design: See subheadings

110-14-02-10
$10 Face Design: Male portrait/St. George slaying dragon/ male portrait
Back Design: See subheadings

Photo Not Available

110-14-02-12
$20 Face Design: Male portrait/livestock by stream/ male portrait
Back Design: See subheadings

2. ORANGE BACK

DESIGNS AND COLOURS
  Face Colour: Black with no tint

Back Design: Scrollwork with "CITY BANK/MONTREAL"
Colour: Orange

IMPRINT
  Toppan, Carpenter & Co., Montreal

SIGNATURES
left	right
none	mss. Geo. Ruthven
none	mss. Fred MacCulloch
none	mss. Wm. G. Benson

ISSUE DATING
  Engraved
  Jany, 1st, 1857
  January 1st, 1857

OVERPRINT
  "TORONTO" in blue

STAMP
  "MINES" in blue

PROTECTOR
  Green "word" on face and in mirror image on the back of some notes.

Cat.No.	Denom.	Date	VG	F	VF	EF	Unc
14-02-02	$1	1857	300.	400.	-	-	-
14-02-04	$2	1857	350.	450.	850.	-	-
14-02-06	$4	1957	550.	900.	-	-	-
14-02-08	$5	1857	450.	700.	-	-	-
14-02-10	$10	1857	900.	1,200.	-	-	-
14-02-12	$20	1857	900.	1,200.	-	-	-

4. PLAIN BACK

DESIGNS AND COLOURS
  Face Colour: Black with no tint
  Back Design: Plain

IMPRINT
  Toppan, Carpenter & Co., Montreal

SIGNATURES
left	right
none	mss. Geo. Ruthven
none	mss. Fred MacCulloch
none	mss. Wm. Benson

ISSUE DATING
  Engraved
  Jan 1st, 1857
  January 1st 1857

OVERPRINT
  "QUEBEC" in blue
  "TORONTO" in blue

PROTECTOR
  Green "word" on face, $1 and $2 mirror image on back.

Cat.No.	Denom.	Date	VG	F	VF	EF	Unc
14-04-02	$1	1857	240.	335.	500.	-	-
14-04-04	$2	1857	300.	425.	650.	-	-
14-04-06	$4	1857	400.	550.	-	-	-
14-04-08	$5	1857	400.	550.	-	-	-
14-04-10	$10	1857	500.	700.	-	-	-

6. GREEN BACK

DESIGNS AND COLOURS
  Face Colours: Black with green V V and panel with FIVE tint
  Back Design: Scrollwork with "CITY BANK" centre and "MONTREAL" above and below
  Colour: Green

IMPRINT
  Toppan, Carpenter & Co., Montreal

SIGNATURES
left	right
none	mss. Geo. Ruthven
none	mss. Fred MacCulloch
none	mss. Wm.G. Benson

CITY BANK

ISSUE DATING
   Engraved
      January 1st, 1857
OVERPRINT
   "ST. CATHARINES" in red

Cat.No.	Denom.	Date	VG	F	VF	EF	Unc
14-06-02	$5	1857	800.	1,000.	-	-	-

110-16. SPURIOUS NOTE ISSUE

Fraudulent notes with design different from genuine issues of the bank.

DESIGNS AND COLOURS

110-16-02
   $4 Face Design: Cherub and lion/seated man with sledge hammer
                     Royal Crest; Indian Princess
      Colour: Black with no tint

   Back Design: Plain

IMPRINT
   Toppan Carpenter & Co. Montreal

SIGNATURES
left	right
mss. various	mss. W. Workman

ISSUE DATING
   Engraved
      Jan. 1st, 1857

Cat.No.	Denom.	Date	VG	F	VF	EF	Unc
110-16-02	$4	1857	150.	200.	300.	-	-

CITY BANK
1836 - 1839
ST. JOHN, NEW BRUNSWICK

BANK NUMBER 115   **REDEEMABLE**

With a capital of £100,000, the City Bank was established in Saint John, New Brunswick in 1836. The bank merged with The Bank of New Brunswick in 1839. Its charter provided for the first time that no shareholder should own more than 20% of the capital stock.

115-10. NEW ENGLAND BANK NOTE CO. PRINTINGS 1836 - 1838

DESIGNS AND COLOURS

115-10-02
   2s 6d Face Design: —/early train; steamboat below/—
      Colour: Black with no tint

   Back Design: Plain

115-10-04
   5s Face Design: —/two moose flanking Crest/—
      Colour: Black with no tint

   Back Design: Lathework
      Colour: Black

115-10-06
   £1 Face Design: —/waterfront scene/—
      Colour: Black with no tint

CITY BANK

Back Design: Lathework
Colour: Black

IMPRINT
New England Bank Note Co. Boston

SIGNATURES

left	right
mss. Thos. Jones	mss. illegible
mss. Thos. Jones	mss. John V. Thurgar

ISSUE DATING
Partially Engraved __18__:
16 July, 1836
1 Jany, 1838

Cat.No.	Denom.	Date	VG	F	VF	EF	Unc
10-02	2s6d	1838	1,500.	2,000.	-	-	-
10-04	5s	1836	1,500.	2,000.	-	-	-
10-06	£1	1836	1,500.	2,000.	-	-	-
10-08P	£5	18__			FACE PROOF		900.
10-10P	£10	18__			FACE PROOF		900.
10-12P	£20	18__			FACE PROOF		900.

115-10-08P
£5 Face Design: —/town, fence and cattle in foreground/—
Colour: Black with no tint

Back Design: Plain

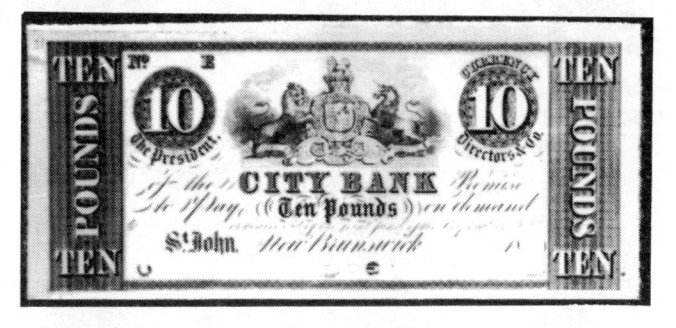

115-10-10P
£10 Face Design: —/Royal Crest/—
Colour: Black with no tint

Back Design: Plain

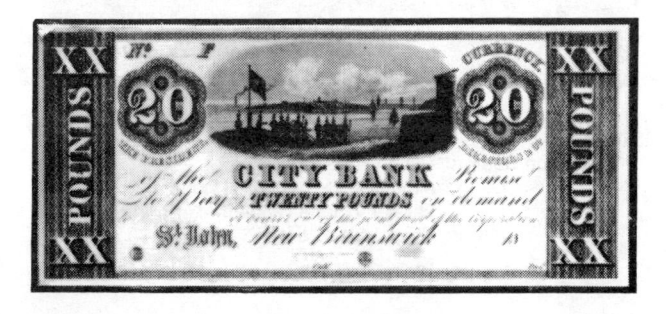

115-10-12P
£20 Face Design: —/soldiers, cannons and Union Jack/—
Colour: Black with no tint

Back Design: Plain

THE CITY BANK OF MONTREAL

18__

TORONTO (CANADA WEST)

BANK NUMBER 120 **NONREDEEMABLE**

No such bank is known; the note is altered from the Colonial Bank of Canada.

120-10. **ISSUE OF 18(59)**

DESIGNS AND COLOURS

120-10-02
- **$5 Face Design:** Farm family under tree/—/ Cornelia Jocelyn
- **Colour:** Orange-brown tint
- **Back Design:** Plain

IMRPINT
Jocelyn, Draper, Welsh & Co.
American Bank Note Company, New York

SIGNATURES

right only
F. MaCulloch
F. Workman

ISSUE DATING
Partially Engraved: __18__
Febr. 9, 1861

Cat.No.	Denom.	Date	Variety	VG	F	VF	EF	Unc
10-02	$5	1861	two signatures	200.	350.	-	-	-

THE BANK OF CLIFTON

1859 - 1863

CLIFTON, PROVINCE OF CANADA

BANK NUMBER 125 **NONREDEEMABLE**

On May 31, 1858, a petition was submitted by The Zimmerman Bank asking the Legislative Assembly for amendments to their charter, one of which was a change of name. On June 2nd, an act was passed granting the petition and the corporate name was changed to The Bank of Clifton. The bank, in reality, was the old Zimmerman Bank, the officers and shareholders remaining nearly the same. In 1859 the stock was transferred to Hubbard & Co. of Chicago with control then going to Callaway and Reed. Reed was the major shareholder in The International Bank of Canada at the time of its collapse. The notes issued under the new owners were never meant to be redeemed.

The charter was withdrawn by an act of the Legislature on August 31, 1863, with Royal assent given on October 15, 1863.

125-10. **ISSUE OF 1859**

DESIGNS AND COLOURS

125-10-02-02
- **$1 Face Design:** Clifton House Hotel/Roebling Suspension Bridge/seated allegorical female
- **Colour:** Black with no tint
- **Back Design:** Plain

125-10-04-04
- **$3 Face Design:** Clifton House Hotel /Roebling Suspension Bridge/ Queen Victoria (Winterhalter portrait) in oval
- **Colour:** Black with no tint
- **Back Design:** Plain

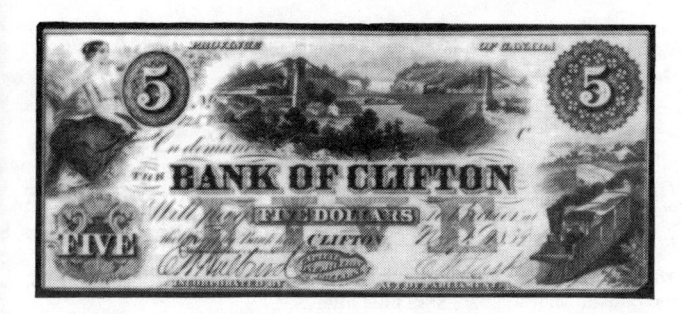

THE BANK OF CLIFTON

125-10-02-06
    $5 Face Design: Seated female with sickle/
                       Roebling Suspension Bridge/train
    Colour: Black with no tint
    Back Design: Plain

Note: Photo above shows a Citizens Bank Delaware note altered from a $5 Bank of Clifton note.

IMPRINT
American Bank Note Co. New York

2.   PARTIALLY ENGRAVED DATE
TWO SIGNATURES

SIGNATURES
left	right
mss. E.W. Hulburd	mss. E.W. Lusk

ISSUE DATING
    Partially Engraved ___185_:
    1859: Oct. 1, Nov. 1

PROTECTOR
Red "word" on face and in mirror image on the back.

OVERPRINT
"OTTAWA, ILL." and 13 - 15 stars in black

Cat.No.	Denom.	Date	VG	F	VF	EF	Unc
10-02-02	$1	1859	30.	40.	60.	90.	150.
10-02-04	$3	1859	60.	100.	150.	200.	300.
10-02-06	$5	1859	30.	45.	65.	100.	175.

4.   FULLY ENGRAVED DATE
ONE SIGNATURE

SIGNATURES
                      right only
                      mss. E.W. Lusk or Evert W. Lusk

ISSUE DATING
    Engraved
    Octr. 1st, 1859

PROTECTOR
Red "word" on face and in mirror image on the back

OVERPRINT
"OTTAWA, ILL." and 13 - 14 stars in black

Cat.No.	Denom.	Date	VG	F	VF	EF	Unc
10-04-02	$1	1859	25.	35.	45.	80.	140.
10-04-04	$3	1859	55.	90.	120.	200.	275.
10-04-06	$5	1859	25.	35.	45.	80.	140.

125-12.   **ISSUE OF 1860 - 1861**

DESIGNS AND COLOURS

125-12-04
    $1 Face Design: —/St. George slaying dragon/—
    Colour: Black with red tint
    Back Design: Plain

125-12-12
    $2 Face Design: —/St. George slaying dragon/—
    Colour: Black with red tint
    Back Design: Plain

85

THE COLONIAL BANK OF CANADA

125-12-18
 $5 Face Design: —/St. George slaying dragon/—
  Colour: Black with red tint
 Back Design: Plain

IMPRINT
 New York Bank Note Co. 50 Wall St.

SIGNATURES
                             right only
                             mss. J. Brown or James Brown

ISSUE DATING
 Engraved
  Sept. 1, 1860
  Sept. 1, 1861

OVERPRINTS
 "Sassenberg & Co, Buenos Ayres" in an oval in blue
 "Reedemed by Frederick Lau & Co. Bankers, 162 Fulton St. N.Y.
 at 3/4 per cent" in an oval in black
 "Redeemable in Chicago at the office of Chadwick & Co."
 "Redeemable in bankable funds at the office of Chadwick
 & Co. 5 Clark Street under the __house Chicago, Ill."

STAMPS
 3 in blue

VARIETY
 1861 Issue Date: Mss. 1 over the engraved 0 in 1860
 1861 Issue Date: Engraved second 1 in 1861

Cat.No.	Denom.	Date	Variety	VG	F	VF	EF	Unc
12-02	$1	1860		20.	30.	40.	75.	130.
12-04	$1	1861	Mss. 1 in date	15.	25.	35.	70.	110.
12-06	$1	1861	Engr. 1 in date	15.	25.	35.	70.	110.
12-08	$2	1860		20.	30.	40.	75.	130.
12-10	$2	1861	Mss. 1 in date	15.	25.	35.	70.	110.
12-12	$2	1861	Engr. 1 in date	15.	25.	35.	70.	110.
12-14	$5	1860		20.	30.	40.	75.	130.
12-16	$5	1861	Mss. 1 in date	15.	25.	35.	70.	110.
12-18	$5	1861	Engr. 1 in date	15.	25.	35.	70.	110.

Note: A $2 note (12-12) has been seen with the colour a rusty red-brown. It may be a trial colour or the original colour has been oxidized.

The 1859 issues were used as sources for altered United States obsolete notes, i.e. Connecticut, Delaware and Massachusetts notes.

THE COLONIAL BANK OF CANADA
1856 - 1863
TORONTO, CANADA WEST

BANK NUMBER 130   **NONREDEEMABLE**

The Colonial Bank of Canada received its charter from a petition read to the Legislature on April 23, 1856, with Royal assent given on July 1, 1856. After several amendments to the bank's charter in 1857 and 1858, the original shareholders sold their interests.

In 1859 the new owners finally opened for business with notes put into circulation. The bank lasted only six months before its failure as a result of a run on it precipitated by the failure of The International Bank. An Advertisement in the October 28, 1859 issue of the Toronto Globe stated that the bank had suspended operation. The bank's charter was repealed on August 31, 1863.

130-10.   **ISSUE OF 1859**
DESIGNS AND COLOURS

130-10-02-02
 $1 Face Design: Bust of young woman/woodsman/—
  Colour: See subheadings
 Back Design: Plain

130-10-02-04
 $2 Face Design: Indians on bluff/—/bust of young woman
  Colour: See subheadings
 Back Design: Plain

THE COLONIAL BANK OF CANADA

130-10-02-06
   $3 Face Design: St. George slaying dragon/three allegorical women/Cornelia Jocelyn
       Colour: See subheadings
   Back Design: Plain

130-10-02-08
   $4 Face Design: "Justice" figure/Queen Victoria (Winterhalter portrait)/—
       Colour: See subheadings
   Back Design: Plain

130-10-02-10
   $5 Face Design: Farm family under tree/—/Cornelia Jocelyn
      Colour: See subheadings
   Back Design: Plain

130-10-02-12
   $10 Face Design: Train at station/—/Indian maiden
      Colour: See subheadings
   Beck Design: Plain

130-10-02-14R
   $20 Face Design: St. George slaying dragon/loading hay/Cornelia Jocelyn
      Colour: See subheadings
   Back Design: Plain

130-10-02-16
   $50 Face Design: St. George slaying dragon/sailing ship/Cornelia Jocelyn
      Colour: See subheadings
   Back Design: Plain

THE COLONIAL BANK OF CANADA

130-10-02-18R
    $100 Face Design: Steamship/—/Queen Victoria (Winterhalter portrait)
    Colour: See subheadings
    Back Design: Plain

2. TWO SIGNATURE NOTES, ORANGE-BROWN TINT

IMPRINT
    Jocelyn, Draper, Welch & Co.
    American Bank Note Company, New York

SIGNATURES

left	right
mss. E.C. Hopkins	mss. Wm. Bettes
mss. E.C. Hopkins	mss. G.G. Moss (p.)
mss. T. Hough	mss. Geo. G. Moss (p.)
mss. T. Hough	mss. Wm. Bettes

ISSUE DATING
    Partially Engraved__18__:
    $1 1859: April 4,26,27,28,29; May 4,8; May, July 7,8,12
    $2 1859: April 4,26,27,29; May 4,7,8,9,16,17,24,25; July 4,8,12,13,14
    $3 1859: April 4,6; May 3,4,8,31; June 2,28; July 6
    $4 1859: April 4; June 4,6,8,9,18,24
    $5 1859: April 4,29; May 4,7,18; June 14,24,28,29; July 1,4
    $10 1859: April 4; May 1st
    $20 1859: May 2,21; Aug. 4
    $50 1859: May 2,21; Aug. 4
    $100 1859: May 2; Aug. 4

STAMP
    Notes occur with various letters, numbers, etc. stamped on the face and back: Blue Y, X, 8; Black X, ZT

Cat.No.	Denom.	Date	Variety	VG	F	VF	EF	Unc
10-02-02	$1	1859	Two signatures	25.	40.	60.	90.	150.
10-02-02R	$1	1859	Two signatures	-	-	-	75.	100.
10-02-04	$2	1859	Two signatures	25.	40.	60.	90.	150.
10-02-04R	$2	1859	Two signatures	-	-	-	75.	100.
10-02-06	$3	1859	Two signatures	75.	125.	175.	225.	425.
10-02-06R	$3	1859	Two signatures	-	-	-	100.	150.
10-02-08	$4	1859	Two signatures	65.	100.	160.	200.	325.
10-02-08R	$4	1859	Two signatures	-	-	-	100.	150.
10-02-10	$5	1859	Two signatures	25.	40.	60.	90.	150.
10-02-10R	$5	1859	Two signatures	-	-	-	75.	100.
10-02-12	$10	1859	Two signatures	70.	100.	140.	225.	425.
10-02-14	$20	1859	Completed note	1,200.	1,600.	2,500.	-	-
10-02-14R	$20	18__	Remainder*	500.	700.	1,000.	-	-
10-02-16	$50	1859	Completed note	600.	900.	1,200.	-	-
10-02-16R	$50	18__	Remainder*	150.	200.	325.	450.	-
10-02-18	$100	1859	Completed note	600.	900.	1,200.	-	-
10-02-18R	$100	18__	Remainder*	150.	200.	325.	450.	-

*Incomplete or spurious dates and signatures - authentically completed notes are dated May 2 or Aug. 4, 1859.
Uncut sheets exist, each sheet consisting of: $20, 20, 50, 100 notes.

Note: See "BANK OF TORONTO", "BANK OF UPPER CANADA" and "CITY BANK OF MONTREAL" for altered Colonial Bank notes.

4. ONE SIGNATURE NOTES, PINK TINT

DESIGNS AND COLOURS
See previous two signature issue.

130-10-04-02

130-10-04-04

130-10-04-06

130-10-04-08

130-10-04-10

130-10-04-12

IMPRINT
Jocelyn Draper, Welch & Co.
American Bank Note Company, New York
ABNCo (monogram)

SIGNATURES

right only
mss. T. Hough
mss. G.G. Moss

ISSUE DATING
Engraved
$1 - $5: May 4th 1859
Partially Engraved __18__:
$10 1859: Oct. 20

STAMP
Notes occur with various letters, numbers, etc. stamped on the face and back. For more information see CPMS Journal April 1978.

Cat.No.	Denom.	Date	VG	F	VF	EF	Unc
10-04-02	$1	1859	25.	40.	60.	90.	150.
10-04-04	$2	1859	125.	175.	250.	400.	800.
10-04-06	$3	1859	60.	100.	150.	225.	300.
10-04-08	$4	1859	60.	100.	150.	225.	300.
10-04-10	$5	1859	25.	40.	60.	90.	150.
10-04-12	$10	1859	70.	100.	150.	225.	500.

Note: The orange-brown tint and the pink tint notes were used as altered sources for United States obsolete notes, i.e. Pennsylvania.

THE COLONIAL BANK OF CHATHAM

1837 - 1839

CHATHAM, U. C.(UPPER CANADA)

BANK NUMBER 135   **NONREDEEMABLE**

This "spurious bank" was established in 1837 in Chatham, Upper Canada, by a group of individuals, principally from Buffalo, for the purpose of circulating its "notes" in the Buffalo area.

135-10.   **ISSUE OF 1837**
DESIGNS AND COLOURS

Photo Not Available

135-10-02
$1 (5s) **Face Design:** Unknown
       Colour: Black with no tint
       Back Design: Plain

135-10-04R
$2 (10s) **Face Design:** Winged male figure/standing "Justice" figure, ornate shield, seated "Agriculture" figure/winged child in clouds. Engraved "Will pay - to Sir Francis Head"
       Colour: Black with no tint
       Back Design: Plain

135-10-06
$3 (15s) **Face Design:** —/seated "Justice" figure, lion; lion below/Indian with headdress Engraved "Will pay - to Sir Francis Head"
       Colour: Black with no tint
       Back Design: Plain

COMMERCIAL BANK

135-10-08
$5 (25s) Face Design: —/Royal Crest; lion below/King William IV
Engraved "Will pay - to Sir Francis Head"
Colour: Black with no tint

Back Design: Plain

135-10-10
$10 (50s) Face Design: —/Britannia in chariot drawn by lions; lion below/female with grain
Engraved "Payable - to Sir Francis Head"
Colour: Black with no tint

Back Design: Plain

IMPRINT
Rawdon, Wright & Hatch New York

SIGNATURES
	left	right
$1 (5s):	mss. Unknown	mss. Unknown
$2 (10s):	mss. W.A. Chamberlin	mss. Unknown
$3 (15s):	mss. W.A. Chamberlin	mss. John Clifford
$5 (25s):	mss. W.A. Chamberlin	mss. A.J. Douglas (v.)
$5 (25s):	mss. W.A. Chamberlin	mss. John Clifford
$10 (50s):	mss. W.A. Chamberlin	mss. John Clifford

ISSUE DATING
Partially Engraved __18__:
$1 (5s) 1837: Unknown
$2 (10s) 1837: Feby. 3
$3 (15s) 1837: Feby. 3, Feb. 15
$5 (25s) 1837: Jany 4, Feby. 3
$10 (50s) 1837: January 4

Cat.No.	Denom.	Date	G	VG	F	VF	EF	Unc
10-02	$1(5s)	1837			NOTE NOT CONFIRMED			
10-04R	$2(10S)	1837*	-	2,000.	2,800.	-	-	-
10-06	$3(15s)	1837	-	2,000.	2,800.	-	-	-
10-08	$5(25s)	1837	-	2,000.	2,800.	-	-	-
10-10	$10(50s)	1837	-	2,000.	2,800.	-	-	-

*Remainder: left signature only

COMMERCIAL BANK
1837
BROCKVILLE, UPPER CANADA

BANK NUMBER 140   **NONREDEEMABLE**

The Commercial Bank at Brockville was a "spurious bank" whose fictitious notes were circulated by swindlers. The public was alerted by the watchful press in January of 1837 when the worthless notes first appeared. Despite this, the notes circulated in Upper Canada, Ohio, and Michigan.

140-10.   DRAFT ISSUE OF 1834 - 1836
Engraved: "For Messrs Sims, Colburn and Co."
DESIGNS AND COLOURS

140-10-02
$5 (25s) Face Design: Sailing ship/seated allegorical figure with lute, urn (water god); cask, bales and ship below/sailing ship; Engraved "For Mess'rs Sims, Colburn & Co"
Colour: Black with no tint

Back Design: Plain

140-10-04
$10 (50s) Face Design: Allegorical female/King William IV; crown below/seated woman with grain, cattle; Engraved "For Mess'rs Sims, Colburn & Co"
Colour: Black with no tint

Back Design: Plain

IMPRINT
Burton, & Edmonds, N. York

SIGNATURES
left	right
mss. Luther R. Sims	mss. W. Colburn

ISSUE DATING
Partially Engraved __18__:
1834: Sept. 2
1836: Nov. 3

Cat.No.	Denom.	Date	VG	F	VF	EF	Unc
10-02	$5(25s)	1836	1,200.	-	-	-	-
10-04	$10(50s)	1834	1,200.	-	-	-	-

COMMERCIAL BANK

1837

KINGSTON, UPPER CANADA

BANK NUMBER 145   **NONREDEEMABLE**

This bank appears to be a "spurious bank", trading on the name of The Commercial Bank of the Midland District established in 1831 in Kingston, Upper Canada.

145-10. DRAFT ISSUE

- **$1:** Engraved: "For the FOREIGN and DOMESTIC Exchange Company"
- **$2 (10s):** Engraved: "For the FOREIGN and DOMESTIC EXCHANGE COMPANY"
- **$3 (15s):** Engraved: "for the Foreign & Domestic Exchange Company"

DESIGNS AND COLOURS

145-10-02-02
- **$1 Face Design:** Portrait of Washington/seated Mercury, ship in background; Indian paddling canoe below/portrait of Franklin
  See subheadings
- **Colour:** Black with no tint
- **Back Design:** Plain

145-10-04-02
- **$1 Face Design:** Portrait of Washington/seated Mercury, ship in background; Indian paddling canoe below/portrait of Franklin
  See subheadings
- **Colour:** Black with no tint
- **Back Design:** Plain

145-10-02-04
- **$2 (10s) Face Design:** Sheaves/woman with grain
  See subheadings
- **Colour:** Black with no tint
- **Back Design:** Plain

145-10-02-06
- **$3 (15s) Face Design:** Horse's head/seated female, mill in background; casks, bales and ship below/-
  See subheadings
- **Colour:** Black with no tint
- **Back Design:** Plain

IMPRINT
Jas. Harris, Engravr N.Y.
Jas. Harris, Engraver, N.Y.

SIGNATURES
left	right
mss. Wm. Holdridge	mss. A.V. Hammond

2. MANUSCRIPT "Commercial" IN BANK NAME

ISSUE DATING
Partially Engraved __18__:
- **$1 1837:** July 18
- **$2 (10s) 1837:** Jany 31, July 30
- **$3 (15s) 1837:** June 21, June 26

Cat.No.	Denom.	Date	VG	F	VF	EF	Unc
10-02-02	$1	1837	800.	1,200.	-	-	-
10-02-04	$2(10s)	1837	800.	1,200.	-	-	-
10-02-06	$3(15s)	1837	800.	1,200.	-	-	-
10-02-08	$5	1837	800.	1,200.	-	-	-
10-20-10	$10	1837	800.	1,200.	-	-	-

4. ENGRAVED "COMMERCIAL" IN BANK NAME

ISSUE DATING
Partially Engraved ___18___:
1837: July 25

Cat.No.	Denom.	Date	VG	F	VF	EF	Unc
10-04-02	$1	1837	900.	1,300.	-	-	-

THE COMMERCIAL BANK

1837

MONTREAL, LOWER CANADA

BANK NUMBER 150 **NONREDEMABLE**

The Commercial Bank in Montreal appears to be another spurious bank of the period. Its notes were produced from the same plate as those of the Mechanics Bank in Montreal and have the same signatures.

150-10. **ISSUE OF 1837**
DESIGNS AND COLOURS

Photo Not Available

150-10-02
- **$3 Face Design:** Dock scene/blacksmith and two women (Industry, agriculture and commerce); arm and hammer in shield below/woman with wheat leaning on pillar
- **Colour:** Black with no tint
- **Back Design:** Plain

Photo Not Available

150-10-04
- **$5 Face Design:** Seated youth with mechanics' tools/seated woman resting on cogwheel: arm and hammer in shield below/blacksmith "Industry"
- **Colour:** Black with no tint
- **Back Design:** Plain

150-10-06
- **$10 Face Design:** Seated woman with rake, leaning on shield/blacksmith and two women; crouching lion in oval below/kneeling cherub inscribing rock.
- **Colour:** Black with no tint
- **Back Design:** Plain

IMPRINT
Rawdon, Wright & Hatch New-York

SIGNATURES
- **left** mss: F.E. Whiting
- **right** mss: W. Morris

ISSUE DATING
Partially Engraved __18__:
$10: June 1 1837

Cat.No.	Denom.	Date	VG	F	VF	EF	Unc
10-02	$3	1837				Not confirmed	
10-04	$5	1837				Not confirmed	
10-06	$10	1837	100.	150.	200.	300.	-

THE COMMERCIAL BANK OF CANADA

1856 - 1868

KINGSTON, PROVINCE OF CANADA

BANK NUMBER 155 **REDEEMABLE**

Originally incorporated as The Commercial Bank of the Midland District in 1831, in Kingston, Canada West, this bank operated until 1868. Its name was changed to The Commercial Bank of Canada in 1856. It suspended specie payment in October, 1867 and in the following year was taken over by The Merchants' Bank of Canada without loss to creditors. The shareholders received about one third of the par value of the paid-up capital. The main reasons for this bank's failure were its involvement in speculation and its large extension of credit to the Detroit and Milwaukee Railway.

155-10. **"YELLOW" ISSUE**
CANADA WEST BRANCHES
1857
DESIGNS AND COLOURS

155-10-06-02
- **$1 Face Design:** Seated Indian with rifle/train and hay field/Indian maiden in oval
- **Colour:** Black with overall yellow tint
- **Back Design:** Plain

155-10-06-04
- **$2 Face Design:** Chickens/cow and calf in stream woman feeding chickens
- **Colour:** Black with overall yellow tint
- **Back Design:** Plain

THE COMMERCIAL BANK OF CANADA

155-10-08-02
- **$5 Face Design:** Surveyors/train/man with pick and shovel
- **Colour:** Black with overall yellow tint
- **Back Design:** See Varieties
- **Colour:** See varieties

155-10-04-02
- **$10 Face Design:** Queen Victoria (Winterhalter portrait) men on dock by anchor/Princess Eugenie
- **Colour:** Black with overall yellow tint
- **Back Design:** Lathework and bank name
- **Colour:** Brown

IMPRINT
Toppan, Carpenter & Co. Montreal

SIGNATURES
right only
mss. W. Griffin

ISSUE DATING
Engraved
2nd Jan'y 1857

2. BROCKVILLE ISSUE

Engraved "BROCKVILLE" in frame at bottom of notes

Cat.No.	Denom.	Date	VG	F	VF	EF	Unc
10-02-02	$1	1857	700.	950.	-	-	-

4. GALT ISSUE

Engraved "GALT" in frame at ends of notes.

Cat.No.	Denom.	Date	VG	F	VF	EF	Unc
10-04-02	$10	1857	800.	1,100.	-	-	-

6. HAMILTON ISSUE

- **$1:** Engraved "HAMILTON" in frame at bottom of notes.
- **$2:** Engraved "HAMILTON" in frame at ends of notes.

Cat.No.	Denom.	Date	VG	F	VF	EF	Unc
10-06-02	$1	1857	700.	950.	-	-	-
10-06-04	$2	1857	700.	950.	-	-	-

10. KINGSTON ISSUE BROWN BACK

Engraved "KINGSTON" in frame at ends of notes.

OVERPRINT
"LONDON" in red and H in black

DESIGNS AND COLOURS

- **$5 Back Design:** Lathework and bank name
- **Colour:** Brown

Cat.No.	Denom.	Date	VG	F	VF	EF	Unc
10-10-02	$5	1857	700.	950.	-	-	-

12. LONDON ISSUE PLAIN BACK

- **$1:** Engraved: "LONDON" in frame at bottom of notes.
- **$2:** Engraved: "LONDON" in frame at ends of notes.

STAMP
- **$1:** "C" in back
- **$2:** "S" in black

Cat.No.	Denom.	Date	VG	F	VF	EF	Unc
10-12-02	$1	1857	700.	950.	-	-	-
10-12-04	$2	1857	700.	950.	-	-	-

14. LONDON ISSUE BROWN BACK

DESIGNS AND COLOURS
- **$5:** Engraved "LONDON" in frame at ends of notes.

155-10-14-04
- **$5 Back Design:** Lathework and bank name
- **Colour:** Brown

OVERPRINT
"S", "CL" in black

Cat.No.	Denom.	Date	VG	F	VF	EF	Unc
10-14-04	$5	1857	700.	950.	-	-	-

THE COMMERCIAL BANK OF CANADA

16. TORONTO ISSUE
Engraved "TORONTO" in frame at bottom of notes
STAMP
  "W" in black

Cat.No.	Denom.	Date	VG	F	VF	EF	Unc
10-16-02	$1	1857	600.	1,000.	-	-	-

155-12. "GREEN" ISSUE
CANADA WEST BRANCHES
1860 - 1861

DESIGNS AND COLOURS

155-12-16-02
  $1 Face Design: Bank Crest; seated Indian with rifle/train and hay field/Indian maiden in oval
  Colour: Black with green tint
  Back Design: Plain

155-12-18-02P
  $2 Face Design: Bank Crest; chickens/cow and calf in stream/woman feeding chickens
  Colour: Black with green tint
  Back Design: Plain

155-12-06-02P
  $5 Face Design: Bank Crest; surveyors/train and hay field/man with pick and shovel
  Colour: Black with green tint
  Back Design: Plain

IMPRINT
  American Bank Note Co. New York
  American Bank Note Company

SIGNATURES
  left — none
  right — mss. J.Davidson

ISSUE DATING
  Engraved
  2nd Jany. 1860
  Jan. 2, 1861

PROTECTOR
  Green outlined "word" on face and back
  Green "numeral" on face and back

2. BELLEVILLE ISSUE
Engraved "BELLEVILLE" in frame at ends of notes.

Cat.No.	Denom.	Date	VG	F	VF	EF	Unc
12-02-02	$1	1860	500.	700.	-	-	-
12-02-04	$2	1860	500.	700.	-	-	-

4. BROCKVILLE ISSUE
Engraved "BROCKVILLE" in frame at ends of notes.
STAMP
  "K" in black

Cat.No.	Denom.	Date	VG	F	VF	EF	Unc
12-04-02	$1	1860	500.	700.	-	-	-

6. CHATHAM ISSUE
Engraved "CHATHAM" in frame at ends of notes.

Cat.No.	Denom.	Date	VG	F	VF	EF	Unc
12-06-02P	$5	1860				PROOF	400.

8. HAMILTON ISSUE
Engraved "HAMILTON" in frame at ends of notes.

Cat.No.	Denom.	Date	VG	F	VF	EF	Unc
12-08-04	$2	1860	400.	600.	-	-	-

10. INGERSOLL ISSUE
Engraved "Ingersoll" in frame at ends of notes.

Cat.No.	Denom.	Date	VG	F	VF	EF	Unc
12-10-02	$1	1860	500.	700.	-	-	-

12. KINGSTON ISSUE
Engraved "KINGSTON" in frame at ends of notes.

Cat.No.	Denom.	Date	VG	F	VF	EF	Unc
12-12-02	$1	1860	500.	700.	-	-	-
12-12-04P	$1	1861				PROOF	400.
12-12-06	$2	1860	500.	700.	-	-	-
12-12-08P	$5	1860				PROOF	400.

14. LONDON ISSUE

Engraved "LONDON" in frame at ends of notes.

Cat.No.	Denom.	Date	VG	F	VF	EF	Unc
12-14-02	$1	1860	500.	700.	-	-	-
12-14-04	$2	1860	500.	700.	-	-	-

16. PERTH ISSUE

Engraved "PERTH" in frame at ends of notes.

Cat.No.	Denom.	Date	VG	F	VF	EF	Unc
12-16-02	$1	1860	500.	700.	-	-	-

18. PORT HOPE ISSUE

Engraved "PORT HOPE" in frame at ends of notes.

Cat.No.	Denom.	Date					Unc
12-18-04P	$2	1860				PROOF	400.

20. PRESCOTT ISSUE

Engraved "PRESCOTT" in frame at ends of notes.

Cat.No.	Denom.	Date					Unc
12-20-02P	$2	1860				PROOF	400.

22. TORONTO ISSUE

Engraved "TORONTO" in frame at ends of notes.

Cat.No.	Denom.	Date	VG	F	VF	EF	Unc
12-22-02	$1	1860	500.	700.	-	-	-

24. WINDSOR ISSUE

Engraved "WINDSOR" in frame at ends of notes.

Cat.No.	Denom.	Date	VG	F	VF	EF	Unc
12-24-02	$1	1860	500.	700.	-	-	-
12-24-04	$2	1860	500.	700.	-	-	-

155-14. "YELLOW" ISSUE MONTREAL BRANCH 1857

$1, $10 & $100: Engraved "MONTREAL" at bottom centre.
$2 & $5: Engraved "MONTREAL" in the frame at ends.
$1000: Engraved "MONTREAL" at right centre.

DESIGNS AND COLOURS

155-14-02
- **$1 Face Design:** Indian/seated farmer with scythe/woman with sheaf over shoulder
- **Colour:** Black with overall yellow tint
- **Back Design:** Plain

Photo Not Available

155-14-04P
- **$2 Face Design:** Seated Indian maiden with shield cattle and sheep near water/—
- **Colour:** Black with overall yellow tint
- **Back Design:** Plain

Photo Not Available

155-14-06P
- **$5 Face Design:** Portrait of Columbus/ships in harbour/sailor with sextant
- **Colour:** black with overall yellow tint
- **Back Design:** Lathework and bank name
- **Colour:** Brown

155-14-08
- **$10 Face Design:** Woman and Arms of Montreal/busy harbour scene/bust of Wellington
- **Colour:** Black with overall yellow tint
- **Back Design:** Lathework and bank name
- **Colour:** Brown

155-14-10P
- **$100 Face Design:** —/bank building/Princess Eugenie
- **Colour:** Black with overall yellow tint
- **Back Design:** Lathework and bank name
- **Colour:** Brown

THE COMMERCIAL BANK OF CANADA

155-14-12P
$1000: (£250)
Face Design: —/Princess Eugenie/—
Colour: Black with overall yellow tint

Back Design: Lathework and bank name
Colour: Brown

IMPRINT
Toppan, Carpenter & Co., Montreal

SIGNATURES
right only
mss. Tho. Kirby

ISSUE DATING
Engraved
2nd Jan'y 1857

Cat.No.	Denom.	Date	VG	F	VF	EF	Unc
14-02	$1	1857	800.	1,200.	-		-
14-04P	$2	1857			FACE PROOF		500.
14-06P	$5	1857			FACE PROOF		500.
14-08	$10	1857	800.	1,200.	-		-
14-10P	$100	1857			FACE PROOF		600.
14-12P	$1000(£250)	1857			FACE PROOF		900.

155-16. "GREEN" ISSUE
MONTREAL BRANCH
1860 - 1862

$1 - $100: Engraved "MONTREAL" at bottom centre.
$1000: Engraved "MONTREAL" at right centre.

DESIGNS AND COLOURS
Counters at the upper left of notes in the 1857 issue were replaced by vignettes.

155-16-02P
$1 Face Design: Indian/seated farmer with scythe/ small bank crest and counter
Colour: Black with overall green tint

Back Design: Plain

155-16-04P
$2 Face Design: Seated Indian maiden with shield/ cattle and sheep near water/ small bank crest and counter
Colour: Black with overall green tint

Back Design: Plain

155-16-06P
$5 Face Design: Small bank crest; portrait of Columbus/ ships in harbour/sailor with sextant
Colour: Black with overall green tint

Back Design: Plain

155-16-10P
$10 Face Design: Bank Crest; woman and Arms of Montreal/ busy harbour scene/bust of Wellington in oval
Colour: Black with overall green tint

Back Design: Plain

Photo Not Available

155-16-12P
$100 Face Design: —/bank building/portrait of young woman wearing hat
Colour: Black with overall green tint

Back Design: Plain

155-16-14P
$1000 **Face Design:** —/Princess Eugenie/—
Colour: Black with overall green tint

Back Design: Plain

IMPRINT
- **$1-$5:** Toppan, Carpenter & Co. Montreal
- **$10:** Toppan, Carpenter & Co. and American Bank Note Co. (monogram)
- **$100:** American Bank Note Company
- **$1000:** None

SIGNATURES
right only
mss. W. Griffin

DATING
Engraved
2nd January 1860
2nd Jany 1860
Jan. 2, 1862

Cat.No.	Denom.	Date	VG	F	VF	EF	Unc
16-02P	$1	1860				PROOF	500.
16-04P	$2	1860				PROOF	500.
16-06P	$5	1860				PROOF	500.
16-10P	$10	1860				PROOF	600.
16-12P	$100	1862				PROOF	750.
16-14P	$1000	1860				PROOF	1,250.

THE COMMERCIAL BANK OF FORT ERIE
1836 - 1839
FORT ERIE, UPPER CANADA

BANK NUMBER 160   **NONREDEEMABLE**

Probably another of the many "spurious banks", whose worthless notes appeared during the winter and spring of 1837. The swindlers preyed with some success on the unwary, mainly in the border states.

160-10.   **ISSUE OF 1836 - 1837**

DESIGNS AND COLOURS

160-10-02
$1 (5s) **Face Design:** St. George slaying dragon/steamboat with U.S. flag; running deer below/ King William IV
Colour: Black with no tint

Back Design: Plain

160-10-04
$2 (10s) **Face Design:** St. George slaying dragon/Royal Crest; early train below/—
Colour: Black with no tint

Back Design: Plain

160-10-06
$3 (15s) **Face Design:** Britannia and anchor/planting scene; paddlewheeler below/St. George slaying dragon
Colour: Black with no tint

Back Design: Plain

THE COMMERCIAL BANK OF FORT ERIE

160-10-08
$4 (20s) Face Design: —/Royal Crest; paddlewheeler below/ men cutting and women carring sheaves
Colour: Black with no tint
Back Design: Plain

160-10-10
$5 (25s) Face Design: —/King William IV; beaver below/ St. George slaying dragon
Colour: Black with no tint
Back Design: Plain

160-10-18R
$10 Face Design: —/Royal Crest; dog's head "Fidelity" below/cherub in clouds
Colour: Black with no tint
Back Design: Plain

160-10-20R
$20 Face Design: —/ships and seated allegorical women, with shield and produce; dog's head "Fidelity" below/ Royal Crest (sideways)
Colour: Black with no tint
Back Design: Plain

IMPRINT
Rawdon, Wright & Hatch New York

SIGNATURES
left
mss. V. Forsyth

right
mss. M.B. Sherwood

ISSUE DATING
Partially Engraved __18__:
- **$1 1837:** Jan. 10
- **$2 1837:** Jan. 10
- **$3 1837:** Jan. 10
- **$4 1836:** July 20
- **1837:** Jany. 20
- **$5 1836:** July 20
- **1837:** Jany 20
- **1837:** Aug. 20

Cat.No.	Denom.	Date	Variety	VG	F	VF	EF	Unc
10-02	$1	1837**		140.	190.	275.	-	-
10-04	$2	1837**	Spurious	140.	190.	275.	-	-
10-06	$3	1837**		250.	325.	475.	-	-
10-08	$4	1836		200.	275.	400.	-	-
10-10	$4	1837		200.	275.	400.	-	-
10-12	$5	1836		140.	190.	275.	-	-
10-14	$5	1837	Jany 20	140.	190.	275.	-	-
10-16	$5	1837	Aug 20	140.	190.	275.	-	-
10-18R	$10	18__*	Remainder	400.	550.	850.	-	-
10-20R	$20	18__**	Remainder	400.	550.	850.	-	-

*unsigned, undated and unnumbered.
**spurious signatures and dates.

Note: Remainder notes are those with spurious signatures and dates.

THE COMMERCIAL BANK OF LAKE ONTARIO

1837

NIAGARA FALLS, UPPER CANADA

BANK NUMBER 165   *NONREDEEMABLE*

Bank notes were ordered in February of 1837; however, there is no record of any notes or proofs having survived.

THE COMMERCIAL BANK OF MANITOBA

1885 - 1893

WINNIPEG, MANITOBA

BANK NUMBER 170   *REDEEMABLE*

This bank was established in Winnipeg, Manitoba, in 1885, as an outgrowth of the private banking and finance business of McArthur, Boyle and Campbell. Its lending policies were very liberal. After the severe winter of 1892-1893, anxiety developed among the depositors which culminated in a run on the bank in July and payments were stopped. Creditors were paid in full but shareholders lost their entire equity.

170-10.   **ISSUE OF 1885**

DESIGNS AND COLOURS

170-10-02
- **$5 Face Design:** Female figure "Ceres"/Indian camp (F.O.C. Darley design) Queen Victoria in oval
- **Colour:** Black with green tint

Back Design: Flowers, Lathework, counters and bank name, flowers
Colour: Brown

170-10-04
- **$10 Face Design:** Female figure "Ceres"/—/farmers reaping grain
- **Colour:** Black with ochre tint

Back Design: Lathework, counters and bank name
Colour: Green

IMPRINT
Canada Bank Note Co. Montreal

SIGNATURES

left	right
mss. A.A. Jackson	engr. D. MacArthur

ISSUE DATING
Engraved
May 1, 1885

Cat.No.	Denom.	Date	VG	F	VF	EF	Unc
10-02	$5	1885	4,500.	-	-	-	-
10-04	$10	1885	4,500.	-	-	-	-

Note: Issued notes of 1885 are extremely rare. Proofs exist and sell for about $1,000 to $1,500.

170-12.   **ISSUE OF 1891**

DESIGNS AND COLOURS

170-12-02
- **$5 Face Design:** Head office/Binder and horses /D. MacArthur
- **Colour:** Black with green tint

COMMERCIAL BANK OF MONTREAL

Back Design: Lathework, counters, bank name and train at prairie station
Colour: Green

170-12-04
$10 Face Design: Head office/ploughing with team of horses/D. MacArthur
Colour: Black with green tint

Back Design: lathework, counters, bank name and Crest
Colour: Green

IMPRINT
British American Bank Note Co. Ottawa

SIGNATURES
left — mss. various
right — engr. D. MacArthur

ISSUE DATING
Engraved
2nd Jan 1891

Cat.No.	Denom.	Date	VG	F	VF	EF	Unc
12-02	$5	1891	4,500.	-	-	-	-
12-04	$10	1891	4,500.	-	-	-	-

COMMERCIAL BANK OF MONTREAL

1835 - 1837

MONTREAL, LOWER CANADA

BANK NUMBER 175   **NONREDEEMABLE**

Established as a private company in Montreal, the Commercial Bank of Montreal operated for only a short period of time until 1837. Little is known of its operation. An 1841 counterfeit detector listed the notes as genuine, noting it was John E. Mills Bank and that all others were frauds.

175-10.   **DRAFT ISSUE OF 1835**

Engraved: "for John E. Mills & Co." at bottom
DESIGNS AND COLOURS

175-10-02
$5 (£1.5) Face Design: St. George slaying dragon/—/ early train
Colour: Black with no tint
Back Design: Plain

175-10-04
$10 (£2.10) Face Design: Indian maiden/—/train
Colour: Black with no tint
Back Design: Plain

175-10-06
$20 (£5) Face Design: Allegorical "Vulcan" and "Industry" —/allegorical "Plenty" and "Commerce"
Colour: Black with no tint
Back Design: Plain

175-10-08
$50 (£12.10) **Face Design:** Allegorical scene: nude woman and cupid
in clouds, sea, horses below/-/-
Colour: Black with no tint

Back Design: Plain

IMPRINT
Rawdon, Wright, Hatch & Edson, New York

SIGNATURES
left
mss. G.B. Rolleston
right
mss. Jno. E. Mills

ISSUE DATING
Partially Engraved __18__:
$5 (£1.5): 1 Sep., 21 Aug.
$10 (£2.10): 1835. 1 Sep.
$20 (£5) & $50 (£12.10): 1835: 10 Oct.

Cat.No.	Denom.	Date	Variety	VG	F	VF	EF	Unc
10-02	$5(£1.5)	1835	21 Aug	900.	1,300.	-	-	-
10-02a	$5(£1.5)	1835	1 Sep	900.	1,300.	-	-	-
10-04	$10(£2.10)	1835	1 Sep	900.	1,300.	-	-	-
10-04a	$10(£2.10)	1835	21 Aug	900.	1,300.	-	-	-
10-06	$20(£5)	1835		950.	1,400.	-	-	-
10-08	$50(£12.10)	1835		950.	1,400.	-	-	-

175-12   DRAFT ISSUE OF 1836

Engraved: "Accepted for John E. Mills & Co." at the bottom and "To John E. Mills & Co." or "To John E. Mills & Company" across top of the face.

DESIGNS AND COLOURS

175-12-02
$1 **Face Design:** Woman with sickle/man with whip and dog/farm girl leaning on fence
Colour: Black with no tint

Back Design: Plain

175-12-04
$2 **Face Design:** Woman with sickle, cornucopia/
early train passing house/
"Justice" figure
Colour: Black with no tint

Back Design: Plain

IMPRINT
Underwood, Bald, Spencer & Hufty, N. York & Philada.

SIGNATURES
left
mss. G.B. Rolleston
right
mss. Jno E. Mills

ISSUE DATING
Engraved
1st June 1836

Cat.No.	Denom.	Date	Variety	VG	F	VF	EF	Unc
12-02R	$1	1836	Remainder*	700.	1,000.	1,500.	-	-
12-04	$2	1836		900.	1,300.	-	-	-

* lacks right-hand signature.

THE COMMERCIAL BANK OF NEW BRUNSWICK

THE COMMERCIAL BANK OF NEW BRUNSWICK

1834 - 1868

"SAINT JOHN, N.B." (NEW BRUNSWICK)

BANK NUMBER 180   **NONREDEEMABLE**

Established in 1834 in Saint John, New Brunswick, this bank failed in 1868 due to gross corruption in management. All creditors of the bank were paid in ful, but its shareholders' losses amount to $495,000.

180-10.   **"FREDERICTON BRANCH" ISSUE POUNDS & SHILLINGS**

Engraved: "BRANCH BANK IN FREDERICTON" across centre and "FREDERICTON" engraved at lower centre.

DESIGNS AND COLOURS

180-10-02
- **£1 Face Design:** Ships/Crest/—
- **Colour:** Black with no tint
- **Back Design:** Unknown
- **Colour:** Green

180-10-04
- **£2 Face Design:** Ships/Crest, lion on crown below/—
- **Colour:** Black with no tint
- **Back Design:** Unknown
- **Colour:** Green

180-10-06
- **£5 Face Design:** Britannia/Crest; lion on crown below/—
- **Colour:** Black with no tint
- **Back Design:** Unknown
- **Colour:** Green

IMPRINT
New England Bank Note Company

SIGNATURES
left	right
none	none

ISSUE DATING
Partially Engraved __18__:

Cat.No.	Denom.	Date	VG	F	VF	EF	Unc
10-02P	£1	18__			FACE PROOF		500.
10-04P	£2	18__			FACE PROOF		500.
10-06P	£5	18__			FACE PROOF		500.

180-12.   **"MIRAMICHI BRANCH" ISSUE POUNDS, SHILLINGS & PENCE**

Branch name engraved at lower left. Engraved "CHECK" at right.

DESIGNS AND COLOURS

180-12-02
- **5s Face Design:** Allegorical female/Crest/-
- **Colour:** Black with no tint
- **Back Design:** Lathework with ships at ends
- **Colour:** Green

180-12-04
- **7s6d Face Design:** Allegorical woman with lyre and cornucopia/Crest/-
- **Colour:** Black with no tint

- **Back Design:** Lathework with ships at ends
- **Colour:** Green

IMPRINT
New England Bank Note Co. Boston

THE COMMERCIAL BANK OF NEW BRUNSWICK

SIGNATURES
    left   right
    none   mss. Thomas C. Allan

ISSUE DATING
    Partially Engraved __18__:
    1837: 4 December

Cat.No.	Denom.	Date	VG	F	VF	EF	Unc
12-02	5s	1837	1,000.	1,500.	-	-	-
12-04	7s6d	1837	1,000.	1,500.	-	-	-

180-14.   **"ST. JOHN" ISSUE**
                     POUNDS & SHILLINGS

Branch name enraved at bottom centre.

DESIGNS AND COLOURS

180-14-02P
    5s Face Design: Ships, lighthouse/Crest; lion on crown below/ two men harvesting grain
        Colour: Black with no tint
    Back Design: Lathework with ships at ends
        Colour: Green

180-14-06P
    £1 Face Design: Ship, cargo, fasces and scroll/Crest; lion on crown below/—
        Colour: Black with no tint

    Back Design: Lathework and "Commercial Bank"
        Colour: Green

180-14-10P
    £2 Face Design: Ships/Crest; lion on crown below/—
        Colour: Black with no tint
    Back Design: Unknown
        Colour: Green

180-14-12P
    £5 Face Design: Seated Britannia/Crest; lion on crown below/—
        Colour: Black with no tint
    Back Design: Lathework and bank name
        Colour: Green

180-14-14P
    £10 Face Design: Ship in oval/Crest; lion on crown below/—
        Colour: Black with no tint
    Back Design: Unknown
        Colour: Green

180-14-16P
    £25 Face Design: Two ships in oval/Crest; lion on crown below/—
        Colour: Black with no tint
    Back Design: Unknown
        Colour: Green

THE COMMERCIAL BANK OF NEW BRUNSWICK

IMPRINT
New England Bank Note Co. Boston

SIGNATURES

left	right
mss. G.P. Sancton	mss. D.J. McLaughlin
mss. G.P. Sancton	mss. Gilbert

ISSUE DATING
Partially Engraved __18__:
- £1 1850: 1 June
- 1852: 1 July
- 1853: 1 June, 1 Novr
- £5 1853: June 1

Cat.No.	Denom.	Date	Variety	VG	F	VF	EF	Unc
14-02P	5s	18__				FACE PROOF		500.
14-04	£1	1850		1,000.	1,500.	-	-	-
14-06	£1	1852		1,000.	1,500.	-	-	-
14-08	£1	1853	1 June	1,000.	1,500.	-	-	-
14-08a	£1	1853	1 Novr	1,000.	1,500.	-	-	-
14-10P	£2	18__				FACE PROOF		500.
14-12	£5	1853		1,000.	1,500.	-	-	-
14-14P	£10	18__				FACE PROOF		500.
14-16P	£25	18__				FACE PROOF		600.

180-16.   DOLLAR/POUNDS & SHILLINGS ISSUE 1860

DESIGNS AND COLOURS

180-16-02
$1 (5s) Face Design: Ships/Crest; lion on crown below/—
Colour: Black with green tint

Back Design: Lathework, bank name with ships vertically at ends
Colour: Green

180-16-04
$2 (10s) Face Design —/Crest; lion on crown below/ shipbuilding scene
Colour: Black with green tint

Back Design: Lathework, bank name with ships vertically at ends
Colour: Green

180-16-06
$4 (£1) Face Design: Ship, cargo, fasces, and scroll/ Crest; lion on crown below/—
Colour: Black with green tint

Back Design: Lathework, bank name with ships vertically at ends
Colour: Green

180-16-08P
$8 (£2) Face Design: —/Crest; lion on crown below/ young girl with flower basket
Colour: Black with green tint

Back Design: Lathework, counters and bank name
Colour: Green

180-16-10
$20 (£5) Face Design: Ship/Crest; lion on crown below/ sailor at ship's wheel
Colour: Black with green tint

Back Design: Lathework, counters and bank name
Colour: Green

180-16-12P
$50 (£12.10) **Face Design:** —/Crest; lion on crown below/ seated allegorical woman
Colour: Black with green tint

Back Design: Lathework, counters and bank name
Colour: Green

180-16-14P
$100 (£25) **Face Design:** —/Crest; lion on crown below/ fishermen on schooner in rough sea
Colour: Black with green tint

Back Design: Lathework, counters and bank name
Colour: Green

IMPRINT
American Bank Note Co. Boston

SIGNATURES
left	right
mss. G.P. Sancton	mss. D.J. McLaughlin
mss. G.P. Sancton	mss. W.M. Parks
mss. G.P. Sancton	mss. A.M.L. Seely

ISSUE DATING
Engraved
Nov. 1st 1860

Cat.No.	Denom.	Date	VG	F	VF	EF	Unc
16-02	$1(5s)	1860		700.	1,000.	1,500.	-
16-04	$2(10s)	1860		900.	1,000.	1,500.	-
16-06	$4(£1)	1860		900.	1,100.	1,600.	-
16-08	$8(£2)	1860				FACE PROOF	1,200.
16-10	$20(£5)	1860				FACE PROOF	500.
16-12	$50(£12.10)	1860				FACE PROOF	500.
16-14	$100(£25)	1860				FACE PROOF	500.

COMMERCIAL BANK OF NEWFOUNDLAND
1857 - 1894
SAINT JOHNS, (NEWFOUNDLAND)

BANK NUMBER 185   **REDEEMABLE**

Established in 1857, this bank, and the Union Bank of Newfoundland, failed in December of 1894 due to mismanagement and poor economic conditions. Almost the entire currency then in use in Newfoundland consisted of notes issued by these two banks. Upon their failure, business was at a stand-still and the people in a state of panic until the Canadian banks opened their first branches in Newfoundland. The Newfoundland government assumed the responsibility for the redemption of the failed banks' notes, and the notes of the Commercial Bank continued to be redeemable for 20 cents on the dollar.

185-10.   **ISSUE OF 1857 - 1858**
POUND ISSUE LARGE SIZE NOTES
(19.5 x 10.5 cm.)

DESIGNS AND COLOURS

185-10-02
£1 **Face Design:** —/seated "Commerce" figure with cask, bales, cornucopia and ships/—
Colour: Black with no tint

Back Design: Plain

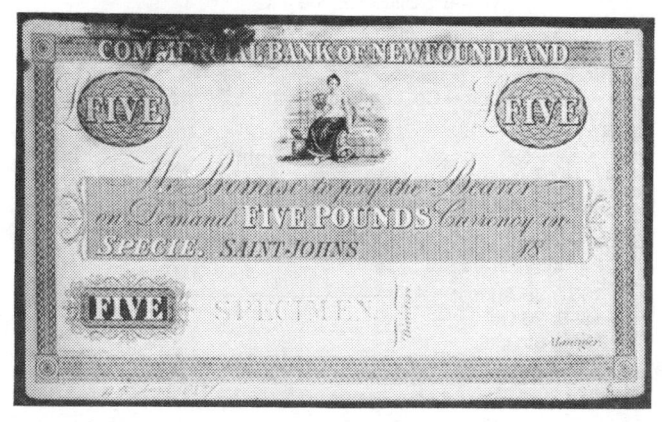

185-10-04
£5 **Face Design:** —/seated "Commerce" figure with cask, bales, cornucopia and ships/—
Colour: Black with no tint

Back Design: Plain

COMMERCIAL BANK OF NEWFOUNDLAND

185-10-06
  £10 **Face Design:** —/seated "Commerce" figure with cask, bales, cornucopia and ships/—
  Colour: Black with no tint
  Back Design: Plain

185-10-08
  £20 **Face Design:** —/seated "Commerce" figure with cask, bales, cornucopia and ships/—
  Colour: Black with no tint
  Back Design: Plain

IMPRINT
Perkins, Bacon & Co. London

SIGNATURES
left	right
mss. Francis Hepburn	mss. R. Brown
mss. G. Ehlers	

ISSUE DATING
Partially Engraved __18__:
1857: 25 August
1858: 20 Oct
1859: 5th Oct.

PROTECTOR
Red mock coins on face only

Cat.No.	Denom.	Date	VG	F	VF	EF	Unc
10-02P	£1	18__				PROOF	500.
10-02	£1	1857	3,000.	4,000.	-	-	-
10-04	£1	1858	3,000.	4,000.	-	-	-
10-12P	£5	18__				PROOF	750.
10-18P	£10	18__				PROOF	750.
10-24P	£20	18__				PROOF	750.

185-12.   **ISSUE OF 1865 - 1867**
TWO SIGNATURE SPACES AT LEFT
POUNDS DOLLAR ISSUE
SMALL SIZE NOTES
(17.5 x 8.5 cm.)

DESIGNS AND COLOURS

185-12-02
  £1 ($4) **Face Design:** Seal in oval/seated "Commerce" figure/ codfish in oval
  Colour: Black with no tint
  Back Design: Plain

185-12-04
  £5 ($20) **Face Design:** Seal in oval/seated "Commerce" figure codfish in oval
  Colour: Black with no tint
  Back Design: Plain

185-12-08
  £10 ($40) **Face Design:** Seal in oval/seated "Commerce" figure codfish in oval
  Colour: Black with no tint
  Back Design: Plain

IMPRINT
Perkins, Bacon & Co. London

SIGNATURES
left	right
mss. Henry Cooke	mss. R. Brown
mss. various	

COMMERCIAL BANK OF NEWFOUNDLAND

ISSUE DATING
 Engraved
  Unknown, 1865
  1st Jany, 1867
PROTECTOR
 £1: Blue "FOUR DOLLARS" on mock coins on face only
 £5: Red-brown "20" on mock coins on face only
 £10: Green "40" on mock coins on face only

Cat.No.	Denom.	Date	VG	F	VF	EF	Unc
12-02	£1 ($4)	1867	1,200.	1,800.	-	-	-
12-04	£5 ($20)	1867	1,200.	1,800.	-	-	-
12-06	£10 ($40)	1865	2,000.	3,000.	-	-	-
12-08	£10 ($40)	1867	2,000.	3,000.	-	-	-

**185-14.   ISSUE OF 1874-1885
ONE SIGNATURE SPACE AT LEFT**

DESIGNS AND COLOURS
See previous issue.

185-14-04

185-14-08

185-14-10P

SIGNATURES
           left   right
  mss. Henry Cooke or   mss. R. Brown
  H Cooke
  mss. H.D. Carter   mss. Henry Cooke

ISSUE DATING
 Engraved
  1st Jan'y 1874
  1st March 1882
  1st July 1884
  1st July 1885
PROTECTOR
 £1: Blue "FOUR DOLLARS" on mock coins on face only
 £5: Red-brown "TWENTY DOLLARS" on mock coins on face only

Cat.No.	Denom.	Date	VG	F	VF	EF	Unc
14-02	£1 ($4)	1874	1,200.	1,800.	-	-	-
14-04	£1 ($4)	1882	1,200.	1,800.	-	-	-
14-06	£1 ($4)	1884	1,100.	1,600.	-	-	-
14-08	£5 ($20)	1874	1,100.	1,600.	-	-	-
14-10P	£5 ($20)	1885				PROOF	500

**185-16. $2 ISSUE OF 1881 - 1884
SMALL SIZE NOTES**

DESIGNS AND COLOURS

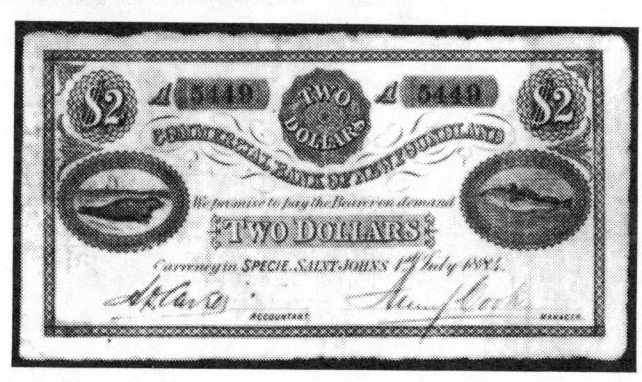

185-16-06
 $2 Face Design: Seal in oval/—/codfish in oval
 Colour: Black with no tint

 Back Design: Plain

IMPRINT
 Perkins, Bacon & Co. London
SIGNATURES
           left   right
  1881-1882: mss. Henry Cooke   mss. R. Brown
  1884: mss. H.D. Carter   mss. Henry Cooke
ISSUE DATING
 Engraved
  1st Jan., 1881
  Unknown, 1882
  1st July 1884
PROTECTOR
 Blue mock coins and TWO DOLLARS on back only

Cat.No.	Denom.	Date	VG	F	VF	EF	Unc
16-02	$2	1881	1,000.	1,400.	-	-	-
16-04	$2	1882	1,000.	1,400.	-	-	-
16-06	$2	1884	900.	1,200.	-	-	-

COMMERCIAL BANK OF NEWFOUNDLAND

185-18. **ISSUE OF 1888**
DOLLAR ISSUE LARGE SIZE NOTES

DESIGNS AND COLOURS

185-18-02
$2 Face Design: Young sailor climbing rigging "Going aloft"/ seated "Commerce" figure/fishermen "Cod fishing"
Colour: See varieties

Back Design: Lathework, counters, bank name and classical motif
Colour: Green

185-18-06
$5 Face Design: Portrait of sailor "young Tar"/seated "Commerce" figure/seals in oval
Colour: Black with green tint

Back Design: Lathework, counters and bank name
Colour: Green

185-18-08
$10 Face Design: Portrait of Queen Victoria "HBM"/ seated "Commerce" figure/ sailor standing by capstan "Charlies Sailor"
Colour: Black with green tint

Back Design: Lathework, counters and bank name
Colour: Green

185-18-10
$20 Face Design: Fisherman with wife, baby and telescope "Old Salt"/seated "Commerce" figure/ "Newfoundland" dog's head "My dog" (Landseer)
Colour: Black with green tint

Back Design: Lathework, counters and bank name
Colour: Green

108

185-18-12
$50 **Face Design:** Boy and dog on ship "Young Fisher"/
seated "Commerce" figure/anchor, box,
barrels and ship "Anchor"
Colour: Black with green tint

Back Design: Lathework, counters and bank name
Colour: Green

IMPRINT
British American Bank Note Co. Montreal

SIGNATURES
left	right
mss. H.D. Carter	mss. Henry Cooke

ISSUE DATING
Engraved
Jany 3rd 1888

VARIETIES
$2 **Face Colour:** Black with green tint
$2 **Face Colour:** Black with orange tint

Cat.No.	Denom.	Date	Variety	VG	F	VF	EF	Unc
18-02	$2	1888	Green tint	400.	550.	900.	1,300.	-
18-04	$2	1888	Orange tint	175.	275.	400.	700.	-
18-06	$5	1888		150.	225.	300.	575.	-
18-08	$10	1888		400.	550.	900.	1,300.	-
18-10	$20	1888		3,000.	4,000.	6,000.	-	-
18-12	$50	1888		3,000.	4,000.	6,000.	-	-

Note: Prices are all for notes without "Paid" or other cancellation stamps or writing on the face.

THE COMMERCIAL BANK OF THE MIDLAND DISTRICT

1831 - 1856

KINGSTON, UPPER CANADA

BANK NUMBER 190   **REDEEMABLE**

After repeated attempts, this bank finally obtained its charter in 1831 with an authorized capital of £100,000. It opened for business in the summer of 1832. In 1856, the bank changed its name to The Commercial Bank of Canada.

190-10.   **ISSUE OF 1832 - 1835**
             PAYABLE AT KINGSTON

DESIGNS AND COLOURS

190-10-04
$1 (5s) **Face Design:** —/paddlewheel steam-boat, coin below/
two smiling cherubs' faces
Colour: Black with no tint

Back Design: Plain

190-10-06
$2 (10s) **Face Design:** Seated woman in oval, figure 2/two
women and shield with figure 2:
"Speed the Plough" under shield; two
coins below/view of town from
harbour (sideways)
Colour: Black with no tint

Back Design: Plain

IMPRINT
Rawdon, Clark & Co. Albany

SIGNATURES
left	right
mss. F.A. Harper	mss. John S. Cartwright
mss. F.A. Harper	mss. J. Watkins (v.)
mss. F.A. Harper	mss. illegible

THE COMMERCIAL BANK OF THE MIDLAND DISTRICT

ISSUE DATING
Partially Engraved __18__:
$1 1832: Aug. 2
1833: 1 Novr.
$2 1833: 1st March
1835: 1 Jany.

Cat.No.	Denom.	Date	VG	F	VF	EF	Unc
10-02P	$1 (5s)	1832				PROOF	500.
10-04	$1 (5s)	1833	1,000.	1,500.	-	-	-
10-06	$2 (10s)	1833	1,000.	1,500.	-	-	-
10-08	$2 (10s)	1835	1,000.	1,500.	-	-	-

190.12. ISSUE OF 1836
PAYABLE AT KINGSTON

DESIGNS AND COLOURS

190-12-02
$1 (5s) **Face Design:** Seated Indian/maid churning butter/ woman with grain
Engraved payee: Alex McNabb
Colour: Black with no tint
Back Design: Plain

190-12-04
$2 (10s) **Face Design:** Harbour scene/allegorical man, urn/ allegorical man and woman
Engraved payee: Alex McNabb
Colour: Black with no tint
Back Design: Plain

IMPRINT
Rawdon, Wright, Hatch & Edson, New-York.

SIGNATURES
left	right
mss. F.A. Harper	mss. W. Logie (v.)
mss. F.A. Harper	mss. M. McCauley (v.)
mss. F.A. Harper	mss. J. Hamilton

ISSUE DATING
Engraved
March 1st 1836

Cat.No.	Denom.	Date	VG	F	VF	EF	Unc
12-02	$1 (5s)	1836	1,000.	1,500.	-	-	-
12-04	$2 (10s)	1836	1,000.	1,500.	-	-	-

190-14. ISSUE OF 1843
PAYABLE AT MONTREAL

DESIGNS AND COLOURS

All notes have a miniature Royal Crest with the lion and unicorn on all fours at the bottom centre.

190-14-02
$1 (5s) **Face Design:** Prince Consort in oval, cherub in ornate I/ semi-nude Indian woman stepping out of canoe/cherub in ornate I; Queen Victoria (Chalon portrait) in oval
Colour: Black with no tint
Back Design: Plain

190-14-04
$2 (10s) **Face Design:** Prince Consort/allegorical women, "Commerce and Agriculture"/Queen Victoria (Chalon portrait)
Colour: Black with no tint
Back Design: Plain

190-14-06
$5 (25s) **Face Design:** Prince Consort/cherubs in ornate 5/ woman and cherubs with ornate 5/ cherubs in ornate 5/Queen Victoria (Chalon Portrait)
Colour: Black with no tint
Back Design: Plain

THE COMMERCIAL BANK OF THE MIDLAND DISTRICT

Photo Not Available

190-14-08P
$10 (50s) Face Design: Queen Victoria (Chalon Portrait)/—/—
Colour: Black with no tint
Back Design: Plain

IMPRINT
Rawdon, Wright & Hatch, New-York
Rawdon, Wright, Hatch and Edson, New-York

SIGNATURES
left	right
mss. Jno. V. Noel	mss. A.H. Campbell

ISSUE DATING
Engraved
1st July 1843

Cat.No.	Denom.	Date	VG	F	VF	EF	Unc
14-02	$1 (5s)	1843	1,000.	1,500.	-	-	-
14-04	$2 (10s)	1843	1,000.	1,500.	-	-	-
14-06	$5 (25s)	1843	1,000.	1,500.	-	-	-
14-08P	$10 (50s)	1843				PROOF	500.

**190-16.   ISSUE OF 1846 - 1854
PAYABLE AT KINGSTON**

DESIGNS AND COLOURS

190-16-02
$1 (5s) Face Design: Man with sickle and sheaves/ reclining woman and ornate 1/ sailor with telescope
Colour: Black with no tint
Back Design: Plain

Photo Not Available

190-16-12
$2 (10s) Face Design: "Justice" and "Liberty" figures/ two seated allegorical women with cornucopia/"Agricultural" and "Commerce" figures
Colour: Black with no tint
Back Design: Plain

190-16-14
$5 (£1.5) Face Design: Queen Victoria (Chalon portrait)/ woman on large 5 supported by four cherubs/Prince Consort
Colour: Black with no tint
Back Design: Plain

190-16-16P
$10 (£2.10) Face Design: Queen Victoria (Chalon portrait)/ seated woman with ornate 10/ Prince consort
Colour: Black with no tint
Back Design: Plain

Photo Not Available

190-16-18P
$20 (£5) Face Design: Queen Victoria (Chalon portrait)/ seated woman with ornate 20/ Prince Consort
Colour: Black with no tint
Back Design: Plain

Photo Not Available

190-16-20P
$50 (£12.10) Face Design: Queen Victoria (Chalon portrait) on Royal Crest/—/—
Colour: Black with no tint
Back Design: Plain

Photo Not Available

190-16-22P
$100 (£25) Face Design: —/allegorical woman/Royal Crest
Colour: Black with no tint
Back Design: Plain

111

THE COMMERCIAL BANK OF THE MIDLAND DISTRICT

IMPRINT
- Rawdon, Wright & Hatch, New York
- Rawdon, Wright, Hatch & Edson, New York

SIGNATURES

left	right
mss. J. Rourke	mss. J.E. Pearce
mss. J. Rourke	mss. Jno. V. Noel
mss. Wm. J. Yarker	mss. C.W. Hamilton

ISSUE DATING
Partially Engraved July 18__:
- 1846: 1 July
- 1847: 1 July
- 1848: 1 July
- 1853: 1 July
- 1854: 1 July

OVERPRINTS
- TORONTO in red
- BELLEVILLE in red
- BROCKVILLE in red

Cat.No.	Denom.	Date	VG	F	VF	EF	Unc
16-02	$1 (5s)	1846	1,000.	1,500.	-	-	-
16-04	$1 (5s)	1847	1,000.	1,500.	-	-	-
16-06	$1 (5s)	1848	1,000.	1,500.	-	-	-
16-08	$1 (5s)	1853	1,000.	1,500.	-	-	-
16-10	$1 (5s)	1854	1,000.	1,500.	-	-	-
16-12	$2 (10s)	18__	1,000.	1,500.	-	-	-
16-14P	$5 (£1.5)	18__				PROOF	500.
16-16P	$10 (£2.10)	18__				PROOF	500.
16-18P	$20 (£5)	18__				PROOF	600.
16-20P	$50 (£12.10)	18__				PROOF	600.
16-22P	$100 (£25)	18__				PROOF	600.

190.-18.   ISSUE OF 185? - 1854
PAYABLE AT KINGSTON

DESIGN AND COLOURS

Photo Not Available

190-18-02P
- **$5 Face Design:** —/seated Mercury with lion/portrait of woman
- **Colour:** Black with no tint
- **Back Design:** Plain

190-18-04
- **$10 Face Design:** Floral panel/flying allegorical male dropping coins from cornucopia/ships
- **Colour:** Black with no tint
- **Back Design:** Plain

IMPRINT
- Rawdon, Wright & Hatch, New York

SIGNATURES

left	right
mss. J.G. Harper	mss. Jno. Hamilton

ISSUE DATING
Partially Engraved __18__:
- 1854: 2 Jany.

Cat.No.	Denom.	Date	VG	F	VF	EF	Unc
18-02P	$5	18__				PROOF	500.
18-04	$10*	1854	120.	175.	225.	-	-

*all known surviving notes are conterfeit.

190-20.   TOPPAN CARPENTER CASILEAR
$4 ISSUES OF 1854
PAYABLE AT VARIOUS BRANCHES

The branch names are engraved in vertical panels flanking the central vignette.

DESIGNS AND COLOURS

190-20-10-02
- **$4 Face Design:** Portrait of young woman/train and farming scene/portrait of young woman
- **Colour:** Black with no tint
- **Back Design:** Plain

IMPRINT
- Toppan, Carpenter, Casilear & Co. Montreal

SIGNATURES

left	right
mss. J. Rourke	mss. Jno. V. Noel

ISSUE DATING
Partially Engraved __185_:
Engraved
2nd May, 185_

PROTECTOR
Green panel with outlined "word" on the face and back

2.   BROCKVILLE ISSUE

Cat.No.	Denom.	Date	VG	F	VF	EF	Unc
20-02-02	$4	1854	600.	900.	1,200.	-	-

4.   HAMILTON ISSUE

Cat.No.	Denom.	Date	VG	F	VF	EF	Unc
20-04-02	$4	1854	600.	900.	1,200.	-	-

6.   **LONDON ISSUE**

Cat.No.	Denom.	Date	VG	F	VF	EF	Unc
20-06-02	$4	1854	600.	900.	1,200.	-	-

10.   **ST. CATHARINES ISSUE**

Cat.No.	Denom.	Date	VG	F	VF	EF	Unc
20-10-02	$4	1854	600.	900.	1,200.	-	-

12.   **TORONTO ISSUE**

190-20-08-02P

Cat.No.	Denom.	Date			Unc
20-12-02P	$4	185		PROOF	500.

THE COMMERCIAL BANK OF WINDSOR

1864 - 1902

WINDSOR, NOVA SCOTIA

BANK NUMBER 195   **REDEEMABLE**

Established in 1864 in Windsor, Nova Scotia, this bank was a small institution with assets totalling $1,688,000 and seven branches in operation. It was taken over by The Union Bank of Halifax in 1902 without any loss to creditors.

195-10.   **ISSUE OF THE 1860's**

DESIGNS AND COLOURS

195-10-02P
    $20 Face Design: Two children holding sheaves train sitting in station/sailor holding flag, bales and lion
             Colour: Black with green tint

       Back Design: Lathework, counters, bank name and floral designs
            Colour: Green

IMPRINT
    American Bank Note Co. N.Y. and Boston

SIGNATURES
left	right
none	none

ISSUE DATING
    Partially Engraved __186__:

Cat.No.	Denom.	Date		Unc
10-02P	$20	186-	FACE PROOF	1,000.

THE COMMERCIAL BANK OF WINDSOR

195-12.   **ISSUE OF 1870**
DESIGNS AND COLOURS

195-12-02P
   $4 Face Design: —/reclining woman and water jar, Niagara Falls/—
   Colour: Black with green tint

   Back Design: Latheworks, counters and bank name
   Colour: Green

195-12-04P
   $5 Face Design: Seated woman on wharf in oval "EXPORTS"/ Royal Crest/anchor, box, barrel and ships in oval
   Colour: Black with green tint

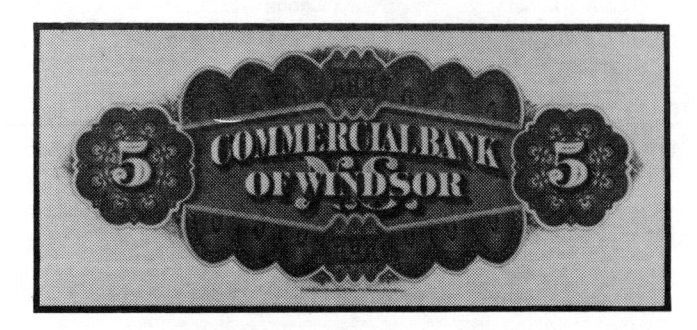

   Back Design: Lathework, counters and bank name
   Colour: Green

195-12-06P
   $10 Face Design: —/train coming out of tunnel/—
   Colour: Black with green tint

   Back Design: Lathework, counters and bank name
   Colour: Green

IMPRINT
British American Bank Note Co. Montreal & Ottawa

SIGNATURES
left	right
none	none

ISSUE DATING
Engraved
September 1st 1870
Sept. 1st 1870

Cat.No.	Denom.	Date		Unc
12-02P	$4	1870	FACE PROOF	900.
12-04P	$5	1870	FACE PROOF	900.
12-06P	$10	1870	FACE PROOF	900.

195-14.   **ISSUES OF 1871 and 1898**
DESIGNS AND COLOURS

195-14-02
   $4 Face Design: —/reclining woman and water jar, Niagara Falls/—
   Colour: Black with green tint

   Back Design: Lathework, counters and bank name
   Colour: Green

195-14-04P
$5 **Face Design:** Seated woman on wharf in oval "exports"/
Royal Crest/anchor, box,
barrel and ships in oval
Colour: Black with green tint
Back Design: Lathework, counters and bank name
Colour: Green

195-14-08
$10 **Face Design:** —/train coming out of tunnel/—
Colour: Black with green tint
Back Design: Lathework, counters and bank name
Colour: Green

IMPRINT
British American Bank Note Co. Montreal & Ottawa

SIGNATURES
left	right
mss. Walter Lawson	mss. G.P. Payzant
mss. Walter Lawson	mss. A.P. Shand

ISSUE DATING
Engraved
July 1st 1871
July 1st 1898

Cat.No.	Denom.	Date	VG	F	VF	EF	Unc
14-02	$4	1871	3,000.	-	-	-	-
14-04P	$5	1871			FACE PROOF		900.
14-06P	$5	1898			FACE PROOF		900.
14-08	$10	1871	3,000.	-	-	-	-
14-10P	$10	1898			FACE PROOF		900.

COMMERCIAL BRANCH BANK OF CANADA

COMMERCIAL BRANCH BANK OF CANADA
1861 - 1862
COLLINGWOOD, PROVINCE OF CANADA

BANK NUMBER 200   **NONREDEEMABLE**

There is no record of a charter being granted to the Commercial Branch Bank of Canada by the Legislature and the institution is considered a phantom bank. From the design of its "notes" they were meant to trade on the credibility of The Commercial Bank of Canada and the supposed credibility of the Bank of Western Canada.

200-10.   **ISSUE OF 1861 - 1862**
DESIGNS AND COLOURS

200-10-02
$3 **Face Design:** Woodsmen clearing forest/-/woman feeding horse. Inscribed "For the Bank of Western Canada"
Colour: Black with overall green tint
Back Design: Plain

200-10-04
$5 **Face Design:** Farmer and child resting under tree, cattle/—/ woman holding child. Inscribed "For the Bank of Western Canada"
Colour: Black with overall green tint
Back Design: Plain

IMPRINT
Union Bank Note Company

SIGNATURES
left	right
none	mss. C.H. Holland
none	mss. A.O. Walter

ISSUE DATING
Partially Engraved __18__:
1861: Sept. 10
1862: July 10

Cat.No.	Denom.	Date	VG	F	VF	EF	Unc
10-02	$3	1861	600.	800.	1,250.	-	-
10-04	$5	1861	700.	900.	1,250.	-	-
10-06	$5	1862	700.	900.	1,250.	-	-

THE CONSOLIDATED BANK OF CANADA

1876 - 1879

MONTREAL, QUEBEC

BANK NUMBER 205 **NONREDEEMABLE**

The Consolidated Bank of Canada was created out of the merger of the City Bank, Montreal, and The Royal Canadian Bank, Toronto, on April 12, 1876. It was an amalgamation of two very weak institutions, and Sir Francis Hinck had taken on the impossible task of trying to make the new bank work.

Within two years the true state of affairs was beginning to show. The losses reported not only wiped out the profits for the year but reserve and contingent funds as well. There was, in fact, a deficit of approximately $450,000. It was decided to carry on but the bank's credit was so impaired that it had lost all credibility with the public.

On August 1, 1879, the bank suspended and in March, 1880, a bill was introduced in Parliament to provide for the winding up of The Consolidated Bank of Canada. All depositors were paid in full and the shareholders recovered 23 cents on the dollar.

205-10. **ISSUE OF 1876**

DESIGNS AND COLOURS

205-10-02
  $4 Face Design: —/Bank Seal in modified Royal Crest/—
  Colour: Black with green tint

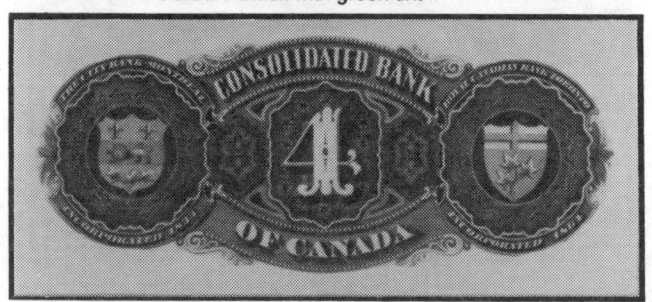

  Back Design: Lathework, counters, seals and bank name
  Colour: Green

205-10-04
  $5 Face Design: —/Bank Seal in modified Royal Crest/—
  Colour: Black with green tint

  Back Design: Lathework, counters, seals and bank name
  Colour: Green

205-10-06
  $10 Face Design: —/Bank Seal in modified Royal Crest/—
  Colour: Black with green tint

  Back Design: Lathework, counters, seals and bank name
  Colour: Green

205-10-08P
  $20 Face Design: —/Bank Seal in modified Royal Crest/—
  Colour: Black with green tint

THE CONSOLIDATED BANK OF CANADA

Back Design: Lathework, counters, seals and bank name
Colour: Green

Back Design: Lathework, counters, seals and bank name
Colour: Green

IMPRINT
British American Bank Note Co. Montreal

SIGNATURES
left	right
mss. various	engr. F. Hincks

ISSUE DATING
Engraved
1s July, 1876

OVERPRINT
"B" in blue	"NH" in blue
"BELLEVILLE" in blue	"ST. CATHARINES" in blue
"C" in blue	"SEAFORTH" in blue
"D" in blue	"SHERBROOKE" in blue
"GALT" in blue	"TORONTO" in blue
"HAMILTON" in blue	"WOODSTOCK" in blue
"N" in blue	

205-10-10P
  $50 **Face Design:** —/Bank Seal in modified Royal Crest/—
  Colour: Black with green tint

Cat.No.	Denom.	Date	VG	F	VF	EF	Unc
10-02	$4	1876	400.	700.	1,000.	-	-
10-04	$5	1876	200.	300.	450.	-	-
10-06	$10	1876	200.	300.	450.	-	-
10-08	$20	1876	1,000.	1,400.	2,100.	-	-
10-10P	$50	1876				FACE PROOF 600.	
10-12	$100	1876	1,000.	1,400.	2,100.	-	-

Note I: $10 notes sheet numbers 12001-13000, with A,B,C & D plate letters were stolen from the bank.

Note II: Back design has at left, "THE CITY BANK - MONTREAL, INCORPORATED 1833." around City Bank Seal and at the right "Royal Canadian Bank - Toronto, incorporated 1864" around Royal Canadian Bank Seal.

Back Design: Lathework, counters, seals and bank name
Colour: Green

205-10-12
  $100 **Face Design:** —/Bank Seal in modified Royal Crest/—
  Colour: Black with green tint

THE BANK OF THE COUNTY OF ELGIN

1855 - 1862

ST. THOMAS, PROVINCE OF CANADA

BANK NUMBER 210   **NONREDEEMABLE**

This bank was one of the five banks organized under The Free Banking Act and it operated during the period of 1855-1862 in St. Thomas, Canada West. It started business with $100,000 deposited for Provincial securities, against which it had drew a like amount in registered notes, but never gained any great strength. The bank struggled against the competition and prestige of the chartered banks and then retired its note issue and wound up.

210.10.   ISSUE OF 1856 - 1857

DESIGNS AND COLOURS

210-10-02
- **$1 Face Design:** Building/farmer driving livestock hens and chickens
- **Colour:** Black with no tint
- **Back Design:** Plain

210-10-04
- **$2 Face Design:** Edward Ermatinger/town, bridge and train/building
- **Colour:** Black with no tint
- **Back Design:** Plain

210-10-08
- **$5 Face Design:** Duke of Wellington in oval/farmer with livestock/building
- **Colour:** Black with no tint
- **Back Design:** Plain

210-10-10C
- **$10 Face Design:** Edward Ermatinger/farm family waving to passing train/building
- **Colour:** Black with no tint
- **Back Design:** Plain

IMPRINT
- Toppan, Carpenter & Co. Montreal

SIGNATURES

left	right
mss. Colin Munro	mss. Edw. Ermatinger
mss. Colin Munro	mss. Jas. Pollock
mss. Jas. Pollock	mss. Edw. Ermatinger

ISSUE DATING
- **Partially Engraved __18__:**
  - **$1 1856:** 25 June, 1 July, 1 Augt, 1 Sept, 1 Decr.
  - **$2 1856:** 1 Augt., 1 Dec'r.
  -     **1857:** 31st Jany
  - **$5 1856:** 25 June, 1 Augt.
  - **$10 1856:** — Feb, 1 July, 1 Augt.

PROTECTOR
- Red "word" on face and in mirror image on the back

Cat.No.	Denom.	Date	Variety	VG	F	VF	EF	Unc
10-02	$1	1856		1,200.	1,700.	-	-	-
10-02C	$1	1856	Cancelled	900.	1,200.	-	-	-
10-04	$2	1856		1,500.	2,000.	-	-	-
10-04C	$2	1856	Cancelled	900.	1,500.	-	-	-
10-06	$2	1857		1,500.	2,000.	-	-	-
10-06C	$2	1857	Cancelled	900.	1,500.	-	-	-
10-08	$5	1856		1,800.	2,500.	-	-	-
10-08C	$5	1856	Cancelled	1,200.	1,800.	-	-	-
10-10	$10	1856		1,900.	2,600.	-	-	-
10-10C	$10	1856	Cancelled	1,200.	1,700.	-	-	-

Note: Notes of this bank are often encountered cancelled, having the right signature area removed.

THE CROWN BANK OF CANADA

1904 - 1908

TORONTO, (ONTARIO)

BANK NUMBER 215 **REDEEMABLE**

Established in Toronto in 1904, this bank amalgamated with The Northern Bank in July of 1908 to become The Northern Crown Bank which was, in turn, absorbed by The Royal Bank of Canada in July of 1918.

215-10. ISSUE OF 1904

DESIGNS AND COLOURS

215-10-02
  $5 Face Design: —/cattle in pasture/—
  Colour: Black with orange and yellow tint

  Back Design: Bank name, crown and floral symbols, lathework
  Colour: Brown

215-10-04P
  $10 Face Design: Lion on mountain/—/—
  Colour: Black with brown and yellow and green tint

  Back Design: Bank name, crown and floral symbols, lathework
  Colour: Blue

215-10-06P
  $20 Face Design: Allegorical male, child and females "UNITY"/—/—
  Colour: Black with rose and blue tint

  Back Design: Bank name, crown and floral symbols, lathework
  Colour: Orange

215-10-08P
  $50 Face Design: Parliament buildings/—/—
  Colour: Black with red and yellow tint

  Back Design: Bank name, crown and floral symbols, lathework
  Colour: Red-brown

THE DOMINION BANK

IMPRINT
British American Bank Note Co. Ottawa

SIGNATURES

left	right
engr. Edward Gurney	mss. various

ISSUE DATING
Engraved
June 1st 1904
1st June 1904

Cat.No.	Denom.	Date	VG	F	VF	EF	Unc
10-02	$5	1904	3,500.	-	-	-	-
10-04P	$10	1904			FACE PROOF		1,000.
10-06P	$20	1904			FACE PROOF		1,000.
10-08P	$50	1904			FACE PROOF		1,000.

Note: Proofs are known for faces and backs with colours other than those listed here.

THE DOMINION BANK

1869 - 1955

TORONTO, ONTARIO

BANK NUMBER 220   *REDEEMABLE*

This bank was established in Toronto in 1869 and amalgamated in 1955 with The Bank of Toronto to form The Toronto-Dominion Bank now active as one of the largest banks in Canada. Its charter was obtained without difficulty, but its founders were unable to open the bank's doors to the public until February 1, 1871. In its first year of operation, the bank opened five branches. For the first time in Canadian banking history, the bank decided to open a city branch in Toronto in addition to the head office. This policy was soon followed by other banks. The bank paid dividends in its first year of operation, and by April of 1872, its assets reached the $2,5 million mark with notes in circulation of $540,508. In the years of depression following the financial crisis of 1873, the bank remained sound through good management. With the return of prosperity in 1880 and the beginning of the activities of the Canadian Pacific Railway, the bank shared in the growth in the banking business and expanded rapidly. Throughout the financial upheavals and legislative changes later, the bank had continued "with monotonous, but very comforting regularity to pay substantial dividends." It had never taken over or merged with another bank. At the time of its amalgamation with The Bank of Toronto, the bank had total assets of $538 million and 194 branches. In approving the amalgamation agreement, the Minister of Finance stated that each of the banks was in a strong financial position, but that the amalgamated institution, through a more nation-wide expansion of branch facilities should be able to offer greater competition and more efficient service to its Canadian customers. The shareholders were also informed that the new bank would start with an authorized capital of $30 million with $15 million paid-up, a reserve fund of $30 million, total assets in excess of $1 billion and 450 branches, including offices in New York and London, England. Of the 1,500,000 shares issued by the new bank, The Toronto-Dominion Bank, shareholders of The Bank of Toronto received 800,000 - 4 for each 3 of that bank - and those of The Dominion Bank received share for share, in accordance with the shareholders' equity in the two banks.

220-10.   **ISSUES OF 1871 and 1873**

DESIGNS AND COLOURS

220-10-02
$4 Face Design: Prince Arthur/farmer pumping water for livestock/seated Britannia
Colour: Black with green tint

THE DOMINION BANK

Back Design: Lathework, counters and bank name
Colour: Green

Back Design: Lathework, counters and bank name
Colour: Green

220-10-04
  $5 Face Design: —/Queen Victoria in "widow's weeds" superimposed on Royal Crest/—
  Colour: Black with green tint

220-10-08P
  $20 Face Design: Shoeing horses/"Implements of agriculture"/logger
  Colour: Black with green tint

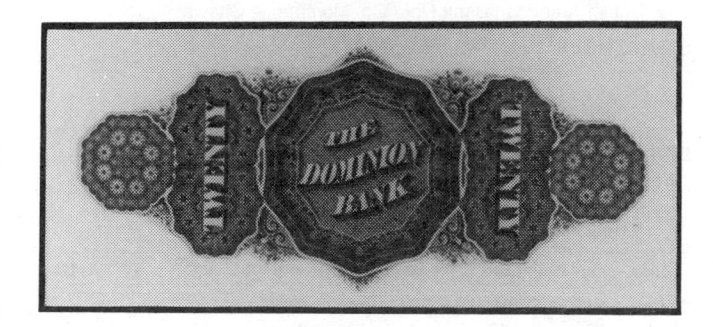

Back Design: Lathework, counters and bank name
Colour: Green

Back Design: Lathework, counters and bank name
Colour: Green

Photo Not Available

220-10-10P
  $50 Face Design: Unknown
  Colour: Black with green tint

  Back Design: Lathework, counters and bank name
  Colour: Green

220-10-06
  $10 Face Design: Girl/paddlewheel steamer "Inland commerce"/woodcutter
  Colour: Black with green tint

121

THE DOMINION BANK

220-10-12
$100 Face Design: —/woman with water jug/—
Colour: Black with green tint

Back Design: Lathework, counters and bank name
Colour: Green

IMPRINT
British American Bank Note Co. Montreal & Ottawa

SIGNATURES
	left	right
$4, $5 & $100:	mss. various	engr. J. Austin

ISSUE DATING
$4 & $5: Feb. 1st, 1871
$10, $20 & $50: May 1st, 1871
$100: 1st October, 1873

Cat.No.	Denom.	Date	VG	F	VF	EF	Unc
10-02	$4*	1871	1,500.	2,000.	2,700.	-	-
10-04	$5	1871	1,500.	2,000.	2,700.	-	-
10-06	$10	1871	1,600.	2,100.	3,000.	-	-
10-08	$20	1871	1,600.	2,100.	3,000.	-	-
10-10P	$50	1871			FACE PROOF		800.
10-12	$100	1873	1,600.	2,100.	3,000.	-	-

* Beware of counterfeits of this note

.220-12.   **ISSUE OF 1876 - 1888**
DESIGNS AND COLOURS

220-12-02
$4 Face Design: Laureate woman's head/
seated woman with children/
woman's head "The Bride"
Colour: Black with green and red-brown tint

Back Design: Lathework and large 4 counter
Colour: Brown

220-12-04
$5 Face Design: Seated woman with sheaf of wheat "Girl with sheaf", tools/—/two seated allegorical women
Colour: Black with blue tint

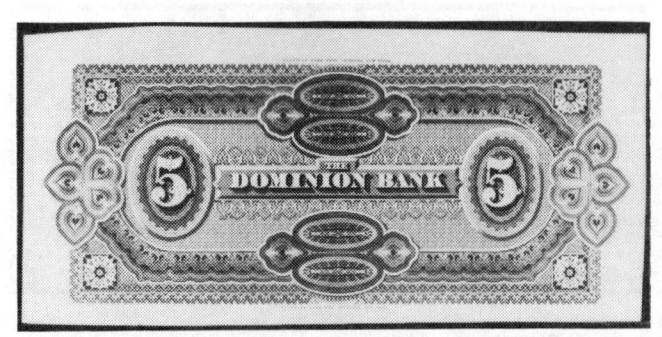

Back Design: Lathework, counters and bank name
Colour: Blue

220-12-06
$10 Face Design: Allegorical female holding fasces/
seated allegorical female with wheat,
sickle, behive
Colour: Black with ochre and green tint

THE DOMINION BANK

Back Design: Lathework, counters, bank name and flowers/reclining Indian/—
Colour: Brown

220-12-08
$50 Face Design: Cartier approaching land "Quebec"/ ships at dock/
Queen Victoria in "widow's weeds"
Colour: Black with green tint

Back Design: Lathework, counters and bank name
Colour: Green

IMPRINT
$4, $5 & $10: American Bank Note Co, New York
American Bank Note Co. N.Y.
$50: British American Bank Note Co. Montreal

SIGNATURES
left	right
mss. various	engr. J. Austin

ISSUE DATING
Engraved
$4: 1st Jany.1876
$5: 1st Jany 1881
$10: 2nd. January, 1888
$50: July 1st, 1881

Cat.No.	Denom.	Date	VG	F	VF	EF	Unc
12-02	$4	1876	1,200.	2,000.	2,700.	-	-
12-04	$5	1881	1,200.	2,000.	2,700.	-	-
12-06	$10	1888	1,600.	2,100.	3,000.	-	-
12-08	$50	1881	1,600.	2,100.	3,000.	-	-

Note: $10 back proof known in green and $10 specimen with all green face tint.

220-14. **ISSUE OF 1891 and 1898**
DESIGNS AND COLOURS

220-14-02
$5 Face Design: "Lighthouse" and boats/binder and horses/power lines and cattle "The drove"
Colour: Black with green tint

Back Design: Lathework, counters and bank name
Colour: Green

220-14-04
$10 Face Design: Frank Smith/cattle in pasture/—
Colour: Black with overall green tint

Back Design: Lathework, counters and bank name
Colour: Green

IMPRINT
British American Bank Note Co. Ottawa

SIGNATURES
	left	right
$5:	mss. various	engr. J. Austin
$10:	mss. various	engr. Frank Smith

123

THE DOMINION BANK

ISSUE DATING
Engraved
1st July, 1891
July 1st, 1898

Cat.No.	Denom.	Date	VG	F	VF	EF	Unc
14-02	$5	1891	1,400.	1,800.	2,600.	-	-
14-04	$10	1898	1,500.	1,900.	3,000.	-	-

220-16. $5 ISSUES OF 1896 - 1925

DESIGNS AND COLOURS

220-16-02
- **$5 Face Design:** Woman kneeling beside anvil/—/ woman seated beside produce. Top counters with fancy scrollwork.
- **Colour:** Black with green tint
- **Back Design:** Unknown
- **Colour:** Unknown

220-16-08
- **$5 Face Design:** Kneeling woman with anvil/—/ seated woman with agricultural produce, top counters plain
- **Colour:** Black with green tint

220-16-14
- **Back Design:** Lathework, counters, bank name and Greek god,
- **Colour:** Green

IMPRINT
American Bank Note Co. Ottawa
Canadian Bank Note Company Limited

SIGNATURES

	left	right
1896:	mss. various	engr. J. Austin
1898:	mss. various	engr. Frank Smith
1900:	mss. various	engr. Frank Smith
1905:	mss. various	typed E.B. Osler
	typed C.A. Bogert	typed E.B. Osler
1925:	typed C.A. Bogert	typed A. Nanton
	typed C.A. Bogert	typed A.W. Austin

ISSUE DATING
Engraved
1st January, 1896
Jan. 1, 1898
2nd January 1900
3rd July 1905
2nd Jany. 1925

Cat.No.	Denom.	Date	Variety	VG	F	VF	EF	Unc
16-02	$5	1896		1,100.	1,400.	2,400.	-	-
16-04	$5	1898		1,100.	1,400.	2,400.	-	-
16-06	$5	1900		1,000.	1,300.	2,200.	-	-
16-08	$5	1905	mss.signat,l.	140.	200.	300.	500.	-
16-10	$5	1905	Bogert,l.	140.	200.	300.	500.	-
16-12	$5	1925	Nanton, r.	100.	140.	225.	375.	900.
16-14	$5	1925	Austin, r.	100.	140.	225.	375.	900.

220-18. $10 ISSUES OF 1900 - 1925

DESIGNS AND COLOURS

220-18-02
- **$10 Face Design:** —/seated Britannia, lion/—
- **1900-1910 Face Colour:** Black with yellow-green and green tint
- **Back Colour:** Maroon, yellow-green and green
- **1925 Face Colour:** Black with yellow and green tint
- **Back Colour:** Yellow and green

- **Back Design:** Lathework, counters, bank name and beaver

IMPRINT
American Bank Note Company, Ottawa
Canadian Bank Note Company Limited

THE DOMINION BANK

SIGNATURES

	left	right
1900:	mss. various	engr. Frank Smith
1910:	mss. various	typed E.B. Osler
	typed C.A. Bogert	typed E.B. Osler
1925:	typed C.A. Bogert	typed A. Nanton
	typed C.A. Bogert	typed A.W. Austin

Note: 18-04 - Engraved "Countersigned" at left. 18-06 - Engraved "General Manager" at left.

ISSUE DATING
Engraved
Jany. 2nd 1900
Jany 3rd 1910
2nd Jany. 1925

Cat.No.	Denom.	Date	Variety	VG	F	VF	EF	Unc
18-02	$10	1900		300.	400.	600.	1,000.	-
18-04	$10	1910	Mss.signature l.	90.	120.	190.	300.	650.
18-06	$10	1910	Bogert, l.	90.	120.	190.	300.	650.
18-08	$10	1925	Nanton, r.	60.	90.	130.	250.	425.
18-10	$10	1925	Austin, r.	60.	90.	130.	250.	425.

220-20 $20 ISSUES OF 1897 - 1925
DESIGNS AND COLOURS

220-20-08
$20 Face Design: Seated woman with sheaf and tools "Girl with sheaf"/two statue-like cherubs surrounding 20/Frank Smith
Colour: Black with blue and yellow-green tint

Back Design: Lathework, counters, bank name and bust of Greek goddess
Colour: Olive-green

IMPRINT
American Bank Note Company, Ottawa
Canadian Bank Note Company, Limited

SIGNATURES

	Left	right
1897:	mss. various	engr. Frank Smith
1909:	mss. various	typed E.B. Osler
	typed various	typed E.B. Osler
1925:	typed C.A. Bogert	typed A.W. Austin

Note: 20-04 - Engraved "countersigned" at left. 20-06 - Engraved "general manager" at left.

ISSUE DATE
Engraved
1st October 1897
1st October 1909
2nd January 1925

Cat.No.	Denom	Date	Variety	VG	F	VF	EF	Unc
20-02	$20	1897		900.	1,400.	2,000.	-	-
20-04	$20	1909	Mss. signat,l.	150.	200.	275.	500.	900.
20-06	$20	1909	Typed signat,l.	150.	200.	275.	500.	900.
20-08	$20	1925		110.	140.	200.	400.	700.

220-22. $50 ISSUES OF 1901 and 1925
DESIGNS AND COLOURS

220-22-04
$50 Face Design: Beehives/—/livestock at stable door
1901 Face Colour: Black with yellow-brown, brown, yellow-green, green and purple tint
Back Colour: Brown, blue, yellow-brown, yellow-green and green
1925 Face Colour: Black with yellow-brown, yellow-green, blue and olive tint
Back Colour: Yellow-brown, yellow-green, blue and olive

Back Design: Lathework, counters, bank name and beaver

IMPRINT
American Bank Note Co. Ottawa
Canadian Bank Note Company, Limited

SIGNATURES

	left	right
1901:	mss. various	typed E.B. Osler
1925:	mss. various	typed A.W. Austin

ISSUE DATING
Engraved
July 2nd 1901
2nd Jany, 1925

Cat.No.	Denom.	Date	VG	F	VF	EF	Unc
22-02	$50	1901	400.	550.	800.	1,400.	-
22-04	$50	1925	275.	400.	500.	900.	

THE DOMINION BANK

220-24. ISSUE OF 1931
DESIGNS AND COLOURS

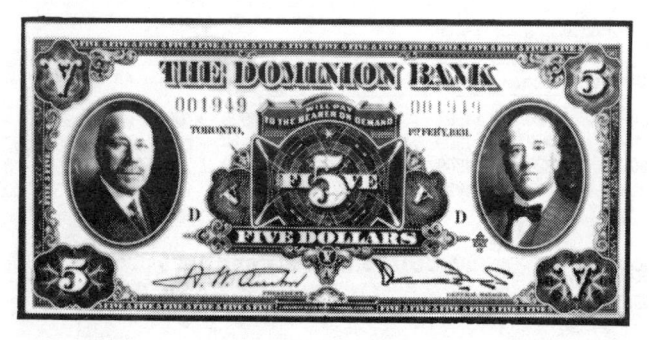

220-24-02
- **$5 Face Design:** A.W. Austin/—/C.A. Bogert
- **Colour:** Black with blue and orange tint 
- **Back Design:** Lathework, counters, bank name and map of Canada
- **Colour:** Green

220-24-06
- **$10 Face Design:** A.W. Austin/—/C.A. Bogert
- **Colour:** Black with blue and orange tint
- **Back Design:** Lathework, counters, bank name and map of Canada
- **Colour:** Blue

220-24-10
- **$20 Face Design:** A.W. Austin/two statue-like cherubs surrounding 20/C.A. Bogert
- **Colour:** Black with purple and orange tint

- **Back Design:** Lathework, counters, bank name and map of Canada
- **Colour:** Purple

220-24-12S
- **$50 Face Design:** A.W. Austin/—/C.A. Bogert
- **Colour:** Black with yellow, pink and orange tint
- **Back Design:** Lathework, counters, bank name and map of Canada
- **Colour:** Orange

220-24-14
- **$100 Face Design:** A.W. Austin/—/C.A. Bogert
- **Colour:** Black with olive-green and orange tint

- **Back Design:** Lathework, counters, bank name and map of Canada
- **Colour:** Red-brown

IMPRINT
Canadian Bank Note Company, Limited

SIGNATURES
left	right
signed A.W. Austin	signed C.A. Bogert
signed C.H. Carlisle	signed D. Dawson

ISSUE DATING
Engraved
1st Feb'y 1931

Cat.No.	Denom.	Date	Variety	VG	F	VF	EF	Unc
24-02	$5	1931	Bogert,r.	60.	80.	110.	190.	375.
24-04	$5	1931	Danson,r.	60.	80.	110.	190.	375.
24-06	$10	1931	Bogert,r.	80.	110.	160.	275.	600.
24-08	$10	1931	Danson,r.	80.	110.	160.	275.	600.
24-10	$20	1931		80.	110.	160.	275.	600.
24-12S	$50	1931				SPECIMEN		750.
24-14	$100	1931		400.	600.	900.	1,500.	-

THE DOMINION BANK

220-26. ISSUE OF 1935
SMALL SIZE NOTES

DESIGNS AND COLOURS

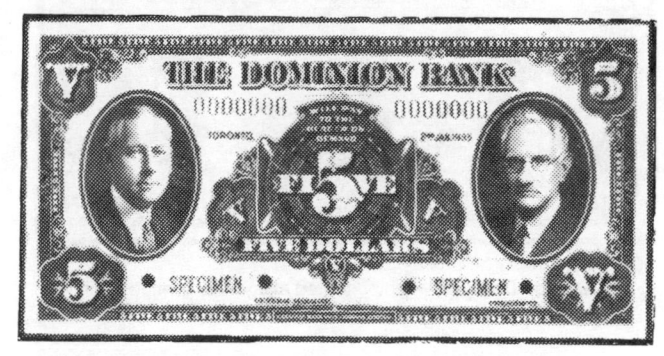

220-26-02
- **$5 Face Design:** Dudley Dawson/—/Clifton H. Carlisle
- **Colour:** Black with green and orange tint
- **Back Design:** Lathework, counters, bank name and map of Canada
- **Colour:** Orange

220-26-04
- **$10 Face Design:** Dudley Dawson/—/Clifton H. Carlisle
- **Colour:** Black with yellow, pink and orange tint
- **Back Design:** Lathework, counters, bank name and map of Canada
- **Colour:** Orange

IMPRINT
Canadian Bank Note Company, Limited

SIGNATURES
left	right
typed D. Dawson	typed C.H. Carlisle

ISSUE DATING
Engraved
2nd Jan. 1935

Cat.No.	Denom.	Date	VG	F	VF	EF	Unc
26-02	$5	1935	25.	40.	55.	90.	175.
26-04	$10	1935	30.	50.	75.	125.	225.

220-28. ISSUE OF 1938
SMALL SIZE NOTES

DESIGNS AND COLOURS

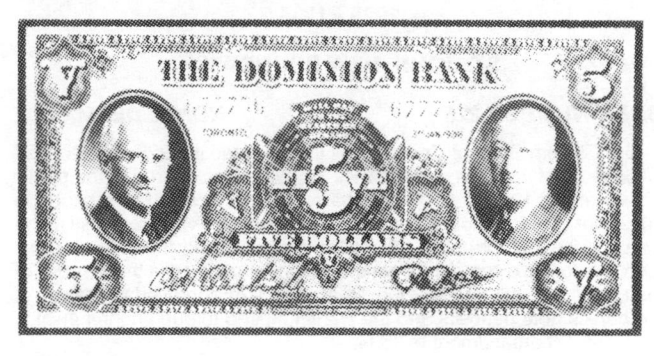

220-28-02
- **$5 Face Design:** Clifton H. Carlisle/—/Robert Rae
- **Colour:** Black with orange and brown tint
- **Back Design:** Lathework, counters, bank name and map of Canada
- **Colour:** Brown

220-28-04
- **$10 Face Design:** Clifton H. Carlisle/—/Robert Rae
- **Colour:** Black with blue and yellow tint

- **Back Design:** Lathework, counters, bank name and map of Canada
- **Colour:** Olive-green

IMPRINT
Canadian Bank Note Company, Limited

SIGNATURES
left	right
typed C.H. Carlisle	typed R. Rae

ISSUE DATING
Engraved
3rd Jan. 1938

Cat.No.	Denom.	Date	VG	F	VF	EF	Unc
28-02	$5	1938	30.	40.	60.	110.	210.
28-04	$10	1938	40.	55.	85.	150.	275.

EASTERN BANK OF CANADA

1928 - 1934

ST. JOHN, NEW BRUNSWICK

BANK NUMBER 225 **NONREDEEMABLE**

The Eastern Bank of Canada was incorporated in 1928 with its head office in Saint John, New Brunswick. Its stock was offered to the public in January of 1927 at $200 per share. Sufficient capital was raised to qualify for certificate to start operations, but the stock market crash in the fall of 1929, lack of public interest in the bank, and the inability of its founders to find a competent general manager resulted in the non-use of the charter. In July of 1932 the Treasury Board approved the return of the bank's note deposits and the charter lapsed through nonrenewal in the Bank Act amendment of 1934.

225-10.   DESIGNS OF 1929

Notes were printed, but all were later destroyed unissued, with only proofs having survived.

DESIGNS AND COLOURS

225-10-02P
- **$5 Face Design:** —/wharf scene with truck, train and steamship/—
- **Colour:** Black with green tint

Back Design: Lalthework, counters, bank name and bank seal
Colour: Orange

225-10-04P
- **$10 Face Design:** —/ship, seated allegorical female, train/—
- **Colour:** Black with brown tint

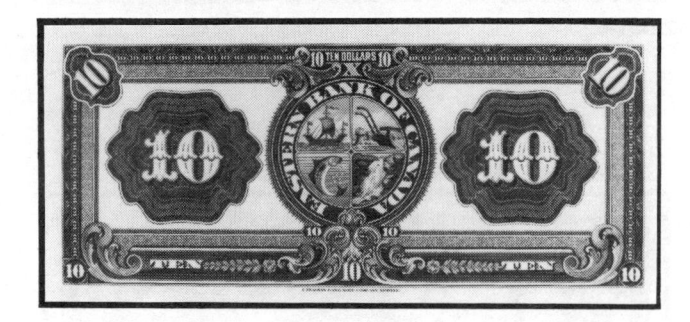

Back Design: Lathework, counters, bank name and bank seal
Colour: Blue

IMPRINT
Canadian Bank Note Company, Limited

SIGNATURES
left	right
none	none

ISSUE DATING
Engraved
15th May 1929

Cat.No.	Denom.	Date	EF	Unc
10-02P	$5	1929	PROOF	850.
10-04P	$10	1929	PROOF	850.

THE EASTERN TOWNSHIPS BANK

1855 - 1912

SHERBROOKE, PROVINCE OF CANADA
SHERBROOKE, PROVINCE OF QUEBEC

BANK NUMBER 230   **REDEEMABLE**

This bank was chartered in 1855 and began operations in 1859 in Sherbrooke, P.Q. Its shareholders were mainly residents of the U.S. and the Eastern Township region of Quebec. The bank operated successfully until it was taken over by The Canadian Bank of Commerce in 1912. The latter acquired about 100 branches and a large number of shareholders abroad as a result of this merger.

230-10.   **"GREEN" ISSUE OF 1859 AND 1861**

DESIGNS AND COLOURS

230-10-04-04
- **$1 Face Design:** Queen Victoria (Chalon portrait)/Magog River Falls (Sherbrooke Mills)/Indian on bluff
- **Colour:** Black with overall green tint
- **Back Design:** Plain

230-10-04-08
- **$2 Face Design:** Queen Victoria (Chalon portrait)/men on horseback with livestock/Prince Consort
- **Colour:** Black with overall green tint
- **Back Design:** Plain

230-10-02-06
- **$4 Face Design:** Prince of Wales/Magog River Falls (Sherbrooke Mills)/Benjamin Pomroy
- **Colour:** Black with overall green tint
- **Back Design:** Plain

230-10-04-16
- **$5 Face Design:** Allegorical female/horse and colt, farmer carrying sack of grain/farmer with scythe
- **Colour:** Black with overall green tint
- **Back Design:** Plain

230-10-04-20
- **$10 Face Design:** Hunter and dog at campfire/reclining shepherd boy/train
- **Colour:** Black with overall green tint
- **Back Design:** Plain

230-10-04-24
- **$20 Face Design:** Allegorical female, machinery/ploughing with team of horses/Britannia, shield: XX on shield
- **Colour:** Black with overall green tint
- **Back Design:** Plain

IMPRINT
American Bank Note Company

THE EASTERN TOWNSHIPS BANK

2. PARTIALLY ENGRAVED DATE 1859

SIGNATURES
left	right
mss. Wm. S. Foster	mss. B. Pomroy

ISSUE DATING
Partially Engraved__18__:
1859: Aug. 1

PROTECTOR
Red "word" on back only

OVERPRINT
"WATERLOO" twice in red

Cat.No.	Denom.	Date	VG	F	VF	EF	Unc
10-02-02	$1	1859	1,900.	2,600.	-	-	-
10-02-04	$2	1859	1,900.	2,600.	-	-	-
10-02-06	$4	1859	1,900.	2,600.	-	-	-
10-02-08	$5	1859	2,000.	2,700.	-	-	-
10-02-10	$10	1859	2,100.	3,000.	-	-	-
10-02-12	$20	1859	2,100.	3,000.	-	-	-

4. ENGRAVED DATE 1859 AND 1861

SIGNATURES
left	right
mss. various	mss. B. Pomroy
mss. William Farwell (per)	engr. B. Pomroy

ISSUE DATING
Engraved
August 1st 1859
1st February 1861

PROTECTOR
Red word on back only.

OVERPRINT
"STANBRIDGE" in red
"STANSTEAD" in red
"WATERLOO" in red

Cat.No.	Denom.	Date	Variety	VG	F	VF	EF	Unc
10-04-02	$1	1859	Mss. Pomroy, r.	1,800.	2,600.	-	-	-
10-04-04	$1	1859	Engr. Pomroy, r.	1,800.	2,600.	-	-	-
10-04-06	$2	1859	Mss. Pomroy, r.	1,800.	2,600.	-	-	-
10-04-08	$2	1859	Engr. Pomroy, r.	1,800.	2,600.	-	-	-
10-04-10	$4	1861	Mss. Pomroy, r.	1,800.	2,600.	-	-	-
10-04-12	$4	1861	Engr. Pomroy, r.	1,800.	2,600.	-	-	-
10-04-14	$5	1859	Mss. Pomroy, r.	2,000.	2,700.	-	-	-
10-04-16	$5	1859	Engr. Pomroy, r.	2,000.	2,700.	-	-	-
10-04-18	$10	1859	Mss. Pomroy, r.	2,100.	3,000.	-	-	-
10-04-20	$10	1859	Engr. Pomroy, r.	2,100.	3,000.	-	-	-
10-04-22	$20	1859	Mss. Pomroy, r.	2,100.	3,000.	-	-	-
10-04-24	$20	1859	Engr. Pomroy, r.	2,100.	3,000.	-	-	-

230-12. ISSUES OF 1873 AND 1974

DESIGNS AND COLOURS

230-12-02P
$4 Face Design: Farm animals in barn "Stable Door" Magog River Falls (Sherbrooke Mills)/ Benjamin Pomroy
Colour: Black with green tint

Back Design: Smithy shoeing white horse in stable; Lathework, counters, bank name and Sherbrooke, P.Q.
Colour: Green

230-12-04P
$5 Face Design: Wm. Farwell/paddlewheel steamer/ wood cutter
Colour: Black with green tint

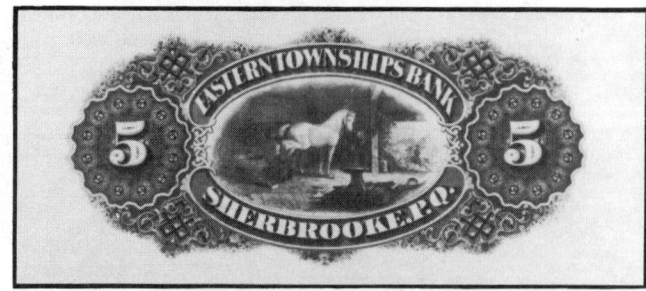

Back Design: Smithy shoeing white horse in stable; Lathework, counters, bank name and Sherbrooke, P.Q.
Colour: Green

230-12-06P
$10 Face Design: Wm. Farwell/farmer pumping water for livestock/Benjamin Pomroy
Colour: Black with green tint

THE EASTERN TOWNSHIPS BANK

Back Design: Smithy shoeing white horse in stable; Lathework, counters, bank name and Sherbrooke, P.Q.
Colour: Green

230-12-08
$50 Face Design: Train emerging from tunnel/ Wm. Farwell/Benjamin Pomroy
Colour: Black with green tint

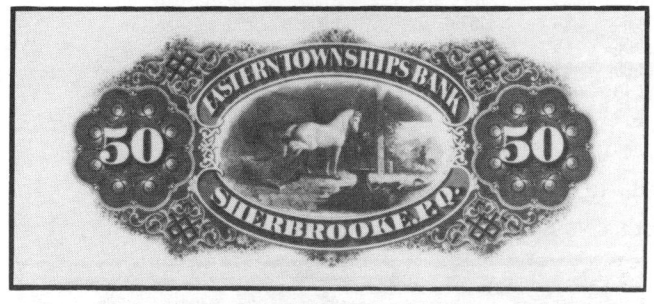

Back Design: Smithy shoeing white horse in stable; Lathework, counters, bank name and Sherbrooke, P.Q.
Colour: Green

230-12-14
$100 Face Design: Wm. Farwell/Magog River Falls (Sherbrooke Mills) Benjamin Pomroy
Colour: Black with green tint

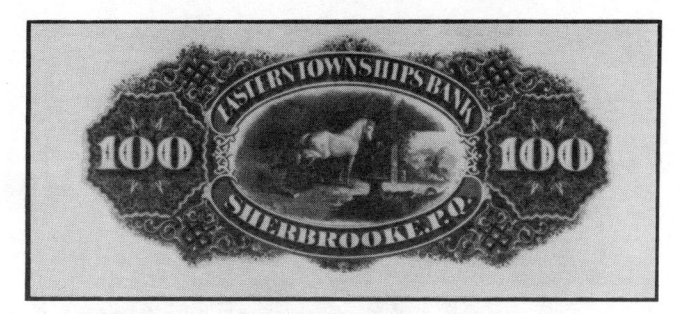

Back Design: Smithy shoeing white horse in stable; Lathework, counters, bank name and Sherbrooke, P.Q.
Colour: Green

IMPRINT
British American Bank Note Co. Montreal

SIGNATURES

left	right
mss. Neil Dinning	engr. B. Pomroy
mss. illegible	engr. B. Pomroy

ISSUE DATING
Engraved
1st July, 1873
1st July, 1874

Cat.No.	Denom.	Date	VG	F	VF	EF	Unc
12-02	$40	1873	2,000.	3,000.	-	-	-
12-04	$5	1873	2,000.	3,000.	-	-	-
12-06	$10	1873	2,000.	3,000.	-	-	-
12-08	$50	1873	2,200.	3,200.	-	-	-
12-10	$50	1874	2,200.	3,200.	-	-	-
12-12	$100	1873	2,200.	3,200.	-	-	-
12-14	$100	1874	2,200.	3,200.	-	-	-

230-14.   ISSUES OF 1879 - 1902

DESIGNS AND COLOURS

230-14-02
$4 Face Design: Farm animals in barn/Magog River Falls (Sherbrooke Mills)/R.W. Heneker
Colour: Black with green tint

Back Design: Smithy shoeing white horse in stable; lathework, counters, bank name and Sherbrooke, P.Q.
Colour: Green

THE EASTERN TOWNSHIPS BANK

230-14-04
$5 **Face Design:** Wm. Farwell/paddlewheel steamer "Inland Commerce"/wood cutter
Colour: Black with green tint

Back Design: Smithy shoeing white horse in stable; Lathework, counters, bank name and Sherbrooke, P.Q.
Colour: Green

230-14-08
$10 **Face Design:** Wm. Farwell/farmer pumping water for livestock/R.W. Heneker
Colour: Black with green tint

Back Design: Smithy shoeing white horse in stable; Lathework, counters, bank name and Sherbrooke, P.Q.
Colour: Green

230-14-12
$20 **Face Design:** Steers (From E. Landseer's painting of the "Wild cattle of Chillingham place")/—/R.W. Heneker
Colour: Black with green tint

Back Design: Lathework, counters, bank name and bull's head
Colour: Green

IMPRINT
British American Bank Note Co. Montreal

SIGNATURES
left	right
mss. Neil Dinning	engr. R.W. Heneker
mss. illegible	engr. R.W. Heneker
mss. Neil Dinning	engr. Wm. Farwell
mss. illegible	engr. Wm. Farwell

ISSUE DATING
Engraved
1st July 1879
2nd Jan. 1893
2nd July 1902

Cat.No.	Denom.	Date	VG	F	VF	EF	Unc
14-02	$4	1879	2,000.	2,700.	-	-	-
14-04	$5	1879	1,900.	2,700.	-	-	-
14-06	$5	1902	1,400.	1,700.	-	-	-
14-08	$10	1879	2,000.	3,000.	-	-	-
14-10	$10	1893	2,000.	3,000.	-	-	-
14-12	$20	1893	2,000.	3,000.	-	-	-

230-16.   **ISSUE OF 1906**
DESIGNS AND COLOURS

230-16-02
$5 **Face Design:** James Mackinnon/train passing hay field/-
Colour: Black with ochre and yellow tint

Back Design: Lathework, counters, bank name and bank crest
Colour: olive green with red, violet and pale yellow tint

THE EXCHANGE BANK

230-16-04
  $10 Face Design: Wm. Farwell/mining scene
  Colour: Black with red and green tint

Back Design: Lathework, counters, bank name and bank crest
Colour: Green with red, violet and pale yellow tint

IMPRINT
American Bank Note Co. Ottawa

SIGNATURES
  left
    typed Wm. Farwell
  right
    mss. various

ISSUE DATING
  Engraved
    January 2d, 1906
    January 2nd, 1906

Cat.No.	Denom.	Date	VG	F	VF	EF	Unc
16-02	$5	1906	800.	1,300.	1,900.	2,550.	-
16-04	$10	1906	800.	1,300.	1,900.	2,550.	-

THE EXCHANGE BANK
1840's
QUEBEC, LOWER CANADA

BANK NUMBER 235   **NONREDEEMABLE**

235-10.   **ISSUE OF 1839-44**
DESIGNS AND COLOURS

235-10-04
  $1 Face Design: —/seated allegorical female; small steamboat below/—
  Colour: Black with no tint

Back Design: Plain

IMPRINT
  None

SIGNATURES
  left
    mss. J. Williams
    mss. J. Weeks
  right
    mss. S. Davis
    mss. D. Purfes

ISSUE DATING
  Partially Engraved __18__:
    1839: September 29
    1844: May 21st

Cat.No.	Denom.	Date	VG	F	VF	EF	Unc
10-02	$1	1839	1,600.	-	-	-	-
10-04	$1	1844	1,600.	-	-	-	-

THE EXCHANGE BANK COMPANY OF CHIPPEWA

1837

CHIPPEWA, UPPER CANADA

BANK NUMBER 240 **NONREDEEMABLE**

Notes purporting to be the issues of this "spurious bank" circulated in the Buffalo area in the early months of 1837. The fraud was promptly reported by the press which limited the success of this particular venture by the swindlers.

240-10. **ISSUE OF 1837**
DESIGNS AND COLOURS

24-10-02
$5 **Face Design:** —/produce and implements; beaver below/ seated Indian with gun
Colour: Black with no tint
Back Design: Plain

240-10-04R
$10 **Face Design:** —/cattle, pigs; small steamboat below/ seated "Commerce" figure leaning on shield depicting anchor
Colour: Black with no tint
Back Design: Plain

IMPRINT
Rawdon, Wright, Hatch, New-York

SIGNATURES

left	right
mss. buffalo (spurious)	mss. buffalo (spurious)
mss. Unknown	mss. Unknown

ISSUE DATING
Partially Engraved __18__:
1837: Jan. 2

Cat.No.	Denom.	Date	Variety	VG	F	VF	EF	Unc
10-02	$5	1837		1,000.	1,500.	-	-	-
10-02R	$5	18__	Remainder*	1,000.	1,500.	-	-	-
10-04R	$10	18__	Remainder*	1,000.	1,500.	-	-	-

*undated and unnumbered.

THE EXCHANGE BANK OF CANADA

1871 - 1883

MONTREAL, QUEBEC

BANK NUMBER 245 **NONREDEEMABLE**

Established in Montreal in 1872, this bank first suspended payment in 1879 but later resumed business. The bank finally failed in 1883. It was badly managed and was accused of being a political bank. The managing director and some of his colleagues on the Board of Directors used funds to manipulate shares and obscure liabilities of the bank. Its notes were paid in full. Double liability was imposed on some of its shareholders and 66 & 1/2% was paid to the creditors.

245-10. **ISSUE OF 1872 AND 1873**
DESIGNS AND COLOURS

245-10-02
$4 **Face Design:** T. Caverhill/seated "Justice" figure/M.H. Gault
Colour: Black with green tint

Back Design: Lathework, counters, bank name and beehive and flowers
Colour: Green

245-10-04
$5 **Face Design:** T. Caverhill/allegorical female, machinery and train/M.H. Gault
Colour: Black with green tint

THE EXCHANGE BANK OF CANADA

Back Design: lathework, counters, bank name and beehive and flowers
Colour: Green

Back Design: Lathework, counters, bank name, beehive and flowers
Colour: Green

245-10-06
$6 Face Design: T. Caverhill/paddlewheel steamship "Inland Commerce"/M.H. Gault
Colour: Black with green tint

245-10-10P
$25 Face Design: T. Caverhill/allegory of trade and transportation/M.H. Gault
Colour: Black with green tint

Back Design: Lathework, counters, bank name, beehive and flowers
Colour: Green

Back Design: Lathework, counters, bank name, beehive and flowers
Colour: Green

245-10-08
$10 Face Design: T. Caverhill/—/M.H. Gault
Colour: Black with green tint

245-10-12P
$50 Face Design: T. Caverhill/M.H. Gault
Colour: Black with green tint

135

THE EXCHANGE BANK OF CANADA

Cat.No.	Denom.	Date	VG	F	VF	EF	Unc
10-02	$4	1872	700.	1,100.	-	-	-
10-04	$5	1872	700.	1,100.	-	-	-
10-06	$6	1872	4,000.	-	-	-	-
10-08	$10	1872	1,500.	2,000.	-	-	-
10-10P	$25	1872			FACE PROOF		1,500.
10-12P	$50	1873			FACE PROOF		700.
10-14P	$100	1873			FACE PROOF		700.

Back Design: Lathework, counters, bank name, beehive and flowers
Colour: Green

245-10-14P
$100 Face Design: T. Caverhill/woman with water jar, Niagara Falls/M.H. Gault
Colour: Black with green tint

Back Design: Lathework, counters, bank name, beehive and flowers
Colour: Green

IMPRINT
British American Bank Note Co. Montreal & Ottawa

SIGNATURES
left	right
mss. various	engr. M.H. Gault

ISSUE DATING
Engraved
1st Oct. 1872   1st November 1872
1st October 1872   2nd Jan. 1873
1st Novr. 1872

OVERPRINT
"A A" in blue   "HAMILTON" in blue
"AYLMER" in blue   "L" in blue
"BEDFORD" in blue   "M M" in blue (sideways)
"BRUSSELS" in blue   "PARKHILL" in blue
"C" in circle in purple   "VALLEYFIELD" in blue
"E E" in blue   "X" over "BRUSSELS" in blue
"EXETER" in blue

THE EXCHANGE BANK OF CANADA

1860's

WINDSOR, ONTARIO

BANK NUMBER 250 **NONREDEEMABLE**

250-10. **ISSUE OF 1864**

DESIGNS AND COLOURS

250-10-02
- **$1 Face Design:** Britannia/early train/Arms
- **Colour:** Black with green tint
- **Back Design:** Plain

IMPRINT
  none

SIGNATURES
  right only
  mss. Ettie G. Gardner

ISSUE DATING
  Partially Engraved __18__:
   1864: June 8th

Cat.No.	Denom.	Date	VG	F	VF	EF	Unc
10-02	$1	1864	500.	750.	-	-	-

THE EXCHANGE BANK OF TORONTO

1855

TORONTO, UPPER CANADA

BANK NUMBER 255 **NONREDEEMABLE**

A firm of foreign exchange dealers named R.H. Brett & Co. in Toronto used the sub-title of "Exchange Bank" in anticipation of establishing a bank with that name under The Free Banking Act of 1855.

255-10. **DESIGNS OF 1855**

DESIGNS AND COLOURS

255-10-02R
- **$1 Face Design:** Crest/seated Indian, deer and counter/ farmer with sheaf and sickle
- **Colour:** Black with no tint
- **Back Design:** Plain

255-10-04R
- **$2 Face Design:** Crest/men with cradles, cutting wheat/ ship sailing toward viewer
- **Colour:** Black with no tint
- **Back Design:** Plain

255-10-06R
- **$5 Face Design:** Crest/sailing ship/woman standing with large anchor
- **Colour:** Black with no tint
- **Back Design:** Plain

THE EXCHANGE BANK OF YARMOUTH

255-10-08R
- **$10 Face Design:** Crest/steamers and sailing ships/deer, 10 and bison
- **Colour:** Black with no tint
- **Back Design:** Plain

IMPRINT
Rawdon, Wright, Hatch & Edson, New-York

SIGNATURES
left	right
none	none

ISSUE DATING
Engraved
May 1st 1855

Cat.No.	Denom.	Date	Variety	VG	F	VF	EF	Unc
10-02R	$1	1855	Remainder*	30.	45.	60.	100.	200.
10-04R	$2	1855	Remainder*	30.	45.	60.	100.	200.
10-06R	$5	1855	Remainder*	30.	45.	60.	100.	200.
10-08R	$10	1855	Remainder*	30.	45.	60.	100.	200.
Full Sheet	$1,2,5,10	1855	Remainder*	-	-	-	375.	750.

*unsigned and unnumbered.

Note: Some $2 notes have spurious numbers and signatures, some $2 and $5 notes are numbered.

THE EXCHANGE BANK OF YARMOUTH

1867 - 1903

YARMOUTH, NOVA SCOTIA

BANK NUMBER 260 **REDEEMABLE**

Established in 1867 in Yarmouth, Nova Scotia, this bank operated successfully but found competition with larger banks difficult. The Bank of Montreal expanded its operations in the Atlantic provinces in 1903 by absorbing The Exchange Bank of Yarmouth which had assets of $680,303.

260-10. **ISSUES OF 1869 - 1902**

DESIGNS AND COLOURS

260-10-06
- **$5 Face Design:** Sailing ships/sailor talking to man and child on shore, anchor, fisherman and small boat/young sailor seated on ship's rail "On the look out"
- **Back Design:** Lathework, counters and bank name

260-10-16
- **$10 Face Design:** "Justice and commerce" figure on seashore/wharf scene, bales in foreground/shipwright chopping timbers "The ship carpenter"
- **Back Design:** Lathework, counters and bank name

260-10-20
$20 **Face Design:** Two sailors on wharf "Mech's & Commerce"/ wharf scene with trains and wagons in foreground/farmer on horse drinking from trough, sheep
Back Design: Lathework, counters and bank name
1869 **Face Colour:** Black with orange tint
: Black with blue tint
Back Colour: Blue
1870 **Face Colour:** Unknown
Back Colour: Uknown
1871 **Face Colour:** Black with green tint
Back Colour: Green
1890 **Face Colour:** Black with green tint
Back Colour: Green
$5 1900 **Face Colour:** Black with red-orange tint
Back Colour: Green
$10 1900 **Face Colour:** Black with ochre tint
Back Colour: Green
1902 **Face Colour:** Black with orange tint
Back Colour: Green

IMPRINT
American Bank Note Co. N.Y.
American Bank Note Co. New York

SIGNATURES
left	right
mss. T.V.B. Bingay	mss. Robert Caie

ISSUE DATING
Engraved
Aug. 1st 1869   July 1st 1890
Aug. 1st 1870   July 1st 1900
July 1st 1871   July 1st 1902

OVERPRINT
1871: "S" in red
"CANADIAN CURRENCY" in red
1890-1902: "S" in red

Cat.No.	Denom.	Date	VG	F	VF	EF	Unc
10-02P	$5	1870			FACE PROOF		1,000.
10-04	$5	1871	4,500.	-	-	-	-
10-06	$5	1890	4,500.	-	-	-	-
10-08	$5	1900	4,500.	-	-	-	-
10-10P	$10	1870			FACE PROOF		1,000.
10-12	$10	1871	4,500.	-	-	-	-
10-14	$10	1890	4,500.	-	-	-	-
10-16	$10	1900	4,500.	-	-	-	-
10-18P	$20	1869			FACE PROOF		1,000.
10-20	$20	1871	4,500.	-	-	-	-
10-22	$20	1902	4,500.	-	-	-	-

THE FARMER'S BANK
1840's
TORONTO, UPPER CANADA

BANK NUMBER 265   **NONREDEEMABLE**

This bank traded on the colloquial name of the Farmers' Joint Stock Banking Company. Like the Commercial Bank (Kingston) notes, these are inscribed "For the Foreign & Domestic Exchange Company," and like those "notes", they were a fraud.

265-10.   **DRAFT ISSUE OF 1843**
Engraved: "New York Exchange" at top
DESIGNS AND COLOURS

265-10-02
$5 (£1.5) **Face Design:** Plough in oval (sideways)/kneeling cherub writing on stone/woman with bow
Colour: Black with no tint
Back Design: Plain

IMPRINT
SC .N.Y. - under centre vignette

SIGNATURES
left	right
mss. illegible	mss. illegible

ISSUE DATING
Partially Engraved __18__:
1843: Aug. 3

Cat.No.	Denom.	Date	VG	F	VF	EF	Unc
10-02	$5(£1.5)	1843	1,000.	-	-	-	-

THE FARMERS BANK OF CANADA

1906 - 1910

TORONTO, (ONTARIO)

BANK NUMBER 270 **REDEEMABLE**

The Farmers Bank of Canada was established in Toronto in 1906 and failed in 1910 after suspending payments with total liabilities of about $2 million of which over $400,000 consisted of note circulation. Dishonest and incompetent management resulted in the entire loss of the paid-up capital and the deposits.

270-10.   **ISSUES OF 1907 and 1908**

DESIGNS AND COLOURS

270-10-04
- **$5 Face Design:** Farmer pumping water for livestock/—/—
- **Colour:** Black with green tint

Back Design: Lathework, counters and bank name
Colour: Green

270-10-06
- **$10 Face Design:** —/sheep grazing/—
- **Colour:** Black with orange tint

Back Design: Counter's, lathework, bank name and bull's head
Colour: Green

270-10-10
- **$25 Face Design:** Sir Wilfrid Laurier/—/Premier James P. Whitney
- **Colour:** Black with gold tint

Back Design: Lathework, counters and bank name
Colour: Gold

270-10-12P
- **$50 Face Design:** —/ploughing with horses/—
- **Colour:** Black with olive tint

Back Design: lathework, counters, bank name and woman with sickle in field
Colour: Green

270-10-14P
$100 Face Design: —/farmer unloading hay into barn/—
Colour Black with red tint

Back Design: Lathework, counters, bank name and man and boy working at grindstone
Colour: 1. Green
: 2. Brown

IMPRINT
British American Bank Note Co. Ottawa

SIGNATURES

	left	right
1907:	engr. W. B. Nesbitt	mss. A.W. Kersell
1908:	engr. James Munro	mss. A.W. Kersell
	engr. James Munro	mss. T.H. Weir
	engr. James Munro	mss. H.A. Rinshaw

ISSUE DATING
Engraved
Jan. 2nd 1907
Sept. 1st 1908

Cat.No.	Denom.	Date	VG	F	VF	EF	Unc
10-02	$5	1907	2,500.	-	-	-	
10-04	$5	1908	2,500.	-	-	-	
10-06	$10	1907	4,500.	-	-	-	
10-08P	$25	1907			FACE PROOF		1,500.
10-10	$25	1908	6,000.	-	-	-	
10-12P	$50	1907			FACE PROOF		900.
10-14P	$100	1907			FACE PROOF		1,000.

THE FARMERS' BANK OF MALDEN

1840's

MALDEN, UPPER CANADA

BANK NUMBER 275   **NONREDEEMABLE**

275-10.   **DRAPER, TOPPAN**
LONGACRE PRINTINGS

DESIGNS AND COLOURS

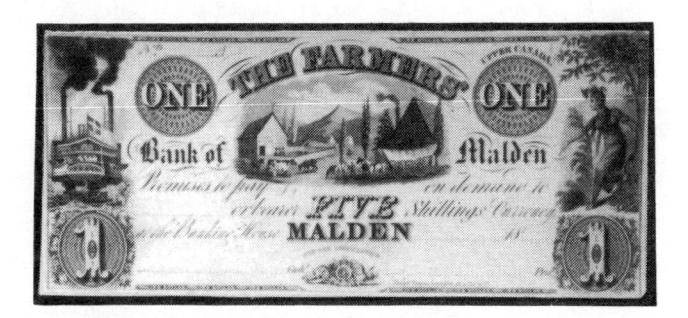

275-10-02P
$1 (5s) Face Design: Steamboat/Pioneer scene; arms below/ Indian maiden
Colour: Black with no tint
Back Design: Plain

275-10-04P
$2 (10s) Face Design: Indian in canoe/seated woman and early train; small coat of arms below/sailboat and view of city (see vignette of $1 note Bank of The People, Toronto)
Colour: Black with no tint
Back Design: Plain

275-10-06P
$3 (15s) Face Design: Seated man with flag/"Commerce" figure, livestock; arms below "Commerce" figure/woman with sickle and sheaf "Agriculture"
Colour: Black with no tint
Back Design: Plain

THE FARMER'S JOINT STOCK BANKING CO.

IMPRINT
Draper, Toppan, Longacre & Co. Phila & N.Y.

SIGNATURES
left	right
none	none

ISSUE DATING
Partially Engraved __18__:

Cat.No.	Denom.	Date			Unc
10-02P	$1(5s)	18__		PROOF	1,200.
10-04P	$2(10s)	18__		PROOF	1,200.
10-06P	$3(15s)	18__		PROOF	1,200.

THE FARMER'S JOINT STOCK BANKING CO.

1835 - 1849

TORONTO, UPPER CANADA

BANK NUMBER 280   **NONREDEEMABLE**

Established in Toronto in 1835 as a private company, it issued its own notes, even after the passage of a legislation in 1837 prohibiting note issue without legislative authority. This bank was one of the four private banks authorized to issue notes without legislative authority on an exception basis. Early in the 1840's it quietly wound up, conducting little business apart from the redemption of its circulation. In 1849 the stock was sold to unscrupulous operators who turned the business into a wildcat bank, pushing as many of its notes as possible, particularly in the United States. The notes soon fell into disrepute in Toronto and Buffalo, but the bank continued a few years more, issuing notes payable at Green Bay, Wisconsin, before finally collapsing.

280-10.   **ISSUE OF 1835 - 1840's**

DESIGNS AND COLOURS

280-10-02
$1 (5s) **Face Design:** Seated girl in bushes/cattle/two men gathering sheaves/men and dog herding sheep/woman at window
Colour: Black with no tint
Back Design: Plain

280-10-04
$2 (10s) **Face Design:** Ship, cargo, fasces in oval/seated woman, haying in background/Britannia
Colour: Black with no tint
Back Design: Plain

THE FARMER'S JOINT STOCK BANKING CO.

280-10-06
$4 (£) Face Design: Indian with bow/woman with grain stalks resting with a dog; haying scene below/ seated Britannia in oval
Colour: Black with no tint
Back Design: Plain

280-10-08
$5 (25s) Face Design: Allegorical female/sailing ship/ haying scene steamship/Britannia
Colour: Black with no tint
Back Design: Plain

280-10-10
$10 (£2.10) Face Design: Cherubs with grapes, grain/ cattle and sheep on hilltop/ beehive in oval
Colour: Black with no tint
Back Design: Plain

Photo Not Available

280-10-12P
$50 (£12.10) Face Design: Woman with flowers planting scene/ man sowing/milk-maids and cows in oval/sheaf and plough
Colour: Black with no tint
Back Design: Plain

IMPRINT
New England Bank Note Co. Boston

SIGNATURES
left	right
mss. H. Dupuy	mss. J. Elmsley
mss. W. Rose	mss. J. Elmsley

ISSUE DATING
Partially Engraved __18__:
$1 1835: 1 Sep'r
$2 1837: 11th Sept.
$4 1836: 1 Feb
$5 1835: 1 Nov.
$10 1830: Dec.

Cat.No.	Denom.	Date	VG	F	VF	EF	Unc
10-02	$1 (5s)	1835	350.	500.	-	-	-
10-04	$2 (10s)	1837	350.	500.	-	-	-
10-06	$4 (£1)	1836	350.	500.	-	-	-
10-06R	$4 (£1)	18__	150.	200.	-	-	-
10-08	$5 (25s)	1835	350.	500.	-	-	-
10-10	$10 (£2.10)	1830	350.	500.	-	-	-
10-12R	$50 (£12.10)	18__					400.

Note: Some notes have "one year after date" written on them.

280-12.   **ISSUE OF 1849 DENOMINATIONS IN DOLLARS AND SHILLINGS, NO PROTECTORS**

DESIGNS AND COLOURS

280-12-02
$1 (5s) Face Design: Britannia/Royal Crest, griffin with key below/ allegorical female
Colour: Black with no tint
Back Design: Plain

280-12-04
$2 (10s) Face Design: Blacksmith at anvil/Prince Consort on Royal Crest; lion, shield and unicorn below/woman with flowers and anchor
Colour: Black with no tint
Back Design: Plain

THE FARMER'S JOINT STOCK BANKING CO.

280-12-06

$5 (25s) Face Design: Britannia and "Justice" figure/Queen Victoria (Chalon portrait) on Royal Crest; crown and swords on cushion below/allegorical women, coins and 5
Colour: Back with no tint
Back Design: Plain

IMPRINT
Rawdon, Wright, Hatch & Edson, New York

SIGNATURES
left	right
mss. Wm. Phipps	mss. J.W. Sherwood

ISSUE DATING
Engraved
Feb'y 1st 1849

STAMP
"KINGSTON" in red
various letters and numbers: C, RY, Z, 7, 8.

Cat.No.	Denom.	Date	VG	F	VF	EF	Unc
12-02	$1(5s)	1849	30.	45.	55.	90.	175.
12-04	$2(10s)	1849	30.	45.	55.	90.	175.
12-06	$5(25s)	1849	30.	45.	55.	90.	175.

280-14. **DENOMINATIONS IN DOLLARS ONLY**

2. **ENGRAVED "THE BRANCH OF" & "... Office in Green Bay Wisconsin"; NO PROTECTORS**

DESIGNS AND COLOURS

280-14-02-02

$1 Face Design: Britannia/Royal Crest: griffin with key below/allegorical female
Colour: Black with no tint
Back Design: Plain

280-14-02-04

$2 (10s) Face Design: Blacksmith at anvil/Prince Consort on Royal Crest; lion, shield and unicorn below/woman with flowers and anchor
Colour: Black with no tint
Back Design: Plain

280-14-02-06

$5 (25s) Face Design: Britannia and "Justice" figure/Queen Victoria (Chalon portrait) on Royal Crest; crown on swords below/allegorical women, coins and 5
Colour: Black with no tint
Back Design: Plain

Cat.No.	Denom.	Date	VG	F	VF	EF	Unc
14-02-02	$1	1849	2,000.	-	-	-	-
14-02-04	$2	1849	2,000.	-	-	-	-
14-02-06	$5	1849	2,000.	-	-	-	-

4. **ENGRAVED "at their Office in"; RED PROTECTORS**

DESIGNS AND COLOURS
See previous listing.

280-14-04-02

280-14-04-04

280-14-04-06

$3 (15s) Face Design: Britannia and "Justice" figure/ Neptune group, crown on swords below/three men and ornate 3
Colour: Black with no tint

Back Design: Plain

280-14-04-08

$5 (25s) Face Design: Britannia and "Justice" figure/Queen Victoria (Chalon portrait) on Royal Crest; crown and swords on cushion below/allegorical women, coins and 5
Colour: Black with no tint

Back Design: Plain

PROTECTOR
Red "word" on face and in mirror image on back.

STAMP
Various letters and numbers: C, RY, X, 0.

Cat.No.	Denom.	Date	Variety	VG	F	VF	EF	Unc
14-04-02	$1	1849	Toronto, red ptr.	20.	30.	45.	70.	125.
14-04-04	$2	1849	Toronto, red ptr.	20.	30.	45.	70.	125.
14-04-06	$3	1849	Toronto, red ptr.	50.	75.	110.	150.	225.
14-04-08	$5	1849	Toronto, red ptr.	20.	30.	45.	70.	125.

THE FARMERS J.S. BANKING CO.

1830's

TORONTO, UPPER CANADA

BANK NUMBER 285   **NONREDEEMABLE**

The Farmers J.S. Banking Co., a "spurious bank", evidently traded on the name of The Farmer's Joint Stock Banking Co.

285-10.   **CASILEAR, DURAND, BURTON & EDMONDS DESIGN**

DESIGNS AND COLOURS

285-10-02R

$10 Face Design: James Fox/seated female and plaque depicting lion; crown below/farm girl with wheat
Colour: Black with no tint

Back Design: Plain

IMPRINT
Casilear, Durand, Burton & Edmonds, N. York

SIGNATURES

left	right
none	none
Wm. Phipps (forged)	J.W. Sherwood (forged)

ISSUE DATING
Partially Engraved __18__:
$10 1849: Feb 1

Note: Denomination also written in French and German.
For the possible origin of the design for this note, see $10 note of the Peoples Bank of Toronto.

Cat.No.	Denom.	Date	Variety	VG	F	VF	EF	Unc
10-02R	$10	18__	Remainder*	-	-	-	50.	100.
10-02	$10	1849		-	-	-	75.	125.

*unsigned, undated and unnumbered.

145

THE FARMERS BANK OF RUSTICO

1862 - 1892

RUSTICO, PROVINCE OF PRINCE EDWARD ISLAND

BANK NUMBER 290 **NONREDEEMABLE**

This bank was established in 1862 and was chartered by the Colonial Legislature of P.E.I. in 1863. It was by far the smallest bank, measured by share capital, ever to operate in Canada. By The Bank Act of 1871, Canada made a decision to do away with small, local branchless banks and adopt a policy of nationwide banking. Some banks were forced to sell out, but the Federal government found it difficult to put The Farmers Bank of Rustico out of business. It survived on frugality and devotion. After extreme pressures and delay, the bank managed to renew its charter in 1883 and almost ubelievably, again on June 24, 1891. But the pressure was on to put this bank out of existence. The terms of this last charter were so harsh and unrealistic that they rendered effective liquidation almost impossible. The bank was authorized to amalgamate with or sell its property to any loan company but wound up its operations about 1892.

290-10.   DENOMINATIONS IN DOLLARS/STERLING 1864

DESIGNS AND COLOURS

290-12-02
$1 (4s) **Face Design:** Sheaf of wheat, scythes/ploughing with team of horses/men shearing sheep
Colour: Black with overall green tint
Back Design: Plain

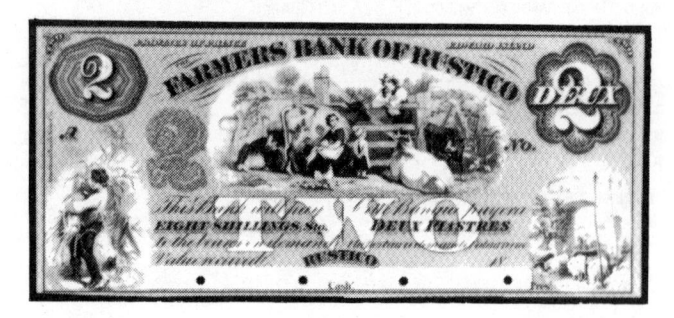

290-10-04P
$2 (8s) **Face Design:** Boy carrying corn stocks "Corn cob Jr."/ pastoral scene: people and animals beside fence/cattle being driven under a bridge "The Drove"
Colour: Black with overall green tint
Back Design Plain

290-10-06P
$5 (£1) **Face Design:** Hens and chickens/farmer pumping water for livestock/milkmaid, cow, calf and duck
Colour: Black with overall green tint
Back Design: Plain

IMPRINT
American Bank Note Co.

SIGNATURES
left   right
mss. Marin J. Blanchard   mss. Jerome Doiron

ISSUE DATING
Engraved
2nd November 1864

Cat.No.	Denom.	Date	VG	F	VF	EF	Unc
10-02	$1(4s)	1864	2,500.	-		-	
10-04P	$2(8s)	1864				PROOF	1,200.
10-06P	$5(£1)	1864				PROOF	1,200.

290-12.   DENOMINATIONS IN DOLLARS ONLY 1872

DESIGNS AND COLOURS
See previous listings.

290-12-02

290-12-04

290-12-06
IMPRINT
American Bank Note Co.
British American Bank Note Co. Montreal & Ottawa
SIGNATURES
left	right
mss. Marin J. Blanchard	mss. Jerome Doiron
mss. Adrien Doiron	mss. Joseph Gallant

ISSUE DATING
Engraved
2nd Jany 1872
Notes are issued with blue or red (rare) sheet numbers.

Cat.No.	Denom.	Date	VG	F	VF	EF	Unc
12-02	$1	1872	1,800.	-	-	-	-
12-04	$2	1872	2,000.	-	-	-	-
12-06	$5	1872	2,500.	-	-	-	-

THE FARMERS BANK OF ST. JOHNS
1837 - 1838
ST. JOHNS, LOWER CANADA

BANK NUMBER 295 **NONREDEEMABLE**

295-10. **DRAFT ISSUE 1837**
Engraved: "To Messrs Brooks, Gridley & Co."
DESIGNS AND COLOURS

295-10-02
 $1 Face Design: Britannia/train; farm tools below/
sheaf of wheat in oval
 Colour: Black with no tint
 Back Design: Plain

295-10-04
 $1.25 Face Design: —/seated "Agriculture" figure,
steamboat in background/standing
Indian with rifle
 Colour: Black with no tint
 Back Design: Plain

295-10-06
 $1.50 Face Design: Two seated allegorical figures/seated
women with globe, standing Indian;
paddlewheel steamboat below/farmer
ploughing with horses
 Colour: Black with no tint
 Back Design: Plain

THE FARMERS BANK OF ST. JOHNS

295-10-08
$2 **Face Design:** Mercury and sailing ship/cherubs sculpting; dog below/Phoenix bird
Colour: Black with no tint
Back Design: Plain

IMPRINT
None

SIGNATURES
left	right
none	mss. J.B. Gridley
none	mss. Cossins

ISSUE DATING
Engraved
$1: Dec. 4, 1837; Dec. 5, 1837
$1.25: Dec. 5, 1837
$1.50: Dec. 5, 1837
$2: Dec. 4, 1837

Cat.No.	Denom.	Date	VG	F	VF	EF	Unc
10-02	$1	1837	700.	-	-	-	-
10-04	$1.25	1837	1,400.	-	-	-	-
10-06	$1.50	1837	1,400.	-	-	-	-
10-08	$2	1837	700.	-	-	-	-

295-12. NOTE ISSUE 1838
DESIGNS AND COLOURS

295-12-01R
$1 **Face Design:** Native standing with rifle/Archimedes lifting the world, bulls head below/seated Commerce and Britannia figures
Colour: Black with no tint
Back design: Plain

Photo Not Available

295-12-02R
$3 **Face Design:** Indian woman standing with bow & arrow/ male seated, with papers; building in background/Indian seated with plaque
Colour: Black with no tint
Back Design: Plain

295-12-04
$5 **Face Design:** —/farmer with cattle and sheep/ seated "Agriculture" figure
Colour: Black with no tint
Back Design: Plain

295-12-06R
$10 **Face Design:** —/farmer ploughing with horses/ seated allegorical male
Colour: Black with no tint
Back Design: Plain

IMPRINT
Lowe 146 B. Way N.Y.

SIGNATURES
left	right
none	none

ISSUE DATING
Partially Engraved __18__:
1838: May 21

Cat.No.	Denom.	Date	Variety	VG	F	VF	EF	Unc
12-01R	$1	18__	Remainder	-	-	400.	775.	-
12-02R	$3	18__	Remainder*	-	-	400.	775.	-
12-04	$5	1838		700.	-	-	-	-
12-06R	$10	18__	Remainder*	-	-	400.	775.	-

*unsigned, undated and unnumbered, some notes with spurious signatures.

THE FEDERAL BANK OF CANADA

1874 - 1888

TORONTO, PROVINCE OF ONTARIO

BANK NUMBER 300 **NONREDEEMABLE**

This bank was originally chartered in 1872 as The Superior Bank, but it did not operate under this name. It was chartered again in 1874 under The Federal Bank of Canada with an ambitious and enterprising management. The bank's business went well until 1884 when it suffered losses in lumber deals and other weak transactions. Other banks came to its aid but to no avail. In 1885, by an Act of Parliament, its capital was reduced and $1 million was wiped out. In 1887 the bank suffered serious deposit withdrawals and note redemptions. To avoid panic, other banks again came to the rescue and advanced $2.7 million out of which all liabilities were paid off including its outstanding circulation. Assets were sufficient to wind up operations without loss.

300-10. **ISSUES OF 1874 - 1882**

DESIGNS AND COLOURS

300-10-02
    $4 Face Design: H.S. Strathy/cherubs and ornate 4/ N.Alexandra
    Colour: Black with green tint

    Back Design: Lathework, counters and bank name
    Colour: Green

300-10-04
    $5 Face Design: H.S. Strathy/workmen, ornate 5 and factories/N. Alexandra
    Colour: Black with green tint

    Back Design: Lathework, counters and bank name
    Colour: Green

300-10-06
    $10 Face Design: H.S. Strathy/two allegorical women and ornate X/N. Alexandra
    Colour: Black with green tint

    Back Design: Lathework, counters and bank name
    Colour: Green

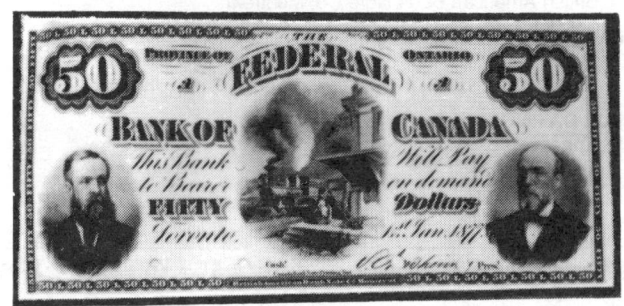

300-10-10P
    $50 Face Design: H.S. Strathy/train at station N. Alexandra/
    Colour: Black with green tint

THE FEDERAL BANK OF CANADA

Back Design: Lathework, counters and bank name
Colour: Green

300-10-12P
$100 Face Design: H.S. Strathy/Canadian Coat of Arms/ N. Alexandra
Colour: Black with green tint

Back Design: Lathework, counters and bank name
Colour: Green

IMPRINT
British American Bank Note Co. Montreal

SIGNATURES
left	right
mss. various	engr. S. Nordheimer

ISSUE DATING
Engraved
1st July, 1874
1st Jan. 1877
Septr 1st, 1882

Cat.No.	Denom.	Date	VG	F	VF	EF	Unc
10-02	$4	1874	500.	700.	-	-	-
10-04	$5	1874	350.	450.	-	-	-
10-06	$10	1874	500.	700.	-	-	-
10-08	$10	1877	500.	700.	-	-	-
10-10P	$50	1877			FACE PROOF		600.
10-12P	$100	1882			FACE PROOF		600.

300-12. **ISSUE OF 1884**
DESIGNS AND COLOURS

300-12-02P
$5 Face Design: S. Nordheimer/workmen, ornate 5 and factories/H.S. Strathy
Colour: Black with green tint

Back Design: Lathework, counters and bank name
Colour: Green

300-12-04P
$10 Face Design: S. Nordheimer/two allegorical women and ornate X/H.S. Strathy
Colour: Black with green tint

Back Design: Lathework, counters and bank name
Colour: Green

IMPRINT
British American Bank Note Co. Montreal

SIGNATURES
left	right
mss. various	engr. S. Nordheimer

ISSUE DATING
Engraved
1st Jan. 1884

Cat.No.	Denom.	Date		Unc
12-02P	$5	1884	FACE PROOF	700.
12-04P	$10	1884	FACE PROOF	700.

THE BANK OF FREDERICTON

1836 - 1839

FREDERICTON, NEW BRUNSWICK

BANK NUMBER 305　　　　　　　**NONREDEEMABLE**

On September 19, 1836, at a meeting of interested citizens, several resolutions were passed founding The Bank of Fredericton. In 1837 a charter was applied for through the Provincial Legislature, but it was never granted. On January 22, 1839 the shareholders of the bank voted to merge with The Commercial Bank of New Brunswick

**305-10.　　NEW ENGLAND BANK NOTE CO.
　　　　　　　　PRINTINGS 1837 - 1838**

DESIGNS AND COLOURS

305-10-02
　1837 5s Face Design: Girl seated on ground/steamboat and sailboats/seated Indian
　　　　Colour: Black with no tint

　　Back Design: Lathework and bank name
　　　　Colour: Blue

305-10-04
　1838 5s Face Design: Girl seated on ground/steamboat and sailboats/standing hunter
　　　　Colour: Black with no tint

　　Back Design: Lathework and bank name
　　　　Colour: Blue

305-10-06P
　10s Face Design: Man with hammer/ships at sea lion and shield in oval
　　　Colour: Black with no tint

　　Back Design: Plain

305-10-08P
　£1 Face Design: Two men harvesting grain/man sowing seeds, team of horses in background/—
　　　Colour: Black with no tint

　　Back Design: Plain

305-10-10P
　£5 Face Design: Seated "Justice" figure/farmer, man on horseback, livestock/—
　　　Colour: Black with no tint

　　Back Design: Plain

IMPRINT
　　left　　　　　　　　　　**right**
　　mss. illegible　　　　　mss. Asa Coy

ISSUE DATING
　　Partially Engraved __18__:
　　　1837: 8th May
　　　1838: 6th March

Cat.No.	Denom.	Date	Variety	VG	F	VF	EF	Unc
10-02	5s	1837	Indian r.	2,000.	-	-	-	-
10-04	5s	1838	Hunter r.	2,000.	-	-	-	-
10-06P	10s	18__					PROOF	900.
10-08P	£1	18__					PROOF	900.
10-10P	£5	18__					PROOF	900.

THE FREE HOLDERS BANK OF THE MIDLAND DISTRICT
1837
BATH, UPPER CANADA

BANK NUMBER 310   *NONREDEEMABLE*

This joint stock banking company was started shortly before the financial panic of 1837. Less than a month after starting up, the Legislature of Upper Canada passed a law prohibiting the formation of any further banks of this type. Therefore, before it could open for business, the firm was forced to wind up its affairs.

310-10.   **RAWDON, WRIGHT & HATCH PRINTINGS**

DESIGNS AND COLOURS

310-10-02R
- **$1 (5s) Face Design:** —/Royal Crest; reclining "agriculture" figure below/female with sheaf; farmers and livestock
- **Colour:** Black with no tint
- **Back Design:** Plain

310-10-04R
- **$5 (25s) Face Design:** —/beehive, cornucopia, sheaf, spinning wheel; child riding deer below/—
- **Colour:** Black with no tint
- **Back Design:** Plain

IMPRINT
Rawdon, Wright & Hatch New-York

SIGNATURES
Rawdon, Wright & Hatch New-York

SIGNATURES
left	right
none	none

ISSUE DATING
Partially Engraved __18__:

Cat.No.	Denom.	Date	Variety	VG	F	VF	EF	Unc
10-02R	$1 (5s)	18__	Remainder*	800.	-	-	-	-
10-04R	$5 (25s)	18__	Remainder*	800.	-	-	-	-

Note I: *Unsigned, undated and unnumbered.
     2: Notes were payable "Twelve months after date".

GODERICH BANK
1834
GODERICH, UPPER CANADA

BANK NUMBER 315   *NONREDEEMABLE*

The status of this bank has never been authoritatively established. It has been contended the bank was a legitimate private bank, but speculation still remains that it was a "spurious bank" intended to circulate fictitious notes.

315-10.   **ISSUE OF 1834**

DESIGNS AND COLOURS

Photo Not Available

315-10-02
- **$1 (5s) Face Design:** Unknown
- **Colour:** Black with no tint
- **Back Design:** Plain

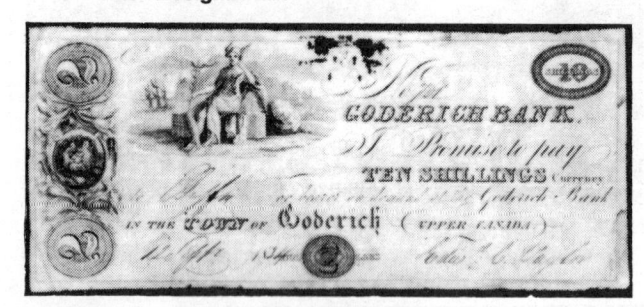

315-10-04
- **$2 (10s) Face Design:** Lion/seated Mercury, ships in background/—
- **Colour:** Black with no tint
- **Back Design:** Plain

IMPRINT
C.P. Harrison Sct N. York

SIGNATURES
left	right
none	mss. Edw. C. Taylor

ISSUE DATING
Partially Engraved __18__:
1834: 12 Sept.

Cat.No.	Denom.	Date	VG	F	VF	EF	Unc
10-02	$1(5s)	1834	1,200.	-	-	-	-
10-04	$2(10s)	1834	1,200.	-	-	-	-

THE GORE BANK
1835 - 1870
HAMILTON, U.C. (UPPER CANADA)

BANK NUMBER 320   **REDEEMABLE**

Established in Hamilton, Upper Canada in 1835, this bank's charter, unlike any of those passed in Upper or Lower Canada, prohibited any incorporated company from holding shares of the bank and imposed double liability on its shareholders. The bank operated successfully, but tied up its funds unwisely in real estate and was hard-hit by withdrawals of deposits when its larger rivals failed. Following the collapse of the land boom in the late 1850's and the subsequent depression, the bank was absorbed by The Canadian Bank of Commerce in 1870, at about 57% on its nominal capital, after its shareholders had already effected a 40% reduction in the value of their shares.

320-10. NEW ENGLAND BANK NOTE CO. PRINTINGS 1836 - 1856

DESIGNS AND COLOURS

320-10-04-06
$1 Face Design: —/Wentworth County Court House/—
Colour: Black with no tint
Back Design: Plain

320-10-02-32
$2 Face Design: —/lion, two seated women, unicorn/—
Colour: Black with no tint
Back Design: Plain

320-10-02-56
$4 Face Design: —/Royal Crest/—
Colour: Black with no tint
Back Design: Plain

320-10-02-66
$10 Face Design: Ship, fasces and produce in oval /St. George slaying the dragon/—
Colour: Black with no tint
Back Design: Plain

IMPRINT
New England Bank Note Co. Boston

SIGNATURES

left	right
mss. A. Steven	mss. Colin C. Ferrie
mss. Wm. G. Crawford	mss. A. Steven
mss. A. Steven	mss. Wm. White

2. PARTIALLY ENGRAVED DATE 1836 - 1850 PAYEE'S NAME IS MANUSCRIPT

ISSUE DATING
Partially Engraved __18__:
- **$1 1840:** 6 Feb.
- **1849:** 1 Nov.
- **1850:** 1 Mar.
- **$2 1845:** Dec. 9
- **1839:** Jan. 3
- **$4 1836:** Nov. 7
- **1839:** July
- **1850:** 1 Mar.
- **$10 1836:** Nov. 16

Cat.No.	Denom.	Date	VG	F	VF	EF	Unc
10-02-10	$1	1840	900.	1,200.	-	-	-
10-02-20	$1	1849	900.	1,200.	-	-	-
10-02-22	$1	1850	900.	1,200.	-	-	-
10-02-32	$2	1845	1,000.	1,400.	-	-	-
10-02-40	$4	1836	1,000.	1,400.	-	-	-
10-02-46	$4	1839	1,000.	1,400.	-	-	-
10-02-56	$4	1850	1,000.	1,400.	-	-	-
10-02-60	$10	1836	1,100.	1,500.	-	-	-
10-02-66	$10	1839	1,100.	1,500.	-	-	-

4. FULLY ENGRAVED DATE 1850 - 1856 PAYEE'S NAME IS ENGRAVED

All 1850 and some 1852 notes have manuscript sheet numbers; some 1852 and all 1856 notes have printed numbers.

ISSUE DATING
Engraved
2nd Sept. 1850
2nd Septr. 1852
2nd June, 1856

Almost all $4 notes of this date are extremley deceptive counterfeits. They can be identified by a doubling of the letter I in QUI in the Royal Crest and by the 52 of date 1852 being slightly higher than the 18. All counterfeits have check letter A. The prices given are for genuine notes.

Cat.No.	Denom.	Date	VG	F	VF	EF	Unc
10-04-02	$1	1850	500.	1,000.	1,300.	-	-
10-04-06	$1	1856	500.	1,000.	1,300.	-	-
10-04-08	$2	1850	500.	1,000.	1,300.	-	-
10-04-10	$2	1852	500.	1,000.	1,300.	-	-
10-04-12	$2	1856	500.	1,000.	1,300.	-	-
10-04-16	$4	1852	600.	1,100.	1,500.	-	-
10-04-22	$10	1852	600.	1,100.	1,500.	-	-

THE GORE BANK OF HAMILTON

ca. 1837

HAMILTON, UPPER CANADA

BANK NUMBER 325 **NONREDEEMABLE**

This is a "spurious bank", evidently intended to trade on the name of The Gore Bank. The notes are crudely engraved, and printed on low quality paper. The parties behind this particular project appear to have been unsuccessful in circulating their productions, as only remainder notes are generally encountered. The $10 note is similar to the equally spurious Farmers' J.S. Banking Co. $10 note, and it is believed that all of the notes of these two "banks" were printed from the same plate.

325-10. CASILEAR, DURAND, BURTON AND EDMONDS PRINTINGS

DESIGNS AND COLOURS

325-10-02R
- **$10 Face Design:** James Fox/seated female with plaque depicting lion; crown below/farm girl with wheat
- **Colour:** Black with no tint
- **Back Design:** Plain

325-10-04R
- **$20 Face Design:** Female with spear/King William IV farm implements below/cattle
- **Colour:** Black with no tint
- **Back Design:** Plain

325-10-06R
- **$50 Face Design:** Allegorical female/King William IV on Royal Arms; head of a deer below/allegorical female
- **Colour:** Black with no tint
- **Back Design:** Plain

IMPRINT
Casilear, Durand, Burton and Edmonds, N. York

SIGNATURES
left	right
none	none

ISSUE DATING
Partially Engraved __18__:

Cat.No.	Denom.	Date	Variety	VG	F	VF	EF	Unc
10-02R	$10	18__	Remainder*	-	60.	85.	175.	-
10-04R	$20	18__	Remainder*	-	60.	85.	175.	-
10-06R	$50	18__	Remainder*	-	60.	85.	175.	-

*unsigned, undated and unnumbered.

Note: Denominations are also printed in French and German. Some notes with spurious dates, serial numbers and signatures.

THE GRENVILLE COUNTY BANK

1856

PRESCOTT, CANADA WEST

BANK NUMBER 330 **NONREDEEMABLE**

Bank notes were ordered by W.D. Dickinson and S. Stanton of Prescott on Nov. 4, 1856; however, there is no record of any notes or proofs having survived. The plate has survived, and the $1 portion was used in the production of the Interpam Souvenir Sheet (1981). It was intended that the bank issue notes under the Free Banking Act, secured by the deposit of provincial securities.

330.10.   WELLSTOOD, HAY & WHITING PRINTINGS

DESIGNS AND COLOURS

330-10-02
- **$1 Face Design:** Jacques Cartier/train/farmer with basket of corn
- **Colour:** Black with no tint
- **Back Design:** Plain

330-10-04
- **$2 Face Design:** Christopher Columbus/dock scene; beaver below/woman and ornate 2
- **Colour:** Black with no tint
- **Back Design:** Plain

330-10-06
- **$5 Face Design:** Prince Consort/steamship; small train below/waterfall, train on bridge and large 5
- **Colour:** Black with no tint
- **Back Design:** Plain

330-10-08
- **$10 Face Design:** Queen Victoria (Chalon portrait) farmer on horseback, cattle and sheep; beehive and flowers below/seated woman and ornate X, cow
- **Colour:** Black with no tint
- **Back Design:** Plain

IMPRINT
Wellstood, Hay & Whiting, New York

SIGNATURES

left	right
none	none

ISSUE DATING
Partially Engraved __18__:

Cat.No.	Denom.	Date	Variety	Unc
10-02	$1	18__		None Available PROOF
10-02a	$1	18__	Interpam reprint, 1981 $5.00	
10-04	$2	18__		None Available PROOF
10-06	$5	18__		None Available PROOF
10-08	$10	18__		None Available PROOF

THE HALIFAX BANKING COMPANY
1825 - 1903
HALIFAX, NOVA SCOTIA

BANK NUMBER 335 **REDEEMABLE**

This Institution commenced business as a private bank in Halifax in 1825. It was the first to give a regular banking service in Nova Scotia and its wealthy owners tried to keep the banking business to themselves. This institution continued to operate as a private company until 1872, and then as a chartered bank until 1903 when it merged with The Canadian Bank of Commerce. The bank enjoyed continuous prosperity, but its growth was hampered by lack of representation in larger financial centres.

335-10.   **MAVERICK PRINTINGS**
              1825 - ca. 1832

DESIGNS AND COLOURS

335-10-02
 £1.10 **Face Design:** Rose, thistle and shamrock/—/ fish, ox and ship
       Colour: Black with no tint
       Back Design: Plain

IMPRINT
 Maverick

SIGNATURES
 left   right
 mss. P.C. Hill   mss. H.H. Cogswell

ISSUE DATING
 Partially Engraved __18__:
 1825: 1st September
 1826: Sept. 1

Cat.No.	Denom.	Date	VG	F	VF	EF	Unc
10-02	£1.10	1825	2,500.	4,500.	-	-	-
10-04	£1.10	1826	2,500.	4,500.	-	-	-

335-12.   **NEW ENGLAND BANK NOTE CO.**
              PRINTINGS - ca. 1833 - 1850's

DESIGNS AND COLOURS

335-12-02R
 £5 **Face Design:** Cattle/ship/cask, bales and cornucopia below/farm implements and sheaf/ whaling scene; ships
    Colour: Black with blue tint
    Back Design: Plain

335-12-04R
 £6.0.0 **Face Design:** Ship; whaling scene/Britannia; farm tools/ harvesting scene
        Colour: Black with blue tint
        Back Design: Plain

335-12-06R
 £6.10.0 **Face Design:** Ship with men fishing/beehive; farm tools below/whaling scene; cattle; whaling scene
         Colour: Black with blue tint
         Back Design: Plain

335-12-08R
 £7.10.0 **Face Design:** Allegorical female/ships; casks and ship below/cattle
         Colour: Black with blue tint
         Back Design: Plain

THE HALIFAX BANKING COMPANY

IMPRINT
New England Bank Note Company, Boston

SIGNATURES
left	right
none	none

ISSUE DATING
Partially Engraved __18__:

Cat.No.	Denom.	Date	Variety	VG	F	VF	EF	Unc
12-02R	£5	18__	Remainder*	-	-	-	-	1,600.
12-04R	£6	18__	Remainder*	-	-	-	-	1,600.
12-06R	£6.10	18__	Remainder*	-	-	-	-	1,600.
12-08R	£7.10	18__	Remainder*	-	-	-	-	1,600.
Full Sheet 5,6,6.10,7.10		18__	Remainder*	-	-	-	-	6,000.

* unsigned, undated and unnumbered.

335-14.   ABNC
$20 ISSUE OF 1863 AND 1871

DESIGNS AND COLOURS

335-14-02-02a
  $20 Face Design: —/ships in Halifax harbour/—
     See subheadings
  Colour: Black with green tint

  Back Design: Lathework, counters and bank name
     Colour: Green

IMPRINT
American Bank Note Co. New York

SIGNATURES
left	right
mss. various	mss. Wm. Pryor

2.   PLAIN COUNTERS 1863 AND 1871

ISSUE DATING
  Partially Engraved __18__:
  1863: 9th Decr.
  Proof dated 14th Septr. (18)71
  Overprinted:
  1871 (July 1)

OVERPRINT
"July 1, 1871" and "CANADA CURRENCY" in red

Cat.No.	Denom.	Date	Variety	VG	F	VF	EF	Unc
14-02-02	$20	1863	Mss. sheet #'s	4,000.	-	-	-	-
14-02-02a	$20	1863	Printed sheet #'s	4,000.	-	-	-	-
14-02-04	$20	1871	Date as red o/p	4,000.	-	-	-	-

4.   "CANADA CURRENCY" ENGRAVED
IN COUNTERS 1871

335-14-04-02

ISSUE DATING
  Engraved
  Septr. 14th, 1871

Cat.No.	Denom.	Date	Variety	VG	F	VF	EF	Unc
14-04-02	$20	1871	Engr. date	4,000.	-	-	-	-

ISSUES OF 1872 AND 1880

DESIGNS AND COLOURS

335-16-02
  $4 Face Design: —/ships in Halifax harbour/—
    Colour: Black with green tint

  Back Design: Lathework, counters and bank name
    Colour: Green

335-16-06
  $5 Face Design: —/Ships in Halifax harbour/—top 5 counters
     differ from 1880 note
    Colour: Black with green tint. (larger than on 1880 notes)

  Back Design: lathework, counters and bank name
    Colour: Green

THE HALIFAX BANKING COMPANY

335-16-08
 $5 **Face Design:** —/ships in Halifax harbour/—
    Colour: Black with green tint

  Back Design: Lathework, counters and bank name
    Colour: Green

335-16-12
 $10 **Face Design:** —/ships in Halifax harbour/—
    Colour: Black with green tint

  Back Design: Lathework, counters and bank name
    Colour: Green

335-16.   **ABNC PRINTINGS 1872 and 1880**

IMPRINT
 American Bank Note Co. New York
 American Bank Note Co. N.Y.

SIGNATURES
left	right
mss. various	mss. Wm. Pryor

ISSUE DATING
 Engraved
 October 1st, 1872
 October 1st, 1880

Cat.No.	Denom.	Date	VG	F	VF	EF	Unc
16-02	$4	1872	4,500.	-	-	-	-
16-04	$4	1880	4,500.	-	-	-	-
16-06	$5	1872	4,500.	-	-	-	-
16-08	$5	1880	4,500.	-	-	-	-
16-10	$10	1872	4,500.	-	-	-	-
16-12	$10	1880	4,500.	-	-	-	-

335-18.   **CANADA BN CO. AND ABNC PRINTINGS 1880**

DESIGNS AND COLOURS

Photo Not Available

335-18-02
 $10 **Face Design:** —/ships in Halifax harbour/—
    Colour: Black with green tint

  Back Design: Lathework, counters and bank name
    Colour: Green

Photo Not Available

335-18-04
 $20 **Face Design:** —/ships in Halifax harbour/—
    Colour: Black with green tint

  Back Design: Lathework, counters and bank name
    Colour: Green

IMPRINT
 American Bank Note Company
 and Canada Bank Note Company

SIGNATURES
left	right
mss. various	mss. R. Uniacke

USSUE DATING
 Engraved
 Oct. 1, 1880

Cat.No.	Denom.	Date	Variety	VG	F	VF	EF	Unc
18-02	$10	1880	Canada BN Co.	4,500.	-	-	-	-
18-04	$20	1880					PROOF	500.

158

335-20. BABNC AND ABNC PRINTINGS 1880
DESIGNS AND COLOURS

Photo Not Available

335-20-01
   $4 **Face Design:** —/ships in Halifax harbour/—
   Colour: Black with green tint

Back Design: lathework, counters and bank name
Colour: Green

335-20-02
   $5 **Face Design:** —/ships in Halifax harbour/—
   Colour: Black with green tint

Back Design: Lathework, counters and bank name
Colour: Green

The tint has been modified and the upper counters have been reduced in size and the panel changed from plain FIVE to FIVE with a background of V5V5V5 etc.

IMPRINT
British American Bank Note Co. Montreal
American Bank Note Co. New York

SIGNATURES
left	right
mss. various	mss. R. Uniacke

ISSUE DATING
   Engraved
   October 1st, 1880

Cat.No.	Denom.	Date	Variety	VG	F	VF	EF	Unc
20-01	$4	1880	BABN Co.				PROOF	500.
20-02	$5	1880	BABN Co.	4,500.	-	-	-	-

335-22. CANADA BN CO. AND BABNC PRINTINGS OF 1887 - 1894
DESIGNS AND COLOURS

335-22-04-02
   $5 **Face Design:** Fishermen and sailing ships "Fishing"/ships in Halifax harbour/Crest of Halifax

Back Design: Lathework, counters and bank name

335-22-02-06
   $10 **Face Design:** Fishermen and sailing ships "Fishing"/ships in Halifax harbour/Crest of Halifax

Back Design: Lathework, counters, bank name, crest and two griffins

THE HALIFAX BANKING COMPANY

335-22-02-08
$20 Face Design: Fishermen and sailing ships "Fishing"/ships in Halifax harbour/Crest of Halifax

Back Design: Lathework, counters, bank name, crest and two winged sphinxes

2. CANADA BN CO. PRINTINGS
1887 and 1890

$5 Face Colour: See varieties
Back Colour: See varieties
$10 Face Colour: Black with green tint
Back Colour: Green
$20 Face Colour: Black with green tint
Back Colour: Green

IMPRINT
Canada Bank Note Co. Montreal
Canada Bank Note Co. Ltd. Montreal

SIGNATURES
left — mss. various
right — engr. R. Uniacke

ISSUE DATING
Engraved
Jan. 1st 1887
July 2nd 1890

VARIETIES
$5 Face colour: Blue
Back Colour: Brown
$5 Face Colour: Black with green tint
Back Colour: Green
$5 Face Colour: Black with red tint
Back Colour: Brown

Cat.No.	Denom.	Date	Variety	VG	F	VF	EF	Unc
22-02-02	$5	1887	Green tint	4,500.	-	-	-	-
22-02-03	$5	1887	Blue tint				PROOF	500.
22-02-04	$5	1887	Red tint	4,500.	-	-	-	-
22-02-06	$10	1890		4,500.	-	-	-	-
22-02-08	$20	1890		4,500.	-	-	-	-

4. BABNC PRINTINGS 1894

DESIGNS AND COLOURS
Same designs as 1887 issue.
$5 Face Colour: Black with blue tint
Back Colour: Blue

IMPRINT
British American Bank Note Co. Ottawa

SIGNATURES
left — mss. various
right — engr. R. Uniacke

ISSUE DATING
Engraved
Jan. 1st 1894

Cat.No.	Denom.	Date	VG	F	VF	EF	Unc
22-04-02	$5	1894	4,500.	-	-	-	-

335-24. "UNIACKE PORTRAIT" ISSUES
1896 and 1898

DESIGNS AND COLOURS

335-24-01
$5 Face Design: H.N. Wallace/ships in Halifax harbour/R.Uniacke
Colour: Black with green tint
Back Design: Lathework, counters, bank name and Halifax Coat of Arms

335-24-02
$5 Face Design: Ornate lathework with V & head of Mercury/ships in Halifax harbour/R. Uniacke
Colour: Black with green tint

Back Design: Lathework, counters and bank name, Halifax coat of Arms
Colour: Green

335-24-04
$10 Face Design: Ships and pilot boats/—R. Uniacke
Colour: Black with green tint

Back Design: Lathework, counters and bank name
Colour: Green

335-24-06
$20 Face Design: Crest of Halifax/—/R. Uniacke
Colour: Black with ochre tint

Back Design: Lathework, counters and bank name
Colour: Green

IMPRINT
British American Bank Note Co. Ottawa

SIGNATURES

left	right
mss. various	engr. Robie Uniacke

ISSUE DATING
  Engraved
  July, 2nd 1896
  July 1st 1898

Cat.No.	Denom.	Date	Variety	VG	F	VF	EF	Unc
24-01P	$5	1896	Portrait I			PROOF		500.
24-02	$5	1896	Ornate V I	4,500.	-	-	-	-
24-04	$10	1898		4,500.	-	-	-	-
24-06	$20	1898		4,500.	-	-	-	-

Note: $10 proof with orange face, brown back

THE HAMILTON BANK

1835

HAMILTON, LOWER CANADA

BANK NUMBER 340 **NONREDEEMABLE**

Bank notes were ordered in November of 1835; however, there is no record of any notes or proofs having survived.

THE BANK OF HAMILTON

1872 - 1923

HAMILTON, (ONTARIO) DOMINION OF CANADA

BANK NUMBER 345 **REDEEMABLE**

The bill chartering The Bank of Hamilton received Royal assent on June 14, 1872 and the bank opened its doors for business in Hamilton, Ontario the following September, a capital stock of $1 million having been subscribed. At its first Annual Meeting, June 17, 1873, a profit of $23,951.27 was declared for the preceding nine months. During the later part of 1873 the bank opened its first two agencies in Ontario, at Listowel and Port Elgin, the former being located on the Wellington, Grey and Bruce Railway, now the C.N.R. By the spring of 1877 money was becoming more plentiful and rates of discount were reduced. In spite of several setbacks that year, including the failure of some long standing banks, the bank managed to show a profit. After 30 years of operation, assets had reached almost 20 million. The bank continued to grow until 1912 when the recession that affected most other financial institutions began to make its presence known. With the signing of the Armistice, however, the bank joined the rush of chartered banks to open more branches. At its 50th anniversary in 1922, amidst post-war depression, it was represented in 157 locations. With the burden of high taxation and increasing competition, The Bank of Hamilton amalgamated with The Canadian Bank of Commerce in 1923.

345-10.   ISSUES OF 1872 AND 1873

DESIGNS AND COLOURS

345-10-02
   $4 Face Designs: D. McInnes/train/machinist at lathe
   Colour: Black with green tint

Back Design: Lathework, counters, bank name and crest
Colour: Green

345-10-04
   $5 Face Design: D. McInnes/factories, blacksmith, women, workers and ornate 5
   Colour: Black with green tint

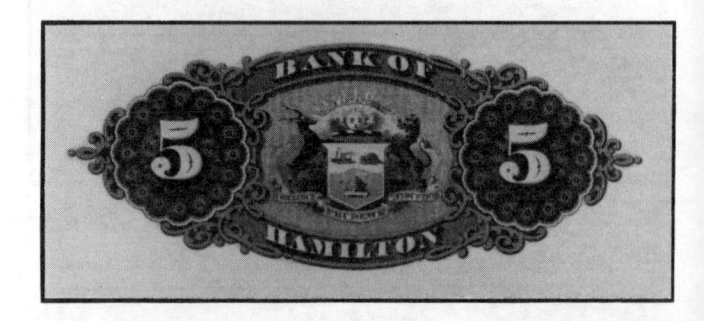

Back Design: Lathework, counters, bank name and crest
Colour: Green

345-10-06
   $10 Face Design: Ornate X and two seated allegorical women/ D. McInnes/—
   Colour: Black with green tint

THE BANK OF HAMILTON

Back Design: Lathework, counters, bank name and crest
Colour: Green

Back Design: Lathework, counters, bank name and crest
Colour: Green

345-10-08P
$20 Face Design: D.McInnes/seated allegorical female with symbols of commerce and industry
Colour: Black with green tint

345-10-12P
$100 Face Design: —/D.McInnes/—
Colour: Black with green tint

Back Design: —/Crest of Hamilton/—
Colour: Green

IMPRINT
British American Bank Note Co. Montreal & Ottawa

SIGNATURES
left	right
mss. various	engr. D McInnes

ISSUE DATING
Engraved
1st Sept. 1872
2nd Sept. 1872
2nd January 1873

Cat.No.	Denom.	Date	VG	F	VF	EF	Unc
10-02	$4	1872	1,400.	2,000.	3,000.	-	-
10-04	$5	1872	1,400.	2,000.	3,000.	-	-
10-06	$10	1872	1,400.	2,000.	3,000.	-	-
10-08P	$20	1873			FACE PROOF		700.
10-10P	$50	1873			FACE PROOF		700.
10-12P	$100	1873			FACE PROOF		700.

Back Design: Lathework, counters, bank name and crest
Colour: Green

345-10-10P
$50 Face Design: D.McInnes/—/farm scene
Colour: Black with green tint

THE BANK OF HAMILTON

345-12.   **ISSUE OF MARCH 1, 1887**
DESIGNS AND COLOURS

345-12-02
  $5 Face Design: John Stuart/—/factories, workers and ornate 5
  Colour: Black with green tint

  Back Design: —/Crest of Hamilton/—
  Colour: Green

IMPRINT
  British American Bank Note Company, Montreal and Ottawa

SIGNATURE
  left   right
  none   engr. John Stuart

ISSUE DATING
  Engraved
  1st March, 1887

Cat.No.	Denom.	Date		Unc
12-02	$5	1887	FACE PROOF	700.

*No surviving issued notes known.

345-14.   **ISSUE OF DECEMBER 1, 1887**

345-14-02
  $5 Face Design: John Stuart/view of Hamilton from the mountain/—
  Colour: Black with ochre tint

  Back Design: —/Crest of Hamilton/—
  Colour: Green

IMPRINT
  Canada Bank Note Co. Montreal

SIGNATURE
  left   right
  mss. various   engr. John Stuart

ISSUE DATING
  Engraved
  Dec. 1st 1887

Cat.No.	Denom	Date	Variety	VG	F	VF	EF	Unc
14-02	$5	1887		1,400.	2,000.	3,000.	-	-
14-04P	$5	1887	Blue face tint				PROOF	700.
14-06P	$5	1887	Green face tint				PROOF	700.

345-16.   **ISSUE OF 1892**
DESIGNS AND COLOURS

345-16-02
  $5 Face Design: "Agriculture" figure/—/John Stuart
  Colour: Black with green tint

  Back Design: Lathework, counters, bank name, griffins and head office
  Colour: Green

345-16-04
  $10 Face Design: John Stuart/Niagara Falls/"Commerce" figure
  Colour: Black with pink tint

164

THE BANK OF HAMILTON

Back Design: Lathework, counters, bank name and head office
Colour: Red-brown

Back Design: Lathework, counters, bank name and Indians hunting buffalo, train crossing prairie
Colour: Olive green

345-16-06S
$20 Face Design: Ploughing scene/John Stuart/—
Colour: Black with ochre tint

345-16-10S
$100 Face Design: Train "Pullman Vestibule Train/—/John Stuart
Colour: Black with red-brown tint

Back Design: Lathework, counters, bank name and stag's head
Colour: Brown

Back Design: Lathework, counters and bank name
Colour: Dull red

IMPRINT
Western Bank Note Co. Chicago

SIGNATURES
left	right
mss. various	engr. John Stuart

ISSUE DATING
Engraved
1st June, 1892

Cat.No.	Denom.	Date	VG	F	VF	EF	Unc
16-02	$5	1892	350.	450.	-	-	-
16-04	$10	1892	500.	700.	-	-	-
16-06S	$20	1892				SPECIMEN	900.
16-08S	$50	1892				SPECIMEN	900.
16-10S	$100	1892				SPECIMEN	900.

345-16-08S
$50 Face Design: John Stuart/tugboat/—
Colour: Black with olive green tint

165

THE BANK OF HAMILTON

345-18.   **ISSUE OF 1904**

DESIGNS AND COLOURS

345-18-02
    $5 Face Design: Queen Alexandra seated on throne/—/—
    Colour: Black with green tint

    Back Design: Lathework, counters and bank name
    Colour: Green

345-18-04
    $10 Face Design: —/Queen Alexandra seated on throne/—
    Colour: Black with orange tint
    Back Design: Lathework, counters and bank name
    Colour: Orange

345-18-06
    $20 Face Design: —/King Edward VII/—
    Colour: Black with olive green tint

    Back Design: Lathework, counters and bank name
    Colour: Brown

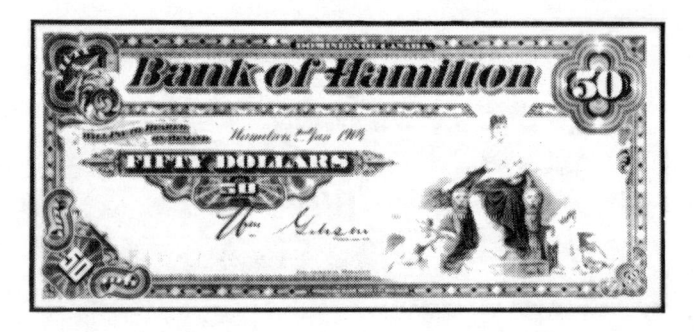

345-18-08
    $50 Face Design: —/—/Queen Alexandra seated on throne
    Colour: Black with blue tint

    Back Design: Lathework, counters and bank name
    Colour: Blue

345-18-10
    $100 Face Design: King Edward VII/—/—
    Colour: Brown

    Back Design: Lathework, counters and bank name
    Colour: Brown

IMPRINT
    Western Bank Note Co. Chicago
    Western Bank Note Company, Chicago

SIGNATURES
left	right
engr. William Gibson	mss. various

ISSUE DATING
    Engraved
    2nd Jan. 1904

Cat.No.	Denom.	Date	VG	F	VF	EF	Unc
18-02	$5	1904	600.	-	-	-	-
18-04	$10	1904	1,200.	-	-	-	-
18-06	$20	1904	1,600.	-	-	-	-
18-08	$50	1904	2,400.	-	-	-	-
18-10	$100	1904	4,000.	-	-	-	-

Specimens exist $800.00 - $1,000.00

345-20. ISSUES OF 1909 AND 1914
DESIGNS AND COLOURS

345-20-02
 $5 Face Design: —/seated Britannia, Agriculture and Industry allegory in background/—
 Colour: Black with green tint

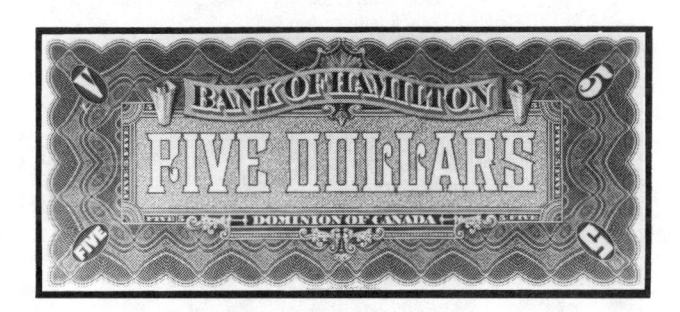

 Back Design: Lathework, counters and bank name
 Colour: Green

345-20-10
 $10 Face Design: Seated allegorical female, Agriculture and Commerce allegory in background/—/—
 Colour: Black with brown and yellow tint

 Back Design: Lathework, counters and bank name
 Colour: Red-brown

345-20-18
 $20 Face Design: —/—/seated Britannia, Agriculture and Industry allegory in background
 Colour: Black with blue tint

 Back Design: Lathework, counters and bank name
 Colour: Slate

345-20-20P
 $50 Face Design: —/seated allegorical female, Agriculture and Commerce allegory in background
 Colour: Black with red tint

 Back Design: Lathework, counters and bank name, woman's head in ornate frame
 Colour: Red-orange

THE BANK OF HAMILTON

345-20-26
  $100 Face Design: Seated Britannia, Agriculture and Commerce allegory in background/—/
  Colour: Black with green tint

  Back Design: Lathework, counters and bank name
  Colour: Olive green

IMPRINT
  American Bank Note Co. Ottawa

SIGNATURES
	left	right
1909:	typed William Gibson	mss. various
	typed John S. Hendrie	mss. various
1914:	typed John S. Hendrie	mss. various
	typed John S. Hendrie	typed J.P. Bell

ISSUE DATING
  Engraved
  1st June 1909
  1st June 1914

OVERPRINT
  1909: "E" twice in red
  "S" twice in red
  1914: "C" twice in red
  "E" twice in red

VARIETIES
  1914: "Pro general manager" with mss. signatures
  "General Manager" with Bell signature

Cat.No.	Denom.	Date	Variety	VG	F	VF	EF	Unc
20-02	$5	1909		100.	175.	300.	500.	-
20-04	$5	1914	Mss.signature,r.	80.	125.	175.	325.	-
20-06	$5	1914	Bell,r.	80.	125.	175.	325.	-
20-08	$10	1909		175.	250.	350.	600.	-
20-10	$10	1914	Mss.signature,r.	175.	250.	350.	600.	-
20-12	$10	1914	Bell,r.	175.	250.	350.	600.	-
20-14S	$20	1909				SPECIMEN		750.
20-16	$20	1914	Mss.signature,r.	300.	425.	650.	-	-
20-18	$20	1914	Bell,r.	300.	425.	650.	-	-
20-20P	$50	1909				FACE PROOF		500.
20-22	$50	1914	Mss.signature,r.	550.	750.	1,125.	-	-
20-24	$50	1914	Bell,r.	550.	750.	1,125.	-	-
20-26	$100	1909		1,500.	2,500.	-	-	-
20-28	$100	1914	Mss.signature,r.	1,500.	2,500.	-	-	-
20-30	$100	1914	Bell,r.	1,300.	2,200.	-	-	-

345-22. "JUBILEE" ISSUE 1922
Issued for the 50th anniversary of the founding of the bank.
DESIGNS AND COLOURS

345-22-02
  $5 Face Design: —/seated Britannia, Agriculture and Commerce allegory in background/—
  Colour: Black with green tint
  Back Design: Lathework, counters and bank name
  Colour: Green

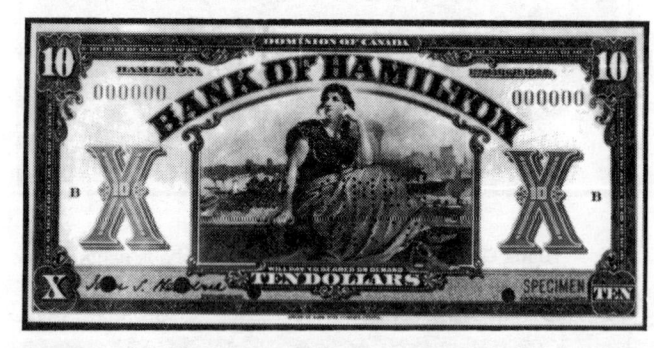

345-22-04
  $10 Face Design: —/seated allegorical female, Agriculture and Commerce allegory in background/—
  Colour: Black with orange tint
  Back Design: Lathework, counters and bank name
  Colour: Orange

345-22-06
  $25 Face Design: Two allegorical women/—/
  Colour: Black with green, pink and purple tint

Back Design: Lathework, counters and bank name
Colour: Purple

IMPRINT
American Bank Note Company, Ottawa

SIGNATURES
left — typed John S. Hendrie
right — typed J.P. Bell

ISSUE DATING
Engraved
1st March 1922

Cat.No.	Denom.	Date	VG	F	VF	EF	Unc
22-02	$5	1922	400.	600.	900.	-	-
22-04	$10	1922	800.	1,000.	1,600.	-	-
22-06	$25	1922	4,000.	5,000.	-	-	-

HART'S BANK
1835 - 1847
THREE RIVERS, L. (LOWER) CANADA

BANK NUMBER 350   *NONREDEEMABLE*

Moses Hart, a respected member of society in Three Rivers, was one of the first bankers in Lower Canada. His application for a charter was turned down but he opened a private bank in 1835. Notes issued by private banks, consisting mostly of wealthy merchants, circulated mainly among French Canadians and were accepted more readily than those of The Bank of Montreal, since the owners of the private institution, including Moses Hart, were known and trusted members of the community. The bank finished its dealings after Hart's death in 1847.

350-10.   **SCRIP ISSUE 1837**
                     SMALL SIZE NOTES

DESIGNS AND COLOURS

350-10-02R
5d (10 sous) Face Design: No vignettes
Colour: Black with no tint
Back Design: Plain

Photo Not Available

350-10-04R
10d (20 sous) Face Design: No vignettes
Colour: Black with no tint
Back Design: Plain

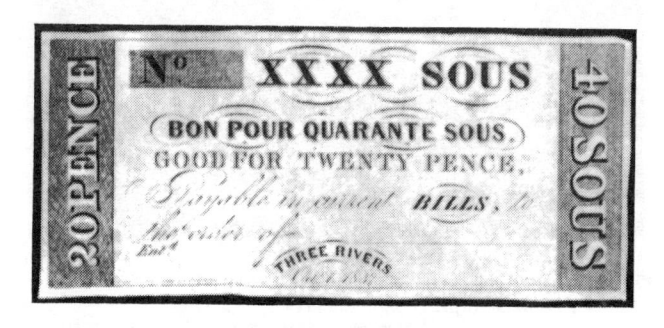

350-10-06R
20d (40 sous) Face Design: No vignettes
Colour: Black with no tint
Back Design: Plain

HART'S BANK

350-10-08R
3 Francs Face Design: ($1/2)
(60 sous) —/—habitant smoking pipe
Colour: Black with no tint

Back Design: Plain

IMPRINT
Bourne

SIGNATURES
left	right
none	none

ISSUE DATING
Engraved
Oct. 1, 1837

Cat.No.	Denom.	Date	Variety	VF	EF	Unc
10-02R	5d(10 sous)	1837	Remainder*	75.	120.	220.
10-04R	10d(20 sous)	1837	Remainder*	75.	120.	220.
10-06R	20d(40 sous)	1837	Remainder*	75.	120.	220.
10-06R	$1/2(60 sous)	1837	Remainder*	75.	120.	220.

*unsigned and unnumbered.

**350-12. DOLLAR ISSUE 1838
LARGE SIZE NOTES**

Reprints of this issue were produced from the original face plate in the early 20th century. (See subheads.)

ORIGINAL PRINTINGS - ORANGE BACK, NORMAL PAPER 1838

DESIGNS AND COLOURS

350-12-02
$1 Face Design: Steamboat in oval (sideways)/
habitants in horse-drawn sleigh; small steamboat below/seated Indian maiden
Colour: Black with no tint

Back Design: Lathework surrounding two male portraits (sideways)
Colour: Orange

350-12-04
$3 Face Design: Seated Indian maiden/habitants in horse-drawn sleigh; ship, casks etc. below/steamboat in oval (sideways)
Colour: Black with no tint

Back Design: Lathework surrounding two male portraits (sideways)
Colour: See subheadings

350-12-06a
$5 Face Design: Seated Indian maiden/habitants in horse-drawn sleigh; ship, casks etc. below/steamboat in oval (sideways)
Colour: Black with no tint

Back Design: Lathework surrounding two male portraits (sideways)
Colour: See subheadings

REPRINTS - PLAIN BACK, THIN PAPER
DESIGNS AND COLOURS
Face Design: See original printings
Back Design: Plain

350-12-04a

IMPRINT
Bourne

SIGNATURES
Originals	
left	right
mss. A.T. Hart	mss. M. Hart

REPRINTS
left	right
none	none

ISSUE DATING
Originals
Partially Engraved __18__:
$1 1838: 28 July
$3 1838: Aug' 20th

REPRINTS
Partially Engraved __18__:

Cat.No.	Denom.	Date	Variety	VG	F	VF	EF	Unc
12-02	$1	1838		600.	800.	-	-	-
12-02a	$1	18__	Reprints*	-	-	60.	100.	175.
12-04	$3	1838		650.	900.	-	-	-
12-04a	$3	18__	Reprints*	-	-	100.	150.	300.
12-06	$5	1838		NOT YET CONFIRMED				
12-06a	$5	18__	Reprints*	-	-	60.	100.	175.

*unsigned, undated and unnumbered.

THE HATLEY BANK
1837
HATLEY, LOWER CANADA

BANK NUMBER 355   **REDEEMABLE**

This bank is presumably a phantom bank with notes, produced to circulate in the New England area. No Bank of North America existed with similar notes in this period. The imprint has not been known for other bank notes. The note has typical United States of America obsolete vignettes.

355-10-10

$10 Face Design: Ships/ sailor seated on bales, flag and ships/ Washington
Back Design: Plain

IMPRINT
W. W. Wilson. Engr. and Pr. Boston

SIGNATURES
Left	Right
Unknown	Unknown

ISSUE DATING
Partially Engraved __18__:

Cat.No.	Denom	Date	VG	F	VF	EF	Unc
10-10	$10	—			ONLY ONE NOTE KNOWN		

HENRY'S BANK

1837

LA PRAIRIE and MONTREAL, LOWER CANADA

BANK NUMBER 357   **NONREDEEMABLE**

This bank, established as a private bank in 1837 in Montreal, operated for only a short period of time. It went into liquidation as a result of an embezzlement by its cashier.

357-10. SCRIP ISSUE OF 1837
DESIGNS AND COLOURS

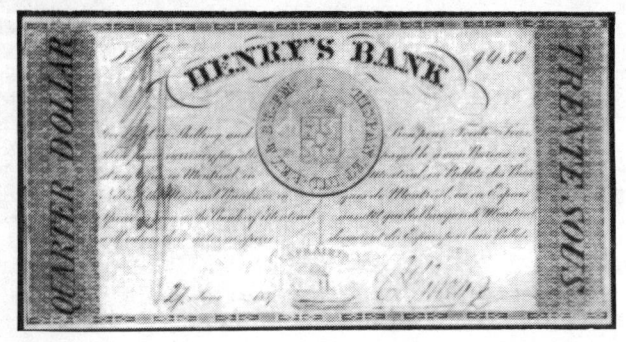

357-10-02
$1/4 (1s.3d.; 30 Sous)
- **Face Design:** —/reverse of Mexican 2 Reales; steamboat below/—
- **Colour:** Black with no tint
- **Back Design:** Plain

357-10-04
$1/2 (2s.6d.; 1 Ecu)
- **Face Design:** —/obverse of Spanish coin; sheaf and agricultural tools below/—
- **Colour:** Black with no tint
- **Back Design:** Plain

IMPRINT
None

SIGNATURES
left	right
none	mss. E. Henry

ISSUE DATING
Partially Engraved ___18___:
Juin 1837
27 Juin 1837

Cat.No.	Denom.	Date	Variety	VG	F	VF	EF	Unc
10-02	$1/4	1837		30.	40.	65.	100.	175.
10-02RP	$1/4	1837	Reprint	-	-	-	-	40.
10-04	$1/2	1837		30.	40.	65.	100.	175.
10-04RP	$1/2	1837	Reprint	-	-	-	-	40.
Sheet of reprints $1/4, $1/4, $1/2				-	-	-	-	125.

357-12. DRAFT ISSUE OF 1837
Engraved: "To Edmund Henry" at upper left.
DESIGNS AND COLOURS

357-12-02
$1 **Face Design:** Allegorical female/seated allegorical male; small steamboat below/allegorical female
- **Colour:** Black with no tint
- **Back Design:** Plain

357-12-04
$2 **Face Design:** Female with wheat/seated female, sheaves and cattle; small shield with 2 below/ cow and sheep
- **Colour:** Black with no tint
- **Back Design:** Plain

IMPRINT
Burton, Gurley & Edmunds, N. York & Bourne Agent Montreal.

SIGNATURES
left	right
mss. E. Henry & Cie	mss. L.A. Moreau

ISSUE DATING
Partially Engraved ___18___:
1837: 19 Juin, 27 Juin

Cat.No.	Denom.	Date	VG	F	VF	EF	Unc
12-02	$1	1837	50.	70.	100.	175.	300.
12-04	$2	1837	50.	70.	100.	175.	300.

355-14. NOTE ISSUE OF 1837
DESIGNS AND COLOURS

357-14-02
- **$5 Face Design:** Ships, town in background (sideways) seated Mercury, ship in background, bales, cask and ship below/farmer standing under tree
- **Colour:** Black with no tint
- **Back Design:** Plain

357-14-04
- **$10 Face Design:** —/allegorical female and eagle, small shield with X below/ornate design with TEN sideways
- **Colour:** Black with no tint
- **Back Design:** Plain

IMPRINT
Burton, Gurley & Edmunds, N.Y. and Bourne, Agent Montreal

SIGNATURES

left	right
mss. L.A. Moreau (Cr.)	mss. E. Henry & Cie

ISSUE DATING
Partially Engraved __18__:
27 Juin 1837

Cat.No.	Denom.	Date	VG	F	VF	EF	Unc
14-02	$5	1837	150.	200.	275.	500.	-
14-04	$10	1837	175.	240.	350.	600.	-

BANQUE D'HOCHELAGA
1873 - 1925

BANK NUMBER 360   **REDEEMABLE**

On May 3, 1873, Parliament passed a law incorporating the Banque d'Hochelaga and the institution opened for business in 1874 in the Place d'Arms in Montreal, the same year the Montreal Stock Exchange opened. During its first year of operations the bank began establishing branches and associating itself with other financial institutions which acted as agents in areas where the bank was not directly represented. After a modest start and slow early progress due to the short-term financial crisis between 1875 and 1896, the bank increased steadily in strength.

The decade from 1910 to 1920 was a booming one for the Banque d'Hochelaga, as it was for most Canadian banks. By the end of 1924 it had 197 branches, the largest number of banks established and administered by Francophone bankers in Quebec. In 1924, the bank merged with La Banque Nationale, having sufficient assets to assume most obligations for losses incurred by La Banque Nationale during an unsuccessful wartime financing scheme. The Quebec government made the merger possible by the unusual step of conveying to the Banque d'Hochelaga, in full ownership, its bonds for $15 million bearing interest at 5% and maturing in 40 years. On February 1, 1925 the Banque d'Hochelaga had its name changed to Banque Canadienne Nationale. Although its branch network remained largely in Quebec, it had operations across Canada and in other countries. Some of the note issues are completely in French, while others are bilingual.

360-10. ISSUES OF 1874 - 1877
DESIGNS AND COLOURS

360-10-04
- **$4 Face Design:** Tree horses heads/milking scene "Dairy Maid"/L. Tourville
- **Colour:** Black with green tint

- **Back Design:** Lathework, counters and bank name
- **Colour:** Green

BANQUE D'HOCHELAGA

360-10-06P
    $5 Face Design: —/train, ships at dockside/—
                      L.Tourville
    Colour: Black with green tint

    Back Design: Lathework, counters and bank name
    Colour: Green

360-10-08P
    $10 Face Design: Shepherd by/Cartier approaching land/
                       L. Tourville
    Colour: Black with green tint

    Back Design: Lathework, counters and bank name
    Colour: Green

360-10-10P
    $20 Face Design: Dog on strongbox/female operating telegraph/L. Tourville
    Colour: Black with green tint

Back Design: Lathework, counters and bank name
Colour: Green

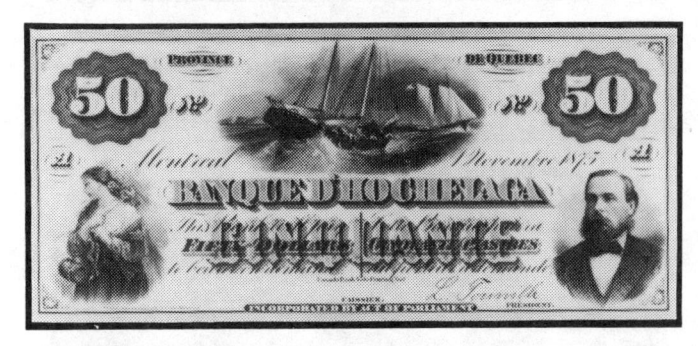

360-10-12P
    $50 Face Design: Female with sheaf/fisherman and ships/
                       L. Tourville
    Colour: Black with green tint

Back Design: Lathework, counters and bank name
Colour: Green

360-10-14P
    $100 Face Design: Dog beside safe/ships at dockside, factories/
                        L. Tourville
    Colour: Black with green tint

BANQUE D'HOCHELAGA

Back Design: Lathework, counters and bank name
Colour: Green

IMPRINT
British American Bank Note Co. Montreal

SIGNATURES
left	right
mss. various	engr. L. Tourville

ISSUE DATING
Engraved
2 Janvier 1874
1 Novembre 1875
2 Juillet 1877

OVERPRINT
$4 1877: "TROIS-RIVIERES" in blue

Cat.No.	Denom.	Date	VG	F	VF	EF	Unc
10-02	$4	1874	1,400.	1,800.	2,800.	-	-
10-04	$4	1877	1,200.	1,700.	2,600.	-	-
10-06P	$5	1874			FACE PROOF		500.
10-08P	$10	1874			FACE PROOF		500.
10-10P	$20	1875			FACE PROOF		500.
10-12P	$50	1875			FACE PROOF		500.
10-14P	$100	1875			FACE PROOF		500.

360-12. ISSUE OF 1880

DESIGNS AND COLOURS

360-12-02P
$5 Face Design: —/train, ships at dockside/
Queen Victoria in "widow's weeds"
Colour: Black with green tint

Back Design: Lathework, counters and bank name
Colour: Green

360-12-04P
$10 Face Design: Shepherd boy/Cartier approaching land/
Queen Victoria in "widow's weeds"
Colour: Black with green tint

Back Design: Lathework, counters and bank name
Colour: Green

360-12-06P
$20 Face Design: Dog on strongbox/female operating telegraph/
Queen Victoria in "widow's weeds"
Colour: Black with green tint

Back Design: Lathework, counters and bank name
Colour: Green

360-12-08P
$50 Face Design: Female with sheaf/fisherman and
ships/Queen Victoria in "widow's weeds"
Colour: Black with green tint

Back Design: Lathework, counters and bank name
Colour: Green

BANQUE D'HOCHELAGA

360-12-10P
$100 **Face Design:** Dog beside safe/ships at dockside, factories/ Queen Victoria in "widow's weeds"
Colour: Black with green tint

Back Design: Lathework, counters and bank name
Colour: Green

IMPRINT
British American Bank Note Co. Montreal

SIGNATURES
left	right
mss. various	engr. F.X. St. Charles

ISSUE DATING
Engraved
1 Sept. 1880
1st September 1880

Cat.No.	Denom.	Date		Unc
12-02P	$5	1880	FACE PROOF	500.
12-04P	$10	1880	FACE PROOF	500.
12-06P	$20	1880	FACE PROOF	500.
12-08P	$50	1880	FACE PROOF	500.
12-10P	$100	1880	FACE PROOF	500.

360-14. "MULTICOLOUR" ISSUE OF 1889
DESIGNS AND COLOURS

360-14-02Pa
$5 **Face Design:** Steamship and sailing ships/—/—
Colour: Black with ochre, blue and orange tint

Back Design: —/Lathework, counters and Provincial Crest/—
Colour: Blue

360-14-04P
$10 **Face Design:** Farmers ploughing with horses/ Samuel de Champlain
Colour: Black with blue, orange and gold tint

Back Design: —/Lathework, counters and Provincial Crest/—
Colour: Orange or blue

360-14-06P
$20 **Face Design:** Black and white horses in front of Roebling suspension bridge/—/Prince of Wales
Colour: Black with blue, red and gold tint

Back Design: —/Lathework, counters and Provincial Crest/—
Colour: Green or orange

BANQUE D'HOCHELAGA

360-14-08P
$50 **Face Design:** Prince of Wales/—/family on house raft
Colour: Black with blue, red and mustard yellow tint

Back Design: —/Lathework, counters and Provincial Crest/—
Colour: Green

360-14-10P
$100 **Face Design:** Samuel de Champlain/—/Indians on bluff "Past and Present"
Colour: Black with blue, red and yellow-brown tint

Back Design: —/Lathework, counters and Provincial Crest/—
Colour: Green

IMPRINT
Canada Bank Note Co. Montreal

SIGNATURES
left	right
engr. F.X. St. Charles	mss. various

ISSUE DATING
Engraved
1889, 1er Juin

Cat.No.	Denom.	Date	Variety	VG	F	VF	EF	Unc
14-02P	$5	1889	(B & W)			FACE PROOF		300.
14-02Pa	$5	1889	(Coloured)			FACE PROOF		750.
14-02S	$5	1889				SPECIMEN		1,000.
14-02	$5	1889		1,400.	1,800.	2,800.	-	-
14-04P	$10	1889	(B & W)			FACE PROOF		400.
14-04Pa	$10	1889	(Coloured)			FACE PROOF		750.
14-04S	$10	1889				SPECIMEN		1,000.
14-06P	$20	1889	(Coloured)			FACE PROOF		750.
14-06S	$20	1889				SPECIMEN		1,000.
14-08P	$50	1889	(Coloured)			FACE PROOF		750.
14-08S	$50	1889				SPECIMEN		1,000.
14-10P	$100	1889	(Coloured)			FACE PROOF		750.
14-10S	$100	1889				SPECIMEN		1,000.

360-16.   **ISSUES OF 1894**

DESIGNS AND COLOURS

360-16-02P
$5 **Face Design:** M.J.A. Pendergast/Montreal harbour/F.X. St. Charles
Colour: Black with green tint

Back Design: Lathework, counters and provincial crest
Colour: Green

360-16-04P
$10 **Face Design:** M.J.A. Pendergast/Cartier approaching land/ F.X. St. Charles
Colour: Black with green tint

BANQUE D'HOCHELAGA

Back Design: Lathework, counters and provincial crest
Colour: Green

IMPRINT
British American Bank Note Co. Ottawa

SIGNATURES
left
mss. various

right
engr. F.X. St. Charles

ISSUE DATING
Engraved
1 Juin, 1894

Cat.No.	Denom.	Date	G	VG	F	VF	EF	Unc
16-02P	$5	1894*				FACE PROOF		500.
16-04P	$10	1894*				FACE PROOF		500.

*Known face proofs have no tint.

360-18. ISSUES OF 1898 and 1907

DESIGNS AND COLOURS

360-18-04
$5 Face Design: M.J.A. Pendergast/steamship/F.X. St. Charles
Colour: Black with olive green tint

Back Design: Lathework, counters, bank name and Provincial Arms
Colour: Green

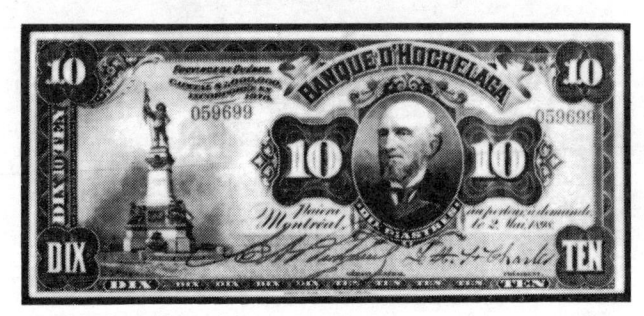

360-18-06P
$10 Face Design: Maissoneuve monument/F.X. St. Charles/—
Colour: Black with olive tint

Back Design: Lathework, counters, bank name and Provincial Arms
Colour: Carmine

360-18-10Pa
$20 Face Design: Loading hay/—/F.X. St. Charles
Colour: Black with olive tint

Back Design: lathework, counters, bank name; Coat of arms/Maissoneuve monument/—
Colour: Blue

360-18-16P
$50 Face Design: M.J.A. Pendergast/—/F.X. St. Charles
Colour: Black with green and olive green tint

178

BANQUE D'HOCHELAGA

Back Design: Lathework, counters, bank name; Coat of Arms/Maissoneuve monument/—
Colour: Olive

360-18-20Pa
$100 Face Design: Dock scene/-/F.X. St. Charles
Colour: Black with olive tint

Back Design: Lathework, counters, bank name; Coat of Arms/Maissoneuve monument/—
Colour: Green

IMPRINT
American Bank Note Company. Ottawa

SIGNATURES
left	right
mss. various	typed F.X. St. Charles

ISSUE DATING
Engraved
Le 1er Mai, 1898
Le 2 Mai, 1898
Le 1er Mars, 1907

Cat.No.	Denom.	Date	Variety	VG	F	VF	EF	Unc
18-02	$5	1898		1,600.	2,400.	-	-	-
18-04	$5	1907		1,600.	2,400.	-	-	-
18-06P	$10	1898	(Coloured*)			FACE PROOF		400.
18-06	$10	1898		1,600.	2,400.	-	-	-
18-08P	$10	1907	(B & W)			FACE PROOF		250.
18-08Pa	$10	1907	(Coloured*)			FACE PROOF		400.
18-10P	$20	1898	(B & W)			FACE PROOF		250.
18-10Pa	$20	1898	(Coloured*)			FACE PROOF		500.
18-12P	$20	1907	(B & W)			FACE PROOF		250.
18-14P	$50	1898	(Coloured*)			FACE PROOF		500.
18-16P	$50	1907	(B & W)			FACE PROOF		250.
18-16Pa	$50	1907	(Coloured*)			FACE PROOF		500.
18-18P	$100	1898	(Coloured*)			FACE PROOF		500.
18-20P	$100	1907	(B & W)			FACE PROOF		300.
18-20Pa	$100	1907	(Coloured*)			FACE PROOF		500.

* Black with an olive or green tint.

360-20. **ISSUE OF 1911**
DESIGNS AND COLOURS

360-20-02P
$5 Face Design: J.A. Pendergast/steamship/J.D. Rolland
Colour: Black with olive green tint

Back Design: Lathework, counters and Provincial Arms
Colour: Green

360-20-04
$10 Face Design: Maissoneuve monument/J.D. Rolland/—
Colour: Black with olive tint

Back Design: Lathework, counters and Provincial Arms
Colour: Carmine

360-20-06P
$20 Face Design: Loading hay/—/J.D. Rolland
Colour: Black with olive tint

Back Design: Lathework, counters and Provincial Arms
Colour: Blue

179

BANQUE D'HOCHELAGA

360-20-08P
$50 Face Design: J.A. Pendergast/—/J.D. Rolland
Colour: Black with green and olive green tint

Back Design: Lathework, counters, bank name, Coat of Arms/Maissoneuve monument/—
Colour: Olive

360-20-10P
$100 Face Design: Dock scene/—/J.D. Rolland
Colour: Black with olive tint

Back Design: Lathework, counters, bank name, Coat of Arms/Maissoneuve monument/—
Colour: Green

IMPRINT
American Bank Note Company, Ottawa

SIGNATURES
left	right
mss. various	typed J.D. Rolland

ISSUE DATING
Engraved
Le 23 Fevrier, 1911
Le 23 Fev. 1911

Cat.No.	Denom.	Date	Variety	VG	F	VF	EF	Unc
20-02	$5	1911		1,600.	2,200.	3,100.	-	-
20-02S	$5	1911				SPECIMEN		450.
20-04	$10	1911		1,600.	2,200.	3,100.	-	-
20-06P	$20	1911	(Coloured*)			FACE PROOF		350.
20-08P	$50	1911	(Coloured*)			FACE PROOF		350.
20-10P	$100	1911	(B & W)			FACE PROOF		350.

*black with an olive or green tint

360-22.   ISSUE OF 1914
DESIGNS AND COLOURS

360-22-02
$5 Face Design: J.A. Vaillancourt/Place d'Arms/Maissoneuve monument
Colour: Black with light blue tint

Back Design: Lathwork, counters, bank name and Provincial Arms
Colour: Blue-green

360-22-04
$10 Face Design: J.A. Vaillancourt/Quebec City/Champlain monument
Colour: Black with yellow-orange tint

Back Design: Lathework, counters, bank name and Provincial Arms
Colour: Red-brown

360-22-06
$20 Face Design: J.A. Vaillancourt/Parliament Buildings, Ottawa/Jacques Cartier
Colour: Black with blue green tint

Back Design: Lathework, counters, bank name and Provincial Arms
Colour: Green

BANQUE D'HOCHELAGA

360-22-08
  $50 Face Design: J.A. Vaillancourt/horse-drawn combine in wheat field/farmer sowing seeds
  Colour Black with salmon tint
  Back Design: Lathework, counters, bank name and Provincial Arms
  Colour: Brown

360-22-10
  $100 Face Design: J.A. Vaillancourt/Moraine Lake/ De La Verendrye monument
  Colour: Black with lilac tint
  Back Design: Lathework, counters, bank name and Provincial Arms
  Colour: Slate

IMPRINT
Waterlow & Sons, Ld London
Waterlow & Sons Ltd. London Wall, London

SIGNATURES
left	right
engr. J.A. Vaillancourt	mss. various

ISSUE DATING
  Engraved
  Le 1er Janvier, 1914

Cat.No.	Denom.	Date	VG	F	VF	EF	Unc
22-02	$5	1914	90.	110.	175.	325.	-
22-04	$10	1914	125.	175.	225.	400.	-
22-06	$20	1914	1,000.	1,400.	2,100.	-	-
22-08	$50	1914	1,000.	1,400.	2,100.	-	-
22-10	$100	1914	1,000.	1,400.	2,100.	-	-

NOTE: Some specimen and proof notes of 1914 issue have different tints from issued notes

  $5: Green Face, Green Back
  $10: Blue Face, Blue Back
  $10: Lilac Face, Brown Back
  $20: Rose Face, Green Back
  $50: Red Face, Red Back
  $100: Orange Face, Brown Back

360-24. **ISSUE OF 1917 AND 1920**
DESIGNS AND COLOURS

360-24-04
  $5 Face Design: J.A. Vaillancourt/statue with four figures/ Beaudry Leman
  Colour: Black with olive tint
  Back Design: Lathework, counters, bank name and Provincial Arms
  Colour: Olive

360-24-08
  $10 Face Design: J.A. Vaillancourt/statue with four figures/ Beaudry Leman
  Colour: Black with brown tint
  Back Design: Lathework, counters, bank name and Provincial Arms
  Colour: Brown

360-24-18
  $20 Face Design: J.A. Vaillancourt/statue with seated allegorical female, Arms of Canada and flag/Beaudry Leman
  Colour: Black with blue tint

BANQUE D'HOCHELAGA

Back Design: Lathework, counters, bank name and Provincial Arms
Colour: Blue

360-24-24
$50 Face Design: J.A. Vaillancourt/Maissoneuve statue/ Beaudry Leman
Colour: Black with red tint

Back Design: Lathework, counters, bank name and Provincial Arms
Colour: Orange-red

360-24-30
$100 Face Design: J.A. Vaillancourt/—/Beaudry Leman
Colour: Black with purple tint

Back Design: Lathework, counters, bank name and Provincial Arms
Colour: Purple

IMPRINT
American Bank Note Company, Ottawa

SIGNATURES

left	right
engr. J.A. Vaillancourt	mss. various
engr. J.A. Vaillancourt	typed Beaudry Leman

ISSUE DATING
Engraved
Jan. 2nd, 1917/le 2 Jan 1917
Jan. 2nd, 1920/le 2 Jan 1920

Cat.No.	Denom.	Date	Variety	VG	F	VF	EF	Unc
24-02	$5	1917	mss. sign,r*	110.	160.	225.	400.	-
24-04	$5	1917	Leman typed,r	110.	160.	225.	400.	-
24-06	$5	1917	Leman engr,r	110.	160.	225.	400.	-
24-08	$10	1917	mss. sign,r	140.	190.	275.	500.	-
24-10	$10	1917	Leman typed,r	140.	190.	275.	500.	-
24-12	$10	1917	Leman engr,r	140.	190.	275.	500.	-
24-18	$20	1917		400.	600.	900.	1,500.	-
24-24	$50	1920		800.	1,100.	1,700.	-	-
24-30	$100	1920		800.	1,100.	1,700.	-	-

*This variety comes with red or blue sheet numbers.

THE HOME BANK OF CANADA

1903 - 1923

TORONTO (ONTARIO)

BANK NUMBER 365   **REDEEMABLE**

Originally a loan and building company, The Home Bank of Canada operated under a charter from 1905, with its head office in Toronto. Its failure in 1923 caused the largest loss to shareholders and creditors recorded up to that time in Canada. The Government of Canada, pursuant to an investigation by a Royal Commission into the responsibilities for and causes of the failure, granted relief to the extent of 35% of the claims of those individuals with claims less than $500. In addition, those with larger claims who were found upon inquiry to be in special need as a result of the failure, were also granted relief at 35%. This assistance involved a total outlay of about $3,460,000.

365-10. ISSUES OF 1904 - 1920
DESIGNS AND COLOURS

365-10-02
- **$5 Face Design:** Maj. Gen Sir Isaac Brock K.B./seated allegorical "commerce" female, ships in background/—
- **Colour:** Black with red tint

- **Back Design:** Lathework, counters, bank name and three students "Mutual improvement"
- **Colour:** Black with red, green and brown tint

365-10-14
- **$10 Face Design:** The Ridgeway monument (1866)(Fenian Raid) woman with horse, poultry/—
- **Colour:** Black with green tint

- **Back Design:** Lathework, counters, bank name and three students "Mutual Improvement"
- **Colour:** Black with red, green and brown tint

365-10-20S
- **$20 Face Design:** Riel Rebellion monument (1885) haying scene, barge and train in background/—
- **Colour:** Black with brown tint

- **Back Design:** Lathework, counters, bank name and three students "Mutual Improvement"
- **Colour:** Black with red, green and brown tint

365-10-26S
- **$50 Face Design:** Boer War monument (1900)/ farmer with horse and children/—
- **Colour:** Black with blue tint

- **Back Design:** Lathework, counters, bank name and three students "Mutual Improvement"
- **Colour:** Black with red, green and brown tint

365-10-36
- **$100 Face Design:** Champlain monument/ helmeted female in oval frame/—
- **Colour:** Black with olive green tint

- **Back Design:** Lathework, counters, bank name and three students "Mutual Improvement"
- **Colour:** Black with red, green and brown tint

THE BANK OF HULL

IMPRINT
American Bank Note Co. Ottawa

SIGNATURES

	left	right
1904:	typed E. O'Keefe	mss. various
1914:	typed James Mason	mss. various
1917:	typed M.J. Haney	mss. various
$5 & $10:		
1920:	typed S. Young	typed J. Cooper Mason
$20 1920:	typed S. Young	mss. various

ISSUE DATING
Engraved
March 1st 1904
March 2nd 1914
March 1st 1917
March 1st 1920

OVERPRINT
$5 1904: "S S" in blue
$10 1904: "S S" in red

Cat.No.	Denom	Date	VG	F	VF	EF	Unc
10-02	$5	1904	1,500.	2,000.	-	-	-
10-04	$5	1914	1,600.	2,000.	-	-	-
10-06	$5	1917	1,500.	2,000.	-	-	-
10-08	$5	1920	1,500.	2,000.	-	-	-
10-10	$10	1904	1,500.	2,000.	-	-	-
10-12	$10	1914	1,500.	2,000.	-	-	-
10-14	$10	1917	1,200.	2,000.	-	-	-
10-16	$10	1920	1,000.	2,000.	-	-	-
10-18S	$20	1904			SPECIMEN		1,000.
10-20S	$20	1914			SPECIMEN		1,000.
10-24	$20	1920	1,800.	2,500.	-	-	-
10-26S	$50	1904			SPECIMEN		1,200.
10-28S	$50	1914			SPECIMEN		1,200.
10-32S	$100	1904			SPECIMEN		1,200.
10-34P	$100	1914			FACE PROOF		600.
10-36	$100	1917	1,800.	2,500.	3,700.	-	-

THE BANK OF HULL

1837

HULL, LOWER CANADA

BANK NUMBER 370 **NONREDEEMABLE**

Orders for bank-notes were placed with Rawdon, Wright, Hatch and Edson on Sept. 28th, 1837. A sheet of Proof notes is in the municipal offices of the city of Hull, Quebec. The denominations are - 30 sous or quarter dollar, 3 francs or half dollar, $1.00 or 5 shillings, $2.00 or 10 shillings, $3.00 or 15 shillings, $5.00 or 25 shillings and $10.00 or 50 shillings.

No other notes are known.

THE IMPERIAL BANK OF CANADA

1873 - 1961

TORONTO (ONTARIO)

BANK NUMBER 375 **REDEEMABLE**

Established in 1873 in Toronto by a group of businessmen, The Imperial Bank of Canada was one of the 28 banks established in the seven years following Confederation. By December of 1874, the Provisional Board was formed to raise the required capital. Of the 432 shareholders, only 160 resided in Toronto. The first office opened for business in Toronto in March of 1875. With the absorption of The Niagara District Bank the same year, branches were acquired elsewhere in Ontario.

The new branches were opened very cautiously. After 10 years the bank had 10 branches, including two in the West. In 1886 a branch was established in Calgary and in 1891 another opened in Edmonton. For some years the Alberta branch was the most northerly bank in Canada. By 1895 there were 12 branches in the West and 20 in the East. In 1899, attracted by lumbering and mining activity, the bank opened its first branch in northern Ontario. The Imperial Bank of Canada absorbed The Wyeburg Security Bank in 1931 extending its operations into Saskatchewan, and in 1956 it absorbed Barclay's Bank (Canada).

In February of 1961, the government announced it had approved an amalgamation agreement between The Canadian Bank of Commerce and the Imperial Bank of Canada, the new institution to be known as the Canadian Imperial Bank of Commerce. In due course the agreement received the required approval of the shareholders of both banks and the merger took effect in June of 1961. At this time, the two banks had 1,242 branches and total assets in excess of $4 billion. Under the agreement, shareholders of The Canadian Bank of Commerce received one share in the new bank for each share already in possession and those of The Imperial Bank of Canada received seven shares in the new bank for each six shares held in The Imperial Bank of Canada.

375-10. **BABN PRINTINGS**
1875 - 1906

DESIGNS AND COLOURS

375-10-02
$4 Face Design: Hon. W.H. Merritt/ornate 4 over Royal Crest/H.S. Howland
Colour: Black with green tint

Back Design: Lathework, counters and bank name
Colour: Green

THE IMPERIAL BANK OF CANADA

375-10-06
- **$5 Face Design:** Hon. W.H. Merritt/ploughing scene/H.S. Howland. Bank name above central vignette
- **Colour:** Black with green tint

- **Back Design:** Lathework, counters and bank name
- **Colour:** Green

375-10-12
- **$5 Face Design:** Hon. W.H. Merritt/ploughing scene/H.S. Howland. Bank name below central vignette
- **Colour:** Black with green tint

- **Back Design:** Lathework, counters and bank name
- **Colour:** Green

375-10-18
- **$5 Face Design:** Hon. W.H. Merritt/Royal Crest with ornate 5/H.S. Howland
- **Colour 1890:** Black with green tint
- **1895-96:** Black with ochre tint

- **Back Design:** Lathework, counters and bank name
- **Colour:** Orange

375-10-22
- **$10 Face Design:** Hon. W.H. Merritt/Bank Crest flanked by lion and Indian/H.S. Howland
- **Colour:** Black with green tint

- **Back Design:** Lathework, counters and bank name
- **Colour:** Green

375-10-24
- **$20 Face Design:** Farmer with horse-drawn mower/—/H.S. Howland
- **Colour:** Black with green tint

- **Back Design:** Lathework, counters and bank name
- **Colour:** Green

185

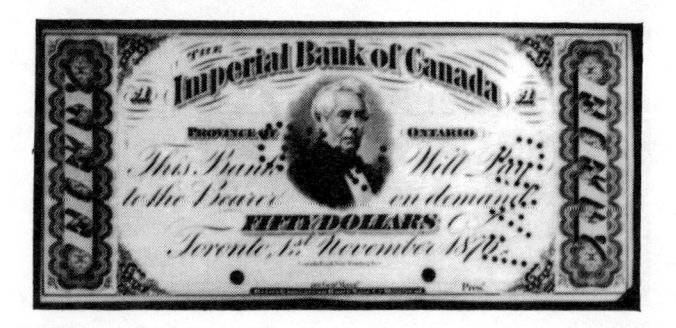

THE IMPERIAL BANK OF CANADA

375-10-28P
  $50 Face Design: —/Hon. W.H. Merritt/—
  Colour: Black with green tint

Back Design: Lathework, counters and bank name
Colour: Green

375-10-30P
  $100 Face Design: —/Canadian Crest/—
  Colour: Black with green tint

Back Design: Lathework, counters and bank name
Colour: Green

IMPRINT
  British American Bank Note Co. Montreal
  British American Bank Note Co. Ottawa

SIGNATURES

	left	right
1875:	mss. various	mss. various
1875:	mss. various	mss. H.S. Howland
1875-1896:	mss. various	engr. H.S. Howland
1906:	mss. various	engr. D.R. Wilkie

ISSUE DATING
  Engraved
  March 1st 1875
  1st March 1875
  1st November 1876
  1st Nov 1876
  Aug. 2nd 1886
  Aug. 2nd 1890
  Oct. 1, 1895
  Oct. 1st 1896
  1st May 1906

OVERPRINT
  1875: "Z Z" in blue

Cat.No.	Denom.	Date	Variety	VG	F	VF	EF	Unc
10-02	$4	1875	Mss. r.	1,200.	1,600.	2,400.	-	-
10-04	$4	1875	Engr.Howland,r.	1,200.	1,600.	2,400.	-	-
10-06	$5	1875	Mss. r.	800.	1,000.	1,500.	-	-
10-08	$5	1875	Engr.Howland,r.	800.	1,000.	1,500.	-	-
10-10	$5	1876		800.	1,000.	1,500.	-	-
10-12	$5	1886		800.	1,000.	1,500.	-	-
10-14	$5	1890	Green tint	800.	1,000.	1,500.	-	-
10-16	$5	1895	Ochre tint	900.	1,200.	2,000.	-	-
10-18	$5	1896	Ochre tint	800.	1,000.	1,500.	-	-
10-20	$10	1875	Mss.Howland,r.	800.	1,100.	1,600.	-	-
10-22	$10	1875	Engr.Howland,r.	800.	1,100.	1,600.	-	-
10-24	$20	1876		900.	1,200.	2,000.	-	-
10-26	$20	1906		900.	1,200.	2,000.	-	-
10-28P	$50	1876				FACE PROOF	500.	
10-30P	$100	1876				FACE PROOF	500.	

THE IMPERIAL BANK OF CANADA

375-12. **WATERLOW PRINTINGS**
1902 - 1910

Some notes of 1902 and 1907 are of extra large size.

DESIGNS AND COLOURS

375-12-04
    $5 Face Design: Woman counting bags in chest/
                          Edward VIII as a boy/Canadian Crest
        Colour: Black with ochre tint

Back Design: seated woman with tablet
Colour: Green

375-12-10
    $10 Face Design: Queen Alexandra and cherubs/
                           Royal Crest/—
        Colour: Black with blue tint

Back Design: —/seated woman with cherub/—
Colour: Yellow-brown

375-12-12
    $20 Face Design: Seated woman and child/
                            George V as Duke of York/—
        Colour: Blue with gold, orange and violet tint

Back Design: —/woman with fruit basket/—
Colour: Green

187

THE IMPERIAL BANK OF CANADA

375-12-16
$50 Face Design: —/Queen Alexandra/seated allegorical female
Colour: Black with gold and green tint

Back Design: —/standing "Commerce" figure/—
Colour: Carmine

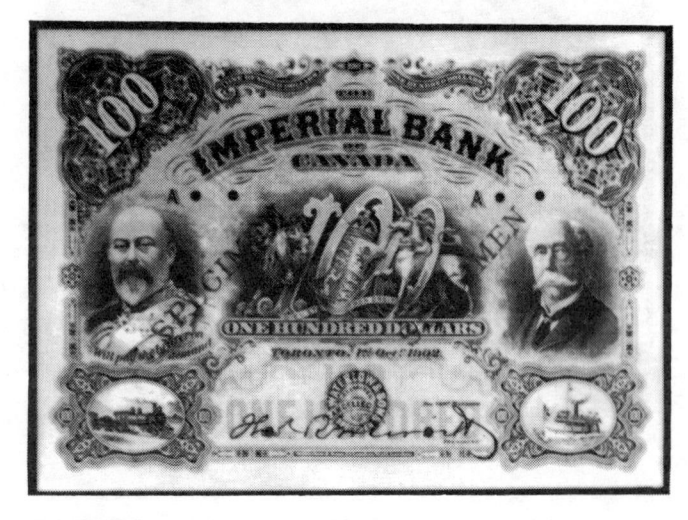

375-12-18S
$100 Face Design: King Edward VII, train/ornate 100 and Royal Crest/Thomas R. Merritt, ship
1902 Colour: Blue with yellow, brown and lilac tint
1907 Colour: Black with red and gold tint

Back Design: —/bank building/—
1902 Colour: Ochre
1907 Colour: Blue

Note: Some specimen notes have different tint from issued notes. $10 ochre face, green back.

IMPRINT
Waterlow & Sons Ld., London Wall, London

SIGNATURES
	left	right
1902:	mss. various	engr. Thos. R.Merritt
1906-1910:	mss. various	engr. D.R. Wilkie

ISSUE DATING
Engraved
1st Octr 1902
1st May 1906
Jan. 2, 1907
1st Jan 1910

Note: Counterfeits of 12-10 exist

Cat.No.	Denom.	Date	Variety	VG	F	VF	EF	Unc
12-02	$5	1902		450.	550.	900.	-	-
12-04	$5	1906		450.	550.	900.	-	-
12-06	$5	1910		350.	400.	700.	-	-
12-08S	$10	1902				SPECIMEN		900.
12-10	$10	1910		300.	550.	800.	-	-
12-12	$20	1902	Extra large size	7,000.10,000.		-	-	-
12-14S	$50	1902	Extra large size			SPECIMEN		3,500.
12-16	$50	1907	Extra large size	7,000.10,000.		-	-	-
12-18S	$100	1902	Extra large size			SPECIMEN		3,500.
12-20S	$100	1907	Extra large size			SPECIMEN		3,500.

THE IMPERIAL BANK OF CANADA

375-14. WATERLOW ESSAYS OF 1914

The following notes are essay and models. They are housed in an institutional collection. The $20 and $50 notes are dated 1st January, 1914.

DESIGNS AND COLOURS

375-14-02E
- **$5 Face Design:** Woman counting bags in chest/Edward VIII as young man/Canadian crest
- **Colour:** Black with ochre tint
- **Back Design:** Unknown
- **Colour:** Unknown

375-14-04E
- **$10 Face Design:** Queen Alexandra in large ornate frame/ Royal Crest
- **Colour:** Black (no tint)
- **Back Design:** Unknown
- **Colour:** Unknown

375-14-06E
- **$20 Face Design:** George V as Duke of York/beaver in ornate 20, forest, factory/crest
- **Colour:** Blue with brown and ochre tint 
- **Back Design:** 20/Bank name, ornate 20 over farm scene/20
- **Colour:** Olive Green

375-14-08E
- **$50 Face Design:** Seated Britannia figure, standing "Commerce" figure at dockside/ three warships/—
- **Colour:** Brown with blue and orange tint

Note: $20 and $50 notes are dated 1st January, 1914.

Cat.No.	Denom	Date	Unc
14-02E	$5	none	in institutional collection SPECIMEN
14-04E	$10	none	in institutional collection PROOF
14-06E	$20	1914	in institutional collection SPECIMEN
14-08E	$50	1914	in institutional collection MODEL

189

THE IMPERIAL BANK OF CANADA

375-16. OLD BABN PRINTINGS
RESUMED 1915 - 1920

DESIGNS AND COLOURS

375-16-04
- **$5 Face Design:** Hon. W.M. Merritt/Royal Crest with ornate 5/ H.S. Howland
- **1915 Colour:** Black with yellow, green and orange tint
- **1916-20 Colour:** Black with green tint
- **Back Design:** Lathework, counters and bank name
- **Colour:** Green

375-16-10
- **$10 Face Design:** Hon. W.H. Merritt/Bank/Arms/H.S. Howland
- **Colour:** Black with green tint
- **Back Design:** Lathework, counters and bank name
- **Colour:** Green

375-16-18
- **$20 Face Design:** Farmer with horse-drawn mower/—/ H.S. Howland
- **Colour:** Black with green tint
- **Back Design:** Lathework, counters and bank name
- **Colour:** Green

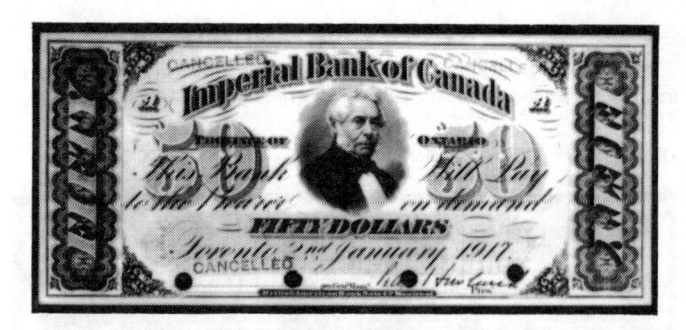

375-16-22
- **$50 Face Design:** —/Hon. W.H. Merritt/—
- **Colour:** Black with green tint
- **Back Design:** Lathework, counters and bank name
- **Colour:** Green

375-16-26
- **$100 Face Design:** —/Canadian Crest/—
- **Colour:** Black with green tint
- **Back Design:** Lathework, counters and bank name
- **Colour:** Green

IMPRINT
British American Bank Note Co. Montreal
British American Bank Note Co. Ottawa

SIGNATURES

left	right
mss. various	engr. Peleg Howland
Typed A.E. Phipps	engr. Peleg Howland

ISSUE DATING
Engraved
1st Oct. 1915
October 1st 1915
Oct 1st 1915
3rd Jan. 1916
2nd January 1917
2nd Jany 1917
2nd Jan. 1920

Note: Beware of counterfeits of 16-24.

Cat.No.	Denom.	Date	Variety	VG	F	VF	EF	Unc
16-02	$5	1915		400.	550.	825.	1,500.	-
16-04	$5	1916		125.	175.	250.	425.	-
16-06	$5	1920		125.	175.	250.	425.	-
16-10	$10	1915		125.	175.	250.	425.	-
16-12	$10	1920	mss.l.	90.	125.	175.	325.	-
16-14	$10	1920	Phipps,l.	90.	125.	175.	325.	-
16-16	$20	1915		225.	325.	500.	850.	-
16-18	$20	1920		225.	325.	500.	850.	-
16-22	$50	1917		1,000.	1,700.	-	-	-
16-24	$100	1917		1,000.	1,700.	-	-	-
16-26	$100	1920		1,000.	1,700.	-	-	-

THE IMPERIAL BANK OF CANADA

375-18.   **ISSUE OF 1923**

DESIGNS AND COLOURS

375-18-02
    $5 Face Design: Peleg Howland/—/A.E. Phipps
         Colour: Black with green tint

    Back Design: Lathework, counters, bank name and lion over crown
         Colour: Green

375-18-06
    $10 Face Design: Peleg Howland/—/A.E. Phipps
         Colour: Black with blue tint

    Back Design: Lathework, counters, bank name and lion over crown
         Colour: Blue

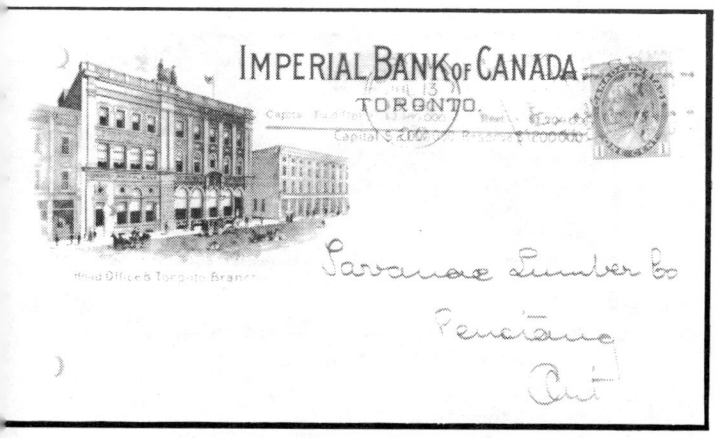

375-18-10
    $20 Face Design: —/Peleg Howland/—
         Colour: Black with brown tint

    Back Design: Lathework, counters, bank name and lion over crown
         Colour: Brown

375-18-14
    $50 Face Design: —/—/Peleg Howland
         Colour: Black with orange tint

    Back Design: Lathework, counters, bank name and lion over crown
         Colour: Orange

375-18-18S
    $100 Face Design: Peleg Howland/—/—
         Colour: Black with olive tint

    Back Design: Lathework, counters, bank name and lion over crown
         Colour: Olive

THE IMPERIAL BANK OF CANADA

IMPRINT
Canadian Bank Note Company Limited

SIGNATURES
left	right
engr. Peleg Howland	typed A.E. Phipps
typed F.A. Rolph	typed A.E. Phipps

ISSUE DATING
Engraved
Nov. 1st 1923

Cat.No.	Denom.	Date	Variety	VG	F	VF	EF	Unc
18-02	$5	1923	Howland,l.	70.	90.	140.	210.	400.
18-04	$5	1923	Rolph,l.	70.	90.	140.	210.	400.
18-06	$10	1923	Howland,l.	70.	90.	140.	210.	400.
18-08	$10	1923	Rolph,l.	70.	90.	140.	210.	400.
18-10	$20	1923	Howland,l.	80.	100.	160.	240.	500.
18-12	$20	1923	Rolph,l.	80.	100.	160.	240.	500.
18-14	$50	1923	Howland,l.	275.	325.	500.	-	-
18-16	$50	1923	Rolph,l.	275.	325.	500.	-	-
18-18S	$100	1923	Howland,l.			SPECIMEN		1,000.

375-20. ISSUE OF 1933
DESIGNS AND COLOURS

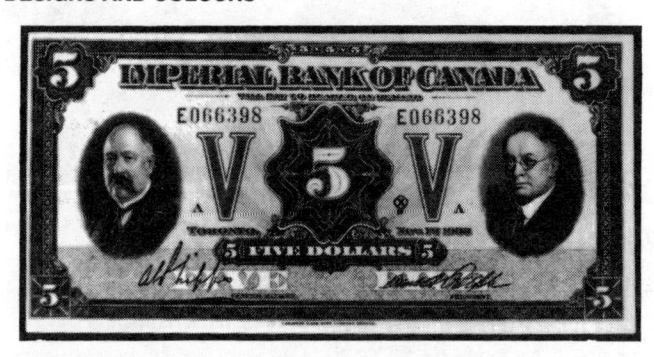

375-20-02
$5 **Face Design:** A.E. Phipps/—/F.A. Rolph
Colour: Black with green tint

Back Design: —/lion over crown/—
Colour: Green

375-20-04
$10 **Face Design:** A.E. Phipps/—/F.A. Rolph
Colour: Black with blue tint

Back Design: —/lion over crown/
Colour: Blue

375-20-06S
$20 **Face Design:** F.A. Rolph
Colour: Black with brown tint

Back Design: —/lion over crown/—
Colour: Brown

IMPRINT
Canadian Bank Note Company, Limited

SIGNATURES
left	right
engr. A.E. Phipps	typed F.A. Rolph

ISSUE DATING
Engraved
Nov. 1st 1933

Cat.No.	Denom.	Date	VG	F	VF	EF	Unc
20-02	$5	1933	60.	80.	120.	225.	450.
20-04	$10	1933	110.	150.	200.	400.	800.
20-06S	$20	1933			SPECIMEN		500.

375-22. ISSUE OF 1934
SMALL SIZE NOTES

DESIGNS AND COLOURS

375-22-04
$5 **Face Design:** A.E. Phipps/—/Frank A. Rolph
Colour: Black with green tint

Back Design: —/lion over crown/—
Colour: Green

375-22-08
$10 **Face Design:** A.E. Phipps/—/Frank A. Rolph
Colour: Black with blue tint

Back Design: —/lion over crown/—
Colour: Blue

IMPRINT
Canadian Bank Note Company, Limited

SIGNATURES
left	right
signed A.E. Phipps	signed F.A. Rolph
signed H.T. Jaffray	signed F.A. Rolph

ISSUE DATING
Engraved
1st Nov. 1934

Cat.No.	Denom.	Date	Variety	VG	F	VF	EF	Unc
22-02	$5	1934	Phipps,l.	22.	30.	45.	80.	150.
22-04	$5	1934	Jaffray,l.	22.	30.	45.	80.	150.
22-06	$10	1934	Phipps,l.	30.	40.	55.	100.	200.
22-08	$10	1934	Jaffray,l.	35.	45.	70.	125.	250.

375-24.   ISSUE OF 1939
DESIGNS AND COLOURS

375-24-02
$5 Face Design: H.T. Jaffray/—/A.E. Phipps
Colour: Black with green tint

Back Design: —/lion over crown/—
Colour: Green

375-24-04
$10 Face Design: H.T. Jaffray/—/A.E. Phipps
Colour: Black with blue tint

Back Design: —/lion over crown/—
Colour: Blue

IMPRINT
Canadian Bank Note Company, Limited

SIGNATURES
left	right
typed H.T. Jaffray	typed A.E. Phipps

ISSUE DATING
Engraved
3rd Jan. 1939

Cat.No.	Denom.	Date	VG	F	VF	EF	Unc
24-02	$5	1939	30.	40.	55.	100.	225.
24-04	$10	1939	35.	45.	65.	120.	250.

THE INTERNATIONAL BANK OF CANADA

1858 - 1859

TORONTO, CANADA WEST

BANK NUMBER 380   NONREDEEMABLE

Originally chartered in 1857 to provide banking services in Cayuga, Ontario, amendments to the charter in 1858 permitted the bank to open in Toronto, where it operated as a "wildcat bank" for about a year before failing in October of 1859. All of the shares were owned by a Mr. Reed when it failed. A man of disreputable character, Reed was also connected with The Bank of Clifton.

The International Bank of Canada was a small local bank and records of September of 1859 indicate notes in circulation of about $119,000. Although it failed in 1859, its charter wasn't repealed until 1863.

380-10.   ISSUE OF 1858
DESIGNS AND COLOURS

380-10-02-02
$1 Face Design: Queen Victoria (Chalon portrait)
Niagara Falls/Prince Consort
Colour: Black with no tint

Back Design: Plain

380-10-02-04
$1 Face Design: Queen Victoria (Chalon portrait)
Roebling Suspension Bridge/Prince Consort
Colour: Black with no tint

Back Design: Plain

380-10-02-06
$2 Face Design: Allegorical female/Royal Crest/—
Colour: Black with no tint

Back Design: Plain

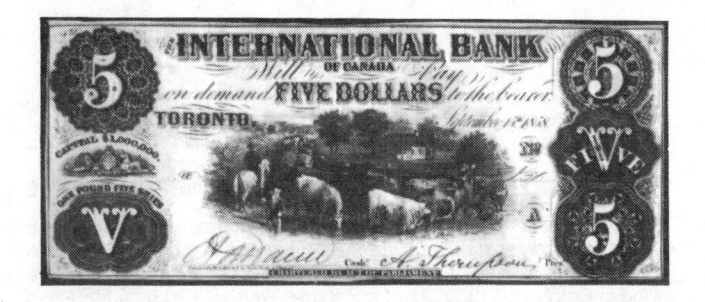

THE INTERNATIONAL BANK OF CANADA

380-10-02-08

$5 Face Design: Cattle drinking at river/—
Colour: Black with no tint

Back Design: Plain

IMPRINT
Danforth, Wright & Co., New York & Philada
ABN Co. Logo

ISSUE DATING
Engraved
September 15th, 1858

2.   TWO SIGNATURES, NO PROTECTORS

SIGNATURES
  left   right
  mss. A.W. Dunn   engr. A. Thompson

SHEET NUMBERS
  Mss. 1-2000

Cat.No.	Denom.	Date	Variety	VG	F	VF	EF	Unc
10-02-02	$1 Falls	1858		90.	125.	175.	290.	550.
10-02-02R	$1 Falls	1858	Remainder	-	-	-	-	325.
10-02-04	$1 Bridge	1858		90.	125.	175.	290.	550.
10-02-04R	$1 Bridge	1858	Remainder	-	-	-	-	325.
10-02-06	$2	1858		120.	160.	225.	375.	800.
10-02-06R	$2	1858	Remainder	-	-	-	-	375.
10-02-08	$5	1858		120.	160.	225.	375.	800.
10-02-08R	$5	1858	Remainder	-	-	-	-	375.

4.   TWO SIGNATURES, RED PROTECTORS

380-10-04-02R

380-10-04-04R

380-10-04-06R

380-10-04-08R

SIGNATURES
  left   right
  mss. A.W. Dunn   engr. A.Thompson

PROTECTOR
  $1 Falls: Red "numeral" on face and back
  $1 Bridge, $2 & $5: Red "word" on face and back

SHEET NUMBERS
  Mss. 1-2000

Note: Do not confuse with the commoner one signature notes of type 10-10.

Cat.No.	Denom.	Date	Variety	VG	F	VF	EF	Unc
10-04-02	$1 Falls	1858		100.	150.	225.	350.	700.
10-04-02R	$1 Falls	1858	Remainder	-	-	-	-	400.
10-04-04	$1 Bridge	1858		100.	150.	225.	350.	700.
10-04-04R	$1 Bridge	1858	Remainder	-	-	-	-	400.
10-04-06	$2	1858		100.	150.	225.	350.	700.
10-04-06R	$2	1858	Remainder	-	-	-	-	400.
10-04-08	$5	1858		100.	150.	225.	350.	700.
10-04-08R	$5	1858	Remainder	-	-	-	-	400.
Full sheet	$1,1,2,5	1858		-	-	-	-	1,800.

ONE SIGNATURE, VARIOUS COLOURED PROTECTORS

One signature space at right. "For the International Bank" in left signature space.

380-10-08-04
- **$1 Face Design:** Queen Victoria (Chalon portrait)/ Niagara Falls/Prince Consort
- **Colour:** Black with no tint
- **Back Design:** Plain

380-10-10-06
- **$1 Face Design:** Queen Victoria (Chalon portrait)/ Roebling Suspension Bridge/Prince Consort
- **Colour:** Black with no tint
- **Back Design:** Plain

380-10-10-12
- **$2 Face Design:** Allegorical female/Royal Crest/—
- **Colour:** Black with no tint
- **Back Design:** Plain

380-10-08-16
- **$5 Face Design:** —/cattle drinking at river/—
- **Colour:** Black with no tint
- **Back Design:** Plain 

STAMPS:
Numerous letters and numbers can be found on types 06 through 14. eg: 1,2,3,5,9,10,13,20.21.80,a,s,t,w.

6. ONE SIGNATURE, GREEN PROTECTORS

SIGNATURES

right only
mss. J.H. Markell
mss. J.R. Fitch

SHEET NUMBERS
Markell - Small blue: 1 - 1000
Fitch - Small red: 9001 - 10000, 14001 - 15000

Cat.No.	Denom.	Date	Variety	VG	F	VF	EF	Unc
10-06-02	$1 Falls	1858	Markell-blue #s	30.	40.	60.	110.	210.
10-06-04	$1 Falls	1858	Fitch-red #s	15.	20.	40.	60.	100.
10-06-06	$1 Bridge	1858	Markell-blue #s	40.	55.	75.	135.	240.
10-06-08	$1 Bridge	1858	Fitch0red #s	20.	30.	40.	70.	140.
10-06-10	$2	1858	Markell-blue #s	40.	55.	75.	125.	240.
10-06-12	$2	1858	Fitch-red #s	20.	30.	45.	70.	140.
10-06-14	$5	1858	Markell-blue #s	40.	55.	75.	125.	240.
10-06-16	$5	1858	Fitch-red #s	15.	20.	40.	40.	100.

THE INTERNATIONAL BANK OF CANADA

8. ONE SIGNATURE, BROWN PROTECTORS

SIGNATURES

right only
mss. J.H. Markell
mss. J.R. Fitch

SHEET NUMBERS
Markell - small blue: 1001-2000
Markell - small red: 7001-8000
Fitch - Small red: 7001-8000, 15001-16000

Note: There is an overlapping or duplication of Markell and Fitch red sheet numbers in 7001-8000 range

Cat.No.	Denom.	Date	Variety	VG	F	VF	EF	Unc
10-08-02	$1 Falls	1858	Markell-blue #s	30.	40.	60.	110.	210.
10-08-02a	$1 Falls	1858	Markell-red #s	30.	40.	60.	110.	210.
10-08-04	$1 Falls	1858	Fitch-red #s	15.	20.	30.	45.	100.
10-08-06	$1 Bridge	1858	Markell-blue #s	30.	40.	60.	110.	210.
10-08-06a	$1 Bridge	1858	Markell-red #s	35.	50.	70.	120.	240.
10-08-08	$1 Bridge	1858	Fitch-red #s	15.	20.	30.	45.	100.
10-08-10	$2	1858	Markell-blue #s	30.	40.	60.	110.	210.
10-08-10a	$2	1858	Markell-red #s	35.	50.	70.	120.	240.
10-08-12	$2	1858	Fitch-red #s	15.	20.	30.	45.	100.
10-08-14	$5	1858	Markell-blue #s	25.	35.	50.	80.	170.
10-08-14a	$5	1858	Markell-red #s	35.	50.	70.	120.	240.
10-08-16	$5	1858	Fitch-red #s	15.	20.	30.	45.	100.

10. ONE SIGNATURE, RED PROTECTORS

SIGNATURES

right only
mss. J.H. Markell
mss. J.R. Fitch

SHEET NUMBERS
Markell small blue 2001-3000
Markell small blue 5001-6000
Fitch small blue 5001-6000, 11001-14000
Fitch large blue 16001-18000

Note: There is an overlapping or duplication of Markell and Fitch blue sheet numbers in the 5001-6000 range.

Cat.No.	Denom.	Date	Variety	VG	F	VF	EF	Unc
10-10-02	$1 Falls	1858	Markell-sm.blue	25.	35.	50.	80.	160.
10-10-04	$1 Falls	1858	Fitch-sm.blue	30.	40.	60.	110.	210.
10-10-04a	$1 Falls	1858	Fitch-lg.blue	15.	20.	30.	50.	100.
10-10-06	$1 Bridge	1858	Markell-sm.blue	30.	40.	60.	110.	210.
10-10-08	$1 Bridge	1858	Fitch-sm.blue	35.	55.	75.	120.	240.
10-10-08a	$1 Bridge	1858	Fitch-lg.blue	15.	20.	30.	45.	100.
10-10-10	$2	1858	Markell-sm.blue	35.	50.	75.	120.	240.
10-10-12	$2	1858	Fitch-sm.blue	30.	40.	60.	110.	210.
10-10-12a	$2	1858	Fitch-lg.blue	15.	20.	30.	45.	100.
10-10-14	$5	1858	Markell-sm.blue	25.	35.	50.	80.	160.
10-10-16	$5	1858	Fitch-sm.blue	15.	20.	30.	45.	100.
10-10-16a	$5	1858	Fitch-lg.blue	15.	20.	30.	45.	100.

12. ONE SIGNATURE, OCHRE PROTECTORS

SIGNATURES

right only
mss. J.H. Markell
mss. J.R. Fitch

SHEET NUMBERS
Markell small red 3001-4000
Fitch small red 6001-7000
Fitch small blue 10001-11000
Fitch large blue 18001-

Cat.No.	Denom.	Date	Variety	VG	F	VF	EF	Unc
10-12-02	$1 Falls	1858	Markell-sm.red	35.	50.	70.	120.	240.
10-12-04	$1 Falls	1858	Fitch-sm.red	35.	50.	70.	120.	240.
10-12-04a	$1 Falls	1858	Fitch-sm.blue	30.	45.	60.	110.	210.
10-12-04b	$1 Falls	1858	Fitch-lg.blue	35.	50.	70.	120.	240.
10-12-06	$1 Bridge	1858	Markell-sm.red	35.	50.	70.	120.	240.
10-12-08	$1 Bridge	1858	Fitch-sm.red	35.	50.	70.	120.	240.
10-12-08a	$1 Bridge	1858	Fitch-sm.blue	25.	35.	55.	90.	160.
10-12-08b	$1 Bridge	1858	Fitch-lg.blue	35.	50.	70.	120.	240.
10-12-10	$2	1858	Markell-sm.red	35.	50.	70.	120.	240.
10-12-12	$2	1858	Fitch-sm.red	35.	50.	70.	120.	240.
10-12-12a	$2	1858	Fitch-sm.blue	25.	35.	55.	90.	160.
10-12-12b	$2	1858	Fitch-lg.blue	35.	50.	70.	120.	240.
10-12-14	$5	1858	Markell-sm.red	30.	40.	60.	110.	220.
10-12-16	$5	1858	Fitch-sm.red	35.	50.	70.	120.	240.
10-12-16a	$5	1858	Fitch-sm.blue	20.	25.	45.	70.	130.
10-12-16b	$5	1858	Fitch-lg.blue	35.	50.	70.	120.	240.

14. ONE SIGNATURE, BLUE PROTECTORS

SIGNATURES

right only
mss. J.H. Markell
mss. J.R. Fitch

SHEET NUMBERS
Markell small red 4001-5000
Fitch small red 4001-5000, 8001-9000

STAMPS:
Numerous letters and numbers can be found on types 06 through 14. eg: 1,2,3,5,9,10,13,20,21,80,a,s,t,w.

Note: There is an overlapping or duplication of Markell and Fitch blue sheet numbers in the 4001-5000 range.

Cat.No.	Denom.	Date	Variety	VG	F	VF	EF	Unc
10-14-02	$1 Falls	1858	Markell-sm.red	35.	50.	70.	120.	240.
10-14-04	$1 Falls	1858	Fitch-sm.red	20.	35.	50.	90.	160.
10-14-06	$1 Bridge	1858	Markell-sm.red	35.	50.	70.	120.	240.
10-14-08	$1 Bridge	1858	Fitch-sm.red	20.	35.	50.	90.	160.
10-14-10	$2	1858	Markell-sm.red	35.	50.	70.	120.	240.
10-14-12	$2	1858	Fitch-sm.red	25.	35.	50.	90.	160.
10-14-14	$5	1858	Markell-sm.red	35.	50.	70.	120.	240.
10-14-16	$5	1858	Fitch-sm.red	20.	35.	50.	90.	160.

380-12. ISSUE OF 1859

DESIGNS AND COLOURS
The backs of this issue are green letterpress printed on thin paper.

380-12-02
    $10 Face Design: Crests, book, crown/town and dock ship/ Queen Victoria (after Winterhalter portrait)
    Colour: Black with no tint

    Back Design: Lathework and counters
    Colour: Green

380-12-04
    $20 Face Design: Beavers/paddlewheel steam-ship/ Albert Edward (Prince of Wales) as a five year old child in a sailor suit
    Colour: Black with no tint

    Back Design: Lathework and counters
    Colour: Green

380-12-06
    $50 Face Design: Woman looking out to sea/ buffalo hunting/ seated Britannia with Arms of Upper Canada
    Colour: Black with no tint

    Back Design: Lathework and counters
    Colour: Green

IMPRINT
American Bank Note Company

SIGNATURES
left	right
none	mss. J.R. Fitch

ISSUE DATING
    Engraved
    June 1st 1859

PROTECTOR
Green "word and numeral" on back only

SHEET NUMBERS
All have blue sheet numbers under 1000.
$10 notes have plate letters A & B,
$20 & $50 have plate letters A.

Cat.No.	Denom.	Date	VG	F	VF	EF	Unc
12-02	$10	1859	85.	110.	155.	260.	525.
12-04	$20	1859	800.	1,125.	1,675.	2,850.	-
12-02	$50	1859	85.	110.	155.	260.	525.

BANQUE INTERNATIONALE DU CANADA

1911 - 1913

MONTREAL, (QUEBEC) DOMINION OF CANADA

BANK NUMBER 385 **REDEEMABLE**

Established in 1911 in Montreal, the Banque Internationale du Canada was absorbed by The Home Bank of Canada on April 15, 1913. Although short-lived, it had a successful existance which enabled The Home Bank of Canada to expand in Montreal, the then financial centre of Canada.

385-10 ISSUE OF 191

DESIGNS AND COLOURS

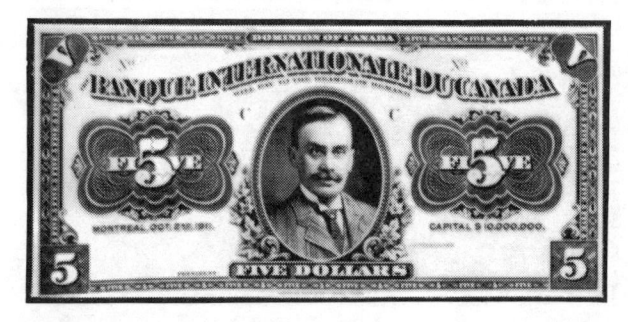

385-10-02P
- **$5 Face Design:** —/R. Forget/—
  Colour: Black with greeen and yellow tint
- **Back Design:** —/globe/—
  Colour: Green

385-10-04
- **$10 Face Design:** R. Forget/—/R. Bickerdike
  Colour: Black with orange and yellow tint
- **Back Design:** —/globe/—
  Colour: Brown

385-10-06P
- **Face Design:** R. Forget/—/R. Bickerdike
  Color: Black with olive green and yellow tint

Back Design: lathework and counters, Bank name surrounding globe
Colour: Peru brown

IMPRINT
  American Bank Note Company, Ottawa
  American Bank Note Co. Ottawa

SIGNATURES
left	right
typed R. Forget	mss. various

ISSUE DATING
  Engraved
  $5: Oct. 2nd, 1911
  $10 & $20: Oct. 17th, 1911

OVERPRINT
  "M M" in red
  "QUEBEC" twice in blue

Cat. No.	Denom.	Date	VG	F	VF	EF	AU	Unc
10-02	$5	1911	4,200.	-	-	-	-	-
10-04	$10	1911	4,200.	-	-	-	-	-
10-06P	$20	1911					PROOF	1,000.

LA BANQUE JACQUES CARTIER
1861 - 1900

MONTREAL, PROVINCE OF CANADA

BANK NUMBER 390 **REDEEMABLE**

Established in 1861 in Montreal, this bank failed in 1899 with heavy losses, but reorganized in 1900 to become La Banque Provinciale du Canada.

390-10 **ISSUE OF 1862**

DESIGN AND COLOURS

390-10-02
- **$1 Face Design:** Queen Victoria (Winterhalter portrait)/ J. Cartier/R. Trudeau
- **Colour:** Black with green tint

- **Back Design:** Lathework and counters
- **Colour:** Green

390-10-04
- **$2 Face Design:** Princess Eugenie/J. Cartier/Prince of Wales
- **Colour:** Black with green tint

- **Back Design:** Lathework and counters
- **Colours:** Green

Photo Not Available

390-10-06
- **$5 Face Design:** Unknown
- **Colour:** Black with green tint

- **Back Design:** Lathework and counters
- **Colour:** Green

Photo Not Available

390-10-08
- **$10 Face Design:** Unknown
- **Colour:** Black with green tint

- **Back Design:** Lathework and counters
- **Colour:** Green

IMPRINT
American Bank Note Co. New York

SIGNATURES
left	right
mss. H Cotte	mss. J.L. Beaudry

ISSUE DATING
Engraved
2 Janvier 1862

Cat. No.	Denom.	Date	VG	F	VF	EF	Unc
10-02	$1	1862	3,000.	4,000.	-	-	-
10-04	$2	1892	3,000.	4,000.	-	-	-
10-06	$5	1862	SURVIVING NOTES NOT CONFIRMED				
10-08	$10	1862	SURVIVING NOTES NOT CONFIRMED				

390-12. **ISSUES OF 1870 AND 1880**

DESIGNS AND COLOURS

390-12-02
- **$4 Face Design:** Ships and seated female "Exports"/ J.Cartier/beaver
- **Colour:** Black with green tint
- **Variety:** Plain black 4's at top

- **Back Design:** Queen Victoria/Bank name over quatre/ Prince Albert
- **Colour:** Green

199

LA BANQUE JACQUES CARTIER

390-12-04
- **$4 Face Design:** Ships and seated female "Exports"/ J. Cartier/beaver
- **Variety:** Four's in green lathework at top
- **Colour:** Black with green tint

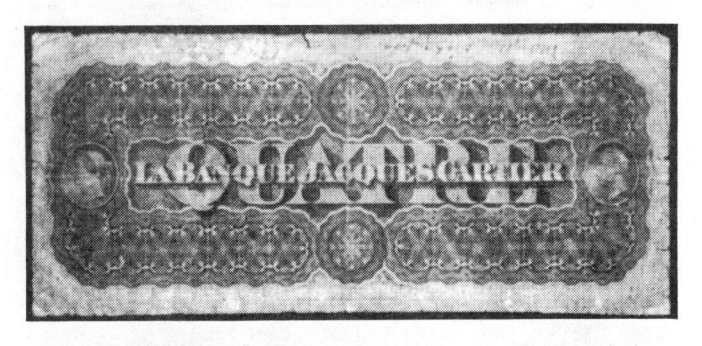

- **Back Design:** Queen Victoria/Bank name over quatre/ Prince Albert
- **Colour:** Green

390-12-08
- **$5 Face Design:** R. Trudeau/J. Cartier/A. Desjardins
- **Colour:** Black with green tint

- **Back Design:** Lathework, counters and bank name
- **Colour:** Green

390-12-10P
- **$20 Face Design:** Dog's head (after landseer)/J. Cartier/ blacksmith and horses
- **Colour:** Black with green tint

- **Back Design:** Lathework, counters and bank name
- **Colour:** Green

390-12-14P
- **$50 Face Design:** Female with parchment/ J.Cartier/ female reaping grain
- **Colour:** Black with green tint

- **Back Design:** Lathework, counters and bank name
- **Colour:** Green

390-12-18P
- **$100 Face Design:** Queen Victoria in "widow's weeds"/ J. Cartier/anchor barrel and bales
- **Colour:** Black with green tint

Back Design: Lathework, counters and bank name
Colour: Green

IMPRINT
British American Bank Note Co. Montreal and Ottawa

SIGNATURES
	left	right
1870:	mss. A. Manseau	engr. R. Turdeau
	mss. A. Manseau	mss. R. Trudeau
1880:	mss. A. Manseau	engr. A. Desjardins

ISSUE DATING
Engraved
2 Mai 1870
2 Mai 1871
1st June 1880

OVERPRINT
$5 1880: "VICTORIAVILLE" twice in blue

VARIETIES
$4: Plain black 4's at top
$4: FOUR's in green lathework over black 4's at top

Cat. No.	Denom.	Date	Variety	VG	F	VF	EF	Unc
12-02	$4	1870	Plain 4's	4,000.	-	-	-	-
12-04	$4	1870	Green FOUR's	4,000.	-	-	-	-
12-06	$5	1870		4,000.	-	-	-	-
12-08	$5	1880		4,000				
12-10P	$20	1870				FACE PROOF		500.
12-12P	$20	1871				FACE PROOF		500.
12-14P	$50	1870				FACE PROOF		500.
12-18P	$100	1870				FACE PROOF		500.

390-14 ISSUES OF 1886 AND 1889

DESIGNS AND COLOURS

390-14-02P
$5 Face Design: J. Cartier/farm family and animals by trough "The Old Well"/bank building

Back Design: Lathework, counters and bank name

390-14-08P
$10 Face Design: J. Cartier/Indians on bluff "Past and Present"/bank building

Back Design: Lathework, counters and bank name

390-14-10P
1886: Face Colour: Black with green tint or black with orange and blue tint
Back Colour: Green, brown or blue
1889: Face Colour: Black with blue-green and ochre tint
Back Colour: Blue-green and ochre

LA BANQUE JACQUES CARTIER

IMPRINT
Canada Bank Note Co. Montreal

SIGNATURES
left	right
none	engr. Alph. Desjardins

ISSUE DATING
Engraved
1st June 1886
1er Juin 1889

OVERPRINT
St. Simon in blue"

Cat. No.	Denom.	Date	Variety	VG	F	VF	EF	Unc
14-02P	$5	1886				FACE PROOF		500.
14-04P	$5	1889				FACE PROOF		600.
14-06	$10	1886	Orange tint	4,000.	-	-	-	-
14-08P	$10	1886	Green tint			FACE PROOF		500.
14-10P	$10	1886	Orange tint			FACE PROOF		600.
14-12P	$10	1889				FACE PROOF		600.

390-16. ISSUE OF 1895
DESIGNS AND COLOURS

390-16-02P
$5 Face Design: A.L. De Martigny/ornate V and J. Cartier superimposed over view of Montreal from mountain/A. Desjardins
Colour: Black with green tint

Back Design: Lathework, counters and Indians on bluff
Colour: Green

390-16-04P
$10 Face Design: A.L. De Martigny/ornate X superimposed over J. Cartier aboard ship/A. Desjardins
Colour: Black with green tint

Back Design: Lathework, counters and Indians on bluff
Colour: Green

IMPRINT
British American Bank Note Co. Ottawa

SIGNATURES
left	right
none	engr. Alph. Desjardins

ISSUE DATING
Engraved
2 Jan. 1895

Cat. No.	Denom.	Date		Unc
16-02P	$5	1895	FACE PROOF	500.
16-04P	$10	1895	FACE PROOF	500.

THE KINGSTON BANK
1837
KINGSTON, LOWER CANADA

BANK NUMBER 395　　　　　　　　　　**NONREDEEMABLE**

Possibly a phantom bank trading on the colloquial name of The Commercial Bank of the Midland District. With the addition of "New York Safety Fund" these notes were also used as supposed notes of the Kingston Bank in New York.

395-10　　　　**ISSUE OF 1837**

These notes occur unsigned or with blue signatures. Rawdon, Wright, Hatch, New York imprint is obviously forged. The printing and engraving is inferior, thus clearly spurious.

DESIGNS AND COLOURS

395-10-02
- **$5 Face Design:** Seated allegorical female/cattle, plough and train; cask, bale, cornucopia and ship below/-
- **Colour:** Black with no tint
- **Back Design:** Plain

IMPRINT
Rawdon, Wright, Hatch, New York (obviously spurious)

SIGNATURES

left	right
mss. W.W. Roy	mss. H.L. Moor
none	none
mss. J. Smith	mss. C. Louusbery

ISSUE DATING
Partialy Engraved_18_:
- **1837:** date incomplete
- **1841:** Oct. 12
- **1843:** Aug. 3

Note: 02R, 08R and 12R are unsigned or signed in blue ink, incomplete date and unnumbered.

Cat. No.	Denom.	Date	Variety	VG	F	VF	EF	Unc
10-02	$5	1837	Fully signed	140.	200.	325.	-	-
10-02R	$5	1837	Remainder	125	175	275	-	-
10-08R	$5	1841	Remainder	125.	175.	275	-	-
10-12R	$5	1843	Remainder	125.	175	275	-	-

THE BANK OF LIVERPOOL
1871-1879
LIVERPOOL, NOVA SCOTIA

BANK NUMBER 400　　　　　　　　　　**NONREDEEMABLE**

Established in Liverpool, Nova Scotia in 1871, The Bank of Liverpool first failed in April of 1873 but was revived in 1878 with an increase in capital. It managed to survive until the autumn of 1879. Its note issue was small and appears to have been redeemed by The Bank of Nova Scotia, its principal creditor. The Bank of Nova Scotia bought the banks assets and paid off its note issue, which amounted to $4000.

400-10.　　　　**ISSUE OF 1871**
DESIGNS AND COLOURS

400-10-02
- **$4 Face Design:** Boy climbing rigging "Going aloft"/ shipbuilders at work/pilot at wheel "Lachine Pilot"
- **Colour:** Black with green tint

Back Design: Lathework, counters and bank name
Colour: Green

400-10-04
- **$5 Face Design:** Lumberjack felling tree/-/loggers at work
- **Colour:** Black with green tint

THE BANK OF LIVERPOOL

Back Design: Lathework, counters and bank name
Colour: Green

400-10-06
$10 Face Design: "Agriculture" figure/fishermen and sailing ships "On the Banks"/sailor aboard ship "Charlies Sailor"
Colour: Black with green tint

Back Design: Lathework, counters and bank name
Colour: Green

400-10-08
$20 Face Design: Bull's head/sailors on shore by mast/ three horses' head
Colour: Black with green tint

Back Design: Lathework, counters and bank name
Colour: Green

IMPRINT
British American Bank Note Co., Montreal & Ottawa

SIGNATURES

left	right
mss. Robie S. Stern	mss. Sylvanus Morton
mss. John A. Leslie, Mgr.	mss. J.F. Forbes
mss. John A. Leslie, Mgr.	mss. Thomas Rees (Vice)
mss. Robie S Stern	mss. Thomas Rees (Vice)

ISSUE DATING
Engraved
1st November 1871
1st Nov. 1871

Cat. No.	Denom	Date	VG	F	VF	EF	Unc
10-02	$4	1871	1,200.	1,600.	-	-	-
10-04	$5	1871	1,100.	1,500.	-	-	-
10-06	$10	1871	1,600.	2,100.	-	-	-
10-08	$20	1871	1,900.	2,500.	-	-	-

THE BANK OF LONDON IN CANADA

1883-1888

LONDON, DOMINION OF CANADA (ONTARIO)

BANK NUMBER 405   **NONREDEEMABLE**

On February 21, 1883 a petition of "William Woodruff, MD. and others" received its third reading in the House of Commons for an act of incorporation in the name of The Bank of London in Canada. The bill was passed by the Commons on April 2, 1883 and received Royal assent on May 25th, 1883. The capital stock was to be $1 million divided into 10,000 shares of $100.00 each. However, the paid-up capital of the bank amounted to $140,000, with a reserve fund of $50,000 of its $1 million subscribed capital.

The bank opened its main office in 1884 with Henry Taylor as president. In 1887, the financial position of the bank appeared so sound that The Bank of Toronto, looking towards expansion, entered into negotiations with The Bank of London in Canada to take over its holdings in southwestern Ontario. Te deal was practically complete when The Bank of London closed down its operations on August 19, 1887 leaving a note on the door saying "The Bank of London has suspended payment." Two days earlier, Mr. Taylor left the country for the U.S., and it was reported that he had withdrawn $20,000. to take with him. Under these circumstances, The Bank of Toronto refused to proceed with negotiations

The financial statements for June and July of 1887 were quite favourable and with the election of a new president, Thomas Kent, The Bank of Toronto offered to assume the business of The Bank of London at par. In October of 1887, the directors of the bank decided to commence the payment of depositors and other creditors. The payment of London depositors was to be made by The Bank of London. The ingersoll, Watford and Brantford depositors were to be paid by The Traders Bank of Canada. Payment of others was carried out by The Bank of Toronto.

The Bank of Toronto opened its doors in London on November 9, 1887 on the same premises as The Bank of London in Canada. The shareholders voted to wind up its affairs of The Bank of London; assent was finally given to the Act on May 22, 1888 and the bank officially wound up.

405-10   **ISSUE OF 1883**

DESIGNS AND COLOURS

405-10-02
    $5 Face Design: "Implements of Agriculture"/ Henry Taylor/ dog on strongbox (after Landseer)
    Colour: Black with green tint

    Back Design: Lathework, counters, bank name and the City of London Crest
    Colour: Green

405-10-04
    $10 Face Design: Henry Taylor/—/allegorical female with flowers
    Colour: Black with green tint

    Back Design: Lathework, counters, bank name and the City of London Crest
    Colour: Green

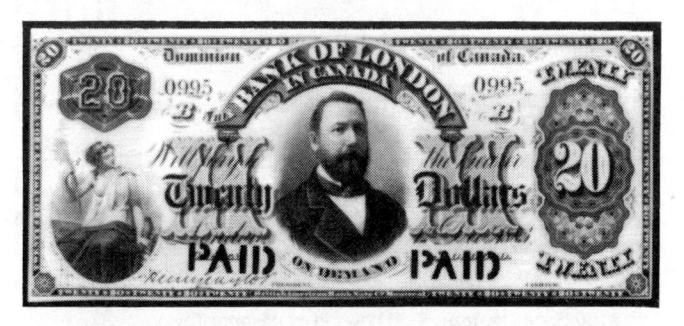

405-10-06R
    $20 Face Design: Allergorical female with "stalks of wheat"/Henry Taylor/—
    Colour: Black with green tint

THE BANK OF LONDON IN CANADA

Back Design: Lathework, counters and bank name
Colour: Green

405-10-08R
$50 Face Design: Horses and pigeons at stable door (after J.F. Herring)/Henry Taylor/ seated allegorical female
Colour: Black with green tint

Back Design: Lathework, counters and bank name
Colour: Green

405-10-10R
$100 Face Design: Two cows in oval/Henry Taylor/ female operating telegragh in oval
Colour: Black with green tint

Back Design: Lathework, counters and bank name
Colour: Green

IMPRINT
British American Bank Note Co., Montreal

SIGNATURES

left	right
engr. Henry Taylor	none
engr. Henry Taylor	mss. A.M. Smart

ISSUE DATING
Engraved
1st Decr. 1883

Cat No.	Demon	Date	Variety	VG	F	VF	EF	Unc
10-02	$5	1883	Issued	3,000.	4,000.	-	-	-
10-02R	$5	1883	Remainder*	-	-	-	3,500.	-
10-04	$10	1883	Issued	4,000.	5,000.	-	-	-
10-04R	$10	1883	Remainder*	-	-	-	3,500.	-
10-06R	$20	1883	Remainder*	-	-	-	3,500.	-
10-08R	$50	1883	Remainder*	-	-	-	3,500.	-
10-10R	$100	1883	Remainder*	-	-	-	3,500.	-

* unsigned at right.

THE BANK OF LOWER CANADA

1830s

QUEBEC, LOWER CANADA

BANK NUMBER 410   NONREDEEMABLE

410-10.   HARRIS & SEALEY PRINTINGS
DESIGNS AND COLOURS

410-10-04
- **$2 Face Design:** Beehive and farm implements/ royal crest, Indian in canoe below/Britannia
  See varieties
- **Colour:** Black with no tint
- **Back Design:** Plain

410-10-06
- **$2 Face Design:** Beehive and farm implements/ Royal Crest, Indian in canoe below/Britannia
- **Colour:** Black with no tint
- **Back Design:** Plain

410-10-08
- **$3 Face Design:** Royal crest/allegorical figures, Indian in canoe below/Britannia
- **Colour:** Black with no tint
- **Back Design:** Plain

410-10-10
- **$5 Face Design:** Standing Indian with rifle/two trains at dock, Royal Crest below/Britannia
- **Colour:** Black with no tint
- **Back Design:** Plain

410-10-12
- **$10 Face Design:** —/Sailboat and "Commerce" figure, small Royal Crest below/Britannia
- **Colour:** Black with no tint
- **Back Design:** Plain

IMPRINT
Harris & Sealey Engravers N. York
Harris & Sealey Engravers N.Y.

SIGNATURES
Various

ISSUE DATING
Partially engraved _____ 18 _____:
Mss. Various dates have been seen between 1839 and 1851
1840: April 4, May 4

VARIETIES
$1 Face Design: Engraved "A Messrs. D. Birdsey & Cie" at lower left
$1 Face Design: "D. Birdsey" omitted

Note: Notes of this bank were altered and issued in various U.S. states. See Haxby CT99-A55.

Cat. No.	Denom.	Date	Variety	VG	F	VF	EF	Unc
10-02P	$1	18_	Engr. Birdsey			PROOF		400.
10-04	$1	18_	Birdsey omitted	200.	300.	425.	500.	600.
10-06	$2	18_		200.	300.	425.	-	-
10-08	$3	18_		250.	350.	-	-	-
10-10	$5	1840's		250.	350.	425.	550.	800.
10-12	$10	1840's		300.	425.	525.	700.	950.

LOWER CANADA BANK

1837

MONTREAL, LOWER CANADA

BANK NUMBER 415   **NONREDEEMABLE**

Apparently this was a "phantom bank." Its function was presumably intended to take advantage of American citizens.

415-10   DRAFT ISSUE OF 1837

Engraved: "To Messrs. D. McDonald & Co. Montreal"

DESIGNS AND COLOURS

415-10-02
- **$1 Face Design:** Ornate design with 1 and sea creatures/ Hercules wrestling lion; clasped hands below/ woman carrying sheaves
- **Colour:** Black with no tint
- **Back Design:** Plain

415-10-04
- **$2 Face Design:** Ornate design with 2 and sea creatures/ men fighting dragons; clasped hand below/ "Commerce" figures
- **Colour:** Black with no tint
- **Back Design:** Plain

415-10-06P
- **$3 Face Design:** Ornate design with 3 and sea creatures/ seated Greek philosopher "Homer"; clasped hands below/cherub with fruit basket in oval
- **Colour:** Black with no tint
- **Back Design:** Plain

IMPRINT
Rawdon, Wright & Hatch New-York

SIGNATURES

left	right
none	mss. G.D. White

ISSUE DATING
     Partially Engraved __18__:
     1837: Nov. 4

Cat.No.	Denom	Date	VG	F	VF	EF	Unc
10-02	$1	18__	500.	700.	-	-	-
10-04	$2	1837	500.	700.	-	-	-
10-06P	$3	18				PROOF	400.

MACDONALD & CO.

1859-1866

VICTORIA, VANCOUVER ISLAND

BANK NUMBER 420 **NONREDEEMABLE**

A private bank founded in 1859 in Victoria, British Columbia, Macdonald & Co. was the first bank west of the Great Lakes. It enjoyed prosperity in its initial years of operation, but with small resources it was increasingly difficult to compete with larger banks. After a serious robbery at its Victoria office, the bank closed its doors in 1864, with substantial losses to note holders and depositors.

ISSUE OF 1863

420-10 INDIAN AT RIGHT, ARM UPRAISED, INDIAN MAIDEN LOOKING LEFT

DESIGN AND COLOURS

420-10-02
- **$1 Face Design:** Indian maiden/Royal Arms/bust of Indian
  See subheadings
- **Colour:** Black with no tint
- **Back Design:** Plain

420-10-04
- **$5 Face Design:** Indian maiden/Royal Arms/bust of Indian
- **Colour:** Black with no tint
- **Back Design:** Plain

420-10-06
- **$10 Face Design:** Indian maiden/Royal Arms/bust of Indian
  See subheadings
- **Colour:** Black with no tint
- **Back Design:** Plain

IMPRINT
Lith. Britton & Co., S.F.; all notes printed by lithography

SIGNATURES

left	right
mss. J.S. Thompson	mss. Macdonald Cy.
mss. Wm. Cocker	mss. Macdonald Cy.
mss. Robt. T. Smith	mss. Macdonald Cy

ISSUE DATING
Manuscript:
  6 Sept. 1863

Cat. No.	Denom.	Date	VG	F	VF	EF	Unc
10-02	$1	1863	120.	180.	275.	-	-
10-04	$5	1863	200.	280.	350.	-	-
10-06	$10	1863	240.	350.	400.	-	-

420-12 INDIAN AT RIGHT, ARM DOWN, INDIAN MAIDEN LOOKING RIGHT

DESIGNS AND COLOURS

420-12-02
- **$1 Face Design:** Indian maiden looking left/Royal Arms/bust of Indian with arm down
- **Colour:** Black with no tint
- **Back Design:** Plain

420-12-04

$5 Face Design: Indian maiden looking left/Royal Arms/ bust of Indian with arm down
Colour: Black with no tint
Back Design: Plain

Cat. No.	Denom.	Date	VG	F	VF	EF	Unc
12-02R	$1	1863*	375.	475.	700.	-	-
12-04	$5	1863	375.	475.	700.	-	-
12-06	$10	1863			Notes not confirmed		

*Remainders only

THE MARITIME BANK OF THE DOMINION OF CANADA

1872-1887

ST. JOHN, NEW BRUNSWICK

BANK NUMBER 425   **NONREDEEMABLE**

A bill to incorporated the bank was introduced on May 7, 1872, and on June 14 the act was given royal assent.

There are two different versions of the bank's early years and difficulties. It has been suggested that the bank was never fully capitalized, and its operations were hindered by lack of funds. By investing in various maritime-based industries, setbacks in the timber industry and the adverse economic conditions of the 1876 depression, the bank found itself in financial difficulty. In an attempt to improve its position, the bank sought to acquire additional capital by making further demands on its shareholders. At this point the Bank of Montreal acquired 15 percent of the shares of the Maritime Bank, which meant that Montreal-based banks now owned 25 percent of the shares.

On June 4, 1880, at the annual meeting, an injunction prevented the Bank of Montreal from voting, since an amendment to the Banking Act prohibited one bank from holding stock in another. At a special general meeting on August 10, 1880, it was resolved to remove the president, vice-president and directors and to set up a new board to wind up the bank's business. A policy of realizing assets was undertaken, but a major task remained in trying to untangle the true financial situation.

It has also been suggested that the course of events leading up to the situation of 1880 resulted from the policy of James Domville, an industrialist from St. John who controlled the bank. Allegedly, he used the bank to finance his own interests. When major losses were suffered in the late 1870s, a number of lockups resulted, all of which were at firms either owned by or associated with Domville's interests, and this precipitated the banking crisis.

The new board of directors marked a change in operational philosophy. The new managers followed traditional policies, but still found the burden of reorganizing the bank too great. Nonetheless, the desire to recoup losses led the stockholders to allow the bank to continue until its final, more costly demise in 1887. While the bank was in the process of regrouping, it found a new source of capital in Freeman's National Bank of Boston. In less than two years, this American bank supplied more than $270,000 on the collateral of notes deposited as security for loans granted to local businessmen. When the Maritime Bank of the Dominion of Canada finally closed its doors, note holders were obliged to redeem their notes through the Boston bank.

425-10   ISSUES OF 1873 AND 1875

DESIGNS AND COLOURS

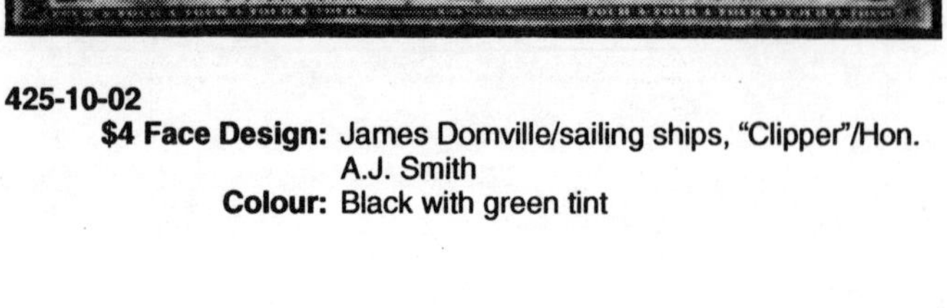

425-10-02

$4 Face Design: James Domville/sailing ships, "Clipper"/Hon. A.J. Smith
Colour: Black with green tint

Back Design: Lathework, counters, bank name, anchor, barrels and bale
Colour: Green

425-10-06P
$5 Face Design: James Domville/sailing steam ship/ Hon. A.J. Smith
Colour Black with green tint

Back Design: Lathework, counters, bank name, anchor barrels and bale

425-10-10P
$10 Face Design: Sailing ship/J. Robertson/boy climbing rigging "Going aloft"
Colour: Black with green tint

Back Design: Lathework, counters, bank name, anchor, barrels and bale

425-10-12P
$50 Face Design: Maj. Gen. J.W. Domville/Great Seal of Canada over Royal Crest/James Domville
Colour: Black with green tint

Back Design: Lathework, counters and bank name

IMPRINT
British American Bank Note Co. Montreal & Ottawa

SIGNATURES
left	right
mss. various	engr. A.J. Smith
mss. various	engr. James Domville

ISSUE DATING
Engraved
2nd. Jan. 1873
1st June 1875

Cat. No.	Denom.	Date	Variety	VG	F	VF	EF	Unc
10-02	$4	1873	Smith, r.	4,000.	-	-	-	-
10-04	$4	1873	Domville, r.	4,000.	-	-	-	-
10-06P	$5	1873	Smith, r.			FACE PROOF		800.
10-08P	$5	1873	Domville, r.			FACE PROOF		800.
10-10P	$10	1873	Smith, r.			FACE PROOF		800.
10-12P	$50	1875	Domville, r.			FACE PROOF		800.

THE MARITIME BANK OF THE DOMINION OF CANADA

425-12 **ISSUES OF 1881 AND 1882**

DESIGNS AND COLOURS

425-12-02
 $5 Face Design: Sailor/dock scene/woman with telescope and 5
  Colour: Black with green tint
 Back Design: Counters, bank name, anchor, barrels and bale

425-12-04
 $10 Face Design: Sailing ship/Queen Victoria in widow's weeds/ boy climbing rigging "Going aloft"
  Colour: Black with green tint
 Back Design: Counters, bank name, anchor, barrels and bale

425-12-06P
 $20 Face Design: Dock scene/steamship/allegorical woman with flag and bale
  Colour: Black with green tint

Back Design: Lathework, counters and bank name

IMPRINT
 British American Bank Note Co. Montreal

SIGNATURES
 left   **right**
 mss. various engr. Thos. Maclellan

ISSUE DATING
 Engraved
 Octr. 3rd 1881
 Nov. 1st 1882

OVERPRINT
 $5: "V" in red

Note: $5 and $10 come with red or blue sheet numbers.

Cat. No.	Denom.	Date	Variety	VG	F	VF	EF	Unc
12-02	$5	1881	No o/p	2,000.	-	-	-	-
12-02a	$5	1881	Red o/p	2,500.	-	-	-	-
12-04	$10	1881		3,000.	-	-	-	-
12-06P	$20	1882				FACE PROOF		800.

212

THE MECHANICS BANK

1865-1879

MONTREAL, CANADA EAST

BANK NUMBER 430   **NONREDEEMABLE**

Established in Montreal in 1865, this bank was managed by corrupt individuals and continued in its later years to be maintained by artificial and improper methods. After its failure in 1879, the shareholders were forced to contribute the whole of the double liability. Even then only 57.5 percent of its liabilities were redeemed. Its loss to creditors amounted to $180,000. The bank went to dangerous extremes to circulate as many of its notes as it could. After suspension, the notes were redeemed at only 57.5 cents on the dollar.

430-10   ISSUE OF 1872
DESIGNS AND COLOURS

430-10-04
- **$4 Face Design:** Two men shoeing horses/men working in carpenter's shop "Carpenters at Work" mechanic at lathe "The Lathe"
- **Colour:** Black with green tint

- **Back Design:** Lathework, counters and bank name
- **Colour:** Blue-green

430-10-08
- **$5 Face Design:** Farmer pumping water for livestock/—/stone cutters
- **Colour:** Black with green tint

- **Back Design:** Lathework, counters and bank name
- **Colour:** Blue-green

430-10-10
- **$10 Face Design:** Farm animals at stable door "Stable Door"/blacksmith shoeing a horse "Horse Shoeing"/arm and hammer "muscle"
- **Colour:** Black with green tint

- **Back Design:** Lathework, counters and bank name
- **Colour:** Blue-green

IMPRINT
British American Bank Note Co. Montreal & Ottawa

SIGNATURES

	left	right
$4 and $5:	mss. W. Dunn	mss. C.J. Brydges
	mss. W. Dunn	mss. W. Shanly
	mss. J.H. Menzies	engr. C.J. Brydges
$10:	mss. W. Dunn	mss. C.J. Brydges
	mss. W. Dunn	mss. Walter Shanly
	mss. J.H. Menzies	engr. C.J. Brydges

THE MECHANICS BANK

ISSUE DATING
 Engraved
  1st June, 1872

OVERPRINT
 Engraved signature notes:
  "A A" in blue
  "B B" in blue
  "L L" in blue
  "ALEXANDRIA" twice vertically in blue
  "BEAUHARNOIS" twice vertically in blue

STAMP
  "A" in circle twice in purple

Cat. No.	Denom.	Date	Variety	VG	F	VF	EF	Unc
10-02	$4	1872	Mss. signat., r.	150.	200.	275.	-	-
10-04	$4	1872	Engr. Brydges, r.	150.	200.	275.	-	-
10-06	$5	1872	Mss. signat., r.	90.	125.	200.	-	-
10-08	$5	1872	Engr. Brydges, r.	90.	125.	200.	-	-
10-10	$10	1872	Mss. signat., r.	800.	1,000.	1,500.	-	-
10-12	$10	1872	Engr. Brydges, r.	800.	1,000.	1,500.	-	-

THE MECHANICS BANK

1837

MONTREAL, LOWER CANADA

BANK NUMBER 435   **NONREDEEMABLE**

The notes of this "spurious bank" appeared briefly during the summer of 1837, centering circulation in Buffalo, but not in Montreal. The true nature of the "bank" was soon exposed by the press and the police.

435-10   **ISSUE OF 1837**

DESIGNS AND COLOURS

435-10-02
 $3 Face Design: Dock scene/blacksmith and two women (Industry, Agriculture, Commerce); arm and hammer in shield below/woman with wheat leaning on pillar
  Colour: Black with no tint
 Back Design: Plain

435-10-04
 $5 Face Design: Seated youth with mechanic's tools/seated woman resting on cogwheel; arm and hammer in shield below/blacksmith "Industry"
  Colour: Black with no tint
 Back Design: Plain

435-10-06
 $10 Face Design: Seated woman with rake, leaning on shield/ blacksmith and two allegorical women (Industry, Agriculture, Commerce); crouching lion in oval below/kneeling cherub inscribing rock
 Colour: Black with no tint
 Back Design: Plain

IMPRINT
 Rawdon, Wright & Hatch, New-York

SIGNATURES
left	right
mss. F.E. Whiting	mss. W. Morris
mss. T.T. Copley	mss. Thos. H. Sprague

ISSUE DATING
 Partially engraved ___ 18___:
 $5 and $10 1837: May 1
 $3, $5 and $10 1837: June 1

Cat. No.	Denom.	Date	VG	F	VF	EF	Unc
10-02	$3	1837	120.	160.	240.	400.	-
10-04	$5	1837	80.	120.	170.	300.	-
10-06	$10	1837	80.	120.	170.	300.	-

THE MECHANICS BANK OF ST. JOHN'S
1837
ST. JOHN'S, LOWER CANADA

BANK NUMBER 440   **NONREDEEMABLE**

The notes of this "spurious bank" appeared briefly during the summer of 1837, entering circulation in Buffalo, but not in St. John's. The true nature of the "bank" was quickly exposed by the press and the police.

440-10   **NOTE ISSUE 1837**
DESIGNS AND COLOURS

440-10-02R
 $5 Face Design: Man ploughing; steamboat with American flag below/allegorical female female and two men (Agriculture, Commerce, Industry)
 Colour: Black with no tint
 Back Design: Plain

440-10-04
 $10 Face Design: Seated woman leaning on cogwheel/train with river and town in background; arm and hammer in shield below/sailing ships (one with American flag), lighthouse
 Colour Black with no tint
 Back Design: Plain

440-10-06R
 $20 Face Design: Blacksmith at anvil/paddlewheel steamship with American flag, lighthouse; old train below/allegorical female
 Colour Black with no tint
 Back Design: Plain

THE MECHANICS BANK OF ST. JOHN'S

IMPRINT
　　Rawdon, Wright & Hatch, New-York

SIGNATURES
　　　　left　　　　　　　　　　right
　　　　mss. G. Hosmer　　　　mss. H.N. Warren

ISSUE DATING
　　Partially engraved ___ 18___:
　　1837: May 20, May 21

Note: 10-02R are remainders with spurious dates and signatures 10-06R and full sheet are remainders unsigned, undated and unnumbered.

Cat. No.	Denom.	Date	VG	F	VF	EF	Unc
10-02R	$5	18_*	250.	325.	475.	800.	-
10-04	$10	1837	275.	400.	575.	1,000.	-
10-04R	$10	18__	275.	400.	575.	1,000	-
10-06R	$20	18_**	275.	400.	575.	1,000.	-
Full Sheet	$5,5,10,20	18_**	-	-	-	-	3,000.

440-12　　　　DRAFT ISSUE, 1837

DESIGNS AND COLOURS

440-12-02-02R
　　$1 Face Design: Seated woman leaning on cogwheel/train, river and town in background; arm and hammer in shield below/seated youth with mechanic's tools
　　　　　　See subheadings
　　Colour: Black with no tint
　　Back Design: Plain

440-12-02-04
　　$2 Face Design: Woman with wheat resting on pillar/blacksmith and two women (Industry, Agriculture, Commerce); steamboat with American flag below/man with scythe in wheat field. See subheadings
　　Colour: Black with no tint
　　Back Design: Plain

440-12-04-06
　　$3 Face Design: —/steamship, one with American flag, lighthouse; old train below/blacksmith and woman (Industry and Agriculture)
　　　　　　See subheadings
　　Colour: Black with no tint
　　Back Design: Plain

IMPRINT
　　Rawdon, Wright & Hatch New-York

2.　　　　ENGRAVED

"A Messrs H.N. Warren & Cie a St. John's" AT LOWER LEFT
Mss. "H.N. Warren & Cie" endorsed vertically across centre

SIGNATURES
　　　　left　　　　　　　　　right
　　　　none　　　　　　　　mss. G. Hosmer

ISSUE DATING
　　Partially engraved ___ 18___:
　　1837: July 1, Novr 29

Cat. No.	Denom.	Date	Variety	VG	F	VF	EF	Unc
12-02-02R	$1	18_	Remainder*	125.	175.	-	-	-
12-02-04	$2	1837		125.	175.	-	-	-
12-02-04R	$2	18_	Remainder*	125.	175.	-	-	-
12-02-06R	$3	18_	Remainder*	175.	240.	-	-	-

*spurious dates

4.　　　　ENGRAVED

"A Messrs T.H. Perry & Cie a St. John's" AT LOWER LEFT
Mss. "T.H. Perry & Cie" endorsed vertically across centre

SIGNATURES
　　　　left　　　　　　　　right
　　　　none　　　　　　　mss. Thos. W. Frink

ISSUE DATING
　　Partially engraved ___ 18___:
　　1837: Nov. 29

Cat. No.	Denom.	Date	Variety	VG	F	VF	EF	Unc
12-04-02	$1	1837		125.	175.	-	-	-
12-04-04	$2	1837		125.	175.	-	-	-
12-04-04R	$2	18_	Remainder*	125.	175.	-	-	-
12-04-06	$3	1837		175.	240.	-	-	-

*unsigned, undated and unnumbered

THE MERCANTILE BANKING CORPORATION

1878

HALIFAX, NOVA SCOTIA

BANK NUMBER 445　　　　　　**NONREDEEMABLE**

445-10　　　**CHAS. SKIPPER & EAST**
　　　　PRINTING OF 1878 LARGE SIZE NOTES

DESIGNS AND COLOURS

445-10-02P
　$10 Face Design —/sailing ships/—
　　Colour: Black with no tint
　Back Design: Unknown

IMPRINT
　Charles Skipper & East, London

SIGNATURES
　left　　　　　　　　right
　none　　　　　　　none

ISSUE DATING
　Engraved
　Jany. 1st 1878

Cat. No.	Denom.	Date		Unc
10-02P	$10	1878	FACE PROOF	1,200.

THE MERCHANTS BANK

1830s

MONTREAL (LOWER CANADA)

BANK NUMBER 448　　　　　　**NONREDEEMABLE**

No information concerning this bank is available. A plate is in existence in the American Bank Note Co. archives.

448-10　　　**RWH PRINTINGS**

DESIGNS AND COLOURS

$5 Face Design: Seated female "Commerce" figure; anchor in shield and ship; child riding deer below/ seated commerce figure
　Colour: Black with no tint
Back Design: Plain

$10 Face Design: Ship and seated male "Commerce" figure; reclining woman below/woman in waves
　Colour: Black with no tint
Back Design: Plain

$20 Face Design Ship and seated male "Commerce" figure; strongbox and dog with key below/dock scene and ships
　Colour Black with no tint
Back Design: Plain

THE MERCHANTS BANK

IMPRINT
Rawdon, Wright & Hatch, New York

SIGNATURES
left	right
none	none
Brooks	Brennan

ISSUE DATING
Partially engraved ___ 18___:
$5 1837: Apr 6

Cat. No.	Denom.	Date	VG	F	VF	EF	Unc
10-02	$5	18_	300.	450.	-	-	-
10-04	$10	18_	SURVIVING NOTES NOT CONFIRMED			
10-06	$20	18_	SURVIVING NOTES NOT CONFIRMED			

THE MERCHANTS BANK
1836-1837
TORONTO, UPPER CANADA

BANK NUMBER 450 **NONREDEEMABLE**

The Merchants Bank was a spurious bank that pushed fictitious notes into public circulation for a limited period in 1836 and 1837.

450-10 ISSUE OF 1836-1837
DESIGNS AND COLOURS

450-10-04
- **$1 Face Design:** Woman with foot on globe, dropping coins/cherub in ornate oval/three allegorical women, produce and ship; sailing ships and small boat below/portrait of young woman in ornate oval
- **Colour:** Black with no tint
- **Back Design:** Plain

450-10-06
- **$2 Face Design:** Sailing ship and tug/two allegorical women; spread eagle below/portrait of young woman in ornate oval
- **Colour:** Black with no tint
- **Back Design:** Plain

450-10-08
- **$3 Face Design:** Two Indians and falls/seated women and Indian; trees and old train below/portrait of young woman
- **Colour:** Black with no tint
- **Back Design:** Plain

450-10-10
- **$5 Face Design:** Seated woman and Indian/dock scene, sailor leaning against large anchor; men and ships below/-
- **Colour:** Black with no tint
- **Back Design:** Plain

The spurious $5 note, above, from Pennsylvania is obviously printed from the same plate, with slight modifications, as the $5 Upper Canada note. The plates for these notes have been used as the sources for printing altered, obsolete notes in Connecticut and Pennsylvania.

IMPRINT
Terry, Pelton and Co. Boston & Prov.

SIGNATURES

left	right
mss. Wm. Firman	mss. N. Wood
mss. J.G. Hunt	mss. H. Hamblin
mss. Wm. Firman	mss. Geo. R. Wait
mss. A.W.G. Rank	mss. N. Wood
mss. A.W.G. Rank	mss. H. Hamblin
mss. J.G. Hunt	mss. Geo. R. Wait

ISSUE DATING
Partially engraved _ 18_:
- **$1 1836:** Dec 5
- **$1 1837:** May 4, June 1, June 14
- **$2 1837:** May 4, June 1, July 4
- **$3 1837:** June 1
- **$5 1837:** June 1, July 4
- **Full Sheet 1837:** May 4

Note: 10-04 R, 10-06R and 10-08R are undated, unsigned and unnumbered. The full sheet is signed and dated, but unnumbered.

Cat. No.	Denom.	Date	VG	F	VF	EF	Unc
10-02	$1	1836	225.	325.	475.	-	-
10-04	$1	1837	225.	325.	475.	-	-
10-04R	$1	1837	-	-	-	550.	750.
10-06	$2	1837	225.	325.	475.	-	-
10-06R	$2	1837	-	-	-	550.	750.
10-08	$3	1837	275.	375.	575.	-	-
10-08R	$3	1837	-	-	-	550.	750.
10-10	$5	1837	800.	1,150.	-	-	-
Full Sheet	$1,1,2,3	1837	-	-	-	-	3,500.
Part Sheet	$1,2,3	1837	-	-	1,500.	-	-

*Remainder
**signed and dated
Remainder - no date, signatures or sheet numbers

THE MERCHANTS BANK
1864-1868
MONTREAL, (CANADA EAST)

BANK NUMBER 455   **REDEEMABLE**

Established in Montreal in 1864, this bank changed its name to the Merchants Bank of Canada in 1868, upon absorbing the Commercial Bank of Canada. The president, Sir Hugh Allan, was destined to become a key figure in the CPR scandal of 1873.

455-10   **ISSUE OF 1864**
DESIGNS AND COLOURS

455-10-02
- **$1 Face Design:** Sailors at dock/wharf scene with train and wagons/Hugh Allan
- **Colour:** Black with green tint

- **Back Design:** Lathework and bank name
- **Colour:** Green

455-10-04
- **$2 Face Design:** Prince of Wales/steamships and sailing ships/Hugh Allan
- **Colour:** Black with green tint

- **Back Design:** Lathework and bank name
- **Colour:** Green

THE MERCHANTS BANK

455-10-06
$5 **Face Design:** Hugh Allan/sailor lying on seashore, anchor/ Albert Edward, (Prince of Wales,) as a small boy in sailor suit
Colour: Back with green tint

Back Design: Lathework and bank name
Colour: Green

455-10-08
$10 **Face Design:** Hugh Allan/train, men and cattle/sailor with telescope "On the look out"
Colour: Black with green tint

Back Design: Lathework and bank name
Colour: Green

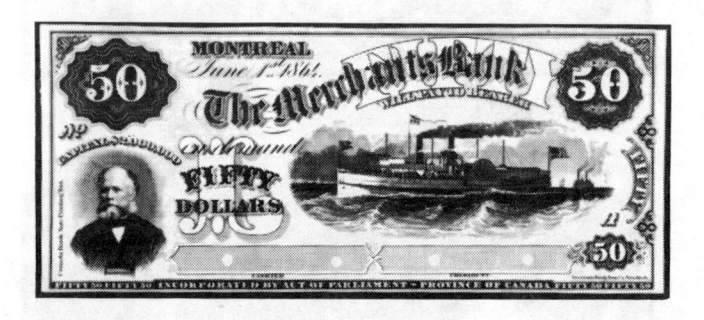

455-10-10P
$50 **Face Design:** Hugh Allan/paddlewheel steamer "Coast Steamer"/—
Colour: Black with green tint

Back Design: Lathework and bank name
Colour: Green

455-10-12P
$100 **Face Design:** Hugh Allan/paddlewheel steamer/ dog seated by strongbox
Colour: Black with green tint

Back Design: Lathework and bank name
Colour: Green

IMPRINT
American Bank Note Co., New York

SIGNATURES
left	right
mss. various	mss. Hugh Allan
mss. various	mss. A. Cameron (p.)

ISSUE DATING
Engraved
June 1st, 1864

Cat. No.	Denom.	Date	VG	F	VF	EF	Unc
10-02	$1	1864	1,000.	1,400.	-	-	-
10-04	$2	1864	1,000.	1,400.	-	-	-
10-06	$5	1864	1,200.	1,600.	-	-	-
10-08	$10	1864	1,500.	2,000.	-	-	-
10-10P	$50	1864			FACE PROOF		800.
10-12P	$100	1864			FACE PROOF		800.

THE MERCHANTS BANK OF CANADA

1868-1923

MONTREAL, QUEBEC

BANK NUMBER 460   **REDEEMABLE**

Established in 1864 in Montreal as the Merchants Bank, the name of the Merchants Bank of Canada was adopted in 1868. The bank lost millions during the depression of the 1870s, and George Hague, the former general manager of the Bank of Toronto, was asked to assume the presidency. Hague accepted and succeeded in restoring the fortunes of the bank. The bank eventually had about 400 branches and sub-agencies in Canada, as well as offices in London, England, and in New York. The bank suffered large losses through bad managerial decisions where unjustified credit was extended.

At the meeting of its shareholders that approved the sale to the Bank of Montreal in 1922, the president stated that the directors had not been aware of the position of the more important accounts in which losses were sustained, and that the general manager and the manager of the Montreal office were responsible. In 1922 the president and the general manager were charged with submitting false returns under the Bank Act, but were acquitted.

460-10   HUGH ALLAN PORTRAIT ISSUES
1868-1873

DESIGNS AND COLOURS

460-10-02
- **$1 Face Design:** Two sailors on wharf "Mech's & Commerce"/train at dockside/Hugh Allan
- **Colour:** Black with overall green tint
- **Back Design:** Lathework, counters and bank name
- **Colour:** Green

460-10-04
- **$2 Face Design:** Prince of Wales/sailing ships and steamship/Hugh Allan
- **Colour:** Black with overall green tint
- **Back Design:** Lathework, counters and bank name
- **Colour:** Green

460-10-06
- **$4 Face Design:** Prince of Wales/cow, cottage and sheep in background/Hugh Allan
- **Colour:** Black with overall green tint 
- **Back Design:** Lathework, counters and bank name
- **Colour:** Green

460-10-10
- **$5 Face Design:** Hugh Allan/sailor on shore with anchor/Albert Edward, (Prince of Wales,) as a child in a sailor suit (after Winterhalter)
- **Colour:** Black with overall green tint
- **Back Design:** Lathework, counters and bank name
- **Colour:** Green

460-10-12P
- **$5 Face Design:** Two sailors on wharf/steamship/Hugh Allan
- **Colour:** Black with overall green tint
- **Back Design:** Lathework, counters and bank name
- **Colour:** Green

THE MERCHANTS BANK OF CANADA

460-10-14
$10 Face Design: River pilot at wheel "Lachine pilot"/ head office/Hugh Allan
Colour: Black with green tint

Back Design: Lathework, counters and bank name
Colour: Green

460-10-16P
$20 Face Design: Earl of Dufferin/train/Hugh Allan
Colour: Black with green tint

Back Design: Lathework, counters and bank name
Colour: Green

IMPRINT
American Bank Note Co. New York on 1868 issues
British American Bank Note Co. Montreal & Ottawa

SIGNATURES
left	right
mss. various	engr. Hugh Allan

ISSUE DATING
Engraved
Mar. 2nd 1868
May 2nd 1870
1st Aug. 1871
$4 and $5: 2nd June 1873
$5 and $20: 1st Aug. 1873

OVERPRINT
1868: "TORONTO" in blue
1868: "PERTH" in blue

Cat. No.	Denom.	Date	VG	F	VF	EF	Unc
10-02	$1	1868	600.	900.	-	-	-
10-04	$2	1868	800.	1,000.	-	-	-
10-06	$4	1870	500.	800.	-	-	-
10-08	$4	1873	500.	700.	900.	-	-
10-10	$5	1868	600	850.	1,275.	-	-
10-12P	$5	1873			FACE PROOF		600.
10-14	$10	1871	1,000.	1,500.	-	-	-
10-16P	$20	1873			FACE PROOF		600.

460-12 ANDREW ALLAN PORTRAIT ISSUE, 1886

DESIGNS AND COLOURS

460-12-02
$5 Face Design: Sailors at dock "Mech's & Commerce"/ steamship/Andrew Allan
Colour: Black with overall green tint

Back Design: Lathework, counters and bank name
Colour: Green

460-12-04
$10 Face Design: River pilot at wheel "Lachine Pilot"/ head office/Andrew Allan
Colour: Black with overall green tint

Back Design: Lathework, counters and bank name
Colour: Green

THE MERCHANTS BANK OF CANADA

460-12-06P
$50 **Face Design:** Lord Dufferin/the paddlewheel steamer "QUEBEC"/Andrew Allan
Colour: Black with overall green tint

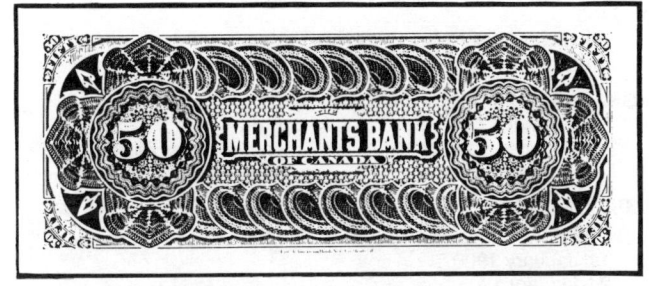

Back Design: Lathework, counters and bank name
Colour: Green

460-12-08P
$100 **Face Design:** Queen Victoria in widow's weeds/ship sailing toward viewer/Andrew Allan
Colour: Black with overall green tint

Back Design: Lathework, counters and bank name
Colour: Green

IMPRINT
British American Bank Note Co. Montreal & Ottawa

SIGNATURES
left	right
mss. various	engr. Andrew Allan

ISSUE DATING
Engraved
2nd July, 1886

Cat. No.	Denom.	Date	VG	F	VF	EF	Unc
12-02	$5	1886	325.	475.	700.	1,100.	-
12-04	$10	1886	400.	500.	700.	1,400.	-
12-06P	$50.	1886			FACE PROOF		600.
12-08P	$100	1886			FACE PROOF		600.

**460-14   MULTICOLOURED TINT ISSUES
1900 AND 1903**

DESIGNS AND COLOURS

460-14-04
$5 **Face Design:** Woman holding sextant "Navigator"/sailing ships "The Clipper"/—
Colour: Black with blue, yellow-brown, yellow-green and lilac tint

Back Design: Lathework, counters, bank name and gypsy woman
Colour: Black with yellow-brown, yellow-green and lilac tint

460-14-08S
$10 **Face Design:** —/two seated allegorical women, factories and train/—
Colour: Black with red-brown, yellow-brown, blue and lilac tint

223

THE MERCHANTS BANK OF CANADA

Back Design: Lathework, counters, bank name and "Justice" figure flanked by allegorical male and female
Colour: Black with red, red-brown, yellow-green and lilac tint

460-14-10S
$20 Face Design: "Steer's head" (after Landseer)/—/—
Colour: Black with green and orange tint

Back Design: Lathework, counters, bank name and Bank Crest
Colour: Black with green, red and yellow-green tint

460-14-12S
$50 Face Design: Stag "Monarch of the Glen" Landseer/—/young woman "Reverie"
Colour: Black with red and olive green tint

Back Design: Lathework, counters, bank name and Bank Crest
Colour: Black with olive, yellow-brown, yellow-green and blue tint

IMPRINT
American Bank Note Co. Ottawa
American Bank Note Company, Ottawa

SIGNATURES
left	right
mss. various	engr. Andrew Allan
mss. various	engr. H. Montagu Allan

ISSUE DATING
Engraved
1st January 1900
2d January 1903

Cat. No.	Denom.	Date	Variety	VG	F	VF	EF	Unc
14-02	$5	1900	Andrew Allan, r.	425.	575.	975.	-	-
14-04	$5	1900	H. Montagu Allan, r.	450.	600.	975.	-	-
14-06S	$10	1900	Andrew Allan, r.			SPECIMEN		500.
14-08	$10	1900	H. Montagu Allan, r.	1,200.	1,600.	2,100.		
14-10S	$20	1903				SPECIMEN		600.
14-12S	$50	1903				SPECIMEN		600.

460-16 ISSUES OF 1906 AND 1907

DESIGNS AND COLOURS

460-16-02
$5 Face Design: River pilot at wheel "Lachine Pilot"/modern steamship/H. Montagu Allan
Colour: Black with overall green tint

Back Design: Lathework, counters, bank name and two beavers

224

THE MERCHANTS BANK OF CANADA

Colour: Green

Type I: Tint surrounds stag and beehive and crest
Type II: Tint leaves white areas around stag and beehive

460-16-04
  $10 Face Design: Indian on horse "Indian Hunter"/horse-drawn reaper/H. Montagu Allan
  Colour: Black with overall green tint
  Back Design: Lathework, counters, bank name and sailor with telescope
  Colour: Green

Back Design: Lathework, counters and bank name
Colour: Green

460-16-06
  $20 Face Design: "Steer's Head" (after Landseer)/—/—
  Colour: Black with overall green tint

460-16-10
  $100 Face Design: Steamship/-/H. Montagu Allan
  Colour: Black with overall green tint

Back Design: Lathework, counters, bank name and sheep at pond
Colour: Green

Back Design: Lathework, counters, bank name and youth painting jug
Colour: Green

460-16-08
  $50 Face Design: Stag "Monarch of the Glen" Landseer/—/Bank Crest
  Colour: Black with overall green tint

225

THE MERCHANTS BANK OF CANADA

IMPRINT
British American Bank Note Co. Ottawa

SIGNATURES
left	right
mss. various	engr. H. Montagu Allan

ISSUE DATING
Engraved
Feb 1st 1906
June 1st 1907

Cat. No.	Denom.	Date	Variety	VG	F	VF	EF	Unc
16-02	$5	1906		125.	175.	250.	450.	-
16-04	$10	1906		125.	175.	250.	450.	-
16-06	$20	1907		450.	700.	950.	-	-
16-08	$50	1907	Type I	1,000.	2,000.	-	-	-
16-09	$50	1907	Type II	1,000.	2,000.	-	-	-
16-10	$100	1907		1,500.	2,000.	-	-	-

460-18   ISSUE OF 1916
DESIGNS AND COLOURS

460-18-02
$5 Face Design: D.C. Macarow/steamship/H. Montague Allan
Colour: Black with overall green tint

Back Design Lathework, counters, bank name and two beavers
Colour: Green

460-18-04
$10 Face Design: D.C. Macarow/horse-drawn reaper/ H. Montague Allan
Colour: Black with overall green tint

Back Design: Lathework, counters, bank name and sailor "On the look out"
Colour: Green

IMPRINT
British American Bank Note Co. Ottawa

SIGNATURES
left	right
mss. various	engr. H. Montague Allan

ISSUE DATING
Engraved
Feb. 1st 1916

Cat. No.	Denom.	Date	VG	F	VF	EF	Unc
18-02	$5	1916	125.	175.	250.	400.	-
18-04	$10	1916	125.	175.	250.	400.	-

460-20   ISSUE OF 1917
DESIGNS AND COLOURS

460-20-02
$5 Face Design: H. Montague Allan/men loading canoes/ E.F. Hebden
Colour: Black with overall green tint

Back Design: Lalthework, counters, bank name and Bank Crest
Colour: Green

THE MERCHANTS BANK OF CANADA

460-20-06
- **$10 Face Design:** H. Montague Allan/steamship, train at dock/E.F. Hebden
- **Colour:** Black with overall green tint
- **Back Design:** Lathework, counters, bank name and Bank Crest
- **Colour:** Green

460-20-10
- **$20 Face Design:** Steer's head (after Landseer)/—/—
- **Colour:** Black with overall green tint
- **Back Design:** Lathework, counters, bank name and Bank Crest
- **Colour:** Green

460-20-14
- **$50 Face Design:** Stag "Monarch of the Glen" Landseer/—/young woman "Reverie"
- **Colour:** Black with overall green tint
- **Back Design:** Lathework, counters, bank name and Bank Crest
- **Colour:** Green

460-20-20
- **$100 Face Design:** H. Montague Allan/seated female with winged wheel and books "Allegory"/ E.F. Hebden
- **Colour:** Black with overall green tint
- **Back Design:** Lathework, counters, bank name and Bank Crest 
- **Colour:** Green

IMPRINT
American Bank Note Co. Ottawa
American Bank Note Company, Ottawa

SIGNATURES

	left	right
$5, $10 and $100:	typed H. Montague Allan	mss. various
	typed H. Montague Allan	typed D.C. Macarow
$20 and $50:	mss. various	typed H. Montague Allan
	typed D.C. Macarow	typed H. Montague Allan

ISSUE DATING
Engraved
3rd January 1917

Cat. No.	Denom.	Date	Variety	VG	F	VF	EF	Unc
20-02	$5	1917	Mss. sig., r.	500.	750.	1,125.	1,300.	-
20-04	$5	1917	D.C. Macarow, r.	500.	750.	1,125.	1,300.	-
20-06	$10	1917	Mss. sig., r.	500.	750.	1,125.	1,300.	-
20-08	$10	1917	D.C. Macarow, r.	500.	750.	1,125.	1,300.	-
20-10	$20	1917	Mss. sig., l.	1,000.	1,400.	1,700.	2,000.	-
20-12	$20	1917	D.C. Macarow, l.	1,000.	1,400.	1,700.	2,000.	-
20-14	$50	1917	Mss. sig., l.	1,400.	1,800.	2,100.	2,800.	-
20-16	$50	1917	D.C. Macarow, l.	1,400.	1,800.	2,100.	2,800.	-
20-18	$100	1917	Mss. sig., r.	1,400.	1,800.	2,100.	2,800.	-
20-20	$100	1917	D.C. Macarow, r.	1,400.	1,800.	2,100.	2,800.	-

THE MERCHANTS BANK OF HALIFAX

460-22 ISSUE OF 1919
DESIGNS AND COLOURS

460-22-02
- **$5 Face Design:** —/Prince of Wales/—
- **Colour:** Black with green tint

- **Back Design:** Lathework, counters, bank name and Bank Crest
- **Colour:** Green

460-22-04
- **$10 Face Design:** —/Late Sir Hugh Allan/—
- **Colour:** Black with blue tint

- **Back Design:** Lathework, counters, bank name and Bank Crest
- **Colour:** Blue

IMPRINT
American Bank Note Company, Ottawa

SIGNATURES
	left	right
$5:	typed D.C. Macarow	typed H. Montague Allan
$10:	typed H. Montague Allan	typed D.C. Macarow

ISSUE DATING
Engraved
1st Nov. 1919

Cat. No.	Denom.	Date	VG	F	VF	EF	Unc
22-02	$5	1919	200.	300.	550.	-	-
22-04	$10	1919	550.	700.	1,000.	-	-

228

THE MERCHANTS BANK OF HALIFAX
1864-1901
HALIFAX, NOVA SCOTIA

BANK NUMBER 465   *REDEEMABLE*

This bank was established in 1864 in Halifax, Nova Scotia, with an authorized capital of $1 million in 10,000 shares of $100.00 each. Its name was changed to the Royal Bank of Canada in 1901. The latter bank is now active as the largest bank in Canada and as one of the largest banks in the world.

465-10 MERCHANTS BANK $20, NO FRAME ISSUE, 1864

The bank title was rendered as MERCHANTS BANK, and the face design lacks a frame.

DESIGNS AND COLOURS

465-10-02
- **$20 Face Design:** —/steamship/—
- **Colour:** Black with orange "TWENTY DOLLARS" tint

- **Back Design:** Lathework and counter
- **Colour:** Black

IMPRINT
Blades, East & Blades, London

SIGNATURES
left	right
mss. Geo. Maclean	mss. J.W. Merkel

ISSUE DATING
Engraved
31st March, 1864

Cat. No.	Denom.	Date	Variety	VG	F	VF	EF	Unc
10-02	$20	1864	No frame	2,500.	3,500.	-	-	-

465-12 MERCHANTS BANK $20, FRAME ISSUE, 1864

Bank title rendered as MERCHANTS BANK, and the face design includes a frame.

DESIGNS AND COLOURS

465-12-02
- **$20 Face Design:** —/steamship/—
  Colour: Black with orange "TWENTY DOLLARS" tint
- **Back Design:** Lathework and counters
  Colour: Black

IMPRINT
Blades, East & Blades, London

SIGNATURES
left	right
mss. various	engr. T.E. Kenny

ISSUE DATING
Engraved
1st October, 1864

Cat. No.	Denom.	Date	Variety	VG	F	VF	EF	Unc
12-02	$20	1864	Frame	2,500.	3,500.	-	-	-

465-14 MERCHANTS' BANK OF HALIFAX, 1869 AND 1870 ISSUES

Bank title rendered as MERCHANTS' BANK OF HALIFAX.

DESIGNS AND COLOURS

465-14-04-02
- **$4 Face Design:** Steamship/steamship/steamship
  Colour: Black with "Four dollars" in green panel
- **Back Design:** Lathework and counter
  Colour: Unknown

465-14-04-04
- **$5 Face Design:** —/steamship/—
  Colour: Black with orange "FIVE DOLLARS" tint
- **Back Design:** Lathework and counter
  Colour: Green

465-14-04-06
- **$20 Face Design:** —/steamship/—
  Colour: Black with orange "TWENTY DOLLARS" tint
- **Back Design:** Lathework and counter
  Colour: Black

IMPRINT
Blades, East & Blades, London

SIGNATURES
left	right
mss. various	engr. T.E. Kenny

ISSUE DATING
Engraved
1st October 1869
July 1st 1870

2. NO GREEN OVERPRINT

Cat. No.	Denom.	Date	VG	F	VF	EF	Unc
14-02-02	$5	1870	2,200.	3,000.	-	-	-
14-02-04	$20	1869	2,200.	3,000.	-	-	-

4. GREEN OVERPRINT

OVERPRINT
"CANADIAN CURRENCY, 1 JULY, 1871" in green

Cat. No.	Denom.	Date	VG	F	VF	EF	Unc
14-04-02	$4	1870	2,200.	3,000.	-	-	-
14-04-04	$5	1870	2,200.	3,000.	-	-	-
14-04-06	$20	1869	2,200.	3,000.	-	-	-

THE MERCHANTS BANK OF HALIFAX

465-16   "CANADA CURRENCY"
ISSUES, 1871-1874

DESIGNS AND COLOURS
     $4 and $5: "CANADA CURRENCY" engraved in frame at top and ends
     $10 and $20: "CANADA CURRENCY" engraved at top only

465-16-06
     $4 Face Design: —/steamship/steamship/steamship/—
         Colour: Black with green "FOUR DOLLARS" and orange "4 4" tint

     Back Design: Lathework and counter
         Colour: Orange

465-16-12
     $5 Face Design: —/steamship/—
         Colour: Black with orange "FIVE DOLLARS" tint

     Back Design: Lathework and counter
         Colour: Green

465-16-14
     $10 Face Design: —/steamship/—
         Colour: Black with green "TEN" and orange "10 10" tint

     Back Design: Lathework and counter
         Colour: Orange

465-16-16
     $20 Face Design: —/steamship/—
         Colour: Black with orange :"TWENTY DOLLARS" tint

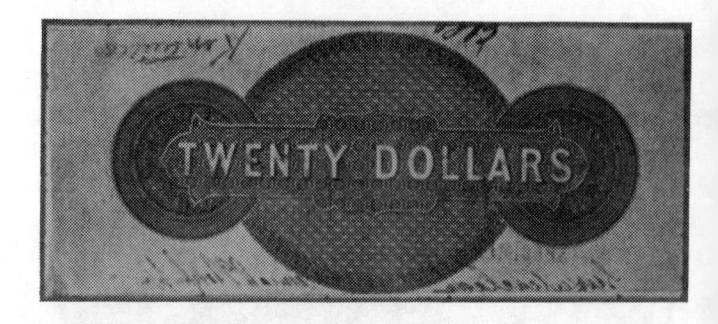

     Back Design: Lathework and counter
         Colour: Black

IMPRINT
     Blades, East & Blades, London

SIGNATURES

	left	right
1871:	mss. Geo. Maclean	mss. Jeremiah Northup
	mss. Geo. Maclean	mss. T.E. Kenny
1871-1874:	mss. Geo. Maclean	engr. T.E. Kenny

THE MERCHANTS BANK OF HALIFAX

ISSUE DATING
Engraved
July 1st 1871
1st Jany. 1872
1st Octr. 1873
1st January 1874

OVERPRINT
"SUMMERSIDE"

Cat. No.	Denom.	Date	VG	F	VF	EF	Unc
16-02	$4	1871	1,800.	2,500.	-	-	-
16-04	$4	1872	1,800.	2,500.	-	-	-
16-06	$4	1873	1,800.	2,500.	-	-	-
16-08	$5	1871	1,800.	2,500.	-	-	-
16-10	$5	1872	1,800.	2,500.	-	-	-
16-12	$5	1873	1,800.	2,500.	-	-	-
16-14	$10	1874	2,000.	2,800.	-	-	-
16-16	$20	1873	2,000.	2,800.	-	-	-

465-18 "DOMINION OF CANADA," ISSUES OF 1878 AND 1879

DESIGNS AND COLOURS

465-18-02
$4 Face Design: Sloop/steamship, entrance to Halifax harbour/bank building
Colour: Black with chartreuse "FOUR DOLLARS" and red "4 4" tint

Back Design: Lathework and counter
Colour: Orange

465-18-04
$10 Face Design: —/steamship/—
Colour: Black with green "TEN" and orange "10 10" tint

Back Design: Lathework and counter
Colour: Orange

IMPRINT
Blades, East & Blades, London E.C.

SIGNATURES
left	right
mss. Geo. Maclean	engr. T.E. Kenny

ISSUE DATING
Engraved
1st January 1878
1st Jany 1879

Cat. No.	Denom.	Date	VG	F	VF	EF	Unc
18-02	$4	1879	1,800.	2,500.	-	-	-
18-04	$10	1878	1,800.	2,500.	-	-	-

465-20 "NO PORTRAIT" ISSUES, 1880-1898

DESIGNS AND COLOURS

465-20-06
$5 Face Design: Seated allegorical female/steamship/ bank building
Colour: Black with orange and green tint

Back Design: Lathework, counters and bank name
Colour: Brown

465-20-10P
$10 Face Design: Small ship sailing away from larger ship "Pilot leaving vessel"/—/bank building
Colour: Black with yellow-orange and blue tint

Back Design: Lathework, counters and bank name
Colour: Green

THE MERCHANTS BANK OF HALIFAX

465-20-16
- **$20 Face Design:** Seated "Agriculture" and "Commerce" figures, ships in harbour/—/—
- **Colour:** Black with blue and orange tint

Back Design: Lathework, counters and bank name
Colour: Brown

IMPRINT
American Bank Note Co. N.Y.
American Bank Note Co., Ottawa

SIGNATURES
	left	right
1880:	mss. various	engr. T.E. Kenny
1883:	mss. D.H. Duncan	mss. Allison Smith
1890-1892:	mss. various	engr. T.E. Kenny
1893:	none	engr. T.E. Kenny
1896:	mss. various	engr. T.E. Kenny
1898:	none	none

ISSUE DATING
Engraved
- 1st July, 1880
- January 1st 1883
- 1st. May. 1890
- 2nd. Jany. 1892
- 2nd. Jany. 1893
- 2nd. Jany. 1896
- January 1st 1898

Cat. No.	Denom.	Date	VG	F	VF	EF	Unc
20-02	$5	1880	1,200.	1,600.	2,400.	-	-
20-04	$5	1890	1,200.	1,600.	2,400.	-	-
20-06	$5	1892	1,300.	1,700.	2,600.	-	-
20-08P	$5	1896			FACE PROOF		600.
20-10P	$10	1880			FACE PROOF		600.
20-12S	$10	1893	1,400.	2,000.	-	-	-
20-14	$10	1896	1,400.	2,000.	-	-	-
20-16	$20	1883	1,400.	2,000.	-	-	-
20-18S	$20	1898			SPECIMEN		1,000.

465-22 "PORTRAIT" ISSUES
1894-1899

DESIGNS AND COLOURS

465-22-04P
- **$5 Face Design:** D.H. Duncan/—/T.E. Kenny
- **Colour:** Black with green tint

Back Design: Lathework, counters, bank name and bank building
Colour: Green

465-22-08S
- **$50 Face Design:** —/miners/T.E. Kenny
- **Colour:** Black with yellow and blue tint

Back Design: Lathework, counters, bank name and bank building
Colour: Blue

465-22-10S
$100 Face Design: Seated woman and baby "History"/—/ T.E. Kenny
Colour: Black with yellow and orange tint

Back Design: Lathework, counters, bank name and bank building
Colour: Orange

IMPRINT
American Bank Note Co. Ottawa

SIGNATURES

	left	right
1894:	mss. John W. Kane	engr. T.E. Kenny
1896-1899:	none	engr. T.E. Kenny

ISSUE DATING
Engraved
1st June 1894
Jan. 2, 1896
2nd Jany. 1899

Letterpress
$50: July 18th 1899
$100: July 3, 1899

Cat. No.	Denom.	Date	VG	F	VF	EF	Unc
22-02	$5	1894	1,400.	2,000.	2,550.	4,500.	-
22-04P	$5	1896			FACE PROOF		700.
22-06	$5	1899	1,400.	2,000.	2,550.	4,500.	-
22-08S	$50	1899				SPECIMEN	1,000.
22-10S	$100	1899				SPECIMEN	1,000.

THE MERCHANTS BANK OF HALIFAX PROPOSED BRITISH WEST INDIES ISSUE

465-24   HAMILTON, BERMUDA, PROPOSED ISSUE, 1880

DESIGNS AND COLOURS

465-24-02S
$5 Face Design: Seated allegorical female/steamship/ bank building
Colour: Black with orange and green tint

Back Design: Lathework, counters and bank name
Colour: Brown

IMPRINT
American Bank Note Co. N.Y.

SIGNATURES

left	right
none	engr. T.E. Kenny

ISSUE DATING
Engraved
1st July 1880

Note: Proofs known with notation "Oct. 6, 1882."

OVERPRINT
"1.1" on upper counters and "The Agency at Hamilton, Bermuda will exchange this note for/ONE POUND ONE SHILLING ST'G." on front and "ONE POUND ONE SHILLING STERLING/AT BERMUDA" on back, all in blue

Cat. No.	Denom.	Date		Unc
24-02S	$5	1880	SPECIMEN	1,400.

THE MERCHANTS BANK OF PRINCE EDWARD ISLAND, 1871-1906

CHARLOTTETOWN, PRINCE EDWARD ISLAND

BANK NUMBER 470　　　　　　　　　　**REDEEMABLE**

This bank was chartered in 1871 with a capital of £30,000 P.E.I. currency, of which one-third was paid in prior to the commencement of business. The failure of a large shipping firm, James Duncan & Co., brought about the suspension of the bank in 1878. Further calls on the shareholders were necessary for the bank to resume business at that time, and again in 1884. Thereafter the bank expanded and prospered, as the other P.E.I. banks vanished one by one. The paid-up capital passed $350,000, and there were six branches when the bank was absorbed by the Canadian Bank of Commerce in 1906.

470-10　　　　**ISSUES OF 1871-1892**

DESIGNS AND COLOURS

470-10-04-04
 $1 Face Design: Farmer ploughing with a team of horses/—/
  sailor standing by rail of ship "Charlies Sailor"
 Colour: Black with green tint

 Back Design: Lathework, counters and bank name
 Colour: Green

470-10-04-06
 $2 Face Design: Anchor with box and bales/
  "Steamboat Canada"/
  three horses' heads in oval
 Colour: Black with green tint

 Back Design: Lathework, counters and bank name
 Colour: Green

470-10-02-06P
 $5 Face Design: Young sailor climbing ship's rigging
  "Going aloft"/woman with cattle and sheep
  "Vogts cattle"/allegorical female
 Colour: Black with green tint

 Back Design: Lathework, counters and bank name
 Colour: Green

470-10-02-08P
 $10 Face Design: Portrait of young woman "Adrienne"/train
  emerging from tunnel/Prince of Wales
 Colour: Black with green tint

Back Design: Lathework, counters and bank name
Colour: Green

470-10-02-10P
$20 Face Design: —/Queen Victoria in widow's weeds/—
Colour: Black with green tint

Back Design: Lathework, counters and bank name
Colour: Green

IMPRINT
British American Bank Note Co. Montreal & Ottawa

SIGNATURES

left	right
mss. Wm. McLean	mss. Robt. Longworth
mss. Wm. McLean	mss. B. Heartz (P)
mss. Wm. McLean	mss. L.H. Davies
mss. J.M. Davison	mss. Benjamin Heartz
mss. J.M. Davison	mss. W.A. Weeks (pro)
mss. J.M. Davison	mss. W.A. Weeks

2. PARTIALLY ENGRAVED DATE, 1871

ISSUE DATING
  Partially engraved ___ 18___:
  $1, 1871: Nov. 6
  $2, 1871: Sept. 1

OVERPRINT
  "CANADA CURRENCY" in red

THE MERCHANTS BANK OF PRINCE EDWARD ISLAND

Cat. No.	Denom.	Date	VG	F	VF	EF	Unc
10-02-02	$1	1871	3,000.	4,000.	-	-	-
10-02-04	$2	1871	3,000.	4,000.	-	-	-
10-02-06P	$5	18_			FACE PROOF		700.
10-02-08P	$10	18_			FACE PROOF		700.
10-02-10P	$20	18_			FACE PROOF		700.

4. FULLY ENGRAVED DATE, 1877-1892

ISSUE DATING
  Engraved
  1st Sept. 1877
  1st September, 1877
  1st August 1889
  6 November 1891
  1st March 1892

OVERPRINT
  "CANADA CURRENCY" in red

Cat. No.	Denom.	Date	VG	F	VF	EF	Unc
10-04-02	$1	1877	3,000.	4,000.	-	-	-
10-04-04	$1	1889	3,000.	4,000.	-	-	-
10-04-06	$2	1877	3,000.	4,000.	-	-	-
10-04-08	$5	1877	3,000.	4,000.	-	-	-
10-04-10S	$5	1892			SPECIMEN		1,200.
10-04-12S	$10	1891			SPECIMEN		1,200.
10-04-14S	$10	1892	3,000.	4,000.			
10-04-16S	$20	1891			SPECIMEN		1,200.
10-04-18S	$20	1892			SPECIMEN		1,200.

470-12 $5 ISSUE OF 1900

DESIGNS AND COLOURS

470-12-02P
$5 Face Design: Two allegorical women "The Reapers"/ steamship at anchor/Indian maiden with spear, leaning on "V" counter
Colour: Black with pink and green tint

Back Design: Lathework, counters and bank name
Colour: Green

MERCHANTS EXCHANGE BANK

IMPRINT
British American Bank Note Co. Ottawa

SIGNATURES
left	right
none	none

ISSUE DATING
Engraved
Jan. 2nd 1900

Cat. No.	Denom.	Date		Unc
12-02P	$5	1900	FACE PROOF	1,000.

MERCHANTS EXCHANGE BANK
1853
GODERICH, CANADA WEST

BANK NUMBER 475   **NONREDEEMABLE**

This was probably a spurious issue, using the plate from the United States note illustrated below.

475-10   ISSUE OF 1853
DESIGNS AND COLOURS

475-10-02

$1 Face Design: Eagle and shield in oval/"Agriculture" and "Justice" figures with eagle and shield; small paddlewheeler below/ship sailing toward viewer Engraved "Will pay ONE DOLLAR on demand to the bearer at their agency in New York"

Colour: Black with no tint

Back Design: Plain

The illustration above of the Merchants Exchange Bank, Anacostia, D.C., is almost identical, except for the placement of the date, the domicile and the red protectors.

IMPRINT
Wellstood, Hanks, Hay and Whiting, New York

SIGNATURES
left	right
mss. illegible	mss. illegible

ISSUE DATING
Engraved
January 1st 1853

Cat. No.	Denom.	Date	VG	F	VF	EF	Unc
10-02	$1	1853	1,200.	1,700.	-	-	-

THE METROPOLITAN BANK

1871-1876

MONTREAL (QUEBEC)

BANK NUMBER 480   **NONREDEEMABLE**

Established in Montreal in 1871, this bank engaged largely in making loans on bank stock and in taking exceptional risks at high rates of interest. The bank did not suspend, but liquidated in 1876. Notes were redeemed at face value at the time of closure, and there was no loss to the creditors. Shareholders received about 75 cents on the dollar.

480-10   **ISSUE OF 1872**
DESIGNS AND COLOURS

480-10-02
    $4 Face Design: Maurice Cuvillier/lion, shield, unicorn and ornate 4/Henry Starnes
    Colour: Black with green tint

    Back Design: Lathework, counters and bank name
    Colour: Green

480-10-04
    $5 Face Design: Maurice Cuvillier/two blacksmiths and ornate 5/Henry Starnes
    Colour: Black with green tint

    Back Design: Lathework, counters and bank name
    Colour: Green

480-10-06
    $10 Face Design: Maurice Cuvillier/two seated allegorical women and ornate X/Henry Starnes
    Colour: Black with green tint

    Back Design: Lathework, counters and bank name
    Colour: Green

480-10-08P
    $50 Face Design: Maurice Cuvillier/—/Henry Starnes
    Colour: Black with green tint

THE METROPOLITAN BANK

1902-1914

TORONTO (ONTARIO)

BANK NUMBER 485   ***REDEEMABLE***

Established in Toronto in 1902 by a group of financiers, the Metropolitan Bank was the first and only Canadian bank to offer its shares at a $100.00 premium. This meant that its authorized capital was, from the beginning, reinforced by an equal sum in reserve fund. In 1914 the bank merged with the Bank of Nova Scotia.

485-10   **ISSUES OF 1902-1912**

DESIGNS AND COLOURS

485-10-06
    $5 Face Design: —/two seated women flanking a standing child/—
    Colour: Black with yellow and red tint

    Back Design: Lathework, counters, bank name and Royal Crest
    Colour: Green

485-10-14
    $10 Face Design: —/steamship/—
    Colour: Black with yellow-green and green tint
    Back Design: Lathework, counters, bank name and Royal Crest
    Colour: Brown

Back Design: Lathework, counters and bank name
Colour: Green

480-10-10P
    $100 Face Design: Maurice Cuvillier/—/Henry Starnes
    Colour: Black with green tint

Back Design: Lathework, counters and bank name
Colour: Green

IMPRINT
    British American Bank Note Co. Montreal & Ottawa

SIGNATURES
    left   **right**
    mss. A.S. Hincks   mss. H. Starnes

ISSUE DATING
    Engraved
        $4 and $5: 1st Feby. 1872
        $10, $50 and $100: 1st May 1872

OVERPRINT
    $5: "O B" in red

Cat. No.	Denom.	Date	VG	F	VF	EF	Unc
10-02	$4	1872	2,500.	-	-	-	-
10-04	$5	1872	2,500.	-	-	-	-
10-06	$10	1872	2,500.	-	-	-	-
10-08P	$50	1872			FACE PROOF		700.
10-10P	$100	1872			FACE PROOF		700.

THE METROPOLITAN BANK

485-10-16S
    $20 Face Design: —/streetcar/—
        Colour: Black with yellow-green and green tint
    Back Design: Lathework, counters, bank name and Royal Crest
        Colour: Olive green

485-10-22S
    $50 Face Design: —/trains, station at left/—
        Colour: Black with brown tint
    Back Design: Lathework, counters, bank name and Royal Crest
        Colour: Orange

485-10-24S
    $100 Face Design: —/mining scene/—
        Colour: Black with yellow-green and red tint
    Back Design: Lathework, counters, bank name and Royal Crest
        Colour: Slate

IMPRINT
    American Bank Note Co. Ottawa

SIGNATURES

	left		right
$5 and $10, 1902:	typed A.E. Ames		mss. various
	typed Robt. H. Warden		mss. various
	typed S.J. Moore		mss. various
$20, $50 and $100 1902:	typed Robt. H. Warden		none
1909:	typed S.J. Moore		mss. various
1912:	typed S.J. Moore		mss. various

ISSUE DATING
    Engraved
        November 5th 1902
        November 5th 1909
        November 5th 1912

OVERPRINT
    $5 and $10, 1902: "S S" in red
    $5 and $10, 1902: "Q Q" in red

Cat. No.	Denom.	Date	Variety	VG	F	VF	EF	Unc
10-02	$5	1902	Ames, l.	1,800.	-	-	-	-
10-04	$5	1902	Warden, l.	1,800.	-	-	-	-
10-06	$5	1902	Moore, l.	1,800.	-	-	-	-
10-08	$10	1902	Ames, l.	2,200.	-	-	-	-
10-10	$10	1902	Warden, l.	2,200.	-	-	-	-
10-12	$10	1902	Moore, l.	2,200.	-	-	-	-
10-14	$10	1909		2,200.	-	-	-	-
10-16S	$20	1902					SPECIMEN	1,200.
10-18	$20	1909		2,500.				
10-20S	$50	1902					SPECIMEN	1,200.
10-22P	$50	1909					FACE PROOF	500.
10-24S	$100	1902					SPECIMEN	1,200.
10-26S	$100	1912					SPECIMEN	1,200.

Note: The 1902 notes are extremely rare in fine or better.

THE MOLSONS BANK

1837-1925

MONTREAL (CANADA EAST)

BANK NUMBER 490   **REDEEMABLE**

The Molsons Bank operated briefly as a private bank from 1837 to 1838. On August 16, 1837, William Molson went to New York to take delivery of some 12,000 bank notes in $1, $2 and $5 denominations, although pounds, shillings and pence were still the official currency in Canada. The government, however, began restricting note issue to chartered banks not engaged in any other business but banking. In response to this policy, Thomas and William Molson applied for a license in March 1839 to engage in the general banking business. Although they had outstanding notes in excess of £6,345 and a capital stock amounting to £120,000, the Molson application was turned down. The government felt that it was not in keeping with the ordinance, as the Molsons were "already being engaged in extensive business as brewers and distillers."

In 1853 the Molsons again entered the banking business under the Free Banking Act. The Molsons Bank operated as a free bank until 1855, when it received a provincial charter. When the Molsons Bank was acquired by the Bank of Montreal in 1925, the purchase price was two shares of Bank of Montreal stock and $10 cash for three shares of the Molsons Bank stock, about $170.00. This transaction was in line with the evolution of Canadian banking, which brought about the disappearance of all but eight major institutions.

490-10   ISSUE OF 1837

DESIGNS AND COLOURS

490-10-02R
- **$1 Face Design:** Men and livestock/allegorical female/paddlewheel steamer; cherub with fruit basket. Engraved "To Messrs. Thos. & William Molson & Compy. Montreal."

Photo Not Available

490-10-04R
- **$2 Face Design:** Unknown
  Engraved "To Messrs. Thos. & William Molson & Compy. Montreal."
- **Colour:** Black with no tint
- **Back Design:** Unknown
- **Colour:** Brown

490-10-06R
- **$5 Face Design:** Steamship/Royal Crest/Archimedes lifting globe with lever
- **Colour:** Black with no tint
- **Back Design:** Lathework
- **Colour:** Brown

IMPRINT
Rawdon Wright & Hatch, New-York

SIGNATURES
left	right
none	none

ISSUE DATING
Engraved
15 Septr. 1837.

Note: Remainders are numbered, but unsigned.

Cat. No.	Denom.	Date	Variety	VG	F	VF	EF	Unc
10-02R	$1	1837	Remainder*	900.	1,100.	1,500.	2,400.	-
10-04R	$2	1837	Remainder*	1,000.	1,200.	1,600.	2,800.	-
10-06R	$5	1837	Remainder*	900.	1,100.	1,500.	2,400.	-

*Numbered, but unsigned

490-12   "FREE BANKING" ISSUE, 1853

DESIGNS AND COLOURS
Some notes have engraved on them "Secured by deposit of Provincial Securities."

490-12-02
- **$1 (5s) Face Design:** Seated allegorical woman "Agriculture," 1 in oval/three ships/1 in oval, seated allegorical woman, "Commerce"
- **Colour:** Black with no tint
- **Back Design:** Lathework, space for Inspector General's registration signature
- **Colour:** Brown

THE MOLSONS BANK

490-12-04
$2 (10s) **Face Design:** Prince Consort in oval in medallion 2/ seated allegorical woman, harvesting scene in background/Queen Victoria (Chalon portrait) in oval
Colour: Black with no tint
Back Design: Lathework, space for Inspector General's registration signature
Colour: Olive

490-12-06
$5 (25s) **Face Design:** Three women and anchor/seated woman, cattle/—
Colour: Black with no tint
Back Design: Lathework, space for Inspector General's registration signature
Colour: Brown

490-12-08R
$20 (£5) **Face Design:** Indian standing in shield/paddlewheel steamship and sailing ships/habitant
Colour: Black with no tint
Back Design: Lathework and counters
Colour: Brown

Photo Not Available

490-12-10P
$50 (£12.10) **Face Design:** Harvesting scene/Queen Victoria (Chalon portrait) in oval/train approaching viewer
Colour: Black with no tint
Back Design: Lathework, space for Inspector General's registration signature
Colour: Brown

IMPRINT
Toppan, Carpenter, Casilear & Co, Montreal

SIGNATURES
left	right
mss. Wm. Sache	mss. Molson & Co.

ISSUE DATING
Engraved
October 1st 1853

OVERPRINT
"PAYABLE AT MONTREAL" in red
"ST. C" in blue

Cat. No.	Denom.	Date	Variety	VG	F	VF	EF	Unc
12-02	$1 (5s)	1853		750.	1,050.	-	-	-
12-04	$2 (10s)	1853		750.	1,050.	-	-	-
12-06	$5 (25s)	1853		850.	1,200.	-	-	-
12-08R	$20 (£5)	1853	Remainder	-	-	900.	-	-
12-10P	$50 (£12.10)	1853				FACE PROOF		500.

FIRST CHARTERED BANK ISSUE, 1855

DESIGNS AND COLOURS
These notes have engraved on them "Chartered by Act of Parliament" at the top or bottom.

490-16-04-02
$1 (5s) **Face Design:** Seated allegorical woman, "Agriculture," 1 in oval/three ships/1 in oval, seated allegorical woman, "Commerce"

Back Design: Lathework, counters and bank name

241

THE MOLSONS BANK

490-14-02-04P
$2 (10s) **Face Design:** Prince Consort in oval in medallion 2/ seated allegorical woman, "Harvesting" allegory in background/Queen Victoria (Chalon portrait) in oval

Back Design: Lathework, counters and bank name

490-16-04-04
$4 (£1) **Face Design:** Portrait of young woman/cherubs and ornate 4; small train below/ three allegorical women and 4

Back Design: Lathework, counters and bank name

490-14-04-06
$5 (25s) **Face Design:** Three women and anchor/ seated woman, cattle; agricultural tools and sheaves below/—

Back Design: Lathework, counters and bank name

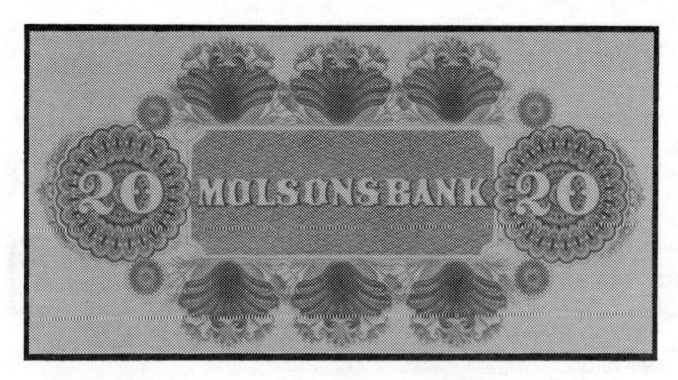

490-14-06-02P
$20 (£5) **Face Design:** Indian standing in shield/paddlewheel steamer, ships; St. George and Dragon below/habitant

Back Design: Lathework, counters and bank name

490-14-06-04P
$50 (£12.10) **Face Design:** Harvesting scene/Queen Victoria (Chalon portrait) in oval/train approaching viewer

Back Design: Lathework, counters and bank name

IMPRINT
Toppan, Carpenter, Casilear & Co. Montreal
Toppan, Carpenter & Co. Montreal
American Bank Note Co. New York.

SIGNATURES
left	right
mss. Wm. Sache	mss. Wm. Molson (pres)
mss. F.J. Foy (p)	mss. Jno. Molson (p)
mss. F.W. Thomas	mss. Jno. Molson (p)

ISSUE DATING
  Engraved
  October 1st 1855
  Octr. 1st 1855

490-14 MONTREAL ISSUE

- **$1:** Branch name engraved at lower left and lower right
- **$4:** Branch name engraved at upper left
- **$5, $20:** Branch name engraved at bottom centre
- **$50:** Branch name engraved at lower left

COLOURS
- **$1 (5s)** Face Colour: Black with no tint
  Back Colour: Orange
- **$2 (10s)** Face Colour: Black with no tint
  Back Colour: Unknown
- **$4 (£1)** Face Colour: Black with no tint
  Back Colour: Green
- **$5 (25s)** Face Colour: Black with no tint
  Back Colour: Green
- **$20 (£5)** Face Colour: See subheadings
  Back Colour: Orange
- **$50 (£12.10)** Face Colour: See subheadings
  Back Colour: Orange

2. No Protector, No Face Tint

Cat. No.	Denom.	Date	Variety	VG	F	VF	EF	Unc
14-02-02	$1 (5s)	1855	Montreal, B&W	800.	1,000.	-	-	-
14-02-04P	$2 (10s)	1855	Montreal, B&W			FACE PROOF		400.
14-02-06	$4 (£1)	1855	Montreal, B&W	1,100.	1,500.	-	-	-
14-02-08	$5 (25s)	1855	Montreal, B&W	1,100.	1,500.	-	-	-
14-02-10P	$20 (£5)	1855	Montreal, B&W			FACE PROOF		400.
14-02-12P	$50 (£12.10)	1855	Montreal, B&W			FACE PROOF		400.

Note: $1 note is known raised to a $5 note.

4. Green Word Protector, No Face Tint

PROTECTOR
Green "word" on face and back

Cat. No.	Denom.	Date	Variety	VG	F	VF	EF	Unc
14-04-02	$1 (5s)	1855	Montreal, green ONE	800.	1,000.	-	-	-
14-04-04	$4 (£1)	1855	Montreal, green FOUR	900.	1,100.	-	-	-
14-04-06	$5 (25s)	1855	Montreal, green FIVE	1,000.	1,300.	-	-	-

6. No Protector, Green Overall Face Tint

Cat. No.	Denom.	Date	Variety					Unc
14-06-02P	$20 (£5)	1855	Montreal, green tint			FACE PROOF		500.
14-06-04P	$50 (£12.10)	1855	Montreal, green tint			FACE PROOF		500.

490-16 TORONTO ISSUE, BRANCH NAME ENGRAVED

COLOURS
- **$1 (5s)** Face Colour: Black with no tint
  Back Colour: Blue
- **$4 (£1)** Face Colour: Black with no tint
  Back Colour: Blue

2. No Protectors

Cat. No.	Denom.	Date	Variety	VG	F	VF	EF	Unc
16-02-06	$1 (5s)	1855	Toronto, B&W	800.	1,000.	-	-	-
16-02-04	$4 (£1)	1855	Toronto, B&W	1,000.	1,300.	-	-	-

4. Green Word Protectors

PROTECTOR
Green "word" on face and back

OVERPRINT
- **$1:** "LONDON" and "PAYABLE/AT/LONDON" in blue near ends
  "PAYABLE AT MONTREAL" in red near ends
- **$4:** "PAYABLE AT LONDON" in blue near ends
- **$5:** "PAYABLE AT LONDON" in blue near ends

Cat. No.	Denom.	Date	Variety	VG	F	VF	EF	Unc
16-04-02	$1 (5s)	1855	Toronto, green ONE	600.	900.	-	-	-
16-04-04	$4 (£1)	1855	Toronto, green FOUR	900.	1,100.	-	-	-
16-04-06	$5 (25s)	1855	Toronto, green FIVE	1,000.	1,300.	-	-	-

490-18 GREEN TINT ISSUE OF 1857

DESIGNS AND COLOURS

490-18-02
- **$1 Face Design:** Portrait of young woman/reclining woman holding ornate 1/sailor with sextant
  Colour: Black with overall green tint
- **Back Design:** Lathework, counters and bank name
  Colour: Green

490-18-04
- **$2 Face Design:** Portrait of young woman/—/Britannia and "Justice" figure flanking ornate 2/—/woman with sheaf and sickle
  Colour: Black with overall green tint
- **Back Design:** Lathework, counters and bank name
  Colour: Green

IMPRINT
Rawdon, Wright, Hatch & Edson, Montreal & N.Y.

SIGNATURES
left: mss. F.W. Thomas
right: mss. Jno. Molson (p)

ISSUE DATING
Engraved
1st Oct. 1857

Cat. No.	Denom.	Date	VG	F	VF	EF	Unc
18-02	$1	1857	800.	1,000.	-	-	-
18-04	$2	1857	800.	1,000.	-	-	-

THE MOLSONS BANK

490-20 ISSUE OF 1871
DESIGNS AND COLOURS

490-20-02
    $6 Face Design: John H.R. Molson/two beavers/Wm. Molson
    Colour: Black with green tint

    Back Design: Lathework, counters and bank name
    Colour: Green

490-20-04
    $7 Face Design: John H.R. Molson/men working on ship's hull "Ship Building"/Wm. Molson
    Colour: Black with green tint

    Back Design: Lathework, counters and bank name
    Colour: Green

IMPRINT
    British American Bank Note Co. Montreal & Ottawa

SIGNATURES
left	right
mss. various	engr. Wm. Molson

ISSUE DATING
    Engraved
    1st Nov. 1871

OVERPRINT
    "TORONTO" in blue

Cat. No.	Denom.	Date	VG	F	VF	EF	Unc
20-02	$6	1871	7,500.	-	-	-	-
20-04	$7	1871	7,500.	-	-	-	-

490-22 ISSUES OF 1872-1901
DESIGNS AND COLOURS

490-22-04
    $4 Face Design: John H.R. Molson/cherubs and ornate 4/Wm. Molson
    Colour: Black with green tint

    Back Design: Lathework, counters and bank name
    Colour: Green

490-22-18
    $5 Face Design: John H.R. Molson/—/Wm. Molson
    Colour: Black with green tint

    Back Design: Lathework, counters and bank name
    Colour: Green

490-22-28
$10 Face Design: John H.R. Molson/cherubs and ornate X/ Wm. Molson
Colour: Black with green tint

Back Design: Lathework, counters and bank name
Colour: Green

IMPRINT
British American Bank Note Co. Montreal & Ottawa
British American Bank Note Co., Ottawa

SIGNATURES

	left	right
1872:	mss. various	engr. Wm. Molson
1875:	mss. various	engr. Jno. Molson
1880:	mss. various	engr. Thomas Workman
1890-1893:	mss. various	engr. John H.R. Molson
1898-1901:	mss. various	engr. Wm. M. Macpherson

ISSUE DATING
Engraved

1st June 1872	3rd Jany. 1893
June 1st 1872	2nd July 1898
June 1st 1875	3rd July 1899
1st June 1880	2nd Jany. 1900
2nd July 1890	2nd July 1901

Cat. No.	Denom.	Date	VG	F	VF	EF	Unc
22-02	$4	1872	1,200.	1,600.	-	-	-
22-04	$4	1875	1,200.	1,600.	-	-	-
22-06P	$5	1872			FACE PROOF		450.
22-08	$5	1880	900.	1,200.	-	-	-
22-10	$5	1890	1,000.	1,300.	-	-	-
22-12	$5	1893	1,000.	1,300.	-	-	-
22-14	$5	1898	700.	1,000.	-	-	-
22-16	$5	1899	450.	700.	950.	-	-
22-18	$5	1900	450.	700.	950.	-	-
22-20	$5	1901	450.	700.	950.	-	-
22-22P	$10	1872			FACE PROOF		450.
22-24	$10	1880	1,000.	1,300.	-	-	-
22-26	$10	1890	800.	1,100.	-	-	-
22-28	$10	1898	700.	1,000.	-	-	-
22-30	$10	1899	700.	1,000.	-	-	-
22-32	$10	1900	450.	700.	1,000.	-	-
22-34	$10	1901	450.	700.	1,000.	-	-

490-24 LATE ISSUES OF OLD RWH 1855 DESIGNS, 1891, 1899 AND 1901
DESIGNS AND COLOURS

490-24-02
$20 Face Design: Indian standing on shield/ paddlewheel steamer; St. George and Dragon below/habitant
Colour: Black with green tint

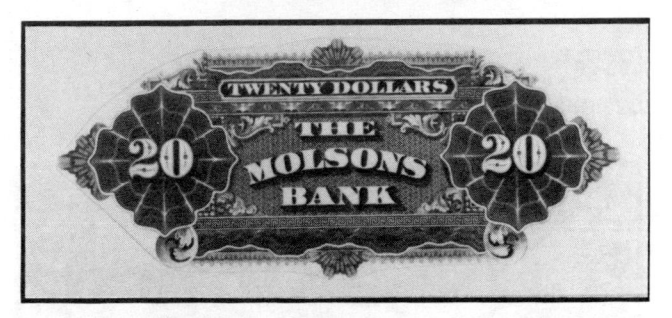

Back Design: Lathework, counters and bank name
Colour: Green

490-24-04
$50 (£12.10) Face Design: Harvesting scene/Queen Victoria/train
Colour: Black with no tint
Back Design: Lathework, counters and bank name
Colour: Unknown

490-24-05
$50 Face Design: Harvesting scene/Queen Victoria (Chalon portrait)/train approaching viewer
Colour: Black with green tint
Back Design: Lathework, counters and bank name
Colour: Green

THE MOLSONS BANK

IMPRINT
British American Bank Note Co. Montreal

SIGNATURES
left	right
1891: mss. Jas. Elliot	engr. John H.R. Molson
1899: mss. Jas. Elliot	engr. Wm. M. Macpherson
1901: mss. Jas. Elliot	engr. Wm. M. Macpherson

ISSUE DATING
Engraved
Jan. 2nd 1891
3rd. July, 1899
1st Oct, 1901

OVERPRINT
ST.T.

Cat. No.	Denom.	Date	VG	F	VF	EF	Unc
24-02	$20	1899	1,600.	2,100.	-	-	-
24-03	$20	1901	1,600	2,100.	-	-	-
24-04P	$50(£12.10	1891				PROOF	500.
24-05	$50	1891	1,600.	2,100.	-	-	-

490-26 ISSUES OF 1903 AND 1904

DESIGNS AND COLOURS

490-26-02
$5 Face Design: Wm. M. Macpherson/ornate 5, woman, cherub/Wm. Molson
Colour: Black with brown and green tint
Back Design: Lathework, counters and bank name
Colour: Green

490-26-06
$10 Face Design: Wm. M. Macpherson/ornate X, Indian, woman/Wm. Molson
Colour: Black with brown and green tint
Back Design: Lathework, counters and bank name
Colour: Green

490-26-10
$20 Face Design: Blacksmith leaning on 20 counter/ steam sailing ship "C.P. LAKE. STEAMER"/ woman with basket of flowers
Colour: Black with green and orange tint
Back Design: Lathework, counters and bank name
Colour: Green

IMPRINT
British American Bank Note Co. Ottawa
British American Bank Note Co. Montreal & Ottawa

SIGNATURES
left	right
mss. various	engr. Wm. M. Macpherson

ISSUE DATING
Engraved
2nd Jan. 1903
2nd May 1904
Jan. 2nd 1904

Cat. No.	Denom.	Date	VG	F	VF	EF	Unc
26-02	$5	1903	225.	350.	475.	-	-
26-04	$5	1904	225.	350.	475.	-	-
26-06	$10	1903	350.	500.	750.	-	-
26-08	$10	1904	350.	500.	750.	-	-
26-10	$20	1904	475.	700.	1,000.	1,700.	3,500.

490-28 ISSUE OF 1905

DESIGN AND COLOURS

490-28-01P
$5 Face Design: Wm. M. MacPherson, shoulder turned to right/woman, cherub, ornate 5/Wm. Molson
Colour: Black with yellow and green tint
Back Design: Lathework, counters and bank name
Colour: Green

THE MOLSONS BANK

490-28-02
- **$5 Face Design:** Wm. M. Macpherson, shoulder turned to right/woman, cherub and ornate 5/ Wm. Molson
- **Colour:** Black with yellow and green tint
- **Back Design:** Lathework, counters and bank name
- **Colour:** Green

490-28-04
- **$5 Face Design:** Wm. M. Macpherson, shoulders turned to front/woman, cherub and ornate 5/ Wm. Molson
- **Colour:** Black with yellow and green tint
- **Back Design:** Lathework, counters and bank name
- **Colour:** Green

490-28-05P
- **$10 Face Design:** Wm. M. MacPherson, shoulders turned to right/Indian and woman flanking ornate X/Wm. Molson
- **Colour:** Black with yellow and green tint
- **Back Design:** Lathework, counters and bank name
- **Colour:** Green

Photo Not Available

490-28-06
- **$10 Face Design:** Wm. M. Macpherson, shoulders turned to right/Indian and woman flanking ornate X/ Wm. Molson
- **Colour:** Black with yellow and green tint
- **Back Design:** Lathework, counters and bank name
- **Colour:** Green

490-28-08
- **$10 Face Design:** Wm. M. Macpherson, shoulders turned to front/Indian and woman flanking ornate X/ Wm. Molson
- **Colour:** Black with yellow and green tint
- **Back Design:** Lathework, counters and bank name
- **Colour:** Green

IMPRINT
British American Bank Note Co. Ottawa

SIGNATURES
left	right
engr. Wm. M. Macpherson	mss. various

ISSUE DATING
Engraved
Oct. 1st 1905
Oct. 2nd 1905

VARIETIES
- **Face Design:** Shoulders turned right in Macpherson portrait
- **Face Design:** Shoulders turned front in Macpherson portrait

Cat. No.	Denom.	Date	Variety	VG	F	VF	EF	Unc
28-01P	$5	1905	Oct. 1				PROOF	500.
28-02	$5	1905	Shoulders right	175.	250.	375.	-	-
28-04	$5	1905	Shoulders front	145.	210.	325.	-	-
28-05P	$10	1905	Oct. 1				PROOF	500.
28-06	$10	1905	Shoulders right	175.	250.	375.	-	-
28-08	$10	1905	Shoulders front	145.	210.	325.	-	-

490-30 ISSUE OF 1908
DESIGNS AND COLOURS

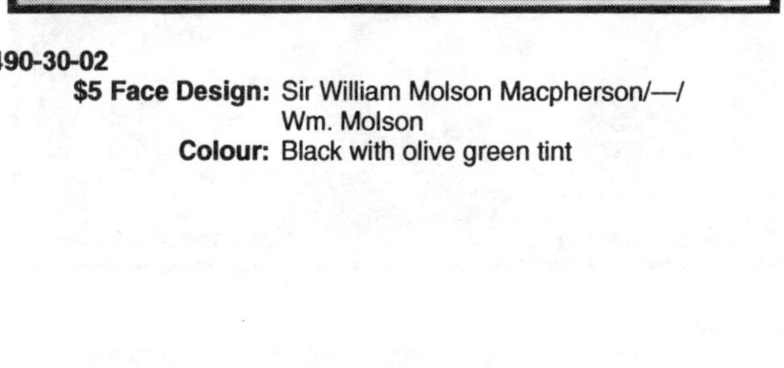

490-30-02
- **$5 Face Design:** Sir William Molson Macpherson/—/ Wm. Molson
- **Colour:** Black with olive green tint

THE MOLSONS BANK

Back Design: Lathework, counters and Bank Crest
Colour: Green

490-30-04
$10 Face Design: Sir William Molson Macpherson/—/Wm. Molson
Colour: Black with olive green tint

Back Design: Lathework, counters and Bank Crest
Colour: Green

IMPRINT
American Bank Note Co. Ottawa

SIGNATURES
left	right
typed Wm. M. Macpherson	mss. various

ISSUE DATING
Engraved
2d. January 1908
2nd. January 1908

Cat. No.	Denom.	Date	VG	F	VF	EF	Unc
30-02	$5	1908	150.	225.	300.	-	-
30-04	$10	1908	160.	240.	325.	-	-

490-32   ISSUE OF 1912
DESIGNS AND COLOURS

490-32-02
$5 Face Design: Two beehives/Wm. Molson/two steers
Colour: Black with green tint

Back Design: lathework, counters, bank name and Bank Crest
Colour: Green

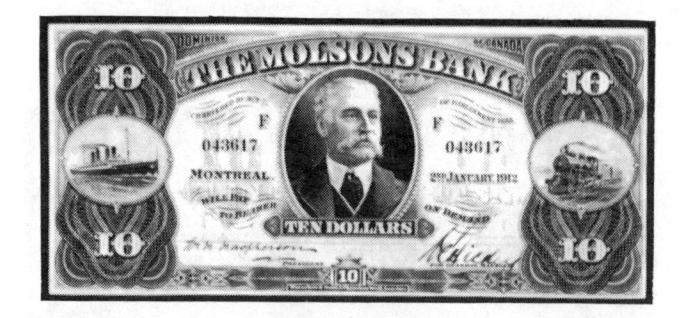

490-32-04
$10 Face Design: Steamship/Sir William Molson Macpherson/train
Colour: Black with lilac tint

Back Design: Lathework, counters, bank name and Bank Crest
Colour: Blue-green

IMPRINT
Waterlow & Sons Ld, London Wall, London

SIGNATURES
left	right
engr. Wm. M. Macpherson	mss. various

ISSUE DATING
Engraved
2nd. January, 1912

Cat. No.	Denom.	Date	VG	F	VF	EF	Unc
32-02	$5	1912	70.	100.	150.	240.	475.
32-04	$10	1912	165.	230.	350.	600.	1,100.

Note: Specimen notes are known with different tints:
$5:   Lilac face, black back
$10: Blue face, brown back
$10: Blue-green face, carmine back

THE MOLSONS BANK

490-34 ISSUE OF 1914
DESIGNS AND COLOURS

490-34-02
  $50 Face Design: Locomotive under bridge/
    Wm. Molson/waterfall and forest
  Colour: Black with green tint

  Back Design: Lathework, counters, bank name and Bank Crest
  Colour: Green

490-34-04E
  $100 Face Design: —/King George V/—
  Colour: Black with orange tint

  Back Design: Lathework, counters, bank name and Bank Crest
  Colour: Green

490-34-06
  $100 Face Design: —/S.H. Ewing/—
  Colour: Black with green tint

  Back Design: Lathework, counters, bank name and Bank Crest
  Colour: Green

IMPRINT
  British American Bank Note Co. Ottawa

SIGNATURES
  left   right
  engr. Wm. M. Macpherson   mss. various

ISSUE DATING
  Engraved
  Jan. 2nd 1914

Cat. No.	Denom.	Date	VG	F	VF	EF	Unc
34-02	$50	1914	1,400.	1,800.	-	-	-
34-04E	$100	1914				ESSAY	1,500.
34-06	$100	1914	1,400.	1,800.	-	-	-

490-36 ISSUE OF 1916
DESIGNS AND COLOURS

490-36-02
  $10 Face Design: —/river and factories/
    Sir William Molson Macpherson
  Colour: Black with green tint

  Back Design: —/Bank Crest/—
  Colour: Blue

IMPRINT
  Waterlow and Sons Ld, London Wall, London

SIGNATURES
  left   right
  engr. Wm. M. Macpherson   mss. various

ISSUE DATING
  Engraved
  3rd. January, 1916

Cat. No.	Denom.	Date	VG	F	VF	EF	Unc
36-02	$10	1916	125.	175.	225.	400.	-

THE MOLSONS BANK

490-38   **1908 DESIGNS RESUMED**
                                1918

DESIGNS AND COLOURS

490-38-02
  $5 Face Design: Wm. M. Macpherson/—/Wm. Molson
  Colour: Black with green tint

  Back Design: Lathework, counters and Bank Crest
  Colour: Green

490-38-04
  $10 Face Design: Wm. M. Macpherson/—/Wm. Molson
  Colour: Black with orange tint

  Back Design: Lalthework, counters and Bank Crest
  Colour: Orange

IMPRINT
American Bank Note Co. Ottawa

SIGNATURES
  left   right
  typed Wm. M. Macpherson   mss. various

ISSUE DATING
  Engraved
  2d. JULY 1918
  2nd JULY 1918

Cat. No.	Denom.	Date	VG	F	VF	EF	Unc
38-02	$5	1918	120.	175.	275.	450.	-
38-04	$10	1918	100.	150.	225.	375.	-

490-40   **ISSUE OF 1922**

DESIGNS AND COLOURS

490-40-02
  $5 Face Design: —/—/F.W. Molson
  Colour: Black with green tint

  Back Design: Lathework, counters, bank name and Bank Crest
  Colour: Green

490-40-04
  $10 Face Design: —/Wm. Molson/—
  Colour: Black with green tint

  Back Design: Lathework, counters, bank name and Bank Crest
  Colour: Green

IMPRINT
British American Bank Note Co. Ottawa

SIGNATURES
  left   right
  typed E.C. Pratt   engr. F.W. Molson

ISSUE DATING
  Engraved
  July 3rd. 1922

Cat. No.	Denom.	Date	VG	F	VF	EF	Unc
40-02	$5	1922	35.	50.	75.	120.	210.
40-04	$10	1922	40.	60.	90.	140.	250.

Note: Proof of $10 exists with yellow tint.

THE MONTREAL BANK
1840s-1850s
MONTREAL, CANADA WEST

BANK NUMBER 495 **NONREDEEMABLE**

This was a phantom bank, trading on the colloquial name for the Bank of Montreal.

495-10 **ISSUE OF 1848**
DESIGNS AND COLOURS

495-10-02
    $5 Face Design: Livestock and farmer by tree in circle/—; seated crown below/paddlewheel steamer
    Colour: Black with no tint
    Back Design: Plain

IMPRINT
  None

SIGNATURES
  left   **right**
  mss. Th. Holmes   mss. J.P. Simm

ISSUE DATING
  Partially engraved ___ 18___:
  1848: Oct. 10
  1853: Apr. 1

Cat. No.	Denom.	Date	VG	F	VF	EF	Unc
10-02	$5	1848	350.	500.	750.	-	-
10-04	$5	1853	350.	500.	750.	-	-

MONTREAL BANK
1817-1822
MONTREAL, LOWER CANADA

BANK NUMBER 500 **REDEEMABLE**

After failing to obtain a charter for 25 years, the founders of the Montreal Bank decided in May 1817 to form a private joint-stock banking corporation. Start-up capital was £250,000, half of which had been raised by sales of stock in the United States. The bank opened its doors for business on November 3, 1817, at 32 Paul Street, Montreal. This institution was the first in British North America to give full banking service.

On July 22, 1822, a charter was granted by the Province of Lower Canada under the name "The President, Directors and Company of the Bank of Montreal."

500-10 **REED ISSUE, 1817-1819**
DESIGN AND COLOURS

500-10-02P
    $5 Face Design: Five coins/view of Montreal, crest in oval below/—
    Colour: Black with no tint
    Back Design: Plain

500-10-10
    $10 Face Design: Nelson's monument/sickle and sheaves below/—
    Colour: Black with no tint
    Back Design: Plain

MONTREAL BANK

500-10-20
- **$20 Face Design:** —/Montreal harbour with ships; Britannia, ship and lion in oval below/—
- **Colour:** Black with no tint
- **Back Design:** Plain

500-10-30P
- **$50 Face Design:** —/Royal Crest/—
- **Colour:** Black with no tint
- **Back Design:** Plain

IMPRINT
A. Reed E.W. Con.

SIGNATURES
left	right
mss. R. Griffin	mss. John Gray

ISSUE DATING
Partially engraved ___ 18___:
- **1817:** 10th October
- **1818:** 1st Jany
- **1819:** 1st January

Note: Many issues of this bank, especially the 500-10 and the 500-12 issues, have been counterfeited, and some of these are of excellent quality.

Cat. No.	Denom.	Date	VG	F	VF	EF	Unc
10-02P	$5	18_				PROOF	400.
10-10	$10	1818	1,350.	1,900.	-	-	-
10-20	$20	1817	1,350.	1,900.	-	-	-
10-22	$20	1818	1,350.	1,900.	-	-	-
10-30P	$50	18_				PROOF	400.

500-12 LENEY & ROLLINSON ISSUE, 1818-1820
DESIGNS AND COLOURS

500-12-04
- **$1 Face Design:** —/Montreal prison/—
- **Colour:** Black with no tint
- **Back Design:** Plain

500-12-10
- **$2 Face Design:** —/paddlewheel steamboat on the St. Lawrence/—
- **Colour:** Black with no tint
- **Back Design:** Plain

500-12-20
- **$5 Face Design:** —/tree and agricultural implements/—
- **Colour:** Black with no tint
- **Back Design:** Plain

500-12-30
- **$10 Face Design:** —/Indian hunting game in forest/—
- **Colour:** Black with no tint
- **Back Design:** Plain

500-12-40P
   $100 Face Design: —/beehive/—
         Colour: Black with no tint
   Back Design: Plain

IMPRINT
   Leney & Rollinson.

SIGNATURES
   left   right
   $1: mss. R. Griffin   mss. G. Garden (v)
   $5-$100: mss. R. Griffin   mss. John Gray

ISSUE DATING
   Partially engraved _ 18_:
      $1, 1819: 1 Mar., Apr. 1
      $2, 1818: 1 Dec
           1819: 1 Mar, 1 April
           1820: Jany 5
      $5, 1819: January 4, 1 Feby, 1 Mar, Mar 5, Mar 11
      $10, 1818: Jan. 1

Cat. No.	Denom.	Date	VG	F	VF	EF	Unc
12-04	$1	1819	1,100.	1,500.	-	-	-
12-10	$2	1818	900.	1,350.	-	-	-
12-12	$2	1819	900.	1,350.	-	-	-
12-14	$2	1820	900.	1,350.	-	-	-
12-20	$5	1819	900.	1,350.	-	-	-
12-30	$10	1818	1,400.	1,900.	-	-	-
12-40P	$100	18_				PROOF	400.

500-14   REED & STILES
              PRINTING, 1821-1822

DESIGNS AND COLOURS

500-14-04P
   $1 Face Design: —/standing Britannia in front of ships and harbour; coin on ornate ONE below/—
         Colour: Black with no tint
   Back Design: Plain

500-14-08
   $5 Face Design: —/woman on shell drawn by sea horses; coin below/—
         Colour: Black with no tint
   Back Design: Plain

IMPRINT
   Reed & Stiles

SIGNATURES
   left   right
   mss. R. Griffin   mss. S. Gerrard

ISSUE DATING
   Partially engraved ___ 18___:
      1821: 7 July, 2 Oct.

STAMP
   Some notes have "PAYABLE AT QUEBEC" stamped vertically near left end.

Cat. No.	Denom.	Date	VG	F	VF	EF	Unc
14-04P	$1	18_				PROOF	400.
14-08	$5	1821	1,100.	1,500.	-	-	-

Note: Beware of counterfeit issues of these notes as in illustration 550-14-08

500-16   GRAPHIC PRINTING
              1820 - 1829

DESIGNS AND COLOURS

500-16-05R
   $5 Face Design: —/hunters, seals/—
         Colour: Black with no tint
   Back Design: Plain

MONTREAL BANK

500-16-10R
    $10 Face Design: —/sheep, shepherd, woman/—
    Colour: Black with no tint
    Back Design: Plain

500-16-20
    $10 Face Design: —/sailing ships/—
    Colour: Black with no tint
    Back Design: Plain

500-16-40
    $20 Face Design: —/seated woman with/—
    Colour: Black with no tint
    Back Design: Plain

500-16-60R
    $50 Face Design: —/seated "Commerce" figure and L/—
    Colour: Black with no tint
    Back Design: Plain

500-16-80
    $100 Face Design: —/woman seated on block bearing/—
    Colour: Black with no tint
    Back Design: Plain

IMPRINT
Graphic Company

SIGNATURES

	left	right
$10:	mss. B. Holmes	mss. J. Molson
$20:	mss. illegible	mss. S. Gerrard
$100:	mss. R. Griffin	mss. S. Gerrard

ISSUE DATING
    Partially engraved ___ 18___:
    1822: June 1
           1 July 1829

STAMP
Some notes are stamped "PAYABLE IN QUEBEC" vertically at the right end.

Cat. No.	Denom.	Date	Variety	VG	F	VF	EF	Unc
16-05R	$5	18__	Remainder*	-	-	1,000.	-	-
16-10R	$10	18__	Remainder*	-	-	1,000.	-	-
16-20	$10	1829		1,100.	1,500.	-	-	-
16-40	$20	1822		1,100.	1,500.	-	-	-
16-60R	$50	18_	Remainder*	-	-	1,100.	-	-
16-80	$100	1822		1,100.	1,500.	-	-	-

* Unsigned, undated and unnumbered.

THE BANK OF MONTREAL
1822 To Date

MONTREAL, LOWER CANADA

BANK NUMBER 505   **REDEEMABLE**

In 1817 nine Montreal merchants signed articles of association of the Montreal Bank, as it was intially called, thereby establishing the first permanent bank in Canada. Under its auspices, the first domestic currency that Canada had known was introduced. Despite its relatively small capital, the bank stood ready to redeem in specie its issue of bank notes at all times. It was also able to bring a degree of order to the market for foreign exchange that had never existed before.

Within a month of its founding, the bank opened an agency in Quebec City to serve two of its most important customers - the government of Lower Canada and the British Army. At the same time, the opening of additional agencies in Toronto, Kingston and elsewhere, set the pattern for branch banking in Canada.

The bank shared in the decline of the fur trade in the late 1820s, but overcame other pre-Confederation upheavals. By buying the Toronto-based Bank of the People in 1840, it expanded its operations to Upper Canada. The bank's entire branch system was centralized by the adoption of the telegraphic message transmission, which had recently been introduced. In 1859 it established its first office in the United States, in New York City. Its first overseas office was opened in London, England, in 1870. In the year of Confederation, on the 50th anniversary of its establishment, the bank found itself acting as the government's depository and fiscal agent and subsequently enjoyed special advantages as the sole issuer of provincial notes.

After Confederation the Dominion of Canada assumed the financial obligations of the various provinces, and while the Bank of Montreal became the federal government's banker, the Dominion took over the sole right to issue notes in denominations of less than four dollars.

When the gigantic project for the building of the Canadian Pacific Railway from Montreal to the Pacific coast was taken up in the 1880s, the bank gave the project its financial support. As western Canada was settled following the building of the railway, local branches were established. The bank's operations then reached from coast to coast.

In 1892 the government of the Dominion withdrew its London fiscal agency from the British houses that had held the Canadian account since the 1839s and awarded it to the Bank of Montreal. From then on the bank not only handled the government's domestic business, but was also responsible for floating Dominion bond issues on the London market. After the turn of the century, British investor confidence in Canada was revived, and the bank's operations through its London branch reached what were then considered immense proportions.

In addition to its underwriting operations, the bank took steps during the first decade of the new century to improve its position in eastern Canada, alongside emerging Canadian industries. To this end, amalgamations were effected with several existing institutions: the Exchange Bank of Yarmouth (1903), the People's Bank of Halifax (1905) and the People's Bank of New Brunswick (1907), all of which had well-established branches and provided the Bank of Montreal with important outlets in the Maritimes and in Quebec. Another acquisition, the Ontario Bank, took place in 1906.

When World War I broke out, the bank was the largest financial institution in Canada. The departure of several staff members to join the armed forces put a strain on the bank at a time when its volume of business was increasing, particularly in connection with its role as the government's banker and fiscal agent in London. This staff depletion led to the hiring of women in large numbers. While mergers effected by the bank in the first decade of the century had greatly strengthened its position in the East, the acquisition of the Bank of British North America in 1918 and the Merchants Bank of Canada in 1922 brought two banks under its direction that had led the way in the opening of the West. In 1925 the Molsons Bank, a Montreal-based institution with good rural representation in Quebec and Ontario, was also absorbed. The drastic deterioration of the economy during the Great Depression was reflected in the balance sheet of the bank, and its assets decreased. All other banks experienced similar declines at this time. For the Bank of Montreal, the establishment of the Bank of Canada had further significance. Since the formation of the Dominion nearly seventy years earlier, the Bank of Montreal had served as banker to the federal government, but after 1935 all chartered banks shared the government account.

During World War II, the bank shared the burden of Canada's war effort with other banks. After the wartime controls were lifted in 1950, Canada entered a period of rapid economic development that has continued, with minor setbacks, to the present day. The bank shared in this development and is now one of the largest banks in Canada.

505-10   **GRAPHIC PRINTING, 1820s**
DESIGNS AND COLOURS

505-10-04
     $1 Face Design: —/seated Britannia, ship, figure 1, female head in oval/—
     Colour: Black with no tint
     Back Design: Plain

505-10-24
     $2 Face Design: —/seated Britannia and Indian; female head in oval below/—
     Colour: Black with no tint
     Back Design: Plain

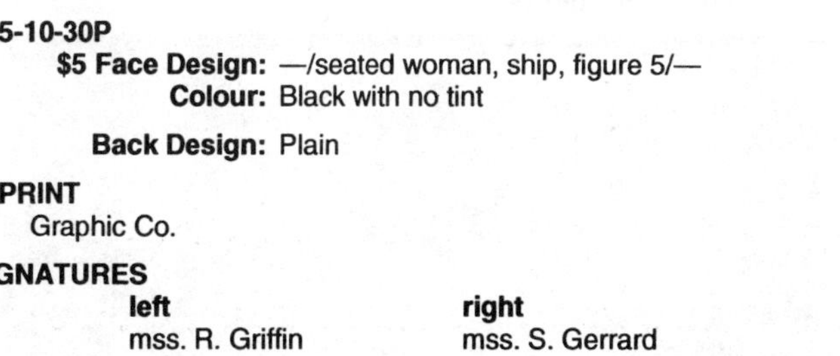

505-10-30P
     $5 Face Design: —/seated woman, ship, figure 5/—
     Colour: Black with no tint
     Back Design: Plain

IMPRINT
     Graphic Co.

SIGNATURES

left	right
mss. R. Griffin	mss. S. Gerrard

THE BANK OF MONTREAL

ISSUE DATING
Partially engraved ___ 18___:
- **1823:** Aug. 1
- **1824:** July 2
- **1825:** 1 Mar, Mar. 1, May 1
- **1826:** Dec. 1

OVERPRINT
"PAYABLE AT QUEBEC" vertically at left end

Cat. No.	Denom.	Date	VG	F	VF	EF	Unc
10-04	$1	1823	1,100.	1,500.	-	-	-
10-12	$1	1825	1,100.	1,500.	-	-	-
10-24	$2	1826	1,100.	1,500.	-	-	-
10-30P	$5	18_				PROOF	500.

505-12 FAIRMAN, DRAPER & UNDERWOOD PRINTING, 1830s

DESIGNS AND COLOURS

505-12-02-10P
- **$1 Face Design:** —/Indian and ornate ONE; child's head below/Walter Ralegh
- **Colour:** Black with no tint
- **Back Design:** Plain

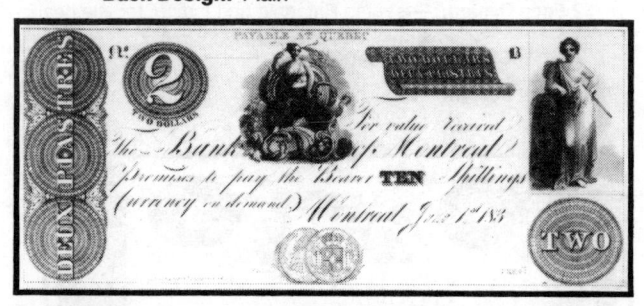

505-12-04-14
- **$2 Face Design:** —/woman on ornate 2, two coins below/standing justice figure
- **Colour:** Black with no tint
- **Back Design:** Plain

505-12-04-18
- **$5 Face Design:** Columbus/two women, child, eagle on ornate 5, bird below/—
- **Colour:** Black with no tint
- **Back Design:** Plain

505-12-04-20
- **$10 (£2.10) Face Design:** Medallion engraved bust/seated woman with ornate TEN; man's head in oval below/medallion engraved bust
- **Colour:** Black with no tint
- **Back Design:** Plain

IMPRINT
Fairman, Draper, Underwood & Co.

SIGNATURES
left	right
mss. B. Holmes	mss. J. Molson (v)
mss. B. Holmes	mss. John Fleming

ISSUE DATING
Partially engraved
- **1831:** 1st July
- **1835:** June 1st 183_
  - 1st June 183_

2. MONTREAL ISSUE

$1: Branch name is engraved at the lower right
$10: Branch name is engraved at the lower left

Cat. No.	Denom.	Date	VG	F	VF	EF	Unc
12-02-10	$1	1831	1,100.	1,500.	-	-	-
12-02-20	$10 (£2.10)	1835	1,100.	1,500.	-	-	-

4. QUEBEC ISSUE

Engraved "PAYABLE AT QUEBEC" at the top.

Cat. No.	Denom.	Date	VG	F	VF	EF	Unc
12-04-10	$1	1831	1,100.	1,500.	-	-	-
12-04-14P	$2 (10s)	183_ June 1st				PROOF	600.
12-04-18P	$5 (£1.5)	183_ June 1st				PROOF	600.
12-04-20	$10 (£2.10)	1835	1,100.	1,500.	-	-	-

505-14 RAWDON, WRIGHT, HATCH PRINTING, 1830s

DESIGNS AND COLOURS

505-14-04-02
- **$1 (5s) Face Design:** Two men and livestock/King William IV; small boat at bottom/St. George slaying the dragon
- **Colour:** Black with no tint
- **Back Design:** Plain

505-14-02-16
- **$2 (10s) Face Design:** Indian women/small crown; sailing ships; small lion on crown below/Indian shooting arrow
- **Colour:** Black with no tint
- **Back Design:** Plain

505-14-04-40P
- **$5 (£1.5) Face Design:** —/small crown, Greek god seated by fountain; small lion on crown below/—
- **Colour:** Black with no tint
- **Back Design:** Plain

505-14-04-50P
- **$10 (£2.10) Face Design:** Two ships in circles/small crown; griffin, allegorical man and woman; small lion on crown below/—
- **Colour:** Black with no tint
- **Back Design:** Plain

505-14-02-40P
- **$20 (£5) Face Design:** Seated Indian man/woman seated by shield; swan feeding its young below/seated "Justice" figure, lion
- **Colour:** Black with no tint
- **Back Design:**

Photo Not Available

505-14-02-50P
- **$50 (£12.10) Face Design:** Unknown
- **Colour:** Unknown
- **Back Design:** Unknown

Photo Not Available

505-14-02-60P
- **$100 (£25) Face Design:** Unknown
- **Colour:** Unknown
- **Back Design:** Unknown

THE BANK OF MONTREAL

505-14-02-70P
£ (Postnote) Face Design: Standing "Commerce" figure/child riding deer, female in chariot pulled by lions, child riding deer/standing "Commerce" figure
Colour: Black with no tint
Back Design: Plain

IMPRINT
Rawdon, Wright, Hatch & Co. New York.
Rawdon, Wright & Hatch New-York

SIGNATURES

left	right
mss. B. Holmes	mss. J. Molson
mss. A. Simpson	mss. J. Molson
mss. B. Holmes	mss. P. McGill

ISSUE DATING
Partially engraved ___ 18___:

$1: 1st January 18__:
1st January 1835
1st January 1836
$2: 1837: June 3

2. MONTREAL ISSUE

STAMP
$1 (5s) and $2 (10s): "PAYABLE AT QUEBEC" in black

Cat. No.	Denom.	Date	VG	F	VF	EF	Unc
14-02-02	$1 (5s)	1835-37	900.	1,300.	-	-	-
14-02-04	$1 (5s)	1836	900.	1,300.	-	-	-
14-02-06	$1 (5s)	1837	900.	1,300.	-	-	-
14-02-16	$2 (10s)	1837	900.	1,300.	-	-	-
14-02-20P	$5 (£1.5)	18_				PROOF	500.
14-02-30P	$10 (£2.10)	18_				PROOF	500.
14-02-40P	$20 (£5)	18_				PROOF	500.
14-02-50P	$50 (£12.10)	18_				PROOF	500.
14-02-60P	$100 (£25)	18_				PROOF	500.
14-02-70P	$100 (£) Postnote	18_				PROOF	300.

4. QUEBEC ISSUE

VARIETIES
The notes are engraved "PAYABLE AT QUEBEC" at the top. They are engraved with "PAYABLE AT THE OFFICE OF THE BANK IN QUEBEC" at the bottom.

Cat. No.	Denom.	Date	Variety	VG	F	VF	EF	Unc
14-04-02	$1 (5s)	18_	At top	900.	1,300.	-	-	-
14-04-10	$1 (5s)	18_	At bottom	900.	1,300.	-	-	-
14-04-20	$2 (10s)	18_	At top	900.	1,300.	-	-	-
14-04-30	$2 (10s)	18_	At bottom	900.	1,300.	-	-	-
14-04-40P	$5 (£1.5)	18_	At bottom				PROOF	500.
14-04-50P	$10 (£2.10)	18_	At bottom				PROOF	500.

"MONTREAL ARMS" ISSUE, ISSUES 505-16, 18 AND 20

The notes have a miniature Montreal Coat of Arms at the bottom centre.

DESIGNS AND COLOURS

505-18-02-02
$1 (5s) Face Design: Woman with anchor in ornate 1/ships in harbour/woman with sheaf and sickle in ornate 1
Colour: Black with no tint
Back Design: Plain

505-20-06-02
$2 (10s) Face Design: Woman with spear and cornucopia standing on ornate 2/Britannia and "Justice" figure flanking ornate 2/woman with sheaf and sickle standing on ornate 2
Colour: Black with no tint
Back Design: Plain

505-16-04-30
$3 (15s) Face Design: Woman standing in ornate 3/allegorical woman with Crest/woman standing in ornate 3
Colour: Black with no tint
Back Design: Plain

505-16-02-30P
 $4 (£1) Face Design: Britannia standing in ornate 4/ Royal Crest/"Justice" figure standing in ornate 4
  Colour: Black with no tint
 Back Design: Plain

505-16-02-40
 $5 (£1.5) Face Design: Young woman with wheat stalks/ woman seated in ornate V/ young woman with sickle
  Colour: Black with no tint
 Back Design: Plain

505-16-02-50
 $10 (£2.10) Face Design: Semi-nude seated woman/two women in ornate X/semi-nude seated woman
  Colour: Black with no tint
 Back Design: Plain

505-16-02-60P
 $20 (£5) Face Design: Standing Indian man with drawn bow/ wilderness scene with deer and Indians/standing Indian princess with bow and arrows
  Colour: Black with no tint
 Back Design: Plain

Photo Not Available

505-16-02-70P
 $50 (£12.10) Face Design: Queen Victoria (Chalon portrait)/ ship/Prince Consort
  Colour: Black with no tint
 Back Design: Plain

505-16-02-80
 $100 (£25) Face Design: Standing "Justice" figure in oval/ Queen Victoria seated on throne/ seated "Commerce" figure
  Colour: Black with no tint
 Back Design: Plain

505-16	**PARTIALLY ENGRAVED DATE, 1844-1860s**

IMPRINT
 Rawdon, Wright & Hatch New-York

SIGNATURES

left	right
mss. illegible	mss. J. Bolton
mss. C.G. Brown	mss. R. Angus
mss. J. Bolton	mss. A. Simpson

2. **MONTREAL ISSUE, 1844-1861**

The branch name is engraved at the ends or at the top.

ISSUE DATING
 Partially engraved ___ 18___:
 1844: Jan. 1
 1849: Jan. 1
 1861: 1 Augt.

THE BANK OF MONTREAL

PROTECTOR
  $5: Red "numeral" on face and back
  $10 and $100: Green "word" on face and back

OVERPRINT
  $10: "T T" in blue and "M" in green

Cat. No.	Denom.	Date	VG	F	VF	EF	Unc
16-02-02P	$1 (5s)	18_			PROOF	600.	
16-02-10P	$2 (10s)	18_			PROOF	600.	
16-02-20	$3 (15s)	1844	2,500.	3,300.	-	-	-
16-02-30P	$4 (£1)	18_			PROOF	600.	
16-02-40	$5 (£1.5)	1844	950.	1,250.	-	-	-
16-02-50	$10 (£2.10)	1849	950.	1,250.	-	-	-
16-02-60P	$20 (£5)	18_			PROOF	600.	
16-02-70P	$50 (£12.10)	18_			PROOF	600.	
16-02-80	$100 (£25)	1861	1,100.	1,500.	-	-	-

4. QUEBEC ISSUE, 1844-1852

The branch name is engraved vertically at the ends.

505-16-04-40

ISSUE DATING
  Partially engraved _ 18_:
  1 May 1844
  1 May 1846
  1 May 1852

PROTECTOR
  $1 (5s) and $2 (10s): Red "numeral" on face and back

Cat. No.	Denom.	Date	VG	F	VF	EF	Unc
16-04-10	$1 (5s)	1846	650.	1,000.	-	-	-
16-04-20	$2 (10s)	1846	650.	1,000.	-	-	-
16-04-30	$3 (15s)	1844	2,500.	3,300.	-	-	-
16-04-40	$10 (£2.10)	1846	950.	1,250.	-	-	-
16-04-50	$10 (£2.10)	1852	950.	1,250.	-	-	-

505-18 ENGRAVED DATE, RED PROTECTOR, TWO SIGNATURES, 1849

These notes have a miniature Montreal Coat of Arms at the bottom centre. The branch names are engraved vertically at the ends.

505-18-04-02

505-18-02-04

505-18-02-06

IMPRINT
  Rawdon, Wright & Hatch, New York

SIGNATURES
  left   right
  mss. various   mss. various

ISSUE DATING
  Engraved
  Jany. 1st 1849

PROTECTOR
  Red "word" on face and back

2. MONTREAL ISSUE

Cat. No.	Denom.	Date	VG	F	VF	EF	Unc
18-02-02	$1 (5s)	1849	650.	1,000.	-	-	-
18-02-04	$2 (10s)	1849	650.	1,000.	-	-	-
18-02-06	$4 (£1)	1849	950.	1,500.	-	-	-

4. QUEBEC ISSUE

Cat. No.	Denom.	Date	VG	F	VF	EF	Unc
18-04-02	$1 (5s)	1849	500.	700.	-	-	-

505-20 ENGRAVED DATE, GREEN PROTECTOR, ONE SIGNATURE, 1849

These notes have a miniature Montreal Coat of Arms at the bottom centre. The branch names are engraved vertically at the ends. Red printed numbers are to the right of the centre vignette, near the left signature space or above the right signature space.

IMPRINT
  Rawdon, Wright, Hatch & Edson, Montreal & N.Y.
  "ABNCo." Mono on some notes

SIGNATURES
  right only
  mss. C.J. Brown
  mss. R. Angus

ISSUE DATING
  Engraved
  Jany. 1st 1849

THE BANK OF MONTREAL

505-20-06-02

PROTECTOR
Green "word" on face and back
Green "word" and "numeral" on face of some notes.

2. COBOURG ISSUE

OVERPRINT
"LINDSAY" in red

Cat. No.	Denom.	Date	VG	F	VF	EF	Unc
20-02-02	$2 (10s)	1849	550.	800.	-	-	-

4. HAMILTON ISSUE

OVERPRINT
"BRANTFORD" in red

Cat. No.	Denom.	Date	VG	F	VF	EF	Unc
20-04-02	$1 (5s)	1849	450.	650.	-	-	-

6. MONTREAL ISSUE

505-20-06-04

OVERPRINT
$1 (5s): "LONDON" in green, in medium or in large letters

STAMP
$1 (5s), with overprint: "S" in blue

Cat. No.	Denom.	Date	VG	F	VF	EF	Unc
20-06-02	$1 (5s)	1849	500.	750.	-	-	-
20-06-04	$2 (10s)	1849	500.	750.	-	-	-

8. QUEBEC ISSUE

505-20-08-04

Cat. No.	Denom.	Date	VG	F	VF	EF	Unc
20-08-02	$1 (5s)	1849	500.	750.	-	-	-
20-08-04	$1 (10s)	1849	500.	750.	-	-	-

10. TORONTO ISSUE

505-20-10-02

OVERPRINT
$1 (5s): "BRANTFORD" twice in red
"COBOURG" in red

$2 (10s): "SIMCOE" in red
"HAMILTON" in green

Cat. No.	Denom.	Date	VG	F	VF	EF	Unc
20-10-02	$1 (5s)	1849	500.	750.	-	-	-
20-10-04	$2 (10s)	1849	500.	750.	-	-	-

THE BANK OF MONTREAL

"DOG AND SAFE" ISSUES

Numbers 505-22 and 505-24 were issued for the Toronto branch. There is a vignette of a small dog and a safe on the bottom centre of all denominations.

DESIGNS AND COLOURS

505-22   PARTIALLY ENGRAVED DATE
NO PROTECTOR, 1842-1847

2.   RAWDON, WRIGHT, HATCH PRINTINGS
2nd APRIL 184—

505-22-02-04P
$2 (10s) **Face Design:** —/seated Mercury, lion/—
    Colour: Black with no tint
  Back Design: Plain

505-22-02-08P
$10 (£2.10) **Face Design:** Allegorical female, anchor/seated Indian (from Death of Wolfe by West) and "Ruins of Jamestown"/roses, shamrocks, thistles, counter
    Colour: Black with no tint
  Back Design: Plain

IMPRINT
Rawdon, Wright & Hatch, New York

SIGNATURES
left	right
none	none

ISSUE DATING
Partially Engraved 2nd April 184__

Cat.No.	Denom	Date	VG	F	VF	EF	Unc
22-02-02P	$1 (5s)	184-				PROOF	750.
22-02-04P	$2 (10s)	184-				PROOF	750.
22-02-06P	$5 (£1.5)	184-				PROOF	750.
22-02-08P	$10 (£2.10)	184-				PROOF	750.

4.   RAWDON, WRIGHT, HATCH PRINTINGS
2nd AUGT 184__

Photo Not Available

IMPRINT
Rawdon, Wright, Hatch New York

SIGNATURES
left	right
mss. B. Thorne	mss. W. Wilson

ISSUE DATING
Partially Engraved 2nd Augt. 184___
1842
1843

STAMP
"BELLEVILLE" in red

Cat.No.	Denom	Date	G	VG	F	VF	EF	Unc
22-04-02	$1(5s)	1842	400.	800.	1,125.	-		
22-04-10P	$2(10s)	184-					PROOF	750.
22-04-20P	$5(£1.5)	184-					PROOF	750.
22-04-30	$10(£2.10)	1842	400.	800.	1,125.	-		

6.   DANFORTH/UNDERWOOD PRINTINGS,
2ND AUGT. 184_

505-22-06-10P
$1 (5s) **Face Design:** —bison/roses, shamrocks, thistles, counter
    Colour: Black with no tint
  Back Design: Plain

505-22-06-20P
$2 (10s) **Face Design:** —/seated Mercury, lion/—
    Colour: Black with no tint
  Back Design: Plain

THE BANK OF MONTREAL

505-22-06-30P
    $5 Face Design: Roses, shamrocks, thistles, counter/ Royal Crest/roses, shamrocks, thistles, counter
    Colour: Black with no tint
    Back Design: Plain

IMPRINT
Underwood, Bald, Spencer & Hufty, Philada
Danforth, Underwood & Co. New York-A.Bourne Agent
Danforth, Spencer & Hufty. New York-A.Bourne Agent and
Spencer, Hufty & Danforth, Philada.

SIGNATURES
left	right
J.S. Smith	W. Wilson

ISSUE DATING
Partially Engraved 2nd Augt. 184__:
1843
1847

STAMP
"BELLEVILLE" in red

Cat.No.	Denom.	Date	VG	F	VF	EF	Unc
22-06-10	$1(5s)	1847	950.	1,400.	-	-	-
22-06-20	$2(10s)	1847	950.	1,400.	-	-	-
22-06-20P	$2(10s)	1847				PROOF	600.
22-06-30	$5(£1.5)	1843	950.	1,400.	-	-	-
22-06-40	$5(£1.5)	1847	950.	1,400.	-	-	-

505-24   **ENGRAVED DATE, RED PROTECTORS, 1849**

505-24-04

505-24-06
    $5 (£1.5) Face Design: Roses, shamrocks, thistles, counter/ Royal Crest/roses, shamrocks, thistles, counter
    Colour: Black with no tint
    Back Design: Plain

IMPRINT
Rawdon, Wright, Hatch & Edson, New York

SIGNATURES
left	right
mss. illegible	mss. W. Wilson
mss. G.H. Wilson	mss. J.F. Smith

ISSUE DATING
Engraved
1st MAY, 1849

PROTECTOR
Red "word" on face and back

ENGRAVED PAYABLE
John G. Horne
J.G. Horne

OVERPRINT
"BROCKVILLE" in red
"BYTOWN" in red
"COBOURG" in red
"HAMILTON" in red
"LONDON" in red
"ST. THOMAS" in red

Cat. No.	Denom.	Date	VG	F	VF	EF	Unc
24-02	$1 (5s)	1849	950.	1,400.	-	-	-
24-04	$2 (10s)	1849	950.	1,400.	-	-	-
24-06	$5 (£1.5)	1849	850.	1,200.	-	-	-
24-08	$10 (£2.10)	1849	950.	1,400.	-	-	-

505-26   **"BANK CREST" ISSUE, 1852-1856**

These notes were printed on watermarked paper, with the date and the branch in red, blue or black letterpress. All notes of these designs dated 1858 or 1864 are counterfeits, and there are counterfeits of other dates as well. The notes have the bank crest design at the top left corner.

    1. Branch name at centre
        Montreal   Quebec
        Ottawa   Toronto

    2. Branch name at ends
        Brantford   Perth
        Bytown   Peterboro
        Hamilton   Quebec
        Kingston   St. Thomas
        London   Toronto
        Montreal

THE BANK OF MONTREAL

DESIGNS AND COLOURS

505-26-04
    Type I (1852)
    $1 (5s) Face Design: Bank Crest/—/sailing ships and 1 counter
        Colour: Black with no tint
    Back Design: Plain

505-26-02-10
    Type II (1852)

505-26-02-16E
    Type I (1851)
    $2 (10s) Face Design: Bank Crest/—/allegorical female, ships, 2 counter
        Colour: Black with no tint
    Back Design: Plain

505-26-02-18
    Type I (1852)

505-26-04-02
    Type II (1852)

505-26-02-30E
    Type I (1851)
    $4 (20s) Face Design: Bank Crest/—/allegorical female, sheep, 4 counter
        Colour: Black with no tint
    Back Design: Plain

505-26-02-32
    Type I (1852)

Photo Not Available

505-26-02-42
    Type II (1856)

THE BANK OF MONTREAL

505-26-02-46
Type I (1852)
$5 (25s) Face Design: Bank Crest/—/Indians and 5 counter
Colour: Black with no tint
Back Design: Plain

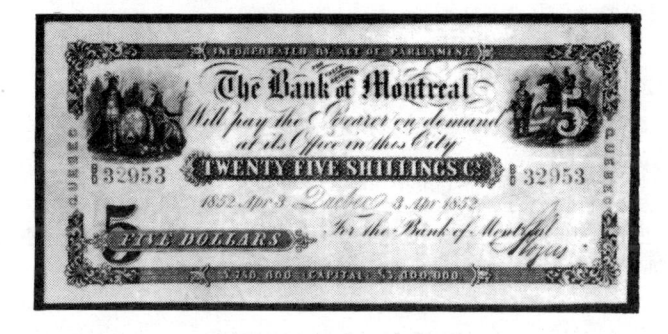

505-26-02-52
Type II (1852)

505-26-02-60
Type I (1852)
$10 (50s) Face Design: Bank Crest /—/paddlewheel steamboat and 10 counter
Colour: Black with no tint
Back Design: Plain

505-26-02-66
Type II (1852)

IMPRINT
Perkins, Bacon & Co. London

SIGNATURES
right only
mss. J. Reed
mss. R. Angus

2. NO PROTECTOR

ISSUE DATING
The entire date added letterpress with serial number:
- **$1 (5s):** 3 Jan 1852; 6 June 1852
- **$2 (10s):** 5 Mar 1852; 1 July 1852
- **$4 (20s):** 1 Apr 1852; 1 Aug 1856
- **$5 (25s):** 3 Apr., 1852; 5 Apr., 1852; 1 Sept 1852; 1 Mar 1853
- **$10 (50s):** 5 May 1852

OVERPRINT
"THREE RIVERS" twice vertically in red

VARIETIES
Type I: Notes have denominations spelled out in a panel at the lower left.
Type II: Notes have a numeral engraved at the left end of the type I panel.

Cat. No.	Denom.	Date	Variety	VG	F	VF	EF	Unc
26-02-04	$1 (5s)	1852	Type I	700.	1,000.	-	-	-
26-02-10	$1 (5s)	1852	Type II	700.	1,000.	-	-	-
26-02-16E	$2 (10s)	1851	Type I			ESSAY		600.
26-02-18	$2 (10s)	1852	Type I	700.	1,000.	-	-	-
26-02-30E	$4 (20s)	1851	Type I			ESSAY		600.
26-02-32	$4 (20s)	1852	Type I	950.	1,400.	-	-	-
26-02-38	$4 (20s)	1852	Type II	950.	1,400.	-	-	-
26-02-42	$4 (20s)	1856	Type II		NOT CONFIRMED			
26-02-46	$5 (25s)	1852	Type I	700.	1,000.	-	-	-
26-02-48	$5 (25s)	1853	Type I	700.	1,000.	-	-	-
26-02-52	$5 (25s)	1852	Type II	700.	1,000.	-	-	-
26-02-54	$5 (25s)	1853	Type II	700.	1,000.	-	-	-
26-02-60	$10 (50s)	1852	Type I	950.	1,400.	-	-	-
26-02-66	$10 (50s)	1852	Type II	950.	1,400.	-	-	-

4. GREEN WORD PROTECTOR

DESIGNS AND COLOURS

505-26-04-02
$2 (10s) Face Design: Bank Crest/—/allegorical female, ships, 2 counter
Colour: Black with no tint
Back Design: Plain

ISSUE DATING
The entire date added letterpress with serial numbers:
$2 (10s): 1 Mar. 1852

OVERPRINT
"LONDON" in green

PROTECTOR
Green "word" on face

Cat. No.	Denom.	Date	Variety	VG	F	VF	EF	Unc
26-04-02	$2 (10s)	1852	Type II	950.	1,400.	-	-	-

THE BANK OF MONTREAL

505-28   "BLUE BACK" ISSUE, 1853-1857

The principal branch name is engraved vertically in black at the ends of the centre panel. Sometimes an additional branch name is overprinted horizontally below the bank title.

DESIGNS AND COLOURS

505-28-60-02R
$1 Face Design: Bank Crest/—/Queen Victoria (Winterhalter portrait)
Colour: Black with no tint

Back Design: Lathework, counters and bank name
Colour: Blue

505-28-56-02
$2 Face Design: Bank Crest/—/Prince Consort
Colour: Black with no tint

Back Design: Lathework, counters and bank name
Colour: Blue

IMPRINT
Toppan, Carpenter, Casilear & Co.
Toppen, Carpenter & Co. Montreal

SIGNATURES
right only
none
mss. R. Angus

ISSUE DATING
The entire date added letterpress in red with serial numbers:
1 Feb 1853
1 Aug 1856
2 Jan 1857
2 Feb 1857

2.   ENGRAVED "BROCKVILLE"

The letterpress "BROCKVILLE" is in red in the date.

Cat. No.	Denom.	Date	VG	F	VF	EF	Unc
28-02-02	$1	1857	600.	800.	-	-	-

12.   ENGRAVED "GODERICH"

"LONDON" is overprinted in red in the date.

OVERPRINT
"BRANTFORD" in green

Cat. No.	Denom.	Date	VG	F	VF	EF	Unc
28-12-02	$1	1856	600.	800.	-	-	-

22.   ENGRAVED "LONDON"

The letterpress "LONDON" is in red in the date, with "T T" at the top.

Cat. No.	Denom.	Date	VG	F	VF	EF	Unc
28-22-02	$1	1857	600.	800.	-	-	-
28-22-04	$2	1856	600.	800.	-	-	-

30.   ENGRAVED "MONTREAL"

There is no overprinted branch name.

Cat. No.	Denom.	Date					Unc
28-30-02P	$1	Undated			FACE PROOF		500.

36.   ENGRAVED "OTTAWA"

"OTTAWA" is overprinted in red in the date.

Cat. No.	Denom.	Date	VG	F	VF	EF	Unc
28-36-02	$1	1857	600.	800.	-	-	-
28-36-04	$2	1857	600.	800.	-	-	-

40.   ENGRAVED "PERTH"

"OTTAWA" is overprinted in red in the date.

Cat. No.	Denom.	Date	VG	F	VF	EF	Unc
28-40-02	$2	1856	600.	800.	-	-	-

44.   ENGRAVED "PICTON"

"KINGSTON" is overprinted in red in the date.

Cat. No.	Denom.	Date	VG	F	VF	EF	Unc
28-44-02	$1	1856	600.	800.	-	-	-
28-44-04	$2	1856	600.	800.	-	-	-

48.　　　ENGRAVED "PORT HOPE"

The letterpress "COBOURG" is in red in the date.
OVERPRINT
　　"LINDSAY" in red

Cat. No.	Denom.	Date	VG	F	VF	EF	Unc
28-48-02	$1	1857	600.	800.	-	-	-

52.　　　ENGRAVED "QUEBEC"

No overprinted branch name.

Cat. No.	Denom.	Date					Unc
28-52-02P	$2	Undated				FACE PROOF	400.

56.　　　ENGRAVED "SIMCOE"

"BRANTFORD" is overprinted in red in the date.

Cat. No.	Denom.	Date	VG	F	VF	EF	Unc
28-56-02	$2	1856	600.	800.	-	-	-

60.　　　ENGRAVED "TORONTO"

"TORONTO" is overprinted in red in the date.

Cat. No.	Denom.	Date	Variety	VG	F	VF	EF	Unc
28-60-02R	$1	1853	Remainder*	-	-	-	850.	-

*Unsigned, dated and numbered.

64.　　　ENGRAVED "WHITBY"

The letterpress "BOWMANVILLE" is in red in the date.

Cat. No.	Denom.	Date	VG	F	VF	EF	Unc
28-64-02	$1	1856	600.	850.	-	-	-

68.　　　ENGRAVED "WOODSTOCK"

"LONDON" is overprinted in red in the date.

Cat. No.	Denom.	Date	VG	F	VF	EF	Unc
28-68-02	$1	1856	600.	850.	-	-	-

505-30　　　"GREEN" ISSUE OF 1859

　　The branch name was added letterpress in red or blue across the lower centre. Additional branch names may be overprinted vertically at each end of the note and in larger print below the bank title.
1. Branch name at centre

Belleville	Kingston	Peterboro
Brantford	Lindsay	Quebec
Brockville	London	Toronto
Cobourg	Montreal	Waterloo
Hamilton	Ottawa	Whitby

2. Branch name above the date line, at the ends or both places.

Cornwall	Perth	Stratford
Goderich	Peterboro	Waterloo
Guelph	Picton	Whitby
Lindsay	Quebec	

DESIGNS AND COLOURS

505-30-02-02
White outlined numerals

505-30-04-02
Full tint numerals
$1 Face Design: Portrait of Queen Victoria/Bank Crest/reclining woman with produce "Ceres"
Colour: Black with overall green tint

Back Design: See subheadings
Colour: See subheadings

505-30-02-04
$2 Face Design: St. George slaying the dragon/Victoria and Albert/Bank Crest
Colour: Black with overall green tint

Back Design: See subheadings
Colour: See subheadings

505-30-04-06
$4 Face Design: Bank Crest/Wellington/seated Britannia
Colour: Black with overall green tint

Back Design: See subheadings
Colour: See subheadings

THE BANK OF MONTREAL

505-30-04-08
$5 Face Design: Bank Crest/front view of head office building/ seated blacksmith
Colour: Black with overall green tint

Back Design: See subheadings
Colour: See subheadings

505-30-04-10
$10 Face Design: Seated female on dock "Commerce"/ Robert Peel/Bank Crest
Colour: Black with overall green tint

Back Design: St. George slaying the dragon
Colour: Green

IMPRINT
Rawdon, Wright, Hatch & Edson
Rawdon, Wright, Hatch & Edson, Montreal & N.Y.
American Bank Note Co.
American Bank Note Co. New York

SIGNATURES

right only
mss. R. Angus
mss. C.G. Brown

ISSUE DATING
Entire date added letterpress:
3 Jan. 1859

2. WHITE OUTLINED NUMERALS, ST. GEORGE BACK DESIGNS

Cat. No.	Denom.	Date	VG	F	VF	EF	Unc
30-02-02	$1	1859	900.	1,250.	1,900.	-	-
30-02-04	$2	1859	900.	1,250.	1,900.	-	-
30-02-06	$4	1859	900.	1,400.	2,100.	-	-
30-02-08	$5	1859	900.	1,250.	1,900.	-	-
30-02-10	$10	1859	900.	1,250.	1,900.	-	-

4. FULL TINT NUMERALS, ST. GEORGE BACK DESIGNS

Cat. No.	Denom.	Date	VG	F	VF	EF	Unc
30-04-02	$1	1859	900.	1,250.	1,900.	-	-
30-04-04	$2	1859	900.	1,250.	1,900.	-	-
30-04-06	$4	1859	900.	1,250.	1,900.	-	-
30-04-08	$5	1859	900.	1,250.	1,900.	-	-
30-04-10	$10	1859	900.	1,250.	1,900.	-	-

6. WHITE OUTLINED NUMERALS, PLAIN BACKS

Cat. No.	Denom.	Date	VG	F	VF	EF	Unc
30-06-02	$1	1859	850.	1,100.	1,600.	-	-
30-06-04	$2	1859	850.	1,100.	1,600.	-	-
30-06-06	$4	1859	850.	1,100.	1,600.	-	-
30-06-08	$5	1859	850.	1,100.	1,600.	-	-

8. FULL TINT NUMERALS, PLAIN BACKS

Cat. No.	Denom.	Date	VG	F	VF	EF	Unc
30-08-02	$1	1859	850.	1,100.	1,600.	-	-
30-08-04	$2	1859	850.	1,100.	1,600.	-	-
30-08-06	$4	1859	850.	1,100.	1,600.	-	-
30-08-08	$5	1859	850.	1,100.	1,600.	-	-

505-32   **ISSUE OF 1862**

The branch names were added letterpress across the lower centre in red or blue. Sometimes an additional branch name is added vertically at the ends or across the upper centre.

1. Branch names added across lower centre
   Brantford   Quebec
   London   Toronto

2. Branch names added vertically at ends
   Goderich   Whitby

DESIGNS AND COLOURS

The tint in this issue is greatly reduced from the 1859 issue to become a panel and two counters.

505-32-02
$1 Face Design: Portrait of Queen Victoria/Bank Crest/ reclining woman with produce "Ceres"
Colour: Black with green tint

Back Design: Plain

505-32-04
 $2 Face Design: St. George slaying the dragon/ Victoria and Albert/Bank Crest
 Colour: Black with green tint
 Back Design: Plain

505-32-06
 $5 Face Design: Bank Crest/corner view of head office building/seated blacksmith
 Colour: Black with green tint
 Back Design: Plain

505-32-08
 $10 Face Design: Seated female on dock "Commerce"/ Robert Peel/Bank Crest
 Colour: Black with green tint
 Back Design: Plain

IMPRINT
 American Bank Note Co.

SIGNATURES
 right only
 mss. C.G. Brown
 mss. R. Angus

ISSUE DATING
 Entire date added letterpress:
 1 Aug. 1862

Cat. No.	Denom.	Date	VG	F	VF	EF	Unc
32-02	$1	1862	550.	800.	1,000.	1,600.	-
32-04	$2	1862	950.	1,300.	1,900.	3,200.	-
32-06	$5	1862	950.	1,300.	1,900.	3,200.	-
32-08	$10	1862	950.	1,300.	1,900.	3,200.	-

505-34   **ISSUE OF 1871**
DESIGNS AND COLOURS

505-34-02
 $4 Face Design: R.B. Angus/woman, cherubs and ornate 4/ E.H. King
 Colour: Black with green tint

 Back Design: Lathework, counters and bank name, St. George slaying the dragon
 Colour: Green

505-34-04
 $5 Face Design: Hon. T. Ryan/Britannia, lion and ornate V/ E.H. King
 Colour: Black with green tint
 Back Design: Lathework, counters, bank name and crest
 Colour: Green

THE BANK OF MONTREAL

505-34-06
$10 Face Design: Hon. T. Ryan/cherubs and ornate X/E.H. King
Colour: Black with green tint

Back Design: Lathework, counters, bank name and crest
Colour: Green

505-34-08
$20 Face Design: —/E.H. King/—
Colour: Black with green tint

Back Design: Lathework, counters, bank name and crest
Colour: Green

505-34-10
$50 Face Design: R.B. Angus/allegorical female and ornate L/ E.H. King
Colour: Black with green tint

Back Design: Lathework, counters, bank name and crest
Colour: Green

505-34-12
$100 Face Design: R.B. Angus/"Justice" figure seated in ornate C/E.H. King
Colour: Black with green tint

Back Design: Lathework, counters, bank name and crest
Colour: Green

IMPRINT
British American Bank Note Co. Montreal & Ottawa

SIGNATURES
left
mss. various

right
engr. E.H. King

ISSUE DATING
Engraved
$4: 6th Feby 1871
$5: 2nd Jany 1871
$10: 1st March 1871
$20: 3rd April 1871
$50: 5th May 1871
$100: 6th June 1871

Cat. No.	Denom.	Date	VG	F	VF	EF	Unc
34-02	$4	1871	1,000.	1,500.	-	-	-
34-04	$5	1871	1,100.	1,550.	-	-	-
34-06	$10	1871	1,200.	1,600.	-	-	-
34-08	$20	1871	1,500.	2,000.	-	-	-
34-10	$50	1871	1,500.	2,000.	-	-	-
34-12	$100	1871	1,500.	2,000.	-	-	-

THE BANK OF MONTREAL

505-36 ISSUE OF 1882
DESIGNS AND COLOURS

505-36-02
$5 Face Design: W.J. Buchanan/Britannia, lion and ornate V/C.F. Smithers
Colour: Black with green tint

Back Design: Lathework, counters and bank name, St. George slaying the dragon
Colour: Green

505-36-04
$10 Face Design: Dr. G.W. Campbell/cherubs and ornate X/C.F. Smithers
Colour: Black with green tint

Back Design: Lathework, counters and bank name, St. George slaying the dragon
Colour: Green

505-36-06
$20 Face Design: C.F. Smithers
Colours: Black with green tint

Back Design: Lathework, counters and bank name, St. George slaying the dragon
Colour: Green

IMPRINT
British American Bank Note Co. Montreal
British American Bank Note Co. Monteal & Ottawa

SIGNATURES
left	right
mss. various	engr. C.F. Smithers

ISSUE DATING
Engraved
2nd January 1882
Jany. 2nd 1882

Cat. No.	Denom.	Date	VG	F	VF	EF	Unc
36-02	$5	1882	1,500.	2,100.	-	-	-
36-04	$10	1882	1,400.	1,900.	-	-	-
36-06	$20	1882	1,800.	2,500.	-	-	-

505-38 ISSUE OF 1888
DESIGNS AND COLOURS

505-38-02
$5 Face Design: W.J. Buchanan/Britannia, lion and ornate V/Donald Smith
Colour: Black with green tint

Back Design: Lathework, counters, bank name and crest
Colour: Green

505-38-04
$10 Face Design: Geo. Drummond/cherubs and ornate X/Donald Smith
Colour: Black with green tint

Back Design: Lathework, counters, bank name and crest
Colour: Green

THE BANK OF MONTREAL

IMPRINT
British American Bank Note Co. Montreal

SIGNATURES
left	right
mss. various	engr. Donald Smith

ISSUE DATING
Engraved
Jany. 2nd 1888

Cat. No.	Denom.	Date	VG	F	VF	EF	Unc
38-02	$5	1888	1,200.	1,700.	-	-	-
38-04	$10	1888	1,500.	2,000.	-	-	-

505-40   ISSUE OF 1891

DESIGNS AND COLOURS

505-40-02
$5 Face Design: Edw. Clouston/Bank Crest/Donald Smith
Colour: Black with green tint

Back Design: Lathework, counters, bank name and Toronto branch building
Colour: Green

505-40-04
$10 Face Design: Geo. Drummond/Bank Crest/Donald Smith
Colour: Black with green tint

Back Design: Lathework, counters, bank name and head office
Colour: Green

505-40-06
$20 Face Design: Edw. Clouston/Bank Crest/Donald Smith
Colour: Black with green tint

Back Design: Lathework, counters, bank name and head office
Colour: Green

505-40-08
$50 Face Design: Geo. Drummond/—/Donald Smith
Colour: Black with green tint

THE BANK OF MONTREAL

Back Design: Lathework, counters, bank name and head office
Colour: Green

IMPRINT
American Bank Note Co. N.Y.

SIGNATURES
left
mss. various

right
engr. Donald Smith

ISSUE DATING
Engraved
Jany. 2nd 1891

Cat. No.	Denom.	Date	VG	F	VF	EF	Unc
40-02	$5	1891	1,200.	1,800.	2,700.	-	-
40-04	$10	1891	1,500.	2,100.	2,700.	-	-
40-06	$20	1891	1,500.	2,100.	2,700.	-	-
40-08	$50	1891	1,500.	2,100.	2,700.	-	-

505-42   **ISSUE OF 1892**

DESIGNS AND COLOURS

505-42-04
$50 Face Design: E.S. Clouston/Donald Smith/Bank Crest
Colour: Black with green tint

Back Design: Lathework, counters, bank name and head office
Colour: Green

505-42-08
$100 Face Design: E.S. Clouston/Bank Crest/Donald Smith
Colour: Black with green tint

Back Design: Lathework, counters, bank name and head office between ornate pillars
Colour: Green

IMPRINT
Canada Bank Note Co. Montreal

SIGNATURES
left
mss. various

right
engr. Donald Smith

ISSUE DATING
Engraved
Jan. 2nd, 1892

Cat. No.	Denom.	Date	VG	F	VF	EF	Unc
42-04	$50	1892	2,200.	2,800.	4,000.	-	-
42-08	$100	1892	2,200.	2,800.	4,000.	-	-

Note: $100 proof notes exist with the face tint in gold and the back tint in red-brown.

505-44   **ISSUE OF 1895**

DESIGNS AND COLOURS

505-44-02
$5 Face Design: E.S. Clouston/counter and Bank Crest/Donald Smith
Colour: Black with green tint

THE BANK OF MONTREAL

Back Design: Latheworks, counters, bank name and Toronto branch building
Colour: Green

505-44-04
$10 Face Design: Bank Crest and Donald Smith/—/George Drummond
Colour: Black with green tint

Back Design: Lathework, counters, bank name and head office
Colour: Green

505-44-06
$20 Face Design: Donald Smith/Bank Crest and ornate XX/ E.S. Clouston
Colour: Black with green tint

Back Design: Lathework, counters, bank name and head office
Colour: Green

IMPRINT
British American Bank Note Co. Ottawa

SIGNATURES
left — mss. various
right — engr. Donald Smith

ISSUE DATING
Engraved
Jan. 2nd 1895
Jany. 2nd 1895

Cat. No.	Denom.	Date	VG	F	VF	EF	Unc
44-02	$5	1895	650.	950.	1,400.	-	-
44-04	$10	1895	1,100.	1,600.	2,400.	-	-
44-06	$20	1895	1,100.	1,600.	2,400.	-	-

505-46   "DOUBLE-SIZE" NOTE (19.5 CM. X 16.5 CM.), ISSUE OF 1903

DESIGNS AND COLOURS

505-46-02
$50 Face Design: Donald Smith/Bank Crest/Geo. Drummond
Colour: Black with orange and green tint

274

THE BANK OF MONTREAL

Back Design: Head office/—/Toronto branch
Colour: Black with green

Back Design: —/head office/—
Colour: Black and green

IMPRINT
Waterlow & Sons, Ld. London Wall, London

SIGNATURES
bottom centre	below strathcona
engr. (Donald Smith) Lord Strathcona	mss. various

ISSUE DATING
Engraved
2nd, January, 1903

Cat. No.	Denom.	Date	VG	F	VF	EF	Unc
46-02	$50	1903	5,000.	8,000.	11,000.	-	-
46-04	$100	1903	5,500.	8,500.	12,000.	-	-

505-48   **ISSUE OF 1904**

DESIGNS AND COLOURS

505-46-04
$100 Face Design: Donald Smith/Bank Crest/Geo. Drummond
Colour: Black with gold and rose tint

505-48-02
$5 Face Design: E.S. Clouston/Bank Crest/Geo. Drummond
Colour: Black with olive green tint

Back Design: Lathework, counters, bank name and head office
Colour: Green

275

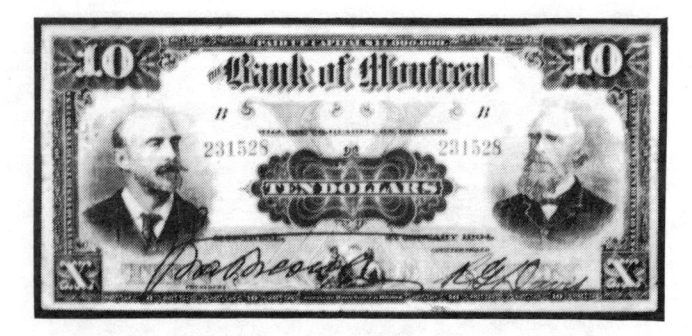

THE BANK OF MONTREAL

505-48-04
$10 Face Design: E.S. Clouston/Bank Crest/Donald Smith
Colour: Black with olive green tint

Back Design: Lathework, counters, bank name and Toronto branch
Colour: Green

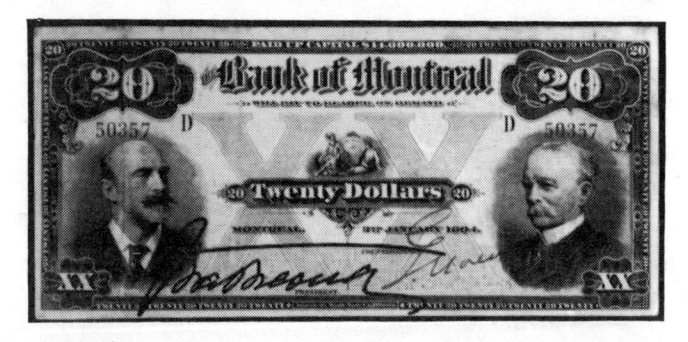

505-48-06
$20 Face Design: E.S. Clouston/Bank Crest/Geo. Drummond
Colour: Black with olive green tint

Back Design: Lathework, counters, bank name and head office
Colour: Green

IMPRINT
American Bank Note Company, Ottawa

SIGNATURES
left	right
typed Donald Smith (as Lord Strathcona)	mss. various

ISSUE DATING
Engraved
2d January 1904
2nd January 1904

Cat. No.	Denom.	Date	VG	F	VF	EF	Unc
48-02	$5	1904	120.	175.	240.	400.	800.
48-04	$10	1904	140.	200.	300.	475.	1,000.
48-06	$20	1904	140.	200.	300.	475.	1,000.

505-50 ISSUE OF 1911
DESIGNS AND COLOURS

505-50-02
$5 Face Design: E.S. Clouston/Bank Crest/R.B. Angus
Colour: Black with olive green tint

Back Design: Lathework, counters, bank name and head office
Colour: Olive green

505-50-04
$20 Face Design: E.S. Clouston/Bank Crest/R.B. Angus
Colour: Black with olive green tint

Back Design: Lathework, counters, bank name and head office
Colour: Olive green

IMPRINT
American Bank Note Company. Ottawa

SIGNATURES
left	right
typed R.B. Angus	mss. various

ISSUE DATING
Engraved
3rd January 1911

Cat. No.	Denom.	Date	VG	F	VF	EF	Unc
50-02	$5	1911	175.	240.	350.	650.	1,150
50-04	$20	1911	200.	300.	450.	800.	1,400

505-52 ISSUE OF 1912
DESIGNS AND COLOURS

505-52-02P
- **$5 Face Design:** Vincent Meredith/Bank Crest/R.B. Angus
  - **Colour:** Black with olive green tint
- **Back Design:** Lathework, counters, bank name and head office
  - **Colour:** Green

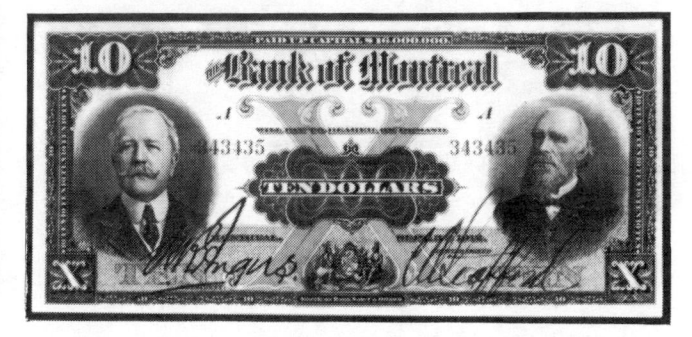

505-52-04
- **$10 Face Design:** Vincent Meredith/Bank Crest/Donald Smith
  - **Colour:** Black with olive green tint
- **Back Design:** Lathework, counters, bank name and Toronto branch
  - **Colour:** Green

505-52-06P
- **$20 Face Design:** Vincent Meredity/Bank Crest/R.B. Angus
  - **Colour:** Black with olive green tint
- **Back Design:** Lathework, counters, bank name and head office
  - **Colour:** Green

505-52-08
- **$50 Face Design:** Vincent Meredith/Bank Crest/Donald Smith
  - **Colour:** Black with olive green tint
- **Back Design:** Lathework, counters, bank name and bank building (Toronto branch)
  - **Colour:** Green

505-52-10
- **$100 Face Design:** Vincent Meredith/Bank Crest/R.B. Angus
  - **Colour:** Black with olive green tint
- **Back Design:** Lathework, counters, bank name and head office 
  - **Colour:** Green

IMPRINT
American Bank Note Company, Ottawa.

SIGNATURES
left	right
typed R.B. Angus	mss. various

ISSUE DATING
Engraved
Sept. 3rd 1912

Cat. No.	Denom.	Date	VG	F	VF	EF	Unc
52-02	$5	1912	175.	250.	400.	600.	1,200.
52-04	$10	1912	240.	325.	500.	850.	1,700.
52-06	$20	1912	225.	400.	550.	900.	2,000.
52-08	$50	1912	375.	500.	700.	1,200.	-
52-10	$100	1912	375.	500.	700.	1,200.	-

THE BANK OF MONTREAL

505-54 ISSUE OF 1914
DESIGNS AND COLOURS

505-54-04
- **$5 Face Design:** Sir Frederick Williams-Taylor/Bank Crest in large V/Vincent Meredith
- **Colour:** Black with olive green tint
- **Back Design:** Lathework, counters, bank name and head office
- **Colour:** Green

505-54-08
- **$10 Face Design:** Sir Frederick Williams-Taylor/Bank Crest under large X/Vincent Meredith
- **Colour:** Black with olive green tint
- **Back Design:** Lathework, counters, bank name and Toronto branch
- **Colour:** Green

505-54-12
- **$20 Face Design:** Sir Frederick Williams-Taylor/Bank Crest between large XX/Vincent Meredith
- **Colour:** Black with olive green tint
- **Back Design:** Lathework, counters, bank name and head office
- **Colour:** Green

505-54-16
- **$50 Face Design:** Sir Frederick Williams-Taylor/Bank Crest under large L/Vincent Meredith
- **Colour:** Black with olive green tint
- **Back Design:** Lathework, counters, bank name and Toronto branch
- **Colour:** Green

505-54-20
- **$100 Face Design:** Sir Frederick Williams-Taylor/Bank Crest inside large C/Vincent Meredith
- **Colour:** Black with olive green tint
- **Back Design:** Lathework, counters, bank name and head office
- **Colour:** Green

IMPRINT
American Bank Note Company, Ottawa
American Bank Note Co. Ottawa

SIGNATURES
left	right
mss. various	typed H.V. Meredith
typed F. Williams-Taylor	typed Vincent Meredith

ISSUE DATING
Engraved
Nov. 3rd 1914

Cat. No.	Denom.	Date	Variety	VG	F	VF	EF	Unc
54-02	$5	1914	Mss. sig., l.	20.	30.	50.	80.	150.
54-04	$5	1914	Typed sig., l.	20.	30.	50.	80.	150.
54-06	$10	1914	Mss. sig., l.	25.	35.	60.	90.	200.
54-08	$10	1914	Typed sig., l.	25.	35.	60.	90.	200.
54-10	$20	1914	Mss. sig., l.	60.	85.	120.	200.	400.
54-12	$20	1914	Typed sig., l.	60.	85.	120.	200.	400.
54-14	$50	1914	Mss. sig., l.	225.	300.	425.	700.	1,500.
54-16	$50	1914	Typed sig., l.	225.	300.	425.	700.	1,500.
54-18	$100	1914	Mss. sig., l.	250.	325.	500.	850.	1,700.
54-20	$100	1914	Typed sig., l.	250.	325.	500.	850.	1,700.

THE BANK OF MONTREAL

505-56   **ISSUE OF 1923**

DESIGNS AND COLOURS
This issue is similar to that of 1914.

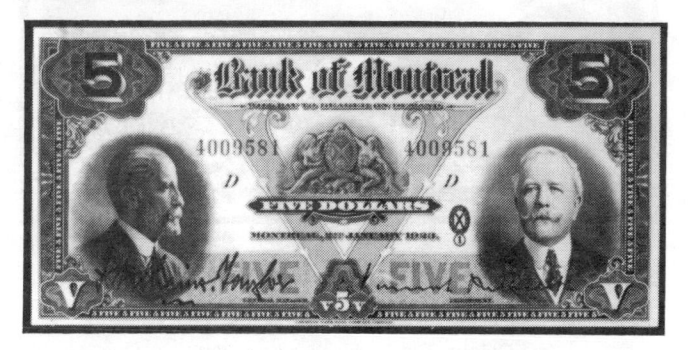

505-56-02
    $5 Face Design: Sir F. Williams-Taylor/Bank Crest, in large V/Vincent Meredith
    Colour: Black with olive green tint

    Back Design: Lathework, counters, bank name and head office
    Colour: Green

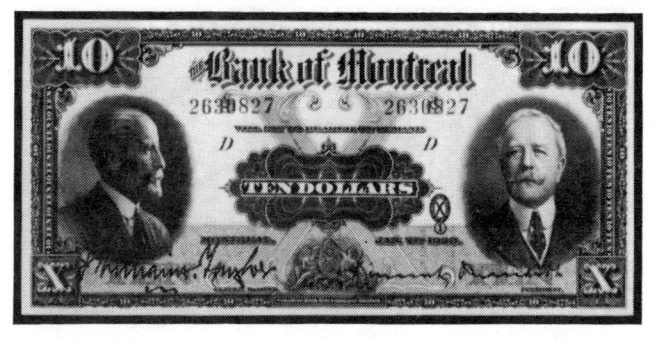

505-56-04
    $10 Face Design: Sir F. Williams-Taylor/Bank Crest under large X/Vincent Meredith
    Colour: Black with olive green tint

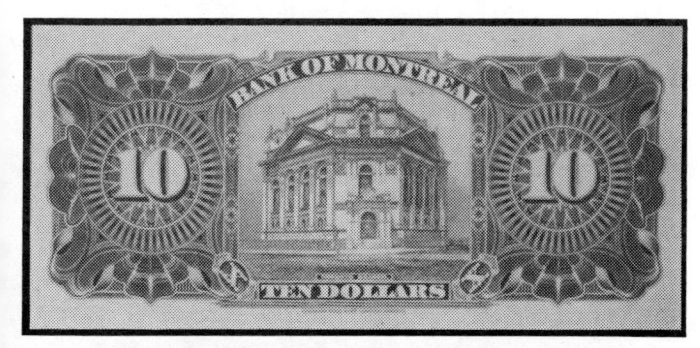

    Back Design: Lathework, counters, bank name, and Toronto branch
    Colour: Green

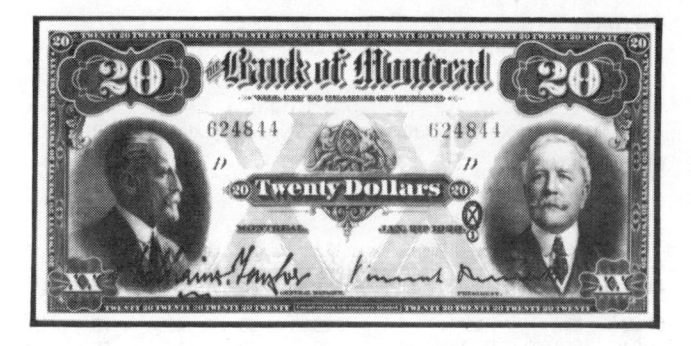

505-56-06
    $20 Face Design: Sir F. Williams-Taylor/Bank Crest between large XX/Vincent Meredith
    Colour: Black with olive green tint

    Back Design: Lathework, counters, bank name and head office
    Colour: Green

505-56-08
    $50 Face Design: Sir F. Williams-Taylor/Bank Crest under large L/Vincent Meredith
    Colour: Black with olive green tint

    Back Design: Lathework, counters, bank name and Toronto branch
    Colour: Green

505-56-10
    $100 Face Design: Sir F. Williams-Taylor/Bank Crest inside large C/Vincent Meredith
    Colour: Black with olive green tint

    Back Design: Lathework, counters, bank name and head office
    Colour: Green

THE BANK OF MONTREAL

IMPRINT
  Canadian Bank Note Company, Limited

SIGNATURES
  left — typed R. Williams-Taylor
  right — typed Vincent Meredith

ISSUE DATING
  Engraved
  2nd January 1923
  Jan. 2nd 1923

Cat. No.	Denom.	Date	VG	F	VF	EF	Unc
56-02	$5	1923	20.	30.	45.	75.	150.
56-04	$10	1923	30.	40.	55.	85.	175.
56-06	$20	1923	40.	55.	75.	120.	275.
56-08	$50	1923	225.	310.	475.	800.	1,600.
56-10	$100	1923	225.	310.	475.	800.	1,600.

505-58 ISSUE OF 1931

DESIGNS AND COLOURS

505-58-02
  $5 Face Design: W.A. Bog/Bank Crest in large V/C.B. Gordon
  Colour: Black with olive green tint

  Back Design: —/head office/—
  Colour: Green

505-58-04
  $10 Face Design: Jackson Dodds/Bank Crest under large X/C.B. Gordon
  Colour: Black with olive green tint

  Back Design: —/Toronto branch/—
  Colour: Green

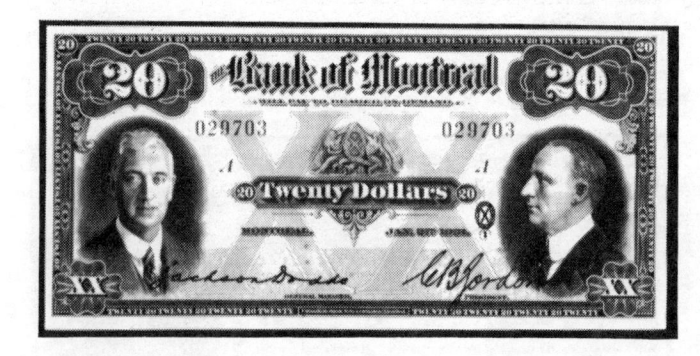

505-58-06
  $20 Face Design: Jackson Dodds/small Bank Crest/C.B. Gordon
  Colour: Black with olive green tint

  Back Design: —/head office/—
  Colour: Green

505-58-08
  $50 Face Design: Jackson Dodds/small Bank Crest/C.B. Gordon
  Colour: Black with olive green tint

  Back Design: Lathework, counters, bank name and Toronto branch
  Colour: Green

THE BANK OF MONTREAL

505-58-10
$100 Face Design: W.A. Bog/small Bank Crest/C.B. Gordon
Colour: Black with olive green tint
Back Design: Lathework, counters, bank name and head office
Colour: Green

IMPRINT
Canadian Bank Note Company, Limited

SIGNATURES
left	right
typed W.A. Bog	typed C.B. Gordon
typed Jackson Dodds	typed C.B. Gordon

ISSUE DATING
Engraved
2nd January 1931
Jan. 2nd 1931

Cat. No.	Denom.	Date	VG	F	VF	EF	Unc
58-02	$5	1931	20.	30.	40.	70.	130.
58-04	$10	1931	25.	40.	60.	90.	175.
58-06	$20	1931	60.	100.	150.	200.	300.
58-08	$50	1931	115.	160.	225.	375.	800.
58-10	$100	1931	140.	200.	320.	525.	1,000.

505-60   **FIRST SMALL-SIZE NOTE, ISSUE 1935**

DESIGNS AND COLOURS

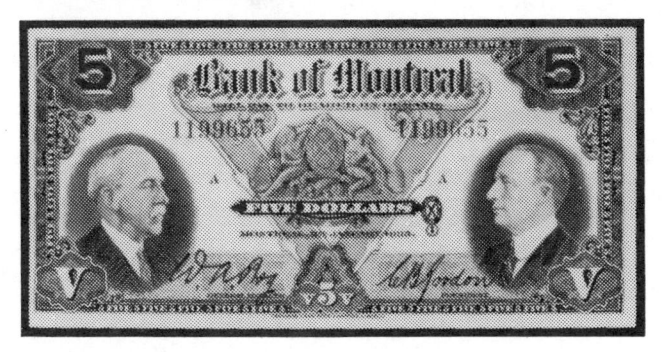

505-60-02
$5 Face Design: W.A. Bog/Bank Crest/C.B. Gordon
Colour: Black with olive green tint
Back Design: Lathework, counters, bank name and head office
Colour: Green

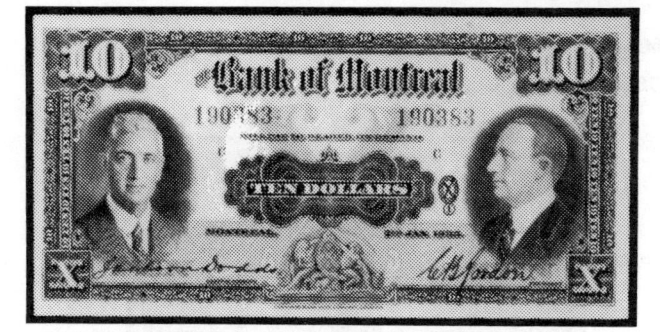

505-60-04
$10 Face Design: Jackson Dodds/small Bank Crest/C.B. Gordon
Colour: Black with olive green tint

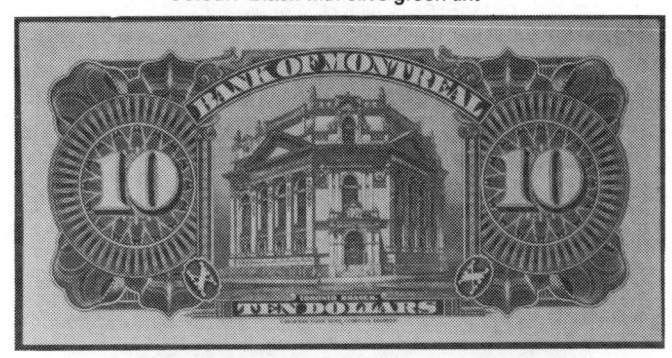

Back Design: Lathework, counters, bank name and Toronto branch
Colour: Green

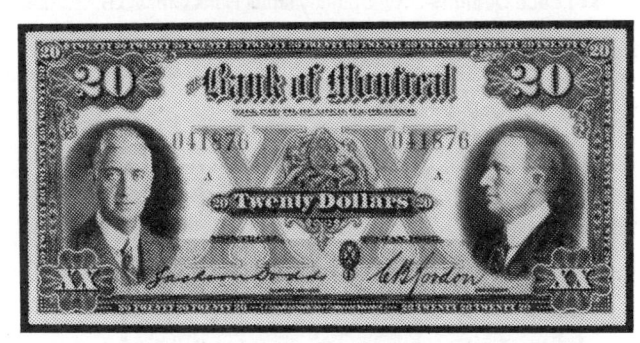

505-60-06
$20 Face Design: Jackson Dodds/Bank Crest/C.B. Gordon
Colour: Black with olive green tint
Back Design: Lathework, counters, bank name and head office
Colour: Green

IMPRINT
Canadian Bank Note Company

SIGNATURES
left	right
typed W.A. Bog	typed C.B. Gordon
typed Jackson Dodds	typed C.B. Gordon

ISSUE DATING
Engraved
2nd Jan. 1935
2nd January 1935

Cat. No.	Denom.	Date	F	VF	EF	Unc
60-02	$5	1935	18.	25.	45.	80.
60-04	$10	1935	25.	35.	60.	100.
60-06	$20	1935	35.	45.	75.	110.

THE BANK OF MONTREAL

505-62   ISSUE OF 1938
DESIGNS AND COLOURS

505-62-02
- **$5 Face Design:** Jackson Dodds/Bank Crest/C.B. Gordon
- **Colour:** Black with olive green tint
- **Back Design:** Lathework, counters, bank name and head office
- **Colour:** Green

505-62-04
- **$10 Face Design:** G.W. Spinney/small Bank Crest/C.B. Gordon
- **Colour:** Black with olive green tint
- **Back Design:** Lathework, counters, bank name and Toronto branch
- **Colour:** Green

505-62-06
- **$20 Face Design:** G.W. Spinney/Bank Crest/C.B. Gordon
- **Colour:** Black with olive green tint
- **Back Design:** Lathework, counters, bank name and head office
- **Colour:** Green

IMPRINT
Canadian Bank Company Limited

SIGNATURES

left	right
typed Jackson Dodds	typed C.B. Gordon
typed G.W. Spinney	typed C.B. Gordon

ISSUE DATING
Engraved
3rd January 1938
3rd Jan. 1938

Cat. No.	Denom.	Date	F	VF	EF	Unc
62-02	$5	1938	18.	25.	45.	80.
62-04	$10	1938	25.	35.	60.	90.
62-06	$20	1938	30.	40.	55.	90.

505-64   ISSUE OF 1942
DESIGNS AND COLOURS

505-64-02
- **$5 Face Design:** B.C. Gardner/Bank Crest/G.W. Spinney
- **Colour:** Black with olive green tint
- **Back Design:** Lathework, counters, bank name and head office
- **Colour:** Green

IMPRINT
Canadian Bank Note Company, Limited

SIGNATURES

left	right
typed B.C. Gardner	typed G.W. Spinney

ISSUE DATING
Engraved
7th December 1942

Cat. No.	Denom.	Date	VG	F	VF	EF	Unc
64-02	$5	1942	18.	25.	40.	65.	120.

LA BANQUE NATIONALE

1860-1925

QUEBEC CITY, QUEBEC

BANK NUMBER 510   **REDEEMABLE**

La Banque Nationale was founded in 1860 with 1,456 shareholders, all with the double liability on the existing 30,000 shares. After World War I, the bank appeared to be failing, despite the fact that it had 230,000 customers, $6 million in circulating notes and over $40 million in deposits. Rather than declaring bankruptcy, an attempt was made to merge La Banque Nationale, La Banque d'Hochelaga and the Provincial Bank. The Provincial Bank declined, the directors of the other two banks asked the premier of Quebec for assistance.

On January 31, 1924, the Legislative Council granted a $15-million provincial bond to assist the merger. It was sanctioned by the Lieutenant-Governor on February 15, 1924.

The merged banks were to be given 40 years to reimburse the bonds. La Banque d'Hochelaga was to assume the liabilities of La Banque Nationale, as well as its assets, and in February 1925 the two banks formally merged under the name La Banque Canadienne Nationale.

Despite the market crash and the depression of the 1930s, the new bank was able to reimburse the government in 20 years, half the time originally allotted.

510-10   **ISSUE OF 1860**

DESIGNS AND COLOURS

510-10-04-04
     $1 Face Design: Habitant/Arms of Quebec City/ Jacques Cartier
     Colour: Black with overall green tint
     Back Design: Plain

510-10-04-08
     $2 Face Design: Two allegorical women, "The Reapers"/ Arms of Quebec City/ bust of Jacques Cartier in oval
     Colour: Black with overall green tint
     Back Design: Plain

510-10-04-10
     $5 Face Design: Agricultural implements/two men ploughing/ young woman with cornucopia
     Colour: Black with overall green tint
     Back Design: Plain

510-10-04-12
     $10 Face Design: St. John the Baptist/train/ Britannia, Arms of Upper Canada
     Colour: Black with overall green tint
     Back Design: Plain

IMPRINT
     American Bank Note Company

SIGNATURES
     left   **right**
     mss. various   mss. various

2.   **PARTIALLY ENGRAVED DATE, MSS. SHEET NUMBERS**

ISSUE DATING
     Partially engraved ___ 18___:
     28 Avril 1860

Cat. No.	Denom.	Date	VG	F	VF	EF	Unc
10-02-02	$1	1860	800.	1,000.	1,400.	2,200.	-
10-02-04	$2	1860	800.	1,000.	1,400.	2,200.	-
10-02-06	$5	1860	900.	1,200.	1,600.	2,400.	-
10-02-08	$10	1860	900.	1,200.	1,600.	2,400.	-

LA BANQUE NATIONALE

4. ENGRAVED DATE, PRINTED SHEET NUMBERS

ISSUE DATING
Engraved
28 Avril 1860
25 Mai 1860

OVERPRINT
$10: "G G" twice at ends and "OTTAWA" twice vertically in red
$1: Red A at top right

Note: Prices listed are for punch-cancelled notes or for those cancelled with a large X. Notes not punch cancelled or without pen cancellation probably command a 25 to 50 percent premium.

Cat. No.	Denom.	Date	Variety	VG	F	VF	EF	Unc
10-04-02	$1	1860	Avril	500.	600.	800.	1,300.	-
10-04-04	$1	1860	Mai	600.	800.	1,000.	1,500.	-
10-04-06	$2	1860	Avril	600.	800.	1,100.	1,600.	-
10-04-08	$2	1860	Mai	1,000.	1,100.	1,500.	2,200.	-
10-04-10	$5	1860	Avril	1,000.	1,100.	1,500.	2,200.	-
10-04-12	$10	1860	Avril	1,000.	1,100.	1,500.	2,200.	-

510-12 ISSUES OF 1870 AND 1871

DESIGNS AND COLOURS

510-12-02
  $4 Face Design: Beehive and flowers/
    paddlewheel steamer "Quebec"/
    sailor leaning on sail, "Charlies Sailor"
  Colour: Black with green tint

  Back Design: Lathework, counters and bank name
  Colour: Green

510-12-06
  $6 Face Design: Woman teaching granddaughter
    to knit "The first lesson"/
    girl watering livestock "Vogts cattle"/
    Samuel de Champlain
  Colour: Black with green tint

  Back Design: Lathework, counters and bank name
  Colour: Green

510-12-08
  $20 Face Design: Farmer feeding horses "Old Burhans"/
    Crest/boy climbing rigging "Going Aloft"
  Colour: Black with green tint

  Back Design: Lathework, counters and bank name
  Colour: Green

510-12-10
  $50 Face Design: Farmer with cornstalks/reclining female with
    water jar, Niagara Falls "Power"/
    "Agriculture" figure
  Colour: Black with green tint

  Back Design: Lathework, counters and bank name
  Colour: Green

510-12-12
$100 **Face Design:** —/sailors looking to sea "Coast scene"/—
Colour: Black with green tint

Back Design: Lathework, counters and bank name
Colour: Green

IMPRINT
British American Bank Note Co. Montreal & Ottawa

SIGNATURES
	left	right
$4 and $6:	none	mss. various
$20, $50 and $100:	none	mss. R. Audette

ISSUE DATING
Engraved
28 Mai 1870
28 Mai 1871
2 Octobre 1871

OVERPRINT
$4 and $6: "SHERBROOKE" in red
"OTTAWA" in red
"M M" in red

$20, $50 and $100: "XX XX" vertically in black

Note: See "note" on 1860 issues.

Cat. No.	Denom.	Date	VG	F	VF	EF	Unc
12-02	$4	1870	700.	1,000.	1,300.	2,100.	-
12-04S	$4	1871			SPECIMEN		1,000.
12-06	$6	1870	4,000.	6,000.	-	-	-
12-08	$20	1871	1,200.	1,500.	2,200.	4,000.	-
12-10	$50	1871	1,200.	1,500.	2,200.	4,000.	-
12-12	$100	1871	1,400.	1,800.	2,500.	3,900.	-

510-14   **ISSUE OF 1873**
DESIGNS AND COLOURS

510-14-02
$5 **Face Design:** Agricultural produce and implements/ shipbuilders at work "Ship Building"/ Britannia and 5 counter
Colour: Black with green tint

Back Design: Lathework, counters and bank name
Colour: Green

510-14-04P
$10 **Face Design:** St. John the Baptist/agricultural produce and implements/anchor
Colour: Black with green tint

Back Design: Lathework, counters and bank name
Colour: Green

LA BANQUE NATIONALE

IMPRINT
British American Bank Note Co. Montreal & Ottawa

SIGNATURES
left	right
none	mss. Ol. Robitaille

ISSUE DATING
Engraved
2 Janvier 1873

Note: See "note" of 1860 issues, 10-04.

Cat. No.	Denom.	Date	VG	F	VF	EF	Unc
14-02	$5	1873	900.	1,160.	1,650.	2,800.	-
14-04	$10	1873	900.	1,160.	1,650.	2,800.	-

510-16   ISSUE OF 1883

DESIGNS AND COLOURS

510-16-02
$5 Face Design: Samuel de Champlain/paddlewheel steamer "Quebec"/J.R. Thibaudeau
Colour: Black with green tint

Back Design: Lathework, counters and bank name
Colour: Green

510-16-04
$10 Face Design: Jacques Cartier/farmer ploughing/J.R. Thibaudeau
Colour: Black with green tint

Back Design: Lathework, counters and bank name
Colour: Green

IMPRINT
British American Bank Note Co. Montreal

SIGNATURES
left	right
mss. various	engr. J. Thibaudeau

ISSUE DATING
Engraved
1er Mars 1883

OVERPRINT
"A D" twice in red

Cat. No.	Denom.	Date	VG	F	VF	EF	Unc
16-02	$5	1883	1,000.	1,300.	1,900.	-	-
16-04	$10	1883	1,000.	1,300.	1,900.	-	-

510-18   ISSUE OF 1891

DESIGNS AND COLOURS

510-18-02
$5 Face Design: Samuel de Champlain/train/A. Gaboury
Colour: Black with green tint

Back Design: Lathework, counters, bank name and the Arms of the City of Quebec
Colour: Green

510-18-04
$10 Face Design: Jacques Cartier/farmer ploughing/A. Gaboury
Colour: Black with green tint

Back Design: Lathework, counters, bank name and the Arms of the City of Quebec
Colour: Green

IMPRINT
British American Bank Note Co. Montreal

SIGNATURES
left	right
mss. various	engr. A. Gaboury

ISSUE DATING
Engraved
Le 2 Janvier 1891

OVERPRINT
"A D" twice in red
"R" twice in red
"P" twice in blue

Cat. No.	Denom.	Date	VG	F	VF	EF	Unc
18-02	$5	1891	1,000.	1,300.	1,900.	-	-
18-04	$10	1891	1,000.	1,300.	1,900.	-	-

510-20 ISSUE OF 1897
DESIGNS AND COLOURS

510-20-02
$5 Face Design: Samuel de Champlain/train/ Britannia standing by globe and flag
Colour: Black with orange tint (tends to oxidize to brown or yellow)

Back Design: Lathework, counters, bank name and the Arms of the City of Quebec
Colour: Green

510-20-06
$10 Face Design: Jacques Cartier/farmer ploughing/ Queen Victoria in "widow's weeds"
Colour: Black with orange tint (tends to oxidize to brown or yellow)

Back Design: Lathework, counters, bank name and the Arms of the City of Quebec
Colour: Green

IMPRINT
British American Bank Note Co. Montreal

SIGNATURES
left — mss. various
right — engr. R. Audette

ISSUE DATING
Engraved
Le 2 Janvier 1897

VARIETIES
Both denominations were initally printed from rather poorly engraved plates and later from greatly improved plates. Apart from the obvious difference in the the quality of the engraving, there are numerous subtle differences.

The first plate lacks the acute accent over the first E of PRESIDENT at the lower-right signature space and has thin date figures. The second plate includes the accent in PRESIDENT and has thick date figures. The characteristic by which the varieties can be most easily identified is the presence of engraved lines below the sheet numbers on the poorly engraved plate and the absence of such lines on the well-engraved plate.

- **$5:** lines under sheet numbers
- **$5:** no lines under sheet numbers, accent over E
- **$10:** lines under sheet numbers
- **$10:** no lines under sheet numbers, accent over E

Note: Back proofs exist in green, as well as in brown tints.

Cat. No.	Denom.	Date	Variety	VG	F	VF	EF	Unc
20-02	$5	1897	Lines	250.	325.	500.	900.	-
20-04	$5	1897	No lines	200.	275.	400.	700.	-
20-06	$10	1897	Lines	300.	425.	600.	1,100.	-
20-08	$10	1897	No lines	300.	325.	500.	900.	-

510-22 ISSUE OF 1922
DESIGNS AND COLOURS

510-22-02
$5 Face Design: Monument/—/Geo. E. Amyot
Colour: Black with olive tint

Back Design: Lathework, counters, bank name and the Arms of the City of Quebec
Colour: Green

LA BANQUE NATIONALE

510-22-04S
$10 Face Design: Cartier sighting land/—/Geo. E. Amyot
Colour: Black with orange tint

Back Design: Lathework, counters, bank name and the Arms of the City of Quebec
Colour: Green

510-22-06S
$20 Face Design: "Quebec Citadel"/—/Geo. E. Amyot
Colour: Black with orange tint

Back Design: Lathework, counters, bank name and the Arms of the City of Quebec
Colour: Green

510-22-08S
$50 Face Design: —/Geo. E. Amyot/—
Colour: Black with brown tint

Back Design: Lathework, counters, bank name and the Arms of the City of Quebec
Colour: Green

510-22-10S
$100 Face Design: —/—/Geo. E. Amyot
Colour: Black with brown tint

Back Design: Lathework, counters, bank name and the Arms of the City of Quebec
Colour: Green

IMPRINT
British American Bank Note Co. Limited
British American Bank Note Co. Limited, Ottawa

SIGNATURES
left	right
typed H. des Rivieres	engr. Geo. E. Amyot

ISSUE DATING
Engraved
Le 2 Novembre 1922

Cat. No.	Denom.	Date	VG	F	VF	EF	Unc
22-02	$5	1922	1,100.	1,500.	2,200.	-	-
22-04S	$10	1922			SPECIMEN		350.
22-06	$20	1922	1,600.	2,100.	3,300.	-	-
22-08S	$50	1922			SPECIMEN		350.
22-10S	$100	1922			SPECIMEN		350.

THE BANK OF NEW BRUNSWICK

1820-1913

SAINT JOHN, NEW BRUNSWICK

BANK NUMBER 515   **REDEEMABLE**

The Bank of New Brunswick was established in 1820 in Saint John, New Brunswick. The first bank in Canada to operate under a charter, it started business with an initial capital of œ50,000, and its charter was for 20 years. The bank's total liabilities were restricted to twice the paid-up capital, instead of three times, as in the other provinces.

The bank absorbed the City Bank, Saint John, in 1839 and the Summerside Bank in 1901, but remained a small institution. Its expansion was hindered by difficulties in raising more capital, and the directors offered to sell out to the Bank of Nova Scotia. This offer was accepted in 1913.

515-10   **PERKINS FAIRMAN HEATH**
1820-1832
POUNDS AND SHILLINGS PRINTINGS
LARGE SIZE NOTES
(10 CM. X 18.5 CM.)

DESIGNS AND COLOURS

Note: All the notes up to and including 1884 have two cherubs, a cask and a bale at the bottom.

515-10-02
- **5s Face Design:** Small Britannia in lathework/seated Brittania flanked by women and cherubs/—
- **Colour:** Black with green tint

- **Back Design:** Two women's heads on lathework circles/cherubs, cask and bale twice/two women's heads on lathework circles
- **Colour:** Blue

515-10-14
- **£1 Face Design:** Small Britannia in lathework/seated Brittania flanked by women and cherubs/—
- **Colour:** Black with no tint

- **Back Design:** Two women's heads on lathework circles/cherubs, cask and bale twice/two women's heads on lathework circles
- **Colour:** Blue

515-10-24P
- **£2 Face Design:** Small Britannia in lathework/seated Brittania flanked by women and cherubs, two cherubs, casks and bale below/—
- **Colour:** Black with no tint

- **Back Design:** Two women's heads on lathework circles/cherubs, cask and bale twice/two women's heads on lathework circles
- **Colour:** Blue

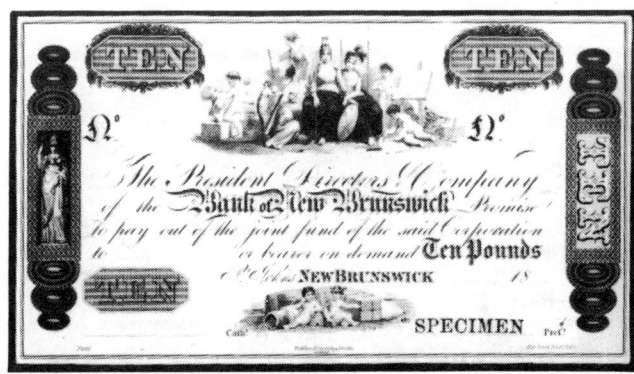

515-10-34P
- **£2 Face Design:** Small Britannia in lathework/seated Brittania flanked by women and cherubs, two cherubs, casks and bale below/—
- **Colour:** Black with no tint

- **Back Design:** Two women's heads on lathework circles/cherubs, cask and bale twice/two women's heads on lathework circles
- **Colour:** Blue

THE BANK OF NEW BRUNSWICK

IMPRINT
　Perkins, Fairman & Heath London

SIGNATURES
	left	right
1820:	mss. H.H. Carmichael	mss. John Robinson
1831:	mss. Z. Wheeler	mss. H. Gilbert

ISSUE DATING
　Partially engraved ___ 18___:
　1820: 26 Dec.
　1831: 1 Jany.
　1832: 1 Octr.

Cat. No.	Denom.	Date	VG	F	VF	EF	Unc
10-02	5s	1820	1,400.	1,800.	-	-	-
10-14	£1	1831	1,400.	1,800.	-	-	-
10-24	£2	1832	1,400.	1,800.	-	-	-
10-34P	£10	18_			FACE PROOF		400.

515-12　　NEBN CO. 1838 - 1859
POUNDS AND SHILLINGS PRINTINGS
REGULAR-SIZE NOTES
(7.2 CM. X 17 CM.)

DESIGNS AND COLOURS

515-12-12
　5s Face Design: Small Britannia in lathework/seated Brittania flanked by women and cherubs, two cherubs, casks and bale below/—
　Colour: Black with no tint
　Back Design: Two women's heads on lathework circles/cherubs, cask and bale twice/two women's heads on lathework circles
　Colour: Blue

515-12-22
　£1 Face Design: Small Britannia in lathework/seated Brittania flanked by women and cherubs, two cherubs, casks and bale below/—
　Colour: Black with no tint
　Back Design: Two women's heads on lathework circles/cherubs, cask and bale twice/two women's heads on lathework circles
　Colour: Blue

515-12-32
　£2 Face Design: Small Britannia in lathework/seated Brittania flanked by women and cherubs, two cherubs, casks and bale below/—
　Colour: Black with no tint
　Back Design: Two women's heads on lathework circles/cherubs, cask and bale twice/two women's heads on lathework circles
　Colour: Blue

515-12-42
　£5 Face Design: Small Britannia in lathework/seated Brittania flanked by women and cherubs, two cherubs, casks and bale below/—
　Colour: Black with no tint
　Back Design: Two women's heads on lathework circles/cherubs, cask and bale twice/two women's heads on lathework circles
　Colour: Blue

515-12-50
　£10 Face Design: Small Britannia in lathework/seated Brittania flanked by women and cherubs, two cherubs, casks and bale below/—
　Colour: Black with no tint
　Back Design: Two women's heads on lathework circles/cherubs, cask and bale twice/two women's heads on lathework circles
　Colour: Blue

THE BANK OF NEW BRUNSWICK

515-12-60
- **£25 Face Design:** Small Britannia in lathework/seated Brittania flanked by women and cherubs, two cherubs, casks and bale below/—
- **Colour:** Black with no tint
- **Back Design:** Two women's heads on lathework circles/ cherubs, cask and bale twice/two women's heads on lathework circles
- **Colour:** Blue

IMPRINT
New England Bank Note Co. Boston
New England Bank Note Co. Boston and ABN Co. Logo

SIGNATURES
left	right
mss. illegible	mss. J.D. Lewin

ISSUE DATING
Partially engraved___ 18___:
- **1838:** Sept. 14
- **1845:** 1 Oct.
- **1849:** June 1, Sept. 1
- **1852:** 1 July
- **1860:** Novr. 1
- **1853:** July 1, Oct. 1
- **1856:** 1 Oct.
- **1858:** Dec. 1
- **1859:** 1 Oct.

PROTECTOR
- **5s, 1858-1859:** Red "ONE DOLLAR" on face only
- **£25, 1860:** Red "ONE HUNDRED DOLLARS" on face only

Note: All known £5 issued notes that were dated and signed are counterfeit.

Cat. No.	Denom.	Date Variety	VG	F	VF	EF	Unc
12-02	5s	1849-56 No ptr.	1,400.	1,800.	-	-	-
12-12	5s	1849-56 Red ptr.	1,400.	1,800.	-	-	-
12-22	£1	1845-52	1,400.	1,800.	-	-	-
12-32P	£2	18_			PROOF		400.
12-42	£5	1838	150.	200.	-	-	-
12-50P	£10	18_			PROOF		400.
12-60	£25	1860	2,000.	2,800.	-	-	-
Full Sheet	£1,2,5,10	18_			PROOF		2,000.

515-14 DOLLAR ISSUES OF 1860-1884

Counters at top
- **A:** Have $ no. and words
- **B:** Have $ no. and $ no.
- **C:** Have words and $ no.

DESIGNS AND COLOURS

515-14-02

515-14-10
- **$1 Face Design:** Small Britannia in lathework/seated Brittania flanked by women and cherubs, two cherubs, casks and bale below/—
- **Colour:** Black with green tint
- **Back Design:** Two women's heads on lathework circles/ cherubs, cask and bale twice/two women's heads on lathework circles
- **Colour:** Blue

515-14-14P
- **$2 Face Design:** Small Britannia in lathework/seated Brittania flanked by women and cherubs, two cherubs, casks and bale below/—
- **Colour:** Black with green tint
- **Back Design:** Two women's heads on lathework circles/ cherubs, cask and bale twice/two women's heads on lathework circles
- **Colour:** Blue

515-14-18

THE BANK OF NEW BRUNSWICK

515-14-22
- **$5 Face Design:** Small Britannia in lathework/seated Brittania flanked by women and cherubs, two cherubs, casks and bale below/—
- **Colour:** Black with green tint
- **Back Design:** Two women's heads on lathework circles/cherubs, cask and bale twice/two women's heads on lathework circles
- **Colour:** Blue

515-14-38P
- **$10 Face Design:** Small Britannia in lathework/seated Brittania flanked by women and cherubs, two cherubs, casks and bale below/—
- **Colour:** Black with green tint
- **Back Design:** Two women's heads on lathework circles/cherubs, cask and bale twice/two women's heads on lathework circles
- **Colour:** Blue

515-14-42
- **$20 Face Design:** Small Britannia in lathework/seated Brittania flanked by women and cherubs, two cherubs, casks and bale below/—
- **Colour:** Black with green tint

- **Back Design:** Two women's heads on lathework circles/cherubs, cask and bale twice/two women's heads on lathework circles
- **Colour:** Blue

515-14-54
- **$50 Face Design:** Small Britannia in lathework/seated Brittania flanked by women and cherubs, two cherubs, casks and bale below/—
- **Colour:** Black with green tint
- **Back Design:** Two women's heads on lathework circles/cherubs, cask and bale twice/two women's heads on lathework circles
- **Colour:** Blue

Photo Not Available

515-14-58
- **$100 Face Design:** Small Britannia in lathework/seated Brittania flanked by women and cherubs, two cherubs, casks and bale below/—
- **Colour:** Black with green tint
- **Back Design:** Two women's heads on lathework circles/cherubs, cask and bale twice/two women's heads on lathework circles
- **Colour:** Blue

IMPRINT
American Bank Note Co. Boston

SIGNATURES

	left	right
1860-1863:	mss. Tho. A. Sancton	mss. J.D. Lewin
	mss. W. Girvan	mss. J.D. Lewin
$1 & $5, 1868:	engr. J.D. Lewin	mss. various
$1 & $2, 1868:	mss	engr. J.D. Lewin
$20, 1868:	engr. J.D. Lewin	mss. various
	mss. A. McDonald	typed James Manchester
1880:	engr. J.D. Lewin	mss. various

THE BANK OF NEW BRUNSWICK

ISSUE DATING
  Engraved
  November 1st 1860
  July 1st 1863
  Sept. 1st 1868
  July 1, 1880
  Jan. 1, 1884

STAMP
  $5, 1860: "$5" in red at right

Note: The counters at the top right and left are different on the 1860 $1 and $5 notes. Most of the later issues seem to have both counters at the top as numerals, except the $10 of 1880.

Cat. No.	Denom.	Date	Variety	VG	F	VF	EF	Unc
14-02	$1	1860		1,500.	2,000.	-	-	-
14-06	$1	1863		1,500.	2,000.	-	-	-
14-10	$1	1868		1,500.	2,000.	-	-	-
14-14P	$2	1868				FACE PROOF		400.
14-18	$5	1860		1,500.	2,000.	-	-	-
14-22	$5	1863		1,500.	2,000.	-	-	-
14-26	$5	1868		1,500.	2,000.	-	-	-
14-30P	$5	1884				FACE PROOF		400.
14-34	$10	1860		1,500.	2,000.	-	-	-
14-38P	$10	1880				FACE PROOF		400.
14-42	$20	1860		1,700.	2,200.	-	-	-
14-46	$20	1868	Lewin, l.	1,700.	2,200.	-	-	-
14-50	$20	1868	Mnchstr, r.	1,700.	2,200.	-	-	-
14-54	$50	1860		1,700.	2,200.	-	-	-
14-58	$100	1860		1,700.	2,200.	-	-	-

Note: Proof sheets in ABN archive sale. $1 (1868), $1 (1868), $5 (1884), $5 (1885), $10 (1880), $20 (1868), $50 (1860)

515-16   ISSUE OF 1892

DESIGNS AND COLOURS

515-16-02
  $5 Face Design: J.S. Lewin/seated Britannia flanked by women and cherubs/Griffin over Bank Crest
  Colour: Black with green and yellow tint

  Back Design: —/bank building/—
  Colour: Blue

515-16-06
  $10 Face Design: Sailor beside Provincial Crest/ seated Britannia flanked by women and cherubs/J.S. Lewin
  Colour: Black with green and yellow tint

  Back Design: —/bank building/—
  Colour: Green

IMPRINT
  American Bank Note Co. New York

SIGNATURES
  left   **right**
  mss. J. Clawson   mss. J.D. Lewin

ISSUE DATING
  Engraved
  March 25th 1892

PROTECTOR
  Some $5 notes: "V V" in red on face only
  Some $10 notes: "X X" in red on face only

Cat. No.	Denom.	Date	Variety	VG	F	VF	EF	Unc
16-02	$5	1892	No ptr.	1,500.	2,000.	3,000.	-	-
16-04	$5	1892	Red ptr.	1,600.	2,100.	3,100.	-	-
16-06	$10	1892	No ptr.	1,600.	2,100.	3,100.	-	-
16-08	$10	1892	Red ptr.	1,700.	2,200.	3,200.	-	-

515-18   ISSUES OF 1903-1906

DESIGNS AND COLOURS

515-18-02
  $5 Face Design: James Manchester/view of St. John/ Griffin over Bank Crest
  Colour: Black with yellow-green and rose tint

  Back Design: —/head office/—
  Colour: Green

515-18-08
  $10 Face Design: Sailor beside Provincial Crest/seated Britannia flanked by women and cherubs/ James Manchester
  Colour: Black with yellow-green and green tint

THE BANK OF NEW BRUNSWICK

Back Design: —/head office/—
Colour: Olive

515-18-12
$20 Face Design: James Manchester/ woman seated by casks and bale/Bank Crest
Colour: Black with blue tint

Back Design: —/head office/—
Colour: Blue

515-18-16
$50 Face Design: Seated "Commerce" figure and cornucopia/Bank Crest/James Manchester
Colour: Black with green tint

Back Design: —/head office/—
Colour: Green

IMPRINT
American Bank Note Co. Ottawa

SIGNATURES
left	right
mss. various	typed James Manchester

ISSUE DATING
Engraved
1st September 1903
2nd January 1904
2nd January 1906

VARIETIES
Left signature space is labelled "MANAGER."
Left signature space is labelled "FOR GENERAL MANAGER."

Cat. No.	Denom.	Date	Variety	VG	F	VF	EF	Unc
18-02	$5	1904	Manager	1,500.	2,000.	3,000.	-	-
18-04	$5	1904	Gen. Mgr.	1,500.	2,000.	3,000.	-	-
18-06	$10	1903	Manager	1,500.	2,000.	3,000.	-	-
18-08	$10	1903	Gen. Mgr.	1,500.	2,000.	3,000.	-	-
18-10	$20	1906	Manager	2,000.	2,500.	-	-	-
18-12	$20	1906	Gen. Mgr.	2,000.	2,500.	-	-	-
18-14	$50	1906	Manager	2,000.	2,500.	-	-	-
18-16	$50	1906	Gen. Mgr.	2,000.	2,500.	-	-	-

THE NEWCASTLE BANKING COMPANY

1836

AMHERST, NEWCASTLE DISTRICT, UPPER CANADA

BANK NUMBER 520   **NONREDEEMABLE**

This bank was established in 1836 at Amherst, Upper Canada, as a private institution. It issued notes, but its application for a charter was refused.

520-10 . ISSUE OF 1836

This issue was in reality a post note. The notes were not convertible into specie until a year after the issue date. They were typographed.

DESIGNS AND COLOURS

520-10-01
 $1 (5s) Face Design: —/Plough and cattle/—
  Colour: Black with no tint
 Back Design: Plain

520-10-02
 $2 (10s) Face Design: —/sheaves of wheat and agricultural implements/—
  Colour: Black with no tint
 Back Design: Plain

520-10-04
 $4 (20s) Face Design: —/seated woman with agricultural implements and produce/—
  Colour: Black with no tint
 Back Design: Plain

IMPRINT
 None

SIGNATURES
 left   right
 none   mss. Wm. Bancks

ISSUE DATING
 Partially engraved ___ 18___:
  1836: 20th January
   15th February

Cat. No.	Denom.	Date	VG	F	VF	EF	Unc
10-01	$1	1836	350.	475.	700.	1,150.	-
10-02	$2	1836	350.	475.	700.	1,150.	-
10-04	$4	1836	425.	575.	850.	1,400.	-

THE NEWCASTLE DISTRICT LOAN COMPANY

1836

PETERBOROUGH, UPPER CANADA

BANK NUMBER 525 **NONREDEEMABLE**

525-10 ISSUE OF 1836

These were post notes, payable 12 months after the issue date.

DESIGNS AND COLOURS

525-10-02R
- **$1 (5s) Face Design:** Naval figure/seated "Agriculture" figure; beaver below/allegorical female, anchor
- **Colour:** Black with no tint
- **Back Design:** Plain

525-10-04
- **$2 (10s) Face Design:** King William IV; man with cradle cutting grain/reclining woman, flowers; arm and hammer below/—
- **Colour:** Black with no tint
- **Back Design:** Plain

525-10-06
- **$4 (20s, £1) Face Design:** Men, cattle and sheep/ King William IV on Royal Crest; ship, cask and bale below/ blacksmith with tools
- **Colour:** Black with no tint
- **Back Design:** Plain

525-10-08
- **$10 (50s) Face Design:** Men, cattle and sheep/ St. George slaying the dragon small paddlewheel steamboat below/ Indian with drawn bow
- **Colour:** Black with no tint
- **Back Design:** Plain

IMPRINT
Rawdon, Wright & Hatch, New-York.

SIGNATURES
left	right
mss. Geo. Cunningham	mss. George Hall

ISSUE DATING
Partially engraved ___ 18___ :
- $2, 1836: 27 Augt., 8th Octr
- $4, 1836: Feb. 15, 6 Augt, 13th Augt, 20 Augt, 27 August, 27 Augt.
- $10, 1836: 6 Augt, 13th Augt, 20 Augt, 27 August

Cat. No.	Denom.	Date	Variety	VG	F	VF	EF	Unc
10-02R	$1 (5s)	18_	Remainder*	250.	325.	500.	-	-
10-04	$2 (10s)	1836		250.	325.	500.	-	-
10-04R	$2 (10s)	18_	Remainder*	300.	400.	600.	850.	-
10-06	$4 (20s, £1)	1836		125.	170.	230.	425.	-
10-08	$10 (50s)	1836		125.	170.	230.	425.	-

* Unsigned, undated and unnumbered.

THE NIAGARA DISTRICT BANK

1853-1875

ST. CATHARINES, CANADA WEST

BANK NUMBER 530   **REDEEMABLE**

The "Bank of the Niagara District" was chartered in 1841, but did not go into operation, being unable to raise sufficient capital. Under the name of the Niagara District Bank it finally went into business in 1853, under the Free Banking Act. In 1855 a charter was applied for and received from the legislature.

The bank operated successfully, with Ontario branches in St. Catharines, Ingersoll and Port Colborne, until it incurred heavy losses through the failure of American correspondents in 1873. It was also affected by the decaying fortunes of St. Catharines, the city in which it had its principal branch. Late in 1874 negotiations began for a merger between the Niagara District Bank and the Imperial Bank of Canada. They officially merged on July 2, 1875, the amalgamation being the first of its kind under the new Bank Act of 1871.

530-10   FREE BANKING ISSUE, 1854-1855

DESIGNS AND COLOURS

530-10-04
- **$1 Face Design:** Milkmaid/royal Crest/—
- **Colour:** Black with no tint
- **Back Design:** Plain

530-10-10

Note: The note shown above is a $1 raised to $10.

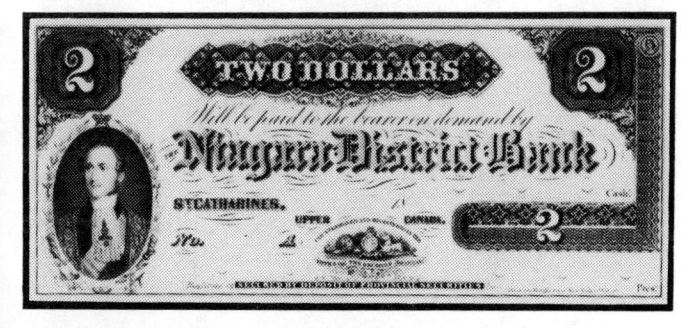

530-10-12P
- **$2 Face Design:** Prince Consort/—/—
- **Colour:** Black with no tint
- **Back Design:** Plain

530-10-14P
- **$5 Face Design:** Shipbuilding scene/Queen Victoria (Chalon portrait)/—
- **Colour:** Black with no tint
- **Back Design:** Plain

IMPRINT
Danforth, Wright & Co., New York & Philada

SIGNATURES

left	right
mss. J.R. Andy	mss. Jno. Smart, Cashr
	and
	mss. Thomas C. Street, Prest.

ISSUE DATING
Partially engraved ___ 18___:
- **1854:** Unknown
- **1855:** Unknown

Cat. No.	Denom.	Date Variety	VG	F	VF	EF	Unc
10-04	$1	1854-55	2,000.	2,800.	-	-	-
10-08	$1	1854-55 Raised to $5	1,100.	1,500.	-	-	-
10-10	$1	1854-55 Raised to $10	1,100.	1,500.	-	-	-
10-12P	$2	18_				PROOF	400.
10-14P	$5	18_				PROOF	400.

530-12   CHARTERED BANK ISSUES
1855 - 1862

DESIGNS AND COLOURS

530-12-02-02P
- **$1 (5s) Face Design:** Niagara Falls/—/—
- **Back Design:** Plain

297

THE NIAGARA DISTRICT BANK

530-12-02-04P
$2 (10s) **Face Design:** Queen Victoria/woman and plaque with shipbuilding scene/locomotive and tender in oval

Back Design: Plain

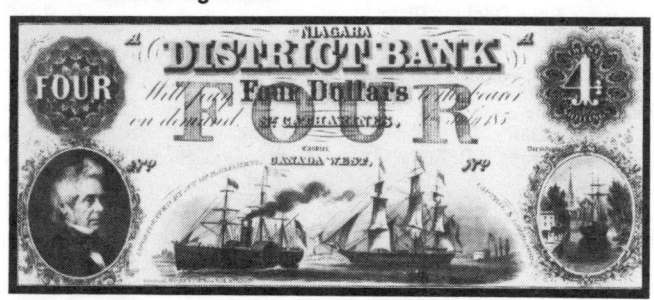

530-12-02-06P
$4 (20s) **Face Design:** Hon. W.H. Merritt/ steamboat and sailing ships/ ship in canal and town in oval

Back Design: Plain

530-12-02-08P
$5 (£1.5) **Face Design:** Hon. W.H. Merritt/three men studying ships' plans at dockside/—

Back Design: Plain

2. PARTIALLY ENGRAVED DATE, RED PROTECTOR, 1855

COLOURS
Face Colour: Black with no tint

IMPRINT
Danforth, Wright & Co. New York & Philada

SIGNATURES
left	right
mss. various	mss. various
none	none

ISSUE DATING
Partially engraved 2nd July 185_:
1855

PROTECTOR
Red "word" on face and back

Cat. No.	Denom.	Date	VG	F	VF	EF	Unc
12-02-02	$1 (5s)	1855	1,400.	2,000.	-	-	-
12-02-04P	$2 (10s)	185				PROOF	400.
12-02-06	$4 (20S)	1855	1,600.	2,200.	-	-	-
12-02-08p	$5 (£1.5)	185				PROOF	400.

4. PARTIALLY ENGRAVED DATE GREEN TINT, 1860s

530-12-04-02P
$10 **Face Design:** Sailor, woman and child "Land Ho!"/ "Justice" figure/reclining woman with basket of produce

Back Design: Plain

COLOURS
Face Colour: Black with green tint

IMPRINT
American Bank Note Co. New York.

SIGNATURES
left	right
none	none

ISSUE DATING
Partially engraved ___ 18___:

Cat. No.	Denom.	Date		Unc
12-04-02P	$10	18_	FACE PROOF	1,000.

6 FULLY ENGRAVED DATE 1862

530-12-06-02
$1 (5s) **Face Design:** Niagara Falls/—/—

Back Design: Plain

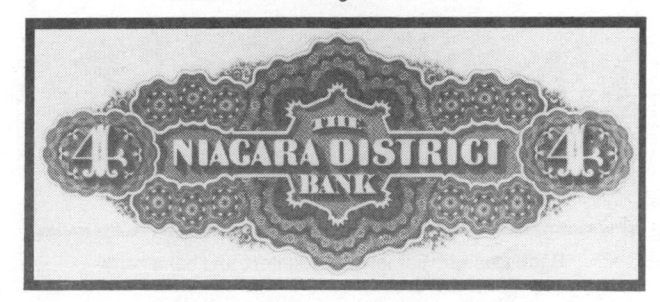

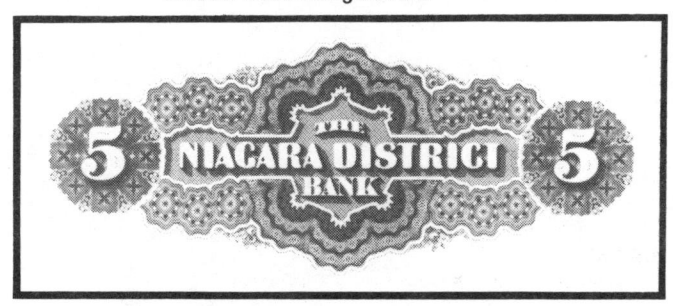

THE NIAGARA DISTRICT BANK

530-12-06-04
$2 (10s) Face Design: Queen Victoria/woman and plaque with shipuilding scene/locomative and tender in oval

Back Design: Plain

530-12-06-06
$4 (20s) Face Deisgn: Hon. W.H. Merritt/steamboat and sailing ships/ship in canal and town in oval

Back Design: Plain

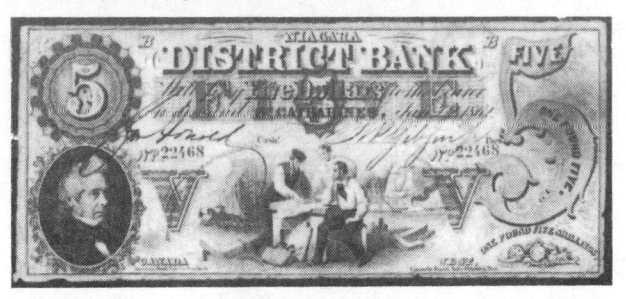

530-12-06-08
$5 (£1.5) Face Design: Hon. W.H. Merritt/three men studing ships plans at dock-side/—

Back Design: Plain

COLOURS
Face Colour: Black with green tint

IMPRINT
Danforth, Wright & Co. New York & Philada and ABNCo. Mono American Bank Note Co. New York

SIGNATURES

left	right
mss. F.W. Gibson	engr. James R. Benson
mss. C.M. Arnold	mss. F.W. Gibson

ISSUE DATING
Engraved
Jan'y. 2 1862.

Cat. No.	Denom.	Date	VG	F	VF	EF	Unc
12-06-02	$1 (5s)	1862	1,300.	1,700.	-	-	-
12-06-04	$2 (10s)	1862	1,300.	1,700.	-	-	-
12-06-06	$4 (20s)*	1862	1,500.	2,000.	-	-	-
12-06-08	$5 (£1.5)	1862	1,300.	1,700.	-	-	-

* Most of the surviving notes are counterfeits, with scratchy engraving and engraved signatures. Prices are for genuine notes.

530-14 ISSUE OF 1872
DESIGNS AND COLOURS

530-14-02
$4 Face Design: Hon. W.H. Merritt/girl watering livestock "Vogt's cattle"/Hon. Jas. R. Benson
Colour: Black with green tint

Back Design: Lathework, counters and bank name
Colour: Green

530-14-04
$5 Face Design: Hon. W.H. Merritt/paddlewheel steamer/Hon. Jas. R. Benson
Colour: Black with green tint

Back Design: Lathework, counters and bank name
Colour: Green

299

THE NIAGARA SUSPENSION BRIDGE BANK

530-14-06
$10 **Face Design:** Hon. W.H. Merritt/Niagara Falls/
Hon. Jas. R. Benson
Colour: Black with green tint

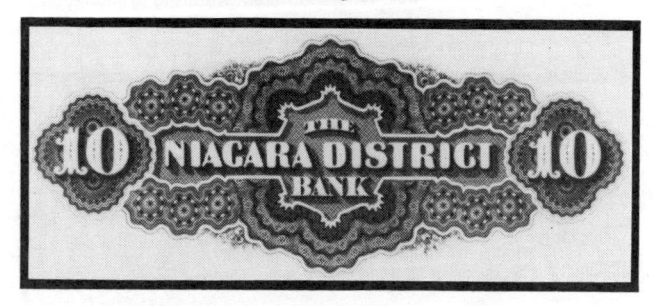

Back Design: Lathework, counters and bank name
Colour: Green

IMPRINT
British American Bank Note Co. Montreal & Ottawa

SIGNATURES

left	right
mss. F.W. Gibson	engr. James R. Benson
mss. C.M. Arnold	engr. James R. Benson

ISSUE DATING
Engraved
July 1st 1872
1st July 1872

Cat. No.	Denom.	Date	VG	F	VF	EF	Unc
14-02	$4*	1872	1,400.	2,000.	-	-	-
14-04	$5*	1872	1,200.	1,600.	-	-	-
14-06	$10*	1872	1,400.	2,000.	-	-	-

* Beware of modern lithographic reproductions of this issue in single notes or in sheets.

THE NIAGARA SUSPENSION BRIDGE BANK
1836-1841
QUEENSTON, UPPER CANADA

BANK NUMBER 535 **NONREDEEMABLE**

This bank went into business on December 20, 1836, as an unincorporated joint-stock bank, at Queenston, Upper Canada. It began with a capital of £7,700, subscribed by a small number of shareholders, most of whom were Americans. It had agencies in Chippewa, Upper Canada, and in Lockport, New York, and did most of its business on the American side of the border. The bank was recognized by the government, and its note issues were taxed. When the bank failed in December 1841, there were $62,384 of its notes in circulation.

535-10 **ISSUE OF 1836-1841**
DESIGNS AND COLOURS

535-10-04-02
$1 (5s) **Face Design:** St. George slaying the dragon/
Niagara suspension bridge; dog's head
below/King William IV
See subheadings
Colour: Black with green tint

Back Design: See subheadings
Colour: See subheadings

535-10-02-04
$3 (15s) **Face Design:** Woman standing with anchor/Niagara
suspension bridge; dog's head below/
Indian paddling canoe
See subheadings
Colour: Black with no tint

Back Design: See subheadings
Colour: See subheadings

THE NIAGARA SUSPENSION BRIDGE BANK

535-10-06-06
$5 (25s) Face Design: —/Niagara suspension bridge; steamboat below/Indian with drawn bow
See subheadings
Colour: Black with no tint

Back Design: See subheadings
Colour: See subheadings

535-10-08-18
$10 Face Design: —/Niagara suspension bridge/ St. George slaying the dragon
See subheadings
Colour: Black with no tint

Back Design: Plain

535-10-08-30
$20 Face Design: Niagara suspension bridge (side view)/ goddess rising from the waves/ Greek god reclining by fountain
See subheadings
Colour: Black with no tint

Back Design: Plain

IMPRINT
Rawdon, Wright & Hatch, New York

2. MSS. "PAYABLE AT THE BANK" AT TOP, PLAIN BACK, 1836

SIGNATURES
 left   right
 mss. P.C.H. Brotherson   mss. Bates Cooke

ISSUE DATING
 Partially engraved ___ 18___ :
 1836: Dec. 20

Cat. No.	Denom.	Date	VG	F	VF	EF	Unc
10-02-02	$1 (5s)	18_	100.	150.	-	-	-
10-02-04	$3 (15s)	1836	150.	250.	-	-	-
10-02-06	$5 (25s)	18_	100.	150.	-	-	-

4. ENGRAVED "PAYABLE AT THE BANK" AT TOP, PLAIN BACK, 1837-1839

SIGNATURES
 left   right
 mss. P.C.H. Brotherson   mss. Bates Cooke

ISSUE DATING
 Partially engraved ___ 18___ :
 1837: Apr. 3
 1839: July 20

Cat. No.	Denom.	Date	VG	F	VF	EF	Unc
10-04-02	$1 (5s)	1837	60.	100.	-	-	-
10-04-06	$3 (15s)	18_	75.	120.	-	-	-
10-04-10	$5 (25s)	1839	60.	100.	-	-	-

6. ENGRAVED "PAYABLE AT THE BANK" AT TOP, ORANGE LATHEWORK ON BACK, 1840

SIGNATURES
 left   right
 mss. G. McMicken   mss. Jos. Hamilton

ISSUE DATING
 Partially engraved ___ 18___ :
 1840: Oct. 13, 13 Oct.

Cat. No.	Denom.	Date	VG	F	VF	EF	Unc
10-06-02	$1 (5s)	1840	50.	90.	175.	-	-
10-06-04	$3 (15s)	1840	60.	105.	200.	-	-
10-06-06	$5 (25s)	1840	50.	90.	175.	-	-

8. PLAIN BACK ISSUE 1841

SIGNATURES
 left   right
 mss. G. McMicken   mss. Jos. Hamilton

ISSUE DATING
 Partially engraved ___ 18___ :
 $1, 1841: 1 July
 $3, 1841: 1 Mar., 1 May, May 1, 1 July
 $5: See varieties
 $10, 1841: Jan. 4, 4 Jany
 $20, 1841: 4 Jany.

THE NORTHERN BANK

VARIETIES

$5 Issue Dating: Engraved "QUEENSTON" on bottom, at left of miniature ship; U.C.: 1841: 1 Mar., May 1, 1 July

$5 Issue Dating: Engraved "QUEENSTON" at bottom, above miniature ship; U.C.: 1841: 4 Jany

$5 Issue Dating: Engraved "QUEENSTON" at bottom, above miniature ship; Upper Canada 18__: Undated remainder

$10 and $20 Face Design: U.C. at bottom

$10 and $20 Face Design: UPPER CANADA at bottom

Cat. No.	Denom.	Date	Variety	VG	F	VF	EF	Unc
10-08-02	$1 (5s)	1841		50.	90.	175.	-	-
10-08-06	$3 (15s)	1841		65.	110.	225.	-	-
10-08-10	$5 (25s)	1841	QUEENSTON above; U.C.	125.	210.	325.	-	-
10-08-10R	$5 (25s)	1841	Remainder	80.	135.	200.	-	-
10-08-12	$5 (25s)	1841	QUEENSTON left; U.C.	50.	90.	175.	-	-
10-08-14R	$5 (25s)	1841	QUEENSTON UPPER CANADA	275.	375.	550.	-	-
10-08-18	$10 (50s)	1841	U.C.	175.	275.	475.	-	-
10-08-18R	$10 (50s)	1841	Remainder	90.	140.	225.	-	-
10-08-22	$10 (50s)	1841	UPPER CANADA	175.	275.	475.	-	-
10-08-22R	$10 (50s)	1841	Remainder	90.	140.	225.	-	-
10-08-26	$20 (£5)	1841	U.C.	200.	325.	600.	-	-
10-08-26R	$20 (£5)	1841	Remainder	175.	250.	400.	-	-
10-08-30	$20 (£5)	1841	UPPER CANADA	200.	325.	600.	-	-
10-08-30R	$20 (£5)	1841	Remainder	175.	250.	400.	-	-

THE NORTHERN BANK

1905-1908

WINNIPEG, MANITOBA

BANK NUMBER 540　　　　　　　　**REDEEMABLE**

Established in Winnipeg, Manitoba, in 1905, this bank amalgamated with the Crown Bank of Canada to become the Northern Crown Bank in 1908.

540-10　　　　　　**ISSUE OF 1905**

DESIGNS AND COLOURS

540-10-02

$5 Face Design: —/farmer, horses and native on prairies/—
Colour: Black with green tint

Back Design: Lathework, counters and bank name
Colour: Green

540-10-04

$10 Face Design: —/farmer cutting wheat with binder/—
Colour: Black with red-brown tint

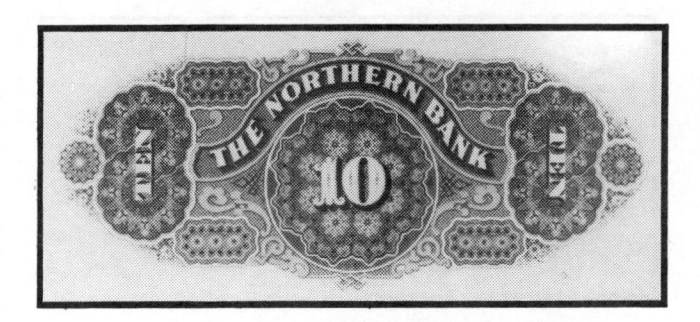

THE NORTHERN BANK

Back Design: Lathework, counters and bank name
Colour: Green

540-10-06
$20 Face Design: —/bison on prairies/—
Colour: Black with brown tint

Back Design: Lathework, counters and bank name
Colour: Green

540-10-08P
$50 Face Design: Agricultural produce and implements/ farmer watering horses at trough/—
Colour: Black with ochre tint

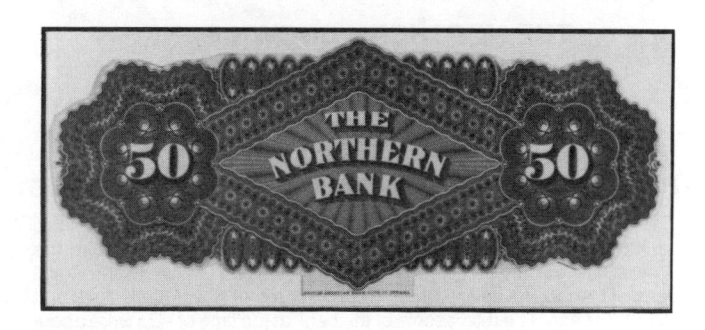

Back Design: Lathework, counters and bank name
Colour: Green

IMPRINT
British American Bank Note Co. Ottawa

SIGNATURES
left	right
mss. various	engr. D.H. McMillan

ISSUE DATING
Engraved
Nov. 1st 1905

Note: A back proof of the $5 note is known with brown tint.

Cat. No.	Denom.	Date	VG	F	VF	EF	Unc
10-02	$5	1905	4,000.	6,500.	-	-	-
10-04	$10	1905	4,000.	5,500.	-	-	-
10-06	$20	1905	4,000.	5,500.	-	-	-
10-08P	$50	1905			FACE PROOF		600.

303

THE NORTHERN CROWN BANK

1908-1918

WINNIPEG, MANITOBA

BANK NUMBER 545   **REDEEMABLE**

Established in Winnipeg, Manitoba, in 1905 as the Northern Bank, this bank became the Northern Crown Bank upon amalgamation with the Crown Bank of Canada (Toronto) in 1908. It was taken over by the Royal Bank of Canada in July 1918 for 10,883 shares of Royal Bank stock and $576,970 cash. The total assets of the bank at the time of sale were about $28 million. The bank had 111 branches and one sub-branch.

545-10   ISSUES OF 1908-1914

DESIGNS AND COLOURS

545-10-02
- **$5 Face Design:** —/farmer and horses on prairies/—
- **Colour:** Black with olive and red tint

- **Back Design:** Lathework, counters, bank name and floral emblems and crown
- **Colour:** Red-brown

545-10-06
- **$10 Face Design:** —/farmer cutting wheat with binder/—
- **Colour:** Black with yellow and green tint

- **Back Design:** Lathework, counters, bank name and floral emblems and crown
- **Colour:** Blue

545-10-10S
- **$20 Face Design:** —/bison on prairies/—
- **Colour:** Black with peach and blue tint

- **Back Design:** Lathework, counters, bank name and floral emblems and crown
- **Colour:** Orange

545-10-12P
- **$50 Face Design:** —/lion in mountains/—
- **Colour:** Black with yellow and red tint

- **Back Design:** Lalthework, counters, bank name and floral emblems and crown
- **Colour:** Purple

IMPRINT
British American Bank Note Co. Ottawa

SIGNATURES
left	right
engr. D.H. McMillan	mss. various

ISSUE DATING
Engraved
July 2nd 1908
July 2nd 1914

Note: A back proof of the $5 note is known with maroon tint.

Cat. No.	Denom.	Date	VG	F	VF	EF	Unc
10-02	$5	1908	1,500.	2,000.	3,200.	-	-
10-04	$5	1914	1,600.	2,400.	3,500.	-	-
10-06	$10	1908	1,600.	2,400.	3,500.	-	-
10-08	$10	1914	1,700.	2,600.	3,300.	-	-
10-10	$20	1908	2,000.	2,900.	-	-	-
10-12P	$50	1908			FACE PROOF		600.

THE BANK OF NOVA SCOTIA

1832 TO DATE

HALIFAX, NOVA SCOTIA

BANK NUMBER 550   **REDEEMABLE**

On December 13, 1831, a group of merchants, ship owners and citizens assembled in Halifax for the purpose of organizing a public bank. After argument, amendment and compromise in the legislature, the bill to incorporate the Bank of Nova Scotia passed on March 30, 1832.

For the first 40-odd years of its existence, the bank was a very small institution by modern standards, but it was by no means unenterprising. For example, it opened the first bank branches in Nova Scotia. The first agency was established in Windsor, Nova Scotia, in 1837, and by the end of 1839, Pictou, Annapolis, Liverpool and Yarmouth also had agencies of the bank. During these early years connections were established with mercantile and private banking firms in Saint John, New Brunswick, New York, Boston and London, England.

The first presidents of the bank were merchants whose businesses, like those of so many of their contemporaries, were founded on the exchange of lumber and fish for West Indian sugar and rum. With the building of the Canadian Pacific Railway in the 1880s, the bank established branches in Winnipeg and Minneapolis. Branches were added in Chicago in 1892 and in Boston in 1899.

During the first two decades of the present century, the bank extended its Caribbean business to Cuba and Puerto Rico and opened its own agency in New York, as well as branches in London, England, and in the Dominican Republic. Business was conducted in Cuba through branches in Havana and at other points on the island, until all foreign banks were closed by arrangement with the Castro government in December 1960.

Mergers with other banks played an important role in the bank's continuing growth as market forces began to reduce the number of Canadian chartered banks. After absorbing the Union Bank of Prince Edward Island in 1833, three additional mergers took place, with the Bank of New Brunswick in 1913, the Metropolitan Bank in 1914 and the Bank of Ottawa in 1919. As the 1920s began, the Bank of Nova Scotia was active in every Canadian province and maintained 30 branches outside Canada. From a sturdy, regional bank, it had become an enterprising and responsible national institution, which served international as well as local needs.

After a consolidation of operations during the Depression and World War II, expansion was renewed through new branches and additional services. In 1958 the bank entered a new phase of business by joining with three British firms to establish the Bank of Nova Scotia Trust Company (Bahamas) Limited, with headquarters in Nassau. The Bahamas Trust has become the parent company for several subsidiaries, and new companies with similar operations have been founded.

A noteworthy feature of the international postwar financial situation was the revival of interest in gold. To facilitate the holding of gold, in 1958 the Bank of Nova Scotia introduced a unique gold certificate, designed as a transferable receipt for gold ingots and bars held for safekeeping in the bank's own vaults. Owners of the certificates made arrangements to take delivery of the metal in Canada, or when conditions permitted at any other office of the bank, or at the office of a correspondent bank in any major gold-trading centre outside Canada where the bank had no office. The bank quickly became Canada's largest gold trader, in both certificates and in bullion, and maintains that position today.

During the 1960s even greater emphasis was placed on international representation. The 1970s saw even further international expansion, with new offices opened in the Middle and Far East. The Pacific Rim continues as a very important area to the bank. Today the Bank of Nova Scotia is recognized as one of the world's leading international financial institutions.

THE BANK OF NOVA SCOTIA

550-10　　RAWDON, WRIGHT, HATCH & CO.
　　　　　　POUNDS & SHILLINGS
　　　　　　PRINTINGS 1832-1852

DESIGNS AND COLOURS

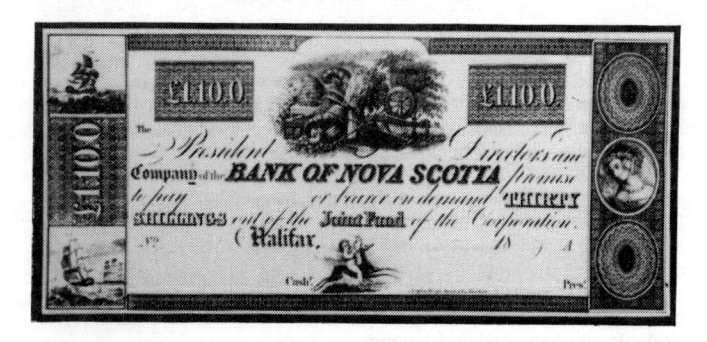

550-10-02P
£1.10.0 (30s)
　Face Design: Sailing ships/farm implements and produce; child riding deer below/bust of young woman "Ceres, Goddess of Corn"
　Colour: Black with no tint
　Back Design: Plain

Photo Not Available

550-10-12P
£2 Face Design: Unknown
　Colour: Black with no tint
　Back Design: Plain

550-10-22P
£2.10.0 Face Design: Two men and livestock/woman; ship; man in canoe below/cherubs face top and bottom
　Colour: Black with no tint
　Back Design: Plain

550-10-32
1837 Issue
　£5 Face Design: Blacksmith/three cherubs and counters; bust of young woman "Ceres, Goddess of Corn" below/alchemist
　Colour: Black with no tint
　Back Design: Plain

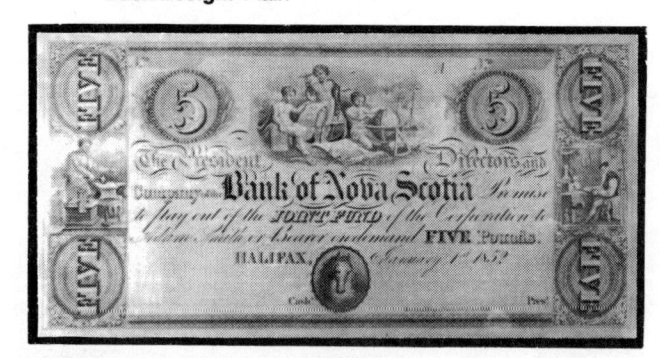

550-10-42
1834, 1839 and 1852 Issues
　£5 Face Design: Blacksmith/three cherubs and counters; horse's head below/alchemist
　Colour: Black with no tint
　Back Design: Plain

550-10-52
　£10 Face Design: King William IV/Royal Crest; flowers below/woman standing with anchor
　Colour: Black with no tint
　Back Design: Plain

IMPRINT
　Rawdon, Wright, Hatch & Co. New York

SIGNATURES

left	right
mss. James Forman	mss. William Lawson
mss. J. Forman	mss. M.B. Almon

THE BANK OF NOVA SCOTIA

ISSUE DATING
Partially engraved ___ 18___:
- **1832:** Aug. 6
- **1834:** 2nd June
- **1837:** 3rd April
- **1839:** 1 Jany

Engraved
January 1st 1852

Cat. No.	Denom.	Date	Variety	VG	F	VF	EF	Unc
10-02P	£1.10	18_					PROOF	500.
10-12P	£2	18_					PROOF	500.
10-22P	£2.10	18_					PROOF	500.
10-32	£5	1837	Woman vign.	1,600.	2,100.	-	-	-
10-42	£5	1832-52	Horse vign.	1,600.	2,100.	-	-	-
10-52	£10	1839-52		1,600.	2,100.	-	-	-

550-12 NEBN PRINTINGS POUNDS & SHILLINGS 1840

DESIGNS AND COLOURS

550-12-02P
- **£5.5 Face Design:** Man and boy in shop/ St. George slaying the dragon; man and horses below/sailing ship
- **Colour:** Black with no tint
- **Back Design:** Plain

550-12-04
- **£6 Face Design:** Men harvesting wheat/ allegorical male on chariot; steamboat below/ man on horse talking to farmer
- **Colour:** Black with no tint
- **Back Design:** Plain

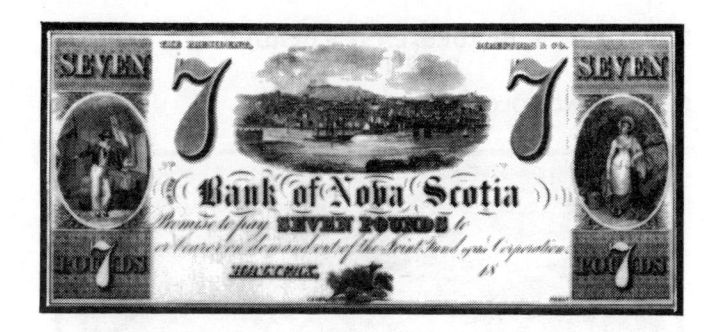

550-12-06
- **£7 Face Design:** Sailor holding flag/Halifax harbour; deer leaping below/dairymaid
- **Colour:** Black with no tint
- **Back Design:** Plain

550-12-08
- **£7.10 Face Design:** "Justice" figure/Crest; dog with key below/ woman supporting lyre
- **Colour:** Black with no tint
- **Back Design:** Plain

IMPRINT
New England Bank Note Co. Boston

SIGNATURES
left	right
unknown	unknown

ISSUE DATING
Partially engraved ___ 18___:
- **£5.5 1840:** May 2

Engraved
- **£6:** 1 July 1840
- **£7:** 1 Augt 1840
- **£7.10:** 1 August 1840

Cat. No.	Denom.	Date	VG	F	VF	EF	Unc
12-02	£5.5	1840	1,700.	2,500.	-	-	-
12-04	£6	1840	1,700.	2,500.	-	-	-
12-06	£7	1840	1,700.	2,500.	-	-	-
12-08	£7.10	1840	1,700.	2,500.	-	-	-

THE BANK OF NOVA SCOTIA

550-14   BLADES, EAST & BLADES PRINTINGS, 1864

DESIGNS AND COLOURS

550-14-02
   $20 Face Design: —/Royal Crest/—
   Colour: Black with green tint

   Back Design: Lathework and bank Crest
   Colour: Unknown

IMPRINT
   Blades, East & Blades, London

SIGNATURES
left	right
unknown	unknown

ISSUE DATING
   Engraved
   1st January 18__

Cat. No.	Denom.	Date	VG	F	VF	EF	Unc
14-10	$20	18_	1,800.	2,400.	3,400.	-	-

550-16 $4, $5 AND $20 ISSUES OF 1870-1877

DESIGNS AND COLOURS

550-16-02
   $4 Face Design: —/beehive and flowers/—
   plain green 4's at top
   Colour: Black with green tint

550-16-03
   $4 Face Design: —/beehive and flowers/—
   green four over 4's at top
   Colour: Black with green tint

550-16-06
   $4 Face Design: —/beehive and flowers/—
   four over 4 and Province of Nova Scotia at top
   Colour: Black with green tint

   Back Design: Lathework, counters, bank name and Crest
   Colour: Green

550-16-10
   $5 Face Design: —/St. George slaying the dragon/—
   Colour: Black with green tint

   Back Design: Lathework, counters, bank name and Crest
   Colour: Green

THE BANK OF NOVA SCOTIA

Photo Not Available

550-16-14
- **$20 Face Design:** Unknown
- **Colour:** Black with green tint
- **Back Design:** Lathework, counters and bank name
- **Colour:** Green

IMPRINT
- **$4 and $5:** British American Bank Note Co. Montreal and Ottawa
- **$20:** American Bank Note Company

SIGNATURES

left	right
mss. various	mss. various

ISSUE DATING
Engraved
- **$4 and $5:** July 1st 1870
- **$4 and $5:** July 1st 1871
- **$4 and $5:** July 2nd 1877
- **$20:** Jan. 1 1877

OVERPRINT
1870 or 1871: "CANADA CURRENCY" twice in red

Cat. No.	Denom.	Date	Variety	VG	F	VF	EF	Unc
16-02	$4	1870	No o/p	1,800.	2,500.	-	-	-
16-02a	$4	1870	Red o/p	1,800.	2,500.	-	-	-
16-03	$4	1870	Four/4	1,800.	2,500.	-	-	-
16-04	$4	1871		1,800.	2,500.	-	-	-
16-06	$4	1877		1,800.	2,500.	-	-	-
16-08	$5	1870	No o/p	1,800.	2,500.	-	-	-
16-08a	$5	1870	Red o/p	1,800.	2,500.	-	-	-
16-10	$5	1871	Red o/p	1,800.	2,500.	-	-	-
16-12	$5	1877		1,800.	2,500.	-	-	-
16-14	$20	1871	SURVIVING NOTES NOT CONFIRMED
16-16	$20	1877	SURVIVING NOTES NOT CONFIRMED

550-18 $10 ISSUES OF 1877-1929

DESIGNS AND COLOURS

550-18-08
- **$10 Face Design:** Mining scene/unicorn, shield and Indian "Arms of Nova Scotia"/ sailing ship
- **Colour:** Black with ochre and blue tint

- **Back Design:** Lathework, counters and bank name
- **1877-1919 Colour:** Green
- **Back Design:** Lathework, counters, bank name and bank seal
- **1924 Colour:** Blue
- **1929 Colour:** Slate

IMPRINT
American Bank Note Co. N.Y.
American Bank Note Co. Ottawa
Canadian Bank Note Company Limited

SIGNATURES

	left	right
1877:	mss. various	engr. Jno. Y. Payzant
	mss. various	engr. Jairus Hart
	mss. various	engr. John Doull
1903:	mss. various	typed Jno. Y. Payzant
1917:	mss. various	typed Jno. Y. Payzant
	typed H.A. Richardson	typed Jno. Y. Payzant
1919:	typed H.A. Richardson	typed Charles Archibald
1924:	typed G.S. Campbell	typed J.S. McLeod
1929:	typed S.J. Moore	typed J.A. McLeod

ISSUE DATING
Engraved
July 2nd 1877
Jany. 2nd 1903
Jany. 2nd 1917
Jany. 2nd 1919
Jany. 2nd 1924
Jany. 2nd 1929

Cat. No.	Denom.	Date	Variety	VG	F	VF	EF	Unc
18-02	$10	1877	Payzant, r.	800.	1,000.	1,400.	-	-
18-04	$10	1877	Hart, r.	800.	1,000.	1,400.	-	-
18-06	$10	1877	Doull, r.	800.	1,000.	1,400.	-	-
18-08	$10	1903		140.	200.	300.	525.	1,100.
18-12	$10	1917	Mss. sig., l.	40.	60.	90.	150.	275.
18-14	$10	1917	Richardson, l.	40.	60.	90.	150.	275.
18-16	$10	1919		30.	40.	70.	110.	200.
18-18	$10	1924		30.	40.	70.	110.	200.
18-20	$10	1929		25.	35.	55.	90.	175.

THE BANK OF NOVA SCOTIA

550-20   **$5 ISSUES OF 1881**

DESIGNS AND COLOURS

550-20-02
- **$5 Face Design:** The Greek goddess Pallas/ Hon. Joseph Howe/Bank seal
- **Colour:** See varieties

550-20-06a

Back Design: Lathework, counters and bank name
Colour: See varieties

550-20-10

IMPRINT
American Bank Note Co. N.Y.

SIGNATURES

left	right
mss. various	mss. Jairus Hart
mss. various	mss. Adam Burns
mss. various	mss. John Doull

ISSUE DATING
Engraved
July 2nd 1881

VARIETIES
1. **Face Colour:** Black with overall blue tint, "FIVE" twice at bottom
   Back Colour: Green
2. **Face Colour:** Black with blue tint, no 5 outlined at bottom
   Back Colour: Brown
3. **Face Colour:** Black with blue, green and ochre tint, "FIVE" under portrait
   Back Colour: Brown
4. **Face Colour:** Black with green and red tint, No "FIVE" under portrait

OVERPRINT
"WINNIPEG" twice in red

Cat. No.	Denom.	Date	Variety	VG	F	VF	EF	Unc
20-02P	$5	1881	Var. 1				PROOF	600.
20-06	$5	1881	Var. 2	2,000.	3,000.	-	-	-
20-06a	$5	1881	Var. 2, Winn.	2,700.	4,000.	-	-	-
20-10	$5	1881	Var. 3	2,000.	3,000.	-	-	-
20-12P	$5	1881	Var. 4				PROOF	600.

550-22   **$20 ISSUE OF 1882**

DESIGNS AND COLOURS

Photo Not Available

550-22-02P
- **$20 Face Design:** Unknown
- **Colour:** Unknown
- **Back Design:** Unknown
- **Colour:** Unknown

IMPRINT
American Bank Note Company

SIGNATURES

left	right
unknown	unknown

ISSUE DATING
Engraved
Jan. 1, 1882

Cat. No.	Denom.	Date	F	Unc
22-02P	$20	1882	FACE PROOF	900.

THE BANK OF NOVA SCOTIA

550-24 $20 ISSUE OF 1896
DESIGNS AND COLOURS

550-24-02
- **$20 Face Design:** —/allegorical female and cherub/—
- **Colour:** Black with pink and blue tint
- **Back Design:** —/bank seal/—
- **Colour:** Blue

IMPRINT
American Bank Note Company, New York

SIGNATURES
left	right
mss. various	engr. John Doull

ISSUE DATING
Engraved
July 2nd 1896

Cat. No. Denom.	Date	VG	F	VF	EF	Unc
550-24-02 $20	1896	2,000.	3,000.	4,200.	-	-

550-26 $20 ISSUE OF 1897
DESIGNS AND COLOURS

550-26-02
- **$20 Face Design:** Allegorical female writing, child "History"/portrait of young woman/allegorical female
- **Colour:** Black with yellow-green and rose tint

- **Back Design:** Lathework, counters, bank name and bank seal
- **Colour:** Olive green

IMPRINT
American Bank Note Company, New York

SIGNATURES
left	right
mss. various	engr. John Doull

ISSUE DATING
Engraved
Novr 1st, 1897

Cat. No. Denom.	Date	VG	F	VF	EF	Unc
26-02 $20	1897	2,000.	3,000.	4,200.	-	-

550-28 SCENIC ISSUES OF 1898-1929
DESIGNS AND COLOURS

550-28-12
- **$5 Face Design:** Allegorical female/mining scene/steamship approaching viewer
- **Colour:** Black with yellow-green and orange tint
  See varieties
- **Back Design:** Lathework, counters, bank name and bank seal
- **Colour:** Olive

550-28-16
- **$20 Face Design:** —/men fishing from two dories/—
- **Colour:** Black with yellow-green and rose tint

- **Back Design:** Lathework, counters, bank name and bank seal
- **Colour:** Rose, green and brown
- **1925 Colour:** Green
- **1929 Colour:** Orange

311

THE BANK OF NOVA SCOTIA

550-28-26
$50 Face Design: —/threshing scene/—
Colour: Black with olive and red tint

Back Design: Lathework, counters, bank name and bank seal
Colour: Slate

550-28-32
$100 Face Design: —/100 counter flanked by Liberty and a lion, and by art and industry figure/—
Colour: Black with yellow-green and rose tint

Back Design: Lathework, counters, bank name and bank seal
Colour: Brown

IMPRINT
American Bank Note Company, Ottawa
Canadian Bank Note Company Limited
American Bank Note Co. Ottawa

SIGNATURES

	left	right
1898:	mss. various	engr. Jairus Hart
	mss. various	typed Jno. Y. Payzant
	mss. various	engr. John Doull
1899:	mss. various	engr. John Doull
1903-1906:	mss. various	typed Jno. Y. Payzant
1908:	mss. various	typed Jno. Y. Payzant
	typed H.A. Richardson	typed Jno. Y. Payzant
1911:	mss. various	typed Jno. Y. Payzant
1918-1920:	mss. various	typed Charles Archibald
	typed Charles Archibald	typed H.A. Richardson
	mss. various	typed G.S. Campbell
1925:	typed J.A. McLeod	typed G.S. Campbell
	mss. various	typed G.S. Campbell
1929:	typed J.A. McLeod	typed S.J. Moore

ISSUE DATING
Engraved

June 1st 1898	1st February 1918
August 1st 1899	January 2nd 1919
January 2nd 1903	July 2nd 1920
May 1st 1906	January 2nd 1925
September 1st 1908	January 2nd 1929
January 3rd 1911	

VARIETIES
$5, 1908 Face Tint: No orange Vs
$5, 1908 Face Tint: Orange Vs at top and "FIVE" twice at bottom

OVERPRINT
$5, 1898: "S S" in red

Cat. No.	Denom.	Date	Variety	VG	F	VF	EF	Unc
28-02	$5	1898	Hart, r.	200.	250.	325.	500.	-
28-04	$5	1898	Doull, r	200.	250.	325.	500.	-
28-06	$5	1898	Payzant, r.	200.	250	325.	500.	-
28-06a	$5	1898	SS o/p	200.	250.	325.	500.	-
28-08	$5	1908	No Vs	75.	110.	150.	250.	500.
28-12	$5	1908	Orange Vs mss'l	80.	120.	200.	225.	450.
28-12a	$5	1908	Orange V'sTyped l.	80.	120.	200.	225.	450.
28-14	$20	1903		200.	250.	375.	600.	1,200.
28-16	$20	1918	mss. l	45.	65.	100.	225.	550.
28-16a	$20	1918	typed l	45.	65.	90.	225.	550.
28-18	$20	1925		40.	60.	90.	175.	400.
28-22	$20	1929		35.	55.	80.	165.	350.
28-24	$50	1906		900.	1,300.	1,400.	3,000.	-
28-26	$50	1920		600.	900.	1,300.	2,100.	4,000.
28-28	$50	1925		700.	1,000.	1,300.	2,400.	4,500.
28-32	$100	1899		1,100.	1,800.	2,500.		
28-34	$100	1911		1,000.	1,600.	2,100.		-
28-36	$100	1919		600.	1,000.	1,400.	2,000.	
28-38	$100	1925		600.	1,000.	1,400.	2,000.	
28-38	$100	1929		600.	1,000.	1,400.	2,000.	-

550-30 $5 ISSUE OF 1918

DESIGNS AND COLOURS

550-30-02
$5 Face Design: John Y. Payzant/—/H.A. Richardson
Colour: Black with green tint

Back Design: Lathework, counters, bank name and bank seal
Colour: Green

IMPRINT
American Bank Note Co. Ottawa

SIGNATURES

left	right
typed Charles Archibald	typed H.A. Richardson

ISSUE DATING
Engraved
July 2nd 1918

Cat. No.	Denom.	Date	VG	F	VF	EF	Unc
30-02	$5	1918	60.	85.	125.	200.	400.

550-32 $5 ISSUE OF 1924

DESIGNS AND COLOURS

550-32-02
- **$5 Face Design:** G.S. Campbell/—/John A. McLeod
- **Colour:** Black with red and green tint
- **Back Design:** Lathework, counters, bank name and bank seal
- **Colour:** Brown

IMPRINT
Canadian Bank Note Company Limited

SIGNATURES
left	right
typed G.S. Campbell	typed J.A. McLeod

ISSUE DATING
Engraved
January 2nd 1924

Cat. No.	Denom.	Date	VG	F	VF	EF	Unc
32-02	$5	1924	22.	30.	50.	80.	160.

550-34 $5 ISSUE OF 1929

DESIGNS AND COLOURS

550-34-02
- **$5 Face Design:** S.J. Moore/—/John A. McLeod
- **Colour:** Black with red and green tint
- **Back Design:** Lathework, counters, bank name and Bank Seal
- **Colour:** Green

IMPRINT
Canadian Bank Note Company Limited

SIGNATURES
left	right
typed S.J. Moore	typed J.A. McLeod

ISSUE DATING
Engraved
January 2nd 1929

Cat. No.	Denom.	Date	VG	F	VF	EF	Unc
34-02	$5	1929	22.	30.	50.	80.	160.

550-36 ISSUE OF 1935, SMALL-SIZE NOTES

DESIGNS AND COLOURS

550-36-02
- **$5 Face Design:** John A. McLeod/—/Harry F. Patterson
- **Colour:** Black with red and green tint 
- **Back Design:** Lathework, counters, bank name and Bank Seal
- **Colour:** Green

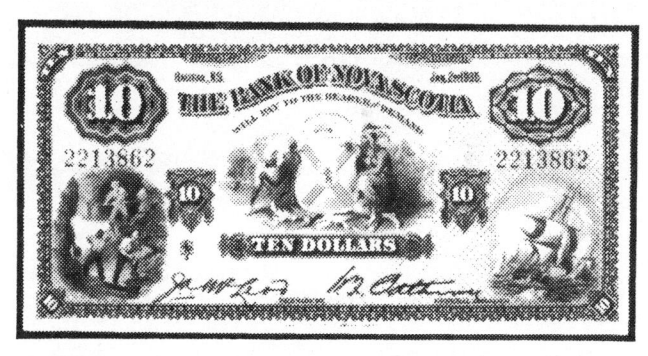

550-36-04
- **$10 Face Design:** Mining scene/unicorn, shield and lion "Arms of Nova Scotia"/ sailing ship
- **Colour:** Black with ochre and blue tint

THE BANK OF NOVA SCOTIA

Back Design: Lathework, counters, bank name and Bank Seal
Colour: Slate

IMPRINT
Canadian Bank Note Co. Limited
Canadian Bank Note Company Limited

SIGNATURES
left	right
typed J.A. McLeod	typed H.F. Patterson

ISSUE DATING
Engraved
Jan. 2nd 1935.

Cat. No.	Denom.	Date	VG	F	VF	EF	Unc
36-02	$5	1935	15.	20.	35.	55.	100.
36-04	$10	1935	20.	25.	40.	60.	110.

THE BANK OF NOVA SCOTIA BRITISH WEST INDIES ISSUES

The trade between the province of Nova Scotia and the West Indies had always been active, as far back as the 1820s. An act of Parliament, passed in July 1899, enabled Canadian banks to issue notes in any British colony other than Canada, and the Bank of Nova Scotia was the first Canadian bank to establish a branch outside Canada.

The Caribbean branch opened in Kingston, Jamaica, in 1889. The notes issued for Jamaica were in denominations of £1 and £5 and were redeemable in that colony. The Bank of Nova Scotia was also the first to open a savings-account business on the island.

550-38   **KINGSTON, JAMAICA, 1900-1930**

2.   **LARGE-SIZE NOTES**

DESIGNS AND COLOURS

550-38-02-02
    £1 Face Design: —/two seated allegorical figures flanking counter/—
    Colour: Black with green and yellow-green tint

Back Design: Lathework, counters, bank name and Bank Crest
Colour: Green

550-38-02-06
    £5 Face Design: —/two allegorical women seated on globe/—
    Colour: Black with orange and yellow-green tint

Back Design: Lathework, counters, bank name and bank crest
Colour: Brown

IMPRINT
American Bank Note Company, N.Y.

SIGNATURES
	left	right
1900:	mss. various	typed Jno. Y. Payzant
1919-1920:	mss. various	typed Charles Archibald

ISSUE DATING
Engraved
January 2nd 1900
January 2nd 1919
Jan. 2, 1920

Cat. No.	Denom.	Date	VG	F	VF	EF	Unc
38-02-02S	£1	1900			SPECIMEN		850.
38-02-04S	£1	1919			SPECIMEN		850.
38-02-06	£5	1900	1,000.	1,500.	2,200.	-	-
38-02-08	£5	1920	700.	950.	1,600.	-	-

4. SMALL-SIZE NOTES
DESIGNS AND COLOURS

550-38-04-04
£1 Face Design: —/woman seated on throne with produce/—
Colour: Black with green, blue and yellow tint
Back Design: Lathework, counters, bank name and Bank Crest
Colour: Green

IMPRINT
Canadian Bank Note Company Limited

SIGNATURES
left	right
typed S.J. Moore	typed John A. McLeod
typed J.A. McLeod	typed Henry F. Patterson

ISSUE DATING
Engraved
January 2nd 1930.

Cat. No.	Denom.	Date	Variety	VG	F	VF	EF	Unc
38-04-02	£1	1930	McLeod, r.	325.	450.	700.	1,250.	-
38-04-04	£1	1930	Patterson, r.	375.	525.	775.	1,300.	-

THE ONTARIO BANK
1857-1906
BOWMANVILLE, PROVINCE OF CANADA

BANK NUMBER 555   **REDEEMABLE**

The Ontario Bank was established in Bowmanville, Canada West, in 1857 (and later in Toronto). It was discovered in 1905 that the general manager had been falsifying the books to hide Wall Street losses that had obliterated the bank's reserves. The bank did not suspend payment, but when difficulties were encountered through some of its lumber accounts, an arrangement was made in 1906 whereby all liabilities were taken over by the Bank of Montreal. Together with certain other banks, the Bank of Montreal assumed all liabilities and paid depositors in full. Criminal charges were laid against the general manager and the president. The former was sentenced to the Kingston Penitentiary, but the president was exonerated of complicity.

555-10   **ISSUES OF 1857 AND 1861**
DESIGNS AND COLOURS

555-10-02-02
$1 Face Design: Agricultural produce/cattle/ sheep shearing scene
See subheadings
Colour: Black with overall green tint
Back Design: Lathework and bank name
Colour: Green

555-10-08-04
$2 Face Design: Blacksmith and anvil/ seated woman with dog and cattle/-
See subheadings
Colour: Black with overall green tint

THE ONTARIO BANK

Back Design: Lathework and bank name
Colour: Green

555-10-06-06P
$5 Face Design: Jacques Cartier/farmer sharpening scythe in grain field/bull's head
See subheadings
Colour: Black with overall green tint

Back Design: Lathework and bank name
Colour: Green

555-10-02-08P
$10 Face Design: Barges and bridge/
seated Indian and Crest/cattle driving scene
See subheadings
Colour: Black with overall green tint

Back Design: Lathework and bank name
Colour: Green

IMPRINT
Rawdon, Wright, Hatch & Edson Montreal & N.Y. and American Bank Note Co. "mono"

SIGNATURES
left	right
mss. various	mss. various

2. ENGRAVED "BOWMANVILLE"
ONE BLUE SHEET NUMBER (AT BOTTOM) 1857

ISSUE DATING
Engraved
Aug't. 15th 1857

OVERPRINT
"GUELPH" twice in red
"MONTREAL" twice in red
"PRESCOTT" in blue
"TORONTO" twice in blue
"ALEXANDRIA" in blue

Cat. No.	Denom.	Date	VG	F	VF	EF	Unc
10-02-02	$1	1857	900.	1,100.	-	-	-
10-02-04	$2	1957	1,000.	1,200.	-	-	-
10-02-06P	$5	1857			FACE PROOF		500.
10-02-08P	$10	1857			FACE PROOF		500.

Note: A $1 1857 face proof is known with red-orange tint.

4. ENGRAVED "MONTREAL"
ONE BLUE SHEET NUMBER (AT BOTTOM) 1857

ISSUE DATING
Engraved
Augt. 15 1857

OVERPRINT
"OSHAWA" twice in red
"TORONTO" in blue

Cat. No.	Denom.	Date	VG	F	VF	EF	Unc
10-04-02	$1	1857	900.	1,100.	-	-	-
10-04-04	$2	1857	1,000.	1,250.	-	-	-
10-04-06P	$5	1857			FACE PROOF		500.
10-04-08P	$10	1857			FACE PROOF		500.

6. ENGRAVED "BOWMANVILLE"
ONE RED SHEET NUMBER (AT BOTTOM) 1861

ISSUE DATING
Engraved
Augt. 15th 1861

OVERPRINT
"GUELPH" twice in red
"DUNDAS" twice in red
"TORONTO" twice in blue

Cat. No.	Denom.	Date	VG	F	VF	EF	Unc
10-06-02	$1	1861	900.	1,250.	-	-	-
10-06-04	$2	1861	900.	1,250.	-	-	-
10-06-06	$5	1861	900.	1,250.	-	-	-
10-06-08	$10	1861	900.	1,250.	-	-	-

8. ENGRAVED "BOWMANVILLE"
TWO RED SHEET NUMBERS (AT TOP) 1861

ISSUE DATING
Engraved
Augt. 15th 1861

OVERPRINT
"HAMILTON" twice in blue
"LINDSAY" twice in red

Cat. No.	Denom.	Date	VG	F	VF	EF	Unc
10-08-02	$1	1861	700.	900.	-	-	-
10-08-04	$2	1861	700.	900.	-	-	-
10-08-06P	$5	1861			FACE PROOF		500.
10-08-08P	$10	1861			FACE PROOF		500.

THE ONTARIO BANK

**10. ENGRAVED "BOWMANVILLE"
TWO BLUE SHEET NUMBERS (AT TOP) 1861**

ISSUE DATING
Engraved
Augt. 15th 1861

OVERPRINT
"GUELPH" twice in red
"WHITBY" twice in blue
"MONTREAL" twice in red

Cat. No.	Denom.	Date	VG	F	VF	EF	Unc
10-10-02	$1	1861	700.	900.	-	-	-
10-10-04	$2	1861	700.	900.	-	-	-
10-10-06P	$5	1861			FACE PROOF		500.
10-10-08P	$10	1861			FACE PROOF		500.

555-12   ISSUE OF 1860

DESIGNS AND COLOURS

555-12-02P
$20 Face Design: Young woman resting on hay/—/farm boy sitting with sheep; Prince Albert
Colour: Black with green tint

Back Design: Lathework, counters and bank name
Colour: Green

555-12-04P
$50 Face Design: Allegorical women with beehive, cornucopia/Prince of Wales/allegorical woman with cornucopia, grapes
Colour: Black with green tint

Back Design: Lathework, counters and bank name
Colour: Green

555-12-06P
$100 Face Design: Prince of Wales/two seated allegorical women "Prosperity"/—
Colour: Black with green tint

Back Design: Lathework, counters and bank name
Colour: Green

IMPRINT
American Bank Note Company

SIGNATURES
left   right
none   none

ISSUE DATING
Engraved
Aug. 3rd 1860
Aug't 3rd 1860

Cat. No.	Denom.	Date		Unc
12-02P	$20	1860	FACE PROOF	600
12-04P	$50	1860	FACE PROOF	600
12-06P	$100	1860	FACE PROOF	600

555-14   ISSUES OF 1870

DESIGNS AND COLOURS

555-14-02
$4 Face Design: Farmer ploughing/—/Prince Arthur
Colour: Black with green tint

Back Design: Lathework, counters and bank name
Colour: Green

THE ONTARIO BANK

555-14-04
$5 Face Design: Prince Arthur/farm woman with sickle/ portrait of woman "Adrienne"
Colour: Black with green tint

Back Design: Lathework, counters and bank name
Colour: Green

555-14-06
$10 Face Design: Woodsman felling tree/—/ girl holding scroll of Confederation
Colour: Black with green tint

Back Design: Lathework, counters and bank name
Colour: Green

IMPRINT
British American Bank Note Co. Montreal & Ottawa

SIGNATURES
left	right
$4: none	mss. illegible
$5 and $10: mss. various	engr. J. Simpson

ISSUE DATING
Engraved
$4:   Augt 1st 1870
$5 and $10:   Novr. 1st 1870

OVERPRINT
"LINDSAY" twice in blue
"PETERBORO" twice in blue
"MONTREAL" twice in blue
"OSHAWA" twice in blue

Note: Beware of counterfeits, some with overprints, that have a crude imprint of the British American Bank Note Co. on the bottom. Prices given are for genuine notes.

Cat. No.	Denom.	Date	VG	F	VF	EF	Unc
14-02	$4	1870	600.	900.	1,200.	-	-
14-04	$5	1870	600.	800.	1,100.	-	-
14-06	$10	1870	600.	800.	1,100.	-	-

555-16   **ISSUE OF 1882**

DESIGNS AND COLOURS

555-16-02
$5 Face Design: Portrait of woman "Lucy"/ Indian girl and Crest/train at station
Colour: Black with green tint

Back Design: Lathework, counters, bank name and Crest
Colour: Green

THE ONTARIO BANK

555-16-04P
$10 **Face Design:** Prince Arthur/dockside scene/
girl with agricultural emblems
Colour: Black with green tint

Back Design: Lathework, counters, bank name and Crest
Colour: Green

555-16-06P
$10 **Face Design:** Cattle grazing/—/
girl with agricultural emblems
Colour: Black with green tint

Back Design: Lathework, counters, bank name and Crest
Colour: Green

555-16-08
$100 **Face Design:** Prince of Wales/
allegorical females "Prosperity"/—
Colour: Black with green tint

Back Design: Lathework, counters, bank name and Crest
Colour: Green

IMPRINT
British American Bank Note Co. Monteal

SIGNATURES
left	right
engr. W.P. Howland	mss. various

ISSUE DATING
Engraved
July 3rd 1882
1st September 1882 ($100)

Cat. No.	Denom.	Date	Variety	VG	F	VF	EF	Unc
16-02	$5	1882		1,600.	-	-	-	-
16-04P	$10	1882	Prince Arthur vign.			FACE PROOF		500.
16-06P	$10	1882	Cattle grazing vign.			FACE PROOF		500.
16-08P	$100	1882				FACE PROOF		500.

555-18   **ISSUE OF 1888**

DESIGNS AND COLOURS

555-18-02
$5 **Face Design:** Farmer feeding hay to horse "Old Burhans"/
Indian brave/woman with hand on wheel
Colour: Black with yellow and orange tint

Back Design: Lathework, counters and bank name
Colour: Orange

555-18-04
$5 **Face Design:** Farmer feeding hay to horse "Old Burhans"/
Indian brave/woman with hand on wheel
(1903 overprint)
Colour: Black with yellow and orange tint

THE ONTARIO BANK

Back Design: Lathework, counters and bank name
Colour: Orange

Back Design: Lathework, counters and bank name
Colour: Green

555-18-06
$10 Face Design: Baby and young girl "Calmady children"/seated allegorical female/sailor boy holding hat
Colour: Black with yellow-green and orange tint

555-18-12P
$50 Face Design: Seated woman with water jar "River Source"/—/sailor, anchor and small boat
Colour: Black with yellow-green and red tint

Back Design: Lathework, counters, bank name and flowers
Colour: Olive

Back Design: Lathework, counters and bank name
Colour: Brown

IMPRINT
American Bank Note Co. Ottawa
American Bank Note Co. N.Y.
American Bank Note Co. New York

OVERPRINTS
"1903" twice in red

SIGNATURES
	left	right
1888:	engr. W.P. Howland	mss. various
1903:	engr. George R.R. Cockburn	mss. various

ISSUE DATING
Engraved
1st June 1888

555-18-10P
$20 Face Design: Laureate busts of two allegorical women "Reapers"/seated woman and sheep/—
Colour: Black with yellow and blue tint

Cat. No.	Denom.	Date	Variety	VG	F	VF	EF	Unc
18-02	$5	1888		1,100.	1,450.	2,100.	-	-
18-04	$5	1888	Red o/p, 1903	1,400.	1,800.	2,600.	-	-
18-06	$10	1888		1,300.	1,700.	2,500.	-	-
18-08	$10	1888	Red o/p, 1903	1,300.	1,700.	2,500.	-	-
18-10P	$20	1888				FACE PROOF		600.
18-12P	$50	1888				FACE PROOF		600.

555-20   **$5 ISSUE OF 1898**

DESIGNS AND COLOURS

555-20-02
- **$5 Face Design:** Portrait of woman "Lucy"/ female figure and cherubs, ornate V/ bull's head
- **Colour:** Black with green tint

- **Back Design:** Lathework, counters and bank name
- **Colour:** Green

IMPRINT
British American Bank Note Co. Ottawa

SIGNATURES
left	right
engr. George R.R. Cockburn	mss. various

ISSUE DATING
Engraved
Jan. 1st 1898.

Cat. No. Denom.	Date	VG	F	VF	EF	Unc
20-02 $5	1898	1,400.	1,900.	-	-	-

Note: Face proof exists with red-brown face tint.

THE BANK OF OTTAWA

1837

MONTREAL, LOWER CANADA

BANK NUMBER 560   **NONREDEEMABLE**

This "spurious" bank was established in 1837 by a group of New York swindlers. Ottawa was known as Bytown until the 1860s.

560-10   **DRAFT ISSUE OF 1837**
FRENCH TEXT

DESIGNS AND COLOURS

560-10-02
- **$5 Face Design:** —/Royal Crest; small horse's head at bottom/ King William IV
- **Colour:** Black with no tint
- **Back Design:** Lathework, miniature vignettes and "steel plate"
- **Colour:** Blue

IMPRINT
Burton, Gurley & Edmonds, N. York

SIGNATURES
left	right
mss. D. Moir Thom	mss. A. Sears

ISSUE DATING
Partially engraved _ 18_:
1837: April 1, Apr. 15, May 15

Cat. No. Denom.	Date	VG	F	VF	EF	Unc
10-02 $5	1837	525.	750.	-	-	-

560-12   **DRAFT ISSUE OF 1837**
ENGLISH TEXT

DESIGNS AND COLOURS

560-02-02
- **$1 Face Design:** Woman pouring wine "Temperance"/ three allegorical women; small crown at bottom/helmeted woman with eagle "Prudence"
- **Colour:** Black with no tint
- **Back Design:** See subheadings
- **Colour:** See subheadings

THE BANK OF OTTAWA

560-04-04
$3 Face Design: Allegorical female with foot on globe/ mill scene, small horse's head at bottom/ bust of young woman
Colour: Black with no tint

Back Design: See subheadings
Colour: See subheadings

560-02-04R
$5 (£1.5) Face Design: Floral panel/semi-nude, reclining Indian maiden; small lion on crown at bottom/ James Fox
See subheadings
Colour: Black with no tint

Back Design: See subheadings
Colour: See subheadings

IMPRINT
Burton, Gurley & Edmonds, N. York

2. "ACCEPTED FOR MESSRS. JOSEPH C. FRINK & CO." AT BOTTOM, BLUE BACK

DESIGNS AND COLOURS
Back Design: Lathework, miniature vignettes of horsehead, deer head, small train, steamboat and "steel plate"
Colour: Blue

SIGNATURES
left — mss. D. Moir Thom
right — mss. Peter Hicker

ISSUE DATING
Partially engraved ___ 18___:
1837: Aug. 10; Oct. 11
1844: Jany

Cat. No.	Denom.	Date	Variety	VG	F	VF	EF	Unc
12-02-02	$1	1837		525.	700.	-	-	-
12-02-04R	$5 (£1.5)	18_	Remainder*	425.	575.	-	-	-

* Signed and numbered, but undated.

3. "ACCEPTED FOR D.F. MERRILL & CO" AT BOTTOM

DESIGNS AND COLOURS
Back Design: Plain

SIGNATURES
left — mss. D. Moir Thom
right — —

ISSUE DATING
Partially Engraved ___ 18___:
1837: May 18

Cat.No.	Denom.	Date	VG	F	VF	EF	Unc
12-03-02	$1	1837	450.	600.	-	-	-

4. "ACCEPTED FOR ____" AT BOTTOM, PLAIN BACK

DESIGNS AND COLOURS
Back Design: Plain

SIGNATURES
left — mss. A. Keith
right — mss. H. Fitch

ISSUE DATING
Partially engraved _ 18_:
1837: Nov. 1
1838: Jan. 4

STAMP
"SECURED BY REAL ESTATE" in black

Cat. No.	Denom.	Date	VG	F	VF	EF	Unc
12-04-02	$1	1837	450.	600.	-	-	-
12-04-04	$3	1838	650.	900.	-	-	-

560-14   ISSUE OF 1837
DESIGNS AND COLOURS

560-14-02
- **$10 Face Design:** Three cherubs with slab bearing "TEN"/ small lion on crown below/ woman with spear
- **Colour:** Black with no tint
- **Back Design:** Lathework, miniature vignettes and steel plate
- **Colour:** Blue

IMPRINT
Burton, Gurley & Edmonds, N. York

SIGNATURES
left	right
mss. D. Moir Thom	mss. A. Sears

ISSUE DATING
Partially engraved ___ 18___:
1837: April 1

Cat. No.	Denom.	Date	VG	F	VF	EF	Unc
14-02	$10	1837	675.	1,000.	-	-	-

THE BANK OF OTTAWA
1874-1919
OTTAWA (ONTARIO) DOMINION OF CANADA

BANK NUMBER 565   **REDEEMABLE**

Established in 1874 in Ottawa, this bank dominated the banking facilities in that city. The Bank of Ottawa had been founded by men who were pioneers in the Ottawa Valley lumber industry. After World War I the bank had reached a point where new capital and vigorous expansion were necessary to maintain its earnings. The offer made by the Bank of Nova Scotia to absorb the bank looked attractive, and the merger was finalized in 1919.

565-10   ISSUE OF 1874
DESIGNS AND COLOURS

565-10-02
- **$4 Face Design:** Hon. George Bryson/Crest of Ottawa/ James Maclaren
- **Colour:** Black with green tint

- **Back Design:** Lathework, counters and bank name
- **Colour:** Green

565-10-04
- **$5 Face Design:** Hon. George Bryson/Crest of Ottawa/ James Maclaren
- **Colour:** Black with green tint

THE BANK OF OTTAWA

Back Design: Lathework, counters and bank name
Colour: Green

565-10-06P
$10 Face Design: Hon. George Bryson/Crest of Ottawa/ James Maclaren
Colour: Black with green tint

Back Design: Lathework, counters and bank name
Colour: Green

IMPRINT
British American Bank Note Co. Montreal

SIGNATURES
left	right
mss. P. Robinson	engr. James Maclaren
mss. Geo. Burn	engr. James Maclaren

ISSUE DATING
Engraved
2nd Novr. 1874

Cat. No.	Denom.	Date	VG	F	VF	EF	Unc
10-02	$4	1874	1,600.	2,100.	-	-	-
10-04	$5	1874	1,500.	2,000.	-	-	-
10-06P	$10	1874			FACE PROOF		500.

565-12   **ISSUE OF 1880**
DESIGNS AND COLOURS

565-12-02
$5 Face Design: Shepherd girl with lamb, ewe/ logging scene/seated woman with pen and book "Trade"
Colour: Black with olive tint

Back Design: —/rafting scene/—
Colour: Brown

565-12-04
$10 Face Design: Bust of blacksmith in oval/"Justice" figure flanked by Crest in oval and loggers in oval/bust of sailor
Colour: Black with olive tint

Back Design: —/Indian maiden/—
Colour: Brown

565-12-04aS
$10 Face Deisgn: Bust of blacksmith in oval/"Justice" figure flanked by Crest in oval adn loggers in oval/ bust of sailor
Colour: Black with olive tint

IMPRINT
American Bank Note Co. New York

SIGNATURES
left	right
mss. Geo. Burn	engr. James Maclaren

ISSUE DATING
Engraved
2nd Novr. 1880

OVERPRINT
"WINNIPEG" twice vertically in blue

Cat. No.	Denom.	Date	VG	F	VF	EF	Unc
12-02	$5	1880	1,400.	1,900.	2,800.	-	-
12-02a	$5	1880	Winnipeg		SPECIMEN		750.
12-04	$10	1880	1,450.	1,950.	2,900.	-	-
12-04a	$10	1880	Winnipeg		SPECIMEN		750.

565-14   ISSUES OF 1888 AND 1891

DESIGNS AND COLOURS

565-14-02P
$5 Face Design: Lumberjack felling tree/cattle/ James Maclaren
Colour: Black with red-brown tint

Back Design: Lathework, counters, bank name and crest
Colour: Green

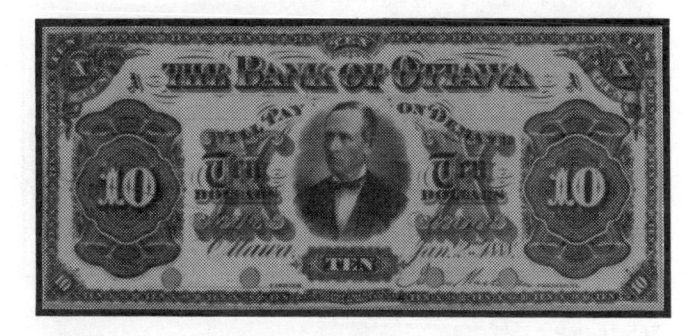

565-14-04P
$10 Face Design: —/James Maclaren/—
Colour: Black with red-brown tint

Back Design: Lathework, counters, bank name and crest
Colour: Green

565-14-06P
$20 Face Design: —/loggers at work, James Maclaren, "Canal Locks No. 2"/—
Colour: Black with overall green tint

THE BANK OF OTTAWA

Back Design: lathework, counters, bank name and Crest of Ottawa
Colour: Green

565-14-08P
$50 Face Design: Farmer with dog/Parliament buildings, James McLaren/three horses heads
Colour: Black with overall green tint

Back Design: Unknown
Colour: Green

IMPRINT
British American Bank Note Company

SIGNATURES
left	right
mss. various	engr. James Maclaren

ISSUE DATING
Engraved
Jan. 2, 1888
Jan. 2, 1891
2nd Jan. 1891

Cat. No.	Denom.	Date	VG	F	VF	EF	Unc
14-02	$5	1888	1,300.	1,800.	2,700.	-	-
14-04P	$10	1888			FACE PROOF		500.
14-06P	$20	1891			FACE PROOF		500.
14-08P	$50	1891			FACE PROOF		500.

565-16 ISSUES OF 1895 AND 1900
DESIGNS AND COLOURS

565-16-02
$5 Face Design: Charles Magee/Parliament Buildings/—
Back Design: Lathework, counters, bank name and Crest of Ottawa

565-16-04
$5 Face Design: Charles Magee/Parliament Buildings/—Dominion of Canada at top
Back Design: Lathework, counters, bank name and Crest of Ottawa

565-16-06P
$5 Face Design: Charles Magee/allegorical female/Parliament Buildings, East Block
Back Design: Lathework, counters, bank name and Crest of Ottawa
1895 Face Colour: Black with green tint
Back Colour: Green

565-16-08
$10 1900 Face Colour: Black with enlarged ochre or olive tint "Dominion of Canada" at the top
Back Colour: Green

THE BANK OF OTTAWA

IMPRINT
British American Bank Note Co. Ottawa

SIGNATURES
left	right
mss. various	engr. Charles Magee

ISSUE DATING
Engraved
Jan. 2nd 1895
June 1st 1900

Note: The tint design and location in the 1900 issues differs from 1895 issues. Also "Dominion of Canada" is engraved at the top of the 1900 issues.

Cat. No.	Denom.	Date	VG	F	VF	EF	Unc
16-02	$5	1895	1,300.	1,800.	2,700.	-	-
16-04	$5	1900	1,300.	1,800.	2,700.	-	-
16-06	$10	1895	1,660.	2,100.	3,300.	-	-
16-08	$10	1900	1,660.	2,100.	3,300.	-	-

565-18   ISSUE OF 1903

DESIGNS AND COLOURS

565-18-02
$5 **Face Design:** Locomotive/Parliament Buildings/—
Colour: Black with ochre tint

Back Design: —/Crest/—
Colour: Green

565-18-03

Photo Not Available

$5 **Face Design:** Locomotive/Parliament Buildings/—
Colour: Black with larger ochre tint (large tint variety)

Back Design: Lathework, counters, bank name and Crest
Colour: Green

565-18-04
$10 **Face Design:** Head office/cattle scene/Parliament Buildings, East Block
Colour: Black with enlarged olive tint

565-18-06
$10 **Face Design:** Head office/cattle scene/Parliament buildings, east block
Colour: Black with modified (less) tint

Back Design: Lathework, counters, bank name and Crest
See varieties
Colour: Green

565-18-11E
$20 **Face Design:** —/logger at work, Hon. George Bryson, canal locks "Canal Locks No. 2"/—
Colour: Black with green tint

Back Design: Lathework, counters, bank name and Crest
Colour: Green

THE BANK OF OTTAWA

565-18-12
- **$20 Face Design:** —/loggers at work, James McLaren, canal locks "Canal Locks No. 2"/—
- **Colour:** Black with green tint
- **Back Design:** Lathework, counters, bank name and Crest
- **Colour:** Green

565-18-16
- **$50 Face Design:** Farmer with horse, dog and hay "Old Burhans"/Parliament Buildings, James Mclaren/three horses' heads
- **Colour:** Black with green tint 
- **Back Design:** —/Crest/—
- **Colour:** Green

565-18-18P
- **$50 Face Design:** Farmer with horse, dog and hay, "Old Burhans"/Parliament buildings James McLaren/three horses' heads
- **Colour:** Black with overall green tint
- **Back Design:** lathework, counters, bank name and Crest
- **Colour:** Green

IMPRINT
British American Bank Note Co. Ottawa

SIGNATURES

left	right
mss. various	engr. Geo. Hay
mss. various	engr. David Maclaren
mss. various	engr. George Bryson

ISSUE DATING
Engraved
Jan. 2nd 1903
2nd Jan 1903

VARIETIES
- **$10 Face Colour:** Large olive tint
- **$10 Face Colour:** Modified olive tint (reduced)

Cat. No.	Denom.	Date	Variety	VG	F	VF	EF	Unc
18-02	$5	1903		1,200.	1,650.	2,400.	-	-
18-03P	$5	1903	Large tint				PROOF	600.
18-04	$10	1903	Large tint	1,300.	1,700.	2,500.	-	-
18-06	$10	1903	Modified tint	1,300.	1,700.	2,500.	-	-
18-08	$20	1903	Hay, r.	1,500.	1,900.	2,900.	-	-
18-10	$20	1903	Maclaren, r.	1,500.	1,900.	2,900.	-	-
18-11E	$20	1903	Bryson, r.				ESSAY	2,000.
18-12	$20	1903	Bryson, r.	1,500.	1,900.	2,900.	-	-
18-14	$50	1903	Hay, r.	1,500.	1,900.	2,900.	-	-
18-16	$50	1903	Maclaren, r.	1,500.	1,900.	2,900.	-	-
18-18	$50	1903	Bryson, r.	1,500.	1,900.	2,900.	-	-

565-20   **ISSUE OF 1906**

DESIGNS AND COLOURS

565-20-04
- **$5 Face Design:** logging camp scene
- **Colour:** See varieties
- **Back Design:** lathework, counters, bank name and Crest of Ottawa 
- **Colour:** Green

THE BANK OF OTTAWA

565-20-10
$10 Face Design: —/dairy farm scene/—
Colour: See varieties

Back Design: Lathework, counters, bank name and Crest of Ottawa
Colour: Green

IMPRINT
American Bank Note Co. Ottawa

SIGNATURES
left	right
mss. various	typed Geo. Hay
mss. various	typed David Maclaren

ISSUE DATING
Engraved
June 1st 1906

VARIETIES
Face Colour: Black with green tint; Hay signature
Black with green tint; Maclaren signature
Black with yellow and green tint; Maclaren signature

Cat. No.	Denom.	Date	Variety	VG	F	VF	EF	Unc
20-02	$5	1906	Hay, r.	750.	1,100.	1,500.	-	-
20-04	$5	1906	Maclaren, r., green	750.	1,100.	1,500.	-	-
20-06	$5	1906	Maclaren, r., yellow	750.	1,100.	1,500.	-	-
20-08	$10	1906	Hay, r., green	750.	1,100.	1,500.	-	-
20-10	$10	1906	Maclaren, r., green	750.	1,100.	1,500.	-	-
20-12	$10	1906	Maclaren, r., yellow	750.	1,100.	1,500.	-	-

565-22   **ISSUE OF 1912**
DESIGNS AND COLOURS

565-22-02
$5 Face Design: —/logging camp scene/—
Colour: Black with blue tint

Back Design: Lathework, counters, bank name and Ottawa Crest
Colour: Olive

IMPRINT
Waterlow & Sons, Ld. London Wall, London

SIGNATURES
left	right
mss. various	engr. David Maclaren

ISSUE DATING
Engraved
June 1st, 1912

Note: A specimen of this issue is known with red face tint and brown back tint.

Cat. No.	Denom.	Date	VG	F	VF	EF	Unc
22-02	$5	1912	750.	1,050.	1,400.	2,300.	-

565-24   **ISSUE OF AUGUST 1, 1913**
DESIGNS AND COLOURS

565-24-02
$10 Face Design: —/dairy farm scene/—
Colour: See varieties

Back Design: —/Crest of Ottawa/—
Colour: Green

THE BANK OF OTTAWA

IMPRINT
American Bank Note Co. Ottawa

SIGNATURES
left	right
mss. various	typed George Bryson

ISSUE DATING
Engraved
August 1st, 1913

VARIETIES
Face Colour: Black with green tint
Face Colour: Black with ochre and green tint

Cat. No.	Denom.	Date	Variety	VG	F	VF	EF	Unc
24-02	$10	1913	Green tint	700.	1,000.	-	-	-
24-04	$10	1913	Ochre tint	700.	1,000.	-	-	-

565-26 ISSUE OF SEPTEMBER 1, 1913

DESIGNS AND COLOURS

565-26-02
$5 Face Design: —/logging camp scene/—
Colour: Black with blue-green plate and ochre tint

Back Design: —/Crest of Ottawa/—
Colour: Brown

565-26-08
$10 Face Design: —/cattle herded under trees/—
Colour: Black with green tint

Back Design: —/Crest of Ottawa/—
Colour: Green

IMPRINT
$5: Waterlow & Sons, Ld. London Wall, London
$10: British American Bank Note Co. Ottawa

SIGNATURES
left	right
mss. various	engr. George Bryson

ISSUE DATING
Engraved
September 1st 1913
Sep. 1st 1913

Note: Specimens of the $5 issue are known with orange face tint and brown back tint and also lilac face plate with orange and green tint and red-brown back tint.

Cat. No.	Denom.	Date	VG	F	VF	EF	Unc
26-02	$5	1913	425.	600.	900.	1,500.	-
26-04	$10	1913	700.	1,000.	1,500.	2,400.	-

565-28 $5 DESIGN OF 1906 RESUMED 1917

DESIGNS AND COLOURS

565-28-02
$5 Face Design: —/logging camp scene/—
Colour: Black with yellow and green tint

Back Design: —/Crest of Ottawa/—
Colour: Green

IMPRINT
American Bank Note Co. Ottawa

SIGNATURES
left	right
mss. various	typed George Bryson

ISSUE DATING
Engraved
June 1st 1917

Cat. No.	Denom.	Date	VG	F	VF	EF	Unc
28-02	$5	1917	700.	1,100.	1,700.	2,800.	-

THE BANK OF THE PEOPLE
1835-1841
TORONTO, UPPER CANADA

BANK NUMBER 570   **REDEEMABLE**

Established in Toronto in 1835 as a joint-stock bank by supporters of the Reform Movememt, this institution was the only bank in Canada that did not suspend specie payment in 1837. Its entire capital stock of £50,000 was bought up by the Bank of Montreal in 1840, giving the latter access to business in Upper Canada through the agency of the Bank of the People. When Upper and Lower Canada were united in 1841, the Bank of Montreal was able to operate in the upper province in its own name, and the process of the absorption of the Bank of the People was completed.

DESIGNS AND COLOURS

570-5   DRAPER, TOPPAN, LONGACRE ISSUE

570-5-02
- **$1 (5s) Face Design:** Three standing women/ships and paddlewheeler, small primitive train below/three standing women
- **Colour:** Black with no tint
- **Back Design:** Plain

570-5-10
- **$5 (25s) Face Design:** Standing justice figure/primitive train pulling stagecoach, dog, safe and key below/seated justice figure
- **Colour:** Black with no tint
- **Back Design:** Plain

IMPRINT
Draper, Toppan, Longacre & Co. Phila & N.Y.

SIGNATURES
Left	Right
Unknown	Unknown

ISSUE DATING
Partially Engraved ___18___:

570-10   ISSUE OF 1836-1840

- Note I: Denominations are listed in English, French and in German.
- Note II: Written in light purple ink on the $10 proof is "April 9, 1842" with sheet number 1106. The left signature is J.C. Walsh and the right signature is illegible.
- Note III: A spurious $10 note with almost the same design and bank title is known. See United States Obsolete Bank Notes, Haxby, NY, 1275-S5
- Note IV: 10-02R exists with spurious dates and signatures.

570-10-02
- **$1 (5s) Face Design:** Allegorical woman seated beside hay/view of Toronto from harbour; small steamboat below/seated allegorical male with chest and anchor
- **Colour:** Black with no tint
- **Back Design:** Plain

570-10-04P
- **$2 (10s) Face Design:** Paddlewheel steamer with U.S. flag/allegorical woman seated beside hay, cattle; small early train below/Toronto harbour
- **Colour:** Black with no tint
- **Back Design:** Plain

570-10-05
- **$3 (15s) Face Design:** —/Three seated allegorical women, crown below/—
- **Colour:** Black with no tint
- **Back Design:** Plain

THE BANK OF THE PEOPLE

Cat. No.	Denom.	Date	VG	F	VF	EF	Unc
10-02P	$1 (5s)	18_				PROOF	900.
10-02R	$1 (5s)	1836	1,800.	2,525.	-	-	-
10-04P	$2 (10s)	18_				PROOF	900.
10-05	$3	1840	2,000.	2,750.	-	-	-
10-06	$4 (20S)	1840	2,000.	2,800.	-	-	-
10-08	$8 (£2)	1840	4,000.	5,600.	-	-	-
10-10P	$10	18_				PROOF	900.
10-20P	$20	18__	SURVIVING EXAMPLES NOT CONFIRMED				
10-30	$50	18__	SURVIVING EXAMPLES NOT CONFIRMED				

570-10-06
$4 (20s) Face Design: James Fox/reclining Indian maiden/—
Colour: Black with no tint

Back Design: Plain

570-10-08
$8 (£2) Face Design: —/royal Crest/—
Colour: Black with no tint

Back Design: Plain

570-10-10P
$10 Face Design: James Fox/farm tools, lion in shield, ships/ young farm girl
Colour: Black with no tint

Back Design: Plain

IMPRINT
Casilear, Durand, Burton & Edmonds N. York

SIGNATURES

left	right
mss. F. Hincks	mss. J. Leslie
mss. J.N. Wenham	mss. Benj. Thorne
mss. J. Hastings	mss. F. Wright

ISSUE DATING
Partially Engraved ___ 18___:
$1, 1836: 12 Dec.
1840: April
$3 1840: 9 Oct
$4 1840: 9 Oct.
$8 1840: 8 June
$10 1842: April 9

LA BANQUE DU PEUPLE

1835-1895

MONTREAL, LOWER CANADA

BANK NUMBER 575   **REDEEMABLE**

Founded in 1835 by Viger, deWitt & Cie, this bank was organized on the en commandite principle, whereby the 12 partners had unlimited liability, while their stockholders were liable only to the extent of their equity. A charter was granted in 1844, setting the authorized capital at £200,000. The failure of several of its debtors precipitated the collapse of the bank in 1895, in which the creditors lost $1,718,284. There followed a wave of failures of Quebec industries that had been supported by the bank.

575-10   **ISSUE OF 1835-1836**

DESIGNS AND COLOURS

575-10-02-02
- **$1 Face Design:** Seated shepherd boy/two men, cattle and sheep; child riding deer below/ kneeling cherub engraving stone
- **Colour:** Black with no tint 
- **Back Design:** Lathework/habitant/lathework
- **Colour:** Blue

575-10-02-06
- **$2 Face Design:** Portrait of man; two allegorical women in clouds; man in canoe below/ seated allegorical female
- **Colour:** Black with no tint
- **Back Design:** Lathework/habitant/lathework
- **Colour:** Blue

575-10-02-10R
- **$5 Face Design:** Louis-Joseph Papineau/ woman in chariot drawn by lions; small sailing ship below/—
- **Colour:** Black with no tint
- **Back Design:** Lathework/habitant/lathework
- **Colour:** Blue

575-10-04-04
- **$10 Face Design:** —/ship and seated allegorical male "Commerce"; small steamboat below/Louis-Joseph Papineau
- **Colour:** Black with no tint
- **Back Design:** Lathework/habitant/lathework
- **Colour:** Blue

IMPRINT
Rawdon, Wright, Hatch & Co. New York

2.   **DRAFTS: "Messrs. Viger, Dewitt & Cie" ENGRAVED AT LOWER LEFT**

The company name is also endorsed vertically across the face on fully completed drafts.

SIGNATURES

	left	right
$1 and $2:	mss. E.R. Fabré, none	mss. various mss. Jogn Donegani
$5 and $10:	none	mss. various

ISSUE DATING
     Partially engraved ___ 18___ :
     1835: 11 Juillet
     1836: 2 Aout

Note: Back proofs known in black.

Cat. No.	Denom.	Date	Variety	VG	F	VF	EF	Unc
10-02-02	$1	1835		650.	900.	-	-	-
10-02-04	$1	1836		650.	900.	-	-	-
10-02-06	$2	1835		750.	1,100.	-	-	-
10-02-10R	$5	18_	Remainder*	-	-	-	350.	700.
10-02-14R	$10	18_	Remainder*	-	-	-	350.	700.
Full sheet	$1,2,5,10	18_	Remainder*	-	-	-	-	2,500.

* Unsigned, undated and unnumbered.

LA BANQUE DU PEUPLE

4. **NOTES: COMPANY NAME REPLACED BY "_____ CAISSIER"**

SIGNATURES
  left
    mss. B.H. Lemoine
  right
    mss. Viger DeWitt & Cie

ISSUE DATING
  Partially engraved ___ 18___:
    1835: 11 Juillet
    1836: 1 Mars, 2 Mai

Cat. No.	Denom.	Date	Variety	VG	F	VF	EF	Unc
10-04-02	$5	1835		850.	1,200.	-	-	-
10-04-04	$10	1836		850.	1,200.	-	-	-

575-12 $5 ISSUE OF 1838
DESIGNS AND COLOURS

575-12-02
  $5 Face Design: Seated woman, lamb/ farm family eating by wheat field/ five Spanish dollars
  Colour: Black with no tint

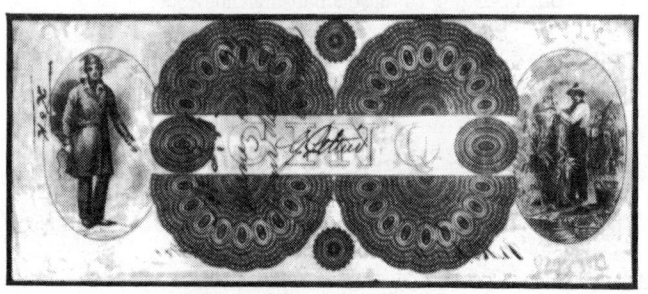

  Back Design: Habitant/lathework and counters/ man picking corn
  Colour: Blue

IMPRINT
  Rawdon, Wright & Hatch, New York

SIGNATURES
  left
    mss. B. Lemoine
  right
    mss. Viger DeWitt & Cie

ISSUE DATING
  Engraved
    1st July 1838

Note: Back proof is known in red and black.

Cat. No.	Denom.	Date	VG	F	VF	EF	Unc
12-02R	$5	18__	300.	500.	-	-	-
12-02	$5	1838	850.	1,200.	-	-	-

575-14 DURAND & CO. PRINTINGS 1839-1845
DESIGNS AND COLOURS

575-14-02-02
  $1 (5s) Face Design: Christ child/angel with cherub and Britannia in shield; agricultural tools below/Christ child
    See subheadings
  Colour: Black with no tint

  Back Design: Spanish dollar/ seated "Agriculture" figure/habitant
  Colour: Blue

575-14-02-04
  $2 Face Design: Woman seated by shield/ angel with cherub and Britannis in shield; agricultural tools below/—
    See subheadings
  Colour: Black with no tint

  Back Design: Reverses of two Spanish dollars/ seated "Agriculture" figure/habitant
  Colour: Blue

575-14-04-04
$2 (10s) Face Design: Woman seated by shield/
angel with cherub and Britannia in shield;
agricultural tools below/—
See subheadings
Colour: Black with no tint

Back Design: Reverses of two Spanish dollars/
seated "Agriculture" figure/habitant
Colour: Blue

IMPRINT
Durand & Compy New York

2. **DRAFTS "A Messrs. Viger Dewitt & Cie"**
    ENGRAVED AT LOWER LEFT
    1839 DOLLARS ONLY

The company name is also endorsed vertically across the right end of the face.

SIGNATURES
                              right only
                              mss. Jogn Donegani

ISSUE DATING
   Engraved
      1st October 1839

Cat. No.	Denom.	Date	VG	F	VF	EF	Unc
14-02-02	$1	1839	700.	1,000.	-	-	-
14-02-04	$2	1839	800.	1,100.	-	-	-

4. **NOTES: COMPANY NAME REPLACED BY**
    "_____ CASH", 1845
    DOLLARS/POUNDS & SHILLINGS

The text is slightly modified to include dual denominations.

SIGNATURES
   left   right
   mss. B.H. Lemoine   mss. J. DeWitt (v)

ISSUE DATING
   Partially engraved ___ 184_:
      1845: 1 Mars

Cat. No.	Denom.	Date	VG	F	VF	EF	Unc
14-04-02	$1 (5s)	1845	700.	1,000.	-	-	-
14-04-04	$2 (10s)	1845	800.	1,100.	-	-	-

TOPPAN CARPENTER PRINTINGS
1845-1892

The basic designs are the same for 575-16, 18 and 20. Only the denominations, tints and imprints change.

DESIGNS AND COLOURS

575-16-02-04
$1 (5s) Face Design: Man constructing barrel/
boy carrying sheaf of wheat and cradle/
four cherubs with numeral 1
Colour: See subheadings

Back Design: Habitant/lathework and counter/habitant
Colour: See subheadings

575-16-02-16
$2 (10s) Face Design: Man sharpening scythe/
two men with sledge and axe/
dog lying by strong box
Colour: See subheadings

LA BANQUE DU PEUPLE

Back Design: Lathework and counters/habitant/ lathework and counters
Colour: See subheadings

575-16-02-22
$4 (20s) Face Design: Seated carpenter/milkmaids and cows, ships; dog's head below/blacksmith
Colour: See subheadings

Back Design: —/portrait of young woman in oval/—
Colour: See subheadings

575-20-02-02
$5 (£1.5) Face Design: "Commerce" figure holding counter/ seated woman with sheaves in ornate V/ allegorical female seated on globe and blowing trumpet
Colour: See subheadings

Back Design: —/man and woman seated by ornate 5/—
Colour: See subheadings

575-20-02-04
$10 (£2.10) Face Design: Two women and ornate X/four cherubs and ornate X, portraits of Victoria and Albert in ovals; sheaves and agricultural tools below/ two women and ornate X
Colour: See subheadings
Back Design: —/six cherubs and 10 counter/—
Colour: See subheadings

575-18-08
$20 (£5) Face Design: Sailor holding telescope/—; small steamboat with sails below/ man ploughing with horses
Colour: See subheadings

Back Design: —/ornate 20/—
Colour: See subheadings

336

LA BANQUE DU PEUPLE

575-16-02-64
$50 (£12.10) **Face Design:** Canal boat/seated sailor with flag; bust of young girl below/ paddlewheel steamship in oval
Colour: See subheadings

Back Design: Blue 50 counter
Colour: See subheadings

Photo Not Available

575-20-04-22P
$100 (£25) **Face Design:** Portrait of woman/Montreal harbour scene; small shield below/portrait of woman
Colour: See subheadings

Back Design: Lathework, counters and bank name
Colour: See subheadings

575-16 **BLUE BACKS**
1845 - 1870
DOLLARS/POUNDS & SHILLINGS

2. NO PROTECTORS
1845-1850

DESIGNS AND COLOURS
Face Colour: Black with no tint
Back Colour: Blue

IMPRINT
Toppan, Carpenter & Co. Philada and New York
Toppan Carpenter & Co. New York & Phila

SIGNATURES
left	right
mss. B.H. Lemoine	mss. J. DeWitt (v)
mss. G. Peltier	mss. J. DeWitt (v)

ISSUE DATING
Partially engraved _ 18_:
$1 and $2, 1846: 1 Septr.
$1 and $2, 1850: 1 Mars
Partially engraved _ 184_:
$4, 1847: 1 Mai.
$20 and $50, 1845: 1 Mars

OVERPRINT
"TORONTO" in blue

Cat. No.	Denom.	Date	VG	F	VF	EF	Unc
16-02-04	$1 (5s)	1846	700.	1,050.	-	-	-
16-02-14	$1 (5s)	1850	700.	1,050.	-	-	-
16-02-16	$2 (10s)	1846	800.	1,100.	-	-	-
16-02-20	$2 (10s)	1850	800.	1,100.	-	-	-
16-02-22	$4 (20s)	1847	900.	1,300.	-	-	-
16-02-30P	$5 (£1.5)	184_			FACE PROOF		500.
16-02-40P	$10 (£2.10)	184_			FACE PROOF		500.
16-02-52	$20 (£5)	1845	1,150.	1,700.	-	-	-
16-02-64	$50 (£12.10)	1845	1,150.	1,700.	-	-	-
16-02-76P	$100 (£25)	184_			FACE PROOF		500.

4. GREEN PROTECTORS
1854, 1870

575-16-04-04
$1 **Face Design:** Man constructing barrel/boy carrying sheaf of wheat and cradle/four cherubs with numeral 1
Colour: See subheadings

DESIGNS AND COLOURS
Face Colour: Black with no tint
Back Colour: Blue

IMPRINT
Toppan, Carpenter & Co. Philada & New York
Toppan, Carpenter & Co. New York & Phila.

SIGNATURES
	left	right
$1 (5s):	mss illegible	mss. J.A. Trottier
	none	mss. L.J. Lamontagne
$2 (10s):	mss. Ed. Fournier	mss. J.A. Trottier
$4 (20s):	mss. J.A. Trottier (cashr)	mss. John Pratt

ISSUE DATING
Partially engraved ___ 18___:
$1 (5s), 1870: 2 May
$2 (10s), 1870: May 2

Engraved
$4 (20s): 2eme Janvier 1854

PROTECTOR
Green "word" on face only

VARIETIES
$1: "Countersigned and Entered/For La Banque de Peuple" inscribed above signature spaces. Blue printed sheet numbers.

$1: Inscriptions deleted above signature spaces. Mss. sheet numbers.

Cat. No.	Denom.	Date	VG	F	VF	EF	Unc
16-04-04	$1 (5s)	1870*	600.	900.	1,500.	-	-
16-04-08	$1 (5s)	1870**	600.	900.	1,500.	-	-
16-04-12	$2 (10s)	1870*	800.	1,050.	-	-	-
16-04-14	$4 (20s)	1854**	900.	1,200.	-	-	-

* Inscription above signature.
** Inscription deleted.

LA BANQUE DU PEUPLE

575-18   **GREEN FACE TINTS,
GREEN BACKS 1870
DOLLARS/ POUNDS & SHILLINGS**

Blue printed sheet numbers.
DESIGNS AND COLOURS

575-18-02
  $4 Face Colour: Black with green tint
  Back Colour: Green

IMPRINT
  $4 (20s): Toppan, Carpenter & Co. New York & Phila.
  British American Bank Note Co. Montreal
  $20 (£5): Toppan, Carpenter & Co. New York & Phila.

SIGNATURES
left	right
$4 (20s): mss. J.A. Trottier	mss. Geo. S. Brush (v.)
$20 (£5): mss. J.A. Trottier	engr. J. Grenier

ISSUE DATING
  Engraved
  2eme Mai 1870
  2nd May 1870

OVERPRINT
  $20 (£5): "S" twice in red

Cat. No.	Denom.	Date	VG	F	VF	EF	Unc
18-02	$4 (20s)	1870	900.	1,250.	-	-	-
18-04	$5 (£1.5)	1870		NOT YET CONFIRMED			
18-06	$10 (£2.10)	1870		NOT YET CONFIRMED			
18-08	$20 (£5)	1870	1,100.	1,600.	-	-	-

570-20   **GREEN FACE TINTS
BLUE BACKS
1882-1892**

**2.   DOLLAR/POUNDS & SHILLINGS ISSUE
BLUE NUMBERS**

DESIGNS AND COLOURS
  Face Colour: Black with green tint
  Back Colour: Blue

IMPRINT
  Toppan, Carpenter & Co. New York and
  British American Bank Note Co. Montreal

SIGNATURES
left	right
mss. various	engr. C.S. Cherrier

ISSUE DATING
  Engraved
  May 2nd 1882

OVERPRINT
  $5 (£1.5): "QUEBEC" twice in blue
  $10 (£2.10): "DM" twice in red

Cat. No.	Denom.	Date	VG	F	VF	EF	Unc
20-02-02	$5 (£1.5)	1882	900.	1,250.	-	-	-
20-02-04	$10 (£2.10)	1882	1,000.	1,400.	-	-	-

**4.   DOLLAR ONLY ISSUES
BLUE NUMBERS**

DESIGNS AND COLOURS

575-20-04-02
  $5 Face Design: "Commerce" figure holding counter/
  seated woman in ornate V/allegorical female
  seated on globe and blowing trumpet
  Colour: Black with green tint

  Back Design: Counters, bank name and man and woman
  seated by ornate 5/—
  Colour: Blue

575-20-04-8
  $5 Face Design: "Commerce" figure holding counter/
  seated woman in ornate V/allegorical female
  blowing trumpet seated on globe
  Colour: Black with green tint

  Back Design: Counters, bank name and man and women
  seated by ornate 5/—
  Colour: Blue

Note: Central V in this bank note has numerous differences with fancy scrollwork.

LA BANQUE DU PEUPLE

575-20-04-12P
$10 Face Design: Two women and ornate X/four cherubs and ornate X, portraits of Victoria and Albert in ovals; sheaves and agricultural tools below/two women and ornate X
Colour: Blue

Back Design: —/six cherubs and 10 counter/—
Colour: Blue

575-20-06-04
$50 Face Design: Canal boat/seated sailor with flag; bust of young girl below/ paddlewheel steamship in oval
Colour: Black with green tint

Back Design: Lathework, counters and bank name
Colour: Blue

575-20-06-06P
$100 Face Design: Portrait of woman/Montreal harbour scene; small shield below/portrait of woman
Colour: Black with green tint

Back Design: Lathework, counters and bank name
Colour: Blue

IMPRINT
Toppan, Carpenter & Co. New York and Phila.
British American Bank Note Co. Montreal
British American Bank Note Co. Ottawa

SIGNATURES
left	right
mss. various	engr. J. Grenier

ISSUE DATING
Engraved
November 6th, 1885
May 2, 1888
July 2, 1892

OVERPRINT
F.D. twice in blue
$5: "QUEBEC" twice in blue

Cat. No.	Denom.	Date	VG	F	VF	EF	Unc
20-04-02	$5	1885	900.	1,250.	-	-	-
20-04-08	$5	1892	1,000.	1,400.	-	-	-
20-04-12P	$10	1888			FACE PROOF		500.
20-04-16P	$50	1885			FACE PROOF		500.
20-04-22P	$100	1885			FACE PROOF		500.

THE PEOPLE'S BANK OF HALIFAX

6. DOLLAR ONLY ISSUES
RED NUMBERS

575-20-06-02

IMPRINT
Toppan, Carpenter & Co. New York & Phila
Canada Bank Note Co. Montreal.

SIGNATURES
left	right
mss. various	engr. J. Grenier

ISSUE DATING
Engraved
November 6th, 1885

OVERPRINT
$5: "S S" in red

Cat. No.	Denom.	Date	VG	F	VF	EF	Unc
20-06-02	$5	1885	900.	1,250.	-	-	-
20-06-04	$50	1885	1,100.	1,600.	-	-	-
20-06-06P	$100	1885			FACE PROOF		500.

THE PEOPLE'S BANK OF HALIFAX
1864-1905
HALIFAX, NOVA SCOTIA

BANK NUMBER 580 **REDEEMABLE**

Established in 1864 in Halifax, Nova Scotia, this bank was absorbed by the Bank of Montreal in 1905. The bank was well managed, and all of its assets were sold to the Bank of Montreal with "the good will of the banking business." With its 26 branches, the People's Bank of Halifax provided a valuable addition to the Bank of Montreal expansion in Nova Scotia and New Brunswick.

Employees of the bank were guaranteed a minimum of one year of employment at their existing salaries, after which those remaining in the service of the Bank of Montreal were added to its pension list with credit for time spent with both banks.

580-10 **$20 ISSUES OF 1864 - 1903**
DESIGNS AND COLOURS

$20 Face Design: Princess of Wales/lion and Indian woman flanking bust of Victoria/two sailors on shore, one with telescope "Looking Out"
Colour: Black with green tint

Back Design: Lathework, counters and bank name
Colour: Blue

580-10-06P

$20 Face Design: Princess of Wales/lion and Indian woman flanking bust of Victoria/two sailors on shore, one with telescope "Looking Out"
Colour: Black with green tint

Back Design: Lathework, counters and bank name
Colour: Blue

Note: The 1903 issue has "of Halifax" added to "The Peoples Bank."

IMPRINT
American Bank Note Co. N.Y.
American Bank Note Co. Ottawa

SIGNATURES
	left	right
1864:	none	none
1898:	mss. various	typed Patrick O'Mullin
1903:	mss. various	typed J.J. Stewart

ISSUE DATING
Engraved
25th May 1864 2nd July 1903.
1st November 1898.

Cat. No.	Denom.	Date	VG	F	VF	EF	Unc
10-02P	$20	1864			FACE PROOF		600.
10-04	$20	1898	2,500.	3,500.	4,200.	-	-
10-06P	$20	1903			FACE PROOF		600.

580-12 $4, $5 AND $10 ISSUES OF 1870-1903

DESIGNS AND COLOURS

Note: The designs, wording and tints of the issues starting in 1900 vary slightly from previous issues.

580-12-02a
 $4 Face Design: Seated "Commerce" figure "Export"/—/ Royal Crest
 Colour: Black with green tint

 Back Design: Lathework, counters and bank name
 Colour: Green

580-12-04P
 $5 Face Design: Seated woman, ship in drydock/—/ three horses' heads/end frame has "5-fives"
 Colour: Green V's and five

 Back Design: lathework counters and bank name
 Colour: Green

580-12-10
 $5 Face Design: Seated woman holding trident, ship in drydock "Ship building"/three horses' heads
 Colour: green Vs and 5

 Back Design: Lathework, counters and bank name
 Colour: Green

580-12-16
 $5 Face Design: Seated woman holding trident, ship in drydock "Ship building"/ three horses' heads
 Colour: overall green tint

 Back Design: Lathework, counters and bank name
 Colour: Green

580-12-18P
 $10 Face Design: —/female operating telegraphic equipment/—
 Colour: overall green tint

 Back Design: Lathework, counters and bank name
 Colour: Green

THE PEOPLE'S BANK OF HALIFAX

580-12-24
$10 Face Design: —/female operating telegraphic equipment/—
Colour: Green tint

Back Design: Lathework, counters and bank name
colour: Green

Face Colour:
- **$4 and $5, 1870-1871:** Black with green tint
- **$5 and $10, 1882-1899:** Black with green tint
- **$5, 1900:** Black with orange tint
- **$5, 1901:** Black with overall green tint
- **$10, 1880:** Black with overall orange tint
- **$10, 1900:** Black with red-brown tint
- **$10, 1901:** Black with overall orange tint
- **$10, 1903:** Black with green tint

IMPRINT
British American Bank Note Co. Montreal & Ottawa
British American Bank Note Co. Ottawa
British American Bank Note Co. Montreal

SIGNATURES

	left (only)	right (only)
1870-1871:	mss. Geo. H. Starr and mss. Peter Jack	
1880:	none	none
1882:		engr. Augustus W. West and mss. various
1894-1900:	mss. various	engr. Patrick O'Mullin
1901, 1903:	mss. various	engr. J.J. Stewart

ISSUE DATING
Engraved

July 1st 1870	April 1st 1899
July 1st 1871	2nd Jan 1900
1st Sept 1880	1st Oct, 1900
July 1st 1882	1st Oct. 1901
Nov. 1st 1894	July 2, 1903
1st Nov 1894	

OVERPRINT
The bank name and "CANADA CURRENCY issue of July 1871" is in a red seal and "CANADA CURRENCY" appears vertically at the right end.

Cat. No.	Denom.	Date	VG	F	VF	EF	Unc
12-02P	$4	18_*				FACE PROOF	700.
12-02a	$4	1870**	1,800.	2,400.	3,600.	-	
12-04P	$5	18_*				FACE PROOF	700.
12-04a	$5	1870**	1,800.	2,400.	3,600.	-	
12-06	$5	1871*	2,200.	3,100.	4,500.	-	
12-08	$5	1882	2,200.	3,100.	4,500.	-	
12-10	$5	1894	2,200.	3,100.	4,500.	-	
12-12	$5	1899	2,200.	3,100.	4,500.	-	
12-14	$5	1900	2,200.	3,100.	4,500.	-	
12-16	$5	1901	2,200.	3,100.	4,500.	-	
12-18P	$10	1880*				FACE PROOF	700.
12-20	$10	1894	2,600.	3,600.	5,400.	-	
12-22	$10	1900	2,600.	3,600.	5,400.	-	
12-24	$10	1901	2,600.	3,600.	5,400.	-	
12-26P	$10	1903				FACE PROOF	700.

* No o/p.
** Red seal o/p.

THE PEOPLE'S BANK OF NEW BRUNSWICK

1864-1907
FREDERICTON (NEW BRUNSWICK)

BANK NUMBER 585 **REDEEMABLE**

Established in Fredericton, New Brunswick, in 1864, this bank was absorbed by the Bank of Montreal in 1907. The principal shareholders of this small bank, the Randolph family, accepted the offer of the Bank of Montreal of a "very generous price of $350.00 per share."

585-10 ABNC PRINTINGS
1864 - 1873

DESIGNS AND COLOURS

585-10-02
- **$1 Face Design:** Henry George Clopper/lion and shield/Victoria (Winterhalter portrait) in oval
- **Colour:** Black with green tint
- **Back Design:** Plain

Photo Not Available

585-10-24
- **$2 Face Design:** Henry George Clopper/Britannia and "Justice" figure flanking numeral 2/oval portrait of Queen Victoria
- **Colour:** Black with green tint
- **Back Design:** Plain

Photo Not Available

585-10-40P
- **$5 Face Design:** Henry George Clopper/Royal Crest/sailboat
- **Colour:** Black with green tint
- **Back Design:** Plain

IMPRINT
American Bank Note Co. New York

SIGNATURES
left	right
mss. S.W. Babbitt	mss. A.F. Randolph

ISSUE DATING
Partially engraved ___ 1st, 18___:
- 1864: Sep.
- 1867: May
- 1873: Apr.

Cat. No.	Denom.	Date	VG	F	VF	EF	Unc
10-02	$1	1864	1,200.	1,700.	-	-	-
10-10	$1	1867	1,200.	1,700.	-	-	-
10-24	$2	1873	1,200.	1,700.	-	-	-
10-40P	$5	18_				PROOF	500.

585-12 ABNC AND BABN PRINTINGS
1874 AND 1881

DESIGNS AND COLOURS

585-12-02
- **$1 Face Design:** Like previous issue, but counters, lathework and tint are different
- **Colour:** Green

Back Design: Lathework, counters and bank name
Colour: Green

585-12-06
- **$2 Face Design:** Like previous issue 585-10
- **Colour:** Green

Back Design: Lathework, counters and bank name
Colour: Green

THE PEOPLE'S BANK OF NEW BRUNSWICK

585-12-10P
  $5 Face Design: Henry George Clopper/Royal Crest/sailboat
  Colour: Black with green tint

Back Design: lathework, counters and bank name
Colour: Green

585-12-16
  $10 Face Design: Prince of Wales in Highland dress/
    seated woman with book and torch/
    ship/George Clopper
  Colour: Black with green tint

Back Design: Lathework, counters and bank name
Colour: Green

IMPRINT
  American Bank Note Co. New York and British American Bank Note Co. Montreal

SIGNATURES

	left	right
1874:	mss. S.W. Babbitt	mss. A.F. Randolph
	mss. J.W. Spurden	mss. A.F. Randolph
1881:	mss. J.W. Spurden	engr. A.F. Randolph

ISSUE DATING
  Engraved
  2nd Jany 1874
  2nd January 1874
  1st December 1881
  1st Decr 1881

Cat. No.	Denom.	Date	VG	F	VF	EF	Unc
12-02	$1	1874	1,000.	1,400.	2,100.	-	-
12-04	$1	1881	1,200.	1,600.	2,400.	-	-
12-06	$2	1874	1,200.	1,600.	2,400.	-	-
12-08	$2	1881	900.	1,250.	2,100.	-	-
12-10	$5	1874	1,000.	1,400.	2,500.	-	-
12-14	$10	1874	1,400.	2,000.	3,000.	-	-
12-16	$10	1881	1,400.	2,000.	3,000.	-	-

585-14 QUEEN VICTORIA "WIDOW'S WEEDS" ISSUE 1885

DESIGNS AND COLOURS

585-14-02
  $1 Face Design: Anchor with box and kegs/train emerging
    from tunnel "Through the tunnel"/
    Queen Victoria in widow's weeds
  Colour: Black with green tint

Back Design: Lathework, counters and bank name
Colour: Green

585-14-04
  $5 Face Design: Oval portrait of Prince Arthur/sailing ship, "Clipper"/Queen Victoria in widow's weeds
  Colour: Black with green tint

Back Design: Lathework, counters and bank name
Colour: Green

IMPRINT
  British American Bank Note Co. Montreal

SIGNATURES
  left   right
  mss. J.W. Spurden   engr. A.F. Randolph

ISSUE DATING
  Engraved
  $1: 2nd Jany 1885
  $5: 2nd Nov 1885

STAMPS
  Red "A"s left and right

Cat. No.	Denom.	Date	VG	F	VF	EF	Unc
14-02	$1	1885	1,200.	1,600.	2,400.	-	-
14-04	$5	1885	1,400.	2,000.	3,000.	-	-

585-16 "RANDOLPH PORTRAIT" ISSUES 1897 AND 1904

DESIGNS AND COLOURS

585-16-02
  $5 Face Design: Queen Victoria; N.B. legislative building/—/A.F. Randolph

Back Design: Lathework, counters and bank name

585-16-06
  $10 Face Design: N.B. legislative building; Queen Victoria/—/A.F. Randolph

Back Design: Lathework, counters and bank name

585-16-08
  $10 Face Design: N.B. legislative building; Queen Victoria/—/A.F. Randolph

Back Design: Lathework, counters and bank name
1897 Face Colour: Black with red-brown tint
  Back Colour: Green
Proofs of the 1897 $5 and $10 exist with blue tint
1904 Face Colour: Black with ochre tint
  Back Colour: Green

THE PEOPLE'S BANK OF NEW BRUNSWICK

IMPRINT
British American Bank Note Co. Ottawa

SIGNATURES
	left	right
1897:	mss. J.W. Spurden	engr. A.F. Randolph
	mss. W.B. Coulthard	engr. A.F. Randolph
1904:	mss. J.W. Spurden	engr. A.H.F. Randolph

ISSUE DATING
Engraved
June 22nd, 1897
July 1st, 1904

Cat. No.	Denom.	Date	VG	F	VF	EF	Unc
16-02	$5	1897	1,400.	2,000.	2,400.	-	-
16-04	$5	1904	1,800.	2,400.	3,500.	-	-
16-06	$10	1897	1,800.	2,400.	3,500.	-	-
16-08	$10	1904	1,800.	2,400.	3,500.	-	-

585-18 ABNC PRINTINGS 1897 AND 1905

DESIGNS AND COLOURS

585-18-02-02
$20 Face Design: "Justice" figure/
St. George slaying the dragon/
oval portrait of the Duke of Wellington

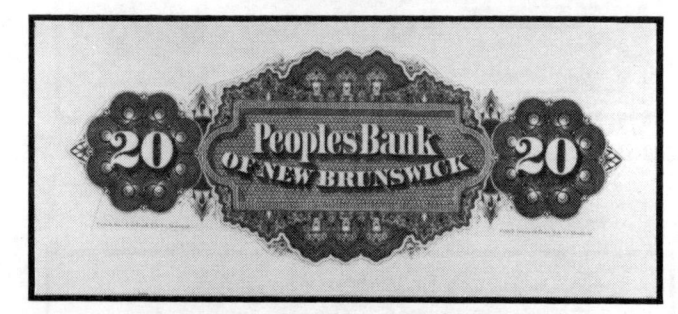

Back Design: Lathework, counters and bank name

585-18-02-04P
$50 Face Design: Queen Victoria (Chalon portrait) in oval/
ship and seated "Commerce" figure with
cornucopia full of produce/train on bridge
with cattle being driven beneath, "The Drove"

Back Design: Lathework, counters and bank name

2. FULLY ENGRAVED DATE, 1897

DESIGNS AND COLOURS
Face Colour: Black with blue tint
Back Colour: Blue

IMPRINT
American Bank Note Company and
British American Bank Note Company

SIGNATURES
left	right
mss. J.W. Spurden	engr. A.F. Randolph

ISSUE DATING
Engraved
June 22nd 1897.

Cat. No.	Denom.	Date	VG	F	VF	EF	Unc
18-02-02	$20	1897	1,800.	2,400.	3,500.	-	-
18-02-04P	$50	1897			FACE PROOF		500.

4. PARTIALLY ENGRAVED DATE, COMPLETED BY RED STAMP, 1905

DESIGNS AND COLOURS

585-18-04-02
Face Colour: Black with green tint
Back Colour: Green

IMPRINT
American Bank Note Co. New York and British American Bank Note Company

SIGNATURES
left	right
mss. W.B. Coulthard	mss. A.H.F. Randolph

ISSUE DATING
Partially engraved _ 18_:
1905: Oct. 6
Nov. 2, 1905 (stamped in red)

Cat. No.	Denom.	Date	VG	F	VF	EF	Unc
18-04-02	$50	1905 (Oct. 6)	1,800.	2,400.	4,000.	-	-
18-04-04	$50	1905 (Nov. 2)	1,800.	2,400.	4,000.	-	-

THE PHENIX BANK

1837-1841

PHILLIPSBURGH, LOWER CANADA

BANK NUMBER 590   **NONREDEEMABLE**

The Phenix Bank is thought to have been a spurious bank of the type that proliferated during the financial crisis of 1837 to 1839. It existed to circulate its paper money at the expense of the public. In the title on the notes there appears in very small letters beside Phillipsburgh, L.C. "The State of Vermont," which led the unwary to believe that these notes were from a U.S. bank. See Haxby VT-170G2, 4 and 6.

590-10   HARRIS ISSUE, 1837-1841
DESIGNS AND COLOURS

590-10-02-02
- **$1 (5s) Face Design:** Steamboat in oval (sideways)/ dog by safe below/Phoenix rising from flames
  See subheadings
- **Colour:** Black with no tint
- **Back Design:** Plain

590-10-02-04R
- **$2 Face Design:** Steamboat in oval (sideways)/ dog by safe below/Phoenix rising from flames
- **Colour:** Black with no tint
- **Back Design:** Plain

590-10-02-06
- **$3 Face Design:** Steamboat in oval (sideways)/ dog by safe below/Phoenix rising from flames
- **Colour:** Black with no tint
- **Back Design:** Plain

IMPRINT
Jas. Harris Eng. N.Y.

SIGNATURES

left	right
mss. H. Reed	mss. Jno. Smith

2. DENOMINATION IN DOLLARS ONLY 1837

ISSUE DATING
Partially engraved ___ 18___:
1837: May 4

Cat. No.	Denom.	Date	Variety	VG	F	VF	EF	Unc
10-02-02	$1	1837		600.	850.	1,200.	-	-
10-02-04R	$2	18_	Remainder*	700.	1,000.	1,400.	-	-
10-02-06	$3	1837		960.	1,300.	2,000.	-	-

* Partially signed, undated and unnumbered.

4. DENOMINATION IN DOLLARS AND SHILLINGS 1841

ISSUE DATING
Partially engraved ___ 18___:
1841: Oct. 8

Cat. No.	Denom.	Date	VG	F	VF	EF	Unc
10-04-02	$1 (5s)	1841	700.	1,000.	1,400.	-	-

THE PICTOU BANK
1873-1887
PICTOU, NOVA SCOTIA

BANK NUMBER 595   **NONREDEEMABLE**

This bank received its charter in 1873. At the time of its collapse, its paid-up capital was $200,000. A series of losses by its main debtors led to lockups. The principal account was with a tannery that used its loans for buildings and equipment. Depositors and noteholders were fully reimbursed, but the shareholders lost $163,970.

595-10   **ISSUES OF 1874 AND 1882**
DESIGNS AND COLOURS

595-10-02R
     $4 Face Design: Anchor/train and ships at dockside "Wharf scene"/ sailor raising flag "Show your colours"
     Colour: Black with green tint

     Back Design: Lathework, counters and bank name
     Colour: Green

595-10-04
     $5 Face Design: Farmer feeding horse "Old Burhans"/ sailing ships "Clipper"/ sailor aboard ship "Charlies Sailor"
     Colour: Black with green tint

     Back Design: Lathework, counters and bank name
     Colour: Green

595-10-08R
     $10 Face Design: —/mining scene "coal mining"/sailing ship
     Colour: Black with green tint

     Back Design: Lathework, counters and bank name
     Colour: Green

IMPRINT
     British American Bank Note Co. Montreal

SIGNATURES
	left	right
1874:	mss. T. Watson	mss. J.R. Noonan
1882:	mss. T. Watson	mss. R.P. Grant

ISSUE DATING
     Engraved
         2nd. Jan. 1874
         2nd. Jan. 1882

Cat. No.	Denom.	Date	Variety	VG	F	VF	EF	Unc
10-02	$4	1874		1,600.	2,200.	3,200.	-	-
10-02R	$4	1874*	Remainder				900.	1,300.
10-04	$5	1874		1,600.	2,200.	3,200.	-	-
10-04R	$5	1874*	Remainder				700.	900.
10-06	$5	1882					600.	850.
10-06R	$5	1882*	Remainder				600.	850.
10-08P	$10	1874					FACE PROOF	500.
10-08R	$10	1874*	Remainder				900.	1,300.
10-10	$10	1882		1,400.	1,950.	2,950.	-	-
10-10R	$10	1882*	Remainder				850.	1,100.
Full sheet	$4,5,5,10	1874*		-	-	-	-	4,400.
Part sheet	$5,5,10	1882*					2,600.	3,000.

* Unsigned remainders.

THE BANK OF PRINCE EDWARD ISLAND

1856-1881

CHARLOTTE TOWN, (PRINCE EDWARD ISLAND)

BANK NUMBER 600   **NONREDEEMABLE**

The first bank in the colony to be incorporated under provincial charter, the Bank of Prince Edward Island was established in 1856. With a capital stock of £30,000 and through conservative management, the bank was prosperous over the next 20 years, until a change of cashiers in 1876 resulted in large advances being made under false pretences. The bank became insolvent as a result and in 1881 was liquidated by the courts, with the Bank of Nova Scotia as liquidator.

600-10   POUNDS, SHILLINGS AND PENCE
ISSUE 1856-1868

DESIGNS AND COLOURS

600-10-04
  5s cy. Face Design   Ship sailing toward viewer/
  (3s 4d stg.):   seated woman with dog and cattle/—
  Colour: Black with no tint
  Back Design: Plain

600-10-20
  10s cy. Face Design   —/man ploughing field; small sailing ship
  (6s 8d stg.):   below/—
  Colour: Black with no tint
  Back Design: Plain

600-10-46
  £1 cy. Face Design   Floral panel/
  (13s 4d stg.):   seated "Agriculture" figure/—
  Colour: Black with no tint
  Back Design: Plain

600-10-48
  £2 cy. Face Design   —/seated farmer with produce; small sailing
  (1.6.8 stg.):   ship below/—
  Colour: Black with no tint
  Back Design: Plain

600-10-64
  £5 cy. Face Design   Queen Victoria (Chalon portrait)/
  (3.6.8 stg.):   Royal Crest/Prince Consort
  Colour: Black with no tint
  Back Design: Plain

IMPRINT
  1856-1857:   New England Bank Note Co. Boston and Rawdon, Wright, Hatch & Edson. New York
  1859-1863:   New England Bank Note Co. Boston and Rawdon, Wright, Hatch & Edson, New York and American Bank Note Company (monogram)

SIGNATURES
	left	right
1856-1857:	mss. Wm. Cundall	mss. R. Brecken
1859-1863:	mss. Wm. Cundall	mss. T.H. Haviland
1868:	mss. Wm. Cundall	mss. Daniel Brenan

THE BANK OF PRINCE EDWARD ISLAND

ISSUE DATING
Partially engraved ___ 18___:

5s cy., 1856: 18 Aug.		**£1 cy., 1856:** 18 Aug.	
1857: 7 April		**1857:** Jany. 1st	
1859: 1 Jan.		**1860:** 2 Jan.	
1863: Dec. 1		**£2 cy., 1856:** 13 Aug., 13 Oct.	
1868: 2 Nov.		**1859:** 1 Jan.	
10s cy., 1856: 13 Aug.		**1863:** Jan. 1st	
1857: 7 April		**£5 cy., 1856:** 13 Aug.	
1859: 1 Jan.			
1860: Jan. 2			
1862: Jan. 1			

PROTECTOR
Red "word" on face and mirror image on the back.

Cat. No.	Denom.	Date	VG	F	VF	EF	Unc
10-02	5s	1856	1,300.	1,700.	-	-	-
10-04	5s	1857	1,300.	1,700.	-	-	-
10-08	5s	1859	1,300.	1,700.	-	-	-
10-16	5s	1863	1,300.	1,700.	-	-	-
10-17	5s	1868	1,300.	1,700.	-	-	-
10-18	10s	1856	1,000.	1,300.	-	-	-
10-20	10s	1857	1,000.	1,300.	-	-	-
10-24	10s	1859	1,000.	1,300.	-	-	-
10-26	10s	1862	1,000.	1,300.	-	-	-
10-34	£1	1856	1,300.	1,700.	-	-	-
10-36	£1	1857	1,300.	1,700.	-	-	-
10-46	£1	1860	1,300.	1,700.	-	-	-
10-48	£2	1856	1,000.	1,300.	-	-	-
10-54	£2	1859	1,000.	1,300.	-	-	-
10-62	£2	1863	1,000.	1,300.	-	-	-
10-64	£5	1856	1,800.	2,400.	-	-	-

600-12   DOLLAR ISSUES, 1872 AND 1877
DESIGNS AND COLOURS

600-12-04
$1 Face Design: —/woman cutting grain with sickle/—
Colour: Black with green tint

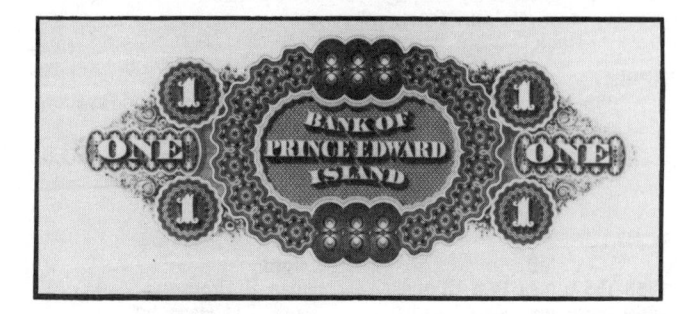

Back Design: Lathework, counters and bank name
Colour: Green

600-12-06a
$2 Face Design: Anchor/horse being watered at stream "At the Brook"/ animals at barn door "Farm Stock"
Colour: Black with green tint

Back Design: Lathework, counters and bank name
Colour: Green

600-12-12a
$5 Face Design: —/farmer watering livestock at pump; young girl's head below "Autumn"/—
Colour: Black with green tint

Back Design: Lathework, counters and bank name
Colour: Green

THE BANK OF PRINCE EDWARD ISLAND

600-12-14R
$10 Face Design: Sailor aboard ship/fishermen and sailing ships "On the Banks"/beehive and flowers
Colour: Black with green tint

Back Design: Lathework, counters and bank name
Colour: Green

600-12-16R
$20 Face Design: Queen Victoria/seated Britannia and ship in dry dock "Ship Building"/Prince of Wales
Colour: Black with green tint

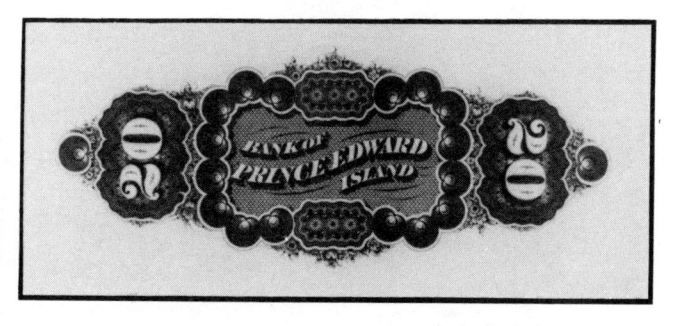

Back Design: Lathework, counters and bank name
Colour: Green

IMPRINT
British American Bank Note Co. Montreal & Ottawa

SIGNATURES

	left	right
1872:	mss. Sam Finlay	mss. Daniel Brenan
	mss. Wm. Cundall	mss. Daniel Brenan
	mss. J.R. Brecken	mss. Joseph Hensley
1877:	mss. Leslie S. McNutt	mss. T. Heath Haviland (p)
	mss. John A. Moore	mss. T. Heath Haviland
	mss. Leslie S. McNutt	mss. Joseph Hensley
	mss. J.R. Brecken	mss. J. Longworth
	mss. John A. Moore	mss. J. Longworth
	mss. J.R. Brecken	mss. Joseph Hensley
	mss. J.R. Brecken	mss. T. Heath Haviland
	mss. Leslie S. McNutt	mss. J. Longworth

ISSUE DATING
  Engraved
    1st Jany. 1872
    1st Jany. 1877

OVERPRINT
  "CANADA CURRENCY" in red

Cat. No.	Denom.	Date	Variety	VG	F	VF	EF	Unc
12-02	$1	1872	No o/p	100.	125.	200.	300.	600.
12-02a	$1	1872	Red o/p	110.	150.	210.	325.	700.
12-04	$1	1877	No o/p	60.	110.	145.	200.	400.
12-04a	$1	1877	Red o/p	110.	150.	210.	325.	700.
12-06	$2	1872	No o/p	110.	150.	210.	325.	700.
12-06a	$2	1872	Red o/p	125.	175.	225.	350.	800.
12-08	$2	1877	No o/p	60.	110.	140.	225.	425.
12-08a	$2	1877	Red o/p	125.	175.	225.	350.	800.
12-10	$5	1872	No o/p	425.	550.	750.	1,300.	2,400.
12-10a	$5	1872	Red o/p	425.	550.	750.	1,300.	2,400.
12-12	$5	1877	No o/p	325.	450.	750.	1,200.	2,300.
12-12a	$5	1877	Red o/p	325.	450.	600.	1,200.	2,300.
12-14	$10	1872*		150.	200.	300.	500.	1,000.
12-14R	$10	1872**		90.	110.	175.	300.	550.
12-16	$20	1872*		160.	225.	325.	500.	1,200.
12-16R	$20	1872**		125.	200.	275.	425.	900.

* Fully signed and issued.
** Remainder with one signature only.

THE PROVINCIAL BANK

1884

LONDON, ONTARIO

BANK NUMBER 605   **NONREDEEMABLE**

The Provincial Bank was incorporated in 1884 in London, Ontario, but did not open for business.

605-10   **DESIGNS OF 1884**

DESIGNS AND COLOURS

605-10-02P
- **$5 Face Design:** Lord Dufferin/farmer watering livestock at pump/barge in locks
- **Colour:** Black with green tint

Back Design: Lathework, counters and bank name
Colour: Green

605-10-04P
- **$10 Face Design:** Lord Dufferin/farm scene "Dairy Maid"/beavers
- **Colour:** Black with green tint

Back Design: Lathework, counters and bank name
Colour: Green

IMPRINT
British American Bank Note Co. Montreal

SIGNATURES

left	right
none	engr. Thos. Fawcett

ISSUE DATING
Engraved
August 1, 1884

Cat. No.	Denom.	Date		Unc
10-02P	$5	1884	FACE PROOF	500.
10-04P	10	1884	FACE PROOF	500.

THE PROVINCIAL BANK OF CANADA

1856-1863

STANSTEAD, PROVINCE OF CANADA

BANK NUMBER 610   **NONREDEEMABLE**

This bank was established under the Free Banking Act of Canada in June 1856 in Stanstead, Canada East. The office was moved to Montreal in 1859. Capital, supplied by a New York firm, was to be $100,000, secured by a deposit of Canada 6% debentures. George W. McCollum purchased $100,000 in municipal debentures and had them deposited with the receiver general of Canada. The notes were printed in New York and Philadelphia and were first shipped to the bank in 1856. Shipments of the notes continued until fall 1860, when approximately $166,500 in face value had been sent.

Even before opening, the bank was under attack. Notes of the bank were placed in circulation in Toronto, Montreal, points in between and the Eastern Townships before the people of Stanstead were aware that a bank had been established. Although notes were in circulation, no office had been set up to redeem them. However, McCollum challenged those concerned to send their notes to Stanstead for redemption. The notes were, in fact, redeemed and confidence in the bank was restored.

In March 1859 a move was made to change the status of the institution, to incorporate it as a chartered bank. McCollum was required to state that he had no interest, past or present, in any bank except the Provincial Bank of Canada. This, however, proved not to be the case, and the application for charter was withdrawn. On December 15, 1863, the receiver general accepted a bond jointly given by J.D. Nutter, Robert Millard and George Warner of Montreal for $12,000 to guarantee the redemption of notes during the time required by law.

Withdrawal of their paper money began in 1862, and the negligible amount not returned became worthless on December 15, 1865.

610-10   **ISSUE OF 1856**

DESIGNS AND COLOURS

610-10-02
- **$1 (5s) Face Design:** Small crest/Royal Crest/—
- **Colour:** Black with no tint
- **Back Design:** Plain

610-10-04
- **$2 (10s) Face Design:** Small crest/Indians with horse/ Queen Victoria (Chalon portrait)
- **Colour:** Black with no tint
- **Back Design:** Plain

610-10-06
- **$5 (£1.5) Face Design:** Three Indians overlooking town/bust of Prince Consort in ornate 5/small crest
- **Colour:** Black with no tint
- **Back Design:** Plain

IMPRINT
Danforth Wright & Co. New York & Philada

SIGNATURES

left	vertically right
engr. J.W. Paterson	mss. C. Cambie
	engr. Wm. Stevens

ISSUE DATING
Engraved
April 1st 1856.

OVERPRINT
"Montreal" in red.

PROTECTOR
$1 and $2: Red "numeral" on face and back
$5: Red Roman numeral on face and back

Cat. No.	Denom.	Date	VG	F	VF	EF	Unc
10-02	$1	1856	600.	850.	1,300.	-	-
10-04	$2	1856	500.	700.	1,150.	-	-
10-06	$5	1856	600.	850.	1,300.	-	-

LA BANQUE PROVINCIALE DU CANADA

1900-1979

MONTREAL, QUEBEC

BANK NUMBER 615 **REDEEMABLE**

This bank was established in Montreal in 1862 as La Banque Jacques Cartier and changed its name in 1900 to La Banque Provinciale du Canada. By the end of the century it had 15 branches, mainly in Quebec, and was growing slowly but successfully despite strong competition from several other banks. Although this bank operated chiefly in Quebec, it had branches in Prince Edward Island, New Brunswick and the French-speaking districts of Ontario.

The bank expanded its operations in Quebec by absorbing the People's Bank in 1907. In Ontario and other provinces expansion occurred through a merger with the Unity Bank of Canada in 1977. On November 1, 1979, La Banque Provinciale du Canada and La Banque Canadienne Nationale amalgamated to form the National Bank (La Banque Nationale). Despite the large assets of the combined institution, it was endangered by having committed funds previously on a long-term basis at a relatively low rate of interest and then, when interest rates soared, having to pay depositors a higher rate than it was receiving.

615-10   ISSUE OF 1900
DESIGNS AND COLOURS

615-10-02
  $5 Face Design: Woman with cow and calf "Alderney"/Bank Crest/man chopping tree, cattle "Logging No. 2"
  Colour: Black with green tint

  Back Design: —/Indians on bluff/—
  Colour: Green

615-10-04
  $10 Face Design: Two women "The Reapers"/Bank Crest/ship
  Colour: Black with green tint

  Back Design: Unknown
  Colour: Green

IMPRINT
  British American Bank Note Co. Montreal
  British American Bank Note Co. Ottawa

SIGNATURES
  left   right
  engr. G.N. Ducharme   mss. various

ISSUE DATING
  Engraved
  July 2nd 1900

Note: A proof of the $5 issue exists with ochre tint.

Cat. No.	Denom.	Date	VG	F	VF	EF	Unc
10-02	$5	1900	1,300.	1,800.	2,500.	4,000.	-
10-04P	$10	1900			FACE PROOF		500.

615-12   ISSUE OF 1907
DESIGNS AND COLOURS

615-12-02
  $5 Face Design: Tancrède Bienvenu/train in station/H. Laporte
  Colour: Black with green tint

Back Design: Lathework, counters, bank name and head office
Colour: Green

615-12-06
$10 Face Design: Tancrède Bienvenu/ steamboat "Montreal"/H. Laporte
Colour: Black with green tint

Back Design: Lathework, counters, bank name and head office
Colour: Green

IMPRINT
British American Bank Note Co. Ottawa

SIGNATURES
left	right
mss. various	engr. H. Laporte

ISSUE DATING
Engraved
Le 1er. Juin 1907

Cat. No.	Denom.	Date	Variety	VG	F	VF	EF	Unc
12-02	$5	1907		650.	900.	1,300.	-	-
12-04P	$5	1907	Brown tint			FACE PROOF	500.	
12-06	$10	1907		1,200.	1,700.	2,500.	-	-

615-14   **ISSUE OF 1913-1928**
DESIGNS AND COLOURS

615-14-08
$5 Face Design: H. Laporte/ornate V/Tancrède Bienvenu

Back Design: Lathework, counters, bank name and head office

615-14-16
$10 Face Design: Ornate X/H. Laporte and Tancrède Bienvenu/ornate X
Back Design: lathework, counters, bank name and head office

615-14-18
$20 Face Design: H. Laporte/ornate XX/J.B. Rolland

LA BANQUE PROVINCIALE DU CANADA

Back Design: Lalthework, counters, bank name and head office
$5, 1913 Face Colour: Black with predominantly orange and green tint
    Back Colour: Green
1919 Face Colour: See varieties
    Back Colour: See varieties
1928 Face Colour: Black with predominantly green and yellow tint
    Back Colour: Green
$10, 1913 Face Colour: Black with predominantly orange and yellow-green tint
    Back Colour: Orange
1919 Face Colour: See varieties
    Back Colour: See varieties
1928 Face Colour: Black with predominantly brown and yellow tint
    Back Colour: Brown
$20, 1928 Face Colour: Black with blue tint
    Back Colour: Blue

IMPRINT
American Bank Note Co. Ottawa
Canadian Bank Note Company, Limited

SIGNATURES
left	right
typed H. Laporte	mss. various

ISSUE DATING
Engraved
Le 2 Janvier 1913
Le 31 Janvier 1919
Le 1er Aout. 1928

VARIETIES
$5, 1919 Face Colour: Black with predominantly orange and green tint
    Back Colour: Green
$5, 1919 Face Colour: Black with predominantly green and yellow tint
    Back Colour: Green
$10, 1919 Face Colour: Black with predominantly orange and yellow-green tint
    Back Colour: Orange
$10, 1919 Face Colour: Black with predominantly brown and yellow tint
    Back Colour: Brown

Cat. No.	Denom.	Date	Variety	VG	F	VF	EF	Unc
14-02	$5	1913		300.	400.	600.	1,000.	2,000.
14-04	$5	1919	Orange tint	150.	225.	300.	500.	1,000.
14-06	$5	1919	Green tint	50.	90.	125.	225.	500.
14-08	$5	1928		35.	50.	100.	160.	325.
14-10	$10	1913		90.	130.	200.	300.	775.
14-12	$10	1919	Orange tint	110.	160.	250.	425.	1,000.
14-14	$10	1919	Brown tint	40.	60.	90.	160.	400.
14-16	$10	1928		40.	60.	90.	160.	400.
14-18	$20	1928		110.	150.	225.	400.	850.

615-16 ISSUE OF 1935
SMALL SIZE NOTES

DESIGNS AND COLOURS

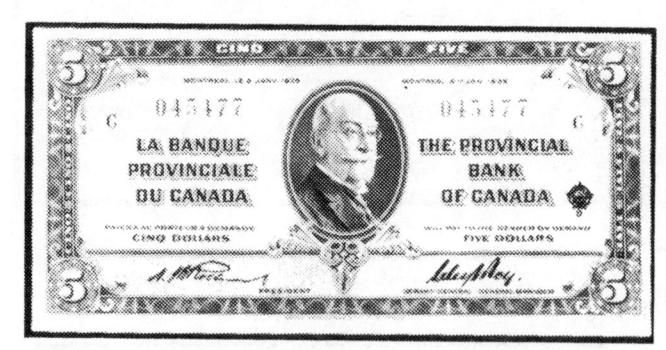

615-16-02
$5 Face Design: —/J.B. Rolland/—
    Colour: Brown tint

Back Design: Lathework, counters, bank name and bank building
Colour: Green

615-16-04
$10 Face Design: —/J.B. Rolland/—
    Colour: Black tint

Back Design: Lathework, counters, bank anme and bank building
Colour: Olive green

356

IMPRINT
British American Bank Note Co Ltd Ottawa

SIGNATURES
left	right
typed S.J.B. Rolland	typed Chs. A. Roy

ISSUE DATING
Engraved
Le 2 Janv. 1935
2nd Jan. 1935

Cat. No.	Denom.	Date	VG	F	VF	EF	Unc
16-02	$5	1935	22.	30.	45.	75.	150.
16-04	$10	1935	27.	35.	50.	80.	160.

615-18 **ISSUE OF 1936**
SMALL SIZE NOTES

DESIGNS AND COLOURS

615-18-04
$5 Face Design: Charles Arthur Roy
Colour: Black with yellow and blue tint

Back Design: Lathework, counters, bank name and bank building
Colour: See varieties

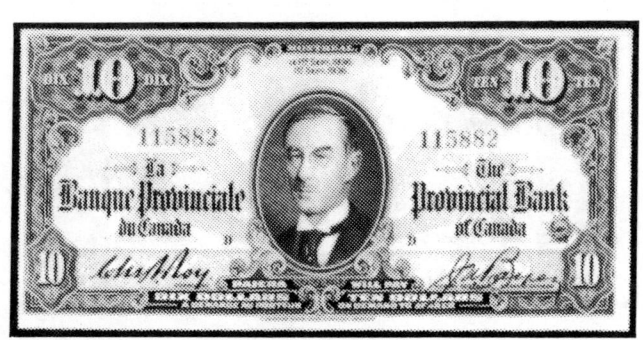

615-18-06
$10 Face Design: Charles Arthur Roy
Colour: Black with yellow and orange tint

Back Design: Lalthework, counters, bank name and bank building
Colour: Orange

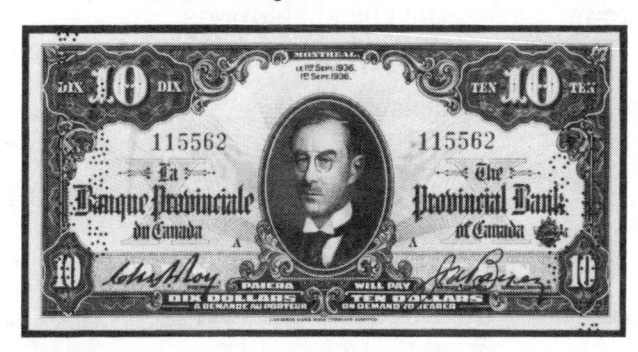

615-18-08
$10 Face Design: Charles Arthur Roy
Colour: Black with green tint and X's

Back Design: Lathework, counters, bank name and bank building
Colour: Green

IMPRINT
Canadian Bank Note Company Limited

SIGNATURES
left	right
typed Charles A. Roy	typed J.U. Boyer

ISSUE DATING
Engraved
Le 1er Sept. 1936
1st Sept. 1936

VARIETIES
$5 Back Colour: Blue
$5 Back Colour: Green
$10 Back Colour: Orange
$10 Back Colour: Green

Cat. No.	Denom.	Date	Variety	VG	F	VF	EF	Unc
18-02	$5	1936	Blue back	25.	35.	55.	80.	200.
18-04	$5	1936	Green back	55.	85.	125.	200.	400.
18-06	$10	1936	Orange back	30.	40.	55.	110.	210.
18-08	$10	1936	Greek back	30.	40.	55.	100.	190.

Note: The $5 note with green back was prepared Jan. 24, 1941; the $10 note with green back was prepared Jan. 17, 1941.

THE QUEBEC BANK
1818-1917
QUEBEC (LOWER CANADA)

BANK NUMBER 620 **REDEEMABLE**

Started as a private partnership in October 1818 in Quebec, Lower Canada, this bank obtained a charter in 1822 from the Province of Lower Canada and obtained a royal charter in May 1837. Its charter from the province was the last one granted by that government. After successful operations as one of the oldest banks in Canada, it merged with the Royal Bank of Canada in 1917, with assets of $22 million and 58 branches. The merger enabled the Royal Bank to expand its operations in Quebec.

620-10 "MAVERICK" PRINTINGS
"ARMY BILL" TYPE NOTES
1818-1819

DESIGNS AND COLOURS

Photo Not Available

620-10-02
$1 **Face Design:** Unknown
Colour: Black with no tint
Back Design: Plain

620-10-06
$3 **Face Design:** Farm and 3/—/—
Colour: Black with no tint
Back Design: Plain

Photo Not Available

620-10-10
$5 **Face Design:** Unknown
Colour: Black with no tint
Back Design: Plain

620-10-14
$10 **Face Design:** Crossed cornucopias/—/—
Colour: Black with no tint
Back Design: Plain

Photo Not Available

620-10-18
$100 **Face Design:** Unknown
Colour: Black with no tint
Back Design: Plain

IMPRINT
Maverick

SIGNATURES
left	right
$3: mss. Noah Freer	mss. J.W. Woolsey

ISSUE DATING
Partially engraved ___ 18___:
$3, 1818: 20th October

Cat. No.	Denom.	Date	VG	F	VF	EF	Unc
10-02	$1	1818	GENUINE NOTES NOT KNOWN				
10-04	$1	1819	GENUINE NOTES NOT KNOWN				
10-06	$3	1818	1,750.	2,400.	-	-	-
10-10	$5	1818	GENUINE NOTES NOT KNOWN				
10-12	$5	1819	GENUINE NOTES NOT KNOWN				
10-14	$10*	1818	GENUINE NOTES NOT KNOWN				
10-16	$10*	1819	GENUINE NOTES NOT KNOWN				
10-18	$100	1818	ALL NOTES REDEEMED				
10-20	$100	1819	ALL NOTES REDEEMED				

* Beware of counterfeits that have engraved signatures and the engraved date of 1 May 1819.

620-12 GRAPHIC PRINTINGS, 1819-1830s

DESIGNS AND COLOURS

620-12-02R
$1 **Face Design:** —/Wheat sheaves, ONE; squirrel below/—
Colour: Black with no tint
Back Design: Plain

620-12-22R
$2 **Face Design:** —/TWO, ship, justice figure,2; racoon below/—
Colour: Black with no tint
Back Design: Plain

THE QUEBEC BANK

620-12-42R
$5 Face Design: —/Ship, female, 5 on pillar, wheat sheaves; fox below/—
Colour: Black with no tint
Back Design: Plain

620-12-62R
$10 Face Design: —/Buildings, TEN over paddlewheel steamer; beaver below/—
Colour: Black with no tint
Back Design: Plain

Photo Not Available

620-12-82
$20 Face Design: Unknown
Colour: Black with no tint
Back Design: Plain

620-12-102R
$50 Face Design: —/Citadel from south shore; bear below/—
Colour: Black with no tint
Back Design: Plain

620-12-122R
$100 Face Design: —/Royal Coat of Arms; Ox below/—
Colour: Black with no tint
Back Design: Plain

620-12-142R
Post Note Design: —/Stagecoach and horses going left; jumping deer below/—
Colour: Black with no tint
Back Design: Plain

IMPRINT
Graphic Company

SIGNATURES
left	right
unknown	unknown

ISSUE DATING
Partially engraved _ 18_:
1819-1837

Cat. No.	Denom.	Date	VG	F	VF	EF	Unc
12-02R	$1	1819-31				PROOF	500.
12-22R	$2	1819-37				PROOF	500.
12-42R	$5	1819-34				PROOF	500.
12-62R	$10	1819-34				PROOF	500.
12-82	$20	1819-33	SURVIVING EXAMPLE NOT CONFIRMED				
12-102R	$50	1819-33				PROOF	500.
12-122R	$100	1819-33				PROOF	500.
12-142R	Post note	1819-37				PROOF	500.

620-14 **ISSUES OF 1833-1841**

DESIGNS AND COLOURS

620-14-02
$1 Face Design: —/three children, man, seated woman, train; small ship below/—
Colour: Black with no tint
Back Design: Plain

Photo Not Available

620-14-06P
$5 Face Design: Unknown
Colour: Black with no tint
Back Design: Plain

359

THE QUEBEC BANK

IMPRINT
  Rawdon, Wright, & Co. N. York

SIGNATURES
left	right
mss. Noah Freer	mss. J. Fraser (v)
mss. Noah Freer	mss. illegible

ISSUE DATING
  Partially engraved 1st June, 18__:
  1835
  1836

Cat. No.	Denom.	Date	VG	F	VF	EF	Unc
14-02	$1	1835	1,100.	1,400.	2,400.	-	-
14-04	$1	1836	1,100.	1,400.	2,400.	-	-
14-06P	$5	18_				PROOF	400.

620-16   JONES PRINTING, 1837

DESIGNS AND COLOURS

620-16-02
  6d (12 sous) Face Design: No vignettes, all text
  Colour: Black with no tint
  Back Design: Plain

IMPRINT
  Jones

SIGNATURES
left	right
none	mss. Jas. Gibb

ISSUE DATING
  Partially engraved 1er Juin 183_:
  1837

Cat. No.	Denom.	Date	VG	F	VF	EF	Unc
16-02	6d (12 sous)	1837	850.	1,150.	-	-	-

620-18   RAWDON, WRIGHT & HATCH PRINTINGS

DESIGNS AND COLOURS

620-18-02
  $1/4 Face Design: Cherub with fruit basket/woman in waves;
  (15d, 30 sous) sheaves and farm tools below/cherub with fruit basket/reverse of Spanish-American 2 reales coin
  Colour: Black with no tint
  Back Design: Plain

620-18-04
  $1/2 Face Design: Reverse of Spanish-American 4 reales
  (2s 6d, 1 ecu, coin/woman in waves, ship, woman in
  3 francs) waves/—
  Colour: Black with no tint
  Back Design: Plain

IMPRINT
  Engr by Rawdon, Wright & Hatch New-York

SIGNATURES
left	right
none	mss. Jas. Gibb
none	mss. illegible

ISSUE DATING
  Engraved
  1er Octobre 1837

Cat. No.	Denom.	Date	VG	F	VF	EF	Unc
18-02	$1/4	1837	1,100.	1,450.	2,100.	-	-
18-04	$1/2	1837	1,100.	1,450.	2,100.	-	-

ISSUE OF 1837-1860s

Note: For the spurious $2 notes of 1857 to 1859 (with Royal Crest at centre), see issue 620-52.

DESIGNS AND COLOURS

Photo Not Available

620-20-02P
  $1 Face Design: Unknown
  Colour: Black with no tint
  Back Design: Plain

Photo Not Available

620-20-14P
  $2 Face Design: Unknown
  Colour: Black with no tint
  Back Design: Plain

Photo Not Available

620-20-28P
  $5 Face Design: Unknown
  Colour: Black with no tint
  Back Design: Plain

Photo Not Available

620-20-42P
  $10 Face Design: Unknown
  Colour: Black with no tint
  Back Design: Plain

THE QUEBEC BANK

620-22-20R
 $20 Face Design: Ships (whaling scene) in circle/
  allegorical women and two men; factory and
  ship below/ship in circle
  Colour: Black with no tint

  Back Design: See subheadings
  Colour: See subheadings

620-22-40R
 $50 Face Design: Dock scene/griffin, allegorical man and
  women; dog by safe below/—
  Colour: Black with no tint

  Back Design: See subheadings
  Colour: See subheadings

620-22-60R
 $100 Face Design: Dock scene/seahorses drawing
  Neptune and woman/schooner
  Colour: Black with no tint

  Back Design: See subheadings
  Colour: See subheadings

IMPRINT
 Rawdon, Wright & Hatch New York

SIGNATURES
  left   right
  mss. Jas. Stevenson mss. D.D. Young

620-20 **ISSUES OF 1837-1842**
     PLAIN BACK

ISSUE DATING
 Partially engraved Nov. 1, 18__:
 1837 - 1842

Cat. No.	Denom.	Date		Unc
20-02P	$1	18_	PROOF	400.
20-14P	$2	18_	PROOF	400.
20-28P	$5	18_	PROOF	400.
20-42P	$10	18_	PROOF	400.
20-56P	$20	18_	PROOF	400.
20-70P	$50	18_	PROOF	400.
20-84P	$100	18_	PROOF	400.

620-22 **ISSUES OF 1860s**
     GREEN LATHEWORK BACK

ISSUE DATING
 Partially engraved 1st Novr. 18__"
 1860's

PROTECTOR
 Olive green "word" on face only

OVERPRINT
 "OTTAWA" twice in blue

Cat. No.	Denom.	Date	Variety	Unc
22-20R	$20	18_	Remainder*	800.
22-40R	$50	18_	Remainder*	800.
22-60R	$100	18_	Remainder*	800.

* Unsigned and undated; blue printed numbers.

620-24 **ISSUES OF 1843-1861**

Note: For the spurious $2 notes of 1857 to 1859 (with the Royal Crest in the centre),
  see issue 620-52.

2. **ISSUES OF 1843 - 1860 PLAIN BACK**
    NO PROTECTOR

DESIGNS AND COLOURS

    Photo Not Available

620-24-02-02P
 $1 (5s) Face Design: —/two women and crowned shield;
  dog's head "Fidelity" below/—
  Colour: Black with no tint

  Back Design: Plain

620-24-02-20
 $2 (10s) Face Design: Britannia/seated allegorical man and
  woman/milkmaid with bucket
  Colour: Black with no tint

  Back Design: Plain

THE QUEBEC BANK

Photo Not Available

620-24-02-40P
$5 (£1.5) Face Design: Seated woman with shield bearing 5/ two men, shield and beehive; 2 small ships below/three cherubs in small oval
Colour: Black with no tint
Back Design: Plain

Photo Not Available

620-24-02-50P
$10 (£2.10) Face Design: Bust of helmeted soldier/sailing ships; dog's head "Fidelity" below/cherub in ornate 10/ Royal Crest over Queen Victoria (Chalon portrait)
Colour: Black with no tint
Back Design: Plain

IMPRINT
Rawdon, Wright & Hatch New York
Rawdon Wright Hatch & Edson. New York

SIGNATURES
	left	right
1852:	mss. C. Gethings	mss. Jas. Gibb
1858-1860:	mss. C. Gethings	mss. W.H. Anderson

ISSUE DATING
Partially engraved Nov. 1st, 18__:
1852
1858-1860

Cat. No.	Denom.	Date	VG	F	VF	EF	Unc
24-02-02P	$1 (5s)	18_				PROOF	400.
24-02-20	$2 (10s)	1852-60	800.	1,100.	1,600.	-	-
24-02-40P	$5 (£1.5)	18_				PROOF	400.
24-02-50P	$10 (£2.10)	18_				PROOF	400.

4. ISSUES OF 1847 - 1861
PLAIN BACK, RED PROTECTOR

DESIGNS AND COLOURS
See 620-24-02

620-24-04-02

620-24-04-20

620-24-04-40

Photo Not Available

620-24-04-50

IMPRINT
Rawdon, Wright & Hatch New York
Rawdon Wright Hatch & Edson New York and ABNCo Mono.

SIGNATURES
	left	right
1847:	mss. Noah Freer	mss. illegible (v)
1849:	mss. Noah Freer	mss. Jas. Gibb
1850:	mss. Noah Freer	mss. Jas Gibb
1850:	mss. C. Gethings	mss. Wm. Petry (v)
1855-1859:	mss. C. Gethings	mss. W.H. Anderson
1860-1861:	mss. W. Dunn	mss. C. Gethings (p)

ISSUE DATING
Partially engraved
1847-1861: November 1st 18_
Novr. 1st 18_

PROTECTOR
Red "word" on face, and red "word" on back in mirror image.

STAMP
"OTTAWA" in blue

Cat. No.	Denom.	Date	VG	F	VF	EF	Unc
24-04-02	$1 (5s)	1855-61	650.	900.	1,300.	2,100.	-
24-04-20	$2 (10s)	1850	850.	1,200.	-	-	-
24-04-40	$5 (£1.5)	1847, 1860-61	750.	1,000.	1,500.	-	-
24-04-50	$10 (£2.10)	1849	850.	1,200.	-	-	-

THE QUEBEC BANK

620-26 ISSUES OF 1865 WITH GREEN LATHEWORK BACK TORONTO ISSUE

620-26-10

IMPRINT
Rawdon, Wright, Hatch & Edson New York

SIGNATURES
left	right
none	mss. J. Price

ISSUE DATING
Partially engraved Nov. 1st, 18__:
1865

PROTECTOR
Red "word" and green "numeral" on face and back
Green "word" and green "numeral" on face only

OVERPRINT
"Payable in Toronto" at top, "TORONTO" at ends and "For the Quebec Bank" in the left signature space, all in black

Cat. No.	Denom.	Date	VG	F	VF	EF	Unc
26-10	$2 (10s)	1865	850.	1,200.	-	-	-

620-28 ISSUES OF 1843-1862

Note: For the spurious $2 notes of 1857 to 1859 (with the Royal Crest in the centre), see issue 620-22.

DESIGNS AND COLOURS

620-28-02-02P
$1 (5s) **Face Design:** Head of Greek god/cherub in ornate 1/ Indians hunting buffalo "Buffalo chase" (after Catlin)/cherub in ornate 1/ woman and anchor in ornate 1
Colour: Black with no tint
Back Design: Plain

620-28-02-06P
$2 (10s) **Face Design:** —/radiant Royal Crest/bust of helmeted soldier
Colour: Black with no tint
Back Design: Plain

620-28-02-10P
$4 (£1) **Face Design:** Bust of helmeted soldier/ ships in harbour; mermaid and sea creature below/bust of helmeted soldier
Colour: Black with no tint
Back Design: Plain

620-28-02-14
$5 (£1.5) **Face Design:** Man standing by shield/cherubs in ornate 5/ two griffins and shield; two small ships below/ cherub in ornate 5/Royal Crest over Queen Victoria (Chalon portrait)
Colour: Black with no tint
Back Design: Plain

620-28-06-32
$10 (£2.10) **Face Design:** Bust of helmeted soldier/sailing ships; dog's head "Fidelity" below/cherub in ornate 10/ Royal Crest over Queen Victoria (Chalon portrait)
Colour: Black with no tint
Back Design: Plain

363

THE QUEBEC BANK

2. ISSUE WITH NO PROTECTOR
DATED NOVEMBER 1843 - 1853

IMPRINT
Rawdon, Wright & Hatch, New-York

SIGNATURES
left	right
mss. C. Gethings	mss. W.H. Anderson
mss. C. Gethings	mss. Jas. Gibb

ISSUE DATING
Partially engraved
1852-1853: 1st November 18__
1st Novr. 18__

STAMP
"BYTOWN" in blue

Cat. No.	Denom.	Date	VG	F	VF	EF	Unc
28-02-02P	$1 (5s)	18_			PROOF		400.
28-02-06P	$2 (10s)	18_			PROOF		400.
28-02-10P	$4 (£1)	18_			PROOF		400.
28-02-14	$5 (£1.5)	1852	750.	1,150.	-	-	
28-02-16	$5 (£1.5)	1853	750.	1,150.	-	-	
28-02-18	$10 (£2.10)	1853	750.	1,150.	-	-	

Note: Most notes are pen or punch cancelled.

4. ISSUE WITH RED PROTECTOR
DATED NOVEMBER 1849-1852

DESIGNS AND COLOURS
Same as previous

620-28-04-02

620-28-04-20

IMPRINT
Rawdon, Wright & Hatch, New York

SIGNATURES
left	right
mss. C. Gethings	mss. illegible (v)

ISSUE DATING
Partially engraved
1849-1852: 1st November 18__
1st Novr

PROTECTOR
Red "word" on face and back

Cat. No.	Denom.	Date	VG	F	VF	EF	Unc
28-04-02	$4	1849-52	750.	1,150.	-	-	-
28-04-10	$5	1849-52			NOT CONFIRMED		
28-04-20	$10	1849-52	750.	1,150.	-	-	-

6. ISSUE WITH NO PROTECTOR
DATED FEBRUARY 1854-1862

DESIGNS AND COLOURS
See previous

620-28-06-14

620-28-06-16

620-28-06-32

IMPRINT
Rawdon, Wright, Hatch & Edson. New York

SIGNATURES
left	right
mss. C. Gethings	mss. W.H. Anderson
mss. W. Dunn	mss. W.H. Anderson
mss. W. Dunn	mss. C. Gethings

ISSUE DATING
Partially engraved
1854 and 1862: 1st February 18__
1st Feby 18__

Cat. No.	Denom.	Date	VG	F	VF	EF	Unc
28-06-14	$4 (£1)	1862	750.	1,100.	1,550.	-	-
28-06-16	$5 (£1.5)	1854	750.	1,100.	1,550.	-	-
28-06-32	$10 (£2.10)	1862	750.	1,100.	1,550.	-	-

THE QUEBEC BANK

620-30 **TOPPAN CARPENTER CASILEAR**
PRINTINGS 1850s
ENGRAVED "PAYABLE IN TORONTO" AT TOP

Note: For the spurious $2 notes of 1857 to 1859 (with the Royal Crest at the centre), see issue 620-52.

2. TORONTO ISSUE NO TINT, NO PROTECTOR, (1856)
DESIGNS AND COLOURS

Photo Not Available

620-30-02-02P
   $1 (5s) Face Design: Anchor with box, bale and barrel/ wood chopper; St. George slaying the dragon below/beehive and flowers
   Colour: See subheadings
   Back Design: Plain

620-30-02-04
   $4 (£1) Face Design: Men, cattle and wagons/ men standing with cattle/ train coming toward viewer
   Colour: See subheadings
   Back Design: Plain

Photo Not Available

620-30-02-06P
   $10 (£2.10) Face Design: Sailor with capstan/—/wood chopper
   Colour: See subheadings
   Back Design: Plain

IMPRINT
   Toppan Carpenter Casilear & Co. Montreal

SIGNATURES
   left   right
   mss. Wm. Manson   mss. Jas. Gibb

ISSUE DATING
   Partially engraved Jany. 2nd, 185__:
   1856

Cat. No.	Denom.	Date	Variety	VG	F	VF	EF	Unc
30-02-02P	$1 (5s)	18_	B&W				PROOF	400.
30-02-04	$4 (£1)	1856	B&W	750.	1,100.	-	-	-
30-02-06P	$10 (£2.10)	18_	B&W				PROOF	400.

4. TORONTO ISSUE NO TINT, GREEN PROTECTOR
SIGNATURES
   left   right
   mss. unknown   mss. unknown

ISSUE DATING
   Partially engraved Jany. 2nd 185__:

PROTECTOR
   Green "word" on face only

Note: A $4 note is known with a green FIVE protector.

Cat. No.	Denom.	Date	Variety	VG	F	VF	EF	Unc
32-04-02	$1 (5s)	185_	Green ptr.	NO ISSUED NOTES KNOWN TO HAVE SURVIVED
32-04-04	$4 (£1)	185_	Green ptr.	NO ISSUED NOTES KNOWN TO HAVE SURVIVED
32-04-06	$10 (£2.10)	185_	Green ptr.	NO ISSUED NOTES KNOWN TO HAVE SURVIVED

620-32 **TOPPAN CARPENTER CASILEAR**
GREEN TINT PRINTINGS OF 1859
ENGRAVED "PAYABLE IN TORONTO" AT TOP

DESIGNS AND COLOURS
   Designs: Same as previous issue
   Colour: Overall green face tint

620-32-02

620-32-04

SIGNATURES
   left   right
   mss. Wm. Manson   mss. W.H. Anderson

ISSUE DATING
   Partially engraved Jany. 2nd 185__:
   1859

Cat. No.	Denom.	Date	Variety	VG	F	VF	EF	Unc
32-02	$1 (5s)	1859	Green tint	900.	1,400.	-	-	-
32-04	$4 (£1)	1859	Green tint	900.	1,400.	-	-	-
32-06	$10 (£2.10)	185_		NO ISSUED NOTES KNOWN TO HAVE SURVIVED

THE QUEBEC BANK

620-34
ISSUE OF 1863
BACK DESIGN LATHEWORK AND BANK NAME ONLY

DESIGNS AND COLOURS

620-34-02
- **$1 Face Design:** Sailor at ship's wheel/Bank Crest/ three loggers in river
- **Colour:** Black with green tint

Back Design: Lathework and bank name
Colour: Green

620-34-04
- **$2 Face Design:** Shipbuilding scene/Bank Crest/three ships
- **Colour:** Black with green tint

Back Design: Lathework and bank name
Colour: Green

620-34-06
- **$4 Face Design:** Sailor, woman and child on shore with telescope "Land Ho!"/Bank Crest/ seated Britannia, shield bearing FOUR and 4
- **Colour:** Black with green tint

Back Design: Lathework and bank name
Colour: Green

620-34-08
- **$5 Face Design:** Two beavers/Bank Crest/ seated woman with telescope and 5
- **Colour:** Black with green tint

Back Design: Lathework and bank name
Colour: Green

620-34-10
- **$10 Face Design:** Reclining woman with navigational equipment/—/Bank Crest
- **Colour:** Black with green tint

Back Design: Lathework and bank name
Colour: Green

IMPRINT
American Bank Note Co. New York

SIGNATURES
Centre on $10
Right only on $1, 2, 4 and 5
mss. various

ISSUE DATING
Engraved
2nd Jany. 1863
2d Jany. 1863

OVERPRINT
Twice vertically towards ends
"GASPE" in blue
"OTTAWA" in blue
"PAYABLE IN TORONTO" in blue
"ST. CATHARINES/PAYABLE IN TORONTO" in blue
"PAYABLE IN MONTREAL" in blue
"THREE RIVERS" in blue
"OTTAWA/PAYABLE IN MONTREAL" in blue

Cat. No.	Denom.	Date	VG	F	VF	EF	Unc
34-02	$1	1863	500.	700.	1,100.	-	-
34-04	$2	1863	850.	1,250.	1,600.	-	-
34-06	$4	1863	850.	1,250.	1,600.	-	-
34-08	$5	1863	1,200.	1,600.	2,300.	-	-
34-10	$10	1863	1,200.	1,600.	2,300.	-	-

THE QUEBEC BANK

620-36 ISSUE OF 1863
BACK DESIGN LATHEWORK COUNTERS AND BANK NAME

DESIGNS AND COLOURS

620-36-02
This issue is the same as 620-34, except for the large green 4s near the top centre, and the green around the 4s in the corners is different.

Photo Not Available

620-36-10
$10 **Face Design:** As 34-10 but top XX counters are like 40-08
Back Design: Lathework, counters and bank name

IMPRINT
American Bank Note Co. New York
British American Bank Note Co. Montreal - Ottawa on the back.

SIGNATURES
right only
mss. various

ISSUE DATING
Engraved
2nd Jany. 1863

OVERPRINT
"TORONTO" twice in blue

Cat. No.	Denom.	Date	VG	F	VF	EF	Unc
36-02	$4	1863	900.	1,200.	1,700.	-	-
36-10	$10	1863					

620-38 ISSUE OF 1870

DESIGNS AND COLOURS

620-38-02
$4 **Face Design:** Sir N.F. Belleau/Bank Crest/
sailor with telescope
Colour: Black with green tint

Back Design: Lathework, counters and bank name
Colour: Green

IMPRINT
British American Bank Note Co. Montreal & Ottawa

SIGNATURES
right only
mss. various

ISSUE DATING
Engraved
Oct. 1st 1870

OVERPRINT
Twice vertically near ends
"OTTAWA" in blue
"TORONTO" in blue
"THREE RIVERS" in blue

Cat. No.	Denom.	Date	VG	F	VF	EF	Unc
38-02	$4	1870	700.	975.	1,475.	-	-

620-40 ISSUES OF 1873 AND 1888
GREEN FACE AND BACK TINT

DESIGNS AND COLOURS

620-40-02
$4 **Face Design:** Sailor with telescope, woman and child on ship "Land Ho!"/Bank Crest/
seated Britannia, shield bearing FOUR and 4
Colour: Green tint

Back Design: Lathework, counters and bank name
Colour: Green tint

367

THE QUEBEC BANK

620-40-04
$5 **Face Design:** Two beavers/Bank Crest/
seated woman with telescope and 5
Colour: Green tint

Back Design: Lathework, counters and bank name
Colour: Green tint

620-40-06
$5 **Face Design:** Two beavers/Bank Crest/
seated woman with telescope and 5
Colour: Green tint, but design around 5s at top is different from 1863 and Jan. 1873 designs

Back Design: Lathework, counters and bank name
Colour: Green tint

620-40-08
$10 **Face Design:** Reclining woman with navigational equipment/—/modified Bank Crest
Colour: Green tint

Back Design: Lathework, counters and bank name
Colour: Green tint

IMPRINT
American Bank Note Co., New York
British American Bank Note Co. Montreal

SIGNATURES

centre on $10	right only on $4 and $5
mss. various	mss. various

ISSUE DATING
Engraved
2d. Jany. 1873.
1st Oct. 1873
3rd Jany. 1888.

OVERPRINT
1888: "A A" in red
"B B" in blue

STAMP
1888: "D" in purple
"B" in purple

Cat. No.	Denom.	Date	VG	F	VF	EF	Unc
40-02	$4	1873	900.	1,200.	1,700.	-	-
40-04	$5	1873 2nd Jan.	1,100.	1,500.	2,100.	-	-
40-05	$5	1873 1st Oct.	1,100.	1,500.	2,100.	-	-
40-06	$5	1888	1,100.	1,500.	2,100.	-	-
40-08	$10	1888	1,300.	1,700.	2,500.	-	-

Note: The $5 Oct. 1873 note has same top counter design as the 1888 note.

620-42 ISSUE OF 1888: BROWN FACE AND BACK TINT

DESIGNS AND COLOURS

Design: Same as 620-40 issue
Colours: The tint colour for this issue is brown

Cat. No.	Denom.	Date	VG	F	VF	EF	Unc
42-02	$5	1888	1,150.	1,550.	2,300.	-	

THE QUEBEC BANK

620-44 ISSUE OF 1898

DESIGNS AND COLOURS

620-44-02
- **$5 Face Design:** —/paddlewheel and modern ship with Quebec Citadel in background/—
- **Colour:** Black with green tint

- **Back Design:** Lathework, counters, bank name and Bank Crest
- **Colour:** Green

620-44-04
- **$10 Face Design:** —/docks at Quebec City/—
- **Colour:** See varieties
- **Back Design:** Lathework, counters, bank name and Bank Crest
- **Colour:** See varieties

620-44-08
- **$20 Face Design:** Cherub on winged wheel and power lines "Coming Light"/—/Montmorency Falls
- **Colour:** Black with yellow and olive tint

- **Back Design:** lathework, counters, bank name and Quebec City, Prescott Gate
- **Colour:** Olive

620-44-12
- **$50 Face Design:** —/seated woman with globe, lyre and fountain globe/—
- **Colour:** Black with yellow and olive tint

- **Back Design:** lathework, counters, bank name and Quebec City, Kent Gate
- **Colour:** Olive

620-44-16
- **$100 Face Design:** Bank Crest in circle, reclining woman with spear "Clione"/—/—
- **Colour:** Black with yellow and olive tint

THE QUEBEC BANK

Back Design: Lathework, counters, bank name and Quebec City, Hope Gate
Colour: Olive

IMPRINT
American Bank Note Company, Ottawa

SIGNATURES
	left	right
$5 and $10:	engr. John Breakey	mss. various
$20, $50	mss. John Breakey	mss. various
and $100:	typed John Breakey	mss. various

ISSUE DATING
Engraved
Jany. 3d, 1898

VARIETIES
$10 **Face Colour:** Black with olive tint
Back Colour: Blue
$10 **Face Colour:** Black with yellow and olive tint
Back Colour: Green

Cat. No.	Denom.	Date	Variety	VG	F	VF	EF	Unc
44-02	$5	1898		900.	1,250.	1,900.	-	-
44-04	$10	1898	Blue back	900.	1,250.	1,900.	-	-
44-06	$10	1898	Green back	900.	1,250.	1,900.	-	-
44-08	$20	1898	Mss. Breakey, l.	1,300.	1,700.	2,500.	-	-
44-10	$20	1898	Typed Breakey, l.	1,300.	1,700.	2,500.	-	-
44-12	$50	1898	Mss. Breakey, l.	1,300.	1,700.	2,500.	-	-
44-14	$50	1898	Typed Breakey, l.	1,300.	1,700.	2,500.	-	-
44-16	$100	1898	Mss. Breakey, l.	1,300.	1,700.	2,500.	-	-
44-18	$100	1898	Typed Breakey, l.	1,300.	1,700.	2,500.	-	-

620-46 ISSUE OF 1901

DESIGNS AND COLOURS

620-46-02
$5 **Face Design:** —/ships, seated woman with shield, lion and globe/—
Colour: Black with green tint

Back Design: Lathework, counters, bank name and Bank Crest
Colour: Green

IMPRINT
American Bank Note Company, Ottawa

SIGNATURES
left	right
engr. John Breakey	mss. various

ISSUE DATING
Engraved
2nd July 1901

OVERPRINT
V V in red

Cat. No.	Denom.	Date	VG	F	VF	EF	Unc
46-02	$5	1901	900.	1,250.	1,900.	-	-

620-48 ISSUES OF 1908 AND 1911

DESIGNS AND COLOURS

620-48-02-02
$5 **Face Design:** —/ships, seated woman with shield and (altered) lion and scroll (improved design)/—
Colour: Black with yellow and olive tint

Back Design: See subheadings
Colour: Green

620-48-04-04
$10 **Face Design:** —/docks at Quebec City/—
See subheadings
Colour: Black with yellow and olive tint

Back Design: See subheadings
Colour: Green

THE QUEBEC BANK

620-48-04-06
- **$20 Face Design:** Cherub on winged wheel and power lines "Coming Light"/—/Montmorency Falls
  See subheadings
- **Colour:** Black with olive and yellow tint
- **Back Design:** See subheadings
- **Colour:** Olive

620-48-08
- **$50 Face Design:** —/seated woman with globe, lyre and fountain/—
  See subheadings
- **Colour:** Black with yellow and olive tint
- **Back Design:** Lathework, counters, bank name and "Kent Gate"
- **Colour:** Olive

620-48-04-10
- **$100 Face Design:** Bank Crest in circle, reclining woman and spear "Clione"/—/—
  See subheadings
- **Colour:** Black with yellow and olive tint
- **Back Design:** Lathework, counters, bank name and "Hope Gate"
- **Colour:** Olive

IMPRINT
American Bank Note Company, Ottawa

SIGNATURES
left	right
typed John T. Ross	mss. various

ISSUE DATING
Engraved
1st June 1908.
Jany. 3d. 1911

2. FACE DESIGNS LACKING "FOUNDED 1818" AT TOP

DESIGNS AND COLOURS
- **$5 Back Design:** Bank Crest
- **$10 Back Design:** Bank Crest

OVERPRINT
- **$5:** "M" twice in red

Cat. No.	Denom.	Date	VG	F	VF	EF	Unc
48-02-02	$5	1908	700.	1,000.	1,450.	2,400.	4,500.
48-02-04	$10	1908	700.	1,000.	1,450.	2,400.	4,500.

4. FACE DESIGN HAVING "FOUNDED 1818" AT TOP

BACK DESIGNS
- **$5 Back Design:** —/Bank Crest/—
- **$10 Back Design:** —/Bank Crest/—
- **$20 Back Design:** —/Quebec City, Prescott Gate/—
- **$50 Back Design:** —/Quebec City, Kent Gate/—
- **$100 Back Design:** —/Quebec City, Hope Gate/—

Cat. No.	Denom.	Date	VG	F	VF	EF	Unc
48-04-02	$5	1908	700.	1,000.	1,400.	2,400.	4,500.
48-04-04	$10	1908	700.	1,000.	1,400.	2,400.	4,500.
48-04-06	$20	1911	1,200.	1,675.	2,525.	-	-
48-04-08	$50	1911	1,200.	1,675.	2,525.	-	-
48-04-10	$100	1911	1,200.	1,675.	2,525.	-	-

620-50 ISSUE OF 1908 AND 1911
"FOUNDED 1818" AT TOP
NEW BACK DESIGNS

BACK DESIGNS

620-50-02
- **Back Design:** Lathework, counters, bank name and Quebec City - Prescott Gate
- **Colour:** Green

620-50-04
- **$10 Back Design:** Lathework, counters, bank name and Quebec City - Hope Gate
- **Green:** Green

BANK OF QUEBEC, LOWER CANADA

620-50-06

    $20 Back Design: Lathework, counters, bank name and Bank Crest
          Colour: Green

Cat. No.	Denom.	Date	VG	F	VF	EF	Unc
50-02	$5	1908	750.	1,000.	1,450.	-	-
50-04	$10	1908	750.	1,000.	1,450.	-	-
50-06	$20	1911	1,450.	1,800.	3,000.	-	-

620-52   **SPURIOUS $2 ISSUE, 1857-1859**
DESIGNS AND COLOURS

620-52-02

    $2 Face Design: Beehive and agricultural implements/ radiant Royal Crest; Indian paddling canoe below/Britannia with spear and shield
          Colour: Black with no tint

    Back Design: Plain

IMPRINT
    Harris & Sealey Engravers N. York

SIGNATURES
    left   **right**
    mss. Chas. Gething   mss. J. Gibb

ISSUE DATING
    Partially engraved ___ 18___:
    1859: Not completed

OVERPRINT
    "QUEBEC" and "C.E." in green

PROTECTOR
    Green "word" on face only

Cat. No.	Denom.	Date	Variety	VG	F	VF	EF	Unc
52-02	$2	1858-59	Spurious	210.	300.	450.	-	-

BANK OF QUEBEC, LOWER CANADA

1841

QUEBEC, LOWER CANADA

BANK NUMBER 625   **NONREDEEMABLE**

This was undoubtedly a phantom bank. These notes were printed from the same plate as the spurious $2 notes for the Quebec Bank and for the Bank of Lower Canada.

625-10   **DESIGN OF 1841**
DESIGNS AND COLOURS

625-10-02R

    $2 Face Design: Beehive and agricultural implements/ radiant Royal Crest; Indian paddling canoe below/Britannia with spear and shield
          Colour: Black with no tint

    Back Design: Plain

IMPRINT
    Harris & Sealey Engravers N. York

SIGNATURES
    left   **right**
    none   none

ISSUE DATING
    Partially engraved ___ 18___:
    1841: Jany. 2

Cat. No.	Denom.	Date	Variety	VG	F	VF	EF	Unc
10-02R	$2	1841	Remainder	325.	475.	700.	-	-

THE ROYAL BANK OF CANADA

1901 TO DATE

MONTREAL, QUEBEC

BANK NUMBER 630   **REDEEMABLE**

The Royal Bank of Canada is the largest Canadian chartered bank in terms of assets and one of the largest in the world.

In April 1864 eight well-to-do merchants in Halifax, Nova Scotia, joined together in a co-partnership called the Merchants Bank, with a capital of $200,000, of which $160,000 was paid up. After Confederation full banking privileges were confirmed by the Royal assent given on June 22, 1869, to a federal charter for the Merchants Bank of Halifax. The new bank had an authorized capital of $1,000,000 in 10,000 shares of $100 each.

Until 1887 the bank's operations were "acceptably profitable," but a marked improvement in business conditions from that date until 1892 lifted the bank from being a small institution of provincial importance to being a large one with some 25 branches in four provinces.

At the 1900 annual general meeting, the president of the bank stated that the expansion of the bank's business throughout Canada and abroad was such that the time had come to adopt a more distinctive and comprehensive designation. Upon the completion of necessary formalities, the name of the bank was changed to the Royal Bank of Canada, effective January 2, 1901. During the period of 1869 to 1900, the bank's growth was cautious, but steady. Rapid expansion came during 1901 to 1913, when Canada experienced a wave of development.

The bank greatly expanded its operations in other provinces and the Caribbean by absorbing other institutions, including a Cuban bank in 1904. Also in 1904, the bank changed its head office from Halifax to Montreal.

During World War I, the bank gave considerable assistance to the government, and despite a preoccupation with the problems of operating under war conditions, expansion continued. Between 1914 and 1918, the number of its branches in Canada increased by 147, but of these, 134 were through the takeovers of two other banks. In terms of total assets, the bank became the second largest bank in Canada by the end of 1918.

The wartime prosperity, which had continued almost uninterrupted through 1919, turned into a depression in 1921 and 1922, during which the bank's assets declined, but its profits kept up remarkably well. With the improvement in business conditions in 1925, prosperity returned until the last quarter of 1929. When the market collapsed in 1929, both the total assets and the profits of the bank were at a record high, and it had become the largest bank in Canada. However, like other banks, the Royal Bank was greatly affected by the Depression. Its assets shrunk, and some of its branches were closed. By 1935 the upward trend in business was firmly established and, in general, continued in that direction during the remainder of the 1930s.

Following the outbreak of war in September 1939, the bank cooperated fully in the execution of the country's war efforts. In this it played its part equally with the other banks and under similar difficulties. Since the end of World War II, the Royal Bank has continued to expand, both in Canada and abroad.

630-10   **ISSUES OF 1901 AND 1909**

2.   **1901 ISSUES**

DESIGNS AND COLOURS

630-10-02-02
    $5 Face Design: Seated woman with two children and dove "Peace"/—/—
    Colour: See varieties

    Back Design: —/Royal Crest/—
    Colour: See varieties

630-10-02-04

630-10-02-06
    $10 Face Design: —/—/seated allegorical female
    Colour: Black with blue, violet, yellow-brown and yellow-green tint
    Back Design: —/Royal Crest/—
    Colour: Blue, violet, yellow-brown and yellow-green

630-10-02-12
    $20 Face Design: —/seated woman with globe, shield and lion/—
    Colour: Black, yellow-brown, green, lilac and gold tint
    Back Design: —/Royal Crest/—
    Colour: Yellow-brown, green, lilac and gold

THE ROYAL BANK OF CANADA

630-10-02-16S
    $50 Face Design: —/—/ships at sea
        Colour: Black with yellow-brown, green, lilac and gold tint

    Back Design: —/Royal Crest/—
        Colour: Yellow-brown, green, lilac and gold

IMPRINT
    American Bank Note Co. Ottawa

SIGNATURES
left	right
mss. various	engr. T.E. Kenny
mss. various	typed T.E. Kenny

ISSUE DATING
    Engraved
    Jan. 2nd 1901

VARIETIES
    Multicoloured Frame - Kenny, engraved right
        Face Colour: Black with green, yellow-green, yellow-brown and lilac tint
        Back Colour: Green, yellow-green, yellow-brown and lilac
    Green Frame - Kenny, typed right
        Face Colour: Black with green and yellow-green tint
        Back Colour: Green

Cat. No.	Denom.	Date	Variety	VG	F	VF	EF	Unc
10-02-02	$5	1901	Kenny engr. r, multi	350.	475.	700.	1,200.	-
10-02-04	$5	1901	Kenny typed r, green	175.	225.	350.	600.	-
10-02-06	$10	1901	Kenny engr. r	400.	550.	800.	1,300.	-
10-02-08	$10	1901	Kenny typed r	400.	550.	800.	1,300.	-
10-02-10P	$20	1901	Kenny, engr. r				PROOF	500.
10-02-12	$20	1901	Kenny, typed r	550.	750.	1,100.	1,800.	-
10-02-14P	$50	1901	Kenny, engr. r				PROOF	500.
10-02-16S	$50	1901	Kenny, typed r				SPECIMEN	1,250.

4. 1909 ISSUES

DESIGNS AND COLOURS

630-10-04-02
    $5 Face Design: Seated woman with two children and dove "Peace"/—/—
        Colour: Black with green and yellow tint, black outlined 5s

    Back Design: —/Royal Crest/—
        Colour: Black with green tint

630-10-04-06
    $5 Face Design: Seated woman with two children and dove "Peace"/—/—
        Colour: Black with green and yellow tint, green outlined 5s

    Back Design: —/Royal Crest/—
        Colour: Black with green tint

630-10-04-10
    $10 Face Design: —/—/seated allegorical female
Multicoloured Frame:
        Colour: Black with green, yellow-green, yellow-brown and lilac tint

    Back Design: —/Royal Crest/—
        Colour: Green, yellow-green, yellow-brown and lilac

630-10-04-14
    $10 Face Design: —/—/seated allegorical female
Black Frame:
        Colour: Black with green-yellow tint

    Back Design: —/Royal Crest/—
        Colour: Olive and yellow

THE ROYAL BANK OF CANADA

630-10-04-18S
  $20 Face Design: —/seated woman with globe, shield and lion/—
  Multicoloured Frame:
    Colour: Black with green, yellow-green, yellow-brown and lilac tint
  Back Design: —/Royal Crest/—
    Colour: Green, yellow-green, yellow-brown and lilac

630-10-04-22
  $20 Face Design: —/seated woman with globe, shield and lion/—
  Black Frame:
    Colour: Black with blue and yellow tint
  Back Design: —/Royal Crest/—
    Colour: Blue and yellow

630-10-04-26S
  $50 Face Design: —/—/ships at sea
    Colour: Black with yellow-brown, green, lilac and gold tint
  Back Design: —/Royal Crest/—
    Colour: Yellow-brown, green, lilac and gold

630-10-04-34P
  $100 Face Design: —/—/seated "Commerce" figure
    Colour: Black with orange tint
  Back Design: —/Royal Crest/—
    Colour: Red-orange

IMPRINT
  American Bank Note Co. Ottawa

SIGNATURES
left	right
mss. various	typed H.S. Holt
typed H.S. Holt	mss. various

ISSUE DATING
  Engraved
    Jan. 2nd 1909

VARIETIES
  $5, 1909 Face Design: Black outlined 5s
  $5, 1909 Face Design: Green outlined 5s
    Back Colour: Green
  Multicoloured Frame:
    Face Colour: Black with green, yellow-green, yellow-brown and lilac tint
    Back Colour: Green, yellow-green, yellow-brown and lilac
  Green Frame:
    Face Colour: Black with green and yellow-green tint
    Back Colour: Green
  Black Frame:
    Face Colour: Black with green and yellow tint
    Back Colour: Olive and yellow
  Blue Frame:
    Face Colour: Black with blue and yellow tint
    Back Colour: Blue and yellow

Cat. No.	Denom.	Date	Variety	VG	F	VF	EF	Unc
10-04-02	$5	1909	Black, Holt, r.	175.	250.	375.	700.	-
10-04-06	$5	1909	Green, Holt, l.	125.	160.	250.	475.	-
10-04-10	$10	1909	Multi, Holt, r.	525.	700.	950.	1,600.	-
10-04-14	$10	1909	Black, Holt, l.	200.	300.	425.	750.	-
10-04-18S	$20	1909	Multi, Holt, l.				SPECIMEN	1,250.
10-04-22	$20	1909	Blue, Holt, r.	600.	950.	1,200.	1,900.	-
10-04-26S	$50	1909	Holt, r.				SPECIMEN	1,250.
10-04-30P	$50	1909					PROOF	500.
10-04-34P	$100	1909					PROOF	500.

THE ROYAL BANK OF CANADA

630-12 ISSUES OF 1913
DESIGNS AND COLOURS

630-12-04
 $5 Face Design: Edson L. Pease/Canadian coat of arms/Herbert S. Holt
 Colour: Black with green tint

 Back Design: Lathework, counters, bank name and Royal Crest
 Colour: Green

630-12-08
 $10 Face Design: —/battleship Bellerophon/—
 Colour: Black with yellow-green and blue tint

 Back Design: —/Royal Crest/—
 Colour: Yellow-orange

630-12-12
 $20 Face Design: —/train on prairies/—
 Colour: Black with blue tint

 Back Design: Lathework, counters, bank name and Royal Crest
 Colour: Blue

630-12-14E
 $50 Face Design: —/Vincent Meridith/—
 Colour: Black with yellow and red tint

 Back Design: Unknown
 Colour: Unknown

630-12-18
 $50 Face Design: Edson L. Pease/—/—
 Colour: Black with green and yellow tint

 Back Design: Lathework, counters, bank name and Royal Crest
 Colour: Olive

630-12-22
 $100 Face Design: —/—/Herbert S. Holt
 Colour: Black with orange and yellow-green tint

 Back Design: Lathework, counters, bank name and Royal Crest
 Colour: Red

IMPRINT
American Bank Note Co. Ottawa or Canadian Bank Note Company, Limited.

SIGNATURES

left	right
mss. various	typed H.S. Holt
typed C.E. Neill	typed H.S. Holt

ISSUE DATING
Engraved
Jan. 2nd 1913

Cat. No.	Denom.	Date	Variety	VG	F	VF	EF	Unc
12-02	$5	1913	Mss. signature, l.	50.	65.	125.	200.	425.
12-04	$5	1913	Typed Neill, l.	50.	65.	125.	200.	425.
12-06	$10	1913	Mss. signature, l.	50.	125.	175.	300.	500.
12-08	$10	1913	Typed Neill, l.	50.	125.	175.	300.	500.
12-10	$20	1913	Mss. signature, l.	100.	200.	250.	275.	550.
12-12	$20	1913	Typed Neill, l.	100.	200.	250.	275.	550.
12-14E	$50	1913					ESSAY	2,000.
12-16	$50	1913	Mss. signature, l.	275.	425.	700.	1,000.	-
12-18	$50	1913	Typed Neill, l.	275.	425.	700.	1,000.	-
12-20	$100	1913	Mss. signature, l.	700.	1,000.	1,400.	2,500.	-
12-22	$100	1913	Typed Neill, l.	700.	1,000.	1,400.	2,500.	-

630-14   **ISSUE OF 1927**

DESIGNS AND COLOURS

630-14-04
 $5 Face Design: C.E. Neill/coat of arms/Herbert S. Holt
 Colour: Black with green tint

 Back Design: —/Royal Crest/—
 Colour: Green

630-14-08
 $10 Face Design: C.E. Neill/coat of arms/Herbert S. Holt
 Colour: Black with orange tint

 Back Design: —/Royal Crest/—
 Colour: Orange

630-14-12
 $20 Face Design: C.E. Neill/coat of arms/Herbert S. Holt
 Colour: Black with blue tint

 Back Design: —/Royal Crest/—
 Colour: Blue

630-14-16
 $50 Face Design: Edson L. Pease/coat of arms/—
 Colour: Black with purple tint

 Back Design: —/Royal Crest/—
 Colour: Purple

630-14-20
 $100 Face Design: —/Canadian coat of arms/Herbert S. Holt
 Colour: Black with olive green tint

 Back Design: —/Royal Crest/—
 Colour: Olive

THE ROYAL BANK OF CANADA

IMPRINT
Canadian Bank Note Company, Limited

SIGNATURES

left	right
typed C.E. Neill	typed H.S. Holt
typed M.W. Wilson	typed H.S. Holt

ISSUE DATING
Engraved
Jan. 3rd 1927

Cat. No.	Denom.	Date	Variety	VG	F	VF	EF	Unc
14-02	$5	1927	Neill, l.	25.	35.	60.	110.	225.
14-04	$5	1927	Wilson, l.	25.	35.	60.	110.	225.
14-06	$10	1927	Neill, l.	25.	35.	60.	110.	225.
14-08	$10	1927	Wilson, l.	25.	35.	60.	110.	225.
14-10	$20	1927	Neill, l.	35.	50.	80.	140.	300.
14-12	$20	1927	Wilson, l.	35.	50.	80.	140.	300.
14-14	$50	1927	Neill, l.	175.	250.	375.	650.	1,300.
14-16	$50	1927	Wilson, l.	175.	250.	375.	650.	1,300.
14-18	$100	1927	Neill, l.	225.	300.	475.	850.	1,600.
14-20	$100	1927	Wilson, l.	225.	300.	475.	850.	1,600.

630-16 ISSUE OF 1933

DESIGNS AND COLOURS

630-16-02
  $5 Face Design: Morris W. Wilson/coat of arms/ Sir Herbert Holt
    Colour: Black with green tint

  Back Design: Lathework, counters, bank name and Royal Crest
    Colour: Green

630-16-04
  $10 Face Design: Morris W. Wilson/coat of arms/ Sir Herbert Holt
    Colour: Black with orange tint

  Back Design: —/Royal Crest/—
    Colour: Orange

630-16-06S
  $20 Face Design: Morris W. Wilson/coat of arms/ Sir Herbert Holt
    Colour: Black with blue tint

  Back Design: —/Royal Crest/—
    Colour: Blue

IMPRINT
Canadian Bank Note Company, Limited

SIGNATURES

left	right
typed M.W. Wilson	typed H.S. Holt

ISSUE DATING
Engraved
July 3rd 1933

Cat. No.	Denom.	Date	VG	F	VF	EF	Unc
16-02	$5	1933	25.	35.	65.	110.	225.
16-04	$10	1933	25.	35.	65.	110.	225.
16-06S	$20	1933			SPECIMEN		750.

378

630-18 ISSUE OF 1935
SMALL-SIZE NOTES

DESIGNS AND COLOURS

630-18-02
- **$5 Face Design:** Morris W. Wilson/coat of arms/Sir Herbert Holt
- **Colour:** Black with green tint
- **Back Design:** Lathework, counters, bank name and Royal Crest
- **Colour:** Green

630-18-04
- **$10 Face Design:** Morris W. Wilson/coat of arms/Sir Herbert Holt
- **Colour:** Black with orange tint
- **Back Design:** Lathework, counters, bank name and Royal Crest
- **Colour:** Orange

630-18-06
- **$20 Face Design:** Morris W. Wilson/coat of arms/Sir Herbert Holt
- **Colour:** Black with blue tint
- **Back Design:** Lathework, counters, bank name and Royal Crest
- **Colour:** Blue

IMPRINT
British American Bank Note Co. Ltd Ottawa

SIGNATURES
left	right
typed S.G. Dobson	typed M.W. Wilson

ISSUE DATING
Engraved
Jan. 2nd 1935

Cat. No.	Denom.	Date	VG	F	VF	EF	Unc
18-02	$5	1935	15.	20.	30.	50.	100.
18-04	$10	1935	20.	25.	35.	60.	125.
18-06	$20	1935	25.	30.	50.	85.	175.

630-20 ISSUE OF 1943

These notes bear the last date of issue of any chartered bank.

DESIGNS AND COLOURS

630-20-02
- **$5 Face Design:** S.G. Dobson/Coat of Arms/Morris W. Wilson
- **Colour:** Black with green tint
- **Back Design:** Lathework, counters, bank name and Royal Crest
- **Colour:** Green

IMPRINT
British American Bank Note Company Limited

SIGNATURES
left	right
typed S.G. Dobson	typed M.W. Wilson

ISSUE DATING
Engraved
Jan. 2nd 1943

Cat. No.	Denom.	Date	VG	F	VF	EF	Unc
20-02	$5	1943	35.	50.	85.	150.	275.

THE ROYAL BANK OF CANADA

BRITISH WEST INDIES ISSUES

In 1902 the Union Bank of Halifax opened a branch in Port of Spain, Trinidad. The Royal Bank took over the Union Bank in 1910 and continued the Caribbean operations. The Royal Bank issued notes dated as early as January 2, 1909, payable on various Caribbean islands.

ISSUES FOR ST. JOHN'S, ANTIGUA

630-22   DESIGNS FOR OVERPRINTED CANADIAN NOTES, 1913

DESIGNS AND COLOURS

630-22-02S
$5 **Face Design:** Edson L. Pease/Canadian Coat of Arms/H.S. Holt
   Colour: Black with green tint
Back Design: Lathework, counters, bank name and Royal Crest
   Colour: Green

IMPRINT
American Bank Note Co. Ottawa

SIGNATURES
left	right
none	typed H.S. Holt

ISSUE DATING
Engraved
Jan. 2nd 1913

OVERPRINT
"ANTIGUA" at ends and "PAYABLE AT ST. JOHN'S/ANTIGUA" at left centre, all in blue

Cat. No.	Denom.	Date		Unc
22-02S	$5	1913	SPECIMEN	750.

630-24   NOTES DESIGNED SPECIFICALLY FOR WEST INDIES, ANTIGUA LARGE SIZE NOTES, 1920

DESIGNS AND COLOURS

630-24-02
$5 (£1.0.10) **Face Design:** —/steamships and sailboat/—
   Colour: Black with green tint
Back Design: —/Royal Crest/—
   Colour: Green

IMPRINT
American Bank Note Company, Ottawa

SIGNATURES
left	right
typed C.E. Neill	typed H.S. Holt

ISSUE DATING
Engraved
January 2nd 1920

Cat. No.	Denom.	Date	VG	F	VF	EF	Unc
24-02	$5 (£1.0.10)	1920	850.	1,200.	1,700.	-	-

630-26   WEST INDIES ANTIGUA DESIGNS SMALL-SIZE NOTES, 1938

DESIGNS AND COLOURS

630-26-02
$5 (£1.0.10) **Face Design:** —/steamships and sailboat/—
   Colour: Black with green tint
Back Design: —/Royal Crest/—
   Colour: Green

IMPRINT
Canadian Bank Note Company Limited

SIGNATURES
left	right
typed S.G. Dobson	typed M.W. Wilson

ISSUE DATING
Engraved
January 3rd 1938

Cat. No.	Denom.	Date	VG	F	VF	EF	Unc
26-02	$5 (£1.0.10)	1938	350.	475.	800.	-	-

THE ROYAL BANK OF CANADA

ISSUES FOR BRIDGETOWN, BARBADOS

630-28 OVERPRINTED CANADIAN NOTES, 1909

DESIGNS AND COLOURS

630-28-02S
- **$5 Face Design:** Seated woman with two children and dove "peace"/—/—
- **Colour:** Black with green and yellow tint
- **Back Design:** —/Royal Crest/—
- **Colour:** Green and yellow

630-28-04
- **$20 Face Design:** —/seated woman and lion/—
- **Colour:** Blue frame, black with blue and yellow tint
- **Back Design:** —/Royal Crest/—
- **Colour:** Blue and yellow

630-28-06S
- **$100 Face Design:** —/—/seated "Commerce" figure
- **Colour:** Black with red-orange, yellow and olive tint
- **Back Design:** —/Royal Crest/—
- **Colour:** Red-orange

IMPRINT
American Bank Note Co. Ottawa

SIGNATURES

	left	right
$5:	typed H.S. Holt	none
$20:	mss. various	typed H.S. Holt
$100:	typed H.S. Holt	none

ISSUE DATING
Engraved
Jan. 2nd 1909.

OVERPRINT
"BARBADOS" at ends and "PAYABLE AT/BRIDGETOWN, BARBADOS" in centre, all in blue

Cat. No.	Denom.	Date	VG	F	VF	EF	Unc
28-02	$5	1909	850.	1,050.	1,800.	3,000.	-
28-04	$20	1909	800.	1,100.	1,700.	-	-
28-06S	$100	1909			SPECIMEN		850.

630-30 NOTES DESIGNED SPECIFICALLY FOR WEST INDIES, BARBADOS LARGE SIZE NOTE DESIGNS, 1920

DESIGNS AND COLOURS

630-30-02
- **$5 (£1.0.10) Face Design:** —/steamships and sailboat/—
- **Colour:** Black with green tint
- **Back Design:** —/Royal Crest/—
- **Colour:** Green

630-30-04S
- **$20 (£4.3.4) Face Design:** —-/harvesting sugar cane/—
- **Colour:** Black with blue tint
- **Back Design:** —/Royal Crest/—
- **Colour:** Blue

630-30-06S
- **$100 (£20.16.8) Face Design:** —/seated "Cleopatra" with tropical island in background,/—
- **Colour:** Black with orange tint
- **Back Design:** —/Royal Crest/—
- **Colour:** Orange

THE ROYAL BANK OF CANADA

IMPRINT
American Bank Note Company, Ottawa

SIGNATURES

left	right
typed C.E. Neill	typed H.S. Holt
typed S.G. Dobson	typed H.S. Holt

ISSUE DATING
Engraved
January 2nd 1920

Cat. No.	Denom.	Date	VG	F	VF	EF	Unc
30-02	$5 (£1.0.10)	1920	800.	1,100.	1,700.	2,900.	5,500.
30-04S	$20 (£4.3.4)	1920			SPECIMEN	1,000.	
30-06S	$100 (£20.16.8.)	1920			SPECIMEN	1,000.	

630-32 NOTES DESIGNED SPECIFICALLY FOR WEST INDIES, BARBADOS SMALL SIZE NOTES, 1938

DESIGNS AND COLOURS

630-32-02
$5 (£1.0.10) **Face Design:** —/steamship/—
Colour: Black with green tint

Back Design: —/Royal Crest/—
Colour: Green

630-32-04
$20 (£4.3.4) **Face Design:** —/harvesting sugar cane/—
Colour: Black with orange tint

Back Design: —/Royal Crest/—
Colour: Rose

IMPRINT
Canadian Bank Note Company Limited

SIGNATURES

left	right
typed S.G. Dobson	typed M.W. Wilson

ISSUE DATING
Engraved
January 3rd 1938

Cat. No.	Denom.	Date	VG	F	VF	EF	Unc
32-02	$5 (£1.0.10)	1938	175.	240.	375.	650.	-
32-04	$20 (£4.3.4.)	1938	650.	900.	1,400.	-	-

ISSUES FOR GEORGETOWN, BRITISH GUIANA

630-34 OVERPRINTED CANADIAN NOTES 1909 AND 1913

DESIGNS AND COLOURS

630-34-02
$5 **Face Design:** Edson L. Pease/Canadian coat of arms/H.S. Holt
Colour: Black with green tint

Back Design: —/Royal Crest/—
Colour: Green

630-34-04
$20 **Face Design:** —/train on prairie/—
Colour: Black with blue tint
Back Design: —/Royal Crest/—
Colour: Blue

Photo Not Available

630-34-06
$100 **Face Design:** —/—/seated "Commerce" figure
Colour: Black with red-orange tint

Back Design: —/Royal Crest/—
Colour: Red-orange

630-34-08S
$100 **Face Design:** —/—/H.S. Holt
Colour: Black with orange and yellow-green tint

Back Design: —/Royal Crest/—
Colour: Red

IMPRINT
American Bank Note Co. Ottawa

SIGNATURES
	left	right
$5 and $20:	mss. various	typed H.S. Holt
$100:	none	typed H.S. Holt

ISSUE DATING
Engraved
Jan. 2, 1909
Jan. 2nd 1913

OVERPRINT
"BRITISH GUIANA" at ends and "PAYABLE AT/GEORGETOWN, BRITISH GUIANA" in centre, all in blue

Cat. No.	Denom.	Date	VG	F	VF	EF	Unc
34-02	$5	1913	500.	675.	1,050.	-	-
34-04	$20	1913	800.	1,150.	1,700.	-	-
34-06S	$100	1909			SPECIMEN		850.
34-08S	$100	1913			SPECIMEN		750.

630-36 NOTES DESIGNED SPECIFICALLY FOR WEST INDIES, BRITISH GUIANA LARGE SIZE NOTES, 1920

DESIGNS AND COLOURS

630-36-02
$5 (£1.0.10) **Face Design:** —/steamship and sailboat/—
Colour: Black with green tint
Back Design: —/Royal Crest/—
Colour: Green

630-36-04S
$20 (£4.3.4) **Face Design:** —/harvesting sugar cane/—
Colour: Black with blue tint
Back Design: —/Royal Crest/—
Colour: Green

630-36-06S
$100 (£20.16.8) **Face Design:** —/seated semi-nude "Cleopatra" with tropical island in background,/—
Colour: Black with orange tint
Back Design: —/Royal Crest/—
Colour: Orange

IMPRINT
American Bank Note Company, Ottawa

SIGNATURES
left	right
typed C.E. Neill	typed H.S. Holt
typed M.W. Wilson	typed H.S. Holt

ISSUE DATING
Engraved
January 2nd 1920

Cat. No.	Denom.	Date	VG	F	VF	EF	Unc
36-02	$5 (£1.0.10)	1920	500.	675.	1,050.	-	-
36-04S	$20 (£4.3.4)	1920			SPECIMEN		750.
36-06S	$100 (£20.16.8)	1920			SPECIMEN		850.

630-38 NOTES DESIGNED SPECIFICALLY FOR WEST INDIES, BRITISH GUIANA SMALL SIZE NOTES 1938

DESIGNS AND COLOURS

630-38-02
$5 (£1.0.10) **Face Design:** —/steamship and sailboat/—
Colour: Black with green tint
Back Design: Lathework, counters, bank name and Royal Crest
Colour: Green

THE ROYAL BANK OF CANADA

630-38-04
$20 (£4.3.4) **Face Design:** —/harvesting sugar cane/—
Colour: Black with orange tint
Back Design: Lathework, counters, bank name and Royal Crest
Colour: Rose

IMPRINT
Canadian Bank Note Company. Limited

SIGNATURES
left	right
typed S.G. Dobson	typed M.W. Wilson

ISSUE DATING
Engraved
January 3rd 1938

Cat. No.	Denom.	Date	VG	F	VF	EF	Unc
38-02	$5 (£1.0.10)	1938	275.	400.	600.	-	-
38-04	$20 (£4.3.4.)	1938	325.	475.	725.	-	-

ISSUES FOR ROSEAU, DOMINICA

630-40   **OVERPRINTED CANADIAN NOTES 1913**

DESIGNS AND COLOURS

630-40-02
$5 **Face Design:** Edson L. Pease/ Canadian Coat of Arms/H.S. Holt
Colour: Black with green tint
Back Design: Lathwork, counters, bank name and Royal Crest
Colour: Green

IMPRINT
American Bank Note Co. Ottawa

SIGNATURES
left	right
mss. various	typed H.S. Holt

ISSUE DATING
Engraved
Jan. 2nd 1913

OVERPRINT
"DOMINICA" at ends and "PAYABLE AT ROSEAU,/DOMINICA" at left centre, all in blue

Cat. No.	Denom.	Date	VG	F	VF	EF	Unc
40-02	$5	1913	850.	1,150.	1,700.	-	-

630-42   **NOTES DESIGNED SPECIFICALLY FOR WEST INDIES, DOMINICA LARGE SIZE NOTES 1920**

DESIGNS AND COLOURS

630-42-02
$5 (£1.0.10) **Face Design:** —/steamships and sailboat/—
Colour: Black with green tint
Back Design: —/Royal Crest/—
Colour: Green

IMPRINT
American Bank Note Company, Ottawa

SIGNATURES
left	right
typed S.G. Dobson	typed H.S. Holt

ISSUE DATING
Engraved
January 2nd 1920

Cat. No.	Denom.	Date	VG	F	VF	EF	Unc
42-02	$5 (£1.0.10)	1920	750.	1,050.	1,575.	-	-

630-44   **NOTES DESIGNED SPECIFICALLY FOR WEST INDIES, DOMINICA SMALL SIZE NOTES, 1938**

DESIGNS AND COLOURS

630-44-02
$5 (£1.0.10) **Face Design:** —/steamships and sailboat/—
Colour: Black with green tint
Back Design: —/Royal Crest/—
Colour: Green

IMPRINT
Canadian Bank Note Company Limited

SIGNATURES
left	right
typed S.G. Dobson	typed M.W. Wilson

ISSUE DATING
Engraved
January 3rd 1938

Cat. No.	Denom.	Date	VG	F	VF	EF	Unc
44-02	$5(£1.0.10)	1938	650.	900.	1,300.	-	-

ISSUES FOR ST. GEORGE'S, GRENADA

630-46 DESIGNS FOR OVERPRINTED CANADIAN NOTES 1909

DESIGNS AND COLOURS

630-46-02s
$5 **Face Design:** Seated woman with two children and dove "Peace"/—/—
Colour: Black with green and yellow tint

Back Design: —/Royal Crest/—
Colour: Green and yellow

IMPRINT
American Bank Note Co. Ottawa

SIGNATURES
left	right
typed H.S. Holt	none

ISSUE DATING
Engraved
Jan. 2nd 1909

OVERPRINT
"GRENADA" at ends and "PAYABLE AT/ST. GEORGE'S, GRENADA" in centre, all in blue

Cat. No.	Denom.	Date		Unc
46-02S	$5	1909	SPECIMEN	850.

630-48 NOTES DESIGNED SPECIFICALLY FOR WEST INDIES, GRENADA LARGE SIZE NOTE DESIGNS 1920

DESIGNS AND COLOURS

630-48-02S
$5 (£1.0.10) **Face Design:** —/steamships and sailboat/—
Colour: Black with green tint

Back Design: —/Royal Crest/—
Colour: Green

IMPRINT
American Bank Note Company, Ottawa

SIGNATURES
left	right
typed C.E. Neill	typed H.S. Holt

ISSUE DATING
Engraved
January 2nd 1920

Cat. No.	Denom.	Date		Unc
48-02S	$5 (£1.0.10)	1920	SPECIMEN	750.

630-50 NOTES DESIGNED SPECIFICALLY FOR WEST INDIES, GRENADA SMALL SIZE NOTES 1938

DESIGNS AND COLOURS

630-50-02
$5 (£1.0.10) **Face Design:** —/steamships and sailboat/—
Colour: Black with green tint

Back Design: —/Royal Crest/—
Colour: Green

IMPRINT
Canadian Bank Note Company, Limited

SIGNATURES
left	right
typed S.G. Dobson	typed M.W. Wilson

ISSUE DATING
Engraved
January 3rd 1938

Cat. No.	Denom.	Date	VG	F	VF	EF	Unc
50-02	$5 (£1.0.10)	1938	800.	1,100.	1,700.	-	-

THE ROYAL BANK OF CANADA

630-52 ISSUES FOR KINGSTON, JAMAICA
LARGE SIZE NOTES 1911

DESIGNS AND COLOURS

630-52-02
  £1 **Face Design:** —/—/seated woman with lyre and model ship
  Colour: Black with orange, yellow and olive tint

  Back Design: Lathework, counters, bank name and Royal Crest
  Colour: Green

630-52-04S
  £5 **Face Design:** Seated woman with pad and palette "Study"/—/—
  Colour: Black with red-orange and yellow-green tint

  Back Design: —/Royal Crest/—
  Colour: Olive

IMPRINT
  American Bank Note Co. Ottawa

SIGNATURES
left	right
typed H.S. Holt	mss. various
typed H.S. Holt	none

ISSUE DATING
  Jan. 2nd 1911

Cat. No.	Denom.	Date	VG	F	VF	EF	Unc
52-02	£1	1911	450.	600.	950.	-	-
52-04	£5	1911	500.	675.	1,050.	-	-

630-54 ISSUES FOR KINGSTON, JAMAICA
SMALL SIZE NOTES 1938

DESIGNS AND COLOURS

630-54-02
  £1 **Face Design:** —/—/seated woman with lyre and model ship
  Colour: Black with green and orange tint

  Back Design: —/Royal Crest/—
  Colour: Green

630-54-04
  £5 **Face Design:** Seated woman with pad and palette "Study"/—/—
  Colour: Black with red-orange and yellow-green tint

  Back Design: —/Royal Crest/—
  Colour: Olive

IMPRINT
  Canadian Bank Note Company, Limited

SIGNATURES
left	right
typed S.G. Dobson	typed M.W. Wilson

ISSUE DATING
  Engraved
  January 3rd, 1938

Cat. No.	Denom.	Date	VG	F	VF	EF	Unc
54-02	£1	1938	650.	900.	1,400.	-	-
54-04	£5	1938	800.	1,150.	1,700.	-	-

THE ROYAL BANK OF CANADA

ISSUES FOR BASSETERRE, ST. KITTS

630-56 OVERPRINTED CANADIAN NOTES 1913

DESIGNS AND COLOURS

630-56-02
  $5 Face Design: Edson L. Pease/Canadian coat of arms/ H.S. Holt
  Colour: Black with green tint

  Back Design: Lathework, counters, bank name and Royal Crest
  Colour: Green

IMPRINT
American Bank Note Co. Ottawa

SIGNATURES
  left — mss. various
  right — typed H.S. Holt

ISSUE DATING
  Engraved
  Jan. 2nd, 1913

OVERPRINT
"ST. KITTS" at ends and "PAYABLE AT BASSETERRE,/ ST. KITTS" at left centre, all in blue

Cat. No.	Denom.	Date	VG	F	VF	EF	Unc
56-02	$5	1913	800.	1,150.	1,700.	-	-

630-58 NOTES DESIGNED SPECIFICALLY FOR WEST INDIES, ST. KITTS LARGE SIZE NOTE DESIGNS, 1920

DESIGNS AND COLOURS

630-58-02S
  $5 (£1.0.10) Face Design: —/steamships and sailboat/—
  Colour: Black with green tint

  Back Design: —/Royal Crest/—
  Colour: Green

IMPRINT
American Bank Note Company, Ottawa

SIGNATURES
  left — mss. various
  right — typed H.S. Holt

ISSUE DATING
  Engraved
  January 2nd, 1920

Cat. No.	Denom.	Date	VG	F	VF	EF	Unc
58-02S	$5 (£1.0.10)	1920				SPECIMEN	750.

630-60 NOTES DESIGNED SPECIFICALLY FOR WEST INDIES, ST. KITTS SMALL SIZE NOTES, 1938

DESIGNS AND COLOURS

630-60-02
  $5 (£1.0.10) Face Design: —/steamships and sailboat/—
  Colour: Black with green tint

  Back Design: —/Royal Crest/—
  Colour: Green

IMPRINT
Canadian Bank Note Company Limited

SIGNATURES
  left — typed S.G. Dobson
  right — typed M.W. Wilson

ISSUE DATING
  Engraved
  January 3rd 1938

Cat. No.	Denom.	Date	VG	F	VF	EF	Unc
60-02	$5 (£1.0.10)	1938	650.	900.	1,350.	-	-

THE ROYAL BANK OF CANADA

630-62 ISSUE FOR CASTRIES, ST. LUCIA

These designs were for large-size notes and were designed specifically for the West Indies.

DESIGNS AND COLOURS

630-62-02S
- **$5 (£1.0.10) Face Design:** —/steamships and sailboat/—
  - **Colour:** Black with green tint
- **Back Design:** —/Royal Crest/—
  - **Colour:** Green

IMPRINT
American Bank Note Company, Ottawa

SIGNATURES
left	right
none	typed H.S. Holt

ISSUE DATING
Engraved
January 2nd 1920

Cat. No.	Denom.	Date				Unc
62-02S	$5 (£1.0.10)	1920			SPECIMEN	1,000.

ISSUES FOR PORT OF SPAIN, TRINIDAD

630-64 OVERPRINTED CANADIAN NOTES 1909

DESIGNS AND COLOURS

630-64-02
- **$5 Face Design:** Seated woman with two children and dove "peace"/—/—
  - **Colour:** Black with green and yellow tint
- **Back Design:** —/Royal Crest/—
  - **Colour:** Green and yellow

630-64-04S
- **$20 Face Design:** —/seated woman, lion, shield and globe/—
  - **Colour:** Blue frame, black with blue and yellow frame
- **Back Design:** —/Royal Crest/—
  - **Colour:** Blue and yellow

630-64-06S
- **$100 Face Design:** —/—/seated "Commerce" figure
  - **Colour:** Black with red-orange, yellow and olive tint
- **Back Design:** —/Royal Crest/—
  - **Colour:** Red-orange

IMPRINT
American Bank Note Co. Ottawa

SIGNATURES
	left	right
$5:	typed H.S. Holt	mss. various
	typed H.S. Holt	none
$20:	mss. various	typed H.S. Holt
$100:	typed H.S. Holt	mss. various
	typed H.S. Holt	none

ISSUE DATING
Engraved
Jan. 2nd 1909

OVERPRINT
"TRINIDAD" at ends and "PAYABLE AT/PORT OF SPAIN, TRINIDAD" in centre, all in red

Cat. No.	Denom.	Date	VG	F	VF	EF	Unc
64-02	$5	1909	650.	900.	1,350.	-	-
64-04S	$20	1909			SPECIMEN		850.
64-06S	$100	1909			SPECIMEN		850.

388

630-66 NOTES DESIGNED SPECIFICALLY FOR WEST INDIES, TRINIDAD LARGE SIZE NOTES 1920

DESIGNS AND COLOURS

630-66-02
- **$5 (£1.0.10) Face Design:** —/steamships and sailboat/—
  - **Colour:** Black with green tint
- **Back Design:** lathework, counters, bank name and Royal Crest
  - **Colour:** Green

630-66-04
- **$20 (£4.3.4) Face Design:** —/harvesting sugar cane/—
  - **Colour:** Black with blue tint 
- **Back Design:** Lathework, counters, bank name and Royal Crest
  - **Colour:** Blue

630-66-06
- **$100 (£20.16.8) Face Design:** —/seated semi-nude "Cleopatra" with tropical island in background/—
  - **Colour:** Black with orange tint
- **Back Design:** Lathework, counters, bank name and Royal Crest
  - **Colour:** Orange

IMPRINT
American Bank Note Company, Ottawa

SIGNATURES

left	right
mss. various	typed H.S. Holt
none	typed H.S. Holt
typed S.G. Dobson	typed M.W. Wilson
typed C.E. Neill	typed H.S. Holt

ISSUE DATING
Engraved
January 2nd 1920

Cat. No.	Denom.	Date	VG	F	VF	EF	Unc
66-02	$5 (£1.0.10)	1920	225.	325.	500.	-	-
66-04	$20 (£4.3.4)	1920	450.	600.	850.	-	-
66-06	$100 (£20.16.8)	1920	800.	1,100.	1,700.	2,900.	-

630-68 NOTES DESIGNED SPECIFICALLY FOR WEST INDIES, TRINIDAD SMALL SIZE NOTES 1938

DESIGNS AND COLOURS

630-68-02
- **$5 (£1.0.10) Face Design:** —/steamships and sailboat/—
  - **Colour:** Black with green tint
- **Back Design:** —/Royal Crest/—
  - **Colour:** Green

THE ROYAL CANADIAN BANK

630-68-04
$20 (£4.3.4) **Face Design:** —/harvesting sugar cane/—
Colour: Black with orange tint

Back Design: —/Royal Crest/—
Colour: Rose

IMPRINT
Canadian Bank Note Company, Limited

SIGNATURES
left	right
typed S.G. Dobson	typed M.W. Wilson

ISSUE DATING
Engraved
January 3rd 1938

Cat. No.	Denom.	Date	VG	F	VF	EF	Unc
68-02	$5 (£1.0.10)	1938	160.	225.	375.	600.	-
68-04	$20 (£4.3.4)	1938	400.	600.	850.	-	-

THE ROYAL CANADIAN BANK
1864-1876
TORONTO, CANADA WEST

BANK NUMBER 635   **NONREDEEMABLE**

Established in Toronto in 1864, this bank had an aggressive management and expanded very rapidly, but soon found dissension and rivalry among its directors. The bank incurred heavy losses through unprofitable branches, fraudulent managers, bad loans and improper favours to political figures. It was reorganized in 1869 and enjoyed prosperity for some time, but again accumulated a substantial number of bad debts. The institution was saved from liquidation by merging with the City Bank in 1876 to become the Consolidated Bank of Canada.

635-10   **ABNC PRINTINGS**
1865

DESIGNS AND COLOURS

635-10-04-04
$1 **Face Design:** Wellington/bank seal flanked by lion and unicorn/sailor standing by capstan
Colour: Black with green tint

Back Design: Lathework and bank name
Colour: Brown

635-10-04-08
$2 **Face Design:** Prince of Wales/bank seal flanked by lion and unicorn/seated woman with basket of produce
Colour: Black with green tint

Back Design: Lathework and bank name
Colour: Brown

THE ROYAL CANADIAN BANK

635-10-02-06P
$5 **Face Design:** Princess of Wales/bank seal flanked by lion and unicorn/seated woman with telescope and large 5
Colour: Black with green tint

Back Design: Lathework and bank name
Colour: Brown

Photo Not Available

635-10-02-08P
$10 **Face Design:** Queen Victoria/bank seal, lion and unicorn/woman with scale and sword on dock
Colour: Black with green tint

Back Design: Lathework and bank name
Colour: Brown

IMPRINT
American Bank Note Co. New York
American Bank Note Co. New York and Continental Bank Note Co. N.Y. print

2. PARTIALLY ENGRAVED DATE

635-10-02-02

SIGNATURES
left	right
mss. T. Woodside	mss. Jas. Metcalfe (v)
mss. T. Woodside	mss. A.M. Smith (p)

ISSUE DATING
Partially engraved ___ 18___:
1865: 4 July

OVERPRINT
"C" in red

STAMP
"K" in black

Cat. No.	Denom.	Date	VG	F	VF	EF	Unc
10-02-02	$1	1865	900.	1,200.	1,700.	-	-
10-02-04	$2	1865	900.	1,200.	1,700.	-	-
10-02-06P	$5	18_			FACE PROOF	450.	
10-02-08P	$10	18_			FACE PROOF	450.	

Note: A back for $5 (10-02-06) is known in green.

4. ENGRAVED DATE

SIGNATURES
left	right
mss. T. Woodside	mss. Jas. Metcalfe
mss. T. Woodside	mss. A.M. Smith
mss. T. Woodside	mss. A.M. Smith

ISSUE DATING
Engraved
26th July 1865

OVERPRINT
"COBOURG" twice in red
"COBOURG" twice in blue
"PARIS" twice in red
"WOODSTOCK" in blue
"OTTAWA" in blue

STAMP
"T T" in blue

VARIETIES
Mss. signature at left: blue sheet number
Engr. signature at left: red sheet number

Note: Some of the $1, $5 notes with engraved date and small blue serial numbers have both the ABN and CON.B.N imprints

Cat. No.	Denom.	Date	Variety	VG	F	VF	EF	Unc
10-04-02	$1	1865	Blue sheet #s	1,000.	1,300.	1,900.	-	-
10-04-04	$1	1865	Red sheet #s	1,000.	1,300.	1,900.	-	-
10-04-06	$2	1865	Blue sheet #s	1,000.	1,300.	1,900.	-	-
10-04-08	$2	1865	Red sheet #s	1,000.	1,300.	1,900.	-	-
10-04-10	$5	1865	Blue sheet #s	1,200.	1,600.	2,400.	-	-

635-12 CONTINENTAL BANK NOTE COMPANY ISSUE OF 1865

DESIGNS AND COLOURS

635-12-02-02
$2 **Face Design:** Prince Albert/bank seal/farmer with scythe
Colour: Black with green tint

Back Design: Bank name, lathework and counters
Colour: Green

THE ROYAL CANADIAN BANK

635-12-02-04
  $5 Face Design: Portrait of young woman/bank seal flanked by lion and unicorn/Indian riding horse
  Colour: Black with green tint

Back design: Bank name, lathework and counters
Colour: Green

635-12-04-06S
  $10 Face Design: Queen Victoria (Chalon portrait)/ bank seal flanked by lion and unicorn/ crouching Indian (after F.O.C. Darley)
  Colour: Black with green tint

Back Design: Bank name, lathework and counters
Colour: Green

IMPRINT
  Continental Bank Note Co. New York

SIGNATURES

left	right
engr. T. Woodside	mss. G.M. Knight
engr. T. Woodside	mss. M.H. Gault (per)
engr. T. Woodside	mss. A.M. Smith
mss. T. Woodside	engr. Hon. J. Crawford

ISSUE DATING
  Engraved
  26th July 1865

STAMP
  "T" twice in blue on face and back

2. "AT ITS BANKING HOUSE IN TORONTO" ABOVE BANK SEAL

Cat. No.	Denom.	Date	VG	F	VF	EF	Unc
12-02-02	$2	1865	1,250.	1,700.	2,500.	-	-
12-02-04	$5	1865	1,250.	1,700.	2,500.	-	-
12-02-06	$10	1865			NOT CONFIRMED		

4. "AT ITS AGENCY IN MONTREAL" ABOVE BANK SEAL

Cat. No.	Denom.	Date	VG	F	VF	EF	Unc
12-04-02	$2	1865			NOT CONFIRMED		
12-04-04	$5	1865	1,000.	1,300.	1,900.	-	-
12-04-04R	$5	1865	-	-	-	850.	-
12-04-06S	$10	1865			SPECIMEN		1,000.
12-04-06R	$10	1865	-	-	-	850.	-

635-14 BRITISH AMERICAN BANK NOTE COMPANY ISSUE 1870 - 1872

DESIGNS AND COLOURS

635-14-02
  $4 Face Design: Sailors at dockside "Mech's & Commerce"/ Crest/beaver
  Colour: Black with green tint
  See varieties: top left 4 in round lathework

Back Design: Lathework, counters and bank name
Colour: Green

392

THE ROYAL CANADIAN BANK

635-14-04
$4 **Face Design:** Sailors at dockside "Mech's & Commerce"/Crest/beaver
Colour: Black with green tint
See varieties: top left 4 in oval lathework

Back Design: Lathework, counters and bank name
Colour: Green

635-14-06
$5 **Face Design:** T. McCracken/Crest/—
Colour: Black with green tint

Back Design: Lathework, counters and bank name
Colour: Green

635-14-08a
$10 **Face Design:** Crest/—/Hon. J. Crawford
Colour: Black with green tint

Back Design: Lathework, counters and bank name
Colour: Green

635-14-10P
$20 **Face Design:** Allegorical female/Crest/sailor aboard ship
Colour: Black with green tint

Back Design: Lathework, counters and bank name
Colour: Green

635-14-12P
$50 **Face Design:** —/Crest/—
Colour: Black with green tint

Back Design: Lathework, counters and bank name
Colour: Green

635-14-14P
$100 **Face Design:** —/Crest/—
Colour: Black with green tint

Back Design: Lathework, counters and bank name
Colour: Green

IMPRINT
British American Bank Note Co. Montreal & Ottawa

THE SAINT FRANCIS BANK

1855

STANSTEAD, PROVINCE OF CANADA

BANK NUMBER 640　　　　　　　　**NONREDEEMABLE**

Intending to have its head office in Stanstead, Canada East, this bank never used its charter and did not operate.

640-10　　　　TC PRINTINGS

"MONTREAL" was engraved twice vertically across the note, flanking the central vignette.

DESIGNS AND COLOURS

640-10-02P
- **$5 Face Design:** Seated Indian brave in oval/Queen Victoria (Chalon portrait) in oval on Royal Crest/Prince Consort in oval
- **Colour:** Black with overall red tin

Back Design: Lathework, counters and bank name
Colour: Blue

640-10-04P
- **$10 Face Design:** Anchor with box, bale and barrel in oval/St. George slaying the dragon/Queen Victoria in oval
- **Colour:** Black with overall red tint
- **Back Design:** Lathework, counters and bank name
- **Colour:** Blue

SIGNATURES
left	right
mss. M. Lang (pro)	engr. Hon. J. Crawford, Jr.

ISSUE DATING
Engraved
- July 1st, 1870
- 2nd Oct. 1871
- 1st July 1872

OVERPRINT
- "MONTREAL" twice in blue
- "BELLEVILLE" in red
- "BELLEVILLE" twice in red and "THE CONSOLIDATED BANK OF CANADA" in red

STAMP
"A" in black

VARIETIES
- **$4:** two sheet numbers, 4 in round lathework at top left
- **$4:** one sheet number (modified tint), 4 in oval lathework at top left

Cat. No.	Denom.	Date	Variety	VG	F	VF	EF	Unc
14-02	$4	1870	Two sheet #s	1,000.	1,300.	1,900.	-	-
14-04	$4	1870	One sheet #	1,000.	1,300.	1,900.	-	-
14-06	$5	1872		1,250.	1,700.	2,500.	-	-
14-08	$10	1872	No o/p	1,400.	1,900.	2,900.	-	-
14-08a	$10	1872	Dual o/p	1,400.	1,900.	2,900.	-	-
14-10P	$20	1871				FACE PROOF		500.
14-12P	$50	1871				FACE PROOF		500.
14-14P	$100	1871				FACE PROOF		500.

IMPRINT
Toppan, Carpenter & Co. New York and Phila.

SIGNATURES
left	right
none	none

ISSUE DATING
Partially engraved ___ 185___:

Cat. No.	Denom.	Date		Unc
10-02P	$5	185_	FACE PROOF	600.
10-04P	$10	185_	FACE PROOF	600.

LA BANQUE DE ST. HYACINTHE
1873-1908
ST. HYACINTHE, QUEBEC

BANK NUMBER 645   **REDEEMABLE**

Established in St. Hyacinthe, Quebec, this bank was small in size and in operating area. In 1908 the bank's large loans to the Southern Counties Railway became generally known, and this raised doubts about its actual strength. The bank was then obliged to suspend payment pending the result of suits against another company that took over this railway. However, the bank failed in the same year, with about $250,000 of notes still in circulation. They were redeemed, but both the creditors and shareholders lost substantial amounts.

645-10   **ISSUE OF 1874**
DESIGNS AND COLOURS

645-10-02P
  $4 Face Design: Farmer with corn stalks/"John Babtist"/ P. Bachand
  Colour: Black with green tint

  Back Design: Lathework, counters and bank name
  Colour: Green

645-10-04P
  $5 Face Design: Allegorical female/farmer watering livestock at pump/P. Bachand
  Colour: Black with green tint

  Back Design: Lathework, counters and bank name
  Colour: Green

LA BANQUE DE ST. HYACINTHE

645-10-06P
$10 Face Design: Shepherd boy/ploughing scene/P. Bachand
Colour: Black with green tint

Back Design: Lathework, counters and bank name
Colour: Green

IMPRINT
British American Bank Note Company

SIGNATURES
left	right
none	none

ISSUE DATING
Engraved
2 Janvier, 1874
2 Jan. 1874

Cat. No.	Denom.	Date		Unc
10-02P	$4	1874	FACE PROOF	500.
10-04P	$5	1874	FACE PROOF	500.
10-06P	$10	1874	FACE PROOF	500.

645-12   ISSUES OF 1880 AND 1892
DESIGNS AND COLOURS

645-12-02
$5 Face Design: Allegorical female/farmer watering livestock at pump/G.C. Dessaulles
Colour: Black with green tint

Back Design: Lathework, counters and bank name
Colour: Green

645-12-04
$10 Face Design: Shepherd boy "John Baptist"/ploughing scene/G.C. Dessaulles
Colour: Black with green tint

Back Design: Lathework, counters and bank name
Colour: Green

645-12-06
$20 Face Design: Shepherdess/Canadian Coat of Arms/allegorical female "Medea"
Colour: Black with yellow-green and green tint

Back Design: Lathework, counters and bank name
Colour: Brown

LA BANQUE DE ST. JEAN

1873-1908

ST. JEAN, QUEBEC

BANK NUMBER 650   ***REDEEMABLE***

Established at St. Jean, Quebec, in 1873, this small bank experienced serious exploitation by its president, who was later sentenced to five years in the penitentiary for making false returns. An amount of $162,000 was collected in respect of double liability, and note holders were paid in full when the bank failed in 1908.

IMPRINT
- **1880:** British American Bank Note Co. Montreal
- **1892:** Canada Bank Note Co. Montreal and British American Bank Note Company

SIGNATURES

	left	right
1880:	mss. illegible	engr. G.C. Dessaulles
1892:	mss. E.R. Blanchard	engr. G.C. Dessaulles

ISSUE DATING
Engraved
1 Juillet 1880
1 Juil. 1880
2 Janvier 1892

Cat. No.	Denom.	Date	Variety	VG	F	VF	EF	Unc
12-02	$5	1880		3,000.	4,200.	6,300.	-	-
12-04	$10	1880		3,200.	4,500.	6,700.	-	-
12-06	$20	1892		3,200.	4,500.	6,700.	-	-
Full sheet	$5,5,5,10	1880	Remainder*	-	-	-	-	8,000.

* No signature at left.

650-10   **ISSUES OF 1873 - 1900**

DESIGNS AND COLOURS

650-10-02P
    $4 Face Design: Crest over ornate 4/L. Molleur/"John Baptist"
    Colour: Black with green tint

    Back Design: Lathework, counters and bank name
    Colour: Green

650-10-06
    $5 Face Design: L. Molleur/factories, workers and ornate 5/ "John Baptist"
    Colour: Black with green tint

LA BANQUE DE ST. JEAN

Back Design: Lathework, counters and bank name
Colour: Green

650-10-10
   $10 Face Design: L. Molleur/allegorical women and ornate X/ "John Baptist"
   Colour: Black with green tint

Back Design: Lathework, counters and bank name
Colour: Green

IMPRINT
British American Bank Note Co. Montreal

SIGNATURES
	left	right
1873:	mss. J. L'Ecuyer	engr. Louis Molleur fils'
1881:	mss. Ph. Baudouin	engr. Louis Molleur fils'
1900:	mss. P.J. L'Heureux	engr. Louis Molleur

ISSUE DATING
Engraved
1 Septembre 1873
1 Septe 1873
1 Avril 1881
1 Avril 1900

Cat. No.	Denom.	Date	VG	F	VF	EF	Unc
10-02	$4	1873	3,000.	4,200.	6,300.	-	-
10-04	$5	1873	3,500.	4,900.	7,350.	-	-
10-06	$5	1900	3,000.	4,200.	6,300.	-	-
10-08	$10	1873	3,500.	4,900.	7,350.	-	-
10-10	$10	1881	3,000.	4,200.	6,300.	-	-

650-12   **ISSUE OF 1906**

DESIGNS AND COLOURS

650-12-02
   $5 Face Design: Jacques Cartier/factories, workers and ornate 5/shepherd boy "John Baptist"
   Colour: Black with green tint

   Back Design: Lathework, counters and bank name
   Colour: Green

650-12-04
   $10 Face Design: Jacques Cartier/allegorical women and ornate X/"John Baptist"
   Colour: Black with green tint

   Back Design: Lathework, counters and bank name
   Colour: Green

IMPRINT
British American Bank Note Co. Montreal

SIGNATURES
left	right
mss. P.J. L'Heureux	engr. P.H. Roy

ISSUE DATING
Engraved
1 Avril 1906

Cat. No.	Denom.	Date	VG	F	VF	EF	Unc
12-02	$5	1906	3,000.	4,200.	6,300.	-	-
12-04	$10	1906	3,000.	4,200.	6,300.	-	-

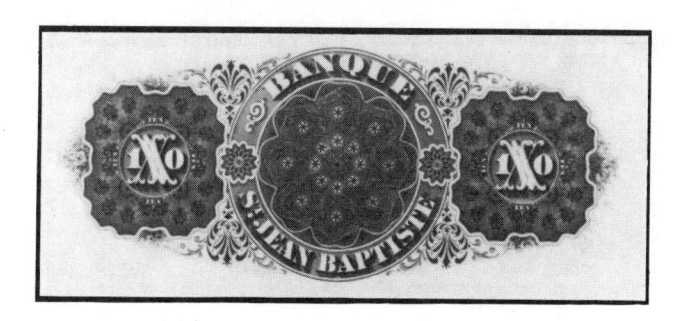

BANQUE ST. JEAN BAPTISTE

1875

MONTREAL, QUEBEC

BANK NUMBER 655 **NONREDEEMABLE**

The founders of this bank did not use their charter, and the bank never opened for business.

655-10 **DESIGNS OF 1875**

DESIGNS AND COLOURS

655-10-02P
- **$4 Face Design:** "St. John Baptiste No. 2"/cupids and ornate 4/ R.A.R. Hubert
- **Colour:** Black with green tint

Back Design: Lathework, counters and bank name
Colour: Green

655-10-04P
- **$5 Face Design:** Allegorical female/"St. Jean Baptiste No. 2"/R.A.R. Hubert
- **Colour:** Black with green tint

Back Design: Lathework, counters and bank name
Colour: Green

655-10-06P
- **$10 Face Design:** —/"St. Jean Baptiste No. 2"/R.A.R. Hubert
- **Colour:** Black with green tint

Back Design: Lathework, counters and bank name
Colour: Green

IMPRINT
British American Bank Note Co. Montreal

SIGNATURES
left	right
none	engr. R.A.R. Hubert

ISSUE DATING
Engraved
24 Juin 1875

Cat. No.	Denom.	Date		Unc
10-02P	$4	1875	FACE PROOF	600.
10-04P	$5	1875	FACE PROOF	600.
10-06P	$10	1875	FACE PROOF	600.

THE ST. LAWRENCE BANK

1872-1876

TORONTO (ONTARIO)

BANK NUMBER 660   **REDEEMABLE**

The charter for the St. Lawrence bank was given Royal assent on June 14, 1872, but when it opened for business in Toronto on March 23, 1873, it became apparent that some bad choices had been made regarding staff and the location of the premises. In addition, the bank's haste in opening other branches in its first year of operation let to early troubles. By June 1874 the bank had 11 agencies in operation, despite the fact that the previous year had seen most banks restricting their loans due to the financial crisis of 1873. The new bank acquired a number of bad risks, and in the latter part of 1874 and the beginning of 1875, Canadian conditions grew worse and the usual dividend was not forthcoming.

At the annual general meeting in June 1875, it was reported that $200,000 was still in arrears on the subscribed stock. At this meeting two directors resigned and a new president, the Honourable Thomas N. Gibbs, who had served as minister of Inland Revenue in the Macdonald Government, was elected to take over from Mr. Fitch, the bank's first president. A new cashier was also engaged. On May 31, 1876, the St. Lawrence Bank changed its name to the Standard Bank of Canada. It was felt the new name would give the bank a fresh start. Permission was granted to reissue St. Lawrence Bank notes until the Standard Bank notes were ready, which took about nine months.

660-10   LOCKHART, FITCH PORTRAIT ISSUE

DESIGNS AND COLOURS

660-10-02P
- **$4 Face Design:** Deer on hillside/oval portrait of K.F. Lockhart/train and ships at dock/—
- **Colour:** Black with green tint
- **Back Design:** Lathework, counters and bank name
- **Colour:** Green

660-10-04P
- **$5 Face Design:** Cartier approaching land "Quebec"/—/oval portrait of J.C. Fitch
- **Colour:** Black with green tint
- **Back Design:** Unknown
- **Colour:** Unknown

660-10-06P
- **$10 Face Design:** Oval portrait of K.F. Lockhart/three cherubs and ornate X/oval portrait of J.C. Fitch
- **Colour:** Black with green tint
- **Back Design:** Lathework, counters and bank name
- **Colour:** Green

IMPRINT
British American Bank Note Co. Montreal & Ottawa

SIGNATURES
left	right
mss. K.F. Lockhart	engr. J.C. Fitch

ISSUE DATING
Engraved
2nd Dec. 1872

Cat. No.	Denom.	Date		Unc
10-02P	$4	1872	FACE PROOF	500.
10-04P	$5	1872	FACE PROOF	500.
10-06P	$10	1872	FACE PROOF	500.

660-12   LOCKHART, FITCH PORTRAITS REMOVED

DESIGNS AND COLOURS

660-12-02P
- **$4 Face Design:** Deer on hillside/train and ships at dock/—
- **Colour:** Black with green tint

Back Design: Lathework, counters and bank name
Colour: Green

660-12-04P
$5 Face Design: Cartier approaching land "Quebec"/—/oval portrait of Prince Arthur
Colour: Black with green tint

Back Design: Lathework, counters and bank name
Colour: Green

660-12-06P
$10 Face Design: Portrait of allegorical female/three cherubs and ornate X/—
Colour: Black with green tint

Back Design: Lathework, counters and bank name
Colour: Green

IMPRINT
British American Bank Note Co. Montreal & Ottawa

SIGNATURES
left	right
mss. K.F. Lockhart	engr. J.C. Fitch

ISSUE DATING
Engraved
2nd Dec. 1872

Cat. No.	Denom.	Date		Unc
12-02P	$4	1872	FACE PROOF	500.
12-04P	$5	1872	FACE PROOF	500.
12-06P	$10	1872	FACE PROOF	500.

THE ST. LAWRENCE BANK & LUMBER CO.

1837

MALBAY, LOWER CANADA

BANK NUMBER 665 **NONREDEEMABLE**

This spurious bank was a fraud perpetuated by some rogues from Buffalo during the summer of 1837. Their paper circulated to some extent in the Buffalo area, but not in Canada.

665-10 **ISSUE OF 1837**

DESIGNS AND COLOURS

665-10-02
- **$1 (5s) Face Design:** 1 over Roman bust twice/sawmills; Indian pointing at bottom/1 over Roman bust twice
- **Colour:** Black with no tint
- **Back Design:** Plain

665-10-04
- **$2 (10s) Face Design:** 2 Roman bust (sideways), 2/TWO over Roman bust/steamship St. Lawrence and two sailing ships, two Spanish dollars below/TWO over Roman bust/2, Roman bust (sideways), 2
- **Colour:** Black with no tint
- **Back Design:** Plain

IMPRINT
Underwood, Bald, Spencer & Hufty N. York & Philada

SIGNATURES
left	right
mss. J. Croft	mss. G.G. McLeod

ISSUE DATING
Partially engraved ___ 18___:
1837: 25th May

Cat. No.	Denom.	Date	VG	F	VF	EF	Unc
10-02	$1	1837	25.	35.	50.	75.	150.
10-04	$2	1837	25.	35.	50.	75.	150.

ST. STEPHENS JOINT STOCK BANKING COMP'Y

1830's

ST. STEPHEN, NEW BRUNSWICK

BANK NUMBER 670 **NONREDEEMABLE**

This bank may have been the forerunner of the St. Stephens Bank.

670-10 **DOLLAR ISSUE, 1830s**

DESIGNS AND COLOURS

670-10-02
- **$3 Face Design:** Man standing on wharf "Lord Byron"/ sailing ships/steamboat and sailboat
- **Colour:** Black with no tint
- **Back Design:** Plain

IMPRINT
New England Bank Note Co. Boston

SIGNATURES
left	right
none	none

ISSUE DATING
Partially engraved ___ 18___:

Cat. No.	Denom.	Date	Variety	VG	F	VF	EF	Unc
10-02R	$3	18_	Remainder	3,500.	-	-	-	-

THE ST. STEPHEN'S BANK

1836-1910

ST. STEPHEN, NEW BRUNSWICK

BANK NUMBER 675   **REDEEMABLE**

This bank was established in St. Stephen, New Brunswick, in 1836, with a charter that contained a provision that no shareholder should own more than 20 percent of the capital stock. The bank operated successfully as a small local institution, but found competition with the larger banks difficult. Upon failing in 1910, its assets were sold to the Bank of British North America, and the president of that bank advanced sufficient funds to permit all liabilities to be paid in full, without resorting to the double liability of its shareholders.

675-10   POUNDS ISSUE 1830's

DESIGNS AND COLOURS

675-10-02P
- **£1 Face Design:** Shipbuilding scene/ Royal Crest; harbour scene below/—
- **Colour:** Black with no tint
- **Back Design:** Plain

675-10-04P
- **£5 Face Design:** Standing Britannia/ Royal Crest; small ships below/—
- **Colour:** Black with no tint
- **Back Design:** Plain

675-10-06P
- **£10 Face Design:** Beehive and flowers/ Royal Crest; dog, key and safe below/—
- **Colour:** Black with no tint
- **Back Design:** Plain

IMPRINT
New England Bank Note Co. Boston

SIGNATURES

left	right
none	none

ISSUE DATING
Partially engraved ___18___:

Cat. No.	Denom.	Date				Unc
10-02P	£1	18_			PROOF	500.
10-04P	£5	18_			PROOF	500.
10-06P	£10	18_			PROOF	500.

675-12   FIRST DOLLAR ISSUE 1830s

DESIGNS AND COLOURS

Photo Not Available

675-12-02P
- **$1 Face Design:** —/ships/seated women
- **Colour:** Black with no tint
- **Back Design:** Plain

675-12-04
- **$2 Face Design:** Allegorical female/seated woman with produce/portrait of woman
- **Colour:** Black with no tint
- **Back Design:** Plain

IMPRINT
New England Bank Note Co. Boston

SIGNATURES

left	right
mss. D. Upton	mss. N. Marks

ISSUE DATING
Partially engraved ___ 18___:
1836: Sept. 1

Cat. No.	Denom.	Date	VG	F	VF	EF	Unc
12-02P	$1	18_				PROOF	500.
12-04	$2	1836	1,250.	1,700.	-	-	-

THE ST. STEPHEN'S BANK

675-14   **ORNATE COUNTER ISSUE**
1846-1853

DESIGNS AND COLOURS

675-14-02-02
- **$1 Face Design:** Ships, ornate 1/seated Indian woman
- **Colour:** Black with no tint
- **Back Design:** Plain

675-14-04-10R
- **$2 Face Design:** Ships/ornate 2/young woman standing by well
- **Colour:** Black with no tint
- **Back Design:** Plain

Photo Not Available

675-14-02-26P
- **$3 Face Design:** Harvest scene/ornate 3/steamboat
- **Colour:** Black with no tint
- **Back Design:** Plain

IMPRINT
New England Bank Note Company, Boston

SIGNATURES

	left	right
1846:	mss. illegible	mss G.D. King
1853:	none	mss. Wm. Todd
	none	none

ISSUE DATING
Partially engraved ___ 18___:
- 1846: January 1
- 1853: Sept. 1

2.   **NO PROTECTOR**

Cat. No.	Denom.	Date	VG	F	VF	EF	Unc
14-02-02	$1	1846	1,250.	1,700.	-	-	-
14-02-14	$1	1853	1,250.	1,700.	-	-	-
14-02-16P	$2	18_				PROOF	500.
14-02-26P	$3	18_				PROOF	500.

4.   **RED PROTECTOR**

PROTECTOR
Red "word" protector on face and back

Cat. No.	Denom.	Date	Variety	VG	F	VF	EF	Unc
14-04-02	$1	18_	Red ptr.		NO SURVIVING NOTES KNOWN			
14-04-10R	$2	18_	Red ptr., remainder*	-	-	-	1,250.
14-04-16	$3	18_	Red ptr.		NO SURVIVING NOTES KNOWN			

* Unsigned, undated and unnumbered.

675-16   **BOSTON BANK NOTE CO.**
PRINTINGS, 1852

DESIGNS AND COLOURS

675-16-02P
- **$5 Face Design:** Tug and sailing ships/two Indians, falls in background; ships below/farmer holding sheaf and sickle
- **Colour:** Black with no tint
- **Back Design:** Lathework and bank name
- **Colour:** Brown

675-16-08P
- **$10 Face Design:** Indian paddling canoe; spread eagle below/shipbuilding scene
- **Colour:** Black with no tint

- **Back Design:** Lathework
- **Colour:** Brown

IMPRINT
Boston Bank Note Co. 39 State St.

SIGNATURES

left	right
none	mss. Wm. Todd
none	none

ISSUE DATING
Partially engraved ___ 18___:
Engraved
June 1st, 1852

Cat. No.	Denom.	Date	VG	F	VF	EF	Unc
16-02P	$5	18_			FACE PROOF		500.
16-04R	$5	1852* **	-	-	-	-	1,250.
16-06P	$10	18_			FACE PROOF		500.
16-08P	$10	1852			FACE PROOF		500.

* Unnumbered and unsigned at left.
** Engraved "WILL PAY ___ ON DEMAND TO CHA'S SPRAGUE OR BEARER."

CANADIAN FUNDS
ISSUES OF 1860-1886

DESIGNS AND COLOURS

675-18-02
$1 Face Design: Wm. Todd/polar bear attacking hunters in boat "The White Bear"/sailor boy holding hat
Colour: Black with green tint

Back Design: See subheadings
Colour: See subheadings

675-18-04P
$2 Face Design: St. George slaying the dragon/—/Wm. Todd
Colour: Black with green tint

Back Design: See subheadings
Colour: See subheadings

675-18-06P
$3 Face Design: Woman writing on tablet, child "History"/ Queen Victoria (Winterhalter portrait)/ seated Britannia with 3
Colour: Black with green tint

Back Design: See subheadings
Colour: See subheadings

675-18-08P
$5 Face Design: Two sailors on dock "Mech's & Commerce"/ lion and shield/portrait of Queen Victoria
Colour: Black with green tint

THE ST. STEPHEN'S BANK

Back Design: See subheadings
Colour: See subheadings

675-18-10P
$10 Face Design: Beehive and flowers/sailor at ship's rail with horn "The Hail"/Royal Crest
Colour: Black with green tint

Back Design: See subheadings
Colour: See subheadings

675-18   ISSUE OF 1860: PLAIN BACK

DESIGNS AND COLOURS
Back Design: Plain

IMPRINT
American Bank Note Company
American Bank Note Co. New-York

SIGNATURES
left	right
mss. R. Watson	mss. Wm. Todd

ISSUE DATING
Engraved
July 1st 1860.

Cat. No.	Denom.	Date	VG	F	VF	EF	Unc
18-02	$1	1860	1,250.	1,700.	2,500.	-	
18-04P	$2	1860			FACE PROOF		500.
18-06	$3	1860	1,250.	1,700.	2,500.	-	
18-08P	$5	1860			FACE PROOF		500.
18-10P	$10	1860			FACE PROOF		500.

675-20   ISSUES OF 1860-1886

2. ISSUE OF 1860: GREEN BACK, SMALL RED SHEET NUMBERS

DESIGNS AND COLOURS
$1, $2 and $3 Back Design: Lathework, counters and bank name
$5 and $10 Back Design: Lathework and counters
Colour: Green

IMPRINT
American Bank Note Co. New York

ISSUE DATING
Engraved
July 1 1860.

Note: A $3 note dated July 1, 1860, has been reported with a brown back.

Cat. No.	Denom.	Date	VG	F	VF	EF	Unc
20-02-02	$1	1860	1,250.	1,700.	2,500.	-	
20-02-04	$2	1860			NO SURVIVING NOTES KNOWN		
20-02-06	$3	1860			NO SURVIVING NOTES KNOWN		
20-02-08P	$5	1860				FACE PROOF	500.
20-02-10P	$10	1860				FACE PROOF	500.

4. LATER ISSUES 1873 - 1886 GREEN BACK, LARGE BLUE SHEET NUMBERS

DESIGNS AND COLOURS
These notes are identical to those of subheading 2, except the face tints are slightly modified.

675-20-04-06

675-20-04-12

406

THE ST. STEPHEN'S BANK

675-20-04-18

675-20-04-20

IMPRINT
American Bank Note Company
British American Bank Note Co. Montreal

SIGNATURES

	left	right
1873:	mss. R. Watson	engr. S.H. Hitchings
1880 and 1886:	mss. J.F. Grant	engr. F.H. Todd
	mss. J.F. Grant	engr. W.H. Todd
	mss. R. Watson	engr. F.H. Todd

ISSUE DATING
  Engraved
  1st Oct. 1873.
  1st March 1880.
  1st Feby. 1886.

Cat. No.	Denom.	Date	VG	F	VF	EF	Unc
20-04-02	$1	1873	900.	1,300.	1,700.	-	-
20-04-04	$1	1880	800.	1,200.	1,600.	-	-
20-04-06	$1	1886	900.	1,300.	1,700.	-	-
20-04-08	$2	1873	950.	1,350.	1,800.	3,000.	-
20-04-10	$2	1880	950.	1,350.	1,800.	-	-
20-04-12	$2	1886	700.	1,000.	1,400.	2,400.	-
20-04-14	$3	1873	700.	1,000.	-	-	-
20-04-16	$3	1880	700.	1,000.	-	-	-
20-04-18	$3	1886	700.	1,000.	-	-	-
20-04-20	$5	1886	1,300.	1,900.	-	-	-
20-04-22	$10	1886	1,300.	1,900.	-	-	-

675-22   "U.S. FUNDS" ISSUES OF 1863

2.   BANK OF NEW YORK ISSUE

Engraved: "To the/BANK OF NEW YORK/New York/Pay . . . in Current/funds of the United States."

DESIGNS AND COLOURS

675-22-02-02
  $1 Face Design: Wm. Todd/—/train
  Colour: Black with green tint
  Back Design: Lathework, counters and bank name
  Colour: Green

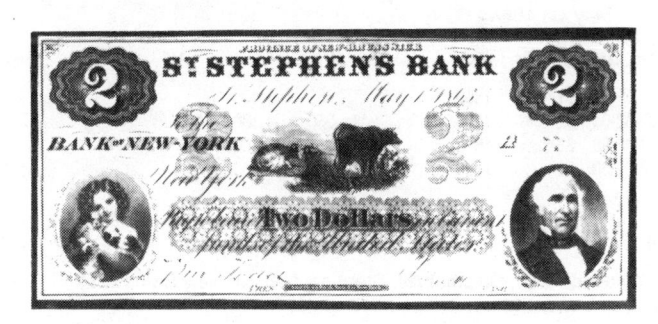

675-22-02-04
  $2 Face Design: Girl with puppies/cattle/Wm. Todd
  Colour: Black with green tint
  Back Design: Lathework, counters and bank name
  Colour: Green

675-22-02-06
  $3 Face Design: Woodcutters/—/Wm. todd
  Colour: Black with green tint
  Back Design: Lathework, counters and bank name
  Colour: Green

THE ST. STEPHEN'S BANK

675-22-02-08
    $5 Face Design: Three Indians by campfire "Indian Camp" (F.O.C. Darley)/—/Wm. Todd
        Colour: Black with green tint

    Back Design: Lathework, counters and bank name
        Colour: Green

IMPRINT
American Bank Note Co. New York

SIGNATURES
left	right
engr. Wm. Todd	mss. R. Watson

ISSUE DATING
  Engraved
  May 1st 1863

Cat. No.	Denom.	Date	VG	F	VF	EF	Unc
22-02-02	$1	1863	950.	1,400.	-	-	-
22-02-04	$2	1863	950.	1,400.	-	-	-
22-02-06	$3	1863	950.	1,400.	-	-	-
22-02-08	$5	1863	950.	1,400.	-	-	-

4. Z. CHIPMAN ISSUE

Engraved:"To/Z. Chipman/St. Stephen, N.B. [or New Brunswick]/Pay in Current/funds of the United States."

DESIGNS AND COLOURS

675-22-04-02
    $1 Face Design: Wm. Todd/—/train
        Colour: Black with no tint

    Back Design: Lathework and counters
        Colour: Green

675-22-04-04
    $2 Face Design: Girl with puppies/cattle/Wm. Todd
        Colour: Black with no tint

    Back Design: Lathework and counters
        Colour: Green

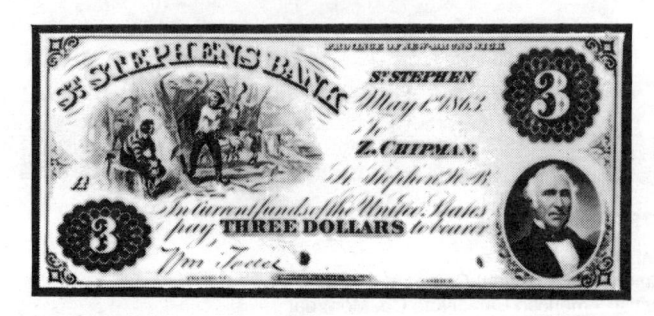

675-22-04-10
    $3 Face Design: Woodcutters/—/Wm Todd
        Colour: Black with no tint

    Back Design: Lathework and counters
        Colour: Green

675-22-04-14
    $5 Face Design: Three Indians by campfire "Indian Camp" (F.O.C. Darley)/—/Wm. Todd
        Colour: Black with no tint

    Back Design: Lathework and counters
        Colour: Green

IMPRINT
American Bank Note Co. New York

SIGNATURES
left	right
engr. Wm. Todd	mss. R. Watson

ISSUE DATING
  Engraved
  May 1st 1863

Note: Notes exist with small and large sheet numbers.

Cat. No.	Denom.	Date	VG	F	VF	EF	Unc
22-04-02	$1	1863	1,100.	1,400.	1,900.	-	-
22-04-06	$2	1863	1,100.	1,400.	1,900.	-	-
22-04-10	$3	1863	1,100.	1,400.	1,900.	-	-
22-04-14	$5	1863	1,100.	1,400.	1,900.	-	-

675-24   ISSUES OF 1892 AND 1903

DESIGNS AND COLOURS

675-24-02
- **$5 Face Design:** Lighthouse and ships "Lighthouse"/ allegorical femal "Arts"/train at station
- **Colour:** Black with green tint
- **Back Design:** Lathework and counters
- **Colour:** Green

675-24-06
- **$10 Face Design:** Ships "Propeller Brig"/C.P.R.R. train, men unloading boxcar no. 43 "The Freight Car"/ Britannia and young Indian girl "Protection"
- **Colour:** Black with green tint
- **Back Design:** Lathework and counters
- **Colour:** Green

675-24-10
- **$20 Face Design:** Allegorical female/farmer watering livestock at pump/sailor
- **Colour:** Black with green tint
- **Back Design:** Lathework and counters
- **Colour:** Green

IMPRINT
British American Bank Note Company and American Bank Note Company
British American Bank Note Co. Ottawa
British American Bank Note Co. Montreal and Ottawa

SIGNATURES

	left	right
1892:	mss. J.F. Brant	mss. W.H. Todd
	engr. J.F. Brant	engr. W.H. Todd
1903:	mss. J.F. Brant	engr. Frank Todd

ISSUE DATING
Engraved
2nd Jan 1892
2nd Jan 1903

Cat. No.	Denom.	Date	VG	F	VF	EF	Unc
24-02	$5	1892	1,360.	1,700.	2,400.	-	-
24-04	$5	1903	1,360.	1,700.	2,400.	-	-
24-06	$10	1892	1,360.	1,700.	2,400.	-	-
24-08	$10	1903	1,360.	1,700.	2,400.	-	-
24-10P	$20	1892			FACE PROOF		500.
24-12P	$20	1903			FACE PROOF		500.

THE BANK OF SASKATCHEWAN

1913

MOOSE JAW (SASKATCHEWAN)

BANK NUMBER 680   **NONREDEEMABLE**

It appears that the Bank of Saskatchewan was meant to be established in 1912 or 1913; however, the charter was never used.

680-10   **DESIGNS OF 1913**

DESIGNS AND COLOURS

680-10-02P
     $5 Face Design: —/discing and prairies, train/—
     Colour: Black with yellow and dark green tint

     Back Design: Lathework, counters, bank name and allegorical female in hayfield
     Colour: Green

680-10-04P
     $10 Face Design: —/railroad construction/—
     Colour: Black with brown and yellow tint

     Back Design: Counters, Lathework and bank name
     Colour: Green

680-10-06P
     $20 Face Design: —/train in grain-storage yard/—
     Colour: Black with red and yellow tint

     Back Design: Lathework, counters, bank name and threshing scene
     Colour: Green

IMPRINT
American Bank Note Co. Ottawa

SIGNATURES

left	right
none	none

ISSUE DATING
     Engraved
     May 1st 1913.

Cat. No.	Denom.	Date		Unc
10-02P	$5	1913	FACE PROOF	1,000.
10-04P	$10	1913	FACE PROOF	1,000.
10-06P	$20	1913	FACE PROOF	1,000.

Note: Back proofs of the $10 in brown and $20 in orange are known.

THE SOVEREIGN BANK OF CANADA

1901-1908

TORONTO, ONTARIO

BANK NUMBER 685 **REDEEMABLE**

Established in 1901 in Montreal by Sir Herbert Holt, in collaboration with J.P. Morgan, the Sovereign Bank of Canada had a brief but spectacular existence. In haste its sponsors succeeded in selling enough shares at a premium to give the bank a paid-up capital of $4 million and a reserve of $1,250,000. Branches opened rapidly until there were over eighty. Among the bank's new and aggressive methods to attract business was the paying of quarterly interest on savings accounts. This was a first in Canadian banking history.

However, the bank sacrificed safety and accumulated a substantial number of bad loan accounts in its drive to attain volume. Inevitably confidence in the bank was weakened and subsequently shattered in the financial crisis precipitated by the Knickerbocker Trust failure of 1907. In January 1908 it was arranged that 12 of the major banks would guarantee the liabilities of the Sovereign Bank of Canada and liquidate its affairs. In carrying out the liquidation, each of the guaranteeing banks took over allotted branches of the failed bank. The depositors and other creditors experienced neither loss nor delay. The notes were redeemable at $1.0056 per dollar.

685-10 ISSUES OF 1902-1907

DESIGNS AND COLOURS

685-10-02
- **$5 Face Design:** Bank seal/King Edward VII/—
- **Colour:** Black with green and yellow-green tint

- **Back Design:** Lathework, counters, bank name and Bank Crest
- **Colour:** Black with yellow-brown, green and lilac tint

685-10-08
- **$10 Face Design:** —/Britannia with laurel crown, lion and produce/—
- **Colour:** Black with red-orange and yellow-green tint
- **Back Design:** Lathework, counters, bank name and bank crest
- **Colour:** Black with red-brown, yellow-brown and lilac tint

685-10-12S
- **$20 Face Design:** Bank seal/—/King Edward VII
- **Colour:** Black with green tint
- **Back Design:** Lathework, counters and bank name
- **Colour:** Orange

685-10-14S
- **$50 Face Design:** King Edward VII/—/bank seal
- **Colour:** Black with blue and yellow-green tint
- **Back Design:** Lathework, counters, bank name and bank building
- **Colour:** Green

THE STADACONA BANK

1872-1879

QUEBEC CITY, QUEBEC

BANK NUMBER 690   **NONREDEEMABLE**

This bank was established in Quebec City in 1872. There was a general panic in Canada in the years that followed and a deep depression set in, notably in the timber market. The shareholders of the bank went into voluntary liquidation in 1879. All creditors and shareholders were paid in full.

IMPRINT
American Bank Note Co. Ottawa

SIGNATURES

	left	right
1902:	typed H.S. Holt	mss. various
1905 &	typed	mss. various
1906:	Randolph Macdonald	
1907:	typed Aemilius Jarvis	mss. various

ISSUE DATING
Engraved
- May 1st 1902
- May 1st 1905
- May 1st 1906
- May 1st 1907

OVERPRINT
1902: Large "M" twice in red

Cat. No.	Denom.	Date	VG	F	VF	EF	Unc
10-02	$5	1902	1,200.	1,500.	2,200.	3,550.	-
10-04	$5	1905	1,300.	1,650.	2,400.	3,900.	-
10-06S	$10	1902				SPECIMEN	1,000.
10-08	$10	1905	1,900.	2,500.	3,750.	-	-
10-10S	$10	1907				SPECIMEN	1,000.
10-12S	$20	1907				SPECIMEN	1,200.
10-14S	$50	1906				SPECIMEN	1,200.
10-16S	$50	1907				SPECIMEN	1,200.

690-10   **ISSUE OF 1874**

DESIGNS AND COLOURS

690-10-02
- **$4 Face Design:** Sailing ship/crest on ornate 4/A. Joseph
- **Colour:** Black with green tint

Back Design: Lathework, counters and bank name
Colour: Green

690-10-04
- **$5 Face Design:** Samuel de Champlain/steamboat "Quebec"/ A. Joseph
- **Colour:** Black with green tint

Back Design: Lathework, counters and bank name
Colour: Green

690-10-06P
$6 Face Design: Train rounding curve/—/A. Joseph
Colour: Black with green tint

Back Design: Lathework, counters and bank name
Colour: Green

690-10-08
$10 Face Design: Jacques Cartier/—/A. Joseph
Colour: Black with green tint

Back Design: Lathework, counters and bank name
Colour: Green

IMPRINT
British American Bank Note Co. Montreal

SIGNATURES
left	right
mss. G. Holt (p)	engr. A. Joseph
mss. Wm. R. Dean	engr. A. Joseph

ISSUE DATING
Engraved
2nd April 1874

OVERPRINT
$4: E twice in red
$4: "L" twice in red
$4: "P" twice in red
$4: "ST. SAUVEUR" twice in red
$5: "E" twice in red
$10: "FRASERVILLE" twice in red

Cat. No.	Denom.	Date	VG	F	VF	EF	Unc
10-02	$4	1874	1,600.	2,250.	-	-	-
10-04	$5	1874	1,800.	2,500.	-	-	-
10-06P	$6	1874			FACE PROOF		900.
10-08	$10	1874	1,800.	2,500.	-	-	-

THE STANDARD BANK OF CANADA

1876-1928

TORONTO, ONTARIO

BANK NUMBER 695   **REDEEMABLE**

On May 31, 1876, the St. Lawrence Bank changed management and became known as the Standard Bank of Canada. Deposits doubled during the next five years of operation, making it possible to establish a small reserve fund. The bank survived another depression from 1896 to 1897, and at the turn of the century, it enjoyed a period of development never before experienced.

By 1907 the assets of the bank reached $20 million, and it was represented by nearly fifty branches. Within another year negotiations had commenced that led to an amalgamation with the Western Bank of Canada, which at that time operated entirely in Ontario. The Standard Bank officially absorbed the Western Bank of Canada in 1909.

In the fall of 1924, the bank amalgamated with the Sterling Bank of Canada and acquired 70 more branches, bringing its total number of offices to 243. Profits for the bank in 1927 were the highest since its inception, with assets reaching $100 million. In 1928 the minister of Finance consented to the union of the Standard Bank of Canada with the Canadian Bank of Commerce on a share for share basis.

695-10   **ISSUES OF 1876 AND 1881**

DESIGNS AND COLOURS

695-10-02
     $4 Face Design: Hon. Thos. N. Gibbs/train and ships at dockside/—

     Back Design: Lathework, counters and bank name
     Colour: Green

695-10-04P
     $5 Face Design: Jacques Cartier approaching land "Quebec"/—/Hon. Thos. N. Gibbs
     Colour: Black with green tint

     Back Design: Lathework, counters and bank name
     Colour: Green

695-10-06P
     $10 Face Design: Farmer feeding cattle "Christmas in the fields"/—/Hon. Thos. N. Gibbs
     Colour: Black with green tint

     Back Design: Lathework, counters and bank name
     Colour: Green

THE STANDARD BANK OF CANADA

695-10-08P
 $50 Face Design: Hon. Thos. N. Gibbs/female operating telegraphic equipment/—
 Colour: Black with green tint

 Back Design: Lathework, counters and bank name
 Colour: Green

IMPRINT
 British American Bank Note Co. Montreal

SIGNATURES
left	right
mss. various	engr. Thos. N. Gibbs

ISSUE DATING
 Engraved
 1st Nov. 1876
 1st Dec. 1881

Cat. No.	Denom.	Date	VG	F	VF	EF	Unc
10-02	$4	1876	1,600.	2,200.	-	-	-
10-04	$5	1876	1,800.	2,525.	-	-	-
10-06	$10	1876	1,800.	2,525.	-	-	-
10-08P	$50	1881			FACE PROOF		500.

695-12   **ISSUE OF 1890**

DESIGNS AND COLOURS

695-12-02
 $10 Face Design: Farmer feeding cattle "Christmas in the fields"/—/Hon. Thos. N. Gibbs
 Colour: Black with green tint

 Back Design: Lathework, counters and bank name
 Colour: Green

695-12-04
 $50 Face Design: W.F. Cowan/female operating telegraphic equipment/—
 Colour: Black with green tint

 Back Design: Lathework, counters and bank name
 Colour: Green

IMPRINT
 British American Bank Note Co. Montreal

SIGNATURES
left	right
mss. various	engr. W.F. Cowan

ISSUE DATING
 Engraved
 1st Dec. 1890

Cat. No.	Denom.	Date	VG	F	VF	EF	Unc
12-02	$10	1890	1,400.	1,900.	-	-	-
12-04	$50	1890	1,400.	1,900.	-	-	-

695-14   **$5 ISSUE OF 1891**

DESIGNS AND COLOURS

695-14-02
 $5 Face Design: Two women/woman smelling flowers, "Innocence"/seated woman with basket of flowers
 Colour: See varieties

415

THE STANDARD BANK OF CANADA

Back Design: Lathework, counters, bank name, bank crest and "Justice" figure
Colour: See varieties

IMPRINT
American Bank Note Co. New York

SIGNATURES
left	right
engr. W.F. Cowan	mss. various

ISSUE DATING
Engraved
1st May 1891

VARIETIES
Face Colour: Black with yellow and blue tint
Back Colour: Brown

Face Colour: Black with yellow and green tint
Back Colour: Green

Face Colour: Black with yellow and red tint
Back Colour: Green

Face Colour: Black with yellow and red tint
Back Colour: Red

Cat. No.	Denom.	Date	Variety	VG	F	VF	EF	Unc
14-02	$5	1891	Blue/brown	1,200.	1,700.	2,500.	-	-
14-04	$5	1891	Green/green	1,200.	1,700.	2,500.	-	-
14-06	$5	1891	Red/green	1,200.	1,700.	2,500.	-	-
14-08	$5	1891	Red/red	400.	650.	1,000.	1,700.	-

695-16 $10 ISSUE OF 1900

DESIGNS AND COLOURS

695-16-02
$10 Face Design: Farmer feeding cattle "Christmas in the fields"/—/W.F. Cowan
Colour: Black with gold tint

Back Design: Lathework, counters and bank name
Colour: Green

IMPRINT
British American Bank Note Co. Montreal

SIGNATURES
left	right
mss. various	engr. W.F. Cowan

ISSUE DATING
Engraved
1st May 1900

Cat. No.	Denom.	Date	VG	F	VF	EF	Unc
16-02	$10	1900	600.	1,000.	1,500.	2,500.	-

695-18 ISSUES OF 1914-1919

DESIGNS AND COLOURS

695-18-02
$5 Face Design: —/allegorical woman wearing wreath/—
Colour: Black with orange tint

Bank Design: Lathework, counters, bank name and bank crest
Colour: Green

416

THE STANDARD BANK OF CANADA

695-18-22
$10 Face Design: —/W.F. Cowan/—
Colour: Black with olive green tint

Back Design: Lathework, counters, bank name and Bank Crest
Colour: Brown

695-18-28
$20 Face Design: —/two allegorical women, one wearing mantilla, the other wearing a wreath of roses/—
Colour: Black with green tint

Back Design: Lathework, counters, bank name and Bank Crest
Colour: Olive green

695-18-34
$100 Face Design: —/W.F. Cowan/—
Colour: Black with yellow-brown tint

Back Design: Lathework, counters, bank name and Bank Crest
Colour: Purple-brown

IMPRINT
American Bank Note Company, Ottawa
Canadian Bank Note Company, Limited

SIGNATURES

	left	right
1914:	typed W.F. Cowan	typed George P. Schofield
	typed W.F. Cowan	typed C.H. Easson
1918:	typed W.F. Cowan	typed C.H. Easson
1919:	typed W. Francis	typed C.H. Easson
	typed W. Francis	typed N.L. McLeod
	typed A.F. White	typed N.L. McLeod

ISSUE DATING
Engraved
2nd January 1914
2nd January 1918
2nd January 1919

Cat. No.	Denom.	Date	Variety	VG	F	VF	EF	Unc
18-02	$5	1914	Cowan/Schofield	350.	425.	420.	-	-
18-04	$5	1914	Cowan/Easson	400.	600.	475.	-	-
18-06	$5	1918		220.	300.	420.	-	-
18-08	$5	1919	Francis/Easson	110.	150.	225.	375.	-
18-10	$5	1919	Francis/McLeod	75.	105.	175.	275.	-
18-12	$5	1919	White/McLeod	50.	70.	125.	180.	425.
18-14	$10	1914	Cowan/Schofield	275.	375.	575.	1,000.	-
18-16	$10	1914	Cowan/Easson	275.	375.	575.	1,000.	-
18-18	$10	1918		275.	375.	575.	1,000.	-
18-20	$10	1919	Francis/Easson	225.	325.	500.	850.	-
18-22	$10	1919	Francis/McLeod	225.	325.	500.	850.	-
18-24	$20	1914	Cowan/Easson	650.	900.	1,300.	2,100.	-
18-26P	$20	1918				PROOF	400.	
18-28	$20	1919	Francis/Easson	600.	850.	1,200.	2,150.	-
18-30	$20	1919	Francis/McLeod	600.	850.	1,200.	2,150.	-
18-32	$20	1919	White/McLeod	400.	600.	900.	1,200.	-
18-34	$100	1914		1,000.	2,000.	-	-	-
18-36P	$100	1918				PROOF	400.	

THE STERLING BANK OF CANADA

695-20   **ISSUE OF 1924**

DESIGNS AND COLOURS

695-20-04
- **$10 Face Design:** "Industry" figure in panel/seated "Britannia No. 2"/"Agriculture" figure in panel
- **Colour:** See varieties

- **Back Design:** Lathework, counters, bank name and Bank Crest
- **Colour:** Green

IMPRINT
British American Bank Note Co. Limited. Ottawa

SIGNATURES

left	right
signed W. Francis	signed N.L. McLeod
signed A.F. White	signed N.L. McLeod

ISSUE DATING
Engraved
2nd January 1924

VARIETIES
- **Face Colour:** Black with yellow-brown tint
- **Face Colour:** Black with yellow-orange tint

Cat. No.	Denom.	Date	Variety	VG	F	VF	EF	Unc
20-02	$10	1924	Francis, l.	150.	200.	275.	425.	-
20-04	$10	1924	White, l.	80.	120.	190.	300.	-

THE STERLING BANK OF CANADA
1905-1924
TORONTO, ONTARIO

BANK NUMBER 700   **REDEEMABLE**

The Sterling Bank of Canada received its charter 1905 and opened for business in the summer of 1906. The principal men behind the bank were Gabriel T. Somers, a private banker and grain exporter, and George B. Woods, managing director of the Continental Life Insurance Company. The bank started with a capital of $1 million, but the failure of some smaller banks at the time caused apprehension with regard to the Sterling's strength in competing with larger and stronger institutions.

In 1922 the bank established its own bond division and is noted for introducing a profit-sharing plan for its employees for the first time in Canadian banking history. The failure of the Home Bank of Canada, coupled with a sizable bank robbery, both in 1923, diminished the Sterling's earning power through the loss of deposits to the point where the ability to continue the existing dividend was uncertain.

On November 17, 1924, a meeting was called at which an offer of merger was presented by the Standard Bank of Canada. This merger came into effect on December 31, 1924, on the basis of two shares of Standard stock for every three shares of Sterling stock.

700-10   **ISSUE OF 1906**

DESIGNS AND COLOURS

700-10-02
- **$5 Face Design:** —/steamships and sailing vessels/—
- **Colour:** Black with green tint

- **Back Design:** Lathework, counters, bank name and Royal Crest
- **Colour:** Green

THE STERLING BANK OF CANADA

700-10-04
$10 Face Design: Seated woman holding flag "Exports"/—/—
Colour: Black with yellow and orange-yellow tint

Back Design: Lathework, counters, bank name and seated Britannia
Colour: Green

700-10-06P
$20 Face Design: —/lion and lioness/—
Colour: Black with green tint

Back Design: Lathework, counters and bank name
Colour: Green

700-10-08P
$50 Face Design: —/Ontario Parliament Buildings, allegorical female with Crest, Niagara Falls/—
Colour: Black with blue tint

Back Design: Lathework, counters and bank name
Colour: Green

IMPRINT
British American Bank Note Co. Ottawa

SIGNATURES
left — mss. various
right — engr. G.T. Somers

ISSUE DATING
Engraved
April 25th, 1906

Cat. No.	Denom.	Date	VG	F	VF	EF	Unc
10-02	$5	1906	800.	1,100.	1,600.	2,300.	-
10-04	$10	1906	500.	700.	1,000.	1,400.	-
10-06	$20	1906	2,000.	3,200.	-	-	-
10-08P	$50	1906			FACE PROOF		500.

700-12   **$5 ISSUE OF 1914**

DESIGNS AND COLOURS

700-12-02
$5 Face Design: Cupid emptying cornucopia/train and station/farm scene with woman in field carrying basket and sheaf
Colour: Black with overall yellow tint

419

THE STERLING BANK OF CANADA

Back Design: —/Princess Patricia of Connaught/—
Colour: Orange-red

IMPRINT
Waterlow & Sons Ld. London Wall, London

SIGNATURES
left	right
mss. various	engr. G.T. Somers

ISSUE DATING
Engraved
1st January 1914

Note: Proofs of the $5 1914 issue are known with yellow face tint and green back tint.

Cat. No.	Denom.	Date	VG	F	VF	EF	Unc
12-02	$5	1914	500.	675.	1,050.	1,700.	3,300.

700-14 $10 ISSUE OF 1921

700-14-02
$10 Face Design: Female with anchor/—/female with cornucopia
Colour: Black with gold tint

Back Design: Lathework, counters, bank name and Indian and woodsman flanking counter
Colour: Blue

IMPRINT
British American Bank Note Co. Ltd. Ottawa Can.

SIGNATURES
left	right
mss. various	engr. G.T. Somers

ISSUE DATING
Engraved
Jan. 3rd 1921

Cat. No.	Denom.	Date	VG	F	VF	EF	Unc
14-02	$10	1921	750.	1,000.	1,500.	-	-

THE SUMMERSIDE BANK OF PRINCE EDWARD ISLAND

1866-1901

SUMMERSIDE, PRINCE EDWARD ISLAND

BANK NUMBER 705   **REDEEMABLE**

Established in 1866 at Summerside, Prince Edward Island, this institution was a small but successful local bank with capital of $48,667. It was one of the few banks to issue notes of $8 denomination. It expanded but could not meet the competition of other, larger banks and was absorbed by the Bank of New Brunswick in 1901.

Records of the Bank of Canada report only $43 in face value of its issue remains outstanding, but this is believed to be lower than the true amount.

ABNC PRINTINGS
1866-1872

DESIGNS AND COLOURS

705-10-02
- **$1 (4s 2d) Face Design:** Three children with a colt; "Feeding the colt"/farmer watching dairymaid milking cow/boy tending sheep in snow; "Sheep feeding"
- **Colour:** Black with no tint
- **Back Design:** Lathework, counters and bank name
- **Colour:** Brown

705-12-04P
- **$2 (8s 4d) Face Design:** Shipbuilding scene/Royal Crest/dog and strongbox
- **Colour:** Black with no tint
- **Back Design:** Lathework, counters and bank name
- **Colour:** Brown

Photo Not Available

705-10-06
- **$4 (16s 8d) Face Design:** Sailor with flag and lion at wharf/paddlewheel steamer/seated Britannia holding shield bearing 4
- **Colour:** Black with no tint
- **Back Design:** Lathework, counters and bank name
- **Colour:** Brown

705-10-08
- **$8 (33s 4d) Face Design:** Man with barrels/fishing boats/two sailing ships, one with 5 on sail
- **Colour:** Black with no tint

Back Design: Lathework, counters and bank name
Colour: Brown

IMPRINT
American Bank Note Co. N.Y. & Boston on face
American Bank Note Co. New York and Boston on back

705-10   **ABNC PRINTINGS DOLLARS/STERLING**

SIGNATURES
- left: mss. E.L. Lydiard
- right: mss. J.R. Gardner

ISSUE DATING
Partially engraved ___ 18 ___:
$1 (4s 2d stg), 1866: 2nd April
$8 (33s 4d stg), 1866: 22nd Jany.

Cat. No.	Denom.	Date	VG	F	VF	EF	Unc
10-02	$1 (4s 2d)	1866		4,000.	7,500.	-	-
10-04P	$2 (8s 4d)	18_				FACE PROOF	700.
10-06	$4 (16s 8d)	18_				ONE NOTE KNOWN	
10-08	$8 (33s 4d)	1866		7,500.	-	-	-

THE SUMMERSIDE BANK OF PRINCE EDWARD ISLAND

705-12 **ABNC PRINTINGS**
DOLLAR ONLY

DESIGNS AND COLOURS

705-12-02
   $1 Face Design: Three children with a colt "Feeding the colt"/ farmer watching dairymaid milking a cow/boy tending sheep in snow "Sheep feeding"
   Colour: Black with no tint

Back Design: Lathework, counters and bank name
Colour: Brown

705-12-04P
   $2 Face Design: Shipbuilding scene/Royal Crest/ dog and strongbox
   Colour: Black with no tint

Back Design: Lathework, counters and bank name
Colour: Brown

705-12-06
   $5 Face Design: Sailor with flag, bales and lion/ paddlewheel steamship/ seated Britannia holding shield bearing 5
   Colour: Black with no tint

Back Design: Lathework, counters and bank name
Colour: Brown

705-12-08
   $10 Face Design: Man with barrels/fishing boats/ two sailing ships, one with 5 on sail
   Colour: Black with no tint

Back Design: Lathework, counters and bank name
Colour: Brown

SIGNATURES
left
mss. Robt. Mc C. Stavert
mss. Robt. Mc C. Stavert

right
mss. Angus McMillan
mss. G. Holman

ISSUE DATING
Engraved
Feby. 1st 1872

PROTECTOR
Green "word" and numeral on face only

OVERPRINT
$1: "CANADA CURRENCY" vertically at ends in red

Cat. No.	Denom.	Date	Variety	VG	F	VF	EF	Unc
12-02	$1	1872	No o/p	4,000.	7,000.	-	-	-
12-02a	$1	1872	Red o/p	4,000.	7,000.	-	-	-
12-04	$2	1872		4,000.	7,000.	-	-	-
12-06	$5	1872		5,000.	7,500.	-	-	-
12-08	$10	1872		5,000.	7,500.	-	-	-

705-14 BABN PRINTINGS, 1884
DESIGNS AND COLOURS

705-14-02
$1 Face Design: Farm girl with cow and calf, "Alderney"/boy on horse with dog at stream "At the Brook"/sailors, one with telescope at seashore "Looking Out"
Colour: Black with green tint

Back Design: See varieties
Colour: See varieties

IMPRINT
British American Bank Note Co. Montreal
British American Bank Note Co. OTTAWA

SIGNATURES
left
mss. Robt. Mc C. Stavert

right
mss. Angus McMillan

ISSUE DATING
Engraved
December 1st 1884

VARIETIES
$1 Back Design: Lathework, counters and bank name
Back Colour: Green
$1 Back Design: Plain

Cat. No.	Denom.	Date	Variety	VG	F	VF	EF	Unc
14-02	$1	1884	Green back	4,000.	7,000.	-	-	-
14-04	$1	1884	Plain back	4,000.	7,000.	-	-	-

705-16 BABN PRINTINGS 1891
DESIGNS AND COLOURS

705-16-02P
$5 Face Design: Farm implements/fishermen and ships;"On the Banks"/seated Britannia and shield bearing 5
Colour: Black with green tint

Back Design: Lathework, counters, bank name and heads of three horses at left
Colour: Green

IMPRINT
British American Bank Note Co. Ottawa

SIGNATURES
left
none

right
engr. Angus McMillan

ISSUE DATING
Engraved
July 1st 1891

Cat. No.	Denom.	Date	VG	F	VF	EF	Unc
16-02	$5	1891			FACE PROOF		700.

THE BANK OF TORONTO

705-18 BABN PRINTINGS 1900

DESIGNS AND COLOURS

705-18-02P
- **$10 Face Design:** Seated woman with cornucopia/ grazing sheep/steamships and sailboats
- **Colour:** Black with olive green tint

- **Back Design:** Lathework, counters and bank name
- **Colour:** Green

IMPRINT
British American Bank Note Co. Ottawa

SIGNATURES
left	right
none	engr. Angus McMillan

ISSUE DATING
Engraved
Sept. 1st 1900

Cat. No.	Denom.	Date	VG	F	VF	EF	Unc
18-02P	$10	1900			FACE PROOF		700.

THE BANK OF TORONTO

1855-1954

TORONTO, PROVINCE OF CANADA

BANK NUMBER 715 *REDEEMABLE*

Toronto was an over-banked city, but for the most part, the rural areas were poorly served. The Millers Association of Canada West, as the bank was known before incorporation, comprised millers, wheat merchants and grain marketers from southern Ontario. They sought to establish a bank with powers to carry on a flour, grain and produce agency, an insurance agency and a banking company. The petition to establish such an institution failed initially, but a charter was finally granted on March 8, 1855, in the name of the Bank of Toronto. It faced difficulties in raising the necessary capital in its first year and did not open its doors to the public until July 8, 1856. Once in operation it completed its first year "with much pleasure" to the shareholders.

The bank was wary of real estate and directed its financing towards the staple industries. From the mid 1850s to the mid 1890s, this policy proved wise in the face of the collapse of the land boom and other national economic failures that saw the demise of some 14 banks.

The Bank of Toronto expanded into the textile and mining industries and opened new branches in other provinces. During World War I, the bank cooperated with the government in raising public loans and closed some of its branches. From 1930 to 1934, the Depression years, the bank was almost at a standstill, but recovered strongly from 1938 on, despite playing its part, as did the other banks, during World War II. Between the end of the war and the amalgamation in 1955 with the Dominion Bank, the bank expanded rapidly. The amalgamation was a "marriage of equals" and was unique in that, of the nine major banks then in operation, neither bank had ever taken over or merged with another institution. The Toronto-Dominion Bank started with an authorized capital of $30 million, with $15 million paid-up, a reserve fund of $30 million, total assets in excess of $1 billion and 450 branches. It is now one of the largest banks in Canada, with operations across Canada and in several other countries.

"PROVINCE OF CANADA" ISSUES OF 1856-1865

DESIGNS AND COLOURS

715-14-02
- **$1 Face Design:** "Justice" figure/reclining farmer, haying in background; small crest of Toronto below/ Indian seated by ornamental 1
- **Colour:** Black with no tint

- **Back Design:** See subheadings
- **Colour:** See subheadings

THE BANK OF TORONTO

715-10-04
$2 **Face Design:** Two children with sheaves/train and wagons at wharf; small crest of Toronto below/ allegorical female
Colour: Black with no tint

Back Design: See subheadings
Colour: See subheadings

715-14-06
$4 **Face Design:** Man with Scythe, three allegorical women; small crest of Toronto below/ Indian chief "Red Jacket"
Colour: Black with no tint

Back Design: See Subheadings
Colour: See Subheadings

715-12-02
$5 **Face Design:** Laureated woman/Royal Crest; small crest of Toronto below/ seated "Commerce" figure and 5, (sideways)
Colour: Black with no tint

Back Design: See subheadings
Colour: See subheadings

715-14-10
$10 **Face Design:** Beaver and maple leaves/ crest of Toronto/train
Colour: Black with no tint

Back Design: See subheadings
Colour: See subheadings

715-10   ISSUE OF 1856
PARTIALLY ENGRAVED DATE
ORANGE BACK, "WORD" PROTECTOR

DESIGNS AND COLOURS

Back Design: Lathework, counters, bank name and Medallion engraved portraits of Queen Victoria and Prince Albert
Colour: Orange

IMPRINT
Rawdon, Wright Hatch & Edson, New York

SIGNATURES
   left   right
   mss. various   mss. J.G. Chewett

ISSUE DATING
Partially engraved 3rd July 185_:
1856

PROTECTOR
Blue "word" on face only
Green "word" on face only

OVERPRINT
"BARRIE"
"PORT HOPE"

Cat. No.	Denom.	Date	VG	F	VF	EF	Unc
10-02	$1	1856	1,100.	1,500.	-	-	-
10-04	$2	1856	1,100.	1,500.	-	-	-
10-06	$4	1856	1,300.	1,800.	-	-	-
10-08	$5	1856	1,100.	1,500.	-	-	-
10-10P	$10	185_				PROOF	500.

THE BANK OF TORONTO

715-12 ISSUE OF 1857
PRINTED DATE, ORANGE BACK
ROMAN NUMERAL PROTECTOR
COBOURG BRANCH

DESIGNS AND COLOURS
  Back Design: Lathework, counters, bank name and Medallion engraved portraits of Queen Victoria and Prince Albert
  Colour: Orange

IMPRINT
Rawdon, Wright, Hatch & Edson, New York

SIGNATURES
  right only
  mss. J.G. Chewett

ISSUE DATING
  Letterpress
  3 Jan'y, 1857

PROTECTOR
Blue Roman Numeral on face only

OVERPRINT
3rd Jan'y COBOURG, 1857

Cat. No.	Denom.	Date	VG	F	VF	EF	Unc
12-02R	$5	1857					ONE KNOWN

715-14 ISSUE OF 1859
ENGRAVED DATE, PLAIN BACK
"WORD" PROTECTOR

DESIGNS AND COLOURS
  Back Design: Plain

IMPRINT
American Bank Note Co. New-York

SIGNATURES
left	right
mss. various	mss. J.G. Chewett
mss. various	mss. Wm. Gooderham
mss. various	mss. Jas. G. Worts

ISSUE DATING
  Engraved
  July 2nd, 1859
  2d July 1859

PROTECTOR
Green "word" on face and back

OVERPRINTS
  "BARRIE" twice in blue
  "COBOURG" twice in blue
  "COLLINGWOOD" twice in blue
  "MONTREAL" twice in blue
  "PETERBORO" twice in red
  "PORT HOPE" twice in blue
  "ST. CATHARINES" twice in blue

Cat. No.	Denom.	Date	VG	F	VF	EF	Unc
14-02	$1	1859	550.	750.	1,100.	-	-
14-04	$2	1859	800.	1,000.	1,400.	-	-
14-06	$4	1859	1,000.	1,400.	2,100.	-	-
14-08	$5	1859	1,000.	1,400.	2,100.	-	-
14-10	$10	1859	1,000.	1,400.	2,100.	-	-

715-16 ISSUE OF 1865
ENGRAVED DATE, PLAIN BACK
"WORD" PROTECTOR

DESIGNS AND COLOURS
  Back Design: Plain

IMPRINT
American Bank Note Co. New-York

SIGNATURES
left	right
mss. various	mss. Wm. Gooderham

ISSUE DATING
  Engraved
  July 3rd, 1865

PROTECTOR
Blue "word" on face and back

Cat. No.	Denom.	Date	VG	F	VF	EF	Unc
16-02	$5	1865	1,000.	1,400.	2,100.	-	-

715-18 DOMINION OF CANADA
ISSUE OF 1876

DESIGNS AND COLOURS

715-18-02
  $4 Face Design: J.G. Worts/allegorical female and two children/Wm. Gooderham
  Colour: Black with green and pink tint
  Back Design: Plain

IMPRINT
American Bank Note Co. New York

SIGNATURES
left	right
mss. various	mss. Wm. Gooderham

ISSUE DATING
  Engraved
  1st January 1876

OVERPRINTS
  "COLLINGWOOD" twice in blue
  "ST. CATHARINES" twice in blue

Cat. No.	Denom.	Date	VG	F	VF	EF	Unc
18-02	$4	1876	1,300.	1,800.	-	-	-

THE BANK OF TORONTO

715-20　　DOMINION OF CANADA
　　　　　ISSUE OF 1880

DESIGNS AND COLOURS

715-20-02
　　$5 Face Design: Woman with laureate/
　　　　　　　　　　Royal Crest; small crest of Toronto below/
　　　　　　　　　　seated "Commerce" figure and 5 (sideways)
　　　　Colour: Black with no tint
　　Back Design: Lathework, counters, bank name and
　　　　　　　　　　Medallion engraved portraits of Queen
　　　　　　　　　　Victoria and Prince Albert
　　　　Colour: Blue

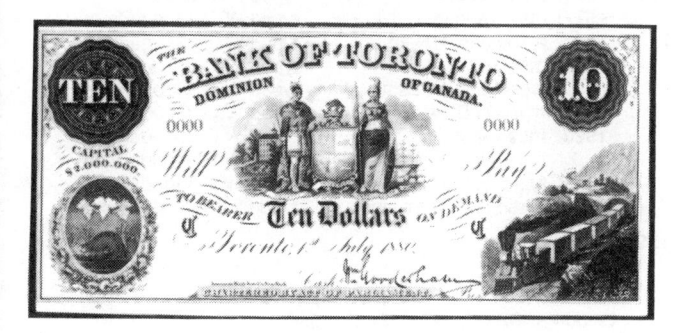

715-20-04P
　　$10 Face Design: Beaver and maple leaves/
　　　　　　　　　　crest of Toronto/train
　　　　Colour: Black with no tint
　　Back Design: Lathework, counters, bank name and
　　　　　　　　　　Medallion engraved portraits of Queen
　　　　　　　　　　Victoria and Prince Albert
　　　　Colour: Blue

715-20-06P
　　$20 Face Design: Portrait of Queen Victoria/train; small crest
　　　　　　　　　　below/milkmaid standing beside cow and calf
　　　　Colour: Black with no tint

　　Back Design: Lathework, counters, bank name and
　　　　　　　　　　Medallion engraved portraits of Queen
　　　　　　　　　　Victoria and Prince Albert
　　　　Colour: Blue

IMPRINT
　American Bank Note Co. New York
　British American Bank Note Co. Montreal

SIGNATURES
left	right
mss. J. Adams (p)	engr. Wm. Gooderham
mss. various	engr. Wm. Gooderham

ISSUE DATING
　Engraved
　July 1st 1880
　1st July 1880

PROTECTOR
　Green "word" on face only

OVERPRINTS
　"ST. CATHARINES" twice in blue

Cat. No.	Denom.	Date	VG	F	VF	EF	Unc
20-02	$5	1880	1,000.	1,400.	2,000.	-	-
20-04P	$10	1880			FACE PROOF		450.
20-06P	$20	1880			FACE PROOF		450.

715-22　　YELLOW ISSUES OF
　　　　　1887-1929

DESIGNS AND COLOURS

715-22-08
　　$5 Face Design: Woman with laureate/Royal Crest; small
　　　　　　　　　　crest of Toronto below/seated "Commerce"
　　　　　　　　　　figure and 5 (sideways)
　　　　Colour: Black with yellow tint
　　Back Design: Lathework, counters, bank name and
　　　　　　　　　　Medallion engraved portraits of Queen
　　　　　　　　　　Victoria and Prince Albert
　　　　Colour: Orange

THE BANK OF TORONTO

715-22-24
- **$10 Face Design:** Beaver and maple leaves/crest of Toronto/train
- **Colour:** Black with yellow tint
- **Back Design:** Lathework, counters, bank name and Medallion engraved portraits of Queen Victoria and Prince Albert
- **Colour:** Orange

715-22-58
- **$20 Face Design:** Queen Victoria/train; small crest below/milkmaid standing beside cow and calf
- **Colour:** Black with yellow tint
- **Back Design:** Lathework, counters, bank name and Medallion engraved portraits of Queen Victoria and Prince Albert
- **Colour:** Orange

715-22-72
- **$50 Face Design:** Bull's head/City Hall/herd of cattle
- **Colour:** Black with yellow tint
- **Back Design:** Lathework, counters, bank name and Medallion engraved portraits of Queen Victoria and Prince Albert 
- **Colour:** Orange

IMPRINT
American Bank Note Co. New York
Canadian Bank Note Company Limited
American Bank Note Co. Ottawa

SIGNATURES

	left	right
1887-1892:	mss. various	engr. Geo. Gooderham
	mss. J.A. Adams	engr. Geo. Gooderham
1906:	mss. various	engr. W.H. Beatty
1911-1914:	mss. various	typed D. Coulson
1917:	mss. various	typed.W.G. Gooderham
	typed Jno. R. Lamb	typed W.G. Gooderham
1920:	mss. various	typed W.G. Gooderham
	typed Jno. R. Lamb	typed W.G. Gooderham
	typed H.B. Henwood	typed W.G. Gooderham
1923:	mss various	typed W.G. Gooderham
	typed Jno. R. Lamb	typed W.G. Gooderham
	typed H.B. Henwood	typed W.G. Gooderham
1929:	typed H.B. Henwood	typed W.G. Gooderham

ISSUE DATING
Engraved

July 1st 1887	1st Feby 1913
1st July 1887	Feb 1 1914
1st July 1890	2nd February 1914
July 1st, 1890	2nd Feb'y 1914
1st June 1892	1st February 1917
1st June 1902	1st Feb. 1917
1st Feb'y 1906	2nd Feb'y 1920
1st February 1906	1st February 1923
1st February 1911	1st Feb'y 1923
Feb 1, 1911	1st October 1929
1st February 1912	1st Oct. 1929
1st Feb'y 1912	Feb 2 1913

PROTECTOR
Green "word" on face only

OVERPRINTS
Issue of 1887:
"LONDON" twice in blue
"LONDON" and "F" twice in blue
"PARRY SOUND" twice in blue
"POINT ST. CHARLES" twice in blue
"WINNIPEG" twice in blue

Issue of 1890:
"BRANTFORD" twice in blue
"CARDINAL" twice in blue
"COLDWATER" twice in blue
"CREEMORE" twice in blue
"ELMVALE" twice in blue
"GANANOQUE" twice in blue
"KEENE" twice in blue
"LONDON" twice in blue
"MILLBROOK" twice in blue
"MONTREAL" twice in blue
"NIAGARA FALLS CENTRE" twice in blue
"OIL SPRINGS" twice in blue
"OMEMEE" twice in blue
"PETERBORO" twice in blue
"POINT ST. CHARLES" twice in blue
"PORT HOPE" twice in blue
"ST. CATHARINES" twice in blue
"SUDBURY" twice in blue
"VICTORIA HARBOUR" twice in blue
"WINNIPEG" twice in blue

Issue of 1892:
"CARTWRIGHT" twice in blue
"COPPER CLIFF" twice in blue
"KING ST. WEST BR." twice in blue
"LONDON" twice in blue

Issue of 1906:
"GASPE" twice in blue
"POINT ST. CHARLES" twice in blue
"ST. CATHARINES" twice in blue
"WATERLOO" twice in blue

Cat. No.	Denom.	Date	Variety	VG	F	VF	EF	Unc
22-01	$5	1887				FACE PROOF		400.
22-02	$5	1890		400.	650.	900.	-	-
22-06	$5	1906		420.	600.	800.	-	-
22-08	$5	1911		500.	700.	1,000.	-	-
22-10	$5	1912		175.	250.	375.	650.	-
22-12	$5	1914		175.	250.	375.	650.	-
22-14	$5	1917	Mss. signature, l.	80.	125.	200.	375.	750.
22-16	$5	1917	Typed Lamb, l.	80.	125.	200.	375.	750.
22-18	$5	1923	Typed Lamb,l.	50.	80.	150.	250.	500.
22-20	$5	1923	Typed Henwood,l.	50.	80.	150.	250.	500.
22-22	$5	1929		50.	80.	150.	250.	500.
22-24	$10	1887		700.	1,000.	-	-	-
22-26	$10	1892		425.	600.	-	-	-
22-27	$10	1902		375.	550.	-	-	-
22-28	$10	1906		375.	550.	-	-	-
22-30	$10	1911		475.	650.	-	-	-
22-32	$10	1912		200.	325.	-	-	-
22-34	$10	1914		200.	325.	-	-	-
22-36	$10	1917	Mss. sign., l.	100.	140.	225.	400.	700.
22-38	$10	1917	Typed Lamb, l.	100.	140.	225.	400.	700.
22-39	$10	1923	mss. sign,.l.	100.	140.	225.	400.	700.
22-40	$10	1923	Typed Lamb, l.	100.	140.	225.	400.	700.
22-42	$10	1923	Typed Henwood, l.	100.	140.	225.	400.	700.
22-44	$10	1929		80.	115.	200.	375.	600.
22-46	$20	1887		800.	1,100.	-	-	-
22-48	$20	1906		550.	800.	-	-	-
22-50	$20	1913		550.	800.	-	-	-
22-52P	$20	1914				FACE PROOF		400.
22-54	$20	1917	Mss. signature, l.	120.	170.	250.	475.	-
22-56	$20	1917	Typed Lamb, l.	120.	170.	250.	475.	-
22-58	$20	1923	Typed Lamb, l.	150.	210.	315.	525.	1,050.
22-60	$20	1923	Typed Henwood, l.	150.	210.	315.	525.	1,050.
22-62	$20	1929		100.	140.	200.	350.	700.
22-64P	$50	1890				FACE PROOF		400.
22-66	$50	1906		1,100.	1,600.	-	-	-
22-68P	$50	1913				FACE PROOF		400.
22-70	$50	1914		1,100.	1,600.	-	-	-
22-72	$50	1920	Mss. signature, l.	500.	700.	1,050.	1,800.	-
22-74	$50	1920	Typed Lamb, l.	500.	700.	1,050.	1,800.	-
22-76	$50	1920	Typed Henwood, l.	500.	700.	1,050.	1,800.	-
22-78	$50	1929		500.	700.	1,050.	1,800.	-

715-24 SMALL-SIZE ISSUES OF 1935 AND 1937

DESIGNS AND COLOURS

715-24-06
$5 Face Design: Woman with laureate/Royal Crest/ seated "Commerce" figure and 5 (sideways)
Colour: Black with yellow tint

Back Design: lathework, counters, bank name and Medallion engraved portraits of Queen Victoria and Prince Albert
Colour: Orange

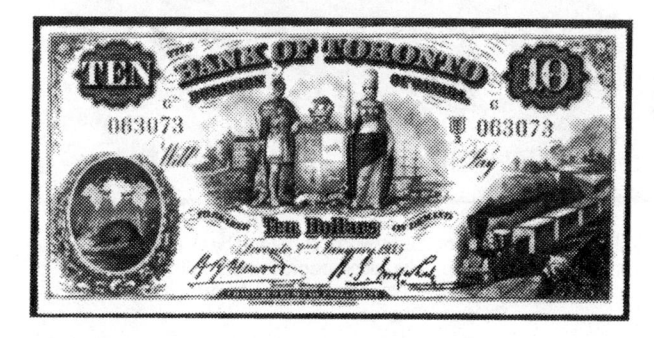

715-24-08
$10 Face Design: Beaver and maple leaves/ crest of Toronto/train
Colour: Black with yellow tint

THE BANK OF TORONTO

Back Design: Lathework, counters, bank name and Medallion engraved portraits of Queen Victoria and Prince Albert
Colour: Orange

715-24-14
$20 Face Design: Queen Victoria/train/dairymaid with cattle
Colour: Black with yellow tint

Back Design: Lathework, counters, bank name and Medallion engraved portraits of Queen Victoria and Prince Albert
Colour: Orange

IMPRINT
Canadian Bank Note Company, Limited

SIGNATURES
	left	right
1935:	typed H.B. Henwood	typed W.G. Gooderham
1937:	typed H.B. Henwood	typed Jno. R. Lamb
	typed F.H. Marsh	typed Jno. R. Lamb

ISSUE DATING
Engraved
2nd Jan. 1935   2nd Jan. 1937
2nd January, 1935   2nd January, 1937

Cat. No.	Denom.	Date	Variety	VG	F	VF	EF	Unc
24-02	$5	1935		30.	40.	65.	110.	200.
24-04	$5	1937	Henwood, l.	30.	40.	65.	110.	200.
24-06	$5	1937	Marsh, l.	30.	40.	65.	110.	200.
24-08	$10	1935		35.	45.	70.	120.	225.
24-10	$10	1937	Henwood, l.	35.	45.	70.	120.	225.
24-12	$10	1937	Marsh, l.	35.	45.	70.	120.	225.
24-14	$20	1935		45.	65.	100.	175.	350.

715-26 NOTES ALTERED FROM THE COLONIAL BANK OF CANADA
DESIGNS AND COLOURS

715-26-02
$1 Face Design: Bust of young women/wood chopper/—
Colour: Black with orange-brown tint
Back Design: Plain

Photo Not Available

715-26-04
$4 Face Design: Helmeted "Justice" figure/Queen Victoria (Winterhalter portrait)/—
Colour: Black with pink tint
Back Design: Plain

IMPRINT
$1: Jocelyn, Draper, Welch & Co. and American Bank Note Company. New York
$4: Jocelyn, Draper & Welch and American Bank Note Co. (monogram)

SIGNATURES
left	right
mss. A. Cameron	mss. J.C. Chewett

ISSUE DATING
Partially engraved ___ 18___:
$1: 1862
Engraved
$4: May 4, 1859

Cat. No.	Denom.	Date	Variety	VG	F	VF	EF	Unc
26-02	$1	1862	Altered	300.	500.	-	-	-
26-04	$4	1859	Altered	375.	600.	-	-	-

715-28 NOTES ALTERED FROM THE INTERNATIONAL BANK OF CANADA

DESIGNS AND COLOURS

715-28-02

$2 Face Design: Allegorical woman/Royal Crest/—
Colour: Black with no tint

Back Design: Plain

IMPRINT
Danforth, Wright & Co.

SIGNATURES
right only
mss. J.C. Fitch

ISSUE DATING
Engraved
Sept. 15, 1858
March 15, 1861

PROTECTOR
Red "word" on face and back

Cat. No.	Denom.	Date	Variety	VG	F	VF	EF	Unc
28-01	$1	1861	Altered	350.	550.	-	-	-
28-02	$2	1858	Altered	350.	550.	-	-	-

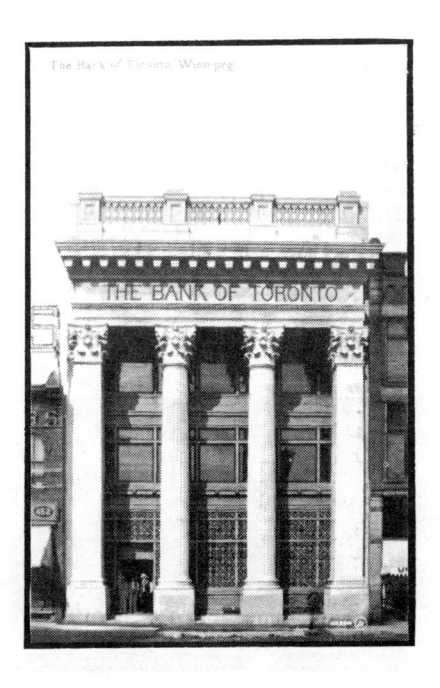

THE TRADERS BANK OF CANADA

1885-1912

TORONTO, ONTARIO

BANK NUMBER 720   **REDEEMABLE**

The Traders Bank opened for business in 1855 with limited capital, but with proper management over a period of years, assets increased and the financial and business communities gained a substantial regard for it. At the time of its takeover by the Royal Bank of Canada in 1912, the Traders Bank of Canada had reserves and capital of $7 million, with total assets of $52 million. The smaller bank also had 126 branches and agencies in operation. A reorganization followed the merger, which saw final acquisition of 90 new branches for the Royal Bank in Ontario, 13 in Alberta, five in Saskatchewan and one in British Columbia. Both the extensive representation and its high reputation of the Traders Bank in Ontario were of particular importance to the purchasing bank, since at this time, the Royal Bank was represented in only 36 places in Ontario.

720-10 ISSUES OF 1885 AND 1886

DESIGNS AND COLOURS

720-10-02P

$5 Face Design: H.S. Strathy/farmer and cattle at barn door, "Milk Producers"/A. Manning
Colour: Black with green tint

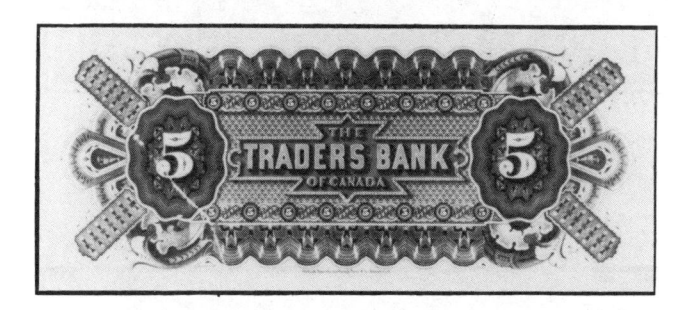

Back Design: Lathework, counters and bank name
Colour: Green

THE TRADERS BANK OF CANADA

720-10-04P
  $10 Face Design: H.S. Strathy/allegorical figures and ornate X/ A. Manning
  Colour: Black with green tint

Back Design: Lathework, counters and bank name
Colour: Green

720-10-06P
  $50 Face Design: H.S. Strathy/allegorical female and globe "Confederation"/A. Manning
  Colour: Black with green tint

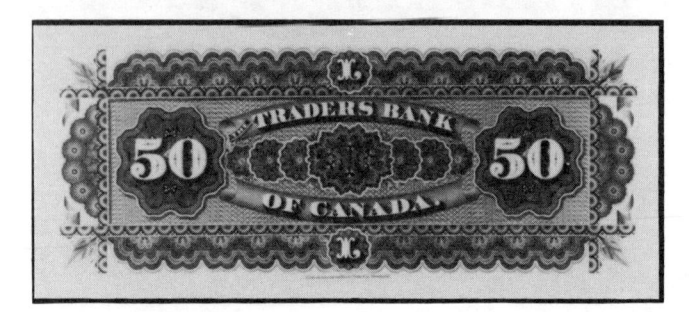

Back Design: Lathework, counters and bank name
Colour: Green

720-10-08P
  $100 Face Design: H.S. Strathy/ships at dock "Allan Line Wharves"/A. Manning
  Colour: Black with green tint

Back Design: Lathework, counters and bank name
Colour: Green

IMPRINT
British American Bank Note Co. Montreal

SIGNATURES
left	right
mss. various	engr. Alex Manning

ISSUE DATING
Engraved
2nd July 1885
Mar. 1st 1886

Cat. No.	Denom.	Date		Unc
10-02P	$5	1885	FACE PROOF	350.
10-04P	$10	1885	FACE PROOF	350.
10-06P	$50	1886	FACE PROOF	500.
10-08P	$100	1886	FACE PROOF	500.

720-12   **ISSUES OF 1890 AND 1893**

DESIGNS AND COLOURS

720-12-02
  $5 Face Design: H.S. Strathy/farmer and cattle at barn door "Milk Producers"/Wm. Bell
  Colour: Black with green tint

  Back Design: Lathework, counters and bank name
  Colour: Green

432

THE TRADERS BANK OF CANADA

720-12-04P
- **$20 Face Design:** H.S. Strathy/seated allegorical female and machinery/Wm. Bell
- **Colour:** Black with green tint
- **Back Design:** Lathework, counters and bank name
- **Colour:** Green

IMPRINT
British American Bank Note Co. Ottawa

SIGNATURES
left	right
mss. various	engr. Wm. Bell

ISSUE DATING
Engraved
Jan. 2, 1890
2nd Jan. 1893

Cat. No.	Denom.	Date	VG	F	VF	EF	Unc
12-02	$5	1893	700.	1,000.	1,500.	2,500.	-
12-04P	$20	1890				FACE PROOF	500.

720-14 ISSUES OF 1897 AND 1907
DESIGNS AND COLOURS

720-14-02a
- **$5 Face Design:** H.S. Strathy/farmer and cattle at barn door "Milk Producers"/Chas. D. Warren
- **Colour:** Black with green tint
- **Back Design:** Lathework, counters and bank name
- **Colour:** Green

720-14-06
- **$10 Face Design:** H.S. Strathy/allegorical figures and ornate X/Chas. D. Warren
- **Colour:** Black with green tint
- **Back Design:** Lathework, counters and bank name
- **Colour:** Green

720-14-10P
- **$20 Face Design:** H.S. Strathy/seated allegorical woman and machinery/Chas. D. Warren
- **Colour:** Black with green tint
- **Back Design:** Lathework, counters and bank name 
- **Colour:** Green

433

THE TRADERS BANK OF CANADA

720-14-12P
  $50 **Face Design:** H.S. Strathy/allegorical female and globe "Confederation"/Chas. D. Warren
  Colour: Black with green tint
  Back Design: Lathework, counters and bank name
  Colour: Green

720-14-14P
  $100 **Face Design:** H.S. Strathy/ships at dock, part of "Allan Line Wharves"/Chas. D. Warren
  Colour: Black with green tint
  Back Design: Lathework, counters and bank name
  Colour: Green

IMPRINT
  British American Bank Note Co. Montreal

SIGNATURES
  left   right
  mss. various   engr. Chas. D. Warren

ISSUE DATING
  Engraved
  Jan. 2, 1897
  2nd July, 1897
  1st Nov. 1907

Cat. No.	Denom.	Date	VG	F	VF	EF	Unc
14-02a	$5	1897	450.	600.	950.	1,600.	3,100.
14-02b	$5	1897	450.	600.	950.	1,600.	3,100.
14-02c	$5	1897	450.	600.	950.	1,600.	3,100.
14-04	$5	1907	500.	700.	1,100.	-	-
14-06	$10	1897	650.	1,100.	1,500.	2,500.	-
14-08	$10	1907	650.	1,100.	1,500.	2,500.	-
14-10P	$20	1907			FACE PROOF		500.
14-12P	$50	1897			FACE PROOF		500.
14-14P	$100	1897			FACE PROOF		500.

Note: $5 1897a Capital 1,000,000 on the note;
  $5 1897b Capital 2,000,000 on the note;
  $5 1897c Capital 3,000,000 on the note.

720-16 ISSUE OF 1909
DESIGNS AND COLOURS

720-16-02P
  $5 **Face Design:** —/"Allan Line Wharves"/—
  Colour: Black with yellow and green tint

  Back Design: Lathework, counters bank name and bank building
  Colour: Green

720-16-04
  $10 **Face Design:** —/men cutting logs/—
  Colour: Black with brown, blue and purple tint
  Back Design: Lathework, counters, bank name and bank building
  Colour: Green, red and brown

720-16-06P
  $20 **Face Design:** —/train at station/—
  Colour: Black with brown, green and red tint

THE TRADERS BANK OF CANADA

Back Design: Lathework, counters, bank name and bank building
Colour: Brown, green and red

720-16-08P
  $50 Face Design: —/steamship in storm/—
  Colour: Black with green, brown and red tint

Back Design: Lathework, counters, bank name and bank building
Colour: Blue with brown and purple

720-16-10P
  $100 Face Design: —/cattle roundup/—
  Colour: Black with yellow-brown, green and brown tint

Back Design: Lathework, counters, bank name and bank building
Colour: Orange with red, green and brown

IMPRINT
  American Bank Note Co. Ottawa — $10,20,50,100.
  British American Bank Note Co. Ottawa — $5

SIGNATURES
left	right
engr. Chas. D. Warren	mss. various

ISSUE DATING
  Engraved
  Jan. 2nd 1909
  2nd January 1909

Note: Proofs of this issue are known to exist with various coloured faces and backs.

Cat. No.	Denom.	Date	VG	F	VF	EF	Unc
16-02P	$5	1909			FACE PROOF		500.
16-04	$10	1909	1,200.	1,680.	2,500.	4,300.	-
16-06P	$20	1909			FACE PROOF		500.
16-08P	$50	1909			FACE PROOF		500.
16-10P	$100	1909			FACE PROOF		500.

720-18   **$5 ISSUE OF 1910**

DESIGNS AND COLOURS

720-18-02
  $5 Face Design: —/farmers reaping grain with horses/—
  Colour: Black with red, green and purple tint

  Back Design: Lathework, counters, bank name and bank building
  Colour: Olive with blue and brown

IMPRINT
  American Bank Note Co. Ottawa

SIGNATURES
left	right
engr. Chas. D. Warren	mss. various

ISSUE DATING
  Engraved
  1st November 1910

Cat. No.	Denom.	Date	VG	F	VF	EF	Unc
18-02	$5	1910	1,200.	1,700.	2,500.	4,000.	-

THE UNION BANK

1838 - CA. 1840

MONTREAL, LOWER CANADA

BANK NUMBER 725 **NONREDEEMABLE**

Established in Montreal, Lower Canada, in 1838 as a private bank, it later became the Union Bank of Montreal.

BURTON & GURLEY PRINTING, 1838

DESIGNS AND COLOURS
Some notes are endorsed vertically across the left end of the face with "H. Gray & Co."

725-10-02
- **$1 Face Design:** —/posing female with sculptures, palette and easel; caduceus, anchor and ship below/—
- **Colour:** Black with no tint
- **Back Design:** See subheadings
- **Colour:** See subheadings

725-10-04
- **$2 Face Design:** —/seated Mercury, ship in background; road and signpost below/—
- **Colour:** Black with no tint
- **Back Design:** See subheadings
- **Colour:** See subheadings

725-14-06
- **$5 Face Design:** —/seated allegorical female and Indian; crown below/—
- **Colour:** Black with no tint
- **Back Design:** See subheadings
- **Colour:** See subheadings

IMPRINT
Burton & Gurley. New York

SIGNATURES
left	right
To H. Gray & Co.	mss. A. Dudley

725-10   **BURTON GURLEY PRINTINGS ISSUE OF 1838 WITH PLAIN BACKS**

DESIGNS AND COLOURS
- **Back Design:** Plain

ISSUE DATING
Partially engraved ___ 18___:
- **$1, 1838:** July 14, Aug. 1
- **$2 and $5, 1838:** July 14

Cat. No.	Denom.	Date	VG	F	VF	EF	Unc
10-02	$1	1838	200.	300.	-	-	-
10-04	$2	1838	200.	300.	-	-	-
10-06	$5	1838	250.	400.	-	-	-

725-12   **ISSUE OF 1838 WITH GREEN BACKS**

DESIGNS AND COLOURS
- **Back Design:** Lathework, miniature vignettes and "STEEL PLATE"
- **Back Colour:** Green

ISSUE DATING
Partially engraved ___ 18___:
- **1838:** Aug. 1
  - August 1

Cat. No.	Denom.	Date	VG	F	VF	EF	Unc
12-02	$1	1838	250.	375.	-	-	-
12-04	$2	1838	250.	375.	-	-	-
12-06	$5	1838	325.	425.	-	-	-

725-14 ISSUE OF 1838 WITH BLUE BACKS

DESIGNS AND COLOURS
   Back Design: Lathework, miniature vignettes and "STEEL PLATE"
   Back Colour: Blue

ISSUE DATING
   Partially engraved ___ 18___:
   1838: August 1, Augt 1.

Cat. No.	Denom.	Date	VG	F	VF	EF	Unc
14-02	$1	1838	250.	375.	-	-	-
14-04	$2	1838	250.	375.	-	-	-
14-06	$5	1838	325.	425.	-	-	-

RWH PRINTINGS 1838

DESIGNS AND COLOURS

725-16-18-02a
   $1 Face Design: —/Indian buffalo-hunting scene "Buffalo chase" (Catlin), man with hammer below/ Indian with drawn bow
   Colour: Black with no tint
   Back Design: Lathework
   Colour: See subheadings

725-16-18-02b
   $2 Face Design: —/Indian in canoe; clasped hands in wreath below/ woman with wheat stalks, leaning on pillar
   Colour: Black with no tint
   Back Design: Lathework
   Colour: See subheadings

725-16-18-02c
   $3 Face Design: —/allegorical figures in clouds; small train below/Indian woman
   Colour: Black with no tint
   Back Design: Lathework
   Colour: See subheadings

725-18-08R
   $5 Face Design: —/train; Mercury's head below/farmer with agricultural implements and plaque
   Colour: Black with no tint
   Back Design: Lathework
   Colour: See subheadings

725-18-10R
   $10 Face Design: Train, bales and barrels/ seated "Wolfes Indian" and "Ruins of Jamestown," griffin with key below/—
   Colour: Black with no tint
   Back Design: Lathework
   Colour: See subheadings

THE UNION BANK OF CANADA

725-16-18-12R
$20 Face Design: Kneeling woman with grain/train at wharf; reclining woman with sheaves below/allegorical female
Colour: Black with no tint

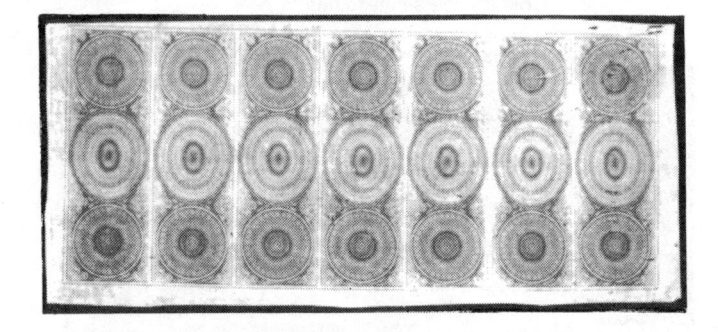

Back Design: Lathework
Colour: See subheadings

IMPRINT
Rawdon, Wright & Hatch. New-York

SIGNATURES
left	right
mss. A. Dudley	mss. Henry Gray

ISSUE DATING
Partially engraved ___ 18___:
1838: August 1

STAMPS AND OVERPRINTS
"COUNTERSIGNED" vertically in black near the left bottom

725-16 ORANGE BACKS

Cat. No.	Denom.	Date	VG	F	VF	EF	Unc
16-02	$1	1838	125.	175.	-	-	-
16-04	$2	1838	100.	140.	-	-	-
16-06	$3	1838	175.	250.	-	-	-
16-06R	$3	18_*	150.	200.	300.	450.	900.
16-08	$5	1838	150.	200.	-	-	-
16-08R	$5	18_*	100.	125.	200.	300.	600.
16-10R	$10	18_*	350.	500.	700.	1,100.	-
16-12R	$20	18_*	300.	450.	650.	900.	-

*These notes are remainders that are unsigned and undated or numbered and dated with no signature or have spurious dates and signatures.

725-18 BLUE BACKS

Cat. No.	Denom.	Date	VG	F	VF	EF	Unc
18-02	$1	1838	100.	140.	-	-	-
18-04	$2	1838	100.	140.	-	-	-
18-06	$3	1838	140.	200.	-	-	-
18-08	$5	1838	200.	350.	-	-	-

Note: The red-brown backs are believed to be oxidized orange backs, and blue-green backs slightly changed blue backs.

THE UNION BANK OF CANADA

1886-1925

QUEBEC CITY, QUEBEC

BANK NUMBER 730   **REDEEMABLE**

This bank commenced business in 1865, under a provincial charter as the Union Bank of Lower Canada; the name was changed to the Union Bank of Canada in 1886. In 1911 the bank acquired the United Empire Bank of Toronto, and the following year it moved its head office to Winnipeg. It was the first chartered bank to open a branch in Alberta. At its peak the bank had 329 branches, with good representation in western Canada. In 1906 negotiations with the Royal Bank of Canada began, but fell through. However, in May 1925 the Royal Bank concluded an agreement with the directors of the Union Bank to purchase that bank for a consideration of 40,000 shares of Royal Bank stock at a par value of $100 each. After all necessary formalities, the purchase was completed and the actual transfer took place on September 1, 1925.

730-10   **ISSUE OF 1886**
DESIGNS AND COLOURS

730-10-02P
$5 Face Design: Quebec Citadel/farmer herding cattle and sheep "The Herd"/Queen Victoria
Colour: Black with red-brown tint

Back Design: Lathework, corner counters and counters with griffins flanking bank name
Colour: Green

438

THE UNION BANK OF CANADA

730-10-04
  $10 Face Design: Quebec Citadel/farmer reaping grain/ Queen Victoria
  Colour: Black with ochre tint

  Back Design: lathework, corner counters and counters with griffins flanking bank name
  Colour: Blue

730-10-06P
  $20 Face Design: Seated allegorical female/ two farmers plowing/Quebec Citadel
  Colour: Black with red-orange tint

  Back Design: Lathework, counters and bank name
  Colour: Brown

730-10-08P
  $50 Face Design: Raphael's angel (minus wings)/—/ Quebec Citadel
  Colour: Black with red-orange tint

730-10-09P
  $50 Face Design: Girl holding feather over head "Juanita"/—/ Quebec Citadel
  Colour: Unknown

  Back Design: Lathework, counters, flowers and bank name
  Colour: Brown

730-10-10P
  $100 Face Design: Allegorical female/winged sphinx-like bust of two women flanking counter/ allegorical female
  Colour: Black with red-orange tint

THE UNION BANK OF CANADA

Back Design: Lathework, counters and bank name
Colour: Brown

IMPRINT
Canada Bank Note Co. Montreal

SIGNATURES
left	right
mss. various	engr. A. Thomson

ISSUE DATING
Engraved
2nd Aug. 1886

Note: Proofs are known of $10 notes with an olive face tint and backs with a brown tint and $50 backs in green.

Cat. No.	Denom.	Date	Variety	VG	F	VF	EF	Unc
10-02P	$5	1886		1,600.	2,000.	-	-	-
10-04	$10	1886		1,600.	2,000.	-	-	-
10-06P	$20	1886				FACE PROOF		600.
10-08P	$50	1886	Angel			FACE PROOF		600.
10-09P	$50	1886	"Juanita"			FACE PROOF		600.
10-10P	$100	1886				FACE PROOF		600.

730-12 ISSUE OF 1893
DESIGNS AND COLOURS

730-12-02
$5 Face Design: Sailing ship/Bank Crest/A. Thomson
Colour: Black with overall green tint

Back Design: Lathework, counters and bank name
Colour: Green

730-12-04
$10 Face Design: Farm implements/Bank Crest/A. Thomson
Colour: Black with overall green tint

Back Design: Lathework, counters and bank name
Colour: Green

730-12-06P
$20 Face Design: Three horses' heads/Bank Crest/A. Thomson
Colour: Black with overall green tint

Back Design: Lathework, counters and bank name
Colour: Green

THE UNION BANK OF CANADA

730-12-08P
    $50 Face Design: —/Bank Crest/A. Thomson
    Colour: Black with overall green tint

Back Design: Lathework, counters and bank name
Colour: Green

730-12-10P
    $100 Face Design: —/Bank Crest/A. Thomson
    Colour: Black with overall green tint

Back Design: Lathework, counters, bank name and three horses' heads
Colour: Green

IMPRINT
    British American Bank Note Co. Ottawa

SIGNATURES
    left   right
    mss. various   engr. A. Thomson

ISSUE DATING
    Engraved
    1st June 1893

Cat. No.	Denom.	Date	VG	F	VF	EF	Unc
12-02	$5	1893	550.	700.	1,000.	1,800.	-
12-04	$10	1893	450.	600.	900.	1,400.	2,500.
12-06P	$20	1893			FACE PROOF		500.
12-08P	$50	1893			FACE PROOF		500.
12-10P	$100	1893			FACE PROOF		500.

730-14   "QUEBEC" $5 AND $10 ISSUES OF 1903 AND 1907

DESIGNS AND COLOURS

730-14-02
    $5 Face Design: —/farmers harvesting with horses "Harvesting"/—
    Back Design: Lathework, counters, bank name and Bank Crest

730-14-08
    $10 Face Design: —/cowboy roping steers "A Round Up"/—

THE UNION BANK OF CANADA

Back Design: Lathework, counters, bank name and Bank Crest
1903 $5 Face Colour: Black with brown frame and brown, olive, red and yellow-green tint
Back Colour: Black with brown, olive, red and yellow-green tint
1907 $5 Face Colour: Black with green frame and blue-green, olive, green and yellow-green tint
Back Colour: Black with blue-green, olive, green and yellow-green tint
$10 Face Colour: Black with black frame and blue, brown, green and yellow-green tint
Back Colour: Black with blue, brown, green and yellow-green tint

IMPRINT
American Bank Note Co. Ottawa
American Bank Note Company, Ottawa

SIGNATURES
	left	right
1903:	typed A. Thomson	mss. various
1907:	typed John Sharples	mss. various

ISSUE DATING
Engraved
1st June 1903
1st June 1907

Cat. No.	Denom.	Date	Variety	VG	F	VF	EF	Unc
14-02	$5	1903*	Blue numbers	550.	800.	1,000.	1,700.	-
14-02a	$5	1903*	Red numbers	550.	800.	1,000.	1,700.	-
14-04	$5	1907		275.	375.	550.	950.	-
14-06	$10	1903		900.	1,100.	1,500.	2,300.	-
14-08	$10	1907		900.	1,100.	1,500.	2,300.	-

730-16   "WINNIPEG" $5 AND $10 ISSUE OF 1912

The head office of the bank changed its location from Quebec City to Winnipeg.

DESIGNS AND COLOURS

730-16-04a
$5 Face Design: —/farmers "Harvesting" with horses/—
Colour: See varieties

Back Design: Lathework, counters, bank name and bank crest
Colour: See varieties

730-16-06
$10 Face Design: —/cowboy roping steers "A Round Up"/—
Colour: Black with blue, olive, green and yellow-green tint

Back Design: Lathework, counters, bank name and bank crest
Colour: Black with blue, olive, green and yellow-green tint

IMPRINT
American Bank Note Co. Ottawa
Canadian Bank Note Company, Limited

VARIETIES
$5 Face Colour: Black frame, black with black, green, olive and yellow-green tint
Back Colour: Black frame, black with black, green, olive and yellow-green tint
$5 Face Colour: Green frame, black with dark green, green, olive and yellow-green tint
Back Colour: Green frame, black with dark green, green, olive and yellow-green tint

SIGNATURES
	left	right
$5, black frame:	typed John Galt	mss. various
	typed John Galt	typed H.B. Shaw
$5, green frame:	typed John Galt	mss. various
	typed John Galt	typed H.B. Shaw
	typed W.R. Allan	typed J.W. Hamilton
$10, green frame:	typed John Galt	mss. various
	typed John Galt	typed H.B. Shaw
	typed W.R. Alla	typed J.W. Hamilton

ISSUE DATING
 Engraved
 July 1st 1912

OVERPRINT
 $5, green frame: Galt signature, "NORTHWEST TERRITORIES" twice vertically in blue

Cat. No.	Denom.	Date	Variety	VG	F	VF	EF	Unc
16-02	$5	1912	Black frame	90.	125.	200.	325.	650.
16-04	$5	1912	Green frame	75.	100.	175.	275.	550.
16-04a	$5	1912	Green frame, blue o/p	1,000.	1,500.	2,000.	3,000.	-
16-06	$10	1912		75.	110.	175.	275.	500.

730-18   **$20, $50 AND $100 DESIGNS SIMILAR TO THE 1886 ISSUE RESUMED 1907 AND 1912**

DESIGNS AND COLOURS

730-18-04
 $20 Face Design: Seated allegorical female/farmers and horses plowing/Quebec Citadel
 Colour: Black with green tint

Back Design: Lathework, counters and bank name

730-18-08
 $50 Face Design: Girl holding feather fan over head "Juanita"/—/Quebec Citadel
 Colour: Black with green tint

Back Design: Lathework, counters, flowers and bank name

730-18-12
 $100 Face Design: Allegorical female/winged sphinx-like bust of two women flanking counter/allegorical female
 Colour: Black with green tint

Back Design: Lathework, counters and bank name

BACK COLOURS
 1907: Back Colour: Brown
 1912: Back Colour: Green

IMPRINT
 British American Bank Note Co. Montreal & Ottawa

SIGNATURES
	left	right
1907:	engr. John Sharples	mss. various
1912:	engr. John Galt	mss. various

ISSUE DATING
 Engraved
 1st June, 1907
 July, 1st 1912

Note: 1907 issues are domiciled in Quebec, later issues in Winnipeg.

Cat. No.	Denom.	Date	Variety	VG	F	VF	EF	Unc
18-02P	$20	1907	Quebec			FACE PROOF		500.
18-04	$20	1912	Winnipeg	700.	1,000.	1,450.	-	-
18-06P	$50	1907	Quebec			FACE PROOF		500.
18-08	$50	1912	Winnipeg	1,000.	1,500.	2,000.	-	-
18-10P	$100	1907	Quebec			FACE PROOF		500.
18-12	$100	1912	Winnipeg	1,300.	1,800.	2,600.	-	-

THE UNION BANK OF CANADA

730-20 ISSUE OF 1921
DESIGNS AND COLOURS

730-20-02
- **$5 Face Design:** H.B. Shaw/—/John Galt
  Colour: Black with lilac, green, gold, red and blue tint
- **Back Design:** Lathework, counters and bank name
  Colour: Green

730-20-04
- **$10 Face Design:** H.B. Shaw/—/John Galt
  Colour: Black with red, lilac, green, orange and blue tint
- **Back Design:** Lathework, counters and bank name
  Colour: Red

730-20-06S
- **$20 Face Design:** H.B. Shaw/—/John Galt
  Colour: Black with orange, green, red, blue and lilac tint 
- **Back Design:** Lathework, counters and bank name
  Colour: Blue

730-20-08S
- **$50 Face Design:** —/John Galt/—
  Colour: Black with blue, lilac, yellow-green, orange and yellow-brown tint
- **Back Design:** Lathework, counters and bank name
  Colour: Brown

730-20-10S
- **$100 Face Design:** —/—/John Galt
  Colour: Black with yellow-green, orange, blue, magenta and green tint
- **Back Design:** Lathework, counters and bank name
  Colour: Olive green

IMPRINT
American Bank Note Company, Ottawa

SIGNATURES
left	right
typed J.W. Hamilton	typed John Galt
typed J.W. Hamilton	typed W.R. Allan

ISSUE DATING
Engraved
July 1st 1921.

Cat. No.	Denom.	Date	VG	F	VF	EF	Unc
20-02	$5	1921	275.	400.	750.	1,000.	-
20-02P	$5	1921			FACE PROOF		500.
20-04	$10	1921	150.	200.	300.	550.	-
20-04P	$10	1921			FACE PROOF		500.
20-06S	$20	1921				SPECIMEN	1,000.
20-06P	$20	1921			FACE PROOF		500.
20-08S	$50	1921				SPECIMEN	1,000.
20-08P	$50	1921			FACE PROOF		500.
20-10S	$100	1921				SPECIMEN	1,000.
20-10P	$100	1921			FACE PROOF		500.

THE UNION BANK OF HALIFAX

1856-1910

HALIFAX, NOVA SCOTIA

BANK NUMBER 735   **REDEEMABLE**

Established in Halifax, Nova Scotia, in 1856, negotiations regarding an amalgamation of this bank with the Merchants Bank of Halifax in 1882 came to nothing. The Union Bank took over the Commercial Bank of Windsor in 1902 and prospered. In 1910 the Union Bank was absorbed by the Royal Bank of Canada, thus expanding the representation of the Royal Bank in the Atlantic provinces and in the Caribbean.

735-10   POUNDS ISSUE, 1861
DESIGNS AND COLOURS

735-10-02
- **œ5 Face Design:** Shipping cargoes top and bottom/ two allegorical women; Queen Victoria (Chalon portrait) below/flowers
- **Colour:** Black with no tint

- **Back Design:** Lalthework, counters, bank name and Medallion engraved portraits of Victoria and Albert
- **Colour:** Red-brown

IMPRINT
Rawdon, Wright, Hatch & Edson, New-York

SIGNATURES
left	right
mss. W.S. Stirling	mss. J.A. Moren

ISSUE DATING
Partially engraved 1st September 18___:___
1861

PROTECTOR
Red "word" on face only

Cat. No.	Denom.	Date	VG	F	VF	EF	Unc
10-02	£5	1861	3,000.	4,500.	-	-	-

735-12   ISSUE OF 1870
DESIGNS AND COLOURS

735-12-02P
- **$4 Face Design:** —/ploughing scene; flower below/—
- **Colour:** Black with green tint

- **Back Design:** Lathework, counters and bank name
- **Colour:** Green

735-12-04P
- **$5 Face Design:** —/head office; flower below/—
- **Colour:** Black with green tint

- **Back Design:** Lathework, counters and bank name
- **Colour:** Green

IMPRINT
British American Bank Note Co. Montreal & Ottawa

SIGNATURES
left	right
none	none

ISSUE DATING
Engraved
June 1st, 1870

Cat. No.	Denom.	Date		Unc
12-02P	$4	1870	FACE PROOF	600.
12-04P	$5	1870	FACE PROOF	500.

THE UNION BANK OF HALIFAX

ISSUES OF 1871-1909

DESIGNS AND COLOURS

735-14-02P
    $4 Face Design: Steamship/—/
                      dog's head "My Dog" (after Landseer)
    Colour: Green 4 and panel outlining 4 FOUR 4

    Back Design: Lathework, counters and bank name
    Colour: Green

735-14-04P
    $5 Face Design: —/head office/—
    Colour: Green V — V

    Back Design: Lathework, counters, bank name and
                      fishermen "Cod Fishing"
    Colour: Green

735-14-09M
    $5 Face Design: Three sailing vessels and one propeller brig
                      in rough seas/—/Halifax crest (no imprint)
    Colour: Black with green wash tint

    Back Design: Plain

735-14-12P
    $10 Face Design: —/Royal Crest/—
    Colour: Green X TEN X

735-16-04P
    $10 Face Design: —/Royal Crest/—
    Colour: Black with ochre tint

    Back Design: Lathework, counters, bank name and
                      fishermen "Cod Fishing"
    Colour: Green

THE UNION BANK OF HALIFAX

735-14-14P
  $20 Face Design: Seated female on deck, ship "Exports"/ fishermen and ship "Union" "Cod Fishing"/ anchor, box, cask and ship
  Colour: Green XX — XX

735-16-06P
  $20 Face Design: Seated female on deck, ship "Exports"/ fishermen and ship "Union" "Cod Fishing"/ anchor, box, cask and ship
  Colour: Black with ochre tint

Back Design: Lathework, counters, bank name and boy, fish and dog on ship
Colour: Green

735-16-08P
  $50 Face Design: "Landing Trinidad"/ Indian and sailor with crest/—
  Colour: Black with overall blue tint

Back Design: Lathework, counters and bank name
Colour: Green

735-16-10P
  $100 Face Design: Fishermen and wife with baby looking out to sea "An Old Salt"/sailor "Young Tar"/—
  Colour: Black with overall brown tint

Back Design: Lathework, counters and bank name
Colour: Green

IMPRINT
British American Bank Note Co. Montreal & Ottawa
British American Bank Note Co. Ottawa

SIGNATURES
	left	right
1871:	none	none
1882:	mss. various	engr. James A. Moren
1886:	unknown	unknown
1900-1909:	mss. various	engr. Wm. Robertson

735-14 ISSUES OF 1871 - 1895
GREEN DENOMINATIONAL FACE TINT

ISSUE DATING
  Engraved
  1st July 1871
  July 1st 1871
  1st July, 1882
  May 1, 1886
  April 1st 1900

Note: These notes all have plate letter u.

Cat. No.	Denom.	Date	VG	F	VF	EF	Unc
14-02P	$4	1871				FACE PROOF	500.
14-04P	$5	1871				FACE PROOF	500.
14-06P	$5	1882				FACE PROOF	500.
14-08	$5	1886	2,500.	4,000.	-	-	-
14-09M	$5	1895				MODEL	2,000.
14-12P	$10	1871				FACE PROOF	500.
14-14P	$20	1871				FACE PROOF	500.

447

THE UNION BANK OF HALIFAX

735-16   ISSUES OF 1900-1909
GENERAL FACE TINTS

DESIGNS AND COLOURS
For designs see previous issues.

735-16-01

735-16-02
- **$5 Face Design:** —/Head office building (different view from earlier issues)/—lathework around inside border has differences.

FACE COLOURS
- **1900 $5:** Black with green V — V and panel
- **1909 $5:** Black with overall green tint
- **$10:** Black with overall ochre tint
- **$20:** Black with ochre tint
- **$50:** Black with overall blue tint
- **$100:** Black with overall brown tint

ISSUE DATING
    Engraved
April 1st 1900
Sept. 1st 1904
May 1st 1909

Cat. No.	Denom.	Date	VG	F	VF	EF	Unc
16-01	$5	1900			FACE PROOF		500.
16-02	$5	1909	2,500.	4,000.	-	-	-
16-04P	$10	1900	2,500.	4,000.	-	-	-
16-06P	$20	1900			FACE PROOF		600.
16-08P	$50	1904			FACE PROOF		500.
16-10P	$100	1904			FACE PROOF		600.

THE UNION BANK OF HALIFAX
PROPOSED BRITISH WEST INDIES ISSUE

735-18   DESIGNS FOR PORT OF SPAIN TRINIDAD, 1904

DESIGNS AND COLOURS

735-18-02P
- **$5 Face Design:** —/bank building/—
  - **Colour:** Black with green tint
- **Back Design:** lathework, counters, bank name and men fishing from end of ship "Cod Fishing"
  - **Colour:** Green

735-18-04P
- **$10 Face Design:** —/Royal Crest/—
  - **Colour:** Black with ochre tint
- **Back Design:** Lathework, counters, bank name and men fishing from end of ship "Cod Fishing"
  - **Colour:** Yellow-orange

735-18-06P
- **$20 Face Design:** woman with flag seated on bale "Exports"/men fishing from end of ship "Cod Fishing"/anchor, box and barrels
  - **Colour:** Black with modified blue tint
- **Back Design:** Lathework, counters, bank name and boy and dog looking over side of ship
  - **Colour:** Blue

735-18-08P
$50 Face Design: Dock and tower "Landing, Trinidad"/ Crest with Indian and sailor/—
Colour: Black with red-brown tint

Back Design: Lathework, counters and bank name
Colour: Red-brown

735-18-10P
$100 Face Design: Fishermen looking through telescope with wife and baby at side "Old Salt"/ sailor "Young Tar"/—
Colour: Black with overall red-brown tint

Back Design: Lathework, counters and bank name
Colour: Red

IMPRINT
British American Bank Note Co. Ottawa
British American Bank Note Co. Montreal and Ottawa

SIGNATURES
left	right
none	engr. Wm. Robertson

THE UNION BANK OF HALIFAX

ISSUE DATING
Engraved
Sept. 1st 1904.

OVERPRINT
"TRINIDAD" at ends and "PAYABLE AT PORT OF SPAIN, TRINIDAD" horizontally across the centre, all in red

Note: A $50 proof is known with a blue tint.

Cat. No.	Denom.	Date		Unc
18-02P	$5	1904	FACE PROOF	750.
18-04P	$10	1904	FACE PROOF	750.
18-06P	$20	1904	FACE PROOF	750.
18-08P	$50	1904	FACE PROOF	750.
18-10P	$100	1904	FACE PROOF	750.

THE UNION BANK OF LOWER CANADA

1865-1886

QUEBEC (CANADA EAST)

BANK NUMBER 740   *REDEEMABLE*

This bank commenced operations under a provincial charter in 1865. In 1872 it purchased the Quebec Provident and Savings Bank, and its name was changed to the Union Bank of Canada in 1886.

ISSUES OF 1866

DESIGNS AND COLOURS

740-10-02
- **$1 Face Design:** Andrew Thomson/Crest flanked by man with flag and Indian "Canadian Arms"/shipbuilder
- **Colour:** See subheadings 
- **Back Design:** Lathework and bank name
- **Colour:** Green

740-10-04
- **$2 Face Design:** Anchor/Crest flanked by man with flag and Indian "Canadian Arms"/Andrew Thomson
- **Colour:** See subheadings
- **Back Design:** Lathework and bank name
- **Colour:** Green

740-10-06
- **$4 Face Design:** Sailors on dock/Crest flanked by man with flag and Indian "Canadian Arms"/Andrew Thomson
- **Colour:** See subheadings
- **Back Design:** Lathework and bank name
- **Colour:** Green

740-10-08
- **$5 Face Design:** Andrew Thomson/Crest flanked by man with flag and Indian "Canadian Arms"/sailors on shore with telescope "Looking Out"
- **Colour:** See subheadings
- **Back Design:** Lathework and bank name
- **Colour:** Green

IMPRINT
American Bank Note Co. N.Y. & Montreal
American Bank Note Co. Montreal and N.Y. on some backs

SIGNATURES

left	right
none	mss. various

ISSUE DATING
Engraved
March 1st 1866

740-10   **ISSUES WITH GREEN "WORD AND NUMERAL" FACE TINT**

OVERPRINT
Large "S" twice in red
"OTTAWA" twice in blue
"MONTREAL" twice in blue

Cat. No.	Denom.	Date	VG	F	VF	EF	Unc
10-02	$1	1866	1,000.	1,400.	2,000.	-	-
10-04	$2	1866	2,200.	2,800.	-	-	-
10-06	$4	1866	2,200.	2,800.	-	-	-
10-08	$5	1866	2,200.	2,800.	-	-	-

THE UNION BANK OF LOWER CANADA

740-12   ISSUES WITH GREEN "WORD" PROTECTOR NO FACE TINT

740-12-02
- **$1 Face Design:** Andrew Thomson/Crest flanked by man with flag and Indian "Canadian Arms"/shipbuilder
- **Colour:** Black with no tint
- **Back Design:** Lathework and bank name
- **Colour:** Green

740-12-04
- **$2 Face Design:** Anchor/Crest flanked by man with flag and Indian "Canadian Arms"/Andrew Thomson
- **Colour:** Black with no tint
- **Back Design:** Lathework and bank name
- **Colour:** Green

PROTECTOR
Green "word" on face only

OVERPRINT
Large "S S" in red
Large "S S" in red and "THREE RIVERS" twice in blue

Cat. No.	Denom.	Date	VG	F	VF	EF	Unc
12-02	$1	1866	1,200.	1,700.	-	-	-
12-04	$2	1866	1,200.	1,700.	-	-	-

740-14   ISSUES OF 1870 AND 1871
DESIGNS AND COLOURS

740-14-02P
- **$4 Face Design:** Queen Victoria in widow's weeds/Bank Crest/sailors at dockside "Mech's & Commerce"
- **Colour:** Black with green tint

- **Back Design:** Lathework, counters and bank name
- **Colour:** Green

740-14-04P
- **$5 Face Design:** Sailors by broken mast with telescope "Coast Scene"/Bank Crest/female at sea being borne aloft by two porpoises
- **Colour:** Black with green tint

- **Back Design:** Lathework, counters and bank name
- **Colour:** Green

THE UNION BANK OF LOWER CANADA

740-14-06P
    $10 Face Design: Ships and female with flag "Exports"/ Crest/sailor climbing rigging "Going Aloft"
    Colour: Black with green tint

Back Design: Lathework, counters and bank name
Colour: Green

740-14-08P
    $20 Face Design: —/Crest/—
    Colour: Black with green tint

Back Design: Lathework, counters and bank name
Colour: Green

740-14-10P
    $50 Face Design: —/Crest/—
    Colour: Black wit green tint

Back Design: Lathework, counters and bank name
Colour: Green

740-14-12P
    $100 Face Design: —/Crest/—
    Colour: Black with green tint

Back Design: Lathework, counters and bank name
Colour: Green

IMPRINT
British American Bank Note Co. Montreal & Ottawa

SIGNATURES
left	right
none	mss. various

ISSUE DATING
Engraved
$4 and $20: Sept. 1st 1870
$5: August 1st 1871
$10: 1st Dec. 1871
$50 and $100: Sept. 1 1870

OVERPRINT
"MONTREAL" twice in red

Cat. No.	Denom.	Date	VG	F	VF	EF	Unc
14-02	$4	1870	1,450.	1,900.	-	-	-
14-04	$5	1871	1,400.	1,850.	-	-	-
14-06P	$10	1871			FACE PROOF		600.
14-08	$20	1870	1,450.	1,900.	-	-	-
14-10P	$50	1870			FACE PROOF		600.
14-12P	$100	1870			FACE PROOF		600.

THE UNION BANK OF MONTREAL

CA. 1840

MONTREAL, LOWER CANADA

BANK NUMBER 745   **NONREDEEMABLE**

Originally established in Montreal as the Union Bank, this bank operated for only a short period of time.

745-10   **ISSUE OF 1840**

DESIGNS AND COLOURS

745-10-02R
$50 Face Design: Kneeling woman with sickle/ships near harbour, flanked by medallion portraits; small crest below/farm boy reclining under sheaves
Colour: Black with no tint

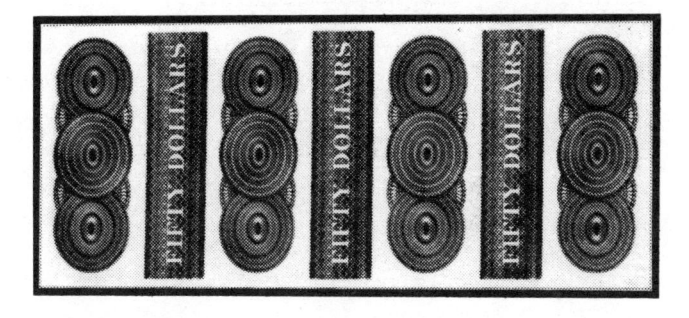

Back Design: Four lathework panels and three panels with "Fifty dollars" outlined in white
Colour: Blue

745-10-04
$100 (£25) Face Design: Seated woman with book/Indians watching steamboat, flanked by medallion portraits; small crest below/man with flag "Lord Byron"
Colour: Black with no tint

UNION BANK OF NEWFOUNDLAND

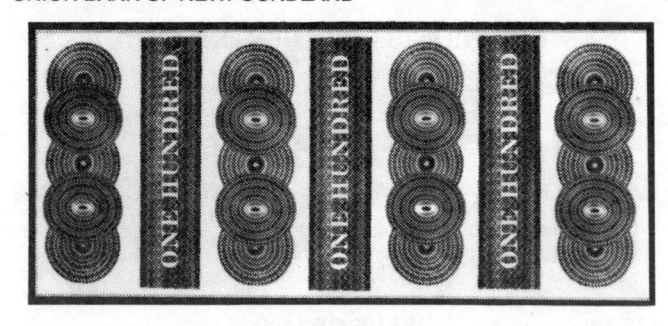

Back Design: Four lathework panels and three panels with "One hundred" outlined in white
Colour: Blue

IMPRINT
Danforth, Underwood & Co. New York
Underwood, Bald, Spencer & Hufty, Philada.

SIGNATURES
left	right
ms. Dudley Blinc	Monny Gray

ISSUE DATING
Partially engraved ___ 184__:
1840: January. 1

OVERPRINT
"G" in red at left

Cat. No.	Denom.	Date	Variety	VG	F	VF	EF	Unc
10-02R	$50	18_	Remainder*	-	-	-	450.	850.
10-02	$50	1840		450.	600.	900.	1,500.	-
10-04	$100 (£25)	1840		450.	600.	900.	1,500.	-

* Unsigned, undated and unnumbered.

UNION BANK OF NEWFOUNDLAND

1854-1894

ST. JOHN'S, NEWFOUNDLAND

BANK NUMBER 750   **REDEEMABLE**

Established in St. John's, Newfoundland, in 1854, this bank failed in 1894 due to disastrous economic conditions and a run on the bank caused by the failure of the Commercial Bank of Newfoundland in the same year. The Newfoundland government assumed the responsibility for redeeming the notes of the failed banks, and the notes of the Union Bank continue to be redeemable for 80 cents on the dollar.

750-10   **LARGE-SIZE POUND NOTES**
              1850s-EARLY 1860s

DESIGNS AND COLOURS

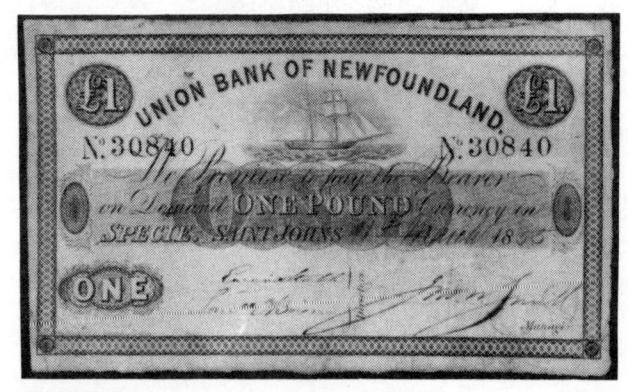

750-10-02
  £1 Face Design: —/sailing ship/—
  Colour: Black with no tint

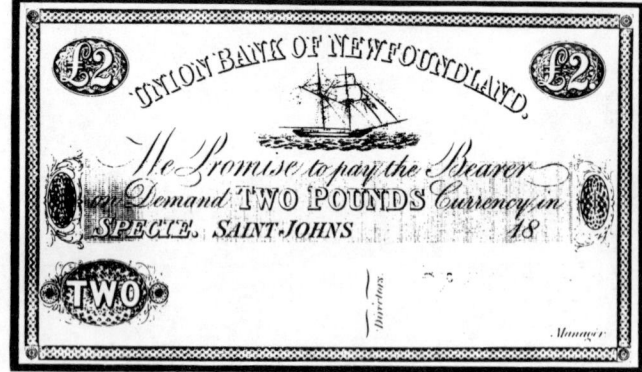

750-10-20
  £2 Face Design: —/sailing ship/—
  Colour: Black with no tint

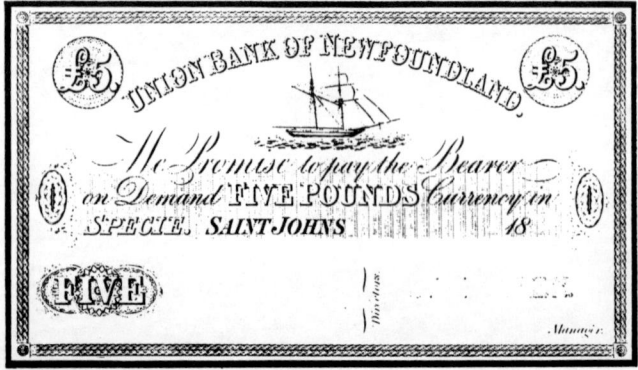

750-10-40
  $5 Face Design: —/sailing ship/—
  Colour: Black with no tint
  Back Design: Plain

UNION BANK OF NEWFOUNDLAND

750-10-60
- **$10 Face Design:** —/sailing ship/—
- **Colour:** Black with no tint
- **Back Design:** Plain

IMPRINT
Perkins, Bacon and Co. London

SIGNATURES

left	right
unknown and	
mss. Jno. W. Smith	mss. Rob't. Prowse
mss. Ewen Stable	
and Lawce O'Brein	mss. Rob't. Prowse

ISSUE DATING
Partially engraved ___ 18___:
- 1854: May 18
- 1855: 1st March

PROTECTOR
- 1854: Red "word" and mock coins on face and back
- 1855: Green "word" and mock coins on face and back

Cat. No.	Denom.	Date	VG	F	VF	EF	Unc
10-02	£1	1854	3,000.	4,000.	-	-	-
10-04	£1	1855	3,000.	4,000.	-	-	-
10-20	£2	18__				PROOF	500.
10-40	£5	18__				PROOF	500.
10-60	£10	18__				PROOF	500.

SMALL-SIZE POUND NOTES, 1865-1883

DESIGNS AND COLOURS

750-14-06
- **£1 Face Design:** Queen Victoria (Winterhalter portrait)/ sailing ship "Fishing Smack"/seal in oval
- **Colour:** Black with no tint
- **Back Design:** Plain

750-14-08
- **£5 Face Design:** Queen Victoria (Winterhalter portrait)/ sailing ship "Fishing Smack"/codfish in oval
- **Colour:** Brown
- **Back Design:** Plain

750-12-12
- **£10 Face Design:** Queen Victoria (Winterhalter portrait)/ sailing ship "Fishing Smack"/codfish in oval
- **Colour:** Blue
- **Back Design:** Plain

IMPRINT
American Bank Note Co. N.Y.
American Bank Note Co. New York

Note: Some £5 notes have a stamped guarantee of $16 and some £10 notes have $32 on the face.

UNION BANK OF NEWFOUNDLAND

750-12 ISSUES OF 1865-1881
PARTIALLY ENGRAVED DATE

SIGNATURES

	left	right
1865-1876:	mss. R. Greene	mss. John Smith
1881:	mss. C.S. Pinsent	mss. James Goldie

ISSUE DATING
Partially engraved ___ 18___:
- £1, 1865: May 1, 4 Oct.
- £5, 1875: 3 Oct.
- £5 and £10, 1865: 2 Oct.
- £5 and £10, 1876: 3 Apr.
- £5 and £10, 1881: 1 Oct.

PROTECTOR
- £1: Green "word" on face and on back in mirror image
- £5: Blue "word" on face and on back in mirror image
- £10: Red "word" on face and on back in mirror image.

Cat. No.	Denom.	Date	VG	F	VF	EF	Unc
12-02	£1	1865	1,200.	1,760.	2,400.	-	-
12-04	£5	1865	1,300.	1,800.	2,700.	-	-
12-05	£5	1875	1,300.	1,800.	2,700.	-	-
12-06	£5	1876	1,300.	1,800.	2,700.	-	-
12-08	£5	1881	1,300.	1,800.	2,700.	-	-
12-10	£10	1865	1,400.	2,100.	3,000.	-	-
12-12	£10	1876	1,400.	2,100.	3,000.	-	-
12-14	£10	1881	1,400.	2,100.	3,000.	-	-

750-14 ISSUES OF 1867-1883
FULLY ENGRAVED DATE

SIGNATURES

	left	right
1867-1880:	mss. C.S. Pinsent	mss. James Goldie
1867:	mss. R. Greene	mss. John Smith
1883:	engr. C.S. Pinsent	engr. James Goldie

ISSUE DATING
Engraved
- 1st March 1867
- 1st Septr 1877
- 1st May 1880
- 1st August 1883

PROTECTOR
- £1: Green "word" on face and back
- £5: Blue "word" on face and back

Cat. No.	Denom.	Date	VG	F	VF	EF	Unc
14-02	£1	1867	800.	1,200.	1,600.	-	-
14-04	£1	1877	800.	1,200.	1,600.	-	-
14-06	£1	1880	500.	700.	1,000.	1,700.	3,200.
14-08	£5	1883	1,000.	1,400.	2,200.	3,500.	-

750-16 DOLLAR ISSUES OF
1882 AND 1889

DESIGNS AND COLOURS

750-16-02
- **$2 Face Design:** Codfish/John W. Smith/dog and safe
- **Colour:** Black with overall green tint
- **Back Design:** Lathework, counters and bank name
- **Colour:** Green

750-16-04
- **$5 Face Design:** Sailing ship "Fishing Smack"/cherub/steamships and sailboats
- **Colour:** Black with green and yellow tint

- **Back Design:** —/cattle at pond/—
- **Colour:** Green

UNION BANK OF NEWFOUNDLAND

750-16-06
$10 Face Design: Newfoundland dog/sailing ship "Sealing"/ sailors hoisting sails "Show your colours"
Colour: Black with orange and yellow tint

Back Design: —/woman and strongbox/—
Colour: Orange

750-16-08
$20 Face Design: 20 counter over front of locomotive /locomotive; small locomotive below/ 20 counter over front of locomotive
Colour: Black with blue and yellow tint

Back Design: —/locomotive/—
Colour: Blue

750-16-10
$50 Face Design: "Justice" figure/bank building/ woman pouring water for sheep "Rebecca"
Colour: Black with brown and yellow tint

Back Design: —/dog by safe (after Landseer)/—
Colour: Brown

IMPRINT
American Bank Note Co. New York

SIGNATURES
left	right
engr. C.S. Pincent	engr. James Goldie

ISSUE DATING
Engraved
1st May 1882
May 1st 1889

Cat. No.	Denom.	Date	VG	F	VF	EF	Unc
16-02	$2	1882	250.	350.	525.	900.	1,800.
16-04	$5	1889	600.	840.	1,260.	2,140.	5,300.
16-06	$10	1889	400.	560.	840.	1,430.	2,850.
16-08	$20	1889	600.	840.	1,260.	2,140.	5,300.
16-10	$50	1889	1,200.	1,700.	2,500.	4,300.	8,550.

THE UNION BANK OF
PRINCE EDWARD ISLAND

1860-1883

CHARLOTTETOWN (PRINCE EDWARD ISLAND)

BANK NUMBER 755 **REDEEMABLE**

Established in Charlottetown, Prince Edward Island, in 1860, this prosperous bank played an important role in bringing the island into Confederation. However, industrial depression and slow liquidation of lumber and shipping forced it to merge with a stronger institution, and on May 25, 1883, an act providing for the absorption of the bank by the Bank of Nova Scotia received royal assent. This enabled the Bank of Nova Scotia to issue, until July 1, 1891, notes in excess of the paid-up capital to the extent of twice the paid-up capital of the Union Bank. The amalgamation became final on October 1, 1883, and that year $130,000 was written off the reserve fund of the Bank of Nova Scotia to cover the losses.

ISSUES OF 1864-1872

DESIGNS AND COLOURS

755-10-02P
$1 (4s 2d) Face Design: Sailors on dock/lion and shield/woman, sheep and sheaves "Agriculture"
See subheadings
Colour: Black with no tint
Back Design: Plain

755-10-04P
$2 (8s 4d) Face Design: Two children with sheaves/Royal Arms, cask and bales below/sailor by capstan "On Deck"
See subheadings
Colour: Black with no tint
Back Design: Plain

755-10-06
$5 (20s 10d) Face Design: St. George slaying the dragon/milkmaid seated in pasture with two cows/steamship and tugboat
See subheadings
Colour: Black with no tint
Back Design: Plain

755-10-08
$20 (£4.3.4) Face Design: Princess of Wales/modified P.E.I. Crest, St. George slaying the dragon below/Prince of Wales
See subheadings
Colour: Black with no tint
Back Design: Plain

IMPRINT
American Bank Note Co. N.Y. & Boston

755-10 **ISSUE OF 1864-1865**
DOLLARS AND STERLING

SIGNATURES
left	right
mss. Jas. Anderson	mss. Chs. Palmer

ISSUE DATING
Partially engraved ___ 18___:
1864: 1 June
1865: Jan. 2

PROTECTOR
Green "word" on face and back
Green "two dollars" on face and back in mirror image
Green "5 FIVE 5" on face and back
Green "TWENTY" on face and back

Cat. No.	Denom.	Date	VG	F	VF	EF	Unc
10-02P	$1 (4s 2d)	185_		FACE PROOF			500.
10-04	$2 (8s 4d)	1864	2,500.	3,500.	-	-	
10-06	$5 (20s 10d)	1865	2,500.	3,500.	-	-	
10-08	$20 (£4.3.4))	185_	3,500.	5,000.	-	-	

755-12 **ISSUE OF 1872**
              DOLLAR ONLY

755-12-02a
    $1 Face Design: Sailors on dock/lion and shield/
        woman, sheep and sheaves "Agriculture"
        See subheadings
    Colour: Black with no tint
    Back Design: Plain

755-12-04
    $2 Face Design: Two children with sheaves/Royal Arms/
        sailor by capstan "On Deck"
        See subheadings
    Colour: Black with no tint
    Back Design: Plain

Photo Not Available

755-12-06P
    $5 Face Design: St. George slaying the dragon/milkmaid
        seated in pasture with two cows/steamship
        and tugboat
        See subheadings
    Colour: Black with no tint
    Back Design: Plain

THE UNION BANK OF PRINCE EDWARD ISLAND

755-12-08P
    $20 Face Design: Princess of Wales/modified P.E.I. Crest,
        St. George slaying the dragon below/
        Prince of Wales
        See subheadings
    Colour: Black with no tint
    Back Design: Plain

IMPRINT
American Bank Note Co. N.Y. and Boston

SIGNATURES

left	right
mss. Jas. Anderson	mss. Chs. Palmer
mss. Wm. Heard	mss. Chs. Palmer
mss. John H. Yeo (p)	mss. Chs. Palmer
mss. Geo. MacLeod	mss. John Ings (v)

ISSUE DATING
    Engraved
    1st January 1872

PROTECTOR
    Green "word" on face and in mirror image on the back

OVERPRINT
    $1: "CANADA CURRENCY" twice vertically in red near the ends

Cat. No.	Denom.	Date	Variety	VG	F	VF	EF	Unc
12-02	$1	1872	No o/p	2,000.	2,600.	-	-	-
12-02a	$1	1872	Red o/p	2,000.	2,600.	-	-	-
12-04	$2	1872		2,000.	2,600.	-	-	-
12-06P	$5	1872				FACE PROOF		500.
12-08	$20	1872		2,500.	3,300.	-	-	-

Note: Beware of $2 counterfeit notes.

755-14 **BABN PRINTINGS**
              1875 AND 1877

DESIGNS AND COLOURS

755-14-02
    $1 Face Design: Two codfish in oval/locomotive/
        two seals in oval
    Colour: Black with green tint

THE UNION BANK OF PRINCE EDWARD ISLAND

Back Design: Lathework, counters and bank name
Colour: Green

755-14-04P
$2 Face Design: River pilot at wheel "Lachine Pilot"/
Landseer's Newfoundland on strongbox
"Dog Trusty"/woman with sheaf of wheat
Colour: Black with green tint

Back Design: Lathework, counters and bank name
Colour: Green

755-14-08P
$5 Face Design: St. George slaying the dragon/
farm implements and produce
"Implements of Agriculture"/
woman with telescope over ornate 5
Colour: Black with green tint

Back Design: Lathework, counters and bank name
Colour: Green

Note: The face tint includes "Canada Currency" twice vertically in green on each note.

IMPRINT
British American Bank Note Co. Montreal

SIGNATURES
left	right
mss. John H. Yeo (p)	mss. John Ings (v)
mss. Geo. MacLeod	mss. Chs. Palmer
mss. John H. Yeo (p)	mss. Chs. Palmer

ISSUE DATING
Engraved
March 1st 1875
Unknown 1877

OVERPRINT
"U" near upper left corner, and "B" at the upper right corner

Cat. No.	Denom.	Date	VG	F	VF	EF	Unc
14-02	$1	1875	1,500.	2,000.	-	-	-
14-04	$2	1875	2,000.	3,000.	-	-	-
14-06	$2	1877	2,000.	3,000.	-	-	-
14-08	$5	1875	2,000.	3,000.	-	-	-
14-10P	$5	1877			FACE PROOF		600.

Note: Beware of counterfeit $2 notes.

UNITED EMPIRE BANK OF CANADA

1906-1911

TORONTO, ONTARIO

BANK NUMBER 760   **REDEEMABLE**

Established in Toronto in 1906 under the name of the Pacific Bank of Canada, it changed its name to the United Empire Bank of Canada later that year and merged with the Union Bank of Canada in 1911. It was a small bank, its growth had been slow and the institution had not held its own with its competitors.

760-10   ISSUE OF 1906

DESIGNS AND COLOURS

760-10-02
$5 Face Design: —/seated Britannia flanked by two world globes/—
Colour: Black with green tint

Back Design: Lathework, counters and bank name
Colour: Green

760-10-04
$10 Face Design: Seated "Justice" figure/—/—
Colour: Black with yellow-green tint

Back Design: Lathework, counters, bank name and beavers
Colour: Blue

IMPRINT
American Bank Note Company, Ottawa

SIGNATURES
left	right
mss. various	typed Saml. Barker

ISSUE DATING
Engraved
1st August, 1906

Cat. No.	Denom.	Date	VG	F	VF	EF	Unc
10-02	$5	1906	4,500.	6,500.	-	-	-
10-04	$10	1906	4,500.	6,500.	-	-	-

BANK OF UPPER CANADA

BANK OF UPPER CANADA

1819 - 1822

KINGSTON, UPPER CANADA

BANK NUMBER 765 **NONREDEEMABLE**

The residents of Kingston, Upper Canada, were the first applicants to apply to the legislature for a charter in the name of the Bank of Upper Canada. Impatient at the delay in receiving royal assent, they began operations without a charter on April 16, 1819. The private bank had a paid-up capital of £12,000 and issued almost £19,000 in notes. It was intended that it be merged with the Bank of Kingston, which received the substitute charter for the Kingston petition; however, bad times followed. The Bank of Kingston never came into existence, and the private Bank of Upper Canada failed on September 23, 1822.

REGULAR NOTE ISSUES, 1819-1822
DESIGNS AND COLOURS

765-10-02
 $1 Face Design: —/steamboat, sheaf and plough, ONE vertically; coin below/—
 Colour: Black with no tint
 Back Design: Plain

765-10-04
 $2 Face Design: —/TWO, seated "Justice" figure and barrels; two coins below/—
 Colour: Black with no tint
 Back Design: Plain

765-10-06
 $5 Face Design: —/fort, harbour area; five coins below/—
 Colour: Black with no tint
 Back Design: Plain

765-10-16
 $10 Face Design: —/fort and Kingston harbour; X over flowers below/—
 Colour: Black with no tint
 Back Design: Plain

IMPRINT
Graphic company

765-10 **REGULAR NOTE ISSUE**
PARTIALLY ENGRAVED DATE 1819 - 1822

SIGNATURES
left	right
mss. S. Bartlett	mss. B. Whitney
mss. S. Bartlett	mss. Henry Murney (v)

ISSUE DATING
 Partially engraved ___ 18___:
 $1 and $2, 1819: May 1, 1 May
 $1 and $5, 1819: 29 March, 1 May
   1822: Apr. 4, May 1, June 3
 $10, 1819: 4 Apr., 1 May
   1822: June 3

OVERPRINT
"Payable at the Bank of Canada in Montreal" in black on some notes.

Cat. No.	Denom.	Date	VG	F	VF	EF	Unc
10-02	$1	1819	110.	150.	225.	-	-
10-02R	$1	18__	-	-	100.	150.	-
10-04	$2	1819	110.	150.	225.	-	-
10-04R	$2	18__	-	-	100.	150.	-
10-06	$5	1819	100.	125.	200.	300.	-
10-06R	$5	18__	-	-	100.	150.	-
10-14	$5	1822	100.	125.	200.	300.	-
10-16	$10	1819	100.	125.	200.	300.	-
10-16R	$10	18__	-	-	100.	150.	-
10-22	$10	1822	100.	125.	200.	300.	-

765-12 REGULAR NOTE ISSUE
FULLY ENGRAVED DATE 1820

DESIGNS AND COLOURS

765-12-02
- **$1 Face Design:** —/steamboat, sheaf and plough and ONE vertically; coin below/—
- **Colour:** Black with no tint
- **Back Design:** Plain

765-12-04
- **$2 Face Design:** —/Numeral 2, seated "Justice" figure and barrels; two coins below/-
- **Colour:** Black with no tint
- **Back Design:** Plain

765-12-06
- **$3 Face Design:** —/sailing ship, lion, Britannia, numeral 3, three coins below/—
- **Colour:** Black with no tint
- **Back Design:** Plain

IMPRINT
Graphic Company

Note: The vignettes and counters are slightly different from the 765-10 issue.

SIGNATURES

left	right
mss. S. Bartlett	mss. Henry Murney (v)
mss. S. Bartlett	mss. B. Whitney

ISSUE DATING
Engraved
Jan. 1 1820

OVERPRINT
"Payable at the Bank of Canada in Montreal" in black on some notes

Note: Counterfeits (photocopies) of $1, $2 and $3 notes have been seen.

Cat. No.	Denom.	Date	VG	F	VF	EF	Unc
12-02	$1	1820	50.	70.	105.	180.	350.
12-04	$2	1820	50.	70.	105.	180.	350.
12-06	$3	1820	75.	100.	125.	200.	375.

765-14 SCRIP ISSUE OF 1820

DESIGNS AND COLOURS

765-14-02
- **6d Face Design:** Seated Britannia/—/— Marked "For Public Accommodation"
- **Colour:** Black with no tint
- **Back Design:** Plain

IMPRINT
None

SIGNATURES

right only
illegible

ISSUE DATING
Letterpress
August 23, 1820

Cat. No.	Denom.	Date	VG	F	VF	EF	Unc
14-02	6d	1820	1,260.	1,600.	-	-	-

THE BANK OF UPPER CANADA

THE BANK OF UPPER CANADA

1821-1866

YORK, UPPER CANADA

BANK NUMBER 770   **NONREDEEMABLE**

This bank was established in York, Upper Canada (now Toronto, Ontario), its charter granted by the Province of Upper Canada in 1819, becoming law on April 21, 1821. The charter was to remain in force until June 1, 1848.

The charter of this bank was different from those of other banks in operation in a few essential respects:

1. The Government of Upper Canada was authorized to subscribe for 2,000 out of 16,000 (later 8,000) shares, which were £12.10 each;
2. The bank was given express authority to establish branches;
3. No limit was placed on the value of real estate that the bank could hold to carry on its business;
4. If the bank refused payment of its notes in specie, it was obliged to cease operations until specie payment was resumed, or forfeit its charter;
5. An annual return, properly sworn, was to be made to the provincial legislature.

Soon after its establishment, the bank was accused of using its power in politics; nonetheless, it had grown steadily and was held in high esteem. It was banker to the government for a number of years. However, it made too many loans secured by real estate, and as a consequence, found itself in difficulties for several years, despite efforts to rehabilitate its affairs.

It failed in 1866 and was the first important bank failure in Canadian history. The insolvency was mainly a result of the land boom in Upper Canada between 1857 and 1858 and the depression that followed. Bank management did not observe sound banking principles, particularly with respect to real-estate loans. When real-estate values declined, the bank was left with many unrealizable assets. The shareholders lost all their capital, which at one time amounted to about $3.3 million. The government lost about $1 million, and the depositors and note holders also suffered heavily.

770-10   **GRAPHIC PRINTINGS**
                                  1826-1832

DESIGNS AND COLOURS

770-10-10
   $1 (5s) Face Design: —/seated Britannia with beehive and ship; one dollar over numeral 1 below/—
           Colour: Black with no tint
   Back Design: Plain

770-10-20
   $2 (10s) Face Design: —/harbour scene and 2 outlined in white; two coins below/—
           Colour: Black with no tint
   Back Design: Plain

770-10-32
   $4 (20s) Face Design: —/St. George slaying the dragon; four coins below/—
           Colour: Black with no tint
   Back Design: Plain

770-10-40
   $5 (25s) Face Design: —/view of York; 5 outlined in bushes below/—
           Colour: Black with no tint
   Back Design: Plain

770-10-76
$10 (50s) Face Design: —/harbour scene; X outlined in bushes below/—
　　　　Colour: Black with no tint
　　Back Design: Plain

IMPRINT
　　Graphic Co.

SIGNATURES
　　left　　　　　　　　　　　　right
　　mss. Thos. G. Ridout　　mss. W. Allan

ISSUE DATING
　　Partially engraved ___ 18___ :
　　$1 (5s), 1829: Mar. 7
　　　　　　　1831: 19 March
　　$2 (10s), 1827: Aug. 3
　　$4 (20s), 1830: 3 Novr.
　　　　　　　1832: 2 Novr.
　　$5 (25s), 1826: 2 Augt.
　　　　　　　1827: 3 Jan.
　　　　　　　1830: 1 Jan., 2d Jan.
　　　　　　　1832: 19 Sept.
　　$10 (50s), 1830: 1 Nov.

VARIETIES
　　$5 (25s): Five Dollars - cinq piastres above counters at top
　　　　　　Five Dollars - cinq piastres below counters at top

Cat. No.	Denom.	Date	Variety	VG	F	VF	EF	Unc
10-10	$1 (5s)	1829		400.	525.	800.	-	-
10-14	$1 (5s)	1831		400.	525.	800.	-	-
10-20	$2 (10s)	1827		450.	600.	950.	-	-
10-32	$4 (20s)	1830		550.	780.	1,150.	-	-
10-36	$5 (25s)	1832		550.	780.	1,150.	-	-
10-40	$5 (25s)	1826	$5 above	400.	550.	800.	-	-
10-42	$5 (25s)	1827	$5 above	400.	550.	800.	-	-
10-48	$5 (25s)	1830	$5 above	400.	550.	800.	-	-
10-52	$5 (25s)	1832	$5 above	450.	650.	950.	-	-
10-64	$5 (25s)	1832	$5 below	450.	650.	950.	-	-
10-76	$10 (50s)	1830		550.	750.	1,150.	-	-

770-12　　ISSUE OF THE 1830s
　　　　　　PAYABLE AT TORONTO
DESIGNS AND COLOURS

770-12-02P
　　$1 Face Design: Seated "Justice" figure/
　　　　　　　　　　Neptune, flying female and horses;
　　　　　　　　　　bust of Indian in oval below/—
　　　　Colour: Black with no tint
　　Back Design: Plain

770-12-08
$2 Face Design:　　Allegorical female and anchor/
　　　　　　　　　　Indian shooting arrow; buffalo below/
　　　　　　　　　　allegorical female in clouds
Colour:　　　　　　Black with no tint
Back Design:　　　Plain

770-12-14
　　$4 Face Design: Indian "Red Jacket"/Royal Crest;
　　　　　　　　　　steamboat below/Sir Walter Raleigh
　　　　Colour: Black with no tint
　　Back Design: Plain

THE BANK OF UPPER CANADA

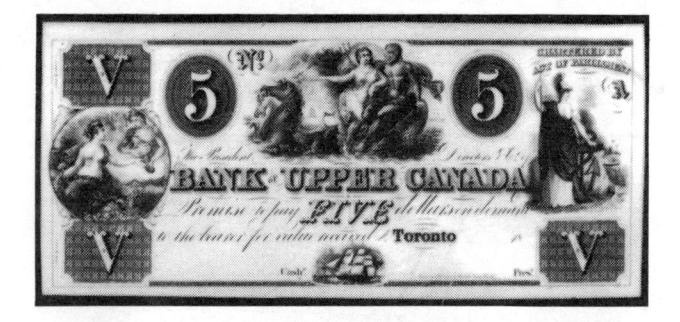

THE BANK OF UPPER CANADA

770-12-18P
    $5 Face Design: Three allegorical figures/Neptune and woman (Commerce) on shell drawn by seahorses; sailing ships below/Britannia, anchor and ship
    Colour: Black with no tint
    Back Design: Plain

770-12-30
    $10 Face Design: Two allegorical females/Neptune and woman (Commerce) on shell drawn by seahorses; sailing ships below/cherub with fruit basket on head in oval
    Colour: Black with no tint
    Back Design: Plain

770-12-32P
    $20 Face Design: —/griffin and three allegorical figures; griffin with key below/obelisk
    Colour: Black with no tint
    Back Design: Plain

770-12-34P
    $20 Face Design: —/griffin and three allegorical figures; griffin with key below/Toronto at right
    Colour: Black with no tint
    Back Design: Plain

770-12-38P
    $50 Face Design: Cherub with fruit basket on head in oval/train and wagons at wharf; griffin with key below/obelisk
    Colour: Black with no tint
    Back Design: Plain

770-12-46P
    $100 Face Design: —/Royal Crest; griffin with key below/obelisk
    Colour: Black with no tint
    Back Design: Plain

THE BANK OF UPPER CANADA

IMPRINT
Rawdon, Wright & Hatch New York or Rawdon, Wright, Hatch & Edson, New York

SIGNATURES
left	right
mss. T.G. Ridout	mss. Wm. Proudfoot

ISSUE DATING
Partially engraved _ 18_:
- 1836: 6 Nov.
- 1837: May 3
- 1838: 1 Jan'y., 10 Jan'y, 5 June

Cat. No.	Denom.	Date		VG	F	VF	EF	Unc
12-02P	$1	18_				PROOF		400.
12-08	$2	1836		650.	850.	1,200.	-	-
12-14	$4	1837		650.	850.	1,200.	-	-
12-18P	$5	18_				PROOF		400.
12-30	$10	1838		650.	850.	1,200.	-	-
12-32P	$20	18_	Toronto l.			PROOF		400.
12-34P	$20	18_	Toronto r.			PROOF		400.
12-38P	$50	18_	Toronto l.			PROOF		400.
12-40p	$50	18_	Toronto r			PROOF		400.
12-46P	$100	18_				PROOF		400.

770-14 ISSUES OF 1849-1856 TORONTO RED PROTECTOR

These issues are engraved "TORONTO" at the bottom centre.

DESIGNS AND COLOURS
All notes have a small image of St. George slaying the dragon at the bottom centre, encircled by "BANK OF U CANADA."

770-14-02
$1 (5s) **Face Design:** Reclining lion in oval (part of Royal Crest)/ seated "Commerce" figure with hand on ornate 1/woman, dog and 1 in oval
Colour: Black with no tint
Back Design: Plain

770-14-20P
$2 (10s) **Face Design:** "Agriculture" figure/two flying griffins flanking 2/portrait of woman
Colour: Black with no tint
Back Design: Plain

770-14-34
$4 (£1) **Face Design:** Queen Victoria (Chalon portrait) in oval/ seated Britannia, lion, cannon and flags/seated "Agricultural Commerce" figure in oval
Colour: Black with no tint
Back Design: Plain

770-14-46
$5 (£1.5) **Face Design:** Queen Victoria (Chalon portrait) in oval/ lion and shield/Prince Consort in oval
Colour: Black with no tint
Back Design: Plain

770-14-62P
$10 (£2.10) **Face Design:** Young woman with wheat stalks/ seated woman with sheaf and harp/ Britannia
Colour: Black with no tint
Back Design: Plain

THE BANK OF UPPER CANADA

770-14-78P
$20 (£5) **Face Design:** Griffin in oval/seated Mercury and woman with caduceus, coins key and sheaf/ Britannia in oval
Colour: Black with no tint
Back Design: Plain

770-14-96P
$50 (£12.10) **Face Design:** Seated "Agriculture" figure/ seated woman with cornucopia and coins on Royal Crest/seated Britannia
Colour: Black with no tint
Back Design: Plain

770-14-104P
$100 (£25) **Face Design:** Queen Victoria (Chalon portrait) in oval/ Queen Victoria (Chalon portrait) in oval on Royal Crest/medallion portrait of helmeted man in oval
Colour: Black with no tint
Back Design: Plain

IMPRINT
Rawdon, Wright & Hatch, New-York

SIGNATURES
left	right
mss. Thos. G. Ridout	mss. Wm. Proudfoot
mss. C.S. Murray	mss. Wm. Proudfoot

ISSUE DATING
Partially engraved ___ 18___ :
$1 (5s) 1849: Sept. 1
$1 (5s) 1855: 4 Sept.
$4 (£1) 1851: 1 Nov.
1852: 5 Aug.
1856: 7 Nov.
$5 (£1.5) 1849: 9 Oct.

PROTECTOR
Issued notes have red "word" on face and back

Cat. No.	Denom.	Date	VG	F	VF	EF	Unc
14-02	$1 (5s)	1849	700.	900.	1,300.	-	-
14-08	$1 (5s)	1855	700.	900.	1,300.	-	-
14-02P	$2 (10s)	18_				PROOF	400.
14-34	$4 (£1)	1851	600.	850.	1,100.	-	-
14-36	$4 (£1)	1852	600.	850.	1,100.	-	-
14-44	$4 (£1)	1856	600.	850.	1,100.	-	-
14-46	$5 (£1.5)	1849	700.	900.	1,300.	-	-
14-62	$10 (£2.10)	18_	700.	900.	1,300.		
14-78P	$20 (£5)	18_				PROOF	400.
14-96P	$50 (£12.10)	18_				PROOF	400.
14-104P	$100 (£25)	18_				PROOF	400.

770-16   **ISSUES OF 1857**
RED PROTECTOR

2.   **MONTREAL ISSUE, 1857**

"Montreal" is engraved at the lower right of these issues, and "OFFICE OF THE BANK OF UPPER CANADA IN MONTREAL" is engraved across the top.

DESIGNS AND COLOURS

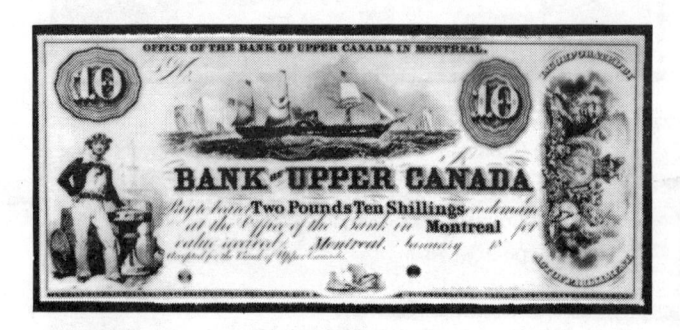

770-16-02-02P
$10 (£2.10) **Face Design:** Sailor with capstan, kegs and bale/ paddlewheel steamship; kegs, bale and anchor below/Royal Crest (sideways)
(check letter A notes)
Colour: Black with no tint
Back Design: Plain

Photo Not Available

770-16-02-04P
$10 (£2.10) **Face Design:** Sailing ships/seated sailor with bale and kegs; bale and kegs below/Royal Crest (sideways) (check letter B notes)
Colour: Black with no tint
Back Design: Plain

THE BANK OF UPPER CANADA

IMPRINT
Rawdon, Wright, Hatch & Edson, New York

SIGNATURES
left	right
none	none

ISSUE DATING
Partially engraved January ___ 18___:

Cat. No.	Denom.	Date	Variety				Unc
16-02-02P	$10 (£2.10)	18_	Steamship			PROOF	450.
16-02-04P	$10 (£2.10)	18_	Seated sailor			PROOF	450.

4. QUEBEC ISSUE, 1857

"Quebec" is engraved at the lower right of these notes, and "OFFICE OF THE BANK OF UPPER CANADA IN QUEBEC" is across the top.

DESIGNS AND COLOURS

770-16-04-02P
- **$10 (£2.10) Face Design:** Sailor with capstan, kegs and bale/ paddlewheel steamship; kegs, bale and anchor below/Royal Crest (sideways) (check letter A notes)
- **Colour:** Black with no tint
- **Back Design:** Plain

770-16-04-04
- **$10 (£2.10) Face Design:** Sailing ships/seated sailor with bale and kegs; bale and kegs below/Royal Crest (sideways) (check letter B notes)
- **Colour:** Black with no tint
- **Back Design:** Plain

IMPRINT
Rawdon, Wright, Hatch & Edson, New York

SIGNATURES
left	right
mss. illegible	mss. F. Boyd
none	none

ISSUE DATING
Partially engraved January ___ 18___ : January ___ 185___ :
1857: January 7

Cat. No.	Denom.	Date	Variety	VG	F	VF	EF	Unc
16-04-02P	$10 (£2.10)	185_	Steamship				PROOF	450.
16-04-04	$10 (£2.10)	185_	Seated sailor	700.	900.	1,300.	-	-

770-18 ISSUES OF 1851-1857
BLUE PROTECTOR

DESIGNS AND COLOURS
All notes have a small image of St. George slaying the dragon at the bottom centre, without the encircling bank name.

770-18-08-06
- **$1 (5s) Face Design:** Crest and Indian/train/ seated Indian woman and shield
- **Colour:** Black with no tint
- **Back Design:** Plain

770-18-06-04P
- **$2 (10s) Face Design:** Train/men on horseback herding livestock/cows being milked
- **Colour:** Black with no tint
- **Back Design:** Plain

THE BANK OF UPPER CANADA

770-18-06-06P
$5 (£1.5) Face Design: Running horse/Queen Victoria (Chalon portrait) in oval on Royal Crest/dog and strongbox
Colour: Black with no tint

Back Design: Plain

IMPRINT
Toppan, Carpenter, Casilear & Co. New York and Phila

2. BROCKVILLE ISSUE, 1851

"BROCKVILLE" is engraved at the lower right of this issue.

SIGNATURES
left	right
mss. R.J. Church	mss. Wm. Proudfoot

ISSUE DATING
Partially engraved January ___ 185___:
1851: January 9

PROTECTOR
Blue "word" on face only

Cat. No.	Denom.	Date	VG	F	VF	EF	Unc
18-02-02	$2 (10s)	1851	500.	750.	900.	-	-

4. KINGSTON ISSUE, 1851

This issue has "KINGSTON, C.W." engraved at the lower right.

SIGNATURES
left	right
mss. various	mss. J.G. Chewett

ISSUE DATING
Partially engraved January ___ 185___:
1851: January. 6

PROTECTOR
Blue "word" on face only

Cat. No.	Denom.	Date	VG	F	VF	EF	Unc
18-04-02	$1 (5s)	1851	600.	900.	1,300.	-	-

6. MONTREAL ISSUE, 1851

"MONTREAL" is engraved at the lower right of these notes.

SIGNATURES
left	right
mss. various	mss. J.G. Chewett

ISSUE DATING
Partially engraved January ___ 185___:
1851: January. 2

PROTECTOR
Blue "word" on face only

Cat. No.	Denom.	Date	VG	F	VF	EF	Unc
18-06-02	$1 (5s)	1851	600.	900.	1,300.	-	-
18-06-04P	$2 (10s)	185_				PROOF	400.
18-06-06P	$5 (£1.5)	185_				PROOF	400.

8. QUEBEC ISSUE, 1852-1857

"QUEBEC" is engraved at the lower right of this issue, and "OFFICE OF THE BANK OF UPPER CANADA IN QUEBEC" or "OFFICE IN QUEBEC" is across the top.

SIGNATURES
left	right
mss. C.S. Murray	mss. F. Boyd
mss. various	mss. J.G. Chewett

ISSUE DATING
Partially engraved _ 185_:
- **$1 (5s) 1853:** 1 Jany.
- **$1 (5s) 1854:** May 2, 3 May, 4 May
- **1856:** Augt., 12 Augt.
- **1857:** 18 May
- **$2 (10s) 1852:** 5 May
- **1853:** June 9, 9 Aout.
- **1854:** May 5
- **1856:** Nov. 7
- **$5 (£1.5) 1857:** 9 May

PROTECTOR
Blue "word" on face only

Cat. No.	Denom.	Date	VG	F	VF	EF	Unc
18-08-04	$1 (5s)	1853	550.	800.	1,100.	-	-
18-08-06	$1 (5s)	1854	550.	800.	1,100.	-	-
18-08-10	$1 (5s)	1856	550.	800.	1,100.	-	-
18-08-12	$1 (5s)	1857	550.	800.	1,100.	-	-
18-08-14	$2 (10s)	1852	550.	800.	1,100.	-	-
18-08-16	$2 (10s)	1853	550.	800.	1,100.	-	-
18-08-18	$2 (10s)	1854	550.	800.	1,100.	-	-
18-08-22	$2 (10s)	1856	550.	800.	1,100.	-	-
18-08-36	$5 (£1.5)	1857	600.	950.	1,250.	-	-

THE BANK OF UPPER CANADA

770-20 **$10 TORONTO BRANCH ISSUE**
LATE 1850s

DESIGNS AND COLOURS

770-20-02P
    $10 (£2.10) Face Design: Portrait of young girl with ringlets "Jessie"/
seated "Commerce" figure and Britannia/
cattle being driven under bridge
         Colour: See varieties

         Back Design: Unknown

IMPRINT
Rawdon, Wright, Hatch & Edson, New York

SIGNATURES
left	right
none	none

ISSUE DATING
    Partially engraved ___ 18___:

VARIETIES
    Face Colour: Black with overall brown-orange tint
    Face Colour: Black with overall green tint

Cat. No.	Denom.	Date	Variety		Unc
20-02P	$10 (£2.10)	18_	Overall brown-orange tint	PROOF	500.
20-04P	$10 (£2.10)	18_	Overall green tint	PROOF	500.

770-22 **GREEN ISSUES OF**
1859 AND 1861

DESIGNS AND COLOURS

770-22-02-02
    $1 Face Design: Seated "Justice" figure/
St. George slaying the dragon/
seated Britannia with Crest of Upper Canada
         Colour: Black with overall green tint

    Back Design: Lathework and counters
         Colour: Green

770-22-02-04P
    $2 Face Design: Portrait of Queen Victoria as a young girl/
sailor reclining on shore by anchor/
seated Britannia with Crest of Upper Canada
         Colour: Black with overall green tint

    Back Design: Lathework and counters
         Colour: Green

770-22-06-06P
    $4 Face Design: Young woman with cornucopia "Autumn"
/two women and Crest/seated blacksmith
         Colour: Black with overall green tint

    Back Design: Lathework and counters
         Colour: Green

770-22-06-08
    $5 Face Design: Sailor leaning on capstan, bale and
barrel/two women and Crest/
Albert, Prince of Wales in oval
         Colour: Black with overall green tint

    Back Design: Lathework and counters
         Colour: Green

THE BANK OF UPPER CANADA

770-22-08-10
 $10 Face Design: Portrait of Queen Victoria as a young girl/ two women and crest/seated Britannia with crest of Upper Canada
 Colour: Black with overall green tint

770-22-10-10
 Back Design: Lathework and counters
 Colour: Green

770-22-02-10
 $20 Face Design: —/"Justice" figure and Britannia flanking Crest of Upper Canada/ stonemason at work
 Colour: Black with overall green tint

 Back Design: Lathework and counters
 Colour: Green

770-22-04-14P
 $50 Face Design: Agricultural implements/ "Justice" figure and Britannia flanking Crest of Upper Canada/ woman with sickle and sheaf in oval
 Colour: Black with overall green tint

 Back Design: Lathework and counters
 Colour: Green

770-22-04-16P
 $100 Face Design: —/"Justice" figure and Britannia flanking Crest of Upper Canada/seated woman leaning on bale
 Colour: Black with overall green tint

 Back Design: Lathework and counters
 Colour: Green

IMPRINT
 Rawdon, Wright, Hatch & Edson. New York
 American Bank Note Company

2. TORONTO ISSUE OVERPRINTED DATE 1859-1861

"TORONTO" is engraved at the bottom centre of this issue.
Date as black overprint on ___ 18___ plates 1859

770-22-02-10P

SIGNATURES

left	right
mss. W.J. Bennetts	mss. M. Scollard
none	none

ISSUE DATING
 Partially engraved ___ 18___ and overprinted:
 $1: 1st July 1859
 $5: 5th July 1859

OVERPRINT
 Various numbers
 "5 5" in blue
 "64 64" in black

Cat. No.	Denom.	Date	Variety	VG	F	VF	EF	Unc
22-02-02	$1	1859	Overprinted date	600.	950.	1,250.	-	-
22-02-04P	$2	18_					PROOF	400.
22-02-06P	$4	18_					PROOF	450.
22-02-08	$5	1859	Overprinted date	600.	950.	1,250.	-	-
22-02-10	$10	18_					PROOF	450.
22-02-12P	$20	18_					PROOF	450.
22-02-14P	$50	18_					PROOF	450.
22-02-16P	$100	18_					PROOF	450.

472

THE BANK OF UPPER CANADA

4. TORONTO ISSUE, ENGRAVED DATE TWO SIGNATURES, 1859

770-22-04-06

SIGNATURES

left	right
mss. W.J. Bennetts	mss. M. Scollard
mss. W.J. Bennetts	mss. C.S. Murray
mss. M. Scollard	mss. C.S. Murray

ISSUE DATING
Engraved

$1: 1st July 1859
$2: 2nd July 1859
$4: 4th July 1859
$5: 5th July 1859
$10: 6th July 1859
$20: 7th July 1859
$50: 8th July 1859
$100: 9th July 1859

OVERPRINT
Numbers in black
Numbers in black and branch names in red
Numbers in red and branch names in red
Branch names in red include:
"52 BROCKVILLE 52"
"49 BROCKVILLE 49"
"GODERICH" twice
"86 KINGSTON 86"
"100 KINGSTON 100"
"08 ST. CATHARINES 08"
"31 ST. CATHARINES 31"
Numbers in black:
"12 12"
"40 40"
"77 77"
"0116 0116"

Cat. No.	Denom.	Date	VG	F	VF	EF	Unc
22-04-02	$1	1859	600.	950.	1,250.	-	-
22-04-04	$2	1859	550.	800.	1,100.	-	-
22-04-06	$4	1859	550.	800.	1,100.	-	-
22-04-08	$5	1859	600.	950.	1,250.	-	-
22-04-10	$10	1859	600.	950.	1,250.	-	-
22-04-12	$20	1859			PROOF		450.
22-04-14P	$50	1859			PROOF		450.
22-04-16P	$100	1859			PROOF		450.

6. TORONTO ISSUE ENGRAVED DATE ONE SIGNATURE, 1861

770-22-06-02

SIGNATURES

right only
mss. C.S. Murray
mss. M. Scollard

ISSUE DATING
Engraved
1st Jany 1861

OVERPRINT
Branch names in black, with or without numbers
Branch names in red, with or without numbers
Branch names in red include:
BARRIE
BELLEVILLE
GODERICH
HAMILTON
KINGS TON
LONDON
OTTAWA
SARNIA
ST. CATHARINES
STRATFORD
WINDSOR C
Branch names and numbers in red:
"B013 LONDON B013"
"B017 ST. CATHARINES B017"
"B023 ST. CATHARINES B023"
KINGSON
"91 KINGSTON 91"

Cat. No.	Denom.	Date	VG	F	VF	EF	Unc
22-06-02	$1	1861	400.	600.	900.	-	-
22-06-04	$2	1861	600.	950.	1,250.	-	-
22-06-06	$4	1861	550.	800.	1,150.	-	-
22-06-08	$5	1861	400.	600.	900.	-	-
22-06-10	$10	1861	550.	800.	1,150.	-	-

8. MONTREAL ISSUE, 1859

770-22-08-10
"MONTREAL" is engraved at the bottom centre.

THE BANK OF UPPER CANADA

SIGNATURES
- left: mss. W.J. Bennetts
- right: mss. C.S. Murray

ISSUE DATING
Engraved
- $1: 1st July 1859
- $2: 2nd July 1859
- $5: 5th July 1859
- $10: 6th July 1859

OVERPRINT
"042 042" in blue

Cat. No.	Denom.	Date	VG	F	VF	EF	Unc
22-08-02	$1	1859	600.	950.	1,250.	-	-
22-08-04	$2	1859	600.	950.	1,250.	-	-
22-08-06	$4	1859			NOT YET CONFIRMED		
22-08-08	$5	1859	600.	950.	1,250.	-	-
22-08-10	$10	1859	600.	950.	1,250.	-	-

10. QUEBEC ISSUE, 1859

"QUEBEC" is engraved at the bottom centre of this issue.

770-22-10-08

770-22-10-10

SIGNATURES
- left: mss. W.J. Bennetts
- right: mss. C.S. Murray

ISSUE DATING
Engraved
- $1: 1st July 1859
- $2: 2nd July 1859
- $5: 5th July 1859
- $10: 6th July 1859

OVERPRINT
Various numbers twice in red, ie. 3, 6, 8, 10, 11, 36, 42, 48, 53, 084, 087

Cat. No.	Denom.	Date	VG	F	VF	EF	Unc
22-10-02	$1	1859	550.	800.	1,100.	-	-
22-10-04	$2	1859	550.	800.	1,100.	-	-
11-10-06	$4	1859			NOT YET CONFIRMED		
22-10-08	$5	1859	600.	950.	1,250.	-	-
22-10-10	$10	1859	550.	800.	1,100.	-	-

770-24 NOTES ALTERED FROM THE COLONIAL BANK OF CANADA

Photo Not Available

770-24-02
- **$1 Face Design:** Bust of young woman/woodsman/-
- **Colour:** Black with orange-brown tint
- **Back Design:** Plain

770-24-08
- **$4 Face Design:** Helmeted "Justice" figure/Queen Victoria (Winterhalter portrait)/-
- **Colour:** Black with orange-brown tint
- **Back Design:** Plain

IMPRINT
Jocelyn, Draper & Welch

SIGNATURES (SPURIOUS)
- left: mss. T.C. Ridout
- right: mss. W. Proudfoot

STAMP
Blue E on face

ISSUE DATING
Partially engraved ___ 18___:
- $1, 1859: July 8
- $4, 1860: Nov. 15

Cat. No.	Denom.	Date	VG	F	VF	EF	Unc
24-02	$1	1859	300.	550.	-	-	-
24-08	$4	1860	300.	550.	-	-	-

770-26 NOTES ALTERED FROM THE BANK OF WESTERN CANADA

DESIGNS AND COLOURS

770-26-08
- **$5 Face Design:** Prince Consort in oval/St. George slaying the dragon/seated Britannia with Crest of Upper Canada
- **Colour:** Black with no tint
- **Back Design:** Plain

IMPRINT
American Bank Note Co.

SIGNATURES
left	right
mss. E.J. Butler	engr. E.J. Richardson

ISSUE DATING
Engraved
Sept. 20th, 1859

PROTECTOR
Red "word" on face and back

Cat. No.	Denom.	Date	VG	F	VF	EF	Unc
26-08	$5	1859	300.	550.	-	-	-

THE BANK OF VANCOUVER

1910-1914

VANCOUVER, BRITISH COLUMBIA

BANK NUMBER 775   **REDEEMABLE**

Organized in 1908, this bank opened for business on July 30, 1910. Its authorized capital was $2 million, and the sum of $1,174,700 was subscribed, of which over $850,000 was paid-up. The bank was riding on the real-estate and industrial boom in British Columbia, which unfortunately did not last. By 1913 the bank was in a weakened condition. There was talk in banking circles of assisting in a peaceful liquidation of this company. This rapidly accelerated the loss of confidence in the Bank of Vancouver, and deposits shrank drastically. On December 14, 1914, it suspended payment. Following this, Mr. Ewing Buchanan was appointed curator and later liquidator. Up until his death in 1918, he collected only $118,911.84, plus $20,940.27 in interest. Mr. R. Kerr Houlgate succeeded as liquidator until the final winding up in 1935. His job was made very difficult in that many debtors simply refused to pay. Their assets shrunk to unmarketable properties. In addition, the War Relief Act meant that some debts could not be collected. The double liability on shareholders amounted to about $150,000. The notes are redeemable at $1.0265 per dollar.

775-10   **ISSUE OF 1910**

DESIGNS AND COLOURS

775-10-02P
  $5 Face Design: —/ships in Vancouver harbour/—
     Colour: Black with yellow-green and green tint

  Back Design: lathework, counters, bank name and Parliament Buildings in Victoria
     Colour: Green

THE BANK OF VANCOUVER

775-10-04P
   $10 Face Design: Two men cutting down fir tree/—/—
   Colour: Black with green and red-brown tint

   Back Design: Lathework, counters, bank name and Parliament Buildings in Victoria
   Colour: Brown

775-10-06P
   $20 Face Design: —/fishing at New Westminster/—
   Colour: Black with yellow-orange and red tint

   Back Design: Lathework, counters, bank name and Parliament Buildings in Victoria
   Colour: Red-brown

775-10-08P
   $50 Face Design: —/miners at work/—
   Colour: Black with blue tint

   Back Design: Lathework, counters, bank name and Parliament Buildings in Victoria
   Colour: Blue

775-10-10P
   $100 Face Design: —/farming B.C./—
   Colour: Black with olive green tint

   Back Design: Lathework, counters, bank name and Parliament Buildings in Victoria
   Colour: Olive green

IMPRINT
British American Bank Note Co. Ottawa

SIGNATURES
left	right
engr. R.P. McLennan	mss. various

ISSUE DATING
Engraved
May 2nd 1910

Cat. No.	Denom.	Date	VG	F	VF	EF	Unc
10-02P	$5	1910			FACE PROOF		1,000.
10-02	$5	1910	6,000.	9,000.	-	-	-
10-04P	$10	1910			FACE PROOF		1,000.
10-04	$10	1910	8,000.	12,000.	-	-	-
10-06P	$20	1910			FACE PROOF		1,000.
10-06	$20	1910	8,000.	12,000.	-	-	-
10-08P	$50	1910			FACE PROOF		1,000.
10-10P	$100	1910			FACE PROOF		1,000.

THE BANK OF VICTORIA

1836

VICTORIA, UPPER CANADA

BANK NUMBER 780   **NONREDEEMABLE**

Bank notes were ordered in July 1836; however, there is no record of any notes or proofs having survived.

LA BANQUE VILLE MARIE

1872-1899

MONTREAL, QUEBEC

BANK NUMBER 785   **REDEEMABLE**

Established in Montreal in 1872, La Banque Ville Marie suspended payment on June 25, 1899, when it was discovered that there was fraudulent over-circulation of notes that had not been shown on the government return. In addition, a substantial number of bad debts arising from fraudulent transactions had not been reported. Some of the officers and directors had been dissipating assets of the bank through heavy speculation many years prior to bankruptcy. Criminal prosecution was taken against several of them for theft, fraud and the filing of false returns, and the president and chief accountant were sentenced to jail.

785-10   **BABN PRINTINGS, 1873 - 1890**

DESIGNS AND COLOURS

785-10-02
$4 **Face Design:** —/Montreal harbour/"John Baptist"
Colour: Black with green tint

Back Design: Lathework, counters and bank name
Colour: Green

LA BANQUE VILLE MARIE

785-10-06
$5 **Face Design:** Samuel de Champlain/Montreal harbour/—
Colour: Black with green tint

Back Design: Lathework, counters and bank name
Colour: Green

785-10-12
$10 **Face Design:** Jacques Cartier approaching land/
Montreal harbour/—
Colour: Black with green tint

Back Design: Lathework, counters and bank name
Colour: Green

785-10-16
$50 **Face Design:** Portrait of woman "Lucy"/
Montreal harbour/"John Baptist"
Colour: Black with green tint

Back Design: Lathework, counters and bank name
Colour: Green

IMPRINT
British American Bank Note Co. Montreal & Ottawa

SIGNATURES
	left	right
1873:	mss. P.A. Fauteux	engr. D.E. Papineau
	engr. A. Fourteur	unknown
	mss. U. Garand	mss. W. Weir

ISSUE DATING
Engraved

2. Janvier 1873
2 Jan. 1873
1er Aout. 1879
1 Octobre 1885
1er Sept. 1890

OVERPRINT
"TROIS-RIVIERES" twice in red
"F" in red
"N N" in blue
"SOREL" in red

Cat. No.	Denom.	Date	VG	F	VF	EF	Unc
10-02	$4	1873	1,800.	2,400.	3,500.	-	-
10-04P	$4	1879			FACE PROOF		600.
10-06	$5	1873	1,900.	2,600.	-	-	-
10-08P	$5	1879			FACE PROOF		600.
10-10	$5	1885	1,900.	2,600.	-	-	-
10-12	$10	1873	1,900.	2,600.	-	-	-
10-14P	$10	1885			FACE PROOF		600.
10-16	$50	1885	2,100.	4,000.	-	-	-
10-18P	$50	1890			FACE PROOF		600.

LA BANQUE VILLE MARIE

785-12 CANADA BNCo PRINTINGS, 1889

DESIGNS AND COLOURS

785-12-02
$5 Face Design: Montreal harbour/—/D. Maisonneuve
Colour: Black with overall green tint

Back Design: Lathework, counters and bank name
Colour: Green

785-12-04
$10 Face Design: Steamship/—/D. Maisonneuve
Colour: Black with overall green tint

Back Design: Lathework, counters and bank name
Colour: Green

785-12-06
$20 Face Design: D. Maisonneuve/griffins surrounding counter/—
Colour: Black with overall green tint

Back Design: Lathework, counters and bank name
Colour: Green

IMPRINT
Canada Bank Note Co. Montreal

SIGNATURES
left	right
mss. U. Garand	mss. W. Weir

ISSUE DATING
Engraved
2me Janvier 1889
2me Jan. 1889
2me Janr 1889

OVERPRINT
"W W" in blue

Cat. No.	Denom.	Date	Variety	VG	F	VF	EF	Unc
12-02	$5	1889	Red numbers	1,700.	2,300.	3,200.	-	-
12-04	$10	1889	Red numbers	1,900.	2,600.	3,700.	-	-
12-06	$20	1889	Red numbers	1,900.	2,600.	3,700.	-	-

785-14 BABN PRINTINGS, 1889

DESIGNS AND COLOURS
They are the same as the Canada BNCo issue.

785-14-02

THE WESTERN BANK OF CANADA

785-14-04

IMPRINT
British American Bank Note Co. Montreal

SIGNATURES
	left	right
$5 and $10:	mss. various	engr. W. Weir
$20:	unknown	unknown

ISSUE DATING
Engraved
2me Jan. 1889
2me Janvier 1889

Cat. No.	Denom.	Date	Variety	VG	F	VF	EF	Unc
14-02	$5	1889	Blue numbers	1,900.	2,600.	3,760.	-	-
14-04	$10	1889	Blue numbers	1,700.	2,600.	3,200.	-	-
14-06	$20	1889	Blue numbers	1,700.	2,600.	3,200.	-	-

THE WESTERN BANK OF CANADA

1882-1909

OSHAWA, ONTARIO

BANK NUMBER 790   **REDEEMABLE**

Chartered on May 17, 1882, this bank operated exclusively in Ontario to promote the manufacturing and exporting interests of the towns along the shores of Lake Ontario. It was a satellite institution of the Ontario Loan and Savings Company, and a number of the directors of the bank sat on the boards of both institutions.

By 1907 the Western Bank of Canada had 26 branches, but the year was characterized by a world-wide stringency in various money markets, from which Canada was not exempt. On November 16, 1908, the Standard Bank of Canada made an offer to purchase the assets of the bank, and a merger took place in 1909.

790-10   **ISSUES OF 1882 AND 1890**

DESIGNS AND COLOURS

790-10-02
     $5 Face Design: R.S. Hamlin/farm implements and produce/ John Cowan
     Colour: Black with green tint

     Back Design: Lathework, counters and bank name
     Colour: Green

790-10-04
     $10 Face Design: R.S. Hamlin/shepherdess with lamb and ewe/ John Cowan
     Colour: Black with green tint

Back Design: Lathework, counters and bank name
Colour: Green

790-10-06
$20 Face Design: R.S. Hamlin/Ceres seated with cornucopia/John Cowan
Colour: Black with green tint

Back Design: Lathework, counters and bank name
Colour: Green

IMPRINT
British American Bank Note Co. Montreal

SIGNATURES
left	right
mss. various	engr. John Cowan

ISSUE DATING
Engraved
Oct. 2nd, 1882
2nd July 1890

Cat. No.	Denom.	Date	VG	F	VF	EF	Unc
10-02	$5	1882	1,800.	2,500.	-	-	-
10-04	$10	1882	2,100.	3,000.	-	-	-
10-06	$20	1890	2,500.	3,500.	-	-	-

Note: $20 face proof exists with yellow-orange tint. $10 back proof exists in blue.

THE BANK OF WESTERN CANADA

1859-1863

CLIFTON, CANADA WEST

BANK NUMBER 795   **NONREDEEMABLE**

Established in Clifton, Canada West, on March 31, 1859, the act incorporating the bank received royal assent on May 4, 1859. The Bank of Western Canada was controlled by a New York tavern keeper by the name of Paddock, who convinced a respectable old gentleman in Clifton to act as president of the bank by paying for his stock. However, the president had no control over the issue of notes, none of which were redeemed. The government reported that it was discreditable to allow the charter to remain in existence, and it was repealed on August 31, 1863.

795-10   **ISSUE OF 1859**
DESIGNS AND COLOURS

795-10-04
$1 Face Design: Queen Victoria/Royal Crest/Prince Consort
Colour: Black with no tint
Back Design: Plain

795-10-08
$2 Face Design: Queen Victoria (Winterhalter portrait)/Britannia, lion and flags/—
Colour: Black with no tint
Back Design: Plain

795-10-12
$4 Face Design: Prince Consort/lion/
Queen Victoria (Winterhalter portrait)
Colour: Black with no tint

THE WESTMORLAND BANK OF NEW BRUNSWICK

Back Design: Plain

795-10-14P

$5 Face Design: Prince Consort/St. George slaying the dragon/Britannia seated with Crest of Upper Canada
Colour: Black with no tint

Back Design: Plain

IMPRINT
American Bank Note Company

SIGNATURES

left	right
mss. E.J. Butler	engr. G. McMicken
mss. E.J. Butler	engr. E.J. Richardson

ISSUE DATING
Engraved
Sept. 20th, 1859

PROTECTOR
Red "word" on face and on the back in a mirror image.

STAMPS
Small "X" in black, small C-W in black
Small "S-W" in black, small K in black
Large "O" in black, N;Y in black
"BANK NOTE REPORTER OFFICE," etc., in black

Cat. No.	Denom.	Date	Variety	VG	F	VF	EF	Unc
10-02P	$1	1859	McMicken, r.	325.	450.	695.	1,150.	-
10-04	$1	1859	Richardson, r.	20.	30.	50.	80.	140.
10-06P	$2	1859	McMicken, r.	325.	450.	675.	1,150.	-
10-08	$2	1859	Richardson, r.	20.	30.	50.	80.	140.
10-10P	$4	1859	McMicken, r.	375.	500.	700.	1,200.	-
10-12	$4	1859	Richardson, r.	45.	70.	90.	150.	300.
10-14P	$5	1859	McMicken, r.	325.	450.	700.	1,150.	-
10-16	$5	1859	Richardson, r.	25.	35.	50.	90.	175.

THE WESTMORLAND BANK OF NEW BRUNSWICK

1854-1867

BEND OF THE PETTICODIAC, NEW BRUNSWICK

BANK NUMBER 800   **NONREDEEMABLE**

Chartered in 1854 with a capital of $60,000, this bank operated in Bend of the Petticodiac, subsequently renamed Moncton. The bank operated agencies at Sackville, N.B., and at Charlottetown, P.E.I. In 1859 a major shipbuilding firm failed and depression struck the area. Debts due to the bank, secured by mortgages on land that could be sold for only a fraction of its former worth, had to be covered from the reserve fund. The position of the bank steadily weakened until its failure on March 13, 1867. The whole capital of the bank was lost, together with an almost equal amount to be covered by the shareholders under the double liability provision in the charter.

800-10   **BEND OF PETTICODIAC (sic)**
ISSUE 1854-1859

DESIGNS AND COLOURS

800-10-02

$1 Face Design: Sailor/shipbuilding scene; casks and bale below/Queen Victoria (Chalon portrait) in oval
Colour: Black with no tint

Back Design: Plain

800-10-20

$2 Face Design: Indian maiden/train; two horses below/sailing ships
Colour: Black with no tint

Back Design: Plain

THE WESTMORLAND BANK OF NEW BRUNSWICK

ISSUE DATING
  Partially engraved ___ 18___:
  1854: 1 May, 1 June, 1 July
  1855: 1 July, 2 Apr.
  1856: 1 May
  1859: 1 November

Cat. No.	Denom.	Date	Variety	VG	F	VF	EF	Unc
10-02	$1	1854	Johnson, l.	300.	425.	625.	-	-
10-06	$1	1855	McAllister, l.	350.	500.	750.	-	-
10-08	$1	1856	McAllister, l.	350.	500.	750.	-	-
10-10	$1	1859	McAllister, l.	300.	500.	750.	-	-
10-16	$2	1854	Johnson, l.	400.	600.	800.	-	-
10-20	$2	1855	McAllister, l.	450.	650.	850.	-	-
10-22	$2	1856	McAllister, l.	450.	650.	850.	-	-
10-28	$2	1859	McAllister, l.	450.	650.	850.	-	-
10-30	$4	1854	Johnson, l.	350.	500.	735.	-	-
10-34	$4	1855	McAllister, l.	350.	650.	750.	-	-
10-36	$4	1856	McAllister, l.	350.	650.	750.	-	-
10-42	$4	1859	McAllister, l.	350.	650.	750.	-	-
10-44	$20	1854	Johnson, l.	4,500.	-	-	-	-
10-50	$20	1856	Johnson, l.	4,500.	-	-	-	-
10-60	$40	18_					PROOF	1,500.

Note: A $20 (Moncton) and $40 (petticodiac) uncut proof pair were in ABN archive sale 1990.

800-10-36
  $4 Face Design: Seated Britannia/farm family with picnic basket; shipbuilding below/ Prince Consort in oval
  Colour: Black with no tint
  Back Design: Plain

800-10-50
  $20 Face Design: Seated Britannia/ornate 20 and woman with rake; swords with crown on cushion below/ seated "Justice" figure and chest
  Colour: Black with no tint
  Back Design: Plain

800-10-60
  $40 Face Design: Oval portrait of young woman/seated "Justice" figure and Britannia flanking Royal badge; shipbuilding below/two women
  Colour: Black with no tint
  Back Design: Plain

IMPRINT
Rawdon, Wright, Hatch & Edson, New York
Rawdon, Wright, Hatch & Edson, New York and American Bank Note Co. Boston

SIGNATURES
	left	right
1854:	mss. J. Johnson	mss. O. Jones
1856-1859:	mss. J. McAllister	mss. O. Jones

800-12 MONCTON ISSUE, 1861

DESIGNS AND COLOURS

800-12-02a
  $1 Face Design: Sailor/shipbuilding scene; casks and bale below/Queen Victoria (Chalon portrait) in oval
  Colour: Black with green tint
  Back Design: Lathework
  Colour: Blue

800-12-04a
  $2 Face Design: Indian maiden/train; two horses below/ sailing ships
  Colour: Black with green tint
  Back Design: Lathework
  Colour: Blue

483

THE WEYBURN SECURITY BANK

800-12-06a
   $5 Face Design: Seated Britannia/farm family with picnic basket; shipbuilding below/ Prince Consort in oval
   Colour: Black with green tint

   Back Design: Lathework
   Colour: Blue

800-12-08
   $20 Face Design: Seated Britannia/ornate 20 and woman with rake; swords with crown on cushion below/ seated "Justice" figure
   Colour: Black with green tint

   Back Design: Lathework
   Colour: Blue

IMPRINT
Rawdon, Wright, Hatch & Edson New York and American Bank Note Co. Boston American Bank Note Co. New York & Boston

SIGNATURES
left	right
mss. J. McAllister	mss. O. Jones
mss. Wm. C. Jones	mss. O. Jones
mss. John S. Trites	mss. O. Jones

ISSUE DATING
   Engraved
      August 1, 1861
      Aug. 1st 1861

Cat. No.	Denom.	Date	Variety	VG	F	VF	EF	Unc
12-02	$1	1861	McAllister, l.	35.	50.	80.	125.	250.
12-02a	$1	1861	Jones, l.	40.	60.	90.	150.	300.
12-02b	$1	1861	Trites, l.	45.	65.	100.	175.	325.
12-02R	$1	1861	Remainder*	-	-	-	125.	250.
12-04	$2	1861	McAllister, l.	35.	50.	80.	125.	250.
12-04a	$2	1861	Jones, l.	40.	60.	90.	150.	300.
12-04b	$2	1861	Trites, l.	45.	65.	100.	175.	325.
12-04R	$2	1861	Remainder*	-	-	-	125.	250.
12-06	$5	1861	McAllister, l.	35.	50.	80.	125.	260.
12-06a	$5	1861	Jones, l.	40.	60.	90.	150.	300.
12-06b	$5	1861	Trites, l.	45.	65.	100.	175.	325.
12-06R	$5	1861	Remainder*	-	-	-	125.	325.
12-08	$20	1861	McAllister, l.	3,000.	4,200.	-	-	-

* These notes are unsigned, have "defunct" in the left signature space or both signature spaces are unsigned.

THE WEYBURN SECURITY BANK

1910-1931

WEYBURN, SASKATCHEWAN

BANK NUMBER 805   **REDEEMABLE**

Established in 1910 in Weyburn, Saskatchewan, this bank was the successor to the Weyburn Security Company, which found competition with the chartered banks very difficult. The new bank decided to take out a charter under the Bank Act and had a successful business until 1931, when it merged with the Imperial Bank of Canada.

805-10   **ISSUE OF 1911**
DESIGNS AND COLOURS

805-10-02S
   $5 Face Design: —/train in city/—
   Colour: Black with green tint

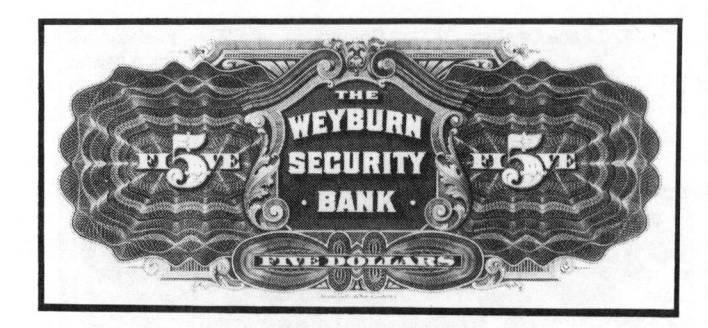

   Back Design: Lathework, counters and bank name
   Colour: Green

805-10-04S
   $10 Face Design: —/allegorical women and children/—
   Colour: Black with yellow-green tint

Back Design: Lathework, counters and bank name
Colour: Green

805-10-06S
$20 Face Design: —/portrait of woman in oval frame supported by two cherubs/—
Colour: Black with orange tint

Back Design: Lathework, counters and bank name
Colour: Orange

IMPRINT
American Bank Note Co. Ottawa
Canadian Bank Note Company, Limited

SIGNATURES
left	right
mss. various	typed Alex Simpson

ISSUE DATING
Engraved
January 3rd 1911.
Jan. 3rd 1911.

Cat. No.	Denom.	Date	VG	F	VF	EF	Unc
10-02	$5	1911	900.	1,200.	1,500.	2,100.	-
10-04	$10	1911	1,000.	1,500.	2,000.	2,500.	-
10-06	$20	1911	2,500.	3,000.	4,000.	-	-

THE BANK OF YARMOUTH

THE BANK OF YARMOUTH

1859-1905

YARMOUTH, NOVA SCOTIA

BANK NUMBER 810　　　　　　　　　　**REDEEMABLE**

The charter for this bank was given in 1859, and it started business in 1865. It failed, however, in 1905, when it was discovered that dividends had continued for years, despite a severe depletion of capital owing to false and deceptive statements filed with the government. The cashier, president and vice-president were charged, and the cashier was convicted. The president and vice-president pleaded ignorance and the charges against them were dismissed. The directors of the bank were held liable for the dividends paid out.

810-10　　　　　　**$20 ISSUE OF 1860**
DESIGNS AND COLOURS

810-10-02
$20 Face Design: Farmer planting seeds/Princess of Wales in oval flanked by lion and unicorn/—ship in drydock
Colour: Black with green tint

Back Design: Lathework, counters and bank name
Colour: Orange

IMPRINT
American Bank Note Co. N.Y.

SIGNATURES
left	right
mss. J.W.H. Rowley	mss. Wm. Hammond

ISSUE DATING
Partially engraved Dec. 1st 186___:
1860: Dec. 1st 186_

OVERPRINT
"CANADIAN CURRENCY" twice in red

Cat. No.	Denom.	Date	Variety	VG	F	VF	EF	Unc
10-02	$20	1860	No o/p	3,000.	4,000.	-	-	-
10-02a	$20	1860	Red o/p	3,000.	4,000.	-	-	-

485

THE BANK OF YARMOUTH

810-12 ISSUES OF 1870 AND 1891
DESIGNS AND COLOURS

810-12-02
$4 Face Design: Allegorical female at sea, borne by two porpoises/—/Indian maiden
Colour: Black with green tint

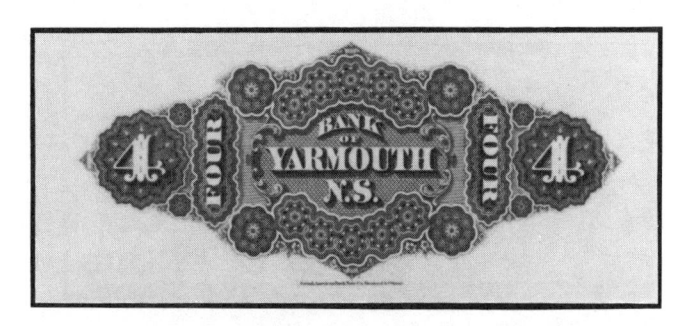

Back Design: Lathework, counters and bank name
Colour: Green

810-12-06
$5 Face Design: Anchor/ships and sea "Great Eastern"/ships and allegorical female with flag, "Exports"
Colour: Black with green tint

Back Design: Lathework, counters and bank name
Colour: Green

810-12-10
$10 Face Design: —/Queen Victoria in widow's weeds flanked by lion and unicorn/—
Colour: Black with green tint

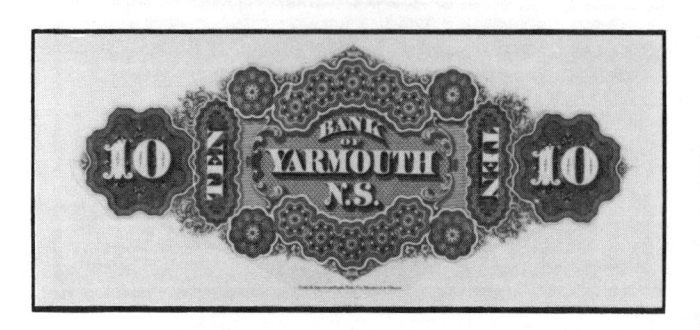

Back Design: Lathework, counters and bank name
Colour: Green

IMPRINT
British American Bank Note Co. Montreal & Ottawa

SIGNATURES
	left	right
1870:	unknown	unknown
1891:	mss. T.W. Johns	mss. L.E. Baker
	mss. T.W. Johns	mss. John Lovitt

ISSUE DATING
Engraved
July 1st 1870
July 1st 1891

OVERPRINT
1870: "CANADIAN CURRENCY" in red

Cat. No.	Denom.	Date	Variety	VG	F	VF	EF	Unc
12-02P	$4	1870	No o/p			FACE PROOF		800.
12-02a	$4	1870	Red o/p	3,000.	4,000.	-	-	-
12-04	$5	1870	No o/p	3,000.	4,000.	-	-	-
12-04a	$5	1870	Red o/p	3,000.	4,000.	-	-	-
12-06	$5	1891		3,000.	4,000.	-	-	-
12-08	$10	1870	No o/p	3,000.	4,000.	-	-	-
12-08a	$10	1870	Red o/p	3,000.	4,000.	-	-	-
12-10	$10	1891		3,000.	4,000.	-	-	-

THE ZIMMERMAN BANK
1854-1859
ELGIN, CANADA WEST, PROVINCE OF CANADA

BANK NUMBER 815 **NONREDEEMABLE**

The Zimmerman Bank began operations in October 1854, under the Free Banking Act of 1850, when debentures totaling $100,000 were deposited with the provincial government on October 11, 1854. The founders were Samuel Zimmerman, the Honourable John Hilyard Cameron, Luther H. Holden, James A. Woodruff, James Oswald, John L. Ranney and Richard Woodruff.

In 1855 the bank obtained a charter with authorized capital of $1 million. Actual business as a chartered bank did not begin until June of the following year.

With the death of the major shareholder, Samuel Zimmerman, on March 12, 1857, operations changed overnight with the decision to wind up the affairs of the bank as quickly as possible. From a peak note circulation of $440,000 in December 1856 (both chartered and registered), the final published return in October 1857 showed only $34,000 in circulation.

In early 1858 the Zimmerman Bank made arrangements with the Bank of Upper Canada to take over its note redemption. In 1859 it changed its name to the Bank of Clifton.

815-10 FREE BANKING ISSUE, 1854-1855

These notes have "ELGIN" engraved at the bottom left and "SECURED BY DEPOSIT OF PROVINCIAL SECURITIES" at the bottom centre. Manuscript numbers.

DESIGNS AND COLOURS

815-10-02
- **$1 Face Design:** Clifton House Hotel/ Roebling Suspension Bridge/ seated allegorical female
- **Colour:** Black with no tint
- **Back Design:** Plain

Photo Not Available

815-10-06P
- **$3 Face Design:** Clifton House Hotel/ Roebling Suspension Bridge/ Queen Victoria (Chalon portrait)
- **Colour:** Black with no tint
- **Back Design:** Plain

815-10-10
- **$5 Face Design:** Seated allegorical female/ Roebling Suspension Bridge/train
- **Colour:** Black with no tint
- **Back Design:** Plain

Photo Not Available

815-10-12P
- **$10 Face Design:** Roebling Suspension Bridge/ Prince Consort/female with sheaf of grain
- **Colour:** Black with no tint
- **Back Design:** Plain

Photo Not Available

815-10-16P
- **$20 Face Design:** Clifton House Hotel/ Roebling Suspension Bridge/ seated woman with telescope
- **Colour:** Black with no tint
- **Back Design:** Plain

IMPRINT
Toppan, Carpenter, Casilear & Co. Montreal

SIGNATURES
left	right
mss. G. McMicken	engr. S. Zimmerman

ISSUE DATING
Partially engraved ___ 185___:
1854: 2 Nov.
1855: 1st Oct.

Cat. No.	Denom.	Date	VG	F	VF	EF	Unc
10-02	$1	1854	425.	650.	800.	-	-
10-06P	$3	185_				PROOF	400.
10-10	$5	1855	425	650.	800.	-	-
10-12P	$10	185_				PROOF	400.
10-16P	$20	185_				PROOF	400.

THE ZIMMERMAN BANK

815-12   "CHARTERED BANK" ISSUE FROM ELGIN, 1856

"ELGIN" and "CAPITAL ONE MILLION DOLLARS" are engraved at the bottom centre. Manuscript numbers.

DESIGNS AND COLOURS

815-12-02-04
    $1 Face Design: Clifton House Hotel/Roebling Suspension Bridge/seated allegorical female
    Colour: Black with no tint

Back Design: Plain, type 2 protector

815-12-02-08R
    $3 Face Design: Clifton House Hotel/
    Roebling Suspension Bridge/
    Queen Victoria (Chalon portrait)
    Colour: Black with no tint

Back Design: Plain, type 2 protector

815-12-02-12R
    $5 Face Design: Seated allegorical female/
    Roebling Suspension Bridge/train
    Colour: Black with no tint

Back Design: Plain, type 2 protector

Photo Not Available

815-12-02-14
    $10 Face Design: Roebling Suspension Bridge/
    Prince Consort/female with sheaf of grain
    Colour: Black with no tint

    Back Design: Plain, Type 1 protector

IMPRINT
Toppan Carpenter & Co. Montreal

SIGNATURES
left	right
mss. G. McMicken	engr. S. Zimmerman
mss. J.W. Dunklee	engr. S. Zimmerman

ISSUE DATING
    Partially engraved _ 185_:
    $1, 1856: June 7, Augt 7, Dec. 1
    $5, 1856: July 7, Augt 7
    $10, 1856: July 7

THE ZIMMERMAN BANK

2. RED "WORD" PROTECTOR ON FACE AND BACK

VARIETIES
- **Type 1:** Face protector normal, back protector reversed (mirror image)
- **Type 2:** Face protector normal, back protector normal

Note: Many remainders have spurious signatures and dates.

Cat. No.	Denom.	Date	Variety	VG	F	VF	EF	Unc
12-02-02R	$1	185_	ONE type 1	125.	175.	250.	400.	800.
12-02-02	$1	1856	ONE type 1	250.	325.	500.	-	-
12-02-04R	$1	185_	ONE type 2	125.	175.	250.	400.	800.
12-02-04	$1	1856	ONE type 2	250.	325.	500.	-	-
12-02-06R	$3	185_	THREE type 1	175.	250.	325.	500.	1,000.
12-02-06	$3	1856	THREE type 1	300.	450.	700.	-	-
12-02-08R	$3	185_	THREE type 2	175.	250.	325.	500.	1,000.
12-02-08	$3	1856	THREE type 2	325.	450.	700.	-	-
12-02-10R	$5	185_	FIVE type 1	125.	175.	250.	400.	800.
12-02-10	$5	1856	FIVE type 1	225.	325.	500.	-	-
12-02-12R	$5	185_	FIVE type 2	125.	175.	250.	400.	800.
12-02-12	$5	1856	FIVE type 2	250.	325.	600.	-	-
12-02-14R	$10	185_	TEN type 1			NOT CONFIRMED		
12-02-14	$10	1856	TEN type 1	500.	650.	850.	1,000.	-
12-02-16R	$10	185_	TEN type 2			NOT CONFIRMED		
12-02-16	$10	1856	TEN type 2			NOT CONFIRMED		

4. BLUE "WORD" PROTECTOR ON FACE AND BACK

Cat. No.	Denom.	Date	Variety	VG	F	VF	EF	Unc
12-04-02R	$1	185_	Blue ONE ptr.*	100.	140.	210.	350.	-
12-04-04R	$3	185_	Blue THREE ptr.*	100.	140.	210.	350.	-
12-04-06R	$5	185_	Blue FIVE ptr.*	100.	140.	210.	350.	-

* Remainder notes. Many notes have spurious signatures and dates.

6. RED "NUMERAL" PROTECTOR ON FACE AND BACK

815-12-08-02

815-12-06-04R

815-12-06-06R

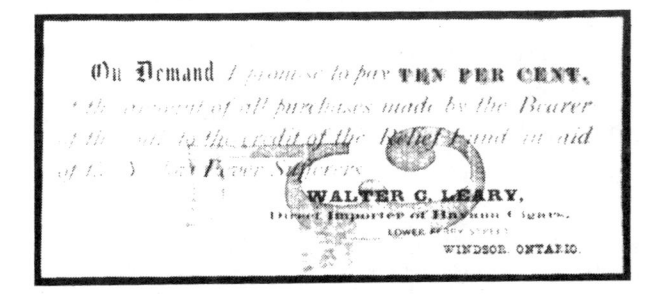

THE ZIMMERMAN BANK

815-12-06-08R

815-12-06-10R

$20 Face Design: Clifton House Hotel/
Roebling Suspension Bridge/
seated woman with telescope
Colour: Black with no tint

Back Design: Plain

Note: Numerals on backs are mirror images.

Cat. No.	Denom.	Date	Variety	VG	F	VF	EF	Unc
12-06-02R	$1	185_	Red 1 ptr.*	125.	175.	250.	425.	-
12-06-04R	$3	185_	Red 3 ptr.*	150.	225.	300.	500.	-
12-06-06R	$5	185_	Red 5 ptr.*	125.	175.	250.	425.	-
12-06-06	$5	1856	Red 5 ptr.**	250.	325.	500.	-	-
12-06-08R	$10	185_	Red 10 ptr.*	200.	275.	400.	-	-
12-06-10R	$20	185_	Red 20 ptr.*	200.	275.	400.	650.	-

* Remainder - many notes have spurious signatures and dates.
** Issued note.

8. BLUE "NUMERAL" PROTECTOR ON FACE AND BACK

Cat. No.	Denom.	Date	Variety	VG	F	VF	EF	Unc
12-08-02R	$1	185_	Blue 1 ptr.*	40.	60.	90.	160.	-
12-08-02	$1	1856		250.	325.	420.	-	-
12-08-04R	$3	185_	Blue 3 ptr.*	100.	175.	250.	325.	-
12-08-06R	$5	185_	Blue 5 ptr.*	30.	60.	90.	160.	-
12-08-08R	$10	185_	Blue 10 ptr.*	55.	80.	120.	225.	-
12-08-10R	$20	185_	Blue 20 ptr.*	55.	80.	120.	225.	-

Sheet of 1,1,3,5 dated Dec. 1, 1856 unsigned
* These are remainder notes. Many have spurious signatures and dates.

815-14 "CHARTERED BANK" ISSUE FROM CLIFTON

"CLIFTON" and "CAPITAL ONE MILLION DOLLARS" are engraved at the bottom centre. There are red printed numbers and faces printed in blue, instead of black. All notes of this type are remainders.

DESIGNS AND COLOURS

185-14-02R

$1 Face Design: Clifton House Hotel/
Roebling Suspension Bridge/
seated allegorical female
Colour: Blue

Back Design: Plain

490

815-14-04R
 $3 **Face Design:** Clifton House Hotel/
  Roebling Suspension Bridge/Queen Victoria
   Colour: Blue

Back Design: Plain

815-14-06R
 $5 **Face Design:** Seated allegorical female/
  Roebling Suspension Bridge/train
   Colour: Blue

Back Design: Plain

Photo Not Available

815-14-08R
 $10 **Face Design:** Roebling Suspension Bridge/
  Prince Consort/female with sheaf of grain
   Colour: Blue
 Back Design: Plain

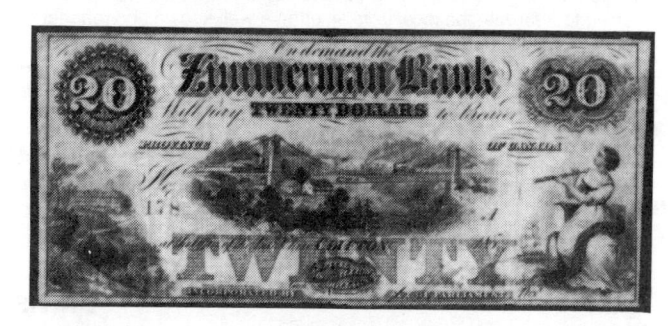

815-14-10R
 $20 **Face Design:** Clifton House Hotel/
  Roebling Suspension Bridge/
  seated woman with telescope
   Colour: Blue
 Back Design: Plain

IMPRINT
 Toppan Carpenter & Co. Montreal
 | left | right |
 | none | none |

ISSUE DATING
 Partially engraved ___ 185___:

PROTECTOR
 Red "word" on face and mirror image on back

Cat. No.	Denom.	Date	Variety	VG	F	VF	EF	Unc
14-02R	$1	185_	Remainder*	40.	55.	80.	130.	300.
14-04R	$3	185_	Remainder*	75.	125.	200.	325.	400.
14-06R	$5	185_	Remainder*	40.	55.	80.	130.	300.
14-08R	$10	185_	Remainder*	150.	200.	300.	450.	-
14-10R	$20	185_	Remainder*	150.	200.	300.	450.	-
Full sheet	$1,1,3,5	185_		-	-	-	1,000.	1,800.

* Many notes have spurious signatures and dates.

PRIVATE BANKS AND BANKERS IN CANADA

Information recently compiled would suggest that private bankers in Canada played a much more significant role in the economic development of Canada than previously realized. There were over five hundred of these bankers (over 425 in Ontario), some with several branches, operating in Canada mainly between 1880 and 1900. It is generally assumed that the majority of financial transactions were carried on through the chartered banks and their branches, and this was probably true in the larger towns and cities. In smaller towns and in rural areas, however, many people preferred to deal with the local banker, often a well-known and respected member of the community.

Competition for capital and customers in the cities often forced the private banker to pay higher interest rates and accept loans of greater risk, resulting in a high failure rate. In rural areas this was not the case, and the chartered banks often resorted to buying out the small banker in order to open and operate a successful branch. As a result, private banks slowly disappeared over the years.

Since private bankers could not issue bank notes, a record of their existence is found in local newspapers, street directories, pass books, cheques, deposit slips and other bank stationery. In addition, lists of these bankers were often included in various bankers' directories, both in Canada and in the United States. These various sources have formed the basis of this preliminary listing, and it is hoped it will stimulate further research into this rewarding, yet neglected, aspect of Canadian banking.

ALBERTA

Name of Bank	Manager or Agent	Paid-up Capital	Town	County
Cowdry Bros.			Fort MacLeod	

BRITISH COLUMBIA

Name of Bank	Manager or Agent	Paid-up Capital	Town	County
Bealey & Co. R. J.			Rossland	
Burke, John M.			Kaslo	
Garesche, Green & Co.	A.A. Green		Victoria	
Green, Worlock & Co.			Victoria	
Retallack J.L.			Sandon	Slocan
Wulffsohn & Bewicke, Ltd	G. Alers Hankey	$300,000	Vancouver	New Westminster
Yorkshire Guar. & Secur. Corp (Banking Department)	L. Neville Smith		Chilliwack	Chilliwack

MANITOBA

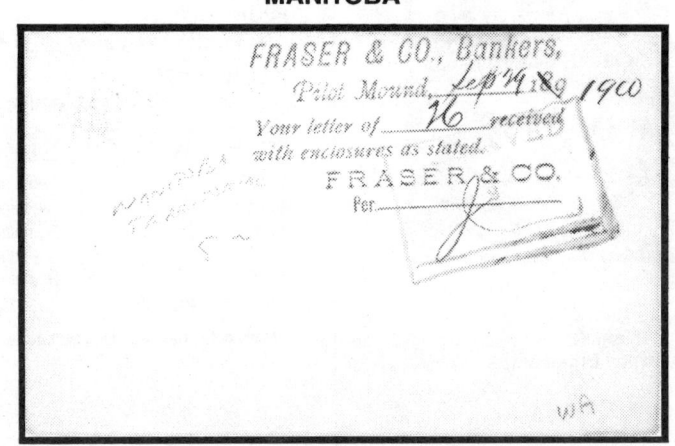

Name of Bank	Manager or Agent	Paid-up Capital	Town	County
Alexander & Co., R.S.			Treherne	Macdonald
Alloway & Champion			Winnipeg	Selkirk
Alloway & Champion			Portage la Prairie	Marquette
Andrew & Co.			Oak Lake	Brandon
Arnold & Co., C.E.	Charles E. Arnold		Rapid City	Minnedosa
Bailey & Co., W.L.			Gladstone	Westbourne
Bailey & Co., W.S.	W.S. Bailey	$25,000	Gladstone	Westbourne
Cowdry Bros.			Birtle	
Cruthers & Co.	S. Cruthers		Manitou	Selkirk
Denison, E. O.			Minnedosa	
Dudley, Leese & Scarth			Russell	
Dunsford & Co.	C.R. Dunsford		Morden	Dufferin
Fraser & Co.	J.M. Fraser	$ 5,000	Pilot Mound	Rock Lake
Gibson, R.W.	R.J. Gomley, Cashier	$50,000	Birtle	Shoal Lake
Haley & Sutton				MordenSelkirk
Harrison's Bank	W.R. Weare, Cashier	$30,000	Neepawa	Beautiful Pl's
Hopper, D.A.			Brandon	Brandon
Harvey & Co.			Dauphin	
Hopper's Banking House	D.A. Hopper		Rapid City	Minnedosa
Ingram, Blain & Co.	D.A. McVicar		Wawanesa	Brandon
Inman & Co., H.	H. Inman		Hamiota	Marquette

MANITOBA

Name of Bank	Manager or Agent	Paid-up Capital	Town	County
Irwin, G.L.			Dauphin	
Ledez, Ch		$25,000	St. Pierre	
Leslie, Ronald			Stonewall	Lisgar
Little, Nathan			Cypress Riv	Marquette
Logan & Co., R.	J.A. Smith		Glenboro	Marquette
Logan & Co., Wm.	Wm. Logan, Cashier		Carberry	Norfolk
Long, M.	N.T. Lee, Cashier	$46,000	Gretna	Manchester
Longan & Co.	W.M. Logan		McGregor	Macdonald
McArthur, D.			Emerson	Manchester
McLenaghen & Co., James			Portage la Prairie	Marquette
McMicken, A.				Fort Gary
Nelson Banking Office	Sutton, Haley & Lafferty		Nelson	Marquette
Newton, F. Y.				Roblin
Nicholls & Co., W.G.			Selkirk	Lisgar
Olser, Hammond & Nanton			Winnipeg	Selkirk
Pickering, Vere H.		$15,000	Minnedosa	Minnedosa
Pickering's Bank				Minnedosa
Ritz & Widmeyer		$320,000	Gretna	Manchester
Robbins & Gill			Miami	Selkirk
Russell, William		$320,000	Winkler	Lisgar
Schimnowski's Bank, A.				Salter
Schimnowski's Bank, A				Selkirk
Schultz' Bank, Frank				Baldur
Stevens, Henry				Bowsman
Strathy & Co., E.K.			Hartney	Selkirk
Stuart, A.P. & F.T.			Deloraine	Turtle Mt'n
Young & Van Someren			Souris	Brandon

NEW BRUNSWICK

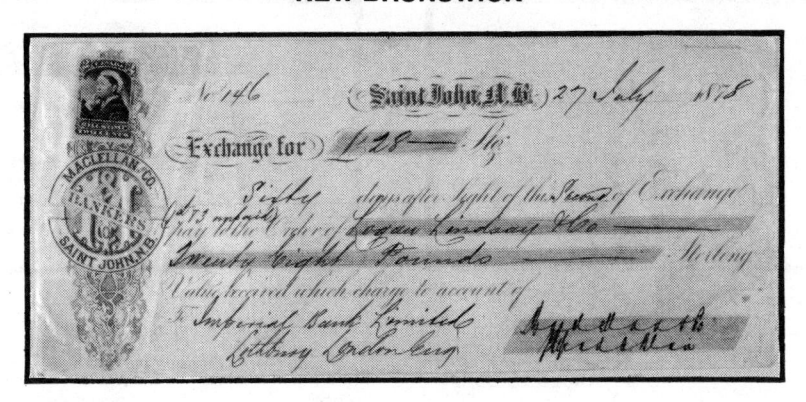

Name of Bank	Manager or Agent	Paid-up Capital	Town	County
Allan, John T.			Woodstock	Carleton
Blair & Co.			St. John	St. John
Clinch, D.C.			St. John	St. John
Halifax Clearing House Ass'n	R.M. Cotton, President		Halifax	Halifax
Jack & Bell			Halifax	Halifax
Jones & Co., S.			St. John	
Mackintosh, James C.			Halifax	Halifax
Maclellan & Co.			Saint John	Saint John
Philps, George			Saint John	Saint John
Robinson, J.M.			Saint John	Saint John

NEWFOUNDLAND

Name of Bank	Manager or Agent	Paid-up Capital	Town	County
Newfoundland Savings Bank	Edwar Morris, Cashier		St. John's	

NORTH WEST TERRITORY

Name of Bank	Manager or Agent	Paid-up Capital	Town	County
Behrends, B.M.			Dawson	
Caswell & Co., S.H.			Qu'Appelle	Assiniboia
Cowdry Bros.	J. Cowdry		Macleod	Alberta
Gibson, R.W.			Wolseley	
Hitchcocke & McCulloch	Harold Jagger	$40,000	Moose Jaw	Assiniboia
MacArthur & Knowles			Prince Albert	
MacDonald, Alexander			Battleford	
McDonald & Co., D.H.			Qu'Appelle	Assiniboia
Morrison & Co.		$ 3,000	Whitewood	Assiniboia
Pease, R.A. & Co.			Wapella	
Pickering, Vere H.			Yorkton	Assiniboia
Skillister & Co., T.A.			Indian Head	Assiniboia
Snow, C.E.			Cardston	
Tryon & Co., C.R.	Percy Bell	$25,000	Grenfell	Assiniboia

NOVA SCOTIA

Name of Bank	Manager or Agent	Paid-up Capital	Town	County
Farquhar, Forrest & Co.			Halifax	Halifax
Jack & Bell			Hollis	Halifax
Jack & Bell			Halifax	Halifax
Lowell & Co., W.L.			Halifax	Halifax
Mackintosh, J.C.			Hollis	Halifax
Pauicy, E.J.H.			Hollis	Halifax

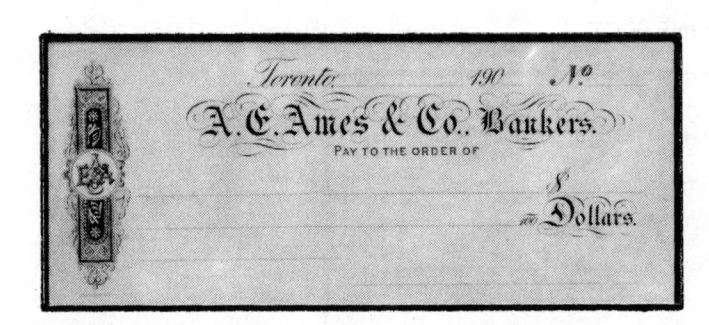

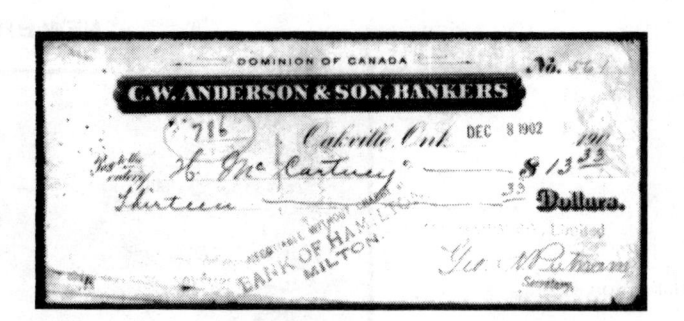

ONTARIO

Name of Bank	Manager or Agent	Paid-up Capital	Town	County
Acton Banking Co.	Storey, Christie & Co.		Acton	Halton
Adams, D.J.		$50,000	Port Perry	Ontario
Agur, Robert			Ingersoll	Oxford
Ainslie & Ainslie		$15,000	Comber	Essex
Aiken, H.C.			Tottenham	Simcoe
Allan, H.W.			Harrow	
Allen & McMahon			Port Elgin	Bruce
Allen, G.L.			Mt. Forest	Wellington
Allen, H.A.	A. Miller		Port Elgin	Bruce
Allison, Adam	A. Allison		Belmont	
Alloway & Champion			Rat Portage	
Ames & Co., A.E.			Toronto	York
Ames & Co., G.W.	G.W. Ames		Wiarton	Bruce
Ames, A.W.			Wiarton	Bruce
Anderson & Co., J.D.		$45,000	Essex	Essex
Anderson & Scott	E.K. Scott		Palmerston	Wellington
Anderson & Son, C.W.			Oakville	Halton
Anderson, C.W.			Oakville	Halton
Anderson, C.W.			Palmerston	Wellington
Anderson, J.D.			Essex	Essex
Andrew & Howarth	Thomas Howarth, Cashier		Oakville	Halton
Annis, David			Woodville	
Armour, Robert			Bowmanville	
Baby & Donelly			Sarnia	Lambton
Baby's Banking House			Sarnia	Lambton
Baby, R.A.			Sarnia	Lambton
Baird, John			Lynden	Wentworth
Baker, John			Harrington	West
Bancroft, James			Hamilton	

ONTARIO

Name of Bank	Manager or Agent	Paid-up Capital	Town	County
Bangs, J.A.			Carleton Place	
Barfoot's Banking Office, S.			Chatham	Kent
Barfoots Bank	A.F. Falls, H.I.I. Campbell		Chatham	Kent
Barker, Joseph			Brechin	
Barnes, S.			Collingwood	
Baxter, R.G.			Burlington	Halton
Bazin Company, The P.I.			Ottawa	Carleton
Bearer, J.			Uxbridge	
Beattie's Banking House	John Beattie		Fergus	Wellington
Beattie, John			Fergus	Wellington
Beaty & Co., K.			Toronto	York
Beaty & Co., Robert			Toronto	York
Beaver Valley Banking Co.	Walter Hunter		Clarksburg	
Bebbington Co., Dean	F. Bebbington		Ottawa	
Becker & Co., L.	L.H. Slaght		Waterford	Norfolk
Beddome, F.B.			London	
Belcher & Company	A.E. Belcher		Southhampton	
Black & Co.	Benjamin Madill		Beaverton	Ontario
Black & Co., W.S.	W.C. Smith		Uxbridge	Ontario
Black, A.N.C.			Dutton	Elgin
Bloomer, E.			Collingwood	
Box & Son, R.			St. Mary's	Perth
Box, R.S.			St. Mary's	Perth
Boyer, John			Kincardine	Bruce
Bredin, R.S.			Mt. Forest	Wellington
Breese, William			Chatsworth	
Bretts Banking House			Toronto	York
Brigden Banking Co.	W.J. Ward		Brigden	Lambton
Brown & Co., W.R.			Toronto	York
Brown's Banking House	Garrett Brown, Cashier		Schomberg	York N.R.
Brown, G.			Schomberg	York, N.R.
Browne & Co., Philip			Toronto	York
Browne, Jas. & Philip			Toronto	York
Bruce Banking House	S.T. Jackson	$26,000	Ripley	Bruce
Bryden, J.			Collingwood	
Burk & Graham			Alliston	
Burk & Graham			Creemore	
Burk & Graham	J.A. Graham	$100,000	Toronto	York
Butler, W.			Walkerton	
Byers, N.			Enniskillen	
Cameron & Campbell			Lucknow	Bruce
Cameron & Curry	John Curry, Cashier		Windsor	Essex
Cameron, John			Toronto	York
Campbell & Cassels			Toronto	York
Campbell's Banking Office	M.S. Campbell		Watford	Lambton
Campbell Bros.			Watford	Lambton
Campbell, J.W.			Glencoe	
Campbell, M.S.			Watford	Lambton
Carrick Banking Co. Charles Schurter	George Curle, President;		Mildmay	Bruce
Carrick Finance Co.			Mildmay	Bruce
Carruthers, J.B.			Kingston	Frontenac
Carscallen & Co., A.W.			Marmora	Hastings
Carscallen, A.W.		$50,000	Marmora	Hastings
Carson, A.S.	Fred Slaven		Picton	Prince Edward
Cassels Son & Co.			Toronto	York

ONTARIO

Name of Bank	Manager or Agent	Paid-up Capital	Town	County
Castles Bros.			Stirling	
Chantry, P.O.			Harlem	
Chatham Savings & Loan Co.			Chatham	
Checkley & Co., E.J.	H.C. Edgar, Cashier; C.R. Hanning, Manager	$10,000	Preston	Waterloo
Christopher, A.N.			Ingersoll	Oxford
Claris' Banking House	George T. Claris		St. Thomas	Elgin
Claris, George T.		$50,000	St. Thomas	Elgin
Clark, J.C.			Kingston	Frontenac
Clarke & Co., T.			Mt. Forest	Wellington
Clarke & Sons	Thomas E. Clarke		Bothwell	Kent
Clay, Sharpe & Co.			Burks Falls	
Collard, Leonard H.			St. Catharines	Lincoln
Collins & Co., T.B.	T.B. Collins		Millbrook	Durham
Collins, T.B.			Millbrook	Durham
Collins, W.B.			Wyoming	
Conn & Co., J.	M. & J. Conn		Alvinston	Lambton
Conn's Banking House	M. & J. Conn		Alvinston	Lambton
Conn's Banking House	R. & J. Conn		Alvinston	Lambton
Cook, B.S.			Fordwich	
Cook, Thos. H.			Sarnia	Lambton
Corbould, W.			Wingham	
Counsell, C.M.			Hamilton	Wentworth
Counsell, Glassco & Co.			Hamilton	Wentworth
Cowdry, N.H.			Waterford	
Crombie, D.B.			St. Catharines	
Cuddy Co.			Bothwell	
Cuddy Falls Company			Amherstburg	Essex
Cuddy, Loftus			Amherstburg	Essex
Curtis, C.L.			Kingston	Frontenac
Cutten, Walter			Guelph	
Dale & Co., J.C.		$30,000	Madoc	Hastings
Dale, J.C.			Madoc	Hastings
Dardis, Thomas			Morrisburg	
Dempsey, S.			Albury	
Denison & Crease			New Hamburg	
Denison, E.R.			Niagara-on-the-Lake	
Dobie & Co., George			Glencoe	
Doble & Co.			Sunderland	Ontario
Doble & Co.	J.B. Vallentyne		Sunderland	Ontario
Dresden Banking Co.			Dresden	
Durval, P.			Collingwood	
Edwards & Co., R.			Cannington	
Edwards & Co., R.	O.E. Weens, Cashier	$50,000	Woodville	Victoria
Elliot & Co.'s Banking House	J.H. Elliot & Co.		Chesley	Bruce
Elliot & Co., J.H.	J.H. Elliot		Chesley	Bruce
Elliot & Company	J.A. Elliot		Ridgetown	Kent
Elliot & Westland	J.A. Elliot		Ridgetown	Kent
Elmira Banking Co.			Elmira	
Emmerton, J.			Clinton	Huron
Essex County Bank	Cameron & Curry, John Curry		Windsor	Essex
Essex County Banking House			Windsor	Essex
Falls Bros			Amherstburg	
Farmer, L.N. & Dep C	Telford & Co.		Owen Sound	
Farmers Bank	Logan & Co.		Seaforth	
Farmers' Banking House	T.A. Gale Gale & Archib		Elora	Wellington
Farran & Archibald			Elora	Wellington
Farran & Tisdall	J.P. Tisdall	$75,000	Clinton	Huron
Farran, W.W.			Clinton	Huron
Farran, W.W.			Elora	Wellington

ONTARIO

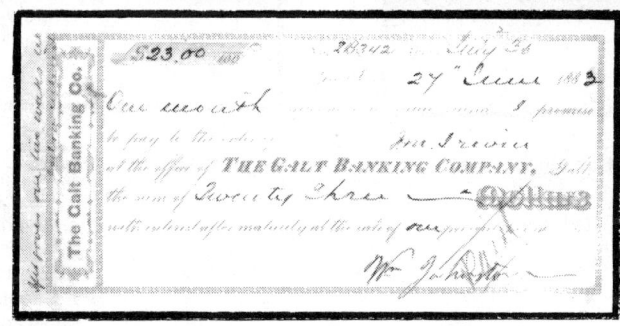

Name of Bank	Manager or Agent	Paid-up Capital	Town	County
Faulkner's Banking House	G.W. Faulkner		Stirling	Hastings
Fawcett & Livingston & Co.			Dresden	
Fawcett & Livingston			Wallaceburg	
Fawcett & Livingston			Wardsville	
Fawcett, Thomas			Listowel	
Fawcett, Thomas			Mitchell	
Fawcett, Thomas			Stratford	
Fawcett, Thomas			Watford	
Fawcett's Bank			Alvinston	Lambton
Fawcett's Bank			Arkona	
Fawcett's Bank			Wyoming	
Fead, J.S.			Orangeville	Dufferin
Finnie			Arnprior	
Fish & Son, Wm. T.	Elbert L. Fish		Cobourg	Northumberland
Fisher, David			Bowmanville	
Fitzgibbon, J.G.			Norwood	
Fleming, M.	Henry Barron		Forest	Lambton
Fleming, M.			Sarnia	
Folger Brothers			Kingston	Frontenac
Forbes & Co.			Toronto	York
Fox, R. & J.	John Fox	$50,000	Lucan	Middlesex
Fraser, Donald			Kingston	Frontenac
Fulford & Co., G.T.			Brockville	Leeds
Fuller & Co., W.S.			Mitchell	
Fuller's Bank	Jacob Fuller	$15,000	Thedford	Lambton
Fuller's Banking Office	P. Phillips, Cashier		Leamington	Essex
Fuller, C.D.			Toronto	York
Fuller, Jacob			Thedford	
Fuller, T.	Maclaughlin		Blenheim	
Fuller, Thomas	P. Phillips		Leamington	Essex
Fuller, W.S.			Alliston	
Galt Banking Company, The			Galt	
Gamble & White			Palmerston	
Gardener, Jas.			Meaford	
Gardiner, Samuel			Chatham	
Gardiner, William E.			Chatham	
Garrett, James			Aylmer	
Gibson, R.C.			Terra Cotta	
Gilberts Bank			St. Thomas	
Gillies & Co.			Teeswater	Bruce
Gillies & Smith			Brussels	
Gillies & Smith			Teeswater	
Gillis & Co., John D.			Highgate	Elgin
Gillis & Reycraft	John D. Gillis		Highgate	Kent
Gordon & Douglas	J.E.W. Branan		Alviston	Lambton
Gordon, A.W.			Orillia	Simcoe
Gould & Bros. I.J.	Isaac J. Gould		Uxbridge	Ontario
Graft, H.H.			Simcoe	Norfolk

ONTARIO

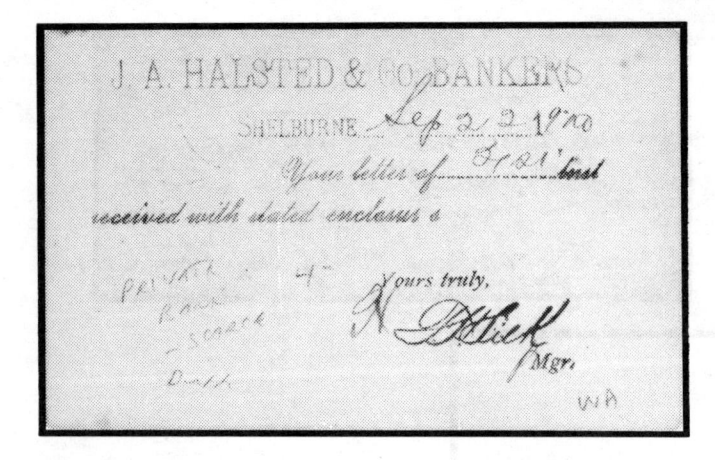

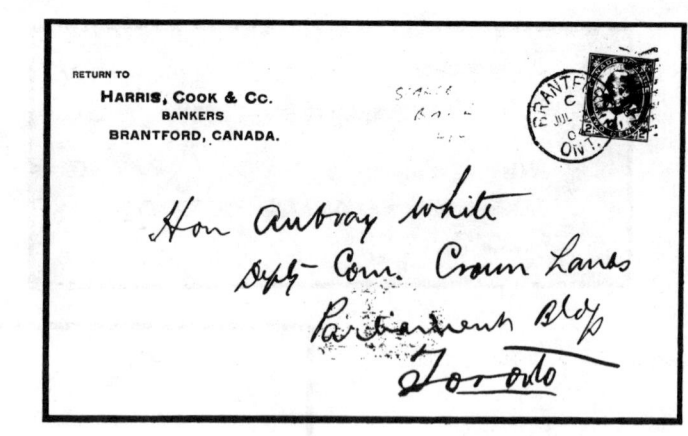

Name of Bank	Manager or Agent	Paid-up Capital	Town	County
Graham & Knight	C.R. Knight	$50,000	Alliston	Simcoe
Graham & Knight	D. McArthur		Creemore	Simcoe
Graham, I.			Uxbridge	
Graham, Joseph C.			Tiverton	
Graydon, W.J.			Streetsville	
Groff, H.H.			Simcoe	Norfolk
Guelph Banking Co.	W.H. Cutten		Guelph	Wellington
Gzowski & Buchan			Toronto	York
Gzowski, C.S., Jr., Broker			Toronto	York
Hale, Horatio			Clinton	
Hallett & Co., J.G.			Woodbridge	
Halliday, Wm.			Pakenham	
Halstead & Co.			Walkerton	
Halstead & Co., J.A.			Orangeville	
Halstead & Scott			Wingham	
Halstead & Co., J.A.	J.A. Halstead		Mt. Forest	Wellington
Halstead & Co., J.A.	E.A. Smith, F.H. Silk, J.F. Miller		Shelburne	Dufferin
Halton & Co., F.J.		$17,000.	Windsor	Essex
Hamer & Co., W.T.			Gravenhurst	Simcoe
Hamilton & Co.	Wm. Lonsdale		Grand Valley	Dufferin
Hamilton Clearing House Asso'n	John Pottenger, Chairman		Hamilton	Wentworth
Hamilton Prov. & Loan Soc.	Geo. H. Gillespie, Pr	$1,100,000.	Hamilton	Wentworth
Hamilton, R.E.			Grand Valley	
Harris, George, F.R.			Emerson	
Harris, Cook & Co.			Brantford	
Harrison & Rathburn			Alvinston	Lambton
Harrison & Rathburn			Glencoe	Middlesex
Hartman & Co.	C.W. Hartman		Clarksburg	Grey
Hartman & Co.	C.W. Hartman		Thornbury	Grey
Hartman & Wilgress			Clarksburg	
Haskins & Co., W.F.	Geo. Wilson	$51,000	Dunnville	Haldimand
Haven & Co., W.C.			Kingston	Frontenac
Hay Bros.			Listowell	Perth
Hay Bros.	A. Miller		Tara	Bruce
Hayes, M.P.			Seaforth	
Hayes, N.			Ingersoll	
Haynes, D. Curtis			St. Catharines	
Hey & Co.			Ailsa Craig	Middlesex
Hey & Jones			Ailsa Craig	Middlesex
Hillhouse, Jas.			Clifford	
Hime, H.L.			Toronto	York
Holtby & Co., F.B.			Mitchell	Perth
Holtby, F.			Mitchell	Perth
Holton & Co., F.J.			Windsor	
Hood, John			Hawkesbury	
Hornibrook & Co.			Beamsville	
House, F.			Cobourg Nort	Humberland
Howard & Co., G.H.			Niagara Falls	Welland
Howard, L.W.			Chesterville	
Howett & Kerr			Guelph	Wellington
Howitt, Charles E.	A. Bradshaw		Guelph	Wellington
Howitt, Charles E.	Geo. Bradshaw		Guelph	Wellington
Howitt, Charles E.	L.C. Mercer		Guelph	Wellington
Howitt, Chas. E.	Chas. Mercer		Guelph	Wellington
Hughes, G.P.		$20,000	Tottenham	Simcoe
Hughes, Geo. P.			Keenansville	Simcoe

ONTARIO

Name of Bank	Manager or Agent	Paid-up Capital	Town	County
Hunt's Bank			Bracebridge	Muskoka
Hunt's Bank	Alfred Hunt		Bradford	Simcoe
Hunt, Alfred			Bracebridge	Muskoka
Huron & Bruce			Goderich	
Hurst & Burk			Thessalon	Ontario
Huxley, G.			Clinton	
Irwin, J.M.			Galt	Waterloo
Irwin, J.M.			Hespeler	Waterloo
Jackson Brothers	S.T. Jackson		Ripley	Bruce
Jackson, Henry			Beeton	
Jackson, T.R.	D. MacLachlan		Blenheim	Kent
James F. Macklem			Chippawa	Welland
Jarvis & Co., Aemilius, Brokers			Toronto	York
Jay & Co., C.H.			Meaford	Grey
Johnson, H.			Springfield	
Johnson, A.			Sarnia	Ontario
Johnston, Alex			Strathroy	
Johnston & Tisdal			Clinton	
Johnston Banking Co.			Amherstburg	
Johnston, G.B.			Goderich	
Johnston, Gale, Tisdal			Clinton	
Jones, Charles T.			Hamilton	Wentworth
Kaine, John			Gorrie	Dufferin
Kemp, D.			Ingersoll	
Kent Bros.			Kingston	Frontenac
Kerr & McKellar			Guelph	
Kilbourne & Co., George S.			Owen Sound	Grey
Killmaster, C.S.			Port Rowan	Norfolk
Kippen & Scarff			Tilbury Centre	Kent
Kirby's Banking House	M.J. Kirby, Cashier		Arthur	Wellington
Kirby, Edward D.			Petrolia	
Kirkpatrick, T.W.			Rodney	Elgin
Kittredge Bros.			Teeswater	
Kittredge Bros.			Walkerton	
Kittredge, H.H.			Parkhill	
Landed Banking & Loan Co.	C.W. Cartwright	$682,000	Hamilton	Wentworth
Larke, C.			Colborne	
Lawrason, J.P.			St. George	Brant
Lemon & Smith			Alvinston	Lampton
Lillico, Peter	C.H. Smith		Drayton	Wellington
Lillico, Peter	R.L. Lillico		Listowel	Perth
Lillicos Banking House			Drayton	
Lillicos Banking House	R.E. Lillico		Arthur	Wellington
Linton & Co., J.			Lakefield	
Linton & Co., James		$35,000	Orono	Durham
Linton & Co., James	W.H. Benson, Cashier	$35,000	Lakefield	Peterborough
Linton, James			Lakefield	Peterborough
Linton, James			Orono	Durham
Loftus Cuddy			Amherstburg	Essex
Logan			Seaforth	
Logan & Weir			Seaforth	
Long, A.			Uxbridge	
Lownsbrough & Co.			Toronto	York
Lucas & Co., William	E.G. Lucas		Dunnville	
Lucas & Co., William	E.G. Lucas		Dundalk	Grey
Lucas & Co., William	William Lucas	$30,000	Markdale	Grey
Lucas, Leacock & Co.	H.J. Leacock		Brigden	Lambton
Lucas, Tanner & Co.	Charles E. Tanner		Blyth	Huron
Lucknow Banking Co.	Geo. A. Siddall		Lucknow	
Lyon, Jr., R.A.			Sault Ste. Marie	
Macarthur & Co.			Zurich	Hay
Macarthur & Co.	John Macarthur, Henry Arnold		Hensall	Huron
MacDonald, W.R.			Hamilton	
Machray & Co.	Robert Machray		Ottawa	
Macklem, James F.			Chippawa	Welland
Madill & Co., B.	Benjamin Madill		Beaverton	
Madoc Banking Co.			Madoc	
Mahon, J.A.			London	
Mair & Siddall	Geo. A. Siddall	$25,000	Lucknow	Bruce
Mair & Smith			Teeswater	
Maitland P., Ketchum			Brighton	Northumberland
Manson, James			Strathroy	
Marten Bros.	C.G. Marten		Leamington	Essex
Matthews & Co., W.H.			Huntsville	Muskoka
Maxon, G.			Leamington	Essex

ONTARIO

Name of Bank	Manager or Agent	Paid-up Capital	Town	County
Mayhew & Harmer			Thamesville	Kent
McCall, William			Sarnia	Lambton
McCullough & Young	W.L. Young		Markdale	Grey
McDonald & Co., A.	David Roy		Listowell	Perth
McDonald, H.F.			London	
McDonald, J.		$5,000	Chatsworth	Grey
McGee			Walkerton	
McGregor & Brother			Windsor	
McGregor, D.			Sault Ste. Marie	
McIntosh & McTaggart	J.M. McIntosh		Brussels	Huron
McIntyre, A.M.			Dutton	
McIntyre & Son, G.			St. Mary's	Perth
McIntyre's Banking Office	G.H. McIntyre		St. Mary's	Perth
McIntyre, Gilbert H.			St. Mary's	Perth
McKay & Jasperson		$4,000	Kingsville	Essex
McKeand, Archibald			Hamilton	Wentworth
McKeggie & Co., J.C.			Coldwater	
McKeggie & Co., J.C.			Fenlon Falls	
McKeggie & Co., J.C.	J. McEachern		Creemore	
McKeggie & Co., J.C.	J. McEachern		Elmvale	Simcoe
McKeggie & Co., J.C.	J.A. Cameron		Staynor	Simcoe
McKeggie & Co., J.C.	J.H. McKeggie		Barrie	Simcoe
McLelland, R.A.			Brockville	
McMahon & Co.			Delhi	
McMurchie & Rance			Blyth	Huron
McNally & Adams			Hanover	Bruce
McTaggart & Co.	D.H. Cameron		Parkhill	Middlesex
McTaggart & Co., A.			Parkhill	Middlesex
McTaggart, Geo. D.			Clinton	Huron
Menzies, Thomas			Peterboro	
Merritt, W.E.			Chatham	Kent
Merritt's Banking Office	W.E. Merritt		Chatham	Kent
Messner & Co., F.X.			Formosa	
Midland Banking Co.	S. Paterson & Bro.	$40,000	Port Hope	Durham
Midland Loan & Savings Co.	Geo. M. Furby		Port Hope	Durham
Midland Trust Co.	S. Patterson/Co.		Port Hope	Durham
Mihell & Co.			Ailsa Craig	Middlesex
Millbrook Banking Co.			Millbrook	
Miller & Co.	W.C. Hamilton		Stouffville	York
Miller & Co.	Walter Miller		Stouffville	York
Miller & Co., J.F.			Shelbourne	
Mills & Cunningham			Kingston	Frontenac
Mills & Kent			Kingston	Frontenac
Milne, John			Essex	Essex
Milner, Wm.			St. Augustine	
Mitchell & Alexander			Ailsa Craig	Middlesex
Mitchell Banking Co.			Mitchell	
Mitchell, George			Flesherton	Grey
Mitchells Banking House	George Mitchell		Flesherton	Grey
Moment, Robert			Orono	Durham
Moore, H.J.			Toronto	York
Morehouse, H.D.			Guelph	
Morgan, Charles E.			Hamilton	Wentworth
Morison, John			Toronto	York
Morris & Co., S.B.	S.B. Morris		Rodney	Elgin

ONTARIO

Name of Bank	Manager or Agent	Paid-up Capital	Town	County
Morris, R.			Petrolia	Lambton
Morton, Geo. K.		$20,000	St. Thomas	Elgin
Mowat & Son, W.	W. Mowat		Stratford	Perth
Mowat, William			Stratford	Perth
Mulholland & Roper	J.H. Roper		Peterboro	Peterboro
Munro, James		$20,000	Embro	Oxford
Murphy, Gordon & Co.	R. Gordon		Tweed	Hastings
Murphy, P. & P.			Stoco	
Murray's Bank	Walter Edgar Murray	$44,000	Aylmer	Elgin
Murray's Bank	W.E. Murray	$44,000	Ayr	Waterloo
Murray, Robert			Embro	Oxford
Murray, W.E.			Aylmer	
Newman & Co., W.P.			Elora	
Norsworthy, J.C.			Ingersoll	Oxford
North American Banking Co.	J.C. Smith		Seaforth	
O'Flynn & Sons, E.D.	E.D. O'Flynn	$150,000	Madoc	Hastings
O'Hara & Co., H., Brokers			Toronto	York
O'Loughlin, B.S.			Yarker	
O'Neil, B.S.		$30,000	Exeter	Huron
O'Neil, R.H.			Lucan	Middlesex
O'Neill & Son, R.H.	F.A. O'Neill		Lucan	Middlesex
Orono Banking House	W.W. Trull		Orono	Durham
Osler & Hammond, Brokers			Toronto	York
Owen & Co.	J.T. Owen		Ailsa Craig	Middlesex
Oxford Banking Co.			Woodstock	
Oxnard, G.A.			Guelph	Wellington
Parish & Son, A.	E.S. Clow		Athens	Leeds
Park Hill Banking Co.			Port Arthur	
Parker Brothers			Stirling	Hastings
Parkhill Banking Co.	Thomas L. Rogers		Parkhill	Middlesex
Patton, F.			Tamworth	
Paxton & Co., R.	Robert Paxton	$10,000	Otterville	Oxford
Paxton, Robert			Otterville	Oxford
Pews Banking House			Welland	
Phipps, W.B.			Toronto	York
Pierce, Howard & Co.			Niagara Falls	Welland
Pool, Hockin & Co.			Dutton	Elgin
Pool, James			Dutton	Elgin
Porteous, R.			Paisley	Bruce
Porteous & Saunders	E. Saunders	$100,000	Paisley	Bruce
Porteous Bank of Canada			Paisley	Bruce
Powell, R.J.			Blenheim	Kent
Preston Banking Co.	E.J. Checkley		Preston	Waterloo
Rae, Robert			Thedford	Lambton
Rae, Robert	R.A. Rae		Oil Springs	Lambton
Ranney & Co., R.			Milverton	Perth
Rapley & Co., J.W.			Kincardine	Bruce
Rapley, J.W.			Kincardine	Bruce
Rathbun Co.	F.S. Rathbun		Deseronto	
Rathbun Company, The	F.S. Rathbun		Deseronto	Hastings
Raven, J.R.			Owen Sound	
Ray, Street & Co.	C.W. Jarvis		Fort William	
Ray, Street & Co.	H.A. McKibbin	$75,000	Port Arthur	Algoma
Ray, Street & Co.	S.W. Ray	$100,000	Port Arthur	Algoma
Reid & Elliot			Essex	Essex
Richardson's Banking Office	Alex. Richardson		Grand Valley	Dufferin
Richardson, A.			Grand Valley	Dufferin
Richardson, Alex			Hillsburgh	
Riddall & Co., R.T.			Wallaceburg	Kent
Ridley & Bury	Thos. H. Ridley		Duart	Kent

ONTARIO

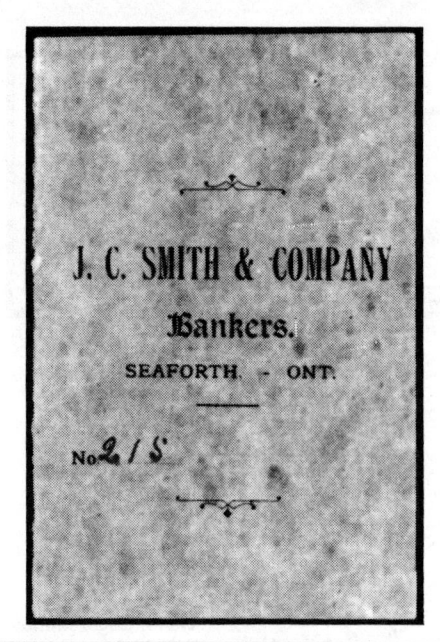

Name of Bank	Manager or Agent	Paid-up Capital	Town	County
Robertson & Son, Samuel			Harriston	Wellington
Robinson & Roberts			Harriston	Wellington
Robinson & Roberts			Mt. Forest	Wellington
Rogers & Co.	R.R. Rogers		Stayner	Simcoe
Rogers, T.L.			Parkhill	Middlesex
Rogers, Thomas L.			Parkhill	Middlesex
Ross, Allan J.		$12,000	Iroquois	Dundas
Ross & Co., J.C.			Aurora	
Rosser, Joseph			Ailsa Craig	Middlesex
Rowland & Co., E.	R.M. Cook, Cas	$66,000	Strathroy	Middlesex
Rowland, E.			Strathroy	Middlesex
Rowley & Co.			St. Thomas	
Salter, J.H.			Hagersville	Haldimand
Scott, C. Tait			Oakville	
Scott, C. Tait			Wingham	
Scott's Banking House	C. Tait Scott		Gorrie	
Scott's Banking House	C. Tait Scott		Oakville	
Scott's Banking House	C. Tait Scott		Wingham	
Scott, J.W.	C.R. Knight		Palmerston	Wellington
Scott, J.W.	G.J. Donaldson		Palmerston	Wellington
Scott, J.W.	G.Y. Donaldson		Listowel	Perth
Scott, J.W.	John Hillhouse, F. Walton		Clifford	Wellington
Sealey, W.O.			Waterdown	
Seaman, S.M.			Harlem	
Shaw & Co.'s Bank, John			Wardsville	Middlesex
Shaw, Jr., S.			Toronto	York
Shipley & Co.			Ailsa Craig	Middlesex
Shipley, James G.			Ailsa Craig	Middlesex
Sharpe, J.W.			Dresden	
Siddall & Mair			Lucknow	
Siddall's Bank			Lucknow	
Simcoe Bank			Port Dover	
Simpson, Isaac			Kingston	Frontenac
Sinasac, A.E.			Harrow	
Skerritt, J.			Arthur	Wellington
Skerritt, J. & Co.		$18,000	Arthur	Wellington
Smart's Banking House	J.H. Smart	$50,000	Kingsville	Essex
Smart, J.H.			Kingsville	Essex
Smart, William F.P.			Goderich	
Smith & Company, J.C.			Seaforth	Huron
Smith & Co., L.H.			Strathroy	
Smith & Co., L.H.	Montague Smith	$100,000	Forest	Lambton
Smith & Co., W.O.			Thornbury	
Smith, H.E.			Wingham	Huron
Smith, J.			Terra Cotta	
Smith, J.C.			Orillia	Simcoe
Smith, J.C.			Seaforth	

ONTARIO

Name of Bank	Manager or Agent	Paid-up Capital	Town	County
Smith, R.O.			Chatham	Kent
Smith, R.O.			Windsor	
Smith, W.O.			Thornbury	
Smith, W.T.			Strathroy	
Snell & Co.	Jos. Snell, Cashier	$10,000	Dashwood	Hay
Snyder, L.P.			North Bay	
Somers, Gabriel T.			Beeton	Simcoe
Somers, Gabriel T.			Cookstown	
South & Co.			Pekin	
Squire & Boughner			Bothwell	Waterloo
Stark & Barnes			Stouffville	York
Steinhoff & Lillie	John Lillie		Wallaceburg	Kent
Stephens, James			Dresden	
Stephenson & Co., J.	M. Stephenson	$20,000	Unionville	York
Stewart, Daniel			Aylmer	
Stewart, J.H.			Trenton	Hastings
Stewart, James	J.W. Hill		Tilbury Centre	Kent
Stewarts Banking House	J.H. Stewart		Trenton	Hastings
Stimson & Co., Geo. A., Brokers			Toronto	York
Stinson, James	Alex H. Moore		Hamilton	Wentworth
Stinsons Bank	James Stinson		Hamilton	Wentworth
Storey, Christie & Co.	D. Henderson		Acton	Halton
Struthers Banking House			Elmira	
Struthers, R.C.			Essex	Essex
Stuart, W.A.			Napierville	
Sutherland, D.F.			Winchester	Dundas
Swaisland & Co., W.	E.O. Swaisland		Glencoe	Middlesex
Swaisland Bros.	E.C. Swaisland		Brantford	Brant
Tanner, J.			Fergus	
Taylor & Minty			Hamilton	Wentworth
Telford & Co.			Owen Sound	
Thomas & Kenward		$16,000	Watford	Lambton
Thompson, H.H.			Penetanguishene	Simcoe
Thompson, U.E.			Belleville	Hastings
Tisdale & Wade			Orillia	Simcoe
Tisdale Private Bank			Orillia	Simcoe
Tisdale, W.B.			Orillia	Simcoe
Tisdale, W.B.			Teeswater	Bruce
Toronto Clearing House	E. Stanger, Secretary		Toronto	York
Townsend, J.			Terra Cotta	
Trow & Sons, J.			Stratford	
Tweed Banking House	Faulknew/McClelland		Tweed	
Unsworth, Isaac			Florence	Lambton
Unsworth, J.			Florence	Lambton
Vandusen, W.	W.J. Fawcett		Tara	Bruce
Vandusen, Whitford			Tara	Bruce
Vaughn & Fairbank	R. Morris		Petrolia	Lambton
Vaughn & Fairbank	W.J. Savage		Petrolia	Lambton
Wadell, Andrew			Goderich	
Ward & Co., W.J.			Brigden	Lambton
Ward & Co., W.J.			New Hamburg	
Ward, W.J.			Brigden	Lambton
Warnock, W.			Aylmer	Elgin
Watson, Chas. W.			Dresden	Kent
Watson, J.			Leamington	Essex
Waugh & Co., Lewis	W.S. Waugh		Orangeville	Dufferin
Webster Bank	W.J. Webster	$20,000	Westport	Leeds
Webster, W.J.			Westport	Leeds
Westcott, F.			Kingsville	Essex
Westland, Alfred			Wyoming	Lambton
Westland & Co., Alfred		$20,000	Wyoming	Lambton
Westland & Nichol	A.J. Westland		Comber	Essex
Westland, E.A.			Wyoming	Lambton
Whealey & Schwendimann	William Salter		Drayton	Wellington
White's Banking Office	W.H. White		Palmerston	Wellington
White, W.H.	J.M. Watson		Luther	Dufferin
Whitelaw, Charles			Paris	
Whittemore, E.F.			Toronto	York
Whyte, John			Ridgetown	Kent
Whyte, Somerville & McDonald			Ridgetown	Kent
Wilcocks, Joseph			Arkona	Lambton
Wilcox, J.			Arkona	Lambton
Williams & Co., J.			Wroxeter	
Willis, A.			Toronto	York

ONTARIO

Name of Bank	Manager or Agent	Paid-up Capital	Town	County
Willson & Co., Benj.			Wingham	
Willson & Co., F.M.			Hamilton	Wentworth
Winkler, A.E.			Elmira	
Wood & Kells			Millbrook	Durham
Wyatt & Co., Brokers			Toronto	York
Wynne, G.H.			Watford	Lambton
Wynnes Banking Office	G.H. Wynne		Watford	Lambton
Yarker, G.W.			Toronto	York

QUEBEC

Name of Bank	Manager or Agent	Paid-up Capital	Town	County
Cartier, Laramie & Co.			St. Fran's du Lac	Yam'ka
Ethier, H.H.			Laurentides	Assomp'n
Garand, Terroux & Co.		$50,000	Montreal	Hochelaga
Gilmour's Bank		$150,000	Stanbridge East	Missisquoi
Gilmour, A.H.			Stanbridge East	Missisquoi
Huntingdon County Bank	Andrew Somerville		Huntingdon	Huntingdon
Marler, G.R.			Montreal	Hochelaga
McGie & Son, Daniel			Quebec	Quebec
Montreal City & Dist. Sav. Bk.	Sir Wm Hingston	$600,000	Montreal	Hochelaga
Montreal Clearing House Asso'n	W.W.L. Chipman, Manager		Montreal	Hochelaga
Panneton, P.E.			Three Rivers	St. Maurice
Picken & Co., J.B.			Montreal	Hochelaga
Strathy Bros., Brokers			Montreal	Hochelaga
Taillon, A.A.			Sorel	Richelieu
Thompson Co., Frank	Frank Thompson		Sherbrooke	Sherbrooke
Weir & Sons, W.			Montreal	Hochelaga

SASKATCHEWAN

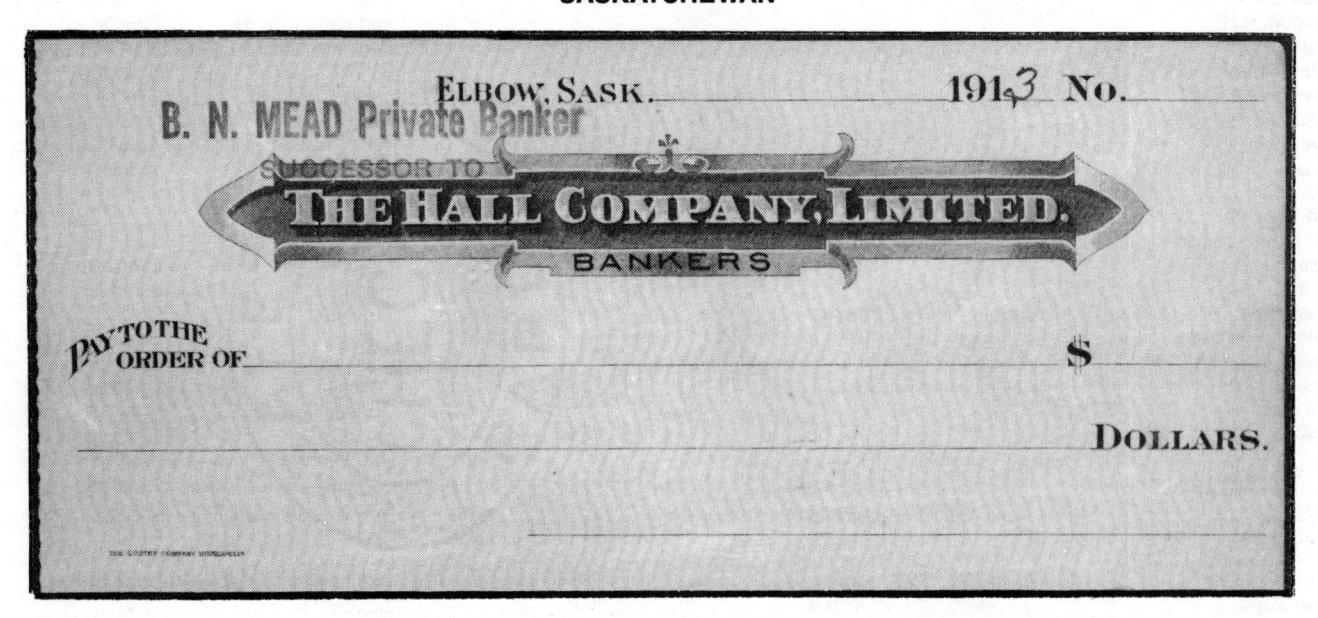

Name of Bank	Manager or Agent	Paid-up Capital	Town	County
Chappel, Son & Co.			Frobisher	
Hall Company, Limited, The			Elbow	
Hettle Co., J. O.			Saskatoon	
Hettle-Drennan Co.			Saskatoon	
McEchinney, O. K.			Glenside	
Mead, B.N.			Elbow	

Table I

CANADIAN CHARTERED BANK NOTES OUTSTANDING

CANADIAN CHARTERED BANK NOTES OUTSTANDING, FEBRUARY 1989
Redeemable by the Bank of Canada

The list includes amalgamated and absorbed banks.

CANADIAN IMPERIAL BANK OF COMMERCE

The Bank of British Columbia	48,727.00
The Bank of Hamilton	125,737.00
Barclays Bank of Canada	18,590.00
The Canadian Bank of Commerce	1,421,636.00
The Eastern Townships Bank	38,660.00
The Gore Bank	
The Halifax Banking Co.	4,597.18
The Imperial Bank of Canada	450,180.00
The Merchants Bank of P.E.I.	8,764.00
The Niagara Districk Bank	
The St. Lawrence Bank	945.00
The Standard Bank of Canada	121,065.00
The Sterling Bank of Canada	18,825.00
The Western Bank of Canada	7,505.00
The Weyburn Security Bank	15,435.00

THE BANK OF MONTREAL

The Bank of British North America	215,212.00
The Bank of Montreal	1,556,227.00
The Commercial Bank of Canada	9,133.00
The Exchange Bank of Yarmouth	1,099.00
The Merchants Bank of Canada	328,502.00
The Molsons Bank	129,103.00
The Peoples Bank of Halifax	1,123.50
The Peoples Bank of New Brunswick	10,509.00

BANQUE CANADIENNE NATIONALE

Banque Canadienne Nationale	195,850.00
Banque d'Hochelaga	99,052.50
La Banque Nationale	73,064.50

THE BANK OF NOVA SCOTIA

The Bank of New Brunswick	32,180.00
The Bank of Nova Scotia	568,127.42
The Bank of Ottawa	94,645.50
The Metropolitan Bank	10,535.00
The Summerside Bank	43.00
The Union Bank of P.E.I.	8,969.76

THE PROVINCIAL BANK OF CANADA

La Banque Jacques Cartier	4,108.00
The Provincial Bank of Canada	129,777.50

THE ROYAL BANK OF CANADA

The Commercial Bank of Windsor	3,324.07
The Crown Bank of Canada	3,325.00
The Merchants Bank of Halifax	10,596.65
The Northern Bank	3,755.00
The Northern Crown Bank	37,207.25
The Quebec Bank	57,394.00
The Royal Bank of Canada	1,310,773.00
The Traders Bank of Canada	39,219.25
The Union Bank of Canada	261,520.50
The Union Bank of Halifax	17,421.52
United Empire Bank of Canada	1,170.00

THE TORONTO-DOMINION BANK

The Bank of Toronto	376,471.00
The Dominion Bank	252,246.50

DEFUNCT BANKS

The Bank of Vancouver	3,376.54
The Bank of Yarmouth	789.82
La Banque de St. Hyacinthe	4,401.00
La Banque du Peuple	7,944.00
Banque Internationale du Canada	1,449.35
La Banque St. Jean	1,847.23
La Banque Ville Marie	5,808.82
The Commercial Bank of Manitoba	5,897.20
The Farmers Bank of Canada	1,883.54
The Home Bank of Canada	35,027.46
The Ontario Bank *	
The St. Stephen's Bank	11,066.67
The Sovereign Bank of Canada	8,664.44

* Redeemable by Royal Trust Co.

The odd cents in the totals are accounted for by some banks having taken over the circulation issued in Halifax currency by earlier institutions. It is also due to the practice of paying only 50 percent of the face value of mutilated notes, of which more than two-fifths of the original was missing, but more than two-fifths remained bearing one signature.

Table II

CURRENT CHARTERED BANKS IN CANADA

Domestic Banks

The Bank of Montreal
The Bank of Nova Scotia
The Canadian Imperial Bank of Commerce
The Canadian Western Bank

The Laurentian Bank of Canada
The National Bank of Canada
The Royal Bank of Canada
The Toronto Dominion Bank

Foreign Bank Subsidiaries

ABN Bank Canada
ANZ Bank Canada
Banca Commerciale Italiana of Canada
Banca Nazionale del Lavoro of Canada
Banco Central of Canada
Bank Hapoalim (Canada)
Bank Leumi le-Israel (Canada)
Bank of America Canada
Bank of Boston Canada
Bank of Credit and Commerce Canada
Bank of Toyko Canada, The
Banque Nationale de Paris (Canada)
Barclays Bank of Canada
BT Bank of Canada
Chase Manhattan Bank of Canada, The
Chemical Bank of Canada
Citibank Canada
Comerica Bank Canada
Credit Commercial de France (Canada)
Credit Lyonnais Canada
Credit Suisse Canada
Dai-Ichi Kangyo Bank (Canada)
Daiwa Bank Canada
Deutsche Bank (Canada)
Dresdner Bank Canada
First Interstate Bank of Canada
First National Bank of Chicago (Canada), The
Fuji Bank Canada
Hanil Bank Canada

Hongkong Bank of Canada
Industrial Bank of Japan (Canada), The
International Commercial Bank of Cathay (Canada)
Irving Bank Canada
Israel Discount Bank of Canada
Korea Exchange Bank of Canada
Manufacturers Hanover Bank of Canada
Mellon Bank Canada
Mitsubishi Bank of Canada
Mitsui Bank of Canada, The
Morgan Bank of Canada
National Bank of Detroit, Canada
National Bank of Greece (Canada)
National Westminster Bank of Canada
Overseas Union Bank of Singapore (Canada)
Paribas Bank of Canada
Republic National Bank of New York (Canada)
Sanwa Bank Canada
Security Pacific Bank Canada
Societe Generale (Canada)
Standard Chartered Bank of Canada
State Bank of India (Canada)
Sumitomo Bank of Canada, The
Swiss Bank Corporation (Canada)
Taiyo Kobe Bank (Canada)
Tokai Bank Canada
Union Bank of Switzerland (Canada)
United Overseas Bank (Canada)

Table III

NON-NOTE ISSUING BANKS

Banks	Established	Remarks
Albert Bank, Saint John, N.B.	1865	Charter not used
Alliance Bank of Canada, Halifax, N.S.	1903	Charter not used
The Anglo-Canadian and Continental Bank, Montreal, Que.	1908	Name changed to Anglo-Canadian Bank in 1909; charter not used
The Anglo-Canadian Bank, Toronto, Ontario	1886	Charter not used
Bank of Agriculture, Hamilton, Ontario	1868	Charter not used
Bank of Kingston, Kingston, Ontario	1819	Charter not used
Bank of London, London, Ontario	1865	Charter not used
Bank of Manitoba, Fort Garry, Manitoba	1872	Charter not used
Bank of Northumberland, Cobourg, Ontario	1865	Charter not used
Bank of Simcoe, Simcoe, Ontario	1865	Charter not used
The Bank of the United Provinces, Toronto, Ontario	1874	Name changed in 1875 from London and Canada Bank: charter not used
Bank of Western Canada, Winnipeg, Manitoba	1966	Charter not used
Bank of Winnipeg, Winnipeg, Manitoba	1884	Charter not used
Bank of Winnipeg, Winnipeg, Manitoba	1903	Charter not used
Bank of Winnipeg, Winnipeg, Manitoba	1908	Charter not used
La Banque des Marchands, Montreal, Quebec	1848	Charter not used
Banque des Trois Rivieres, Trois-Rivieres, Quebec	1841	Charter not used
Bedford District Bank, Waterloo, Ontario	1871	Charter not used
Brant County Bank of Canada, Brantford, Ontario	1883	Charter not used
British Canadian Bank, Winnipeg, Manitoba	1883	Name changed in 1883 from North Western Bank; charter not used
Canadian Commercial and Industrial Bank, Edmonton, Alberta	1975	Failed
Central Bank of Canada, Montreal, Quebec	1873	Charter not used
The Chartered Bank of British Columbia and Vancouver Island	1862	Name changed to Bank of British Columbia
Chartered Bank of London and Canada, Toronto, Ontario	1900	Charter not used
Chartered Bank of London and North America, Montreal, Quebec	1876	Name changed in 1882 to Chartered Bank of London and Winnipeg; charter not used
Citizens Bank of Canada, Toronto, Ontario	1903	Charter not used
City and County Bank of Canada, Ottawa, Ontario	1903	Charter not used
Colonial Bank (Canada), Montreal, Quebec	1915	Charter not used
Colonial Bank of British Columbia, New Westminster, B.C.	1863	Charter not used
Colonial Bank of Canada, Winnipeg, Manitoba	1906	Charter not used
Continental Bank of Canada, Montreal, Quebec	1886	Charter not used
District Bank of Quebec, Quebec, Quebec	1847	Charter not used
Eastern Bank of New Brunswick, Saint John, N.B.	1865	Charter not used
Great West Bank of Canada, Regina, Saskatchewan	1920	Charter not used
Klondike and Dawson City Bank, Montreal, Quebec	1898	Charter not used
London and Canada Bank, Toronto, Ontario	1874	Charter not used
Manitoba Bank, Winnipeg, Manitoba	1882	Charter not used
Manufacturers' Bank of Canada, Montreal, Quebec	1873	Name changed in 1875 from Victoria Bank of Canada; charter not used
Mercantile Bank of Canada, Montreal, Quebec	1953	Active
Miramichi Bank, Chatham, N.B.	1857	Charter not used
Monarch Bank of Canada, Toronto, Ontario	1905	Charter not used
Mutual Bank of Nova Scotia, Halifax, N.S.	1864	Charter not used
Niagara Suspension Bridge Bank, Chippewa, Ontario	1835	Failed in 1840
Northern Bank, Chatham, N.B.	1866	Charter not used
Northland Bank, Winnipeg, Manitoba	1976	Active
North-Western Bank, Winnipeg, Manitoba	1882	Name changed in 1883 to British Canadian Bank; charter not used
The People's Bank, Montreal, Quebec	1969	Merged in 1970 with the Banque Provinciale du Canada
Planters' Bank of Canada, Montreal, Quebec	1882	Charter not used
Quebec District Bank, Quebec, Quebec	1847	Charter not used
The Royal Bank of Canada, Toronto, Ontario	1859	Charter not used
Securities Bank of Canada, Toronto, Ontario	1902	Charter not used
Shediac Bank, Shediac, N.B.	1856	Charter not used
Sterling Bank of Canada, London, Ontario	1903	Charter not used
Superior Bank of Canada, Toronto, Ontario	1872	Charter not used
Three Rivers Bank, Trois-Rivieres, Quebec	1873	Charter not used
Union Bank of Canada, Hamilton, Ontario	1856	Charter not used
Unity Bank of Canada, Toronto, Ontario	1972	Merged in 1977 with La Banque Provinciale du Canada
Victoria Bank of Canada, Montreal, Quebec	1873	Name changed in 1874 to Manufacturers' Bank of Canada; charter not used
Western Bank, Yarmouth, N.S.	1871	Charter not used
Woodstock Bank, Woodstock, N.B.	1865	Charter not used
York County Bank, Toronto, Ontario	1890	Charter not used

Table IV

BANK MERGERS AND AMALGAMATIONS SINCE JULY 1, 1867

Purchasing Bank	Date	Bank Absorbed
The Bank of Montreal	22/05/1868*	The Commercial Bank of Canada
	13/08/1903	The Exchange Bank of Yarmouth
	27/06/1905	The People's Bank of Halifax
	13/04/1907	The People's Bank of New Brunswick
	12/10/1918	The Bank of British North America
	20/03/1922	The Merchants Bank of Canada
	20/01/1925	The Molsons Bank
The Bank of Nova Scotia	01/10/1883	The Union Bank of Price Edward Island
	12/09/1901*	The Summerside Bank
	15/02/1913	The Bank of New Brunswick
	14/11/1914	The Metropolitan Bank
	30/04/1919	The Bank of Ottawa
The Canadian Imperial Bank of Commerce	19/05/1870*	The Gore Bank
	21/06/1875*	The Niagara District Bank
	31/12/1900*	The Bank of British Columbia
	30/05/1903*	The Halifax Banking Company
	31/05/1906*	The Merchants Bank of Prince Edward Island
	13/02/1909*	The Western Bank of Canada
	29/02/1912*	The Eastern Townships Bank
	31/12/1923*	The Bank of Hamilton
	31/12/1924*	The Sterling Bank of Canada
	03/11/1928*	The Standard Bank of Canada
	01/05/1931*	The Weyburn Security Bank
	01/02/1956*	Barclays Bank (Canada)
	01/06/1961	The Canadian Bank of Commerce
	01/06/1961	The Imperial Bank of Canada
The Consolidated Bank of Canada (since failed)	10/05/1876	The City Bank
	10/05/1876	The Royal Canadian Bank
The Home Bank of Canada (since failed)	15/04/1913	Banque Internationale du Canada
The National Bank of Canada	01/11/1979	La Banque Provinciale du Canada
	01/11/1979	Banque Canadienne Nationale **
	03/08/1970*	The People's Bank
	16/06/1977*	Unity Bank of Canada
	30/04/1924*	La Banque Nationale
The Royal Bank of Canada	31/10/1902*	The Commercial Bank of Windsor
	02/07/1908*	The Crown Bank of Canada
	01/11/1910	The Union Bank of Halifax
	31/03/1911*	United Empire Bank of Canada
	03/09/1912	The Traders Bank of Canada
	02/01/1917	The Quebec Bank
	02/07/1918	The Northern Crown Bank
	31/08/1925	The Union Bank of Canada
The Toronto Dominion Bank	01/02/1955	The Bank of Toronto
	01/02/1955	The Dominion Bank

Note: Dates since 1900 are those of the authorizing Order in Council.

* Previously merged or amalgamated with another bank in this listing.

** Formerly the Bank d'Hochelaga.

INDEX

CANADIAN NOTE-ISSUING BANKS

Bank, Issue, Major Alteration	Bank No.	Major Issue No.	Alteration No.	Page No.
Acadia, The Bank of Issue of 1872	5	10	-	1
Accommodation Bank, The Issue of 1837	10	10	-	2
No "_____" above vignette	10	10	02	2
"Redeemable at the UPPER CANADA BANK at Kingston" engraved above vignette	10	10	04	3
Agricultural Bank, The (Montreal)				
Burton and Gurley. New York Printings	15	10		3
Agricultural Bank, The				
Rawdon, Wright, Hatch & Co. Printings Payable at Toronto	20	10		4
New England Bank Note Co. Printing Payable at Montreal	20	12		6
"For GEO. TRUSCOTT . . ." engraved at bottom, 1835-1836	20	12	02	6
"For GEO. TRUSCOTT . . ." omitted and "The" added to bank name	20	12	04	6
Arman's Bank				
Issue of 1837	25	10	-	7
Barclay's Bank (Canada)				
Issue of 1929, large-size notes	30	10	-	8
Issue of 1935, small-size notes	30	12	-	9
Boucherville, La Banque de				
Bourne Printing	35	10	-	9
Brantford, The Bank of				
Payable at Brantford, overall green tint	40	10	-	10
Partially engraved date	40	10	02	11
Engraved date	40	10	04	11
Payable at Sault Ste. Marie, overall red tint	40	12	-	11
British Canadian Bank, The				
BABNC Printings, 1884	45	10	-	12
British Columbia, The Bank of				
Victoria coin issue, 1862-1863, large-size notes	50	10	-	13
Victoria medallion issue, 1863-1875, small-size notes	50	12	-	14
Partially engraved date, 1863	50	12	02	15
Fully engraved date, 1864-1875	50	12	04	15
Issue of 1879	50	14	-	15
Red serial number on face only	50	14	02	16
Black serial number on face, repeated on back	50	14	04	16
Issue of 1894	50	16	-	16
British North America, The Bank of				
Early bank crest issues, 1837-1847	55	10	-	17
Halifax, Nova Scotia, branch issue	55	10	02	17
Montreal, Lower Canada, issue	55	10	04	18
Montreal branch issue				18
Quebec, Lower Canada, issue	55	10	06	18
Quebec branch issue				19
St. John, New Brunswick, issue	55	10	08	19
St. John's, Newfoundland, issue, large-size notes	55	10	10	19
Toronto, Upper Canada, issue	55	10	12	20
Miniature royal crest issues, 1841-1872	55	12	-	20
Brantford issue	55	12	02	21
Fredericton, New Brunswick, issue	55	12	04	21
Halifax issue	55	12	05	21
Hamilton, Brantford agency, issue	55	12	06	22
Hamilton, Dundas agency, issue, 1853 and 1856	55	12	08	22
Hamilton, Simcoe agency, issue	55	12	10	23
Hamilton branch issue	55	12	12	23
Kingston issue	55	12	14	24
London issue	55	12	16	25
Montreal, Bytown agency, issue	55	12	17	26
Montreal issue	55	12	18	26
Quebec issue	55	12	20	27
St. John, New Brunswick, issue	55	12	22	28
St. Stephen, New Brunswick, issue	55	12	24	29
Toronto dollar issue	55	12	26	29
Toronto dollar/pounds and shillings issue	55	12	28	30
Large royal crest issue, 1856	55	13	-	31
Hamilton, Dundas agency, issue, 1856	55	13	10	31

CANADIAN NOTE-ISSUING BANKS

Bank, Issue, Major Alteration	Bank No.	Issue No.	Major Alteration No.	Page No.
British North America, The Bank of (cont.)				
Hamilton issue	55	13	14	31
St. John, New Brunswick, issue	55	13	26	31
No frame $1 and $2 issues, 1852-1868	55	14	-	31
Brantford issue	55	14	02	32
Hamilton issue	55	14	04	32
Kingston issue	55	14	06	32
London issue	55	14	08	33
Montreal issues	55	14	10	33
Quebec issue	55	14	12	34
St. John, New Brunswick, issue	55	14	14	34
Toronto issue	55	14	16	35
Victoria, Vancouver Island, issue	55	14	18	35
Common denomination design, payable at separate branches, 1859-1875				36
Brantford issue	55	16	02	36
Halifax, Nova Scotia, issue	55	16	04	36
Hamilton issue	55	16	06	37
Kingston issue	55	16	08	38
London, Canada West; London, Ontario, issue, 1866-1875	55	16	10	38
Montreal issue	55	16	12	39
Napanee issue				39
Ottawa issue	55	16	14	40
Quebec issue	55	16	16	40
St. John, New Brunswick, issue	55	16	18	41
Toronto issue	55	16	20	41
Victoria, Vancouver Island, issue	55	16	22	42
Branch name to be filled in, manuscript, 1861-1872	55	16	24	43
General issues payable at all branches, 1876-1877	55	18	-	43
$5 issue of 1884	55	20	-	45
Issues of 1886 and 1889	55	22	-	46
Issue of 1911	55	24	-	46
Canada Bank				
Issue of 1792	60	10	-	48
Canada Bank, The				
Danforth, Wright & Co. Printings, 1855	65	10	-	48
Canada, The Bank of				
First issue, 1818-1822	70	10	-	49
Second issue, 1818-1823	70	12	-	51
Engraved date, engraved payee's name	70	12	02	52
Partially engraved date, payee's name not engraved	70	12	04	52
Reed and Stiles issue				52
Graphic issue of 1822	70	14	-	53
Canadian Bank of Commerce, The				
Issues of 1867-1871	75	10	-	53
Issues of 1879 and 1887	75	12	-	55
Issues of 1888-1912	75	14	-	56
Issue of 1917	75	16	-	58
White background on face, tint consists of seal only	75	16	02	58
Overall face tints with seal	75	16	04	59
Issue of 1935, small-size notes	75	18	-	60
Bridgetown, Barbados, issues of 1922 and 1940, large-size notes	75	20	-	61
Bridgetown, Barbados, issue of 1940, small-size notes	75	22	-	62
Kingston, Jamaica, issues of 1921 and 1938, large-size notes	75	24	-	62
Kingston, Jamaica, issue of 1938, small-size notes	75-	26	-	63
Port of Spain, Trinidad, issues of 1921, large-size notes	75	28	-	63
Port of Spain, Trinidad, issues of 1939, small-size notes	75	30	-	64
Canadienne, Banque				
Draft issue of 1836	80	10	-	65
Note issue of 1836	80	12	-	65
Canadienne Nationale, Banque				
Issue of 1925	85	10	-	66
Issue of 1929, large-size notes	85	12	-	67
Issue of 1935, small-size notes	85	14	-	68
Cataract Bank	88	-	-	69
Central Bank of Canada, The				
Issues of 1884 and 1887	90	10	-	69
Central Bank of New Brunswick				
Issue of 1847-1857, pounds, shillings and dollars	95	10	-	70
Black face and blue lathework back, 1847	95	10	02	71

CANADIAN NOTE-ISSUING BANKS

Bank, Issue, Major Alteration	Bank No.	Major Issue No.	Alteration No.	Page No.
Central Bank of New Brunswick (cont.)				
Blue face and grey lathework back, 1847-1851	95	10	04	71
Blue face and orange lathework back, 1852-1853	95	10	06	71
Blue face and green lathework back, 1847	95	10	08	71
Black face and plain back, 1856-1857	95	10	10	71
Issue of 1860	95	12	-	72
Charlotte County Bank				
Perkins and Heath Printings, 1852-1859	100	10	-	73
Charlottetown, Bank of				
Pounds, shillings and pence note issue	105	10	-	75
Dollar draft issue, 1852	105	12	-	75
City Bank, The				
Bilingual issue, 1833-1840s, payable at Montreal, denominations in dollars only	110	10	-	76
Separate branch issues, 1850-1865, dollars/pounds and shillings	110	12	-	78
Montreal issue, 1851-1853	110	12	02	78
Toronto issue, 1850-1865	110	12	04	79
Quebec issue	110	12	06	80
Common branch issue of 1857, Province of Canada	110	14	-	80
Orange back	110	14	02	81
Plain back	110	14	04	81
Green back	110	14	06	81
Spurious note issue	110	16	-	82
City Bank				
New England Bank Note Co. Printings, 1836-1838	115	10	-	82
City Bank of Monteal, The				
Issue of 18(59)	120	10	-	84
Clifton, The Bank of				
Issue of 1859	125	10	-	84
Partially engraved date, two signatures	125	10	02	85
Fully engraved date, one signature	125	10	04	85
Issue of 1860-1861	125	12	-	85
Colonial Bank of Canada, The				
Issue of 1859	130	10	-	86
Two-signature notes, orange-brown tint	130	10	02	88
One-signature notes, pink tint	130	10	04	88
Colonial Bank of Chatham, The				
Issue of 1837	135	10	-	89
Commercial Bank (Brockville)				
Draft issue of 1834-1836	140	10	-	90
Commercial Bank (Kingston)				
Draft issue of 1837	145	10	-	91
Manuscript "Commercial" in bank name	145	10	02	91
Engraved "COMMERCIAL" in bank name	145	10	04	91
Commercial Bank, The (Montreal)				
Issue of 1837	150	10	-	92
Commercial Bank of Canada, The				
Yellow issue, Canada West branches, 1857	155	10	-	92
Brockville issue	155	10	02	93
Galt issue	155	10	04	93
Hamilton issue	155	10	06	93
Kingston issue, brown back	155	10	10	93
London issue, plain back	155	10	12	93
London issue, brown back	155	10	14	93
Toronto issue	155	10	16	94
Green issue, Canada West branches, 1857-1861	155	12	-	94
Belleville issue	155	12	02	94
Brockville issue	155	12	04	94
Chatham issue	155	12	06	94
Hamilton issue	155	12	08	94
Ingersoll issue	155	12	10	94
Kingston issue	155	12	12	94
London issue	155	12	14	95
Perth issue	155	12	16	95
Port Hope issue	155	12	18	95
Prescott issue	155	12	20	95
Toronto issue	155	12	22	95
Windsor issue	155	12	24	95

CANADIAN NOTE-ISSUING BANKS

Bank, Issue, Major Alteration	Bank No.	Major Issue No.	Alteration No.	Page No.
Commercial Bank of Canada, The (cont.)				
Yellow issue, Montreal branch, 1857	155	14	-	95
Green issue, Montreal branch, 1860-1862	155	16	-	96
Commercial Bank of Fort Erie, The				
Issue of 1836-1837	160	10	-	97
Commercial Bank of Lake Ontario, The	165	-	-	99
Commercial Bank of Manitoba, The				
Issue of 1885	170	10	-	99
Issue of 1891	170	12	-	99
Commercial Bank of Montreal				
Draft issue of 1835	175	10	-	100
Draft issue of 1836	175	12	-	101
Commercial Bank of New Brunswick, The				
Fredericton issue, pounds and shillings	180	10	-	102
Miramichi branch issue, pounds, shillings and pence	180	12	-	102
St. John issue, pounds and shillings	180	14	-	103
Dollar/pounds and shillings issue, 1860	180	16	-	104
Commercial Bank of Newfoundland				
Issue of 1857-1858, pound issue, large-size notes	185	10	-	105
Issue of 1865-1867, two signature spaces at left, pounds/dollar issue, small-size notes	185	12	-	106
Issue of 1874-1885, one signature space at left	185	14	-	107
$2 issue of 1881-1884, small-size notes	185	16	-	107
Issue of 1888, dollar issue, large-size notes	185	18	-	108
Commercial Bank of the Midland District, The				
Issue of 1832-1835, payable at Kingston	190	10	-	109
Issue of 1836, payable at Kingston	190	12	-	110
Issue of 1843, payable at Montreal	190	14	-	110
Issue of 1846-1854, payable at Kingston	190	16	-	111
Issue of 185?-1854, payable at Kingston	190	18	-	112
Toppan Carpenter Casilear $4 issues of 1854, payable at various branches	190	20	-	112
Brockville issue	190	20	02	112
Hamilton issue	190	20	04	112
London issue	190	20	06	113
St. Catharines issue	190	20	10	113
Toronto issue	190	20	12	113
Commercial Bank of Windsor, The				
Issue of the 1860s	195	10	-	113
Issue of 1870	195	12	-	114
Issues of 1871 and 1898	195	14	-	114
Commercial Branch Bank of Canada				
Issue of 1861-1862	200	10	-	115
Consolidated Bank of Canada, The				
Issue of 1876	205	10	-	116
County of Elgin, The Bank of the				
Issue of 1856-1857	210	10	-	118
Crown Bank of Canada, The				
Issue of 1904	215	10	-	119
Dominion Bank, The				
Issues of 1871 and 1873	220	10	-	120
Issues of 1876-1888	220	12	-	122
Issues of 1891 and 1898	220	14	-	123
$5 issues of 1896-1925	220	16	-	124
$10 issues of 1900-1925	220	18	-	124
$20 issues of 1897-1925	220	20	-	125
$50 issues of 1901 and 1925	220	22	-	125
Issue of 1931	220	24	-	126
Issue of 1935, small-size notes	220	26	-	127
Issue of 1938, small-size notes	220	28	-	127
Eastern Bank of Canada				
Designs of 1929	225	10	-	128
Eastern Townships Bank, The				
Green issues of 1859 and 1861	230	10	-	129
Partially engraved date, 1859	230	10	02	130
Engraved date, 1859 and 1861	230	10	04	130
Issues of 1873 and 1874	230	12	-	130

CANADIAN NOTE-ISSUING BANKS

Bank, Issue, Major Alteration	Bank No.	Major Issue No.	Alteration No.	Page No.
Eastern Townships Bank, The (cont.)				
Issues of 1879-1902	230	14	-	131
Issue of 1906	230	16	-	132
Exchange Bank, The				
Issue of 1839-1844	235	10	-	133
Exchange Bank Company of Chippewa, The				
Issue of 1837	240	10	-	134
Exchange Bank of Canada, The (Montreal)				
Issue of 1872 and 1873	245	10	-	134
Exchange Bank of Canada, The (Windsor)				
Issue of 1864	250	10	-	137
Exchange Bank of Toronto, The				
Designs of 1855	255	10	-	137
Exchange Bank of Yarmouth, The				
Issues of 1869-1902	260	10	-	138
Farmer's Bank, The				
Draft issue of 1843	265	10	-	139
Farmers Bank of Canada, The				
Issues of 1907 and 1908	270	10	-	140
Farmers' Bank of Malden, The				
Draper, Toppan, Longacre Printings	275	10	-	141
Farmer's Joint Stock Banking Co., The				
Issue of 1835-1840s	280	10	-	142
Issue of 1849, denominations in dollars and shillings, no protectors	280	12	-	143
Denominations in dollars only	280	14	-	144
Engraved "The Branch of" and ". . . Office in Green Bay Wisconsin"; no protectors	280	14	02	144
Engraved "at their Office in"; red protectors	280	14	04	144
Farmers J.S. Banking Co., The				
Casilear, Durand, Burton & Edmonds Design	285	10	-	145
Farmers Bank of Rustico, The				
Denominations in dollars/sterling, 1864	290	10	-	146
Denominations in dollars only, 1872	290	12	-	146
Farmers Bank of St. John's, The				
Draft issue, 1837	295	10	-	147
Note issue, 1838	295	12	-	148
Federal Bank of Canada, The				
Issues of 1874-18820	300	10	-	149
Issue of 1884	300	12	-	150
Fredericton, The Bank of				
New England Bank Note Co. Printings, 1837-1838	305	10	-	151
Free Holders Bank of the Midland District, The				
Rawdon, Wright & Hatch Printings	310	10	-	152
Goderich Bank				
Issue of 1834	315	10	-	152
Gore Bank, The				
New England Bank Note Co. Printings, 1836-1856	320	10	-	153
Partially engraved date, 1836-1850, payee's name is manuscript	320	10	02	153
Fully engraved date, 1850-1856, payee's name is engraved	320	10	04	153
Gore Bank of Hamilton, The				
Casilear, Durand, Burton and Edmonds Printings	325	10	-	154
Grenville County Bank, The				
Wellstood, Hay & Whiting Printings	330	10	-	155
Halifax Banking Company, The				
Maverick Printings, 1825-ca. 1832	335	10	-	156
New England Bank Note Co. Printings, ca. 1833-1850s	335	12	-	156
ABNC $20 issue of 1863 and 1871	335	14	-	157
Plain counters, 1863 and 1871	335	14	02	157
"CANADA CURRENCY" engraved in counters, 1871	335	14	04	157
Issues of 1872 and 1880				157
ABNC Printings, 1872 and 1880	335	16	-	158
Canada BN Co. $10 Printing, 1880	335	18	-	158
BABNC and ABNC Printings 1880	335	20	-	159
Canada BN Co. and BABNC Printings, 1887-1894	335	22	-	159

CANADIAN NOTE-ISSUING BANKS

Bank, Issue, Major Alteration	Bank No.	Major Issue No.	Alteration No.	Page No.
Halifax Banking Company, The (Cont.)				
Canada BN Co. Printings, 1887 and 1890	335	22	02	160
BABNC Printings, 1894	335	22	04	160
Uniacke portrait issues, 1896 and 1898	335	24	-	160
Hamilton Bank, The	340	-	-	162
Hamilton, The Bank of				
Issues of 1872 and 1873	345	10	-	162
Issue of March 1, 1887	345	12	-	164
Issue of December 1, 1887	345	14	-	164
Issue of 1892	345	16	-	164
Issue of 1904	345	18	-	166
Issues of 1909 and 1914	345	20	-	167
Jubilee issue, 1922	345	22	-	168
Hart's Bank				
Scrip issue, 1837, small-size notes	350	10	-	169
Dollar issue, 1838, large-size notes	350	12	-	170
Original Printings - Orange back, normal paper 1838				170
Reprints - plain back, thin paper	350			171
Hatley Bank, The	355	10	-	171
Henry's Bank				
Scrip issue of 1837	357	10	-	172
Draft issue of 1837	357	12	-	172
Note issue of 1837	357	14	-	173
Hochelaga, Banque d'				
Issue of 1874-1877	360	10	-	173
Issue of 1880	360	12	-	175
Multicolour issue of 1889	360	14	-	176
Issues of 1894	360	16	-	177
Issues of 1898 and 1907	360	18	-	178
Issue of 1911	360	20	-	179
Issue of 1914	360	22	-	180
Issues of 1917 and 1920	360	24	-	181
Home Bank of Canada, The				
Issues of 1904-1920	365	10	-	183
Hull, The Bank of	370	-	-	184
Imperial Bank of Canada, The				
BABN printings of 1875-1906	375	10	-	184
Waterlow printings, 1902-1910	375	12	-	187
Waterlow essays of 1914	375	14	-	189
Old BABN printings, resumed 1915-1920	375	16	-	190
Issue of 1923	375	18	-	191
Issue of 1933	375	20	-	192
Issue of 1934, small-size notes	375	22	-	192
Issue of 1939	375	24	-	193
International Bank of Canada, The				
Issue of 1858	380	10	-	193
Two signatures, no protectors	380	10	02	194
Two signatures, red protectors	380	10	04	194
One signature, green protectors	380	10	06	195
One signature, brown protectors	380	10	08	196
One signature, red protectors	380	10	10	196
One signature, ochre protectors	380	10	12	196
One signature, blue protectors	380	10	14	196
Issue of 1859	380	12	-	197
Internationale du Canada, Banque				
Issue of 1911	385	10	-	198
Jacques Cartier, La Banque				
Issue of 1862	390	10	-	199
Issues of 1870 and 1880	390	12	-	199
Issues of 1886 and 1889	390	14	-	201
Issue of 1895	390	16	-	202
Kingston Bank, The				
Issue of 1837	395	10	-	203
Liverpool, The Bank of				
Issue of 1871	400	10	-	203

CANADIAN NOTE-ISSUING BANKS

Bank, Issue, Major Alteration	Bank No.	Major Issue No.	Alteration No.	Page No.
London in Canada, The Bank of				
Issue of 1883	405	10	-	205
Lower Canada, The Bank of				
Harris & Sealy Designs	410	10	-	207
Lower Canada Bank				
Draft issue of 1837	415	10	-	208
Macdonald & Co.				
Indian at right, arm upraised, Indian maiden looking right	420	10	-	209
Indian at right, arm down, Indian maiden looking left	420	12	-	209
Maritime Bank of the Dominion of Canada, The				
Issues of 1873 and 1875	425	10	-	210
Issues of 1881 and 1882	425	12	-	212
Mechanics Bank, The (Montreal, Canada East)				
Issue of 1872	430	10	-	213
Mechanics Bank, The (Montreal, Lower Canada)				
Issue of 1837	435	10	-	214
Mechanics Bank of St. John's, The				
Note issue, 1837	440	10	-	215
Draft issue, 1837	440	12	-	216
Engraved "A Messrs H.N. Warren & Cie a St. John's" at lower left, mss. "H.N. Warren & Cie" endorsed vertically across centre	440	12	02	216
Engraved "A Messrs T.H. Perry & Cie a St. John's" at lower left, mss. "T.H. Perry & Cie" endorsed vertically across centre	440	12	04	216
Mercantile Banking Corporation, The				
Chas. Skipper & East printing of 1878, large-size notes	445	10	-	217
Merchant Bank, The (Montreal, Canada East)				
RWH printings	448	10	-	217
Merchants Bank, The (Toronto)				
Issue of 1836-1837	450	10	-	218
Merchants Bank, The (Montreal, Canada East)				
Issue of 1864	455	10	-	219
Merchants Bank of Canada, The				
Hugh Allan portrait issues, 1868-1873	460	10	-	221
Andrew Allan portrait issue, 1886	460	12	-	222
Multicoloured tint issues, 1900 and 1903	460	14	-	223
Issues of 1906 and 1907	460	16	-	224
Issue of 1916	460	18	-	226
Issue of 1917	460	20	-	226
Issue of 1919	460	22	-	228
Merchants Bank of Halifax, The				
Merchants Bank $20, no frame issue, 1864	465	10	-	228
Merchants Bank $20, frame issue, 1864	465	12	-	229
Merchants' Bank of Halifax issues, 1869 and 1870	465	14	-	229
No green overprint	465	14	02	229
Green overprint	465	14	04	229
"CANADA CURRENCY" issues of 1871-1874	465	16	-	230
"DOMINION OF CANADA" issues of 1878 and 1879	465	18	-	231
No portrait issues, 1880-1898	465	20	-	231
Portrait issues, 1894-1899	465	22	-	232
Hamilton, Bermuda, proposed issue of 1880	465	24	-	233
Merchants Bank of Prince Edward Island, The				
Issues of 1871-1892	470	10	-	234
Partially engraved date, 1871	470	10	02	235
Fully engraved date, 1877-1892	470	10	04	235
$5 issue of 1900	470	12	-	235
Merchants Exchange Bank				
Issue of 1853	475	10	-	236
Metropolitan Bank, The (Montreal)				
Issue of 1872	480	10	-	237
Metropolitan Bank, The (Toronto)				
Issues of 1902-1912	485	10	-	238
Molsons Bank, The				
Issue of 1837	490	10	-	240
Free banking issue, 1853	490	12	-	240

515

CANADIAN NOTE-ISSUING BANKS

Bank, Issue, Major Alteration	Bank No.	Major Issue No.	Alteration No.	Page No.
Molsons Bank, The (cont.)				
First Chartered bank issue 1855	490			241
Montreal issue	490	14	-	243
No protector, no face tint	490	14	02	243
Green word protector, no face tint	490	14	04	243
No protector, green overall face tint	490	14	06	243
Toronto issue, branch name engraved	490	16	-	243
No protectors	490	16	02	243
Green work protectors	490	16	04	243
Green tint issue of 1857	490	18	-	243
Issue of 1871	490	20	-	244
Issues of 1872-1901	490	22	-	244
Late issues of old RWH designs, 1891 and 1899	490	24	-	245
Issues of 1903 and 1904	490	26	-	246
Issue of 1905	490	28	-	246
Issue of 1908	490	30	-	247
Issue of 1912	490	32	-	248
Issue of 1914	490	34	-	249
Issue of 1916	490	36	-	249
1908 designs, resumed 1918	490	38	-	250
Issue of 1922	490	40	-	250
Montreal Bank, The				
Issue of 1848	495	10	-	251
Montreal Bank				
Reed issue, 1817-1818	500	10	-	251
Leney & Rollinson issue, 1818-1820	500	12	-	252
Reed & Stiles printing, 1821-1822	500	14	-	253
Graphic printing, 1822-1829	500	16	-	253
Montreal, The Bank of				
Graphic printing, 1820s	505	10	-	255
Fairman printings, 1830s	505	12	-	256
Montreal issue	505	12	02	256
Quebec issue	505	12	04	256
Rawdon, Wright, Hatch printings, 1830s	505	14	-	257
Montreal issue	505	14	02	258
Quebec issue	505	14	04	258
Montreal arms issue, issues 505-16, 18 & 20	505			258
Partially engraved date, 1844-1860s	505	16	-	259
Montreal issue, 1844-1861	505	16	02	259
Quebec issue, 1844-1852	505	16	04	260
Engraved date, red protector, two signatures, 1849	505	18	-	260
Montreal issue	505	18	02	260
Quebec issue	505	18	04	260
Engraved date, green protector, one signature, 1849	505	20	-	260
Cobourg issue	505	20	02	261
Hamilton issue	505	20	04	261
Montreal issue	505	20	06	261
Quebec issue	505	20	08	261
Toronto issue	505	20	10	261
Dogs and safe issues	505			262
Partially engraved date, no protector, 1842-1847	505	22	-	262
Rawdon, Wright, Hatch printings, 2nd April 184-	505	22	02	262
Rawdon, Wright, Hatch printings, 2nd Augt 184-	505	22	04	262
Danforth/Underwood printings, 2nd Augt 184-	505	22	06	262
Engraved date, red protectors, 1849	505	24	-	263
Bank crest issue, 1852-1856	505	26	-	263
No protector	505	26	02	265
Green word protector	505	26	04	265
Blue back issue, 1853-1857	505	28	-	266
Engraved "Brockville"	505	28	02	266
Engraved "Goderich"	505	28	12	266
Engraved "London"	505	28	22	266
Engraved "Montreal"	505	28	30	266
Engraved "Ottawa"	505	28	36	266
Engraved "Perth"	505	28	40	266
Engraved "Picton"	505	28	44	266
Engraved "Port Hope"	505	28	48	267
Engraved "Quebec"	505	28	52	267
Engraved "Simcoe"	505	28	56	267
Engraved "Toronto"	505	28	60	267
Engraved "Whitby"	505	28	64	267
Engraved "Woodstock"	505	28	68	267

Bank, Issue, Major Alteration	Bank No.	Major Issue No.	Alteration No.	Page No.
Montreal, The Bank of (cont.)				
Green issue of 1859	505	30	-	267
White outlined numerals, St. George back designs	505	30	02	268
Full tint numerals, St. George back designs	505	30	04	268
White outlined numerals, plain backs	505	30	06	268
Full tint numerals, plain backs	505	30	08	268
Issue of 1862	505	32	-	268
Issue of 1871	505	34	-	269
Issue of 1882	505	36	-	271
Issue of 1888	505	38	-	271
Issue of 1891	505	40	-	272
Issue of 1892	505	42	-	273
Issue of 1895	505	44	-	273
Double-size note issue of 1903	505	46	-	274
Issue of 1904	505	48	-	275
Issue of 1911	505	50	-	276
Issue of 1912	505	52	-	277
Issue of 1914	505	54	-	278
Issue of 1923	505	56	-	279
Issue of 1931	505	58	-	280
First small-size note issue, 1935	505	60	-	281
Issue of 1938	505	62	-	282
Issue of 1942	505	64	-	282
Nationale, La Banque				
Issue of 1860	510	10	-	283
Partially engraved date, mss. sheet numbers	510	10	02	283
Engraved date, printed sheet numbers	510	10	04	284
Issues of 1870 and 1871	510	12	-	284
Issue of 1873	510	14	-	285
Issue of 1883	510	16	-	286
Issue of 1891	510	18	-	286
Issue of 1897	510	20	-	287
Issue of 1922	510	22	-	287
New Brunswick, The Bank of				
Perkins Fairman Heath, 1820-1831, pounds and shillings printing, large-size notes	515	10	-	289
NEBN Co., 1838-1859, pounds and shillings printing, regular-size notes	515	12	-	290
Dollar issues of 1860-1884	515	14	-	291
Issue of 1892	515	16	-	293
Issues of 1903-1906	515	18	-	293
Newcastle Banking Company, The				
Issue of 1836	520	10	-	295
Newcastle District Loan Company, The				
Issue of 1836	525	10	-	296
Niagara District Bank, The				
Free banking issue, 1854-1855	530	10	-	297
Chartered bank issues, 1855-1862	530	12	-	297
Partially engraved date, red protector, 1855	530	12	02	298
Partially engraved date, green tint, 1860s	530	12	04	298
Fully engraved date, 1862	530	12	06	298
Issue of 1872	530	14	-	299
Niagara Suspension Bridge Bank, The				
Issue of 1836-1841	535	10	-	300
Mss. "PAYABLE AT THE BANK" at top, plain back, 1836	535	10	02	301
Engraved "PAYABLE AT THE BANK" at top, plain back, 1837-1839	535	10	04	301
Engraved "PAYABLE AT THE BANK" at top, orange lathework back, 1840	535	10	06	301
Plain back issue, 1841	535	10	08	301
Northern Bank, The				
Issue of 1905	540	10	-	302
Northern Crown Bank, The				
Issues of 1908 and 1914	545	10	02	304
Nova Scotia, The Bank of				
Rawdon, Wright, Hatch & Co., pounds and shillings printings, 1832-1852	550	10	-	306
NEBN, 1840, pounds and shillings	550	12	-	307
Blades, East & Blades printings, 1864	550	14	-	308
$4, $5 and $20 issues of 1870-1877	550	16	-	308
$10 issues of 1877-1929	550	18	-	309
$5 issue of 1881	550	20	-	310
$20 issue of 1882	550	22	-	310
$20 issue of 1896	550	24	-	311

CANADIAN NOTE-ISSUING BANKS

Bank, Issue, Major Alteration	Bank No.	Major Issue No.	Alteration No.	Page No.
Nova Scotia, The Bank of (cont.)				
$20 issue of 1897	550	26	-	311
Scenic issues of 1898-1929	550	28	-	311
$5 issue of 1918	550	30	-	312
$5 issue of 1924	550	32	-	313
$5 issue of 1929	550	34	-	313
Issue of 1935, small-size notes	550	36	-	313
Kingston, Jamaica, 1900-1930	550	38	-	314
Large-size notes	550	38	02	314
Small-size notes	550	38	04	315
Ontario Bank, The				
Issues of 1857 and 1861	555	10	-	315
Engraved "Bowmanville," one blue sheet number at bottom, 1857	555	10	02	316
Engraved "Montreal," one blue sheet number at bottom, 1857	555	10	04	316
Engraved "Bowmanville," one red sheet number at bottom, 1861	555	10	06	316
Engraved "Bowmanville," two red sheet numbers at top, 1861	555	10	08	316
Engraved "Bowmanville," two blue sheet numbers at top, 1861	555	10	10	317
Issue of 1860	555	12	-	317
Issues of 1870	555	14	-	317
Issue of 1882	555	16	-	318
Issue of 1888	555	18	-	319
$5 issue of 1898	555	20	-	321
Ottawa, The Bank of (Montreal)				
Draft issue of 1837, French text	560	10	-	321
Draft issue of 1837, English text	560	12	-	321
"Accepted for MESSRS. JOSEPH C. FRINK & CO." at bottom, blue back	560	12	02	322
"Accepted for D.F. Merrill & Co. at Bottom	560			322
"Accepted for _____" at bottom, plain back	560	12	04	322
Note issue of 1837	560	14	-	323
Ottawa, The Bank of (Ottawa)				
Issue of 1874	565	10	-	323
Issue of 1880	565	12	-	324
Issues of 1888 and 1891	565	14	-	325
Issues of 1895 and 1900	565	16	-	326
Issue of 1903	565	18	-	327
Issue of 1906	565	20	-	328
Issue of 1912	565	22	-	329
Issue of Aug. 1, 1913	565	24	-	329
Issue of Sept. 1, 1913	565	26	-	330
$5 design of 1906, resumed 1917	565	28	-	330
People, The Bank of the				
Issue of 1836-1840	570	10	-	331
Peuple, La Banque du				
Issue of 1835-1836	575	10	-	333
"Messrs. Viger, DeWitt & Cie" engraved on drafts at lower left	575	10	02	333
Notes: Company name replaced by "_____ CAISSIER"	575	10	04	334
$5 issue of 1838	575	12	-	334
Durand & Co. printings, 1839-1845	575	14	-	334
On drafts "A Messrs. Viger DeWitt & Cie" engraved at lower left, 1839, dollars only	575	14	02	335
On notes company name replaced by "_____ Cash," 1845, dollars/pounds and shillings	575	14	04	335
Toppan Carpenter printings 1845-1892	575			335
Blue backs, 1845-1892, dollars/pounds and shillings	575	16	-	337
No protectors, 1845-1850	575	16	02	337
Green protectors, 1854, 1870	575	16	04	337
Green face tints, green backs, 1870, dollars/pounds and shillings	575	18	-	338
Green face tints, blue backs, 1882-1892	575	20	-	338
Dollar/pounds and shillings issue, blue numbers, 1882-1892	575	20	02	338
Dollars only issues, blue numbers	575	20	04	338
Dollars only issues, red numbers	575	20	06	340
People's Bank of Halifax, The				
$20 issues of 1864-1903	580	10	-	340
$4, $5 and $10 issues of 1870-1903	580	12	-	341
People's Bank of New Brunswick, The				
ABNC printings, 1864-1873	585	10	-	343
ABNC and BABN printings, 1874 and 1881	585	12	-	343
Queen Victoria widow's weeds issue, 1885	585	14	-	344
Randolph portrait issues, 1897 and 1904	585	16	-	345
ABNC printings, 1897 and 1905	585	18	-	346
Fully engraved date, 1897	585	18	02	346
Partially engraved date, completed by red stamp, 1905	585	18	04	346

… CANADIAN NOTE-ISSUING BANKS

Bank, Issue, Major Alteration	Bank No.	Major Issue No.	Alteration No.	Page No.
Phenix Bank, The				
Harris issue, 1837-1841	590	10	-	347
Denomination in dollars only, 1837	590	10	02	347
Denomination in dollars and shillings	590	10	04	347
Pictou Bank, The				
Issues of 1874 and 1882	595	10	-	348
Prince Edward Island, The Bank of				
Pounds, shillings and pence issue, 1856-1868	600	10	-	349
Dollar issues of 1872 and 1877	600	12	-	350
Provincial Bank, The (London)				
Designs of 1884	605	10	-	352
Provincial Bank of Canada, The				
Issue of 1856	610	10	-	353
Provinciale du Canada, La Banque				
Issue of 1900	615	10	-	354
Issue of 1907	615	12	-	354
Issue of 1913-1928	615	14	-	355
Issue of 1935, small-size notes	615	16	-	356
Issue of 1936, small-size notes	615	18	-	357
Quebec Bank, The				
Maverick printing, army-bill type notes, 1818-1819	620	10	-	358
Graphic printings, 1819-1830s	620	12	-	358
Issues of 1833-1841	620	14		359
Jones printing, 1837	620	16	-	360
Rawdon, Wright & Hatch printings	620	18	-	360
Issues of 1837-1860s	620			360
Issues of 1837-1842, plain back	620	20	-	360
Issues of 1860s, green lathework back	620	22	-	361
Issues of 1843-1861	620	24	-	361
Issues of 1843-1860, plain back, no protector	620	24	02	361
Issues of 1847-1861, plain back, red protector	620	24	04	362
Issues of 1865 with green lathework back, Toronto issue	620	26	-	363
Issues of 1843-1862	620	28	-	363
Issue with no protector, dated November 1843-1853	620	28	02	364
Issue with red protector, dated November 1849-1852	620	28	04	364
Issue with no protector, dated February 1854-1862	620	28	06	364
Toppan Carpenter Casilear printing, 1850s, engraved "Payable in Toronto" at top	620	30	-	365
Toronto issue, no tint, no protector, 1856	620	30	02	365
Toronto issue, no tint, green protector	620	30	04	365
Toppan Carpenter Casilear printing, 1859, engraved "Payable in Toronto" at top	620	32	-	365
Issue of 1863, lathework and bank name on back	620	34	-	366
Issue of 1863, lathework, counters and bank name on back	620	36	-	367
Issue of 1870	620	38	-	367
Issues of 1873 and 1888, green face tint and back	620	40	-	367
Issue of 1888, brown face tint and back	620	42	-	368
Issue of 1898	620	44	-	369
Issue of 1901	620	46	-	370
Issues of 1908 and 1911	620	48	-	370
Face designs lacking "FOUNDED 1818" at top	620	48	02	371
Face designs with "FOUNDED 1818" at top	620	48	04	371
Issue of 1908 and 1911, "FOUNDED 1818" at top, new back designs	620	50	-	371
Spurious $2 issue, 1857-1859	620	52	-	372
Quebec Lower Canada, Bank of				
Design of 1841	625	10	-	372
Royal Bank of Canada, The				
Issues of 1901 and 1909	630	10	-	373
1901 issues	630	10	02	373
1909 issues	630	10	04	374
Issue of 1913	630	12	-	376
Issue of 1927	630	14	-	377
Issue of 1933	630	16	-	378
Issue of 1935, small-size notes	630	18	-	379
Issue of 1943	630	20	-	379
Designs for overprinted Canadian notes, 1913	630	22	-	380
Notes designed specifically for West Indies, Antigua, large-size notes, 1920	630	24	-	380
For West Indies, Antigua designs, small-size notes, 1938	630	26	-	380
Overprinted Canadian notes, 1909	630	28	-	381
Notes designed specifically for West Indies, Barbadoa, large-size note designs, 1920	630	30	-	381
Notes designed specifically for West Indies, Barbados, small-size notes, 1938	630	32	-	382

CANADIAN NOTE-ISSUING BANKS

Bank, Issue, Major Alteration	Bank No.	Major Issue No.	Alteration No.	Page No.
Royal Bank of Canada, The (cont.)				
Overprinted Canadian notes, 1909 and 1913	630	34	-	382
Notes designed specifically for West Indies, British Guiana, large-size notes, 1920	630	36	-	383
Notes designed specifically for West Indies, British Guiana, small-size notes, 1938	630	38	-	383
Overprinted Canadian notes, 1913	630	40	-	384
Notes designed specifically for West Indies, Dominica, large-size notes, 1920	630	42	-	384
Notes designed specifically for West Indies, Dominica, small-size notes, 1938	630	44	-	384
Designs for overprinted Canadian notes, 1909	630	46	-	385
Notes designed specifically for West Indies, Grenada, large-size note designs, 1920	630	48	-	385
Notes designed specifically for West Indies, Grenada, small-size notes, 1938	630	50	-	385
Issues for Kingston, Jamaica, large-size notes, 1911	630	52	-	386
Issues for Kingston, Jamaica, small-size notes, 1938	630	54	-	386
Overprinted Canadian notes, 1913	630	56	-	387
Notes designed specifically for West Indies, St. Kitts, large-size note designs, 1920	630	58	-	387
Notes designed specifically for West Indies, St. Kitts, small-size notes, 1938	630	60	-	387
Issues for Castries, St. Lucia	630	62	-	388
Issues for Port of Spain, Trinidad	630			388
Overprinted Canadian notes, 1909	630	64	-	388
Notes designed specifically for West Indies, Trinidad, large-size notes, 1920	630	66	-	389
Notes designed specifically for West Indies, Trinidad, small-size notes, 1938	630	68	-	389
Royal Canadian Bank, The				
ABNC printings, 1865	635	10	-	390
Partially engraved date	635	10	02	391
Engraved date	635	10	04	391
Continental Bank Note Company issue of 1865	635	12	-	391
"At Its Banking House in Toronto" above bank seal	635	12	02	392
"At Its Agency in Monteal" above bank seal,	635	12	04	392
British American Bank Note Company issue, 1870-1872	635	14	-	392
Saint Francis Bank, The				
RWH printings	640	10	-	394
St. Hyacinthe, La Banque de				
Issue of 1874	645	10	-	395
Issues of 1880 and 1892	645	12	-	396
St. Jean, La Banque de				
Issues of 1873-1900	650	10	-	397
Issue of 1906	650	12	-	398
St. Jean Baptiste, Banque				
Designs of 1875	655	10	-	399
St. Lawrence Bank, The				
Lockhart, Fitch portrait issue	660	10	-	400
Lockhart, Fitch portraits removed	660	12	-	400
St. Lawrence Bank & Lumber Co., The				
Issue of 1837	665	10	-	402
St. Stephens Joint Stock Banking Comp'y				
Dollar issue, 1830s	670	10	-	402
St. Stephen's Bank, The				
Pounds issue, 1830s	675	10	-	403
First dollar issue, 1830s	675	12	-	403
Ornate counter issue, 1846-1853	675	14	-	404
No protector	675	14	02	404
Red protector	675	14	04	404
Boston Bank Note Co. printings, 1852	675	16	-	404
"Canadian Funds" issues of 1860-1886	675			405
Issue of 1860, plain back	675	18	-	406
Issues of 1860-1886	675	20	-	406
Issue of 1860, green back, small red sheet numbers	675	20	02	406
Later issues, 1873-1886, green back, large blue sheet numbers	675	20	04	406
U.S. funds issues of 1863	675	22	-	407
Bank of New York issue	675	22	02	407
Z. Chipman issue	675	22	04	408
Issues of 1892 and 1903	675	24	-	409
Saskatchewan, The Bank of				
Designs of 1913	680	10	-	410
Sovereign Bank of Canada, The				
Issues of 1902-1907	685	10	-	411
Stadacona Bank, The				
Issue of 1874	690	10	-	412

CANADIAN NOTE-ISSUING BANKS

Bank, Issue, Major Alteration	Bank No.	Major Issue No.	Alteration No.	Page No.
Standard Bank of Canada, The				
Issues of 1876 and 1881	695	10	-	414
Issue of 1890	695	12	-	415
$5 issue of 1891	695	14	-	415
$10 issue of 1900	695	16	-	416
Issues of 1914-1919	695	18	-	416
Issue of 1924	695	20	-	418
Sterling Bank of Canada, The				
Issue of 1906	700	10	-	418
$5 issue of 1914	700	12	-	419
$10 issue of 1921	700	14	-	420
Summerside Bank of Prince Edward Island, The				
ABNC Printings 1866-1872	705	10	-	421
ABNC printings, dollars/sterling	705	10	-	421
ABNC printings, dollars only	705	12	-	422
BABN printings, 1884	705	14	-	423
BABN printings, 1891	705	16	-	423
BABN printings, 1900	705	18	-	424
Toronto, The Bank of				
"Province of Canada" issues of 1856-1865	715	10	-	424
Issue of 1856, partially engraved date, orange back, "word" protector	715	10	-	425
Issue of 1857, printed date, orange back, Roman numeral protector, Cobourg branch	715	12	-	426
Issue of 1859, engraved date, plain back, "word" protector	715	14	-	426
Issue of 1865, engraved date, plain back, "word" protector	715	16	-	426
Dominion of Canada issue of 1876	715	18	-	426
Dominion of Canada issue of 1880	715	20	-	427
Yellow issues of 1887-1929	715	22	-	427
Small-size issues of 1935 and 1937	715	24	-	429
Notes altered from the Colonial Bank of Canada	715	26	-	430
Notes altered from the International Bank of Canada	715	28	-	431
Traders Bank of Canada, The				
Issues of 1885 and 1886	720	10	-	431
Issues of 1890 and 1893	720	12	-	432
Issues of 1897 and 1907	720	14	-	433
Issue of 1909	720	16	-	434
$5 Issue of 1910	720	18	-	435
Union Bank, The				
Burton & Gurley printings, 1838	725	10	-	436
Burton Gurley Printings, issue of 1838 Plain backs	725	10	-	436
Issue of 1838, green backs	725	12	-	436
Issue of 1838, blue backs	725	14	-	437
RWH Printings, 1838	725	16	-	437
Orange backs	725	16	-	438
Issue of 1838, blue backs	725	20	-	438
Union Bank of Canada, The				
Issue of 1886	730	10	-	438
Issue of 1893	730	12	-	440
Quebec $5 and $10 issues of 1903 and 1907	730	14	-	441
Winnipeg $5 and $10 issue of 1912	730	16	-	442
$20, $50 and $100 designs similar to the 1886 issue, resumed 1907 and 1912	730	18	-	443
Issue of 1921	730	20	-	444
Union Bank of Halifax, The				
Pounds issue, 1861	735	10	-	445
Issue of 1870	735	12	-	445
Issues of 1871-1909	735			446
Issues of 1871-1895, green denominational face tint	735	14	-	447
Issues of 1900-1909, general face tints	735	16	-	448
Designs for Port of Spain, Trinidad, 1904	735	18	-	448
Union Bank of Lower Canada, The				
Issues of 1866	740			450
Issues with green word and numeral face tint	740	10	-	450
Issues with green "word" protector, no face tint	740	12	-	451
Issues of 1870 and 1871	740	14	-	451
Union Bank of Montreal, The				
Issue of 1840	745	10	-	453
Union Bank of Newfoundland				
Large-size pound notes, 1850s-early 1860s	750	10	-	454
Small-size pound notes, 1865 - 1883	750	14	-	455

521

CANADIAN NOTE-ISSUING BANKS

Bank, Issue, Major Alteration	Bank No.	Major Issue No.	Alteration No.	Page No.
Union Bank of Newfoundland, (cont.)				
Issues of 1865-1881, partially engraved date	750	12	-	456
Issues of 1867-1883, fully engraved date	750	14	-	456
Dollar issues of 1882 and 1889	750	16	-	456
Union Bank of Prince Edward Island, The				
Issues of 1864-1872	755	10	-	458
Issue of 1864-1865, dollars/sterling	755	10	-	458
Issue of 1872, dollars only	755	12	-	459
BABN printings of 1875 and 1877	755	14	-	459
United Empire Bank of Canada				
Issue of 1906	760	10	-	461
Upper Canada, Bank of (Kingston)				
Regular note issue, 1819 - 1822	765	10	-	462
Regular note issue, partially engraved date, 1819-1822	765	10	-	462
Regular note issue, fully engraved date, 1820	765	12	-	463
Scrip issue of 1820	765	14	-	463
Upper Canada, The Bank of (York)				
Graphic printing, 1826-1832	770	10	-	464
Issue of the 1830s, payable at Toronto	770	12	-	465
Issues of 1849-1856, Toronto, red protector	770	14	-	467
Issues of 1857, red protector	770	16	-	468
Montreal issue	770	16	02	468
Quebec issue	770	16	04	469
Issues of 1851-1857, blue protector	770	18	-	469
Brockville issue, 1851	770	18	02	470
Kingston issue, 1851	770	18	04	470
Montreal issue, 1851	770	18	06	470
Quebec issue, 1852-1857	770	18	08	470
$10 Toronto branch issue, late 1850s	770	20	-	471
Green issues of 1859 and 1861	770	22	-	471
Toronto issue, overprinted date, 1859-1861	770	22	02	472
Toronto issue, engraved date, two signatures, 1859	770	22	04	473
Toronto issue, engraved date, one signature, 1861	770	22	06	473
Montreal issue, 1859	770	22	08	473
Quebec issue, 1859	770	22	10	474
Notes altered from the Colonial Bank of Canada	770	24	-	474
Notes altered from the Bank of Western Canada	770	26	-	474
Vancouver, The Bank of				
Issue of 1910	775	10	-	475
Victoria, The Bank of	780	-	-	477
Ville Marie, La Banque				
BABN printings, 1873-1890	785	10	-	477
Canada BNCo printings, 1889	785	12	-	479
BABN printings, 1889	785	14	-	479
Western Bank of Canada, The				
Issues of 1882 and 1890	790	10	-	480
Western Canada, The Bank of				
Issue of 1859	795	10	-	481
Westmorland Bank of New Brunswick, The				
Bend of Petticodiac (sic) issue, 1854-1859	800	10	-	482
Moncton issue, 1861	800	12	-	483
Weyburn Security Bank, The				
Issue of 1911	805	10	-	484
Yarmouth, The Bank of				
$20 issue of 1860	810	10	-	485
Issues of 1870 and 1891	810	12	-	486
Zimmerman Bank, The				
Free banking issue, 1854-1855	815	10	-	487
Chartered bank issue from Elgin, 1856	815	12	-	488
Red "word" protector on face and back	815	12	02	489
Blue "word" protector on face and back	815	12	04	489
Red numeral protector on face and back	815	12	06	489
Blue numeral protector on face and back	815	12	08	490
Chartered bank issue from Clifton	815	14	-	490

SOURCES

Walter D. Allan, Photo and Engraving Archives
Archives of the American Bank Note Co., New York
Archives of the British American Banknote Co., Ottawa
Bradford Rhodes & Co.'s Bankers' Directory and Collection Guide, January 1898
Bank of Canada Numismatic Collection, Ottawa
A History of the Canadian Bank of Commerce, 3 vols., V. Ross, 1922
Canadian Banks and Bank-Notes, A Record, C.S. Howard
Canadian Numismatic Research Society, The Transactions
Centenary of the Bank of Montreal 100 Years, 1817-1917
Charlton Auction Catalogues, various, including the Walter D. Allan sales
The Charlton Standard Catalogue of Canadian Paper Money, 1st edition
The Charlton Press photo archives

The Currency and Medals of Prince Edward Island by the Numismatic Education Society of Canada, 1988
The Essay Proof Society Journals, various
Fiftieth Anniversary of the Royal Bank of Canada 1869-1919
Fifty Years of Banking Service the Dominion Bank, 1871-1921
History of the Bank of Nova Scotia 1832-1900
The House of Joseph in the Life of Quebec, E.C. Woodley, 1946
Journals of the Canadian Paper Money Society, various, 1965-1995
John A. Muscalus, various monographs on the origin of banknote vignettes
The Bank of Nova Scotia 1832-1932
Ontario Private Banks listed by Steven Thorning Town
Rand, McNally & Co.'s Bankers' Directory and List of Bank Attorneys, January 1887
United States Obsolete Bank Notes, James A. Haxby, 1988, 4 vols.
Wrights' 1899 Classified Business Directory

UNION BANK OF NEWFOUNDLAND.

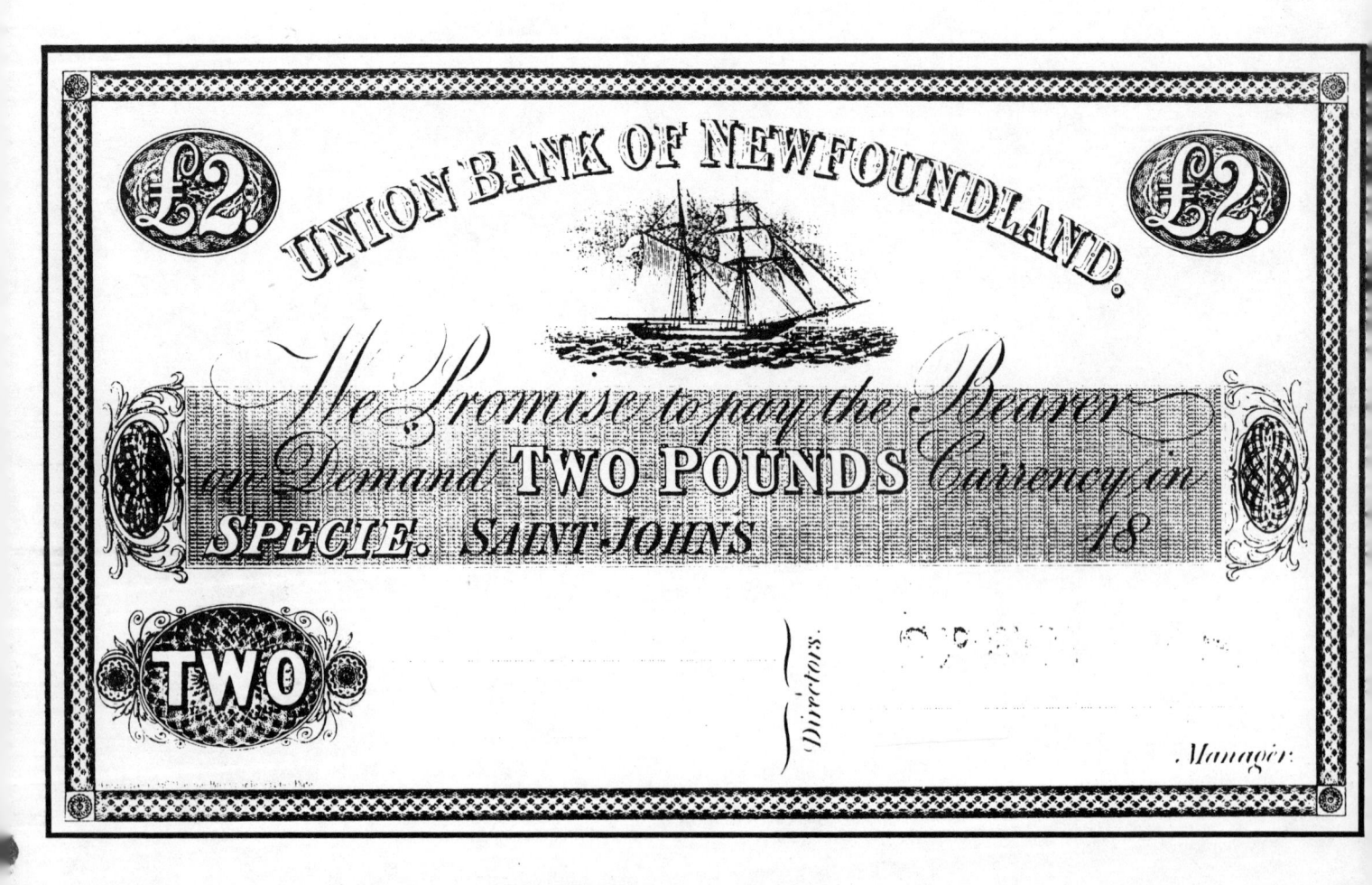

£2 £2

We Promise to pay the Bearer on Demand **TWO POUNDS** *Currency in* **SPECIE. SAINT JOHNS** 18

TWO

Directors.

Manager.